This is a volume in
THE UNIVERSITY OF MICHIGAN HISTORY OF THE MODERN WORLD
Upon completion, the series will consist of the following volumes:

The United States to 1865 *by Michael Kraus*
The United States since 1865 *by Foster Rhea Dulles*
Canada: A Modern History *by John Bartlet Brebner*
Latin America: A Modern History *by J. Fred Rippy*
Great Britain to 1688 *by Maurice Ashley*
Great Britain since 1688 *by K. B. Smellie*
France: A Modern History *by Albert Guérard*
Germany: A Modern History *by Marshall Dill, Jr.*
Italy: A Modern History *by Denis Mack Smith*
Russia and the Soviet Union: A Modern History *by Warren B. Walsh*
The Near East: A Modern History *by William Yale*
The Far East: A Modern History *by Nathaniel Peffer*
India: A Modern History *by Percival Spear*
The Southwest Pacific: A Modern History *by C. Hartley Grattan*
Africa: A Modern History *by Ronald E. Robinson*

RUSSIA AND THE SOVIET UNION

A Modern History

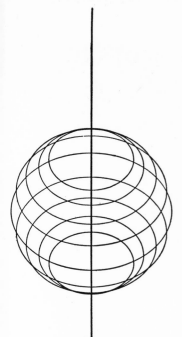

The University of Michigan History of the Modern World

Edited by Allan Nevins and Howard M. Ehrmann

RUSSIA and the Soviet Union

A Modern History

BY WARREN BARTLETT WALSH

Ann Arbor : The University of Michigan Press

TO MY FAMILY
Elizabeth, Lucy, Leza, and Sara

Preface

There are so many ways of looking at history that the writer of "a history" is under some obligation to forewarn the reader as to emphasis and bias. Here, very briefly—more as an enumeration of points than as a discussion of them—is how history looks to me.

History is a story about people; about the vast, undistinguished and indistinguishable majority, and about the famous or notorious few. It is a story based mainly upon imperfect and incomplete written records, supplemented when possible by other sources of information. No history book can be free from either error or bias because the books are written by imperfect men working with imperfect knowledge and data.

History is also an extension of human memory. No living man can recall from personal experience the reform of the Russian Orthodox Church made by Peter the Great, but no literate person who has free access to information needs to be ignorant of that event. History is an air liner of the mind, winging across time. At the take-off—that is, when reviewing the very recent past, the air liner is so close to the ground that very many details are visible, but the wide view is impossible. This is reversed as the air liner of the mind travels farther into the past. Details blur into masses until only the great outlines can be seen and men cannot be sure whether the far-distant shapes are clouds or mountain ranges. This brings up the always difficult problem of how best to tell the story.

Events happen in time sequence; or, if the events are literally simultaneous, human perception of them occurs in time sequence. We find it impossible to tell stories wholly in one tense because we must both recollect and anticipate. This pattern is applicable to the telling of a history. One begins by setting a time limit or chronological span, then one arranges material within that span by topics. The pattern cannot be rigid. The first four chapters of this book, for example, have a time span of several thousand years, whereas the last four cover only a single generation. A chapter which flies over centuries obviously cannot deal with any incident in much detail, but a chapter which saunters through only half a decade cannot avoid details. The justification for this change of pace is that recent events have a more direct bearing on us than do earlier occurrences and therefore need a fuller coverage. This implies that the study of history contributes to an understanding of the present.

What people do today depends in part upon what they did yesterday, and what they will do tomorrow will partly depend upon today's actions and events. Another way of saying this is to describe history as a study of past and present social norms and values. Every group has its accepted social norms. Such norms are both tangibles, such as diet, clothing, housing; and intangibles, such as prejudices and habits of thought. Each group, moreover, places certain judgments or values upon its norms. A monastic community, for example, not only eschews meats on fast days, but also regards this abstinence as a positive good; failure to abstain is a positive wrong. Both norms and values are important determinants of human action. Furthermore, the norms and values of living societies are constantly changing. History tries to find the origins and measure the changes.

Because norms and values change slowly, history has a characteristic dualism. It must record both changes and continuity. To stress either to the exclusion of the other can lead only to unsound judgments. For example, it is equally erroneous to say either that Soviet expansion is something entirely new or that it is merely a prolongation of something done by the tsars. There are elements both old and new in Soviet expansion and in Soviet society.

Four special problems arise in studying the history of Russia and of the U.S.S.R. The first is the relative unfamiliarity of the story. More explanatory asides are necessary than would be the case if we were retreading familiar ground. On the other hand, the reader has the right to expect mature interpretations as well as elementary explanations. Since there isn't room for both, there must be a continuous series of compromises which do not fully satisfy either demand. I wish to state explicitly at this point that I have written for the general reader and not for the professional specialist in Russian history.

The second problem springs from the necessity of changing the Russian alphabet into English. I have tried to use Russian words sparingly. Sometimes either there is no exact English equivalent or it requires a whole string of English words to convey the meaning of one Russian term. In such cases, on the assumption that you would prefer to read (for example) *barshchina* rather than "work done by a serf for his master, or a sort of rent paid in labor," I have used the Russian word, accompanied at its first appearance by an explanation or translation. However, there is no uniformly accepted system of transliteration so that one often finds various spellings of the same word as, for example, in the name of a certain type of city assembly which appears as *vieche, veche,* and *vyeche.* Some such variations will appear in this book, both in quoted passages and in my own work. However they are spelled, if you pronounce the words to yourself as you read, they will soon become familiar acquaintances.

The third difficulty, relatively minor, occurs because the Russians continued until 1918 to use the Julian calendar whereas the West changed to the Gregorian calendar in the sixteenth and seventeenth centuries. The Julian (Old Style) calendar was eleven days behind the Gregorian (New Style) calendar in the eighteenth century; twelve days behind it in the nineteenth century; and thirteen days behind in the twentieth century. This is why what we call the March Revolution is known to the Soviets as the February Revolution. According to the calendar then in use in Russia, the revolution began in late February. By our calendar, the revolution began in early March. Similarly, the Soviets date the Bolshevik Revolution as beginning in October while we place it in November. There is no problem after 1918, of course, and none in the first part of the history. The difficulty arises when dealing with the late nineteenth and early twentieth centuries. It will be met by giving both dates in this manner: February 27/March 9, 1917.

Much more serious, especially in connection with the Soviet period, is the fourth problem—bias and prejudice. My convictions and prejudices—probably including some of which I am not conscious—will be apparent to you. I have tried to be fair and honest, and, although I have not hidden my preferences, I have tried not to obtrude them unreasonably. But in some matters I am neither neutral nor indifferent. I have an implacable antipathy toward those who deny men the right of free inquiry. I hold enserfment and slavery to be moral wrongs which debase both masters and men. I am convinced that the philosophy of ends justifying means is an unmitigated evil which can lead only to greater evils. I unreservedly prefer what is loosely called "the American way" to either "the Russian way" or "the Soviet way."

This history, like all general histories, is a synthesis of many sources. Some of it records the results of my own researches, but much of it rests upon the work of others. I have been taught by many men of widely varying views. I am presenting here what seems to me to be sound and worthy, knowing all the while that another might have chosen differently. As for those materials which I should have seen and used but didn't, I can only paraphrase Dr. Johnson's rejoinder to a critic. The error is due only to my ignorance.

Warren B. Walsh

January 12, 1958

Contents

MAPS

RUSSIA AND THE SOVIET UNION

A Modern History

CHAPTER I

The Wedge and the Pool

The Russian Empire at the time of its greatest extent claimed an area which stretched from the eastern border of Prussia to the coast of California, or considerably more than halfway around the globe. The Union of Soviet Socialist Republics is less extensive, east to west, but its north-south extent is somewhat greater than that of the empire. Sixteen per cent of the total land area of the earth, exclusive of the regions covered by icecaps, lies within the Soviet borders. Three times as big as the continental United States, the Soviet Union is a veritable giant compared to the countries of western Europe: forty times the size of France, one hundred and eighty times the size of England.

These overall measurements are, however, rather misleading. Only about one million of the eight and one-half million square miles of Soviet territory are good farm land. Almost a quarter of the country is north of the Arctic Circle, and a sixth of it lies within the frigid zone. Much of the rest is too dry or too infertile or too inaccessible to be of much use to many people.

THE WEDGE

The part which historically has been the most important and is still the most populous is an area whose general shape is that of a blunt wedge. You can readily trace its rough outlines on a map. Place your finger on Leningrad and run it down the map (that is, south) to Odessa. Now move it diagonally up and to the right until you touch the southern Urals; then, straight up a short distance and, thence, back to Leningrad. Geographers will point out that the thin end of the wedge actually extends eastward beyond the Urals to Lake Baikal. This is true, but though some interesting and important events have taken place east of the Urals, most of the action has been to the west of them.

Compared to the United States, this wedge is a northerly land.

Odessa and Rostov along the southern side of the wedge are as far north, respectively, as Quebec and Seattle. Stalingrad, of World War II fame, is in the same latitude as the capital of Newfoundland. Moscow, more or less in the center of the wedge, is roughly as far north of Washington, D.C., as Washington is north of Miami. And Leningrad lies on the same parallel of latitude as Seward, Alaska. In these last two cities, the longest day in the year lasts almost nineteen hours; the shortest, less than six.

Weather conditions vary markedly from north to south. The Leningrad-Moscow region benefits from the warm winds which blow off the Atlantic Ocean. These bring the summer rains, which make this one of the best-watered sections, and in winter they exercise a moderating effect upon the temperature. Nevertheless, both Moscow and Leningrad expect six to eight weeks during the winter when the temperature is below fourteen degrees Fahrenheit. Snow cover lasts from four to five months with a mean depth of two to three feet. The mean daily temperature does not rise above freezing until early April. About the same conditions obtain at Stalingrad, which is south of Moscow but distant from the Atlantic winds. Odessa and Rostov enjoy much milder climates. They get only a week or two of cold below the fourteen-degree mark, and spring there is expected in January. Snowfall is light, although it may last a month or two. On the other hand, they receive appreciably less rain than the Leningrad-Moscow region. The average rainfall over the wedge is only twenty inches, or less than half the average for New York City. By and large, the people who live in the wedge must put up with both cold and dryness. Their basic social norms of clothing, diet, and housing reflect this fact.

🐟 SOIL AND VEGETATION ZONES

There are within the Soviet Union six distinct zones marked by differences in soils and vegetation. These run across the land, forming strips or belts of varying width. Map makers have to show them set off by distinct lines, but, of course, they really blend one into another. Only three of these zones fall within the wedge. They have been variously labeled, and any choice of names is largely arbitrary. We shall call them, from north to south: the forest zone, the forest steppe, and the feather-grass steppe. Forest lands have always been very important to the people of Russia. They have served as hiding places from invaders and from native rulers. They have provided building materials and fuels to combat the cold. Men have fed upon their game, used the skins and furs for clothing, and feasted upon the wild honey. Furs and honey, together with lumber and other forest products, have been major items of trade from the earliest times. Men have, in fact, drawn upon this treasure house from times unrecorded and in so doing have reduced its wealth. About half the original forest lands have been cut and cleared during the centuries. Kiev today, for example, is in an almost treeless area. But it owed its original settlement and early prosperity partly to its once extensive forests.

The northern forests are mostly spruce, fir, pine, and larch; that is, evergreens or conifers. The soils in this section (called gray by the Russians) are thin, rather acid, and relatively infertile. The technical name for them is podsol. As one goes south, the conifers begin to thin out. Deciduous trees—birches, maples, elms, lindens, and oaks—gradually appear, grow more thickly, and finally replace the conifers. These soils are still thin, but they are somewhat more fertile. Moreover, they have the great advantage of being comparatively well watered. But the most fertile lands are those to the south. Little by little the trees begin to disappear. They no longer form forests but become groves with larger and larger open spaces between, until finally the trees entirely disappear. This is the great steppe where the feather grasses grow. Here are the extremely fertile black soils (*chernozem*) which are comparable to the richest farm lands of the American Middle West. But against the richness of the earth, slightly alkaline and heavy with humus, must be set the frequent lack of moisture. When the snowfall is heavy and the rains adequate, this black-earth belt is a bountiful producer. When, as often happens, the rains do not come and the snowfall is light, then crops fail, and hunger or even famine stalks the land.

⊕ UPLANDS AND RIVERS

The lands within the wedge are generally level or rolling. One of the very important features of the landscape is a relatively narrow strip of uplands and hills which runs roughly north and south across the plains. Actually, it begins on the Arctic shore in the region of Murmansk. The portion of it most important to us starts farther south at a spot about two hundred miles northwest of Moscow and the same distance southeast of Leningrad, but slightly to the west of a straight line between the two. Here, in the space of a hundred square miles, are the Valdai Hills. The highest of them is just over a thousand feet. Running south and slightly east of them is the Smolensk-Moscow Ridge. This continues in the same direction but acquires a new name, the Central Russian Upland. The highlands end in the Donets Ridge some distance north of the Sea of Azov. The importance of these uplands is that they form the watersheds of the great plain. From their waterlogged grounds spring the major rivers. The small area of the Valdai Hills is the birthplace of such important rivers as the Western Dvina, which flows to the Baltic; the great Dnieper, which runs to the Black Sea; and the mighty Volga, which empties into the Caspian Sea. Lesser rivers—some independent, such as the Lovat, and others, tributaries to the larger streams—arise within these elevated lands. The closeness of their sources has made portages easy and has facilitated the linkage of rivers by canals. Because of this, men have been able to travel, by river and portage, across the vast plains and through the pathless forests. Historically, the power that held the Valdai Hills controlled the great routes of trade and travel. The successive states of Kiev, Novgorod, and Muscovy were erected partly on this foundation.

Rivers were of great significance in Russian history. We who live in long-settled, thickly inhabited regions, with their thousands of streets and hundreds of connecting roads, have to make a conscious effort to imagine a land where, even today, there are almost no roads. The straight-line distance from Leningrad to Moscow is four hundred miles; from Moscow to Odessa, over eight hundred. The western side of the wedge is more than a thousand miles long. This is only a matter of minutes to a jet plane, but it is a long horseback ride and a longer walk. Distance was itself a significant barrier.

The southern grasslands offered a relatively easy highway and often served both invaders and migrants. But the heat and dryness in summer are obstacles to travel, and the spring rains turn the land into quagmires. North of the steppe, huge areas of swamp and marsh form almost impassable barriers. Travel through real forests is never swift nor easy. The only ways across much of this land were the waterways. Even where other highways existed, the water roads were usually the best. In the grasslands, they supplied water for men and animals; through the forests, they were the open roads. River travel was not without limitations and difficulties of its own. The rivers are long. They meander in great loops and turns. Sometimes the river route is two or three times as long as a straight-line distance from source to mouth. They are also slow-moving since, except in a few places, the fall from source to mouth is relatively slight. Almost all of them flood every spring, some of the floods spreading out as much as thirty miles from the normal river bed. The additional moisture brought by the floods is beneficial in a dry land. Some sections are also benefited by the deposits of silt, but others are injured by the scouring action of the flood water, which causes erosion. The floods subside as the season changes until, in the dry summer, navigation becomes difficult on most of the rivers and impossible upon some. A few dry up almost completely.

Because of the geology of the land, the right banks of the rivers (which are usually the western banks) are high and steep; the left banks, low. The spring floods submerge the left banks and drown the lands beyond for some distance. This will explain why the towns which grew up along the river trade routes were usually on the right banks. These elevations gave protection both against the recurrent high waters and against marauders from the east. These early settlements, largely made by traders, were often at the juncture of two streams. Nizhni-Novgorod (now Gorki) is an excellent example. It was built at the junction of the Oka and Volga rivers. Moscow illustrates another type of site, one chosen primarily for its defensibility. The city began some eight hundred years ago as a fortified or palisaded camp located on a bluff above the River Moskva (Moscow). The Kremlin now covers this spot. Kiev, its name probably derived from the words *kui ev* meaning "settlement on a river bank," also began as a fortified settlement, on a steep bluff which rises some three hundred feet above the Dnieper River.

🜚 THE POOL

Picture, if you will, a broad but shallow pool shut off from the great waters by a low sand bar. Waves from the great waters constantly lap at the bar. Great waves, created by some disturbance in the larger body of water, wash over the bar into the pool. The force of these invaders disturbs the pool. Very large waves displace some of the water in the pool, driving it onto or even across the bar. The power of the moving water changes the shores of the pool and alters the contour of its bottom. Each incoming wave carries some flotsam and jetsam across the bar and adds it to what was already in the pool. The new waters mingle and mix with the old. Always changing, always different, it nonetheless remains the same pool.

The imagery is obvious. It is also reasonably accurate. The pool represents the peoples whom we find upon the lands of the wedge. The waves are the numerous invasions into and across the wedge. We shall not try to label and describe every wave. Only the most powerful and most significant of the waves need be named. And we shall be less interested in the waves themselves than in the changes they wrought in the pool.

No one knows what peoples made up the pool at the beginning. About all we know of the earliest times is that men first formed a pool in the lands of the wedge some hundred thousand years ago. So far as the archaeologists can tell, the pool has been in continuous existence ever since. Five thousand years ago the lands of the wedge were widely, though sparsely, settled.

⊕ THE SCYTHIANS, SLAVS, AND TURKIC NOMADS

It was from the ancient Greeks that the West got its first recorded information about the pool. The Greeks, who had trading and other connections with the northern coast of the Black Sea, called the people whom they found there Scythians. The name passed into the Western historical tradition and it was long supposed that the Scythians were a single tribe or nation. This was an oversimplification. The Scythians were apparently only a ruling minority; a conquering people who appeared in southern Russia about the seventh century before Christ, and who dominated the land for about five hundred years. Their subjects, if that is the proper term for them, were divided into at least two major groups.

Those who lived west of the Dnieper River were a sedentary and agricultural people of Slavic stock. The Slavs' homeland was apparently an oblong area which lay partly to the west of the wedge but extended well into it. Lying to the northeast of the Carpathian Mountains, and running from the Vistula to the Dnieper, its northern limit was along the Pripet. In the south, it touched the Pruth, the Bug, and the Dniester rivers. The people who occupied this area were known to the West as Veneti, Venedi, or Wends. The name "Slav" was not used at that time. The Slavs were hemmed in by natural obstacles and powerful neighbors. The chief natural barrier was the Carpathian Mountains to the south. The human barriers were the Germanic tribes along the line of the Vistula and, in the east, the Scythian rulers. Boxed in as they were by man and nature, the Slavs remained relatively stable until the Christian Era.

The other major group under Scythian dominion lived east of the Dnieper River. They were probably nomadic peoples of Turkic stock. Peoples of Turkic stocks long played an extremely important part in the story of the Russian lands. They formed a part of the pool, as the West first knew it, and later waves of them included the Huns, the Avars, the Bulgars, and the Khazars in the early period; the Pechenegs, the Kipchaks, and the Tatars in a later time. It is also probable that the Finno-Ugric nomads, whom the Slavs found settled in the northern section of the wedge, were of the same general stock.

The oldest account we have of the people who lived on the steppes between the Volga and the Urals is in Arabic. This gives the name Badjanakia to these people. Greek texts of a much later date speak of a people who lived in that region as Patzinaks. Other sources call them Pechenegs. Were they one people or several? We don't know. Badjanakia may have derived from the the Turkish *badjanak* which means "brother-in-law," and might imply that these were allied peoples. Latin writers referred to a people who lived on the southern borders of Russia about the eleventh century as Cumani, or Comani, or Kumani. The Greek version was Komanoi. From these came the name Cumans, which has been generally used in the West. But Slavic sources of that time and later called these same people Polovtsi, which probably meant "people of the steppes" and may have been simply a Russian translation of the Turkish word *kipchak*. Some scholars believe this to be what these people called themselves and hold, therefore, that it is a more accurate name than either Cuman or Polovtsi.

Many of the peoples of the pool and many of the waves which washed into the pool were of Asiatic origin. All these peoples at some stage in their history were nomads who were attracted by the wealth and resources of the grasslands. Some of them settled down. Between these sedentary peoples and the nomads there was an almost continuous struggle. Repeatedly, the latter swept across the grasslands, destroying or driving out the sedentary peoples. Then the marauders settled down in their turn, associating themselves with whatever had escaped their savagery. A later sweep struck them and the process was repeated.

The Scythians were probably just such an Asiatic invader who were able to establish dominion over their distant kinsfolk east of the Dnieper and over the Slavs to the west of it. The civilization which they built was essentially commercial. They maintained fortified trading posts in the area later called Kiev, and had extensive commercial contacts with the Greek trading cities along the Black Sea. Then, after centuries of prosperity, the Scythian power was broken or replaced by a new conqueror from the east, the Sarmatians, who dominated the lands for about five centuries, beginning in the second century before Christ.

THE GOTHS

Another wave, this time from the west, washed into the pool and gradually displaced the Sarmatian power. The Goths, a Germanic tribe familiar in early west European history, moved into the basins of the Bug and Dniester rivers about the second century A.D. There they remained as masters until driven out by the Asiatic Huns in A.D. 370. The Goths were never numerous. They formed only a small ruling class, but linguistic evidence shows that they had tremendous influence on the Slavs.

This evidence consists of the number of Slavic words which were borrowed or adapted from the Gothic language. The assumption is that the Goths either introduced the things or customs named, or altered existing ones. In the first case, the Slavs had no word of their own to describe the innovation and therefore had to borrow the word as well as the object or custom. In the second case, the Slavic way was submerged or modified by the Gothic, and the label was accordingly changed. Among the borrowings were the words (and presumably the items for which the words stood) for *helmet, armor,* and *sword; debt, purse,* and *to buy; plow, garden,* and *vineyard;* and, also, *doctor* and *scribe.*

Extensive finds of Roman coins of the second and third centuries A.D. show that the Goths not only maintained the old trade relations with the West but also extended them. This is corroborated by another bit of evidence. The Slavic measure *chetverik* is exactly equal to the Roman measure *quadrantalis* (6.9 U.S. gallons); and the Slavic measure *polosmina* is the same as the old Roman *medimnos* (13.8 U.S. gallons). The trade which this evidence indicates did not, however, survive the Hunnic invasions. There was very little commercial contact between these southern Russian lands and the West during the period from the fifth to the eighth centuries (A.D.). This was the period of the dispersion of the Slavs.

🐚 SLAV MIGRATIONS

The great Slavic migrations were slow and ponderous rather than swift and sudden. The waters of the pool rose gradually and flowed over the banks in all directions. Only after the banks were thoroughly broken down did the seepage grow into floods. Sometime early in the Christian Era, the Slavs trickled into the Danube Basin. By the sixth century (A.D.) they were well established there and had begun to move on into the Balkans. Within a century or a little more, they became the most numerous people in that region. But they were not the most powerful, at least in the cultural sense. Those who settled in the western Balkans came under very strong Latin influences; those in the eastern portion, under Byzantine influences. Traces of both these influences are still perceivable in the present-day Yugoslavs, who are the descendants of these early migrants.

The Slavic movement toward the west and northwest began not later than the second century (A.D.) and may have started before that. But the big wave did not come until the early sixth century when the Slavs occupied the lands as far west as the Elbe and Oder rivers. These people were the forerunners of the western Slavs whom we know as the Poles, Czechs, and Slovaks. The Poles and Czechs came under Latin and German cultural dominion; the Slovaks, under Magyar influence. The differences among these early cultural influences partly explain the present variations among these Slavic peoples.

The Slavic migration east must have been in many ways the easiest. The Dnieper, which had been the boundary of the original Slav homeland, did not present much of a physical barrier. When the lands to the east of that river were no longer dominated by strong peoples, the river itself and the network of water roads with which it connected facilitated migration. Moreover, the native peoples of the northern and central portions of the wedge offered little effective resistance. They were few in number and nomadic or seminomadic in habits. Known as the Finno-Ugrians, they were probably of Mongoloid origin (their present descend-

Early Peoples — 2ⁿᵈ to 7ᵗʰ centuries

ants include the Estonians and the Finns). Finno-Ugric culture was more primitive than that of the invading Slavs and was largely submerged by the latter.

By the ninth century (A.D.) these Slavic invaders had scattered over the western half of the wedge. Their area stretched roughly from Lake Ladoga south to the Dniester River and the Black Sea, and eastward to the river Don. They were at this time divided into many tribes in various stages of cultural development. On the basis of their language, they formed three divisions: the northern group, which was the forerunner of the Great Russians; the central group, which eventually split with its eastern members, joining the Great Russians and its western ones, becoming Bielorussians; [1] and the southern group, which evolved into the Malorussians or Ukrainians.

ⓖ NORMS AND VALUES: EASTERN SLAVS

The social norms and values of the eastern Slavs, who came to occupy most of the lands of the wedge, varied considerably among the several tribes. We shall pay much more attention to tangible norms, such as ways of earning a living, than to intangible norms. This is certainly not because the latter are less important. It is because of ignorance. You can dig up pottery and weapons and excavate sites of ancient villages, but you cannot, literally, unearth customs or habits of thought. Most of the eastern Slavs lived in settled communities. Some of these were tiny hamlets, but some, formed by a federation of adjacent villages, attained considerable size. The social organization also varied in relation to both time and place. The tribes along the middle Dnieper, for example, abandoned the patriarchal clan with its blood ties and developed territorial communes long before the tribes along the upper Oka did so. Land tenure in the older communities was usually communal.

Along the frontiers there developed isolated settlements which bore some external resemblance to similar outposts in the early history of the United States. There was perhaps more individualism in the frontier settlements than in the settled lands to the west. Hunting and trapping, the livelihood of the forest peoples, are solitary occupations which require individual enterprise. Property was generally regarded as belonging, if not to an individual, at least to a family rather than to the whole community. As settlement caught up with the old frontiers, and as the small stockades, built originally as places of refuge and defense, developed into centers of trade and community life, these frontier norms and values changed, at least in the steppe zones.

The economic mainstay of the feather-grass steppe was farming. This was also the major occupation of dwellers in the forest steppe, although they probably supplemented it by hunting and by tapping the other resources of the forest. Trade was also an integral part of their economy. There was almost always some trade going on, although it must have been subject to frequent interruptions due to wars and migrations.

Farming, which is hard work even with the most modern tools and up-to-date techniques, must have been a back-breaking task with little sure return. It is a curious comment on human stubbornness that Russia has always been a land of farmers, despite the fact that most of the land is not very well suited to agriculture. The tools and the techniques of these early Slavic farmers were extremely primitive. Their ordinary plow, for example, was a rough "Y" formed by the branching of a tree. One limb, cut short and sharpened, was the plowshare. The contraption was guided by a man holding the tail of the Y, and pulled by men or beasts attached to the longer limb. It could do little more than scratch the surface of the ground. In the forest steppe, lands were cleared partly by cutting but mostly by burning. This method temporarily fertilized the soil, and when it was no longer arable the land was abandoned and the process repeated. On the more fertile lands of the open steppe, the so-called two-field or three-field systems were often used. The two-field system is a division of land in half, with each half alternately growing crops and lying idle. In the three-field system the arable land is divided into thirds, which are rotated on the pattern of two years of crops followed by one year of idleness. An inefficient system by modern standards, it has served to feed hundreds of millions of people who knew nothing either of crop rotation or of soil fertilization.

Crop yields were low in terms of the amount of land used and the labor expended on it, and this remained true of Russian farming for a thousand years or more. The variety of crops was considerable. Of the small grains, barley, wheat, rye, oats, and millet were commonly grown for food. Flax and hemp were raised for their fibers, which were used in making cloth and cordage. Beets and beans were among the most common and important vegetables, and the fruits included apples, pears, cherries, and some others. Horses were raised for hunting, war, and transportation; cattle, for meat, hides, and tallow; sheep, for food and clothing; swine and the familiar domestic fowl—ducks, hens, and geese —for food.

These farm products were supplemented by forest products. Wild animals provided food, furs, and hides. Wild bees supplied honey, which was used directly as a food or as the base of a fermented drink, and beeswax. The forests also furnished wood for buildings, boats, and fuel; and supplied other products from their gums and resins. The rivers, lakes, ponds, and inland seas provided fish.

Manufacturing existed only in its literal and now obsolete meaning of making by hand. The spinning and weaving of cloth, both woolen and linen, were common household crafts. Pottery and metalworking were also fairly common techniques. Gold, silver, lead, and iron were known and used quite early—the first two for adornment, the second two for weapons and implements. Some tribes had developed skill in making fairly large boats by hollowing out the trunks of big trees. But carpentry was still in a crude stage. The earliest houses were dugouts which were roofed with earth-covered logs. These were later modified in some sections by the addition of half walls so that the structures were raised a little above the surrounding ground. Rude log cabins were built sometime later in the forest and forest-steppe zones.

Primitive Slav society did not possess that classless equality which used to be thought the distinguishing characteristic of such groups. But neither was it divided exclusively between slaves and masters. There were slaves, perhaps in some numbers. Many of them were probably prisoners of wars or raids, but slave trading was apparently an ancient habit, and became an important source of wealth. At the other end of the social scale was an ill-defined aristocracy. Between the two, and probably merging with them on both sides, was a fairly large class of freemen. There is no precise information about either the size or the make-up of these three classes. Similarly, we know in general that polygamy and concubinage were common and that the religion of these people was chiefly but not exclusively animistic and anthropomorphic. Beyond these generalizations, it is difficult to go with any certainty.

CHAPTER II

Trade and Politics:
The First Rus States

🌐 SOURCES OF RUSSIAN HISTORY: THE CHRONICLES

The earliest native Russian written sources are the medieval annals, and the oldest of these is an account of the years from the middle of the ninth century to the second decade of the twelfth. This account was long thought to have been written by a monk named Nestor, from whom it derived the name *The Chronicle of Nestor.* Modern scholarship has shown it to be a compilation of earlier sources plus some firsthand information added by the compiler. The work may have been done by several men, though some scholars now believe it the work of an individual, probably of the monk Sylvester. All that is certain, however, is that the material was put into the form which we know about 1113. The work is now generally called either *The Primary Chronicle,* or *The Tale of Bygone Years,* the title which appears at the head of the traditional text.

Two early versions of *The Tale of Bygone Years* have come down to us—both copies of manuscripts which have not survived. The older version is known as the Laurentian text, from the name of the monk Lawrence, who copied it in 1377. The *Tale* is followed in the Laurentian text by annals of the Rostov and Suzdal areas to the year 1305. The other version is called the Hypatian or the Ipatsky, after the name of the monastery where it was found. It dates from the mid-fifteenth century. In it, the *Tale* is followed by a detailed account of Kiev in the twelfth century and by a south Russian chronicle covering the thirteenth century.

Although Peter the Great ordered all texts of the chronicles to be collected and copied in 1722, and, although some parts of them were published in the eighteenth century, no critical study of them was made until the following century. The first English translation of *The Tale of*

Bygone Years was published by the late Professor S. H. Cross in 1930.[1] It is this translation from which the quotations in this book are taken.

Annals were also kept in places other than Kiev. Some of these appear to have been preserved in full. Others survive only as quotations in later works. The most important of these other annals is *The Chronicle of Novgorod,* which records happenings from the early eleventh to late fifteenth centuries. This is also available in an English translation.[2]

All the chronicles are mosaics of different materials. *The Tale of Bygone Years* contains some material taken from a Byzantine chronicle of the ninth century and another of the tenth. It also includes some biblical history from an unidentified source or sources, perhaps some items from Khazar records, and certainly some material which had been preserved as oral traditions. To all these were added information taken from biographies of various saints and, of course, the experiences of the annalists themselves. Modern scholars have identified some of these pieces, but not all of them. Historians supplement what they find in the chronicles by information gleaned from non-Russian sources such as Arabic records and Scandinavian sagas. The Russian annals, especially *The Primary Chronicle,* remain basic to the study of early Russian history. Though we no longer accept its version of the Russian beginnings, we do accept the following entry and attach considerable significance to it:

> When the Polyanians lived by themselves among the hills, a trade-route connected the Varangians with the Greeks. Starting from Greece, this route proceeds along the Dnieper, above which a portage leads to the Lovat. By following the Lovat, the great Lake Ilmen is reached. The river Volkhov flows out of this lake and enters the great lake Nevo. The mouth of this lake opens into the Varangian Sea. Over this sea goes the route to Rome, and on from Rome overseas to Tsargrad [Constantinople]. The Pontus, into which flows the river Dnieper itself rises in the upland forest, and flows southward. The Dvina has its source in this same forest, but flows northward and empties into the Varangian Sea [Baltic Sea]. The Volga rises in this same forest, but flows to the east, and discharges through seventeen mouths into the Caspian Sea. It is possible by this route to the eastward to reach the Bulgars and the Caspians, and thus attain the region of Shem [the eastern regions, according to the ancient legend]. Along the Dvina runs the route to the Varangians, whence one may reach Rome, and go on from there to the race of Ham [according to the legend, the southern region]. But the Dnieper flows through various mouths into the Pontus. This sea, beside which taught St. Andres, Peter's brother, is called the Russian Sea.

🐾 ALIEN IMPACTS

It is appropriate and interesting that this account of the trade routes should stand near the beginning of *The Primary Chronicle.* The unknown chroniclers clearly recognized the significance of the routes and the men who used them.

Three things were happening outside of the Russian lands which vitally affected events within those lands. The first of these was the rise, in the middle of the seventh century, of the Arabian Empire. This created a new "Great Power" just as did the rise of the German and Japanese empires in the nineteenth and twentieth centuries and the rise of Soviet power in our time. The old balance was upset. New alliances and alignments had to be made. Old enmities faded as new clashes took place. The shift in power started new migrations and conquests. It also reopened old trade routes and opened new ones.

The second non-Slavic event was the emergence in the eighth century of Constantinople as the richest, most powerful, and most important city in Europe. This pre-eminence was retained for five hundred years or more. During this time, Constantinople was to Europe what New York is today to the United States: the seat of financial power, the focal center of commerce, the leader in style and fashion. It was also what New York is not, the center of an extensive religious movement and the home of a religious leadership whose influence, if not authority, was steadily expanded.

The third non-Russian happening was the westward drive in the sixth century of conquering peoples from Turkestan. One of the regions which they conquered was the northern Caucasus, where they mastered the many native tribes. For a brief time this great Turkic Empire formed a single unit, but it soon divided into an eastern and a western part, with the western section inferior to the eastern. Apparently there had been, among the native Caucasian tribes who were conquered by these Turks, one particularly vigorous or lucky group, the Khazars. They seem to have joined their conquerors, at least at first, and then, eventually, to have made good on their own. At any rate, the name Khazar or Khazaria came to be applied to what had been the western portion of the Turkic Empire.

☙ KHAZARS AND SLAVS

Operating out of their homeland, the Khazars slowly expanded their power. Neighboring tribes were either forced to become tributaries or allowed to become allies. The Slavic tribes of southern Russia became tributaries to the Khazars, and were dominated by them for about two centuries. Since Khazar culture was relatively advanced, it left a considerable mark on Slavic life. For one thing, the Khazars were traders as well as conquerors. In fact, the existence of trade between northern Russia and Byzantium (Constantinople) and Persia—a trade that had been greatly stimulated by the rise of the Arab Empire—was probably the main attraction which drew the Khazars into southern Russia. They established new military and trading bases in this area, or developed the existing Slavic settlements, such as Kiev, to serve their purposes. And they dominated the trade routes to their considerable profit. They were, so to speak, the keepers of the bridge between the Arabs and the Byzantines, and the north. Skillfully and successfully, they collected toll. In protecting these trading interests, the Khazars also protected the Slavs, some of whom shared in the trade and its profits.

Some of the garrisons grew into trading towns and fortresses of note. The most successful of them gradually extended their power over the surrounding countryside and so developed into town-provinces. (The hyphenated name signifies that the town was the center of power and that the area of its effective control was regional.) At least in their beginnings and probably for some time thereafter, these town-provinces were still subordinate to the Khazars and dependent upon them for protection. But many conflicts with the Arabs, and the incursions of a new Turko-Tataric invader (the Pechenegs or Patzinaks) sapped the strength of Khazaria. It had one last triumph before it faded, but after the middle of the ninth century the town-provinces were increasingly on their own. Meanwhile—this time from the north—the Varangians appeared with increasing frequency and force.

THE VARANGIAN-SWEDES

The Varangians, generically speaking, were the Scandinavian marauders and invaders who are famous in west European history as the Vikings or Normans. They were Swedes, and we may properly use for them the hyphenated name which preserves their traditional label but adds the more accurate characterization. The Varangian-Swedes began to establish themselves along the southern coasts of the Gulf of Riga in the sixth century—at about the time the eastern Slavs were beginning to colonize the northern and central areas of the wedge and the invaders from Turkestan were conquering the northern Caucasus. The Varangian-Swedes found the native Finno-Ugric and other Baltic peoples no harder to conquer than did the Slavs. In fact, in many ways the Varangian-Swedish cultural stage was superior not only to that of the Finno-Ugrians but also to that of the eastern Slavs.

When the Varangian-Swedes entered the Russian lands they were already skilled craftsmen. They regularly built timbered houses in contrast to the ruder dwellings of the Slavs. They also built boats up to fifty feet long and capable of carrying fifty tons of cargo. Their metalwork, particularly the fabrication of weapons, was superior.

Sometime in the seventh century, probably toward the end of it, the Varangian-Swedes began to ascend the Western Dvina, which leads toward the center of the Russian wedge. This movement more or less coincided with the rise of the Arab Empire far to the south; with the early expansion of Khazaria; and with the settlement of the city and area of Novgorod by the Slavs. The Varangian-Swedes had little trouble mastering the native peoples, but when they reached the Slav settlements around Novgorod, they by-passed them and pushed on by portage to the Dnieper. They found this to be blocked by strong Lithuanian and Slav tribes, so they swung northeast toward the upper Volga. But passage down the Volga was also barred by the power of the Bulgars.

The persistent Varangian-Swedes then sought another way and, traveling by small streams and portages, reached the Oka west of its junction with the Volga. It was now about the beginning of the eighth century. The leadership of Constantinople was established and so was the power of the Khazars over the southern Russian lands along the Dnieper. The Varangian-Swedes, moving from the Oka, pushed overland to the rivers Don and Donets. Here they were opposed by the Magyars, but this time they fought it out and gained control of these waterways, which led them to the Sea of Azov. They first reached there about the middle of the eighth century. One of the most recent and best-informed scholarly guesses is that the Varangian-Swedes then mastered the native tribes, the As and the Rus, and adopted the latter's name, setting up a Rus (sian) state early in the ninth century.

Some years after the creation of this Russian state in the Azov area, other Varangian-Swedes conquered the northern Slavs. The ancient chroniclers put it less bluntly: "The Varangians from beyond the sea imposed tribute. . . ." The date now usually given for this conquest is 859. Presumably, these northern conquerors kept close touch through trade and migrations with their kinsmen of the Russian state to the south. Then the Khazars, on the eve of their decline, created a whole series of crises for the Varangian-Swedes by cutting the routes which connected the northern and southern groups.

🐦 THE "COMING OF THE VARANGIANS"

The Russian state in the south suffered a serious decline. The northerners were hurt by the stoppage of trade and by their isolation from their southern kinsmen. But perhaps the most serious problem was caused by the continuing immigration of Varangian-Swedes into the Novgorod area. Finding their way to the south blocked, these newcomers entered into fierce and often violent competition with their established kinsmen. Disorders became extensive as a result of this population pressure. It became absolutely essential to relieve the pressure by reopening the route to the south. Presumably the Novgorod group found that they were unable to do this by themselves and therefore sought the aid of others. This, at least, is one of the most plausible guesses concerning "the coming of the Varangians." *The Primary Chronicle* relates the event in these words:

6368–6370 (860–862). The tributaries of the Varangians drove them back beyond the sea and, refusing them further tribute, set out to govern themselves. There was no law among them, but tribe rose against tribe. Discord thus ensued amongst them, and they began to war against one another. They said to themselves: 'Let us seek a prince who may rule over us, and judge us according to the law.' They accordingly went overseas to the Varangian Russes: these particular Varangians were known as Russes, just as some are called Swedes, and others Normans, Angles, and Goths, for they were thus named. The Chuds, the Slavs, and the Krivichians then said to the people of Rus: 'Our whole land is great and rich, but there is no order in it. Come to rule and reign over us.' They thus selected three brothers, with their kinsfolk, who took with them all the Russes and migrated. The oldest, Rurik, located himself in Novgorod; the second, Sineus, in Byeloozero; and the third, Truvor, in Izborsk. On account of these Varangians, the district of Novgorod became known as the land of Rus. The present inhabitants of Novgorod are descended from the Varangian race, but aforetime they were Slavs.

There were Varangian-Swedes in the Russian lands, not only at Novgorod but also in the Azov region, long before the time set by the legend.[3] There were also organized states in Russia both before the legendary "coming of the Varangians" and even before the actual immigration of the Varangian-Swedes. We also know that there was a Varangian or Viking chieftain named Rurik, famed and feared in the West as a marauder. Sometime in the latter part of the ninth century, Rurik made himself master of Jutland and thus became one of the major powers of the Baltic region. But as far as we know, he had no brothers or associates named Sineus or Truvor.

The northern or Novgorod Slavs, using that as a general geographic rather than as a precise tribal or political designation, hired Rurik to restore domestic order and to lead an expedition against the Khazars for the purpose of reopening the trade route to the south. Rurik took the job and brought his full force to accomplish it. Sometime after his arrival he discovered that he could usurp authority within Novgorod. He did so. Some of his followers he placed in control elsewhere. Rurik ruled Novgorod until his death (873?). Before that time, two members of his retinue, Oskold and Dir, left Rurik's service and made their way down the Dnieper River en route to Tsargrad (Constantinople):

. . . and in the course of their journey they saw a small city on a hill. Upon inquiry as to whose town it was, they were informed that three brothers, Kii, Shchek, and Khoriv, had once built the city, but that since their deaths, their descendants were living there as tributaries of the Khazars.

The two Varangians overcame the rulers and made themselves masters of this city, called Kiev, and, shortly thereafter, of the region. ". . . they established their domination over the country," states *The Primary Chronicle,* "at the same time that Rurik was ruling at Novgorod."

After Rurik's death, power in Novgorod passed to Oleg the Norwegian, whom the annalist speaks of as Rurik's heir. If he was, he had to win his heritage from other aspirants by force. Conquering the cities of Smolensk and Lyubech, he descended upon Kiev. Oskold and Dir fell into a trap which he laid for them and were killed. Oleg then proclaimed himself prince of Kiev and proclaimed Kiev to be "the mother of Russian cities." From his base in Kiev, Oleg then conquered a number of the Slavic tribes and forced them to pay tribute to him. The road from the Varangians to the Greeks thus came under his control.

🐚 KIEVAN RUS

We have again run a little ahead of our story. The reply of the natives to Oskold and Dir very compactly summarized a great deal of history. The city of Kiev, they said, had been built by three brothers. This is a typical medieval legend. It is probably accurate in essence but inaccurate in details. We have noted before that Kiev was on a high bluff above the Dnieper River. The site, a little way below the junction of the Dnieper and the Desna rivers, was originally in the forest steppe. There were sufficient open lands to support some farming, and the forest provided additional resources to sustain life and trade. The river was the highway to the world. We do not know who the original settlers were, but it is entirely likely that the settlement was very early taken over by Slavs even if they were not the founders. One school of thought traces the name Kiev to the man Kii, spoken of by the chronicler. Professor Cross believed that the name was a derivation from the words *kui ev,* and that this label (settlement on the riverbank) was applied by the Khazars. In either case, the settlement may be assumed to have existed before the Khazars made it their tributary.

Skilled and lucky leaders—Khazars or Slavs or both—successfully exploited the favorable location to make Kiev the strongest and richest town on that part of the great trade route. But its prosperity had a price. It attracted Oskold, Dir, and other Varangians. The decline and ultimate failure of the Khazar state created a political vacuum in this area, opening the way for the rise of a new empire. Kiev was drawn into that vacuum. Under Varangian leadership, its prosperity and power expanded. It demonstrated over a period of time that it could protect itself, its associates, and the all-important trade. This in itself must have led some other town-provinces to affiliate voluntarily with Kiev. Each increase made it easier for Kiev to coerce into association those who did not voluntarily seek it. The result was the formation of an agglomeration of states known as Kievan Rus.

There was considerable fluctuation in size and power during the four centuries or so of Kievan Rus, but, since we are not going to tell the story in detail, it will suffice to describe its greatest extent. The southwestern border was formed by Galicia, which reached to the Carpathian Mountains, and abutted on Poland. East and north of Galicia, abutting on Poland in the west and on Kiev itself in the east, was Volhynia. Polotsk, lying north of both Kiev and Volhynia, formed the northwestern border. Its western neighbors were the Lithuanians and Livonians. The northern borderland was Novgorod, whose story must be told separately. It was for a time second only to Kiev. Later it became independent and, still later, fell victim to the rising power of Muscovy. South of Novgorod and east of Polotsk was Smolensk; and south of it, Chernigov and Periaslavl. About in the center of the wedge were the lands called Riazin and Suzdalia; and farther to the east, the backwoods region of Viahtka. Six of these lands—Novgorod, Chernigov, Periaslavl, Smolensk, Polotsk, and Kiev itself—had grown from the town-provinces of early times, and antedated the Varangian power.

🦅 ITS PRINCES

Whether princely power was of Varangian or of Slavic origin, such power existed at one time or another in the Kievan states. It seems likely that whatever authority a prince possessed was personal rather than official. A prince who had only a small private army or whose control over his retinue was weak was, by those facts, a weak prince. Perhaps the nearest modern parallel is a political boss whose influence and authority depend not on holding office but upon his personal political machine.

The businesses of the prince were trade, military defense, and the dispensation of justice. Trade was originally under princely control, and the princes were long ranked among the chief traders. Their position as military leaders enabled them to accumulate wealth from tribute and taxes so that they became important capitalists. Taxes and tribute were often collected in goods which went immediately into trade. Wars and alliances were often made to protect or to further commerce. The trade routes had to be kept clear and as safe as possible. Competitors had to be dealt with in some way, often forcibly, and marauders had to be driven off.

There were some thirty-five princes, more or less, who ruled Kievan Rus during the three and one-half centuries of its active existence. Between 878 and 1015 there were only five princes. Their average reign

Kievan Rus — 12th to 13th centuries

was over twenty-seven years—evidence of their power and of the stability of the regimes. In the next 110 years there were nine princes, with average reigns of a little more than twelve years. Regimes had become markedly less stable. And from 1125 to 1238 there were eleven princes, indicating a continued decline in stability.

In the second quarter of the twelfth century Prince Yaroslav succeeded in establishing a system of succession to the thrones of the Kievan states. Under this system, called the Rota, the eldest prince became the prince of Kiev and overlord of all the other princes. The death or removal of a senior prince meant promotion for all his juniors. Thus, during the years when Novgorod was officially recognized as second to Kiev, the Novgorodian prince automatically became the prince of Kiev upon the death or removal of the reigning prince. All the junior princes then moved up a notch. This really constituted a collective dynasty with individual assignments. Except for the dynastic feature of the succession, it resembled somewhat the promotion of branch managers from smaller to larger branches and eventually into the home office.

The Rota was generally operative for about a hundred years, although there were exceptions to it. The old chronicles record both the practice and its violation:

1054: Yaroslav, Great Prince of Rus, passed away. While he was yet alive, he admonished his sons with these words: '. . . The throne of Kiev I bequeath to my eldest son, your brother Izyaslav. Heed him as ye have heeded me, that he may take my place among you. To Svyatoslav I give Chernigov, to Vsevolod Pereyaslavl, *to Igor the city of Vladimir,* and to Vyacheslav Smolensk.

1056–57. Vyacheslav, son of Yaroslav, died at Smolensk, and Igor took up his abode in Smolensk, moving over from Vladimir.

1064. Rotislav, son of Vladimir and grandson of Yaroslav, fled to Tmutorakan. . . . Upon his arrival, he expelled Gleb [Svyatoslav's son] . . . and occupied his principate himself. Svyatoslav . . . re-established his son Gleb upon the throne, and returned home. Rotislav returned, however, and expelled Gleb, who rejoined his father, while Rotislav remained in Tmutorakan.

1073. The devil stirred up strife among these brothers, the sons of Yaroslav. When disagreement thus ensued among them, Svyatoslav and Vsevolod united against Izyaslav. The latter left Kiev [and fled to Poland]. Svyatoslav thus ruled in Kiev after the expulsion of his brother, and thus broke the injunction of his father and of God.

The exceptions to the Rota became increasingly more frequent. By the latter twelfth century the transfer or promotion of princes was largely at an end; each prince regarded his state as a personal possession to be handed down in his direct line. The annals of the time repeatedly record the princely feuds and the disorders and wars which resulted from them. The following entry in *The Chronicle of Novgorod* is typical:

1135. Miroslav went from Novgorod to make peace between the people of Kiev and those of Chernigov, and he came back without having achieved anything; for the whole Russian land was in great disorder. Yaropolk called the men of Novgorod to his side and the [prince] of Chernigov to his; and they fought. God helped the son of Oleg with the men of Chernigov, and he cut up many of the men of Kiev, and others they captured in the month of August.

THE BOYARS

Associated with the prince were the aristocratic elements: the Boyars' Councils. Probably the councils changed frequently both in their relations to the princes and in their own composition. It is likely that there was usually a sort of inner circle or cabinet, composed of three to five leading members of the prince's private army. These men were the closest associates and advisers of the prince, and the cabinet may be said to have been in permanent session. The whole council was a much larger body, which was called only on special occasions. It consisted of the prince's retinue plus various important persons such as wealthy traders, clan or tribal chieftains or their descendants, and city elders. These people, apparently, were not bound to the service of the prince by anything beyond their own interest. Even the boyars, a title loosely used to designate the members of the princely retinue, had no obligation comparable to the feudal bonds which bound vassals to lords in western Europe. The boyars were free to leave the service of one prince for that of another.

The major function of the Boyars' Councils was to support the prince in his domestic administration and legislation, and in the making of war and peace. They also served sometimes as a supreme court. Professor Vernadsky believes that no important decision could be made nor any important action undertaken without the councils' consent. This must have been true in most cases, since the princes' authority rested upon this group. But there were probably other instances when an unusually strong personality bent the councils to his will. The relative authority of prince and council must have been determined largely by personalities and individual circumstances.

LOCAL GOVERNMENT

Democratic government as we know it did not exist in Kievan Rus any more than it did in ancient Athens. There was no such thing as universal manhood suffrage, and any democratic representation was, at most, rudimentary. The rural areas of the various states were ruled by the capital city (which was called *gorod*). The junior or provincial cities (*prigorodi*) had theoretically some voice in the affairs of the state, but it usually amounted to very little. On the other hand, there were institutions which discussed purely local matters. The basic unit was the mir, the local commune. Rural sections, smaller towns, and cities each had one mir. Larger districts sometimes had several. The cities also had a city assembly (*vieche*) which, in theory though not always in practice, was composed of all freemen who were heads of families. None of these would rank as representative institutions according to our stand-ards. For one thing, there was nothing hierarchical about them. The mirs did not send representatives to the "higher" units, and the mirs, as noted, were concerned only with local affairs.

The city assemblies, except for that of the capital city, were also local bodies. Sometimes it was held that citizens of the junior cities were also citizens of the capital and eligible to the assembly, but distance and the difficulty of travel made this largely meaningless. Decisions by the assembly had to be unanimous. Minorities were overridden, some-times vocally and sometimes by physical violence. The assembly of the capital city had some influence and occasionally some power in the choice of the prince. The most important and powerful assembly was that of Novgorod.

🎐 LORD NOVGOROD

Novgorod, like Kiev, was the name of a city and of a "land." The city was situated on the River Volkhov between Lake Ilmen and Lake La-doga. The land over which the city ruled in its heyday was extensive. Its western limit was the Baltic. Toward the north and east, it stretched off for an indeterminate distance. Novgorod, both land and city, was in the relatively infertile forest zone and the Novgorodians, from an early date, had to import part of their food. Grain trade with Kiev has already been mentioned. The lack of agricultural wealth, however, was balanced by other resources and the commercially strategic location. The economic and to some extent the social and political life of Novgorod reflected these circumstances.

The forests provided an abundance of timber for the building of houses, bridges, and boats. Wood fabrication was a major industry. The Baltic Sea furnished fish and salt, both of which were major trade items. (The coming of Christianity increased the economic importance of the fisheries by introducing fast days, and the use of candles in the churches similarly produced a boom in beeswax.) The wax and the honey were chiefly forest products, as were game and fur-bearing animals. Furs were particularly important both for domestic use in clothing and for export. The expansion of Novgorod to the north and east was partly pioneered by hunters and trappers in search of furs.

Novgorodians were very active in domestic and foreign trade. Merchants from Novgorod appeared sooner or later in virtually all the market places of Kievan Rus. They also traded with the towns of the Hanseatic League, and maintained good-sized commercial fleets on the Baltic. Some of the trade was local, between the city and the rural areas. Some of it was to supply the needs and demands of the Novgorodians themselves. But much of it was a transit trade from the Baltic to the markets of the Caspian and Black Sea regions. This was especially profitable. Some merchants amassed great wealth and exercised a proportionate power. Merchant associations were socially and politically as well as economically prominent.

The Primary Chronicle implies that Novgorod was a populous and thriving land before the "coming of the Varangians," and it explicitly states that the early inhabitants were Slavs. Since this is corroborated by other evidence, we may conclude that the wealth of Novgorod was probably what first attracted the Varangian-Swedes. We know also (from *The Chronicle*) that the Novgorodians had paid tribute to the Varangian-Swedes before the arrival of Rurik. We have already seen that he usurped the power and that his successor, Oleg, having captured Kiev, transferred his capital thither. Novgorod remained inferior to Kiev for many years.

But in 1016, Novgorodians aided Prince Yaroslav to conquer Kiev, and for this aid they exacted a *quid pro quo* in the form of a charter which recognized them as equal to the Kievans and also placed certain limits on the powers of their prince. Under the Rota, Novgorod ranked second to Kiev and throughout most of the eleventh century Novgorodians were relatively content with the arrangement. Late in that century, however, they deposed their Rota prince and, after considerable turmoil, chose another from Suzdal. About half a century later, Novgorod successfully asserted its own sovereignty, taking the title of Lord Novgorod, and making the office of prince elective.

The first contracts between the Novgorodians and their princes were lost long ago, so the terms of the agreements are unknown. But later charters which survived show three major provisions. First, no prince or his retainers could own estates within the land of Novgorod. Second, the city could elect its officials without any interference from the prince. Third, the supreme judicial authority was vested in the city assembly. Historians used to think that the existence of the assemblies indicated the existence of a rudimentary democracy. If that had anywhere been true it would have been in Novgorod.

The Novgorod assembly was composed of all its citizens, but the citizens were only a small part of the population. Slaves, of course, were excluded, and so were other large groups. Technically the assembly could summon and dismiss princes; make war and peace; and generally, exercise top legislative, judicial, and executive power. But in practice the assembly could only vote "yes" or "no" to proposals submitted to it by the Council of Lords. This body numbered about three hundred and was composed entirely of such upper-class men as boyars, agents of the princes, leading city officials, and high church officials. It was, in other words, an oligarchy, and it had the exclusive power of initiating action.

The city was divided into five boroughs, each of which was governed by a mir under the supervision and power of the mayor of the city. The mayor, who was always one of the oligarchy, was elected by the assembly. Each borough also controlled one of the five provinces into which the land of Novgorod was divided. Junior cities were ruled by mayors, who were appointed by the assembly of the capital city. Legally, the citizens of the junior cities were also citizens of the city of Novgorod and were entitled to places in the assembly or on the council. But since they were usually unable to be present at meetings this meant very little in terms of actual political power.

The top social class in Novgorod were the boyars. Originally, these had been the "prince's men," but it appears that later the wealthiest merchants and the richest landowners were also included in the boyar class. On the legal scales, at least, the boyars weighed twice as much as the next lower class, whose label meant "prosperous people." These probably included landowners and employers of labor. Merchants had the same status but formed a separate class. The lowest classes of free men were known as "the younger men" or "the black men." Presumably they were the free workers and craftsmen. Their legal rank was only one-fifth that of the boyars. Perhaps the most numerous class, although that is not quite certain, were the smerdi. It is not clear whether these people ought to be called state peasants or serfs. They lived on state lands and farmed those lands at least partly for the state. They may have been free, but they were not citizens and therefore were not members of the assembly. Some authorities believe that most of the rural population were smerdi. The lowest class were the slaves, who were also very numerous.[3]

CHAPTER III

In the Days of Kievan Rus

🎠 ECONOMIC LIFE

The earliest interpretation, presented by the great historian V. O. Kliuchevskii and long accepted as classic, was that foreign trade was the determining factor in the origin and subsequent developments of Kievan Rus. It held that the Kievan state flourished when trade flourished; decayed when the trade declined. Agriculture was thought to be of relative unimportance. The currently approved Soviet interpretation, by B. D. Grekov, insists that agriculture was the main occupation of the people in the days of Kievan greatness. This interpretation minimizes trade, although it does not wholly exclude it.

Modern historical scholarship and archaeological finds have produced a modification of the classic interpretation. It is now perfectly clear that the Slavs practiced agriculture on a large scale as early as the third century. It is also apparent that there were extensive grain production and grain trade with the Khazars, for example, in the eighth century. Kliuchevskii's minimizing of the importance of agriculture is no longer generally regarded as accurate. Neither is it believed that the evidence we now possess supports his theory that the rise of Muscovy was largely brought about by mass migrations from Kiev.

On the other hand, there is also enough sound historical evidence to show that Kievan Rus was not exclusively agricultural. The estimated population at the time of Kiev's greatest power was seven and a half million people. It is further calculated that about 13 per cent of these were townsmen, about the same percentage of townsmen as in the Russian Empire of the late nineteenth century. We properly speak of nineteenth-century Russia as being predominantly agricultural, but we also recognize the growing importance of trade and industry. This would also seem to be applicable to Kievan Rus. The trade in grain has been mentioned. Other trading items—furs, hides, slaves, timber, honey, and beeswax—were added in later centuries. The relative importance of trade as a determinant of policy was the greater because trade was the major interest and concern of the princes and their retinues. They could not, however, ignore agriculture completely. Farming was not only the way of life of most of their people, it was also a major producer of trade goods.

🐍 AGRICULTURE

The description of agriculture among the Slavs needs only to be modified for the Kievan period. Some of the agricultural settlement was, as before, in the forest zone. Lands there still had to be cleared by cutting and burning. The wood ash served as a temporary fertilizer, but when it was used up or leached out by rains, these lands ceased to be arable and new clearings were made. This laborious process took many hands. It was probably carried out frequently by some sort of a co-operative arrangement.

The very fertile soil of the feather-grass steppe made it possible to grow several crops with only one tilling. Originally, this land was then abandoned, and new fields were plowed and fitted, but this could be done only when there was ever so much more land than people. The growth of population forced the Kievan Russians to develop different patterns of land use. One was private ownership. Because it took less work to till the fertile black soil of the steppe than to clear the forests before farming, it was possible for one man or one family to do the job. There consequently appeared numbers of small, private farms. On the other hand, the great expanse of arable lands made it profitable to farm large tracts by the use of hired, indentured, or slave labor. And in consequence large estates became common. Such estates were owned by the princes, by the boyars, and, later, by the Church. They were worked by slaves, by indentured labor, and by free contract labor. The two- or three-field systems of land use were commonly followed both on the estates and on the small farms. Livestock farming was rather widely practiced—horse breeding, cattle raising, and the breeding of hounds for hunting. The raising of poultry was also general.

🐍 INDUSTRIES

Industry was, on the whole, less developed except for such home crafts as spinning and weaving, but it was by no means negligible. The production of salt was a leading industry. In Galicia, which was the major producer, salt was mined. Along the Crimean coast, it was produced by natural or solar evaporation of sea water. Novgorod also manufactured salt. Its northerly location and frequently cloudy weather made natural evaporation too uncertain, so artificial evaporation of the brine was necessary. Salt was always a major trade item. Kiev, for example, got most of its salt from Galicia.

Metallurgy was also carried on in several sections. Copper, tin, lead, silver, and gold were imported and fabricated. By far the most important metal was iron, from which both tools and weapons were made. Kiev and Novgorod were both centers of the metalworking industry. Novgorod also had a wide reputation for woodworking and was sometimes called the "Carpenters' City." An old chronicle tells of one occasion when the Kievan leader taunted the Novgorodians who had come to fight against him, saying: "Why do you come hither with this crooked-shanks, you carpenters? We shall put you to work on our houses." But woodworking of various sorts, including boatbuilding, was native to the Slavs, and there must have been many carpenters and builders besides those of Novgorod. Masonry was done, but was not originally a native craft. The first masons were probably imported from the Byzantine Empire in the tenth century, but native workmen were subsequently trained.

The making of cloth and cordage was also an ancient skill which was widely practiced. This industry increased in volume and the cloth improved in quality and variety through the years. Woolen fabrics were made in Kiev for trade. Cordage for nets and for boats, sailcloth, and burlap were also produced in commercial quantities. Furriery was a highly developed craft. The industry also included the making of clothing and utensils at home. Most of the people, in fact, depended upon homemade goods.

🝢 TRADE

Trade must be nearly as old as man. The most ancient written records take its existence for granted. This has been repeatedly confirmed by the archaeologists' finds of preliterary remains, and by the studies of the anthropologists. Presumably the reasons for trade are the variations in natural resources and the differences of skills among men. One man has "a way with animals"; another, "an eye for line and form"; a third possesses "a green thumb"; and so on. What could be more natural than that each should follow his bent and exchange his surplus for the superior produce of another? The differences in soil and climate between the three zones which lie within the Russian wedge are other cases in point. The northern lands are less suited to farming than the southern. The south lacks timber. Timber abounds in the north. The southern lands can be made to produce a surplus of grain, which can then be traded for logs from the northern forests. This exchange, not necessarily or exclusively of wood for grain, is still basic in Soviet economy.

It has, in fact, become a commonplace in studies of Russian economy to refer to grain-producing provinces of the south and the bread-consuming provinces of the north. At the time of which we speak, this meant particularly and most significantly: Kiev and Novgorod. At a later time, it meant Novgorod and Suzdalia. After sizable urban settlements had been made, the reciprocal needs of the townsmen for food-stuffs and of the farmers for manufactured goods were productive of trade. Every city in Kievan Rus had its local markets where small-scale, domestic trade could be carried on. In the smaller towns and cities, there were also local merchants with permanent establishments. The larger cities supported both such local merchants and a varying number of alien merchants as well. Extant records show that extensive trade was carried on in cloth, clothing, furs, metals, and metal goods (for example, weapons), salt, pottery, timber, grains, flour, cattle, horses, sheep, fowl, meat, game, wax, and honey. Some of this trade —perhaps most of it—probably took place directly between the maker or producer of the goods and the user. But there was also a considerable trade wherein a merchant bought goods for further exchanges with others.

Foreign trade, so-called, included both the transit trade and what might be differentiated as internation trade. Both traders and trade routes changed with the passage of time. During the eighth and ninth centuries, the most important trade routes were those from the Baltic Sea in the north to Azov and the Caspian in the south. These routes were blocked by a barbarian people, the Cumans, in the eleventh century. Meanwhile, during the tenth century, the trade along the Dnieper developed until it surpassed in importance the older routes. The First Crusade (1096) seriously injured the Russian Black Sea trade. The cities of Novgorod and Pskov engaged in considerable trade within the Baltic area, using both sea and land routes. There was some overland trade between Kiev and Central Europe.

The contrast between exports from Kievan Rus and imports tells a good deal about the Kievan economy. By and large, the exports were of raw materials or of semifinished goods. The raw materials included the now familiar items of furs and honey, and the less familiar goods such as walrus tusks, flax, hemp, hops, and sheepskins. There was also some trade in silver, silverware, textiles, and slaves. The imports varied with their place of origin. In general, they were luxury goods, which must have been available only to the wealthy. Wines, silks, glassware, art objects, and fruits were imported from the Byzantine Empire. From the Orient came spices, silks and satins, Damascus steel, wines, horses, and precious stones. The imports which came over the Baltic routes more nearly matched in character the Kievan exports. Iron, copper, tin, and lead were important. Some manufactured goods such as weapons, needles, and glassware also appear on the lists. In addition there were (in appropriate combinations, one trusts) herring, beer, and salt.

Because of the great distances and because of the dangers from marauders, trade was carried on mostly by groups. For the overland trade, this meant caravans of wagon trains or pack animals. Water-borne commerce employed fleets under convoy. The caravans and convoys were usually operated by associations of merchants, somewhat like the merchant guilds of western Europe. These associations appeared early in Kievan history.

BARTER, MONEY, AND CREDIT

Presumably the earliest trading done in Russia, as elsewhere, was the direct exchange of goods for goods—barter. But the use of money as a medium of exchange is also a relatively ancient practice. Money, in its primary form, was simply a commodity so generally desired that it could readily be exchanged for other commodities. In the northern lands of Russia, before the days of Kievan leadership, the commodity most universally desirable was fur, and this served as currency. The corresponding currency in the southern lands during pre-Kievan days was cattle. During the Kievan period the actual furs and cattle were replaced in trading by silver bars and/or coins. These bore the names of, and sometimes depicted, the commodities which they displaced as media of exchange. This domestic coinage began sometime in the tenth or eleventh century. Foreign coins were also used, and their variety and number increased as trade grew.

It is noteworthy that Kievan Rus had a highly developed system of credit. Proof of this is found in the Kievan legal codes which included a highly developed commercial law. *Russkaia Pravda,* the earliest Russian legal code which has come down to us, contains regulations upon loans, interest charges, primary claims in bankruptcy cases, and so on. The interest rate for loans which covered a year or more was fixed at 50 per cent per annum.

The prince had first claim on the remaining assets of a bankrupt person. This may have been because the princes were the chief money-lenders—at least in the early days. Since the princes' first concern was trade, they were as much merchants as leaders of states, and they were particularly involved in foreign trade, from which most of the capital originally accumulated. Moreover, the princes were the collectors of both taxes and tribute. They must have also acquired very considerable wealth from successful wars and raids: goods, treasure, tribute, and slaves. It seems likely that the princes were the first capitalists in Kievan Rus.

As trade expanded and prospered, merchants other than the princes also accumulated wealth. Members of the princely retinues must also have prospered in varying degree, since they shared in the trade, in the booty, and in the distribution of lands. In medieval Europe, land was the source and the measure of wealth. In medieval Russia there were other sources and other measures besides the land. Capital was represented by money and by credits, by trade goods, by cattle, by slaves, by forest preserves, and so on.

It is characteristic of the records which have survived that they tell more about the few possessors of wealth than about the masses of the people. Our information about labor and labor conditions in Kievan Rus is very limited. We know that there were three general categories: slave labor, indentured labor, and free labor. The *Russkaia Pravda* contains some regulations concerning wages, but wages and conditions of labor were regulated by custom rather than by law. Labor was legally regarded not as individual persons but only as an instrument for the production of capital. And the legal code was designed to protect capital rather than persons. It may also be noted that, although there were numerous workers in industry, there was no industrial labor in the modern sense.

🜃 SLAVIC SOCIETY

There is evidence that the early Slavs had, with different speeds, passed through the tribal and patriarchal clan stages of social organization. But there is no historical evidence that either of these led to the development of the Russian state. The unit from which that grew was probably the large family; that is, not the biological family of parents and offspring, but all the uncles, and the cousins, and the aunts, and the grandparents, as well. Perhaps in pre-Kievan times, certainly by Kievan times, families had grouped into communities, not all of whose members were related to each other. Blood bonds were still important. The large family long remained the primary social unit of Russia. But blood ties were supplemented and sometimes supplanted by the bonds of proximity. Membership in such a group was apparently voluntary.

Three social classes were distinguishable among the eastern Slavs as early as the sixth century. These were the aristocracy, the commoners, and the slaves. The barriers between classes were not insurmountable, even in Kievan times. Slaves could buy or be given their freedom and become commoners. Commoners could sell themselves into slavery or raise themselves to the aristocracy. This was a class but not a caste system. The *Russkaia Pravda* gives specific listing of the classes which were legally recognized in the eleventh century. There were four. First, were the upper-class freemen who were associated with the prince. Below them came the middle-class freemen. Freemen of limited status were third, and slaves, fourth.

This system grew more complex as time went on. The upper-class freemen eventually developed into the boyars. The boyar group (it was not legally a class at this time) seems to have grown from the merging of two streams, the upper-class freemen, and some persons of lower social origin who entered the service of the prince and rose in his employ to become members of his private army or retinue. Some of the boyars remained as members of the prince's immediate retinue. Others retired from constant service and formed a sort of rural or local aristocracy. Eventually, almost all boyars became landowners. Their power and their prestige, which came to rest on land ownership, were often as great or greater than the power and prestige of the junior or minor princes. The boyars had no legal class privileges, although as individuals they had many.

The middle classes must be divided for purposes of definition. The rural middle classes were those between the large-estate owners (mostly boyars) on the one hand, and nonowners on the other. They were free men, and were relatively prosperous farmer-proprietors. Apparently this status had evolved from the middle-class freemen of the earlier day. In the cities, the middle class was composed of the well-to-do, small owners, in distinction to the lower class which, in the cities, was composed of artisans and workers, both those who were self-employed and those who worked for hire. The lower class in the rural areas were freemen of limited status. They seem to have been state peasants, who were personally free but who owed a special obligation to the prince. Apparently they did not own land, but had usufruct, the right to use the land and its produce, though the title to the land remained with another. This usufruct was inheritable. It is rather interesting that peasants on Soviet collective farms today live under a somewhat similar arrangement. The collective farmer has the usufruct of a piece of land (usually two and one-half acres), but he may not own the land.

A measure of the relative value placed upon men of the several classes by the rulers was the bloodwite, decreed by law. The bloodwite was the payment which the murderer had to pay to the prince.

It was distinct from the wergild, which was the payment to the kin of the murdered person. The law required the payment of both the blood-wite and the wergild for males, except slaves. Bloodwite for females was half that for males, but women had a wergild. The bloodwite for upper-class freemen was eighty grivna; for middle-class freemen, forty grivna; for freemen of limited status, five.

Legal serfdom did not exist in Kievan Rus, but debt serfdom was common. The debtor did not carry his family into serfdom with him. It was neither inheritable nor necessarily permanent. The serfdom could be ended by discharging the debt. There appear to have been a large number of debt serfs. Quasi-serfdom was also the lot of those who for any of a number of possible reasons placed themselves under the protection of a prince, a boyar, or, later, the Church. This was not at all an unusual procedure in times of famines and invasions. It had its counterpart in the patron-client relationships of the Roman Empire.

Slavery also existed in Kievan Rus and probably involved a large number of persons. Some of the slaves were those captured in wars and raids, and descendants of captives. But slaves could also be purchased and slave markets existed. Nor was it at all unknown for a person to sell himself into slavery. Slaves could achieve freedom either by manumission on the part of their owner or by redemption payments made to the owner. They had no civil rights. Professor Kliuchevskii was of the opinion that slave-owning and landowning were in cause and effect relationship. The man who worked the land with his slaves came to be regarded as the owner of the land. This supposition seems quite reasonable. The land by itself was a thing of no value. The investment of capital and labor upon the land transformed it.

❧ THE COMING OF CHRISTIANITY

Kievan norms and values were greatly affected by the Christianization of Kievan Rus. Even Marxist historians, whose preoccupation with materialism long led them to ignore or minimize its role, have now recognized that the Orthodox Church was a very important factor in the development of the Russian state and of Russian society. Christianity forced some existing norms and values into the discard, greatly modified others, and introduced many new elements. The ancient chroniclers were right in emphasizing the matter, though their primary motives for doing so were considerably different from ours. They were making a case for the Church—*pro gloria Deo*. One of the longest stories recorded in *The Primary Chronicle*—amounting to about 16 per cent of the whole—deals with "the conversion of Vladimir." This account is preceded by another, less lengthy but covering many pages, of the earlier acceptance of Christianity by the Princess Olga.

According to *The Chronicle,* Olga was the wife of Igor, son of Oleg the Norwegian, who had conquered Kiev from Oskold and Dir. Following Igor's death in battle, Olga distinguished herself by her skilled and vigorous leadership of the Kievan forces. One of her exploits was the burial alive of envoys from the people who had killed her husband. Sometime after this, Olga went to Tsargrad (Constantinople). The emperor, in the words of the annalist, ". . . wondered at her intellect. He conversed with her and remarked that she was worthy to reign with him in his city. When Olga heard his words, she replied that she was still a pagan, and that if he desired to baptize her, he should perform this function himself; otherwise, she was unwilling to accept baptism. The emperor, with the assistance of the patriarch, accordingly baptized her. When Olga was enlightened, she rejoiced in soul and body."

Refusing an imperial offer of marriage, Olga requested permission to return to Kiev. She also sought the patriarch's blessing, saying to him, "My people and my son are heathen. May God protect me from all evil!" The patriarch gave his blessing and she went back to Kiev. But her son Svyatoslav resisted all her urgings that he be baptized, though he permitted those who wished to be baptized to do so. He would not, however, accept Christianity for himself. Olga remained true to her new faith and in the view of the chroniclers, "She was the first from Rus to enter the Kingdom of God."

THE "CONVERSION OF VLADIMIR"

After Svyatoslav's death there was a period of internecine warfare which ended in the dominance of Vladimir. Vladimir was a pagan. He was visited by Bulgarian Moslems who urged him to adopt Mohammedanism. Vladimir listened to them (*The Chronicle* makes great point of the carnal nature of their propaganda) but refused to accept their teachings. The Moslems were followed by emissaries from the pope. They had no better success. The Jewish Khazars also came and urged upon Vladimir the adoption of Judaism. He sent them away, too. Finally the Greeks sent a missionary of their church. Vladimir listened, and questioned the Greek, at length.

Vladimir was impressed but not yet converted. The decisive factor, according to the legendary account, was Vladimir's desire to wed the Christian princess Anna. Her family refused to let her marry a pagan. She promised him that baptism would cure his temporary blindness. Just as Paris was supposedly "worth a mass" to Henry IV, so did

Vladimir apparently deem his sight and a wife worth a baptism. "When Vladimir heard her message, he said, 'If this proves true, then of a surety is the God of the Christians great' and gave order that he should be baptized."

The baptism was immediately followed by the promised cure. This so impressed Vladimir's followers that many of them were also baptized:

Thereafter Vladimir sent heralds throughout the whole city to proclaim that if any inhabitant, rich or poor, did not betake himself to the river, he would risk the Prince's displeasure. When the people heard these words, they wept for joy, and exclaimed in their enthusiasm, 'If this were not good, the Prince and his boyars would not have accepted it.' On the morrow, the Prince went forth to the Dnieper with the priests of the Princess and those from Kherson, and a countless multitude assembled. They all went into the water: some stood up to their neck, others to their breasts, the younger near the bank, some of them holding children in their arms, while the adults waded farther out. The priests stood by and offered prayers. There was joy in heaven and upon earth to behold so many souls saved.

Thus *The Chronicle* records the conversion of Vladimir and his people in the year 988. The legend is interesting, and not so very far removed in spirit from similar legends such as that of the conversion of the Roman Emperor Constantine. It is also quite completely inaccurate.

Christianity first penetrated the Russian lands in the first century A.D. The missionaries had some success, which apparently did not long survive them. Then there seems to have been a hiatus of almost seven hundred years until Christianity again entered Russia in the ninth century. A Christian church (the Church of St. Elias) was established at Kiev by the middle of the ninth century. A minority among the upper classes adopted the religion. In 867 the first Russian metropolitanate was set up by the patriarch at Constantinople. The seat of the metropolitan was probably at the city of Tmutorakan on the Sea of Azov. All this took place about a century before the appearance of Vladimir.

As a matter of fact, Vladimir, in the early years of his reign, had been strongly anti-Christian. During the early 980's he had even attempted the forcible revival of paganism. This failed. Moreover, it contributed to domestic unrest. All available evidence suggests that political reasons were the chief determinants in his decision to adopt Christianity. His conversion not only removed a formidable rival to Christianity but also was doubtless a very important factor in the further spread of that religion. At the very least, it gave the Christians both social and political prestige.

THE EARLY CHURCH

Very little is known about the early organization of the Church in Russia. Its relations with the patriarchate in Constantinople are particularly obscure until the first metropolitan of Kiev was appointed by the patriarch in 1037, but it is certain that the Orthodox Church in the Russian lands was practically self-governing from the beginning. The power of the patriarchs was neither sure nor steady. Shifts in the political scene and changes in personnel at Constantinople produced many shifts in patriarchal power. Sometimes it was extensive; at others, almost nil. This meant that the Russian Church, often left to find its own way, had to become self-reliant. It also meant a steady development toward a national church. Both the Russian rulers and the Russian peoples were satisfied to have it so. Not only were the clergy largely autonomous in relation to the patriarch, they were also relatively autonomous in relation to the Russian state. They were also generally influential, but it was the very rare exception when the Church or the clergy challenged the supremacy of state power. This, of course, is in sharp contrast to the struggle between Church and State, pope and king, which dominated medieval western Europe. The Russian Church and clergy, presumably content with autonomy and influence, accepted a subordinate position from the beginning. Moreover, with very few exceptions, ecclesiastical authority was used to confirm and expand the power of the state.

CONTRIBUTIONS OF THE CHURCH

A major contribution of the Church was the development of a written literary language. Christianity, with its dependence upon the Gospels and the liturgies, greatly increased the need for a written language. The Church supplied the need. The written, literary forms were based upon and developed from Church Slavonic, which was the language of the religious books and churchly services. And the Church determined not only the mechanical tool of writing but also what was written. For centuries all written Russian literature was ecclesiastical in authorship and in tone. The chronicles illustrate one important variety of ecclesiastical writing. A later type related the lives of the saints. The following sample is quoted from a translation of *The Life and Martyrdom of Prince Michael of Chernigov and of his Boyar Feodor*. It deals with the coming of the Tatars, a theme with which we shall shortly be concerned:

> When thou beholdest wars, seditions or any other calamities, think not that these come by chance or are the ordinary events of this temporal world; but know that these visitations are sent by the will of God Almighty

to bring us, sinners, to repentance. . . . Even so happened it with the whole of our land of Russia. When we by our sins and wickedness, had outraged the Lord's mercy, and wished not to turn from our evil ways, He allowed cruel and godless barbarians, named Tatars, with their iniquitous and godless Khan Baty, to invade our country in countless numbers. These Tartars overcame the Christian armies and killed many god-fearing princes; all the towns were sacked and the whole land was destroyed by fire and sword, for no one could resist these godless hordes into whose hands the Lord gave us up, according to the words of His prophet: 'If ye be willing and obedient, ye shall eat the good of the land; but if ye refuse and rebel, ye shall be devoured with the sword.' (Isaiah i: 19–20)

During those times lived the godly and ever to be remembered Michael, Prince of Chernigov. From his earliest years he was a lover of Christ, serving Him in meekness and charity, walking in the ways of the Lord. He had a favorite boyar named Feodor, likewise full of virtues; together they suffered at the hands of the godless Baty, laying down their lives for Christ.

The ancient biographer then describes the whirlwind advance of the Tatars and their conquests of the Russian lands. After the initial conquests, Baty (or Batu, as he is also known) sent word to the Russian princes that they would be left in peace and power if they paid tribute to the Tatars. Many princes accepted the offer and carried it out even though they were forced to worship idolatrously, as did the Tatars, before the khan would receive them. Michael, hearing of these things, ". . . felt sore at heart, and being jealous for the Lord, resolved to go to the most unjust and cruel of all kings and before him fearlessly to confess Christ, and to shed his blood for the Lord." Feodor, his faithful boyar, went with him. And together they stood steadfast against both the entreaties of their fellow princes to give lip service to idolatry, and against the fury of the Tatars. The latter, their threats failing, fell upon Michael and Feodor and killed them. Michael's head was struck off, but:

. . . the holy martyr's lips still repeated, 'I am a Christian.' O wondrous Miracle! The head severed from the body ceased not to confess Christ.

. . . .

After the murder of the holy martyrs the godless Baty again invaded Poland and Hungary, but was killed in battle, thereby receiving a cruel end to his cruel life, but the holy martyrs inherited the Kingdom of Heaven, where they glorify the Father, Son, and Holy Ghost forever. Amen.

The Russian Church, like the Catholic Church of the medieval West, sponsored education and long dominated it. The reasons for this were essentially the same in both cases. The institutional Church had to have a clergy sufficiently literate to read the Scriptures and the liturgies. It needed at least a few scholars. And it also needed administrators who could keep records, carry on correspondence, and generally attend to the business of an expanding and ramifying institution. Schools and education were therefore important to the Church, and it took pains to maintain and control them. There were also some schools for laymen. *The Primary Chronicle,* for example, reports that Vladimir, after his conversion, "took the children of the best families and sent them to schools for instruction in book-learning." Grekov refers to these as "state schools" and argues convincingly that "book-learning" in the usage of that time meant not just reading and writing but advanced studies. He is of the further opinion that these schools, which he thinks existed in other cities besides Kiev—certainly in Novgorod—were to train statesmen. This may well be so, but literacy, schools, and education were mainly for the clergy throughout many generations. The reader has firsthand acquaintance with the pious nature of the annals and the hagiographies.

Judging by the survivals which have come down to us, the Church was the mother of the arts as well as of letters. The best in architecture was apparently devoted to the building of churches; and the highest artistry, to their adornment. The inspiration of both art and architecture was originally Byzantine, but they were not mere slavish imitations. The earliest church building of which we know was St. Elias at Kiev, which was standing in 944. A wooden building, it was completely destroyed by fire. The converted Vladimir built several churches, at least one of which was an elaborate structure of stone and marble. This was destroyed at the time of the Tatar attack in 1240. The oldest Kievan church to have survived until our times was St. Sophia, which was built in the early eleventh century. It was destroyed by the Germans during World War II. Colorful mosaics, some of intricate design, were used in the building, which was further decorated by elaborate frescos. Many of the frescos, but not all of them, were of religious subjects.

The painting of icons was also, of course, religious art, which was highly developed in Kievan times. Grekov speaks of it as beginning in Kiev and spreading throughout the Russian lands. Some of the icons are relatively simple depictions of single figures. Others are very elaborate representations of religious events. Miniatures were also painted. The subjects were most often ecclesiastical, but there were also some which portrayed princes and other secular subjects.

The Orthodox Church, again like its counterpart in the medieval West, was particularly concerned with establishing its hold upon family life and relations. Births, marriages, and deaths were, of course, occasions for sacramental devotions. But jurisdiction was also involved. The protection of widows and orphans, which the Church took upon itself, also involved the disposal or control of property. The ramifications of this, and certain theological doctrines, touched upon the position of women in society. Women in pre-Christian Russia had certain well-defined rights which were generally observed, though a woman was not considered the equal of a man. The bloodwite for females, as previously indicated, was only half that for males, but women had a wergild, which was a crass but real recognition of their place in the family. The Christian Church, with its insistence upon woman's responsibility, through Eve, for original sin, somewhat lowered the regard in which women had been held. This was partly counterbalanced by the worship or veneration of the "Birthgiver to God" (Mary). But on the whole, the evidence indicates that women were less well regarded, less independent, and less well off after the coming of Christianity to Russia than they had been before.

On the other hand, the Christian Church gradually introduced in Russian society and Russian law certain moral concepts. This stands out particularly in the changing values relative to the commission of crime. The earlier attitudes had placed crime as an offense against property or property rights. The bloodwite was compensation to the prince by a murderer for the loss of a valuable resource. The wergild was recompense to the murdered person's family for their material loss. The Church taught that certain crimes were offenses against a moral law. It set up a doctrine of moral responsibility and established moral deterrents to the commission of crime. These new value patterns were slow in gaining ascendancy over the old. Perhaps they never wholly accomplished it.

NORMS OF THE PEOPLE

Very little is known about the everyday life of the masses. There are specific records which describe the physical norms of the privileged minority, but references to the people are only scattered and casual generalizations. We know that the majority of the people were rustics. Perhaps eighty-seven out of every hundred persons lived in the country. Their homes in the northern lands were usually small log cabins. In the south, where wood was less abundant, they lived in houses having timber frames and clay-filled walls. The most prominent furnishing was a large stove made of clay or brick.

The typical Russian stove is totally unlike the ones generally familiar in the West. In the first place, it is more an actual part of the house than an appurtenance. It occupies a large part of the floor space, and it serves as cookstove, furnace, and bedstead. The more elaborate stoves have separate ovens, and places for boiling or frying food. The fire is built in the oven itself. When it has burned to embers, these are thrust aside and the food is put in to be baked by the heat retained in the oven. Shelves or recesses along the upper sides, or the top of the stove itself, serve as sleeping places. Stoves of this sort are still in common use throughout rural Russia.

The usual summer dress of the men consisted of linen shirts and trousers. Women wore linen shirts and woolen skirts, or a kind of sleeveless dress. Woolen caftans, which were long, flowing coats held in place by a sash, and sheepskin coats were used in winter. Bread, wheaten in the south, rye in the north, was the staple of the diet. This was supplemented by game of various kinds; by beef, mutton, and pork; and by fish. The common vegetables and fruits and dairy products were also eaten. For drinks, they had mead made from honey; kvas, a sour drink fermented from grain; and wines. Most of the food was home-grown and most of the clothing was homemade. The wealthy, of course, supplemented the native products with imports from abroad.

Epidemic diseases of several sorts frequently struck the people, and epizootics were equally common among the domesticated animals. Famines due to droughts and to human destruction of crops were also frequent. Fires, either arson or accident, were extremely numerous. And the marauding raids of invaders or brigands, as well as the nearly incessant wars among the princes, were destructive of life and property. It seems reasonable to suppose that, then as now, such goings-on were often harder upon ordinary folks than upon their social, economic, or political superiors.

Kievan Rus was not an isolated community, cut off from the world. The Kievans maintained many, close, and varied contacts with their neighbors on all sides. Lively commercial relations; dynastic marriages, alliances, and conflicts; wars; and cultural interborrowings went on continuously between the Russian peoples and the western Slavs, the Germans, the Scandinavians, the Byzantine Empire, and the Caucasian peoples. Many of these contacts gave added life and vigor to Kievan Rus. But certain others contributed directly to its decline.

❧ DECLINE OF KIEVAN RUS

The downhill slide of Kievan power was long and gradual. Its beginnings can be seen in the eleventh century, though Kiev stood as a major power for another two hundred years. Its climax came in the thirteenth century, though the Kievan state lingered beyond that time. The causes of the decline are matters of conjecture.

Kievan Rus has been variously referred to in the preceding pages as a state or group of states, as a "land of cities," as a "land" or "lands," as a federation, and so on. It is actually difficult to say with precision just what it was. Probably the most accurate terminology is to call the various parts by a literal translation of the word *zemlia,* which means "land." Thus reference would be to the land of Kiev, or the land of Chernigov, or the land of Suzdalia. The whole agglomeration would be called the lands of Kievan Rus. The importance of what may seem to be merely a technical triviality is this. The peoples of Kievan Rus never developed any sense of national unity or solidarity. Neither was there any sense of a general communality of interests. The chief bond among them was the ruling prince. The decline of power was rapid under weaklings, incompetents, and unfortunates, but this trend was checked or even reversed by strong, competent, or lucky rulers. Since there was little genuine, popular support for the state or system, the whole thing could be overthrown with relative ease by an ambitious and determined opponent.

The princely feuds and wars had the long-run effect of weakening not only the princely system itself but also the power of the Kievan lands as a whole. For one thing, the always loose combination came apart at the seams, as it were. The several lands tended to withdraw from the federation. Apart from it they were individually weaker, and the federation was weakened by their defection.

One example will serve to illustrate the nature of the princely wars and their effects upon Kiev. To go back a little, one of the most famous rulers of Kiev was the Prince Vladimir Monomakh (1113–25), who both beat off the Polovtsi and also reunited the lands under his strong rule. Monomakh himself had abided by the Rota and he forced his sons to do so. But after his death, the struggles were renewed, and the principle of the Rota was again violated. One of Monomakh's sons, Yuri, who had served his junior appointment in Suzdalia (as, indeed, had Monomakh himself), eventually possessed himself of Kiev at the cost of civil war. Yuri's son, Andrew of Bogolyubovo, grew up in the northern lands and eventually became the prince of Suzdal. In 1169 he stormed and sacked the city of Kiev—a blow from which it never fully recovered. Ukrainian historians see in this event a proof of their contention that there was an ancient and fundamental cleavage between Muscovy (Suzdalia) and Ukraine (Kiev), and that the two were really separate nations. The evidence does not support this interpretation. But it does dramatically demonstrate the breaking up of the old formation.

The lands themselves became divided into smaller units as this or that princeling or boyar successfully challenged the ruling prince. Thus within each micro-organism was repeated the atomization which took place in the macro-organism.

The wars were costly to the people as a whole. The sum total of resources was gradually whittled away. Destruction of crops, of buildings, and of livestock, even on a small scale, has a most deleterious cumulative effect. Men are not likely to farm or otherwise produce to their fullest ability if they think it likely that war or civic disorders will rob them of the products of their labor.

Trade, particularly trade which is based on credit, likewise declines under such circumstances. Lenders are loath to give credit or loans to men whom circumstances are likely to render unable to repay the advances. Traders shun deferred exchanges when wars are likely to make completion of the deal difficult or impossible. And these effects of the princely feuds were greatly heightened, as will presently be seen, by invasions.

Not all of the difficulty was local, for trade was also injured in very appreciable measure by events which took place entirely outside the Russian lands. The advance of the Seljuk Turks across Asia Minor in the eleventh century reduced the power and prosperity of the Byzantine Empire at least temporarily, and this cut into the trade of Kievan Rus. The first Crusade (1096), though not launched with any intent to do so, also injured Constantinople. The Fourth or Commercial Crusade (1204) sponsored by Venice and aimed against Constantinople—Venice's chief trade rival—ruined that market. Furthermore, the revival and growth of trade in western Europe during these centuries brought new routes into being. This reduced the traffic which had long traveled the roads from the Varangians to the Greeks.

The increasing decline in trade, coupled with the raging internecine wars and concomitant insecurity, led to a gradual depopulation of the southern lands. At once a partial cause and a partial result of the commercial depression and of the increasing insecurity and weakness, this depopulation was also both cause and effect of the alien invasions which climaxed these developments. From the southwest came the Polovtsi, who first raided the borderlands in 1062. Their defeat by Monomakh was only a temporary check. Their raids continued for two centuries, growing more frequent and more disastrous to Kiev as its power dwindled. The impact of the Polovtsi accelerated the flight of the people. Even before the reign of Yuri, many refugees had settled either in Suzdalia or in Galicia, thereby enhancing the strength and increasing the prosperity of these regions.

Meanwhile, at the opposite corner of the Russian lands, i.e., in the northwest, another enemy had appeared. About the middle of the twelfth century Germanic peoples began to move inland along the Western Dvina. These incursions were generally peaceful until the Germans had been converted to Christianity. Then warrior-priests and priestly warriors with their followers began to crusade against the pagan and heretic Slavs. First came the "Livonian Order of Sword-Bearers" and then, beginning in 1230, the "Teutonic Order of Knights." These organizations undertook a military drive to the east at the expense of the Russians.

🔥 THE TATARS

But the most awful and the most important of these invasions was the one which the monkish biographer of Prince Michael of Chernigov explained as visitations sent by Almighty God to bring the Russian sinners to repentance—the coming of the Tatars.

The northeastern lands first felt the Tatar blows, Riazin in particular being exceptionally hard-hit. The city of Kiev was struck and almost destroyed in 1240. It had been one of the largest cities in medieval Europe, with a population of about 100,000 at the beginning of the twelfth century. After the Tatars had finished with it, the city was only ruins and bones. The few who survived the Tatar visitation fled to safer lands. The migrations were now so complete that the whole population east of the Dnieper was removed. In the words of an annalist, "Then the whole of Kiev ran away." The end of Kievan Rus had come.

CHAPTER IV

Tatar and Muscovite

⚙ GENGHIS KHAN

The Tatar conquest of the Russian lands may well stand as one of the markers, not alone in the history of Russia but also, because of its lasting aftereffects, in the history of the world. It has been previously stressed that the Tatars who conquered Russia in the thirteenth century were not the first but the last in a long line of Turkic invaders who time and again overran the steppe lands. It may be noted parenthetically that Tatar was a generic name commonly applied by the Russians to mixed Turkic peoples. In the case of the great invasion which is called Tatar, the leaders were Mongols; the rank and file, Tatars and others. It was leadership that distinguished this invasion from its predecessors. With the exception of Attila the Hun, none of the Turkic tribes had produced a leader of stature. The Tatars had one—a contemporary of that Andrew of Bogolyubovo who captured and sacked the city of Kiev. His name was Temuchin, and his exploits as well as his calculated ruthlessness make Andrew seem insignificant by comparison. In the year 1207 the Mongolian peoples of Asia appointed Temuchin their supreme leader. His title, which is better known in the West than his real name, was Genghis Khan. There is no agreement as to how this title should be translated. It has been variously rendered as "Very Mighty King," "Emperor within the Seas," and "The Perfect Warrior." But whatever its exact meaning, it was the title of a leader who, having mastered the Tatar-Mongol peoples, set out to fulfill a grandiose scheme of world conquest. Within two decades Genghis Khan had made himself master of northern China, Turkestan, part of India, Persia, and Armenia. Part of the credit for these exploits of course properly belongs to Temuchin himself, but a share should also be accorded to his associate, Ye-liu Chu-tsai. Ye-liu's genius for organization and administration matched the military prowess of Genghis Khan.

The westward advance of the Tatars aimed at nothing less than the conquest of all Europe. The Russian lands were not themselves the goals, but only something to be picked up en route. The coming of the Tatars so disturbed the Kievans and the Polovtsi (also a Tataric people) that they suspended their ancient hostilities and formed a common front against the new invaders. In 1223 an allied army opposed itself to the onrushing Tatars in a great battle fought on the steppes between the Don and Dnieper and was most ingloriously defeated. The victorious Tatars pushed on as far as the Dnieper, then suddenly returned the way they had come. The annalist reported, "We do not know from whence these evil Tatars came upon us, nor whither they have betaken themselves again; God alone knows." The explanation of the action which seemed so mysterious to the chronicler was simply that the Tatars had come not to conquer but to reconnoiter. The conquest was briefly delayed during dynastic changes following Temuchin's death. The new khan in 1236 ordered the invasion of Korea, southern China, and Europe. Only the last of these expeditions comes into our story.

THE CONQUEST

The command was given to Batu Khan, grandson of Genghis Khan, and Batu with his ordu moved westward through the Caspian Gate. *Ordu* is not a familiar word. In fact, it is not an English word at all but a Turko-Tataric one, and it meant "a division of an armed force with its headquarters." The Russian version of *ordu* was *orda*. It passed into English as "horde," and the original meaning was shortened to "camp" or "army." Later, horde was used still more loosely to describe any group of nomadic peoples; and it took on a connotation of "swarm" or "rabble." Batu's horde acquired a descriptive adjective, golden (from the color of his tent), and so the name has come down to us as the Golden Horde. This label may give the false impression that it was a mass movement. It wasn't, even though the Novgorod chronicler spoke of the coming of "foreigners called Tatars in countless numbers like locusts." Probably it seemed that to those who suffered the fury of the Tatar attack. The force with which Batu invaded the lands along the Volga has been estimated at anywhere from 120,000 to 500,000. More recent studies incline toward the lower figure. This was a force certainly more powerful but probably not more numerous than those which opposed it. And there is no reason to suppose that the Tatars were ever more than a small ruling minority in comparison to the Slavic population.

Batu's Golden Horde first struck and conquered the Bulgars (another Turkic group), who lived along the Volga. They then established

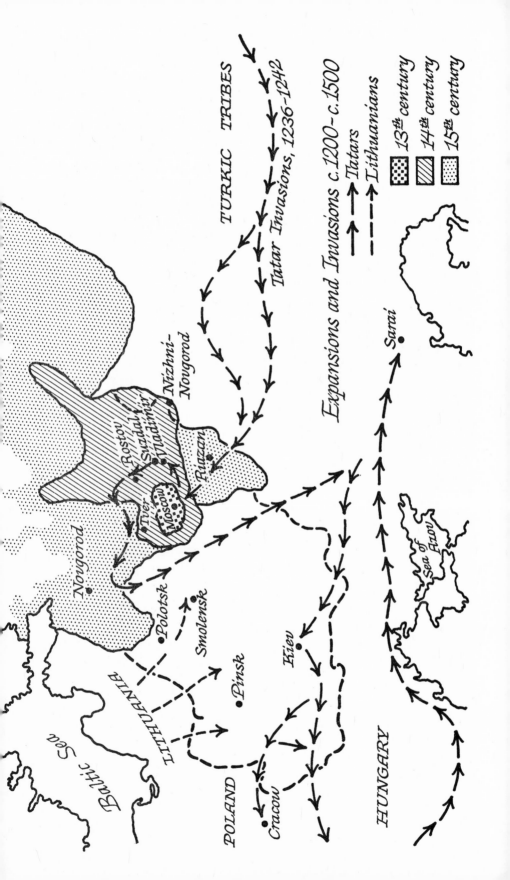

Expansions and Invasions c.1200–c.1500

Tatar Invasions, 1236–1242

TURKIC TRIBES

→ Tatars
⇢ Lithuanians

13th century
14th century
15th century

Baltic Sea

Novgorod

Polotsk

Smolensk

LITHUANIA

Pinsk

POLAND

Cracow

Kiev

HUNGARY

Rostov
Suzdal
Vladimir
Nizhni-
Novgorod
Tver
Moscow
Ryazan

Sea of Azov

Sarai

a state of their own, correctly but infrequently referred to as the Kipchak state of the Golden Horde, in the lands between the Volga and the Don. Their capital, founded by Batu's son, was Sarai on the lower Volga. From this base, the Tatars hurtled westward. Riazan was the first Russian land to fall. Its capital was stormed, captured, and sacked after a five-day siege. The inhabitants were slaughtered and, wrote the annalist, "No eye remained open to weep for the dead." Within a matter of weeks, the towns of Suzdal—including Moscow and Vladimir —were captured. Only Novgorod escaped, presumably because the spring thaw and floods hindered the Tatar advance. This occurred in 1238, and the Tatar campaign and victories were resumed the following year. Kiev and its area fell in 1240, and the Tatar armies then drove westward into Poland and Hungary. They soon withdrew, but they remained masters of the Russian lands, except Novgorod, which they never conquered but which sometimes paid them tribute, until the middle of the fifteenth century.

Nor was this first incursion by any means their last destructive visitation upon Russia. From time to time throughout the period of their power the Tatars scourged the Russians. Sometimes the expeditions were punitive; sometimes, for the apparent purpose of reasserting power; and sometimes, to get captives and plunder. The annals abound in reference to these events. Fairly typical is the following excerpt from *The Chronicle of Novgorod,* which records a Tatar incursion made almost a century after the original invasion: "(A.D. 1327) The same winter a very great force of Tatars came, and they took Tver and Kashin and the Novi-torg district, and to put it simply, laid waste all the Russian land."

A contemporary description of the Tatars, written in 1243, is preserved in Richard Hakluyt's famous account, *Principal Navigations, Voiages, and Discouveries of the English Nation.* The description, slightly abridged and with the spelling given in modern form, was as follows:

They were above all men, covetous, hasty, deceitful and merciless; notwithstanding that, by reason of the rigor and extremity of the punishments to be inflicted on them by their superiors, they are restrained from brawling and from mutual strife and contention. . . . They think that all things are created for themselves alone.

. . . .

They be hardy and strong in the breast; lean and pale-faced; rough and huge-shouldered; having flat and short noses; long and sharp chins; their upper jaws are low and declining; their teeth long and thin; their eyebrows extending from their foreheads down to their noses; their eyes inconstant and black; their countenances writhen (contorted) and terrible; their extreme joints strong with bones and sinews; having thick and great thighs and short legs and yet being equal to us in stature, for that length which is wanting in their legs is supplied in the upper parts of their bodies.

.   .   .   .

Vanquished, they ask no favor; and vanquishing, they show no compassion. . . . Suddenly diffusing themselves over a whole province, and surprising all the people thereof unarmed, unprepared and scattered, they make such horrible slaughters that the king or prince of the invaded land cannot find people sufficient to wage battle against them and to withstand them.

Even allowing for the exaggeration in this account, which was due to shock and perhaps to a desire to excuse Russian defeats, it is not difficult to comprehend the feeling of terror which the Tatars aroused in the people of that day.

This was not a mass conquest, no large body of Asiatic migrants followed the conquering armies into the Russian lands. On the contrary, the Tatars were content to remain a minority which controlled the princes, collected tribute and taxes, and drafted Russian manpower for Tatar use. Some of the Russian princes, notably and most successfully those of Moscow, became the agents of the khans.

The Tatars, at least during the first century of their dominion, built up an extensive and prosperous trade. Some of the Russian peoples, again most notably the Muscovites, shared in this trade and in its profits. Harsh as the Tatar rule was, and, though it imposed a crushing burden upon the peasants especially, there were those Russians who profited from it. Among the Russian institutions which benefited was the Orthodox Church. The Tatars, who were pagans, allowed full religious toleration within the Russian lands, but they gave special privileges to Orthodoxy and to the Orthodox clergy. The khan made the metropolitan of the Russian Orthodox Church the head of all clergy within the Russian lands.

🐚 LEGACIES OF THE TATARS

It would seem reasonably clear that the Tatar dominion isolated Russia to some extent from the West. From one point of view, "insulated" might be substituted for "isolated." Tatar power protected the Russians against attacks which presumably might have been made by the expanding states of Lithuania and Poland. The Tatars also protected Russian Orthodoxy from Roman Catholic missionaries and Roman Catholic conquerors. In short, the Tatars guarded Russia during a time of great Russian weakness. But if they protected Russia, they also cut her off from more advanced Western cultures and so contributed to Russian backwardness.

Perhaps the salient feature was that neither the Renaissance nor the Protestant Revolution ever reached Russia. This was partly because the Russian Orthodox Church so willed it, and partly because of the Tatars. As a result neither the spirit of individualism nor the spirit of free inquiry, both of which were characteristic of the Renaissance and the Revolution, reached the masses of Russia. So sweeping a generalization is subject to exceptions. There were individual Russians who were devoted both to individualism and to a spirit of free inquiry, and also to democracy, which is in a large measure the outgrowth of these two things. But the generalization applies reasonably well to the masses. It may very well be that this is the basic deviation between the developments in Russia and developments in parts of the West. What did develop in Russia was the Tatar theory and practice of state service and/or autocracy.

The alert reader will at once protest that neither Italy, home of the Renaissance, nor the Germanies, first seat of the Protestant Revolution, made much progress toward the development of democracy. This is true. Obviously, it is easy to exaggerate the influence of the Tatars in this respect. There must have been other factors both in the development of democracy in England, France, Scandinavia, and elsewhere, and in the failure to develop democracy in the other nations. Tatar dominion alone is not a sufficient explanation in the case of Russia. But if all this is freely granted, there still remains the long-term and subtle effect of the lack of emphasis upon individualism and an excessive emphasis upon collectivized responsibility and privileges.

The Tatar theory and practice of state service, if it was not built upon the well-developed totalitarian philosophy of the Ch'in dynasty, which the Tatars displaced in northern China, at least owed much to that philosophy. Whatever its origin, the Tatar system rested upon the submission of the individual to the group. It held that every subject, or every member of the group, had a paramount obligation of group service. And it valued a person in terms of this service. This was developed, not without some variations, into the Muscovite system of state service, which demanded that all classes and all persons should serve the state in some fashion. This may be called, though not with literal accuracy, a system of state serfdom. It was closely integrated with authoritarianism.

The khans were completely autocratic, or at least as autocratic as each ruler's personal power permitted him to be. They claimed to hold in their hands not only the absolute ownership of all lands within their domains but also ownership of the persons of all their subjects. The princes of Moscow who set themselves up as heirs of the khans adopted this claim to absolutism. It was the more readily enforceable because of certain economic effects of Tatar action.

It has been noted that some Muscovites profited from participation in Tatar-controlled trade. There is another side to this story. The recurrent Tatar invasions and punitive expeditions were terrible scourges to the Russian peasantry. Their crops were taken or destroyed, their livestock confiscated or killed, their houses burned, their equipment ruined. Many of them, fleeing from the terror, settled in new lands. Others sought to rebuild at home. Many of both groups were literally bankrupted by the Tatar destructiveness. They had to buy or lease new lands, rebuild their homesteads, gather new equipment, find seeds, and restock their farmyards. In order to do this, many besought the aid of wealthy persons or institutions such as monasteries and obligated themselves to repay the advances. Tatar taxation and exaction of tribute, and also the Tatar drafts of men, had the same effect of impoverishing the peasants. Out of this poverty and the efforts to overcome it there came economic and then legal serfdom. Out of it also came a great increase of the power of the few over the many; and chief among the few were the princes.

The passing reference to monasteries requires a little elaboration. During the turbulent years of the fourteenth and fifteenth centuries, particularly, numerous individuals sought respite in flight and in solitude. The flight was both literal and figurative: literal in the sense of actual physical removal to the frontiers away from the Tatars, chiefly in the northeast; and figurative in the sense of withdrawal from the material world to one of spiritual contemplation. Some of these fugitives from the world achieved considerable repute as spiritual leaders, and their hermit cells became nuclei about which followers gathered. Monastic communities sometimes grew from these beginnings. The most famous instance was the Trinity (Troitsa) Monastery which developed from the original solitary settlement of a holy man later canonized as St. Sergius of Radonezh. In this case, as in others less famous, the monastic community attracted settlers to its vicinity. Eventually the Trinity Monastery became a center of ecclesiastical and cultural life and, also, the largest single landowner in Muscovy. Such settlements were the advance guard of Russian expansion into these regions.

Other and more tangible borrowings from the Tatars included certain elements in administrative and military organization, in the collection of taxes and the taking of tribute, and in court ceremonials and customs.

🜄 THE APPANAGE OF MOSCOW

According to tradition, Moscow was founded in the middle of the twelfth century by Prince Dolgoruki as a frontier outpost for the protection of the junior land of Suzdalia. It is probable that the original settlement had been made much earlier and more casually. Perhaps the first formal and effective fortification and garrisoning of the place was as the legend has it. Whoever chose the location chose well. The site is on the Moscow River, which flows into the Oka, which, in turn, is tributary to the Volga. Moreover, the site strategically dominates the riverway which became the major trade route from Novgorod to Riazin and the southeast. But at the time of settlement, Suzdalia was off the main trade routes of the Dnieper and far removed from the main center, Kiev. It was regarded as a remote backwater and its princes were well down on the Rota.

We have already seen the gradual decline of the power of Kiev over its associates and the gradual disruption of the Rota system. Similar decentralization took place within the lands themselves. Their princes came to regard the lands as family property which could be parceled out among their heirs. The physical features of the northern regions and their frontier character favored the growth of small settlements. The isolation of such settlements from each other encouraged their independence. Often they were assigned by the prince of the land to his younger heirs. At first such assignments were usually in the nature of a trust, but later they became the permanent, personal possessions of the assignee and his heirs. Moscow was a case in point. Alexander Nevsky, who won great renown for his successful defense of Novgorod against the Swedes, the Lithuanians, and the Germans, and who was later appointed grand prince by the khans, gave Moscow to his son Daniel. It remained thereafter a separate appanage.

An appanage was a small state or, in many cases, simply an estate. With the growth of princely families, the lands were increasingly redivided and subdivided until many portions were no bigger than a manor. The lord of the manor, i.e., the prince, was an independent or quasi-independent ruler. Geographical isolation temporarily favored such autonomy. By the same token it promoted weakness. The growth of appanages was a process of fragmentation which resulted in a multiplication of petty, weak states. This was similar in results, though not in the detailed process, to feudalism in western Europe. In both Russia and Europe, the multiplicity and the weakness of individual units made possible their reunification by a strong ruler or series of rulers. This, in Russia, was the prince of Moscow.

🜊 MUSCOVITE EXPANSION

Daniel and his son Yuri, for example, were able to bring the whole length of the Moscow River under their control, absorbing several weaker appanages in the process. Their successors were skillful, lucky, and unscrupulous leaders, who were able to establish a reasonable degree of domestic order and security. This accomplishment in itself attracted to their lands more people, wealth, and power. The location of Moscow facilitated such movement; the rivers brought trade and settlers and riches. Success fed upon itself. Some appanage princes decided that they would be better off under the rule of the Muscovite prince and, accordingly, arranged to join their states to his. These accretions also increased Muscovite strength, not only attracting still other additions, but also giving Moscow power to coerce the recalcitrant and the reluctant. A very important boost was given to Muscovite power by the khans in the fourteenth century.

In 1328 the rule of Muscovy passed to Ivan Yurievich (1328–41), who won the nickname Kalita ("Moneybags"). Prince Ivan got from the Tatar khan a commission to collect the tribute which the khan extracted from his Russian subjects. Ivan was also given certain authority. As the khan's agent, Ivan had prestige and power beyond anything possible for a mere prince of Muscovy. Some of the tribute which Ivan collected never left Moscow, and there were times when the delegated power was used more for the benefit of Ivan than of the khan. This situation long survived Ivan, who died in 1341. It was a major contribution to the growth of Muscovite power, although the khans scarcely could have intended such a result.

Ivan also successfully followed the established family policy of expansion. His chief gain was the temporary defeat of Tver, a partial victory which completed Muscovite control over the highly strategic and important Valdai Hills. Closely connected with the victorious campaign against Tver was the removal of the seat of the metropolitanate to Moscow. At the beginning of the fourteenth century, the Metropolitan Maxim moved from the ruined city of Kiev to Vladimir. This was particularly appropriate since Vladimir, partly because of the exploits of Alexander Nevsky and partly because of recognition by the Tatars had come to be regarded as the heir of Kiev. Ivan Kalita, in the year of his accession to the principality of Moscow, succeeded in making himself also the grand prince of Vladimir.

Maxim's successor as metropolitan, Peter, had remained at Vladimir. He supported Ivan Kalita against Tver and, later, moved to Moscow, where Ivan built for him the great Uspenski Cathedral (Cathedral of the

Assumption). Peter's immediate successor, one Theognostus, not only stayed at Moscow but also formally established that city as the seat of the metropolitanate. This made Moscow the ecclesiastical center of Russia, and the princes of Muscovy became the favorite sons of the Church, which greatly enhanced their prestige and increased their authority. The metropolitans sometimes gave active support to the princes, as in the case of Peter and Ivan; and the princes returned the favor. It was a mutually beneficial arrangement which might be roughly compared to the traditional alliance of Church and Crown in France.

To anticipate chronological developments still a little further, the Church also greatly aided the rise of autocracy in Moscow by its contributions to and endorsement of autocratic political theory. The practice of autocracy, as has been said, grew partly out of the Tatar example. Its explanatory theory came largely from ancient biblical and Roman concepts developed in the Byzantine Empire and spread by the Church. The theory was based on the claim that the king or prince was an instrument chosen by God for the maintenance of the true faith. It held that an Orthodox prince was as fully God-ordained and necessary as an Orthodox patriarch or metropolitan. From this to a fully elaborated doctrine of monarchy by divine right is a very short step. This theoretical development was fully compatible with both the Tatar theory and the Tatar practice of autocracy.

🌑 TATAR DECLINE

As a quasi ally of the khans, Ivan Kalita was able to provide a relative security against Tatar attacks. This comparative peace and tranquillity were most attractive to migrants. Many of the people of Tver, after their prince had been defeated by Ivan and the Tatars, followed Ivan back to Muscovy and settled there. Ivan's growing wealth enabled him to buy off the Tatars and, furthermore, to add to his possessions by purchasing appanages. He sometimes used his wealth to ransom prisoners from the Tatars, then built villages for them and settled them on his lands. This transformed the land into an important asset. And still more princelings were encouraged to throw in their lot with Moscow. Ivan Kalita's immediate successor was formally placed over the other Russian princes by the action of the khan. Moscow's star was steadily rising.

Meanwhile, the Tatar power was steadily waning due largely to dynastic and domestic quarrels. By the 1370's, the Russians found that they could flout Tatar authority, though their impudence sometimes brought harsh retribution. But they were able, now and again, unilaterally, to reduce or withhold their tribute; and their troops defeated

Tatar forces at first in skirmishes and later in battles. In 1380 the Muscovite prince Dimitri of the Don (1359–89) defeated a great Tatar army at the battle of Kulikovo. This was a clean-cut single victory but not a final defeat of Tatar power. Tatar forces swept back to punish Moscow. The myth of Tatar military supremacy was broken, however. By taking the lead against the Tatars while his rival Russian princes, notably Michael of Tver, held back, Dimitri established himself and his state as the defender of Russia. The next two princes (Vasili I, 1389–1425; and Vasili II, 1425–62) continued to expand Muscovite power. The first Vasili added the region of Nizhni-Novgorod to his domain. The second Vasili managed to survive a civil war and beat back a major Tatar attack in 1451. He also declined to accept the attempt made in 1439 by the Council of Florence to reunite the Eastern and Western churches. Tatar power never fully recovered from the blows dealt it by the great Turkic conqueror Tamarlane (more accurately, Timur) at the end of the fourteenth century. By then the area of greatest danger had shifted from the east to the west and north, whence Moscow's rising power was challenged by the Lithuanians and the Poles.

LITHUANIANS AND POLES

The Lithuanians were an ancient people of Indo-European stock. The crusading orders of the German knights found them ensconced along the southeastern coast of the Baltic Sea. The Germans also found them an extremely tough and stubborn enemy. But by the fourteenth century, German pressures had turned the Lithuanians toward the weaker Russian states to the east. The Lithuanian Prince Gedymin (1316–41) conquered the old Russian land of Polotsk and extended his power into the area of the middle Dnieper. His son, Olgerd, continued to push eastward and to interfere in Russian affairs. He supported Tver against Moscow, for example, and several times led his troops to the outskirts of Moscow. The struggle continued after his death. In particular, Lithuania contended with Moscow for control of Novgorod. Olgerd's son married Jadwiga of Poland, thus creating a personal union which continued with some interruption until the submergence of Lithuania by Poland in the sixteenth century. As a direct and very important result of the Polish marriage, Lithuania became Roman Catholic in religion and the upper classes, at least, became Polish in culture. National rivalry between Moscow and Lithuania was therefore greatly exacerbated by the hostility between Orthodoxy and Catholicism.

The Grand Prince of Moscow Ivan III (1462–1505) inherited the quarrel with Lithuania as well as the fight with the Tatar remnants and other policies of his family. He acquitted himself with great skill and distinction. First he forced Novgorod to abandon its alliance with Lithuania. Later he conquered Novgorod and added its large territory to Muscovy. The upper classes of the defeated land were killed or driven into exile; the lower classes, forced into complete submission. Lord Novgorod ceased to exist as an independent power. Not long thereafter, Ivan—called "the Great" for obvious reasons—annexed Tver and extended Muscovite power at the expense of Riazin. Dynastic squabbles in Lithuania and Poland at the turn of the century gave him a chance which he did not miss. His victory brought some of the borderlands of Ukraine and Bielorussia into the expanding Muscovite state. It was Ivan the Great, also, who finally and formally broke the hold of the Tatars and freed Russia from their long dominion.

But one of the most consequential things which Ivan the Great did was to marry Sophia Paleologue, niece of the last Byzantine emperor. The marriage, which took place in 1472, was, curiously enough, arranged by a Roman Catholic pope. The last emperor died in the fight against the Turks. His niece and heiress, Zoe (she took the name Sophia after her marriage), became the ward of Pope Paul II. It was in the hope of effecting that union of the Eastern and Western churches, which the Council of Florence had vainly sought, that the pope suggested the marriage. It was duly arranged and carried out, but the result was not the one the pope had desired. Ivan the Great not only clung to his Orthodoxy, he went further and set himself up as the heir of the Byzantine emperor and the special defender of the Orthodox faith. There is a legend, possibly apocryphal, to the effect that when Zoe, accompanied by a papal representative, approached Moscow, the Russian metropolitan threatened to leave if the Roman Catholic legate was allowed to enter carrying the Latin Cross. Ivan heeded the threat, and the cross was put away. There is at least a symbolical accuracy to the story. Ivan remained the strong supporter of Orthodoxy, and the Orthodox clergy on their part remained the staunch defenders of autocracy. One of their efforts was the promulgation of the Theory of the Third Rome.

This theory was first advanced by the monk Philotheus of Pskov. The first Rome (on the Tiber) was the original repository of religious truth. But this Rome fell into error and supported a heresy in the Great Schism which split the Church into Eastern and Western parts. This mistake cost the first Rome its leadership, since it no longer served the truth, and it was punished by destruction of its power. The truth then resided with the patriarch at Tsargrad (Constantinople), which became the second Rome. As long as the true faith was maintained unsullied, Tsargrad prospered. But when it, too, fell into error it paid for its deviation by becoming prey to the infidel Turk. The heir of Tsargrad was Moscow, the third Rome, where the one true faith was maintained pure and undefiled. Therefore to Moscow passed the torch of truth and the obligation to carry this torch to the unenlightened. At the very least, the Theory of the Third Rome implied a Russian responsibility and authority over the Orthodox Christians. At the very most, it was a kind of messianism. Added to the doctrine of divine-right monarchy, it gave ecclesiastical sanction to the growth of autocracy.

⚛ ACCOMPLISHMENTS OF IVAN THE GREAT

No fine-spun theory, however, would have availed if Ivan the Great had been a weakling. Nor would his marriage with Zoe, with all its symbolical meaning of a joining of the Muscovite and Byzantine crowns, have had any effect without Ivan's ability to translate theory and symbols into practical, political facts. He was largely responsible for the administrative system which lasted until the time of Peter the Great. He called himself *Samoderzhets* after the break with the Tatars. The word is derived from the Greek *autokrator,* but it carries the special meaning of an independent sovereign. He also used the titles Tsar (*tsisari,* from the Latin *Caesar*) and Autocrat of All the Russias. He began the creation of bureaus or departments to handle government business, and he borrowed secretaries and undersecretaries from the Church, or from church schools, to staff these bureaus. He encouraged special attention to Byzantine scholarship and leaned heavily upon adepts in this study for advice in drafting the Grand Prince's Code. This code, set forth in 1497, was concerned mainly with the procedures of the administration of justice and with centralization of power. While it is true that Ivan imported Italian architects, artists, and craftsmen, whose work has been preserved in the oldest buildings of the Moscow Kremlin, Byzantium remained the chief mode. The Soviet historian R. Vipper has recently put the matter this way, ". . . the Moscow intelligentsia [in the latter fifteenth century] passed through something in the nature of a Renaissance, but while in the West the writers of the earlier classical period were closely studied, Rus remained faithful to her medieval Byzantine teachers."

The employment of Italian craftsmen was by no means the whole of Ivan's contacts with the West. As part of his drive toward the Baltic, he established friendly relations with Denmark and even signed a treaty with the Danish king. (Denmark at that time controlled the western end of the Baltic.) There was also talk of a dynastic marriage between the two states. Ivan also sent a diplomatic mission to the Turkish sultan in Constantinople and another to the pope.

🐚 THE *Pomestie* SYSTEM

In terms of Russian norms and values, Ivan's most significant single deed was the extension of the system of landholding, which is called *pomestie*. This began not as the first step of a planned reform but as a way of meeting an immediate need. Ivan the Great and his successors faced the same sort of problem which confronted other national monarchs whose power was increasing. The addition of new territories to Muscovy also meant the introduction into Muscovite society of the princes and the aristocracy of the annexed appanages. At the same time, the increased size of the state made it necessary to enlarge both the administration and the military. Moreover, the unseated princes were likely to be unruly and unwilling subjects of the tsar. Certainly they did not always accept a subordinate position gracefully. They jockeyed for position and place and, at times, challenged the power of the national monarch.

The problem had been met in part by allowing the princelings, or some of them anyway, to retain their hereditary estates and their powers of local government. This produced a patchwork similar to that found in France as a result of the expansion of the Capetian holdings. Each locality was usually a law unto itself. There was always a danger that the residual separatism normal to a recently independent but now subordinate state would flare into a successful movement. The continuing feuds and rivalries among the princelings made for chronic disorder. There was also the ever-present threat that, singly or collectively, they might rebel against the tsar. Ivan's Polish contemporaries sought to meet a similar situation by playing off the lesser nobility against the greater. This worked for a short time, but in bidding for the support of the lesser nobles the Polish crown surrendered too much. Its authority was so undermined thereby that it eventually failed.

Ivan took a new approach after the conquest of Novgorod. It has been noted that the native aristocracy of Novgorod was liquidated. Their lands, confiscated by the tsar, gave him a reservoir of treasure which he turned to good account. Sections of the lands were distributed to officers of his army in return for services rendered and anticipated. Failure to render service on demand meant forfeiture of the land. This gave Ivan a force upon which he could rely to raise an army and govern the territory. Since these new landowners, who were called *pomeshchik* from the name of the system and of the estate (*pomestie*), were Moscovites, they acted as a check both upon the remnants of the Novgorodian aristocracy and upon any separatist movement.

As to the appanage princes and their followers, it was not always either possible or politic to eliminate them. Instead, there developed a practice of separating them from their native places. They were brought to Moscow and compelled to reside there. But they were also more or less absorbed into the court and into government service. Their competition for place and power enabled the tsars often to use them to weaken each other. These new systems did not work perfectly nor did they wholly obviate the dangers of separatism and insurrection. There were times when the aristocracy dominated the autocrat. But, by and large, it was autocracy and not aristocracy which won.

🏵 DEVELOPMENT OF SERFDOM

The creation of the *pomestie* had another result, which was the development of serfdom. One of its roots was debt serfdom, which grew out of the Tatar invasions. The connection between serfdom and the new system of land grants in return for service is obvious. The land was of absolutely no value whatever without labor. The *pomeshchiks* had certain fixed obligations to the tsar which they were wholly unable to discharge unless they had peasants to work the land. This was the *raison d'être* of the new development. It was the gradual introduction of new norms and values which partly re-enforced and partly modified or displaced the existent norms and values.

Not much is known about social development during the appanage period. It appears that most Russian peasants were free men, although there may have been variations among them as to the degree of freedom. Most of them are presumed to have been free to bequeath and inherit property, free to contract for employment, and free to change employers at will. Probably long before the coming of the Tatars some of them chose or were forced by poverty into becoming debtors for equipment, seeds, livestock, and so on. Others may have attached themselves to stronger or richer persons for protection and may have paid for this security by giving up some or all of their individual freedom. Both these processes were greatly accelerated and spread as a result of the Tatar conquest and dominion. Peasants who had borrowed money were known in the ancient usage as "silver-men." Those who settled on the estate of a prince or boyar (or monastery) and who were given a homestead by the owner were required to pay a rental which usually amounted to about a quarter of the yearly production of the homestead.

In the early days, the peasant was free to leave whenever he had discharged his obligation either by repaying the "silver" which had been loaned or by payment of the rental. At first such removals could be made at any time, but later they were restricted to a designated period after the harvest and in the spring. The Grand Prince's Code of 1497 set the removal period at the festival of St. George, which came in late November. If the peasant had not fully discharged his obligation at that time, he was forced to remain for at least another year unless he could get some other person to buy him off from his creditor. In the latter case, of course, he could move, but he also assumed a new obligation.

It has been thought by some historians that the peasants on any given estate were very early organized into mirs. These, in one aspect—and they had or developed many aspects—were a sort of corporation which was self-governing, though subject to the landlord. The mirs also acted as intermediary between the peasants and the landlords. The obligations were placed upon the mir which, in turn, apportioned them among its members. It is presumed that the landlord was not unwilling to have individual peasants move so long as the mir as a whole discharged its obligation. The *pomeshchik* had to have adequate labor or lose his holdings.

His problem was made more acute because the same expansion which had brought him into being also provided additional opportunities for peasant movement. The subsiding of the Tatar menace had the same effect, since the borderlands were less subject to recurrent raids. The opening up of new lands and the creation of new estates created a brisk competition for labor while at the same time offering greater chances for personal freedom if the peasant could escape toward the frontiers. It may seem as if these conditions ought to have operated to free peasants from their debt serfdom. It did not. In the long run it led to transforming them from debt serfs to legal serfs, who were held in place not only by economic bondage but also by the whole power of the government.

CHAPTER V

Ivan Grozny, Autocrat of All Russia

⬦ THE SIXTEENTH CENTURY: ITS VIGOR AND ITS VIOLENCE

The sixteenth century appears to have been one of the most vigorous and exciting hundred-year periods in human history. It was a time of great changes and of greater turbulence. It was a period of reaching out, an age of expansion both geographically and intellectually. It was a time of violence and of sudden death for many, as well as a period of glory and power for the few. It was an age of war and of great military conquests. It was a day of astonishing exploits throughout the world.

The sixteenth was the century in which Magellan circumnavigated the globe—a feat which ought to be appreciated rather than forgotten by the century which has seen the circumaviation of the world. It was the day of Drake, of Raleigh, of Jacques Cartier. It saw the establishment in India of the Empire of the Great Mogul; it witnessed the Japanese attacks upon Korea—their first strike toward world dominion; and it saw the expansion of Persian power in the Middle East. It was the time of Suleiman the Magnificent, whose advance of Turkish power across Europe was checked by the Christian West only with the greatest difficulty.

The sixteenth century was the age of the Tudors, of the Great Armada, and of the terrible sack of Rome by the mercenary troops of Charles V. It was also, of course, the century of the Protestant Revolution and of the Catholic Reformation; of Luther, Zwingli, Calvin, and Loyola. It was the age of vicious wars fought in the name of religion, and among its bloody pages are those which record the massacre of St. Bartholomew's Eve.

But though it may have been exciting it can hardly have been glamorous to those ordinary little people whose lives were disrupted and forfeited that the great ones might carry out their grandiose ambitions.

It can scarcely have seemed a day of gladness to the peasants whose lands were devastated, whose hovels were burned, and whose poor livestock were killed by the raging soldiery. Though rulers may have gloried and people perhaps thrilled vicariously to the expansion of power, how far could these feelings have been shared by those upon whose bodies the empires were built? This was the age of the rulers, not of the common people. They manned the ships and filled the ranks of armies, they tilled the fields and worked the mines, they suffered the lash and bore the thrust of lances that their "betters" might build their power *pro gloria patri et deo*. So it was in the England of the Tudors, in the France of the Henrys, in the Spain of Charles and Philip, in the Germany of Luther, and in the Italy of many popes. So it was also in Russia in the days of that Ivan commonly known to the West as "the Terrible." In Russia, too, there was change, and expansion, turbulence, and violence. In Russia, as elsewhere, there was the increasing power of the ruler, and the increasing weight of burdens put upon his people. And in Russia, too, was found a close identification of Church and State.

🗝 CHURCH AND STATE

Somehow it seems curiously fitting that the sixteenth century opened on a bitter struggle within the Russian Church, a struggle which had strong political overtones. One part of this conflict involved the ownership of lands. Over the years the Church had acquired tremendous wealth in land, most of it owned by the monasteries. A minority of churchmen, who were known as the Trans-Volga Elders and who followed the lead of Nilus of Sorsk, protested against this great wealth and urged the Church to strip herself of it. Christian poverty and humility, they thought, were not compatible with the possession and management of great estates. The majority of churchmen, including the hierarchy, rejected this protest. This group, known as the Josephites from the name of their leader, Joseph of Volokolamsk, held that the Church needed its wealth in order properly to fulfill its functions.

The government was inclined to side with the Elders on the land question. This was a period of the expansion of the *pomestie* system, and the rich lands of the Church aroused both the cupidity and the fear of the government. They coveted the acres which, added to their possessions, would have made possible an increase of their supporting *pomeshchiks;* they looked askance at the power which this wealth conferred upon its owners. But there was another issue besides that of land, and on this second matter the sympathy of the government was entirely with the Josephites.

The Josephites were traditionalists, literalists, ritualists, and formalists in religion. Moreover, they believed in the desirability of and necessity for a very close and indissoluble alliance between the Church and the autocracy. They supported the autocracy by precept and by action, as in the promulgation of the Theory of the Third Rome and of divine-right autocracy, as well as in concrete and specific aid to the prince. In return, they asked that the autocrat give them full protection and support, including the persecution and suppression of heretics. The Elders, in contrast, set great store by personal piety and comparatively little by dogmas and rituals. While they were eager for the spread of Christianity and for the acceptance of what they held to be the true religion, they nonetheless rejected compulsion as the way to achieve those ends. Persuasion, not force, was the method they preached. The Elders also believed that the realm of the Church was spiritual; that of the State, physical and violent. The Church, they therefore argued, should not mix in matters of state; and the State should not interfere with religion.

The Elders were bucking the stream of continuity. Throughout most of the preceding five centuries of Church history in Russia, Church and State had been joined in a mutually profitable alliance. The Church had helped mightily in building up the power and prestige of the prince. The princes had reciprocated by favors to the Church. Moreover, the insistence of the Elders on personal piety was tantamount to the championship of individual freedom as opposed to the accepted norm and value of collectivism. Nilus and his followers opposed the demands of Joseph for the violent liquidation of what is known in Russian history as the "Jewish Heresy." The label is derived from the fact that one of its leaders was a Jew. But the heresy which flourished first in Novgorod and later in Moscow was as much Unitarian as it was Judaic. Against these heretics and in the other issues, Joseph had his way. A church council in 1503 condemned the heretics to death. By an informal, unwritten agreement the Josephites promised unqualified support of the autocracy, and the government ceased its secularization of Church lands. It was a deal which stood the grandson of Ivan III in very good stead.

🜨 VASILI III (1505–33)

Ivan's second son and immediate successor, Vasili III, followed the general lines of policy laid down by his father. He continued to expand the *pomestie* system and by this and other means sought successfully to build up the power of his crown. Like his father he still used the titles of *Samoderzhets* and Grand Prince, but sometimes he styled himself as tsar. He undertook three expeditions against the Tatars in Kazan, suffering ignominious defeat in the first two, but winning a limited success in the third. He added to Muscovy the old land of Smolensk, which he conquered from Lithuania, and the lands of Riazin and Pskov. To Vasili and to Muscovy, these last two additions were the climax of a long drive and, therefore, were welcome triumphs. To the conquered lands, it appeared otherwise. In the lament of the chronicler of Pskov:

> Then disappeared the glory of Pskov and our city was taken, not by those of another faith, but by those of our own faith. 'Who would not weep and groan for this disaster, O glorious and great city of Pskov, for what dost thou lament and weep?' And the beautiful city of Pskov answered: 'How can I help weeping and grieving over the desolation which has befallen me? A many-winged eagle has flown to me with lion's claws, and has taken from me all my beauty and wealth and carried off my children.'

As to his relations with the West, Vasili listened to the proposals of the German emperor that Muscovy join a crusade against the Turks and that it ally with the empire against Lithuania, Poland, and Hungary. Vasili also received envoys from the pope, who wished to reunite Christendom under his leadership. Wary and cunning, Vasili used these contacts to bring to Moscow foreign craftsmen, technicians, and men of learning. He accepted papal mediation in order to make a truce with Lithuania. But he did not yield to the importunings of the emissaries. He refused to enter into any negotiations which aimed at ecclesiastical reunion, and he repeatedly stated his faithfulness to Orthodoxy.

The metropolitan repaid him by aiding in the continuation of his dynasty. When his first wife proved childless, Vasili, with the consent of the metropolitan, shut her away in a convent and took for his second wife one Helen Glinskaia, a Lithuanian exile who had found asylum in Muscovy. Two of the Trans-Volga Elders who protested this second marriage were imprisoned—a fate which was not displeasing to the victorious Josephites. Helen bore Vasili two sons: Ivan and Yuri. Yuri was an imbecile. Ivan was a little boy of three when his father died, in 1533. By the dying ruler's will, the little Ivan received the title of grand duke under the regency of a council which was headed by Helen and which included the metropolitan.

Now followed a decade and a half of feud and counterfeud, plot and counterplot, murder and retribution as the boyars contended for power. And who were the boyars? Broadly speaking, they were the nobility who served the prince as councilors, military and civil officials, and so on. Some of them were *pomeshchiks* as well as boyars. Some of them were descendants of families who had long been in the service of the prince. Others were the descendants of the appanage princelings who had "made submission" and so become the "free servants" of the grand prince. These prince-boyars were, in general, an arrogant and haughty lot of troublemakers. Ivan the Great and Vasili III had managed to hold them in check. But what power had a boy of three, or a regent who, though she had the backing of the metropolitan, was a foreigner from an alien, enemy land? Helen and her clique managed to hang on to power for five years. Then she suddenly died and men said, though without proof, that she had been murdered by the prince-boyars.

At any rate, power was taken over by this group and the boy Ivan became a pawn in their murderous game. Chief among the protagonists were the Shuiskis and the Belskis. First victory went to the Shuiskis. In the words of the Russian historian Platonov, ". . . they spared neither Grand Prince, nor Metropolitan, nor common man. They insulted the one, deposed the other, and oppressed the third." Then the Belskis got the upper hand and were no better. The Shuiskis won again and ran the state for their own profit until the day the twelve-year old grand prince ordered his guards to kill the head of the Shuiski family. The order was speedily and brutally obeyed. Others of the Shuiski family were banished from Moscow. But Ivan was still too young to rule, and power was assumed by his relatives. Meanwhile, Ivan had come under the influence of the Metropolitan Maccarius, who genuinely befriended the friendless boy. It was Maccarius who taught Ivan to think of himself as tsar of Russia, as heir to the ancient crowns of Monomakh and the Byzantine Empire, as leader of the Orthodox and champion of the Third Rome.

🐚 IVAN IV (1533–84)

What sort of a person was this Ivan IV, Grand Prince of Moscow and first formally to assume the title of Tsar? It is not easy to characterize him. The Englishman Sir Jerome Horsey, who was in Russia off and on from 1575 to 1591 and who served both Queen Elizabeth and Tsar Ivan as envoy, described him as "comly in person, indued with great witt, excelent gifts and graces, fitt for government of so great a monarchie." Elsewhere in his *Travells* he says that Ivan "was a goodlie man of person and presence, waell favored, high forehead, shrill voice; a right Sithian; full of readie wisdom, cruell, bloudye, merciles." Contemporary pictures show him bearded, and emphasize his oval eyes and his large beaklike nose. Other contemporary descriptions referred to Ivan as brave, shrewd, and cunning, a man of high spirit and subtle mind. But all else about the man is generally overshadowed by the horrendous labels applied to him in the West: Jean le Terrible, Iwan der Schreckliche, Ivan the Terrible— all of which are presumably translations of the Russian, *Ivan Grozny*.

Grozny may be (and usually is) translated as "terrible," but the English connotation is not the same as the Russian, which may carry the sense of "redoubtable" or "stern" or "threatening." Not that there is the slightest question that Ivan was cruel and merciless, but he did some great deeds which were more important than the atrocities he certainly committed.

Two important events in Ivan's life took place in the year 1547: his coronation by Maccarius as Tsar and Autocrat of All the Russias and his marriage to Anastasia Romanov. His bride came from a boyar family which had loyally served the princes of Muscovy. Anastasia's brother, Nikita, was for twenty years one of Ivan's commanders, and it was his grandson, Michael, who became the first Romanov tsar in 1613. Ivan's marriage was a happy one. Some historians have credited Anastasia with the "good years" of Ivan's early reign, and attributed the "black years" after her death to her absence. This explanation appears to rest more on traditional assumptions than on proven facts. Perhaps as significant as Anastasia's early influence was the guidance given Ivan by the priest Sylvester.

Vipper, the Soviet historian, goes so far as to refer to the years from 1547 to 1553 as the period of clerical policy. This is not at all unreasonable. The influence of Maccarius and Sylvester was strong. It was, moreover, a time of vigorous activity in the Church. Maccarius summoned several church councils for the purpose of unifying and strengthening the Church. Local pecularities in ritual and liturgy were attacked, an all-Russian book of saints was prepared, a more rigid discipline was established among the clergy, and efforts were made to expand the influence of clerical leadership. Some of the aims were, as Vipper observes, similar to those of the Council of Trent. But the major aim was to increase the central authority of the metropolitan and the tsar. Sylvester, who served as Ivan's adviser and virtual chancellor, symbolized this alliance. It is noteworthy that Sylvester's protégé, Adashev, became Ivan's intimate councilor and lieutenant. The employment of Adashev, who had been only a minor figure until Ivan charged him with receiving the petitions of the people, also illustrates Ivan's determination to free his power from the restrictions placed on it by the prince-boyars.

✿ REFORMS AND WARS

With the help of these men, Ivan began a series of administrative and other reforms which were designed to enhance his authority. The old Boyars Council was supplanted by a "Chosen Council" which included men of various ranks, such as boyars' sons, officials, and clerks—men who owed their elevation to the tsar and might, therefore, be expected to serve him loyally. In addition, Ivan chose a thousand of the lesser boyars to serve as a special force. Their names were entered in the

Book of the Thousand, and they were rewarded for their services with estates close to Moscow. This was a refinement of the *pomestie* system which had been instituted by Ivan the Great. The system itself was somewhat revised and strengthened by equalizing the rewards given to the *pomeshchiks* on the basis of a careful inventory of lands and estates. Connected with this reform was the abolition of the special powers originally given to the governors of cities and provinces. These officials had been allowed to enrich themselves by taking fees for their legal and administrative services. This right was now withdrawn, partly because it had allowed the officials to become less dependent upon the tsar. Some of the functions which had been carried out by these governors were now transferred to local men who were paid by the tsar out of the proceeds of a special tax which was levied for that purpose. Ivan may have been aiming at the promotion of his subjects' welfare by giving more self-government. Some historians have thought so. But it seems more likely that his primary intention was to increase the centralization of power.

Ivan Grozny was no less keen than his forbears to expand his power both by centralization and by wars of conquest. His first military victory was at the expense of the Tatar peoples, against whom Vasili had contended with little success. Ivan's campaign against Kazan was prepared with great skill and care which included the establishment of frontier outposts and the construction of siege engines. The fortress of Kazan fell to the Russian forces in 1552. Four years later Astrakhan was captured. These conquests broke the Tatar hold upon the Volga region and opened these lands to Russian trade and Russian settlement. The Russian power was temporarily extended into part of Transcaucasia, and it was apparently planned to carry it into the Crimea also. This proved impossible, partly because of the strength of the Crimean Tatars and their backers, the Ottoman Turks, and partly because Ivan committed his major efforts to an attack upon Livonia.

Livonia, gate to the Baltic, had attracted the attention of Ivan III, who had hoped to annex it to his growing state. He was unable to do this, but he did force Livonia to pay him tribute. The Livonians, quite understandably fearful of Russian intentions, sought an alliance with the Hapsburg Emperor Charles V and tried vainly to secure a Russian promise of nonaggression. The alliance was not forthcoming, and the most that could be gotten from Moscow was a limited truce conditioned on the payment of tribute. For Russia was on the march to the Baltic. Russian trade had long gone through Livonian ports and had long been subjected to Livonian interference. Now the rising strength of Russia and the declining power of Livonia encouraged Ivan to reverse the past.

In 1558 Ivan opened his campaign against Livonia, thus beginning
a war which lasted, with some intermissions, for a quarter century. The
first two years were marked by such sweeping Russian successes that
Livonia disintegrated. But it did not surrender to Russia. Estonia attached itself to Sweden; Livonia proper, to Lithuania; Courland, to a
feudatory of the Polish king. The Russian-Livonian War now became

Russia and her Neighbors — *about 1550*

a war of Russia against Sweden and Lithuania. Since the latter was joined to Poland by the Union of Lublin in 1569, Ivan eventually had to fight the Poles as well. He concentrated first against the Lithuanians and won a series of successes which were not, however, decisive. After the Polish-Lithuanian union, the tide slowly turned until finally Ivan was constrained to accept a truce by which he gave up his conquests in Lithuania and his claims to Livonia. This was in 1582, and the Swedes took advantage of Ivan's weakness to invade Russia and to force Ivan to accept a peace which left Estonia and some other lands in Swedish control. The long Livonian War thus ended in a Russian failure. It had, meanwhile, played a considerable part in domestic developments.

🖐 POLITICAL CRISES

Back in 1553, when the twenty-three-year-old Ivan had been tsar for six years, he fell gravely ill—so ill that it was expected that he would die. Calling his Chosen Council to his bedside, Ivan announced to them that he was designating his small son, Dimitri, as his successor, and asked that they swear allegiance to the boy. Some did so readily, but others were extremely reluctant. They argued that the real power would be vested in a regency dominated by the Romanovs, from whom they were not willing to take orders. (Some of them had been very much opposed to Ivan's marriage with the daughter of an ordinary boyar.) Ivan's will finally prevailed but not until their reluctance had convinced him that he could no longer fully trust Sylvester, Adashev, and some of the others of the Chosen Council. There was no open break at the time, however. The men took the required oath. Ivan surprised everyone by recovering his health, and matters apparently went on much as before. Ivan, however, turned less to Sylvester and Adashev than to Prince Kurbski, who was also a member of the select group.

The decision to enter upon the Livonian War apparently was made only after bitter dispute between Ivan, who favored the move, and the party of Sylvester and Adashev, who urged a campaign against the Crimea instead. The tsar again had his way, and the successes of the first five years of the war not only seemed to confirm the correctness of his judgment but also greatly increased his self-confidence. There is much evidence to show that Ivan had long resented the strict tutelage under which Sylvester sought to keep him. There is also some evidence which indicates that the Chosen Council deliberately sought to check the growing authority of the tsar. It appears that Kurbski, in particular, wished to curb the tsar by means of the council just as the Supreme Council of the Polish nobles curbed the power of the Polish king. Ivan, with the initial successes against Livonia, began to feel his oats. Sylvester was the first to go. He was banished to a monastery, but Adashev remained in Ivan's service, as did Kurbski, who as late as 1562 still enjoyed Ivan's absolute confidence.

It has been repeatedly urged that the decisive event in the development of Ivan's character was the death in 1560 of his wife, Anastasia. In fact, the classic interpretation is that this event threw Ivan mentally off balance, or at least completely removed all restraining influences from him. The most recent biographer of the tsar spends page after page embroidering this theme. There can be no doubt that Anastasia's death was a terrible blow to Ivan, and it may be that her gentleness had held his lack of gentleness in check. But there seems to have been more to the story than that.

If 1563 was a year of triumph, 1564 was a year of serious military reverses. Two major campaigns utterly failed—partly, at least, because of the lackadaisical performance of their leaders. Then Kurbski, Ivan's most trusted lieutenant, fled to Poland to serve with the Polish king. These were military and political disasters of the scale which produces crises. It may be, as has been argued, that Kurbski, who had lost a battle to the Poles, simply did not dare to face his despotic and cruel master. But Ivan could scarcely have been expected to take this view of the matter. To Ivan, Kurbski's action was high treason—desertion to the enemy in time of war. The fact of Ivan's confidence in Kurbski and of the effects of the other military reverses must have made Kurbski's action seem doubly damnable to the tsar. Russia was engaged in a major war against very formidable enemies. She had just suffered serious defeats. If the tsar could no longer depend even upon his Chosen Council, the outlook was bleak indeed for Russia and for the tsardom. For it should be remembered that the struggle between the autocrat and the recalcitrant boyars had by no means ended. Treason must have appeared imminent. Drastic action was required not alone to protect the life and person of the tsar but, even more important, to reform and reorder the national strength to meet the foreign menace. These were the chief considerations which led Ivan to create the *Oprichnina* (1565–72).[1]

⊕ THE *Oprichnina*

There were many dramatic aspects of the *Oprichnina,* including a brutal "reign of terror," which have not been overlooked by historians. On the contrary, they have more often so emphasized the melodrama as to lose sight of less spectacular but more significant features. Ivan has been pictured as suddenly making up his mind to undertake a drastic innovation; as suddenly and dramatically leaving Moscow to take refuge in a distant village; and then, as simultaneously threatening to abdicate and appealing to the people for support. These various incidents took place, but they were neither sudden nor unpremeditated.

Late in December, 1564, Ivan gathered about him a certain number of his courtiers together with their families, a selected guard, his second wife and household, all his treasure—money, jewels, gold and silver plate, and his icons—and set out on a roundabout journey to the village of Alexandrovsk. He was no stranger to this place, which had often been his temporary residence between military campaigns and on his trips around the realm. About a month later, an envoy from Ivan arrived in Moscow with one letter to the metropolitan and another addressed to the merchants and "the whole Christian population of Moscow." The theme of the messages was that the tsar had no complaints against the merchants and the people, but many (which he specified at length) against the clergy and the higher officials. So desperate was the situation, the messages said, that Ivan was determined to abdicate. The merchants and the people, and even the boyars whom he had excoriated, now besought the metropolitan to intercede with the tsar to prevent the abdication. It was promised that the tsar might rule as he chose and that he might punish any whom he thought needed punishing.

The emissaries who carried this message back to Alexandrovsk were graciously received. Ivan agreed to continue as tsar on two conditions. The first condition was that he might punish all traitors and rebels and confiscate their wealth. The second was that he should be allowed to divide the realm by establishing an *Oprichnina*. His stipulations were readily accepted. It was the view of the Marxist historian Pokrovskii that this whole "negotiation" had been carefully prearranged during the month immediately following Ivan's departure from Moscow. The letter to the metropolitan and the appeal to the people, as well as their response, were carefully staged to ensure public support of the tsar. Certainly the whole incident is misleading when treated alone or told only in terms of its drama. It needs to be seen in historical perspective.

The establishment of the *Oprichnina* in 1565 was not entirely an innovation. Rather, it was an expansion and refinement of the policy first implemented in 1550 by the creation of the Thousand. This set up in the Moscow district a separate administration with a separate force who owed their place and power to the tsar alone. By a decree of 1562, Ivan had deprived certain prince-boyars and princes of the right to sell or exchange their hereditary estates. The same law also provided that these estates should become the tsar's property should the owner die without male issue. The decree went much further. It declared forfeit to the sovereign all estates of the specified group which had been sold or exchanged ten or more years before the decree. This was an extension of the custom which obtained under Ivan's father and grandfather that the princes' estates could be sold only with the consent of the grand prince. In other words, it had long been held that these lands were the property of the sovereign and were therefore subject to his power.

The arrangement of 1565 greatly extended the area directly under Ivan's control. The *Oprichnina,* which was gradually enlarged, came to include the old appanage lands, the most important commercial and manufacturing centers, and most of the great trade routes. It never included all of Russia. But within the *Oprichnina,* the tsar's authority was as complete and absolute as that of any landlord over his private estate. It is not, in fact, either inaccurate or inappropriate to consider the *Oprichnina* in precisely those terms. Ivan executed or expelled from their hereditary lands most of the prince-boyars whose estates fell within the *Oprichnina.* Some of these people were compensated for the loss of their patrimonies by the grant of estates outside the *Oprichnina* (in the part known as the *Zemshchina*). Some of them sought asylum abroad, and many were simply liquidated. Estates confiscated from those accused of treason were steadily added to the *Oprichnina* (which lost that distinctive title in 1572 and became known as "the Court"). The lands thus acquired served as a treasure which was at Ivan's sole disposal, and by which he paid his chosen followers.

☙ THE *Oprichniki*

These men, known as the *Oprichniki* ("Men of the Apart") originally numbered about one thousand. Eventually this was increased to approximately five thousand. Since each *Oprichnik* was required to furnish a number of men for service, this meant that Ivan had under his command a force many times greater than the number of the *Oprichniki* alone. It was the *Oprichniki,* acting both under Ivan's orders and on their own responsibility, who carried the reign of terror throughout the country. Immediately after the agreement of January, 1565, a considerable number of Ivan's real or suspected enemies were executed, banished to monasteries, or exiled. This process, marked by the most horrible atrocities and excesses, continued for years, reaching a climax in 1570 with an attack upon Novgorod. Ivan, with some of his *Oprichniki* and with many Tatar troops whom he used extensively, had just made a profitable but very vicious campaign against the towns of Livonia. Many prisoners and much loot had been sent back to Novgorod. What happened next was described from hearsay by the Englishman Jerome Horsey:

> But the Emperower returninge to the great cittie of Novgorod, wher all his captives and prisonors remayned, he beinge mightely displeased against this cittie, above all others, the inhabitants, for revenge of their treasons and

treachories, 'as' joining with the discontented nobillitie, he charges it with 30 thowsand Tartors and tenn thowsand gonnors [gunners] of his guard, withowt any respect ravished all of the weomen and maieds, ranzacked, robbed, and spoilled all that wear [were] within it of their jewells, plate and treasur, murthered the people yonge and olde, burnt all their howshold stuff, merchandices and warehowses of wax, flaex, tallow, hieds, salt, wynes, cloth, and silks, sett all one fier, with wax and tallow melted down the kennels in the streats, together with the bloud that rann into the river, and of all other livinge creatures and cattell, their dead carcacesses did stoppe as it wear [were] the stream of the river Volca [Volga], beinge cast therin.

The figure of seven hundred thousand dead is an absurd exaggeration. Kurbski put the figure at fifteen thousand; the Pskov chronicler, at sixty thousand; and modern historians, at two thousand. But the number does not particularly matter now, nor does the traditional exaggeration alter the essential fact that there was an extensive terror between 1565 and 1575.

However, the *Oprichnina* was much more than a reign of terror and the *Oprichniki* was more than terrorists and more than security police. They performed both functions, but, more important, they furthered the expansion of autocratic power at the expense of the boyars. In this respect, the whole business of the *Oprichnina* may be regarded as roughly parallel to the destruction of the old nobility by the Tudors of England. It was part of the process of building a national autocracy out of what had been a disjointed oligarchy. The process was not complete, as the events of the next generation showed.

THE NATIONAL ASSEMBLY

The relationship of these domestic developments to foreign affairs, and particularly to the military crises which precipitated Ivan's action, needs a little further attention. In 1566, Ivan summoned a National Assembly (the *Zemski Sobor*) to drum up support for the war. Limited assemblies had been previously summoned. Ivan the Great, for example, had called one in 1471. But Russian historians are in general agreement that this meeting in 1566 is properly to be regarded as the first true National Assembly. Invited to it were the higher clergy, the Boyars Council, important government officials—both civil and military—merchants, and some minor aristocrats. These last two groups had never been included in preceding assemblages. Most of the members of this assembly were chosen from the original Thousand of 1550; Ivan had skillfully mixed the old and the new. The question placed before the National Assembly was whether to accept a Polish peace offer or to continue the war to secure all of Livonia. It was decided to go on fighting. By associating these others with him in this decision, Ivan both gained their support and strengthened his position as a national monarch.

But foreign affairs did not go well for the Russians. Sweden succeeded in closing off the northern route. Sigismund II, one of the greatest of the Polish kings, effected a union of Poland and Lithuania (the Union of Lublin), thus strengthening his power. He also persuaded the Crimean Tatars to attack Moscow. This they did in 1571 with a result reported in a contemporary letter to England: "The Mosco is burnt every sticke by the Crimme the 24, day of May last. . . ." The Tatars also destroyed much of the area around Moscow.

These setbacks coincided with the most devastating periods of the terror. Some of Ivan's own family and some prominent *Oprichniki* were put to death. Ivan has been judged harshly for these man-hunts and there was undoubtedly a large element of hysteria and personal vindictiveness involved. But, again without excusing his atrocities, it may be pointed out that Ivan's actions were not without some justification. There had been a plot against his life in 1567. The intensification of the war in the north was a very serious challenge to Russia, and the north was linked to the Tatars by the connection between Sigismund and the Crimean Khan. Moreover, the Tatar raid of 1571 was not an isolated incident but part of a larger plan which involved an alliance of Turks and Tatars against Russia. This group launched another large attack in 1572 which was finally beaten off, not by the forces of the *Oprichnina* but by those of the boyar-led *Zemshchina*. Perhaps Ivan was hypersensitive and unduly suspicious, but he had considerable reason to fear treason. The personnel of the *Oprichniki* had proved somewhat faulty. Ivan therefore undertook an extensive reshuffling of men. Some of the *Oprichniki* were banished or killed, their estates reverting to the tsar, and some of the *Zemshchina* were brought in to replace them. The *Oprichnina* continued as a military and administrative device. Under its new name, "the Court," it included at Ivan's death more than half the realm—the richest and most important part.

There are two other series of events which greatly affected Russia during this period. One was the eastward expansion of the Russian state by the actions, in the first instance, of the fur traders. The other is the coming of the English to Ivan's Russia.

EXPANSION INTO SIBERIA

The vast expanses of Siberia were at this time, as they remained for centuries, very lightly peopled. The most important groups in the west were the remnants of the Tatars, who were united in the late sixteenth century into a kingdom which the Russians called Siberia. The name is probably a derivation from the name of their capital, Sibir. These Siberian Tatars were still partly nomadic, although some of them had settled down to agriculture. Hunting, trapping, and the raising of deer were their other main occupations. Several other groups, mostly nomadic hunters and trappers, also lived in Siberia. None of them, except for the Siberian Tatars, could offer much resistance to Russian expansion. And since the Tatars were too uncivilized to know the use of guns, their powers of resistance were limited. The Siberian lands had long been known to some Russians; merchants of Novgorod had made their way there in the fourteenth century. Maps of the area are known to have existed at least as early as the beginning of the sixteenth century. But no effective Russian expansion into Siberia took place before Ivan's reign. The pioneers then were the trading family of the Stroganovs.

Earlier accounts refer to the Stroganovs as wealthy boyars from Novgorod. More recent historical studies identify them as having originally been peasants who by skill and luck acquired great wealth. Whatever their family history, the Stroganovs had become extremely wealthy merchant-manufacturers by the the time of Ivan Grozny. The foundation of the family fortune was salt, but their business had ramified until their interests included many other things as well. It is calculated that they employed fifteen thousand workers in their various enterprises. They sought and got admission to the *Oprichnina,* and generally flourished during Ivan's rule. In 1574 the Stroganovs sent a number of expeditions across the Urals to search for furs. Six years later they dispatched a large expedition, under the command of the Cossack Yermak, against the Siberian kingdom. The kingdom was conquered and its lands were added to those of Ivan. His government now became much more active. Garrisons were established, governors were sent out, and more and more Siberian acres were claimed as part of Russia. The movement continued for some time, however, to be spear-headed by private enterprise. If the undertaking succeeded, the government took over; if it failed, the government disavowed the empire builders. The matter, especially the exploits of Yermak, were more dramatically recorded in a popular folk poem of the type called *bylinas.* The speaker is Yermak:

> I am the robber Hetman of the Don;
> 'Twas I went over the blue sea, the Caspian;
> And I it was who destroyed the ships;
> And now, our hope, our Orthodox Tsar,
> I bring you my traitorous head,
> And with it I bring the empire of Siberia,
> And the Orthodox Tsar will speak,
> He will speak, the formidable Ivan Vasilievich,
> Ah! Thou art Yermak, son of Timofei,

Thou art the Hetman of the warriors of the Don.
I pardon thee and thy band,
I pardon thee for thy trusty service,
And I give the glorious Don as thy inheritance.

🐚 RUSSO-ENGLISH RELATIONS

The coming of the English traders and the opening of formal Anglo-Russian diplomatic relations were important events which make an interesting story. The experiences were carefully recorded by the Englishmen who took part in them. We have, among others, the account of Richard Chancelour, whose expedition reached Moscow via the White Sea in 1553; the supplementary report by Clement Adams, one of Chancelour's pilots; Giles Fletcher's famous account, *Of the Russe Common Wealth;* and the *Relacion or Memoriall abstracted owt of Sir Jerom Horsey his Travells.* Availability of source material certainly had a good deal to do with the fullness of the histories on this matter. The outline of the story goes like this.

Three small ships sailed from England in the spring of 1553. Their plotted course was across the North Sea to the Norwegian coast; thence, north around Novaya Zemlya; and then, they hoped, east or northeast to India. It was a daring attempt to find a northeast passage to the Orient. The little flotilla was separated by a storm and the two smaller ships were lost. But Richard Chancelour in the "Edward Bonaventure" (160 tons) ". . . held on his course toward the unkowen part of the world, and sailed so farre that hee came at last to the place where hee found no night at all, but a continuall light and brightness of the Sunne shining clearely upon the huge and mightie Sea."

This was the White Sea, and Chancelour landed near the site of the present town of Archangel. Incidentally, this town was founded by the English. Chancelour was well received by the people, who assisted him on his journey to Moscow. There he was welcomed by Ivan, who saw in the English a solution to some of his own problems. Troubles with Livonia and the rising power of Poland placed a barrier across the Baltic trade routes. The way discovered by the English made it possible to by-pass the Baltic and its guardians. Moreover, the English were a mercantile and maritime Power who could supply goods which Russia needed and supply carriage for the trade. They could also provide artisans and technicians. For these reasons, Ivan directed that "Richard [Chancelour] and the guests arrived from the English land with wares brought in their ships from beyond the seas might come and go in safety in the Russian dominions and might buy or build houses without hindrance."

Chancelour took Ivan's invitation to engage in trade back to England in 1554 and was then sent again to Russia in the following year to seek trade concessions. These were granted and for some time the English enjoyed a profitable trade monopoly. Within a few years there were English trading centers in five cities, and English agents in others. Early each year, the Muscovy Company, an English joint-stock company which had been formed to carry on the trade, sent out thirteen or fourteen ships laden wtih cloth, pewter, munitions, and other wares. The ships anchored at the mouth of the Northern Dvina River until fall, when they returned with ladings of cordage, timber, and furs. The Swedish king, as early as 1556, sent a special protest to Queen Mary against this supplying of his enemy with arms and ammunition. Three years later, after Ivan's conquests in Livonia had opened up the port of Narva to English trade, Sigismund of Poland blockaded that port. His announcement of this to Queen Elizabeth sounds quite modern. (The quotation is from a contemporary translation of the original Latin.)

. . . so now we write againe to your Majesty, that we know and feele of a surety the Muscovite, enemy to all liberty under the heavens, dayly to be grown mightie by the increase of such things as be brought to the Narve [Narva] . . . by meane whereof he maketh himself strong to vanquish all others. . . . And we perfectly know your Majesty cannot be ignorant how great the cruelty is of the said enemy, of what force he is, what tyranny he useth on his subjects, and in what servile sort they be under him. . . . For now we do forsee . . . the Muscovite, puffed up in pride with those things that be brought to the Narve, and made more perfect in warlike affaires, with engines of warre and shippes, will make assault this way on Christendome, to slay or make bound all that shall withstand him: which God defend.

The English, however, were much more concerned with their trade than with heeding such protests. They had pushed their advantages hard. Seven expeditions were sent out by the company in the hope of opening trade with Persia and the East by way of Russia. But though Ivan welcomed the trade, he was interested in other possibilities. He dispatched an ambassador to England in 1556 and others in later years. In 1567, Ivan proposed "That the Queen's Majestie and he might be to all their enemyes joyned as one. . . ." Specifically he proposed an alliance against Sigismund. He also asked Elizabeth to send him "all kynde of artillerie and things necessarie for warre," and to permit English shipbuilders and masters to work for him. He even asked:

. . . that there may be assurance made by oath and faith betwixt the Queen's Majestie and him, that yf misfortune might fall or chance upon ether [either] of them to go out of their countries, that it might be lawfull to ether of them to come into the others countrey for the safeguard of themselves and their lyves, and there to lyve and have relief without any feare or danger untill such tyme as misfortune be past. . . .

Elizabeth avoided a direct answer on these points, but Ivan persisted and presented a treaty of offensive-defensive alliance for her signature. She wouldn't sign it, but she did send him a signed treaty pledging friendship and mutual assistance against common enemies. She also promised that he might find asylum in England if he needed it. Ivan was not content with this answer and continued to press for an alliance. A lively diplomatic interchange went on between the two monarchs as long as Ivan lived. Near the end of his life he coupled his reiterated request for an alliance with a proposal to take an English bride. That Ivan already had a wife who gave birth to a son during these marriage negotiations did not at all embarrass the tsar. He persisted in his desire "to marry some kinswoman of her Majestie [i.e., of Elizabeth]."

🌀 EVALUATION OF IVAN GROZNY

Ivan Grozny was definitely "the marrying kind." After the death of his first wife, the Anastasia whom he had truly loved, the tsar married and remarried. Some of his wives died, at least one was repudiated, and not all the marriages were sanctified or recognized by the Church. This multiple matrimony did not produce a multiplicity of heirs, an end which was perhaps more important than lust in determining Ivan's actions. Of his three sons by Anastasia, only two, Ivan and Fedor, grew to manhood. Ivan, the heir apparent, was struck down by his father in a fit of rage and died as a result of the blow. Fedor was moronic. A third son, Dimitri (the second of Ivan's sons to bear that name), who was born during the marriage negotiations with England, was not recognized by the Church as a legitimate heir. He was, moreover, only a child when Ivan died. Aware of this dynastic weakness, Ivan had appointed a six-man Council of Regents to rule for Fedor. Prominent among them were Nikita Romanov, brother of Anastasia; and Boris Godunov, brother-in-law of Fedor.

How shall one evaluate this unhappy man, Tsar Ivan Grozny? The problem is the more difficult because most of the surviving records are tainted. Kurbski's letters to Ivan, and Ivan's replies—both of which have been preserved and have been widely used as historical sources—are polemics. The characterization of Ivan by Sigismund was a description by an enemy. The local chronicles were generally exaggerated and prejudiced. There is reason to think that considerable evidence, for example about the plot against Ivan in 1567, was either destroyed by interested persons or lost by misadventure in the troubled period which followed Ivan's death. Nor can the reports of the English observers such as Horsey be taken wholly at face value. The difficulty has been still further increased within recent years by the attempted "rehabilitation" of Ivan at the hands of Soviet historians, acting under orders from the Communist Party.[2]

We may here set down in summary a few of Ivan's accomplishments. He survived a dreadful childhood which must have left its marks upon him. Violence and neglect were his nursemaids; vengeance was his tutor; and fear, his continuous companion. He was brutal partly because he had been brutalized by his upbringing. He was more direct and less subtle in dissembling his cruelties than were his contemporary sovereigns in the West. Perhaps his victims were more numerous than theirs, though this may be doubted. But it is difficult to see Ivan as any more cruel than Charles or Philip or the Henrys of France. Reigns of terror were by no means confined to Russia in the sixteenth century. As Ivan wrote concerning the Massacre of St. Bartholemew: "You, dear Brother, grieve over the blood that was shed; that in the Kingdom of the French King several thousands were slain together with suckling babes; it is quite seemly for a Christian sovereign to grieve over the inhuman treatment of so many people by the French King, and over the blood he has spilt without reason."

At any rate, the child prince survived to become the adolescent tsar and Autocrat of All the Russias. He not only regained the wealth and power from the boyars, but also increased them until Europe counted him its richest and most powerful prince. By skillful opportunism and astute long-range planning, he centralized the power in his own hands. The creation of the Thousand, the extension of the *pomestie,* the establishment of the *Oprichnina,* and the changes in its personnel were all effective steps toward that end. It may have been good or it may have been evil to concentrate power in the hands of one man. At least it avoided the particularisms which cursed Poland with anarchy and eventually made it the prey of other Powers.

Ivan Grozny reformed the local administration, codified the law, and greatly enlarged the scope and action of the central government. This last was apparently done without any plan. When Adashev was first appointed, for example, he was charged with hearing the petitions of Ivan's subjects. This led to the creation of the Bureau (*Prikaz*) of Petitions. Other bureaus were added haphazardly as the need arose; a Bureau of Kazan to administer Siberia; one to look after the *pomestie;* another to take care of the military; still another to handle foreign relations; and so on. By the end of the century there were thirty different bureaus with much confusion of authority and overlapping of function among them.

Ivan also greatly expanded his patrimony and pointed the way for further growth. He annexed Kazan and Astrakhan. Trans-Ural expansion began in his reign, and the conquest of the Siberian Tatars was completed the year he died. He drove hard toward the Baltic road to the West, held it temporarily, and then lost it. The way which Peter the Great later took had already been clearly pointed out by Ivan. The Livonian War aroused the attention and the fears of Europe. Russia under Ivan was not equal in influence or power to France or Spain, but if she had not yet attained the full stature of a Great Power, she was certainly on the road to becoming one.

Ivan's interests were not confined to wars and politics. He was to a limited degree also a patron of arts and letters. He sent to Europe for artists as well as artisans; for printers as well as captains. The first printing press to be operated in Russia was set up in Moscow in 1563 for the printing of ecclesiastical books. To be sure, this so aroused the wrath of reactionaries among civil and Church officials that the printers were driven out five years later. But one of them testified that the opposition to him and his work did not include Ivan. In fact, though Ivan neither prevented the expulsion of the printers nor sought to restore printing in Moscow, he did maintain a press and printers at Alexandrovsk for the printing of such materials as he ordered.

A physical memorial of Ivan's reign is the Church of St. Basil, which still stands beside the Kremlin in Moscow's Red Square. This was built between 1554 and 1560 as a votive church in gratitude for Ivan's victory over Kazan. Its extreme elaboration usually strikes the Westerner as fantastic and bizarre. Its eight bulbous cupolas are all differently decorated. One has alternate red and white vertical stripes; another resembles the outside of a pineapple; a third has green and white wavy stripes; and so on. Inside and out, the building is vividly polychromatic. Older accounts say that the Church of St. Basil was built by an Italian architect whose work so gratified Ivan that he caused the Italian to be blinded so that the poor man might never build a more beautiful structure. Actually this is a myth which gained credence partly because it fitted the dual prejudices about Ivan the Terrible and about Russian backwardness. The church was designed by two Russian architects, Posni and Barma, and neither of them was blinded for his pains.

Whatever the West thought of Ivan Grozny, he was celebrated in glowing words in the folk poems of his people:

> Why, bright moon, father moon
> Dost thou not shine as of Old?

In the Cathedral of the Assumption,
The Cathedral of Archangel Michael,
They beat upon the great bell
And the sound echoed over the whole earth.
All the princes and boyars assembled
All the warrior people came to pray to God
In the Cathedral of the Assumption.
There stood a new-made cypress-wood coffin;
In the coffin lies the Orthodox Tsar,
The Orthodox Tsar, Ivan Vasilievich, the formidable.
The life-giving cross stands at his head.
By the cross lies the imperial crown,
And at his feet, the terrible sword.
Everyone prays to the life-giving cross
Everyone bows to the golden crown.
Everyone trembles at the sight of the terrible sword.
Wax tapers burn around the coffin,
Before it stand the priests and patriarch.
They read. They sing the farewell hymn.
They say farewell to our Orthodox Tsar,
Our formidable Tsar, Ivan Vasilievich.

CHAPTER VI

Relapses, Recoveries, Rebellions, and Romanovs: The Seventeenth Century

🔥 *Votchina* AND *Pomestie*

"The Formidable Tsar" was a revolutionary in the sense that he expedited changes which were revolutionary in scope. This may be seen most clearly in relation to landownership, with its concomitant political power. By the sixteenth century the old common lands of the central regions of Muscovy had been largely swallowed by four kinds of private ownership. The first of these were the personal, hereditary estates (*votchinas*); the second, the *pomestie* ("service-land") estates; the third, lands held by the prince; and the fourth, those owned by the Church. The latter were effectively withdrawn from circulation because lands acquired by the Church could not be alienated. This affected the state, as has been previously noted in connection with the disagreement between the Elders and the Josephites. It is necessary only to recall that the state, in return for Josephite support, generally resisted the temptation to confiscate Church lands. The *pomestie* lands, usually small or middle-sized, were steadily increased during the sixteenth century at the expense of the *votchina* lands. Ivan Grozny greatly accelerated this process through the establishment of the *Oprichnina*.

The boyars and prince-boyars had been the rulers as well as the proprietors of their estates. Even when they submitted to the Muscovite princes, the boyars usually retained their local administrative and judicial powers. In fact, it was possession of these powers which had largely been responsible for the success of the boyars in getting peasants to work for them. The boyars had the wealth to provide land, implements, and seed; the power to guarantee a modicum of security to their people; and enough privilege to free their dependents from certain exactions. The *pomeshchiks,* whose need for labor was equally great, usually had somewhat less to offer. There developed a keen competition for peasants among the boyars, the *pomeshchiks,* and the monasteries. Because of the increased burdens of services and taxes, all who had laborers sought to squeeze as much as possible out of them. The only effective defenses which the peasants had were to work as little as possible or to run away. A very great many peasants did run away. By 1600 almost half the villages in the central provinces had been abandoned, and the arable land of the remaining peasant households had been cut in half. This was an agricultural crisis which weakened the state and led the *pomeshchiks* to try all possible ways of binding the peasants to their lands.

Individual peasants were able to turn this demand for labor to their own advantage, but the majority were not. It may be supposed that many of them were so deeply in debt and so completely dependent that they had no bargaining power even under these circumstances. We know, for example, that 70 per cent of the peasants who rented land from a certain monastery in this period were so poor that they had to borrow seed from the monastery in order to have anything to plant. Such persons were too poor to move. Another factor which operated against the peasants was that the *pomeshchiks* became increasingly influential in the government and were therefore able to enlist the power of the state in their behalf. Little by little they re-enforced and extended by legal bonds the already existent economic ties which bound the peasantry.

ENSERFMENT

Until nearly the end of the sixteenth century, peasants generally had the right to change masters whenever they had discharged their obligations. Gradually, this right of free movement was whittled away. Peasant removals were restricted to set periods in the spring and fall, and eventually these were ended. More and more peasants were bound to the lands upon which they lived. Two factors delayed this process a little. First, many landowners favored the retention of the removal periods, which gave them a chance to secure peasants for themselves by luring them from another owner. This was sometimes done legally by assuming the peasant's obligations to his creditor. At other times it was done by kidnapping peasants with or without their collusion. The second factor in the delay was the devastating effects of wars and famines, which caused owners as well as peasants to move about. Moreover, in hard times, peasants frequently deserted the poorer masters to take service with the wealthier or more fortunate. Legal or not, this was a hard fact which was recognized in practice by the saying that "the peasant shall live with him who fed him in the hungry years."

By the famous Law of 1597, all owners were ordered to return to former masters any runaway peasants who had settled on their estates within the past five years. This is customarily interpreted as an attempt by or in behalf of the lesser landlords to curtail peasant freedom in order to freeze the labor supply. There may have been other, even contrary, purposes. The law specified right of recovery only of peasants who had illegally left their masters after 1592. It might have been intended to protect both the peasants who had legally moved after that date and all who had migrated before then. The law did not abolish the right of peasant removals in the traditional periods. If there may be some question about the purposes of the Law of 1597, there is none about the subsequent extensions of the recovery period to fifteen years. This was done for the landlords.

Not until 1649, however, were all time limits on recovery abolished. This was decreed by the Code of 1649, which marked the beginning of legal serfdom. It gave legal standing to a situation which had long existed. The law of 1649 did not make serfs of all Russians, nor of all peasants, nor even of the majority. The serfs did not number more than half the population until a century later. They were, however, already numerous in the middle seventeenth century. As the Englishman Fletcher put it in his very famous account (1588):

> The number of their vagrant and begging poore is almost infinite, that are so pinched with famine and extreame neede, as that they begge after a violent and desperate manner. . . . This may truly be saide of them, that there is no servant or bond-slave more awed by his maister, nor kept downe in a more servile subjection, than the poore people are, and that universally. . . .

🔥 SERF NORMS AND VALUES

Part of the poverty of the people was certainly due to the unproductiveness of their agriculture. A rudimentary form of the three-field system was used on their "living" fields (those regularly cultivated). But it was still a hit-or-miss affair rather than a regular alternation of spring sowing, winter sowing, and fallow. There had been some advance in tools. The primitive hoe and almost equally primitive plow had been improved. Though most plows were still made of wood, some iron plows were used. Harrows, scythes, and sickles were among the other common tools. There was some knowledge and practice of manuring the fields, but it was not universal. Crop yields were usually very small. Recent studies of the harvest record show that the fields usually returned only two or three times the amount of seed. Very rarely, the rate was five to one. Rye was the chief winter grain. Wheat was less extensively grown. Oats, millet, and buckwheat were common spring-planted grain crops along with barley. Flax and hemp were extensively grown in certain provinces.

Orchard and garden crops (as distinct from the grain fields) included apples, pears, plums, cherries, melons, and berries; cucumbers, cabbage, garlic, onions, and some root vegetables. Oxen and horses were used as draft animals, or were raised for hides and tallow. Sheep, swine, and poultry were raised, at least on the larger estates. Rye bread and cabbage were perhaps the most common and important foodstuffs, supplemented on special occasions by a little meat and by fresh, salt, or dried fish. The usual drinks were mead and a malt beverage, *kvas*.

The houses of the people were generally of logs or adzed beams, roofed with boards and chinked with moss. Some had narrow windows covered with thin skins or hides. Furniture was of the simplest variety, and the main furnishing was the stove. The dress of the common people was equally simple. Summer garb for men and women was a sort of smock. Fletcher calls them "shirtes" and says that the men wore one; the women, two. For winter wear, the women "goeth in a redde or blew gowne" worn over a waistcoat of fur or sheepskin. The men wore a long outer garment "of coarse white or blew cloth" or, among the poorest, "of kowes haire." Under this, the men also wore a fur or sheepskin waistcoat. Men's hats were of fur. Women usually wore kerchiefs on their heads. And, adds Fletcher, "Without earrings of silver or some other mettall, and her crosse about her necke, you shal see no Russe woman, be shee wife or maide."

The servility which Fletcher deplored perhaps was partly a reflection of the obligations which many peasants owed to their economic masters, the landlords. These obligations were chiefly of two kinds: rent in labor (*barshchina*) and rent in kind (*obrok*). The parties to the contracts were, on the one side, the landowner; on the other, a group of peasants or, more rarely, a single peasant. The contract usually bound the landowner to supply seed and a loan in addition to "renting" a designated plot of land. The usual term was from three to five years. Any buildings which the peasants might erect were to become the property of the landowner at the expiration of the agreement. The contracts often specified the materials to be used and the size and type of buildings to be erected.

If repayment was to be by labor for the landowner, specific tasks were allotted. Common assignments were to plow and sow the landowner's fields, to mow his hay, to spread manure on his fields, to make new clearings, to work in his flour mill, to go lumbering or fishing for him, to cart his grain to market. During most of the sixteenth century these tasks took a quarter to a third of the peasants' total labor time. By the beginning of the next century the burden had become much heavier. It now took as much as half of the peasants' labor time. Repayment in kind required the peasants to supply the landowner with a certain quantity of eggs, grain, fish, butter, wool, and so on. As time went on, money was increasingly demanded instead of goods. This also placed a greater burden on the peasants. It was these burdens, plus the extension of the system, from which the peasants sought relief either by not farming so much land or by flight. Those who could not escape were doubly hard-hit, and, understandably, most resentful. The end of the sixteenth century was a time of great social unrest as well as of economic crisis or near crisis. These coincided with a political crisis which was precipitated by the ending of the dynasty. For this, too, Ivan Grozny was partly responsible.

✺ BORIS GODUNOV

When the Formidable Tsar died, his titles passed to the weak and incompetent Fedor (1584–98); the power, to a Council of Regents appointed by Ivan from among his followers. The group included scions of the prince-boyar families of the Shuiski and the Belski, and a lesser noble, almost a parvenu, who had been one of Ivan's chief *Oprichniks*. His name was Boris Godunov, and, beating out his jealous rivals, he became the real ruler of Russia. It was he, acting in the name of the moronic Fedor, who had promulgated the Law of 1597 on the recovery of the runaway peasants. He recovered from Sweden some of the region toward the Baltic. Under his regency, an invasion of the Crimean Tatars was repulsed and the conquest of the Siberian kingdom was completed. Peace and prosperity seemed, for a few years, to have returned to Russia. It was a lull like that found in the eye of a hurricane; a period of peacefulness, relatively speaking, between the storms of Ivan and the Time of Troubles. Two events in these years had immediate bearing upon subsequent happenings. One was the death, or presumed death, of Ivan's youngest son, Dimitri. The other was the establishment of a Russian patriarchate.

Dimitri Ivanovich was only three years old when his father died and he and his mother were sent away from Moscow. Thus begins one of the several unsolved mysteries in Russian history. Did the little prince actually go into exile, or was he abducted by friends and his place taken by a substitute? Sober scholars have suggested this possibility. No one knows. The little boy who did go died of a knife wound. Was it an accidental injury, or was it murder? The evidence is conflicting. If it was murder, was it committed on the orders of Godunov? Many have thought so, and Moussorgsky made it the theme of his opera *Boris Godunov*.

The creation of the patriarchate was the climax of a long series of events. After the Turkish capture of Constantinople, the metropolitan of Moscow, who had long been chosen not by the patriarch but by a council of Russian bishops and archbishops, had gradually assumed a position of leadership among the Orthodox churches. These churches had often appealed to Russia for financial help, and Godunov had tried to capitalize on this to get recognition of a Russian patriarchate. His first try was a failure, but in 1588 he persuaded the patriarch of Constantinople to consecrate the Metropolitan Job as patriarch of Moscow. The Council of Patriarchs subsequently confirmed the action and admitted the new patriarch to their number. Job more than repaid Godunov in the crisis which followed the death of Fedor in 1598. Fedor was childless. His wife, Godunov's sister, refused to accept the crown. The dynasty was extinguished.

THE TIME OF TROUBLES

A Russia without a tsar was unthinkable. The tradition of government by the greater boyars was moribund—mortally wounded by actions of Ivan Grozny and the growth of the *pomestie* system. It was necessary to choose a tsar. Four boyars offered themselves as candidates. Rivalry among them was fierce. It was then that the Patriarch Job influenced the people of Moscow to offer the crown to Godunov. He refused to take it from their hands. So Job then summoned a National Assembly (*Zemski Sobor*), which elected Godunov by a majority vote. He accepted this election and was shortly thereafter crowned Tsar Boris (1598–1605).

His reign was troubled. Some boyars, jealous and rebellious, plotted against him. Boris took strong measures. One of his rivals was exiled. His most formidable opponent, the able and very popular Fedor Romanov, was forced to enter a monastery. He assumed the monastic name of Philaret. Even nature seemed to join the conspiracies against Tsar Boris. A killing frost destroyed the unripened crops in 1601, and the next year both the spring and winter plantings failed. There was grain in storage, but those who had it refused to share it, and Boris' enemies sabotaged his efforts to relieve the famine by distributing government surplus. The people suffered bitterly. The peasants interpreted their misery as a sign of Divine displeasure with their elected tsar, and listened willingly to the rumor that Dimitri Ivanovich was alive and ready to claim his rightful patrimony. The riotous disorders which grew out of the famine were skillfully exploited by Boris' enemies into a political movement against him. Its rallying point was a young man who certainly acted as if he thought himself to be Dimitri. Whether he was is still unsettled.

True tsar or pretender, Dimitri appeared first in Poland, where he won the sponsorship of the Polish king and his attendant Jesuits. With Polish support, which included troops, Dimitri invaded the Russian lands. The people of Russia stirred and muttered, and joined the growing army of the First Pretender. Tsar Boris prepared to meet the challenge but died in the midst of his preparations. Dimitri entered Moscow in triumph with his motley forces in June, 1605, and assumed the crown. It was hardly in place on his head before plots against him began. For reasons unknown, Dimitri did not take strong action against the plotters, who were led by Basil Shuiski, scion of the ancient prince-boyar family. In May, 1606, Tsar Dimitri paid for this forbearance with his life; he was murdered at the instigation of Shuiski.

Basil Shuiski (1606–10) now secured his own "election" as tsar at the hands of the boyars and upper classes of Moscow. His contemporaries said that he had "suddenly and autocratically" seized the throne. Soviet historians have called Basil Shuiski "the Boyars' tsar." This is true insofar as he had to yield to the Moscow boyars who had elected him, but it does not cover the facts that other boyars always opposed him and that many Muscovites became alienated from him.

Many peasants had fled from the burdens and troubles of Moscow to the southern lands on the borders of the state. They, together with some Cossacks and lesser *pomeshchiks,* now gathered around a revolutionary standard raised by a onetime serf, Ivan Bolotnikov. There were also other risings, but "Bolotnikov's Rebellion" was the most important. After initial successes in the south, Bolotnikov led his mixed rabble of the privileged, less-privileged, and unprivileged north toward Moscow. His force grew steadily by the accretion of peasants and lesser *pomeshchiks* from the regions through which he passed. Soviet historians, emphasizing Bolotnikov's peasant origin and the number of peasants who followed him, treat this as an early instance of the "class war." The divisions, however, were not made strictly along class lines. Bolotnikov was temporarily supported by some of the boyars who were discontented with Tsar Shuiski. The rebels reached Moscow and besieged the city. Shuiski rallied all possible forces against the essentially disunited rebels. Lack of real unity played a part, and so did treason. Bolotnikov's forces were routed. He was later captured and killed. The revolt was broken and punishments were meted out, but the conditions which had produced the troubles still remained.

POLISH INTERVENTION

Some of Bolotnikov's followers joined another equally heterogeneous group which had gathered around a second pretender, known as "the Thief." With his Cossacks, his Russians, and with Lithuanian and Polish forces in his train, the Thief advanced upon Moscow, set up his headquarters at the nearby village of Tushino, and encircled the city. Tsar Shuiski, in desperation, sought aid from Sweden. The Swedes agreed to help him if he would return to them the lands captured by Godunov. Meanwhile the Thief's forces had, by their depredations, turned many against them. These people sided with Shuiski, who was able to bring a considerable army, including Swedish troops, to the relief of his capital. The Thief withdrew from Tushino, but this victory of the tsar was more than counterbalanced by the formal appearance of another enemy.

Poland had been actively but secretly intervening for some time. Now the Polish king, Sigismund, used the Swedish alliance as an excuse for open intervention. Polish forces defeated those of Shuiski and moved on Moscow. The Thief, emboldened by Shuiski's weakness and desirous of forestalling the Poles, also turned again toward the city. Shuiski's uncertain support melted away and the people of Moscow, sparked by the boyar Lyapunov, deposed the tsar and forced him to enter a monastery (1610). Moscow now came under the rule of certain boyar groups. They were unable to resist the Polish advance, however, and Polish troops occupied the Kremlin.

A good many powerful boyars had served, for longer or shorter times, under the Thief. Some of them had commuted, so to speak, from Moscow to Tushino and back again. Prominent among them was Philaret (Fedor Romanov). Even before the deposal of Tsar Shuiski and the entrance of the Poles into Moscow, members of this group had invited King Sigismund of Poland to send his son, Wladyslaw, to be their tsar. Negotiations to this end were speeded up after the Polish occupation of the Kremlin. An election of sorts was held by the group and Wladyslaw was chosen tsar, subject to the acceptance of certain conditions. A "Grand Embassy," of which Philaret was an important member, was sent to get Sigismund's consent to the agreement and to bring back the new tsar. The enormity of this action can be seen from its religious implications.

The long and tortuous efforts to achieve a reunion of the Eastern and Western churches under Roman leadership finally gained a limited success at the close of the sixteenth century with the establishment of the Uniate Church. This group retained its Orthodox ritual but accepted the theology and leadership of Rome. Closely connected with this new establishment was Sigismund, an ardent Roman Catholic, who was assisted and strengthened in his attacks upon Orthodoxy by the Jesuits. Under his aegis, the Uniate Church won successes in western Russia. The nationalistic quarrel was thus aggravated by a religious struggle. It became not only Russian against Pole, but also Orthodox against Roman Catholic and Uniate. Both fights were further complicated by the actions of Protestant Sweden, which made the Polish victories the occasion to invade Russia and seize Russian territory.

The "Grand Embassy," partly for religious reasons, refused a proposal to make Sigismund tsar in place of his son, and stood stiff-necked against increasing Polish pressure. Sigismund thereupon arrested them and sent them to Polish prisons. Meanwhile his agents and troops in Moscow were treating it like a conquered city which, indeed, it was. Outside the city, the Thief awaited his chance to strike again. This was the nadir of Russian power. The Russian state had, in fact, ceased to be. Its recovery is one of the most dramatic incidents in a story full of drama.

🈯 RUSSIAN RECOVERY

First to try to rally his countrymen was the Patriarch Hermogen. He absolved the people from any oaths taken to Wladyslaw and urged the faithful to defend Orthodoxy and Russia. The death of the Thief (December, 1610) led to a dissolution of his forces. Early in 1611, the same Lyapunov who had opposed Shuiski gathered troops and moved toward Moscow. He was joined by about a hundred thousand disorganized followers. The Poles and their Russian collaborators retreated into the Kremlin. While they besieged the citadel, the Russian forces tried to create a government, but this emphasized their disunity until —serfs, peasants, Cossacks, boyars, followers of the Thief, and so on— the whole host dissolved. It was now the autumn of 1611. The Poles held Moscow, Smolensk, and other places in the southwest. The Swedes had occupied Novgorod and adjacent lands, and a third "False Dimitri" had appeared in Pskov.

The eastern towns, sparked still by certain of the clergy (including the patriarch, who smuggled letters out of the prison where the Poles had put him), began to exchange correspondence. It was Nizhni-Novgorod which now took the lead under the urgings of one of its citizens, Kuzma Minin. The town pledged a third of its annual income to raise and equip an army. A militia was raised and, at Minin's suggestion, Prince Pozharski was made its commander. Appeals for men, arms, and money went out to other towns, most of which responded generously to this call to fight "against the common enemies, men of Poland and Lithuania and Germans, and Russian 'thieves,' who are causing new bloodshed in the State." Rapidly they gathered—land-owners, tradesmen, serfs, peasants, Cossacks, Russians, Tatars, and others. In the spring of 1612, they paused to consolidate themselves and to set up a provisional government. Detachments went out against the bands of "thieves" (remnants of the Tushino forces) and against the Poles. One group of Cossacks struck at the army of Minin and Pozharski. They were beaten back, and the host now set out for Moscow.

They encamped near the city close by a second Cossack group which temporarily neither joined nor impeded them. A Polish army, reputedly as large as the Russian forces, marched to the relief of their beleaguered comrades. The fight raged fiercely for days. Finally, Trubetzkoi and his Cossacks joined with Minin and Pozharski to defeat the Polish army. The Poles in the Kremlin, now wholly cut off, were starved into sur-render. Moscow was free (November, 1612), but Russia was still in a parlous and disordered condition. It was necessary to establish a gov-ernment immediately and to that end Pozharski summoned a National Assembly (1613).

THE ROMANOVS

This was the fullest assembly ever to meet. Some fifty towns sent repre-sentatives. There were peasants and Cossacks, greater and lesser land-owners, higher and lower clergy—in short, all the *free* classes were represented. Its first and greatest task was to choose a tsar. This proved to be difficult. "For many days there were meetings of the men," wrote the chronicler, "but they could not settle the business and vainly swayed this way and that." Finally their choice turned to the Romanovs, fa-vored by many of the *pomeshchiks* and by the Cossacks, who were particularly influential. Philaret (nee Fedor) Romanov was especially popular with the Cossacks who had known him while he served the Thief at Tushino. Philaret was not available since he was still in a Polish prison. However, his wife (the nun Martha, whom Godunov had forced into a convent) and their son Michael were in Russia. Michael was a rather sickly youth of seventeen or eighteen whom a contemporary described as "kind, mild, gentle, meek and well-inten-tioned." The same source added, "He had not enough strength of mind to govern the country." This was the person whom the National As-sembly finally chose. After some hesitation, Michael accepted and in 1613 was crowned tsar, holding office until his death in 1645.

The Romanov dynasty was very much a family affair in its early years. Philaret did not return from Poland until 1619, but Martha was a strong and capable person in whose hands the tsar was content to leave the power. Immediately upon Philaret's return, he was elected patriarch, and given the title of sovereign with rights equal to his son's. Theoretically, the power was shared by father and son. Practically, the father was completely dominant until his death in 1633.

The first Romanovs, much as the last Romanovs did three hundred years later, had to choose between autocratic rule and government in co-operation with the people. While it is certainly true that the National Assembly was composed of the privileged classes and stood in no close relation to the masses, it represented comparatively broad interests. It sometimes spoke for the people, as on the occasion when it complained to the tsar that his taxes were too heavy and that his officials were abusing their authority. It may also be recalled that, in addition to the National Assembly, the forces which had beaten the Poles were a truly national army. Had the Romanovs been willing to co-operate with these groups, the story of Russia might have been very different. They did not so choose.

During the first years of their regime, while their power was still uncertain, the Romanovs leaned heavily on the National Assembly, which met annually from 1613 to 1623. For a few years, laws and taxes were jointly decreed by the tsar and the assembly. This lasted only as long as the Romanovs' weakness. As long as they did whatever the Romanovs requested, the assemblies were continued; when they became critical, the tsar summoned them only in emergencies. Finally, in the third quarter of the seventeenth century, they were dropped altogether.

The Romanovs chose to rule with men of their own kind. Minin, Pozharski, Trubetzkoi, and many other leaders of the national army were either forgotten or assigned to far-off posts. Most of the Romanov clique were successful opportunists who had left Shuiski for the Thief, the Thief for Wladyslaw, and the Poles for the Romanovs. A few were princes, some were officials who had kept their posts and done their jobs through all the changes, but most of them were *pomeshchiks*.

⚑ TASKS OF THE NEW GOVERNMENT

The tasks which faced this new government were staggering. Sweden still held Novgorod and other regions; Poland held Smolensk and other territories. Neither the Swedes nor the Poles were inclined to leave Michael in undisputed possession of the throne. Trade and agriculture had suffered severely during the Time of Troubles and the country was disorderly in the extreme. The Troubles, it is often said, had bred lawlessness and anarchy. This is an illustration of a recurrent social phenomenon. Self-preservation is one of the mainsprings of human action. When governments fail to maintain a reasonable security so that men can have some hope of making their livings, people must provide for themselves. Something of this sort had happened in the Time of Troubles.

Invasions and civil strife had made farming almost impossible, but men still had to eat. They knew that stores of food had been hoarded by some individuals and by the government, and, in desperation, they plundered the hoards and destroyed the hoarders. These men would join anyone who promised to improve their lot. When one movement failed, they sought another or broke up into marauding bands. The election of a tsar did not automatically cure these ills. Groups of men continued to roam the country, a large one coming even to the gates of Moscow itself. Only gradually were they suppressed by force or undercut by the stabilization of society and economic recovery. The foreign menaces were perhaps less easily removed.

Sweden was the simpler problem largely because Russia was able to enlist the aid of the Dutch and English in arranging a settlement. War was tried as an instrument of national policy, but it proved indecisive and both Sweden and Russia accepted Anglo-Dutch mediation. The mediated Peace of Stolbovo (1617) awarded an indemnity to Sweden and allowed her to keep the lands between the Baltic and Lake Ladoga. Novgorod and its adjacent territories were restored to Russia. Since his treasury was still empty, Michael had to borrow from England in order to pay the indemnity. He repaid the loan within a year. Relations with Poland were much more complicated.

UKRAINE AND POLAND

The southern portions of old Kievan Rus had been largely deserted in the fourteenth century. The centers of economic and political power shifted north and east into Novgorod and Suzdalia; west and north into Galicia and Volhynia. Galicia had a brief period of glory and was then swallowed up by an expanding Poland. Volhynia became attached to Lithuania. The old lands became a wilderness where a few hardy men trapped and fished. Lithuania claimed these borderlands, refuge of the adventurous fugitives, but Lithuanian authority did not extend south or east of the old city of Kiev. There was a slow pushing forward of the frontier by popular migration and by the actions of the Polish and Lithuanian governments. Kiev was gradually repeopled and other frontier garrison towns were built, but the total population of the whole area did not exceed fifty thousand in 1550,

As Lithuania gradually merged with Poland the Lithuanian ruling classes became increasingly Polonized. This meant, among other things, the expansion of the Polish system of a dependent and unfree peasantry. This system was partly an outgrowth of the struggle between the Polish crown and the Polish *magnates* (great nobles). The crown sought to enlist the *szlachta* (lesser nobles) on its side and one of the inducements which it offered was the extension of the *szlachtas'* power over their peasants, who, more and more, were degraded into serfs. The advance of this social pattern into Galicia and Volhynia caused many peasants to run away to the borderlands, where they joined the Cossacks. These frontiersmen of the borderlands (which is the literal meaning of the phrase "Cossacks of Ukraine") had created a certain amount of security along the frontier by repeated victories over the Crimean Tatars. In the middle of the sixteenth century, a Cossack band under the leadership of Vishnevetsky founded a settlement beyond the rapids of the Dnieper River. This group, known as the Zaporogians (from the words *za porogi,* "beyond the rapids") won a wide reputation as fighters and as freemen. The fugitive peasants flocked to join them. There followed a rapid increase in the population and a short period of prosperous independence.

But the Union of Lublin (1569), which officially merged Poland and Lithuania, opened these lands to acquisition by the Polish landlords at a time when western Europe's demand for wheat increased greatly. The fertile lands of the feather-grass steppe suddenly assumed an entirely new importance. The fortunate or far-sighted nobles were able to get tremendous grants of this land, which they hastened to occupy with peasants. This new wave of migration overtook the fugitives. Within half a century, the population of Ukraine increased tenfold, and troubles increased by the hundreds. The landlords were mostly Roman Catholic; the peasants and Cossacks, mostly Orthodox. The Cossacks and their associates had run away from precisely the system of serf labor which the newly arrived landlords were determined to introduce. The Cossacks had been free and independent. It was a tragic defect of the Polish nobility that the only society they could envision was one in which they dominated the townsmen and the peasants. The Cossacks of Ukraine—virtually all the peasants in Ukraine considered themselves to be Cossacks—counted themselves *sui generis* and refused to fit peacefully into the Polish pattern.

The Polish nobility considered itself to be vastly superior in culture to the non-Polish eastern Slavs. Though they had fostered the Uniate Church in several ways, including promising to give the Uniates equality with the Roman Catholics in government jobs, the Polish prelates refused equality to the Uniate prelates, the Roman Catholic nobility scorned their Uniate counterparts, and the promise of job equality was not kept. Under these conditions, the Uniates ceased to be accomplices of the Poles and became their opponents, but the Uniate, nevertheless remained generally suspect to the Orthodox.

Polish efforts to deprive the Cossacks of their free social status were simply ignored as long as the Poles were unable to enforce them. Attempts to enroll the Cossacks in the Polish service attracted only a few thousand men. The majority, spear-headed by the Zaporogians, continued to go their own way until, challenged by an increase in Polish power, they rebelled. The revolt was quelled, but the Ukrainian Cossacks had become an important force in the affairs of eastern Europe. They took an active role in the Time of Troubles. Many of them fought in the army of the first Dimitri and on the side of the Thief. They raided and pillaged the Russian lands and took their booty home to enrich Ukraine. Under the leadership of Sahaydachny they attained a *de facto* alliance and equality with Poland, although this was never legally recognized. Sahaydachny revived the Orthodox Church and removed its hierarchical capital to Kiev, which became a center of ecclesiastical learning from which Moscow soon borrowed. Co-operation with Poland continued after Sahaydachny's death. The Cossacks fought for Poland against Russia when the latter tried to recover Smolensk (1632–34). But it was an insecure alliance, since the interests of the two were often antipathetic. Intermittent rebellions took place, climaxing in a struggle led, for Ukraine, by Bohdan Hmelnetsky (or Bogdan Khmelnitski). His relations with Poland, Sweden, Russia, and Turkey (not to mention the highly complex intra-Cossack and intra-Ukrainian complications) are much too tortuous to relate in detail.

WESTERN INFLUENCES

The problems of rehabilitation with which Michael and his associates had to deal were largely responsible for the speeding up of Westernization. In addition to his Dutch and English connections, Michael signed a treaty of peace and commerce with Sweden and received a Swedish ambassador. The tsar had previously sent an envoy to Paris to seek an alliance. Many years later a French envoy arrived in Moscow with instructions to ask for trading concessions and a political alliance. Nothing came either of the Russian overtures to Louis XIII or of the French overtures to Michael. Diplomats were by no means the only aliens to come to Russia. The number of foreigners greatly increased during the reign. Some were merchants; some, manufacturers; some, soldiers; and some were scholars. A Dutchman named Vinius built the first large-scale, industrial ironworks to process the iron ore mined at Tula. He was soon joined by other foreigners who also erected iron foundries there. A Swede named Koet built a glassworks near Moscow. Copper mines and smelters, armament works, and other enterprises were started or run with the help of foreign technicians. The army was increasingly trained and led by foreign mercenaries. The learned astronomer and geographer Olearius of Holstein was brought to Moscow for a number of years as was Joseph of Alexandria, a scholar of Greek.

✎ REBELLIONS AND WARS

All these things—the modernization of the army on Western models, payment for imported arms and munitions and for instructors and mercenaries, fees and concessions to alien merchants and technicians—cost a good deal of money which had to be raised by the people. The burdens of the rehabilitated and growing state became increasingly heavy and were not offset completely by the economic recovery of the country. And the officials of the Romanovs, "a clique of unscrupulous men, who exercised unrestricted power in the name of the inexperienced and indifferent young Tsar," made matters considerably worse. One of the petitions presented to the tsar by the National Assembly set forth the following indictment:

> Your secretaries and clerks have been favored with your sovereign money in salaries and with estates and patrimonies, and, being unceasingly at your sovereign affairs, and having become rich with great riches by their unrighteous extortions, they have bought many patrimonies and built for themselves many houses, stone dwellings, and mansions, such as it would be hard to relate. Under former Sovereigns of blessed memory, even men of great family, who would have been worthy of living in such houses, have not had them.

The mutterings of discontent evoked by these conditions were loud enough so that one foreign observer predicted a general rising before Michael died (1645). It did not come, however, until the reign of Tsar Alexis (1645–76). The first outbreak was in Moscow, though there were insurrections in other towns as well. Alexis partially checked the movement, having first quelled the "riots" with force, by the Code of 1649, which particularly favored the *pomeshchiks* and the wealthier townsmen. But serious rebellions also flared up in Novgorod and Pskov in 1650 and were put down only with some difficulty.

Sixteen hundred and forty-eight—the year of the Fronde in France, of the climax of the English Civil War, and of the Peace of Westphalia in Europe—saw the first revolt of the Ukrainians under Hmelnetsky against Poland. This celebrated Ukrainian national hero was a descendant of the lesser nobility of Volhynia, a Cossack who had faithfully served the Polish crown for many years. His first revolt, carried out chiefly for personal reasons, made him master of Ukraine and, temporarily, kingmaker in Poland. But he soon broke with the king he helped to elect, suffered a defeat, and accepted an agreement which protected his own interests and those of his class but did nothing for the peasants. Alleging Polish violation of the agreement, Hmelnetsky again rebelled and was again defeated, but his power was not broken. Moscow had been watching these events with close attention. Alexis had refused a Ukrainian bid for aid in 1649, partly because of the rebellions at home and partly because the Russians still resented the part the Ukrainians had played in the Time of Troubles. But in 1653–54 an agreement was reached between Alexis and Hmelnetsky. Just what was agreed upon soon became a matter of violent dispute which has not yet ended. The Russo-Polish conflict flowed from it.

This war was complicated by both Russian and Polish relations with Sweden and also by internal struggles within Ukraine. Russian successes against Poland were followed by a Swedish attack upon that country and by an apparent defection of Hmelnetsky. Catholic Austria, apprehensive lest Protestant Sweden should cut across Poland and effect a juncture with Protestants in Hungary and Transylvania, came to the diplomatic aid of the Poles, who also benefited from Danish intervention against Sweden. Russia now (1656) made war upon Sweden and slacked off its attacks on Poland. The death of Hmelnetsky in 1657 brought to power one Vyhovsky, who soon made an agreement with Poland and rebelled against Russia. Russian influence in Ukraine continued, despite defeats by Vyhovsky and his Polish allies, because the lower classes in Ukraine rebelled. The brief Russo-Polish amity was thus ended and war was resumed in 1660.

Matters did not go well for Tsar Alexis at first. Uprisings at home, similar to those of 1648, crippled his power and he was forced to accept a peace with Sweden which restored to her the Baltic lands he had temporarily held. Civil war became epidemic in Ukraine as now this group and now that alternately supported or fought against both Russia and Poland, both of whom were becoming exhausted from their war against each other and from their efforts to curb the anarchy of Ukraine. Finally, in 1667, Russia and Poland agreed to the Treaty of Andrusovo, an important landmark in the diplomatic history of both countries and of Ukraine. The treaty divided Ukraine between Poland and Russia not so much by an actual partition as by the establishment of a joint rule. To Russia went the lands on the left bank of the Dnieper up to the point where that river turns south. Poland retained the lands on the right bank. The city of Kiev, which is on the right bank, was to be occupied by Russia for two years and then given to Poland. This provision, however, was never carried out. Both powers were to share the services of the Zaporogians, and Russia further agreed to assist the Poles with troops if necessary.

The Ukrainians were struggling for independence from both Poland and Russia. Ukraine was the borderland common to both those Powers and they contested for its control, the residents thereof being only pawns in the struggle. Russia maintained that her agreement with Hmelnetsky had established at least a Russian protectorate over Ukraine if it had not actually joined Ukraine to Russia. But, whatever the formal documents may have said, this had not been Hmelnetsky's intention. He thought of the agreement as an alliance between equals. As for Vyhovsky, part of his motive was to use the Poles against Russia, who seemed the greater threat. Subsequent risings followed the same pattern. An additional factor was introduced by Doroshenko's flirtations with the Turks. Peter Doroshenko had been specifically forbidden by the Treaty of Andrusovo to rule any part of Ukraine. Outlawed by both Russians and Poles, he in turn opposed both and hoped to turn Ukraine into an autonomous vassal of Turkey. Risings and counter-risings were accompanied by Turkish intervention. Ukraine continued to be a troubled and troublesome spot.

In addition to troubles in the borderlands, Tsar Alexis had been confronted by two serious defections at home. Late in the 1660's, Stepan Razin, a Cossack of the Don, gathered about him a large force of poor Cossacks, peasants, and serfs. Early successes in raids and pillage attracted more followers until, in 1670, he had an army of some seven thousand which he led against the Volga town of Tsaritsin (now Stalingrad). Some of the tsar's troops who had been sent against Razin now joined him. Tsaritsin was captured, then Astrakhan, and then town after town, as he successfully advanced up the Volga. Peasants and serfs, made hopeful by Razin's coming, rebelled against their landlords and joined the revolutionary army. After a few months of glory and victory, Razin's force was defeated by the tsar's troops. Razin escaped from the rout but was pursued, caught, and sent back to Moscow, where he was executed in 1671. The insurrection broke into fragments, which Alexis' forces eventually hunted down and punished. Razin's rebellion, a genuine peasant uprising against the landlords, was thus crushed.

RELIGIOUS SCHISM: *Raskol*

The other defection was more stubborn. It was partly a religious schism, but there were also other elements in it. For an understanding of it, we must realize that religion and the Church were not isolated institutions, existing in a vacuum, but part of the norms and values of seventeenth-century Russia.

There developed in the Russian Orthodox Church two distinct classes of clergy. The parish priests, known as the white clergy from their white habiliments, were men of the people in many ways. Poorly educated and poorly trained, they were scarcely less ignorant and superstitious than the peasants among whom they lived. They married, raised families, eked out a living from fees, charity, and farming. They served two masters: the village commune which selected them, paid them (or failed to), and limited their actions; and the higher ecclesiastics whom they were taxed and taxed to maintain. These higher clergy (the black clergy) were all monks or former monks. No white clergy could hope for promotion to the places of power and wealth such as the bishoprics and archbishoprics. These were the monopoly of the black clergy, and between the black and the white was an almost unbridgeable gap. The black clergy were the servants of the absolute tsar, just as the whites were the servants of the villages. Rebellions against the authority of the higher churchmen were not infrequent, and there was a persistent though largely futile opposition on the part of the lower clergy to efforts to increase and centralize clerical authority.

The climax of these efforts came during the patriarchate of Nikon (1652–58). A strict disciplinarian, Nikon sought to reform and revitalize the Church. It needed both, but his despotic methods seriously alienated many and led even the tsar, his patron, to say of him that "he drove men to fast by force, but could not drive anyone by force to believe in God." Nikon was also a scholar, to whom it naturally seemed imperative that a reform of abuses should include a correction of errors in liturgies, texts, and ritual. He was not the first to attempt this, nor did his efforts initially arouse opposition but they became the immediate cause of the *Raskol* (the Great Schism). This was partly because he had many powerful enemies who were glad to use this as an excuse.

For the Russian masses, the organized religion of the Orthodox Church was interwoven with superstition and confused with magic. The liturgies and services were in old Cyrillic, a language wholly incomprehensible to them. Ignorant, unlettered, semipagan, and semi-Christian, the masses regarded prayers and rituals as magic formulae whose efficacy would be destroyed by any variations. The sounds of the liturgies were venerated, even when errors had rendered the words nonsense. Nikon's efforts at correction could readily be made to appear dangerous. Moreover, these corrections could be presented as foreign innovations since, native scholarship failing, Nikon imported Ukrainian and Western scholars. Some of the clergy sincerely feared the taints of Roman Catholicism or Protestantism; others pretended to. The nationalistically minded opposed the changes because they were alien. And many opposed them simply because Nikon promoted them. Opposition to the innovations was also tied to an important psychological factor: the traditional forms were familiar routines which gave an illusion of security. The still small but steadily increasing Westernization of many and varied norms apart from religion had begun seriously to threaten this sense of security by displacing the traditional. The people, insecure enough amid chronic disorders, bitterly opposed new and further efforts to uproot the old.

The specific opposition to Nikon's reforms was at first confined to the higher clergy, but under the leadership of Avvakum the movement spread widely. Nikon lost the favor of Alexis and his enemies displaced him in control of the Church, but still the quarrel raged between those who supported the changes and those who opposed them. Finally a church council, called in 1666, accepted Nikon's reforms, condemned, excommunicated, and punished those who would not agree. Because the power of the tsar stood behind the council, the schismatics (*Raskolniki,* or people of the *Raskol*) were in effect rebels against both Church and State. Many were purged, but still the movement persisted. The schism and purge, however, weakened the Church and made it easier for Peter the Great to subordinate it.

CHAPTER VII

The Dynamic Peter

Peter Alexievich is probably the most widely celebrated of all Russian sovereigns. He compelled the attention of his contemporaries, and his biography has intrigued all succeeding generations. Peter has been damned as a tyrant, eulogized as a genius, decried as a madman, and exalted as the Westernizer of Russia. Whatever their estimates of him, few writers have sought to deny Peter the appellative "Great." There was nothing in his birth or boyhood, however, which so marked him.

🎈 BOYHOOD AND EARLY YOUTH

Peter's father, Alexis, was married twice. His first wife, one of the Miloslavski family, bore him thirteen children of whom only three are of concern to us: the weak and sickly Fedor, tsar from 1676 to 1682; the weaker and sicklier Ivan, co-tsar from 1682 to 1689 and the vigorous Sophia, regent from 1682 to 1689. Alexis' second wife was Natalia Naryshkin, ward of his important adviser, Artamon Matveiev. Natalia's first-born was named Peter Alexievich. He was five years old when his father died; eleven when his half brother, Tsar Fedor III, died. During Fedor's reign, in which the most important event was the expulsion of the Turks from Ukraine, power was chiefly exercised by the Miloslavski family. The Naryshkins and Matveiev were punished and exiled. The death of Fedor gave them an opportunity to renew the struggle, since Ivan was physically and mentally incapable. The Naryshkin party, abetted by the Patriarch Ioakhim, executed a *coup d'état*. The boy Peter was proclaimed from the Kremlin as the sole tsar. It was a transient triumph which lasted no more than a month before it was all undone by Sophia and the *Streltsi*.

The *Streltsi* was a military organization originally founded by Ivan Grozny which, over the years, had won for itself special favors and powers. Its members were paid, equipped, housed, and given various privileges by the government in peace as well as war. During peace times the *Streltsi* policed the capital, served as firemen, and formed the tsars' bodyguard. In war, they were the core of the army. There were twenty regiments of *Streltsi* in Moscow in 1682 and they totaled between sixteen and twenty thousand men, led by their own officers and supervised by a special department. By this time, they had become a state within a state, turbulent and unruly—a sort of Praetorian Guard which more often created disorder than subdued it. Punished by Matviev and the victorious Naryshkins, the *Streltsi* readily became the instruments of Sophia and her intimate associate Basil Golitsin. The latter, an aide to Matviev and head of the Foreign Office (to give it a modern label) under Alexis, was a talented innovator and a devotee of Western ways. He had been largely responsible for the abolition of the ancient "Book of Pedigrees" which determined the service rank a man might hold. He was a frequenter of the "German suburb" (*Nemetskaia sloboda*),[1] that portion of Moscow in which foreigners were required to live, and an associate of many who lived there. His palace was filled with Western furnishings and his library, with Western books. Golitsin, Khovanski (a prominent member of the *Streltsi*), and Sophia first met around the sickbed of Fedor, and together with some others they formed a conspiratorial alliance.

The counterstroke was an affair of violence and blood which took place literally before the eyes of the eleven-year-old Peter, who watched while the *Streltsi* killed Matviev with their pikes and tore Ivan Naryshkin to pieces. The imbecilic Ivan was acclaimed as senior tsar; Peter, as junior tsar; and, a little later, Sophia was made regent over both. The actual ruler, however, was Golitsin. Peter and his mother withdrew to the village of Preobrazhenskoe, just outside of Moscow and close to the German suburb. There for the next several years they lived in obscurity broken only by Peter's infrequent appearances with his co-tsar on a famous double throne which concealed Sophia, who told her puppets what to do and say.

Three events in foreign affairs may be noted before we turn to a further consideration of Peter's boyhood, education, and personality. The first, in 1686, was a peace with Poland confirming the settlement of Andrusovo, with the additional provision that Kiev should be permanently Russian in return for Russian help against the Turks and Tatars. To fulfill this agreement, Sophia and Golitsin sent two expeditions against the Crimean Tatars—the second event. Both expeditions ended in complete failure and the second fiasco was used as an excuse to get rid of its sponsors. The third was the Treaty of Nerchinsk (1689) with China, which established the Russian boundary along the left bank of the Amur River. This was the first treaty which China concluded with any Western Power.

🪬 PETER'S EDUCATION

Peter, living at Preobrazhenskoe, was not at all concerned with these affairs of state. His exclusion from the court at the Kremlin freed him from many of the restrictions which were usually placed about the royal princes and made it possible for him to have a training quite unlike that of any of his predecessors. His formal education came to an abrupt end with his exile from Moscow, but his informal education then began. Like most boys, Peter enjoyed playing war, but Peter played with real, live soldiers. "Play" regiments were formed of soldiers living in the villages of Preobrazhenskoe and Semenovski. Peter's games with them became ever more real. He discovered that to be an artilleryman he had to know something of mathematics and that to build fortresses he needed certain other special information. Accordingly, he learned at least a smattering of these things and his teachers were, in almost every case, foreigners from the German suburb. As Professor Platonov once put it:

In this way it came about that Peter depended on the Germans to help him build his fortress; on the Dutchman Timmerman to teach him arithmetic, geometry and fortification; and on another Dutchman, Brant, to instruct him in the art of sailing. Under the influence of these games and of his foreign instructors, Peter became little by little a soldier and a sailor. He did not obtain the ordinary scholastic education of his time, but acquired instead some special, unusual knowledge, and showed some queer preferences which were not at all what was expected of a tsar. This youthful sovereign represented a cultural type that was quite uncommon in Moscow.

Peter's reputation for "wildness," which was not without foundation, caused many to predict no good end for him. Even his mother felt that some restraint was necessary, and in 1689 married him off to a young woman named Eudoxia. It was in that same year that the smoldering feud between his mother and his half sister broke into the open. In August, 1689, it was falsely reported that Sophia had sent some of the *Streltsi* to assassinate Peter. Under the stimulus of this alarm, Peter was literally pulled out of bed, thrust, half-dressed, on horseback, and taken to a forest hiding place, from which he was later removed to the Trinity monastery. There he was soon joined by his wife, his mother and her party, his "play" regiments, some of the *Streltsi,* and some regular troops. Natalia, his mother, now took the initiative and, in Peter's name, called Sophia to account. Sophia's support melted away; she was sent into a convent and Golitsin was arrested. Peter and Ivan were now rulers of Russia in their own right. But actually neither of them ruled—Ivan because he was incompetent and Peter because he didn't want to. Until her death in 1694, Natalia, supported and counseled by the Patriarch Ioakhim and his successor, the Patriarch Adrian, governed the country. Peter occupied himself with his boats, his soldiers, and his companions in the German suburb.

❧ PETER'S APPEARANCE AND NATURE

Peter had grown into a tremendous man—very strong, large-boned, and with his weight well proportioned to his height of six feet, eight and one-half inches. His hair and eyes were dark; his complexion swarthy. His nose was prominent; his cheeks, round, and on one of them was a wart. He walked with great strides and much arm-swinging and, like many other very tall men, he early developed a marked stoop. Clothing did not interest him, and he habitually was poorly dressed. There is a record of his appearance at a formal function wearing a green cap, an ordinary brown overcoat, heavily darned stockings, and very dirty shoes. One physical characteristic of Peter has given rise to many attempts at posthumous diagnosis. He was afflicted with a sort of spasticity, which was evidenced by a grotesque twitching of his head and by involuntary flailings of his arms and legs. A contemporary description of him reported:

> One of his commonest tricks was to try to look at his sword by bending his head backward over his shoulder, and to raise one of his legs and stretch it out behind him. He sometimes turned his head as if he desired to bring his face above the middle of his shoulders. Those who waited on him asserted that this kind of convulsion always came upon him when his thoughts were very earnestly fixed on any special subject.

Peter's driving energy, his vigor of thought and directness of action, and his fits of wild rage make one wonder if his thyroid was overactive. Perhaps his most outstanding trait was a complete lack of any restraint or moderation. When he was afraid, he was terrified and scuttled away in panic like a timid rabbit. When he was brave, he stood his ground and fought like an enraged lion, careless of personal danger. When he ate, he gormandized; when he drank, he guzzled. Though he enjoyed buffoons and buffoonery, he never suffered fools gladly and was violently impatient with inefficiencies and sloth. His displeasure was like a mountain thunderstorm, and his rages swept all before them like a flash flood. His enthusiasms were quick, great, and often transient, yet his persistence in some things was measured by years. His mind was facile; his curiosity limitless in scope; but both were often superficial. He was essentially childlike in his shifting fancies, his impatience, and in his

THE DYNAMIC PETER
107

capacity for mental and physical cruelty. Many admired Peter and many hated him. Most of his associates feared him, but rarely hesitated to fool him for their own advantage when they could. Even Menshikov, whom Peter lifted from obscurity to be his closest companion and who was genuinely loyal to the tsar, did not scruple to trick him now and again. Perhaps only Catherine, mistress of many before Peter—the Catherine whom he made his wife and his empress and who followed him on the throne—ever managed to soothe and comfort and control this turbulent giant for long.

🏵 TRAVELS AND DIPLOMACY

Peter's reign was long; his actual possession and use of the power, somewhat shorter. From 1682 to 1689 he was the junior co-tsar with Ivan. For the next five years he was virtually the only tsar but took little part in state business. Only after his mother's death in 1694 did he assume the actual responsibilities of his office, and he did not take them on all at once, being content to leave many matters in the hands of others and even to entrust the government to them while he made a journey to Europe. There were differences of opinion in the Moscow of that day as to what motives led Peter so to outrage convention and precedent as to leave his country to go abroad—something that no Russian ruler had done for six hundred years. Historians have continued to disagree about it. Some have thought that the chief purpose was to get an alliance against the Turks, with whom Peter had become involved as a result of a campaign against Azov. Voltaire, who wrote a history of Peter's Russia, thought that the journey was undertaken in order that the tsar might learn how better to govern Russia. Many of Peter's contemporaries were sure that Peter's main purpose was to amuse himself and to escape the few restraints which bound him. Others said that he went to fulfill a vow. Schuyler, whose biography of Peter has been supplemented but not supplanted by later works, said flatly that the tsar went to Europe "simply to become a good shipwright." This is apparently true as far as it goes, but it does not take sufficient account of the reasons, other than personal interest, why Peter thought it desirable to learn shipbuilding. Those reasons were closely connected with foreign policy.

It was necessary both in Russia's self-interest and in fulfillment of the agreement made with Poland in 1686 for Peter to renew the war against the Crimean Tatars and their backers, the Turks. Since Golitsin's direct attacks on the Crimea had ended disastrously, Peter and his advisers adopted a different strategy. A feint was made toward the Crimea, but the main force was sent against the fortress of Azov at the mouth of the Don. This first attempt (1695) failed because Peter could invest the fortress only from the land, and it was re-enforced and supplied by sea. Peter at once had a small fleet built and renewed his attack with combined naval and land forces. This time he won. Azov fell and Peter's ambitions expanded. He proposed to build a real navy and also to form a European alliance system for the purpose of expelling the Turk from Europe. Shipyards were built, foreign craftsmen and technicians were invited to come to work in them, fifty young Russians were sent to Europe to study navigation, and the landowners and cities were ordered to furnish a set number of naval vessels by 1698. Then Peter determined to accomplish several things at once by sending to Europe a "Grand Embassy."

Titular head of the embassy was General Lefort, a Swiss whose association with Peter had begun in the German suburb and who had served in the Azov campaign. Lefort's ranking associates were Golovin, who had made the Treaty of Nerchinsk with China, and another veteran diplomat and administrator, Voznitsin. Twenty nobles and thirty-five "volunteers" to learn the arts of shipbuilding completed the suite. The roster of the volunteers carried the name of Peter Mikhailov, identified as a noncommissioned officer of the Preobrazhenskoe regiment. This alias fooled no one, but it was carefully respected because Peter Mikhailov was the Tsar of All the Russias. The composition of this Grand Embassy suggested that Peter had diplomacy as well as shipyards in mind. So he did. A treaty of friendship was made with Frederick of Prussia, who sought to divert Peter's attention from the Turks to the Swedes, and time was found to intervene in Polish affairs. An interregnum in Poland produced two candidates for the throne: Conti, backed by France, and Augustus, the Elector of Saxony. Peter supported Augustus. En route home, Peter visited Augustus, found him congenial, and laid the foundation for an alliance against Sweden. Nobody, not even the Germanic emperor, who was then at war with the sultan, could he interest in making an alliance against the Turks.

As for the other purposes of the embassy, Peter Mikhailov worked more than four months in an Amsterdam shipyard and almost as long at the English government shipyard at Deptford. He recruited artisans, technicians, naval officers, pilots, and physicians; collected compasses, tools, sailcloth, anchors, pistols, and munitions; and shipped two hundred and sixty cases of such supplies to Moscow. He mingled freely with commoners, but he also met and talked with princes and prelates. At odd moments, this dynamic Peter visited hospitals and asylums, factories and arsenals, observatories and museums. He learned a bit about building bridges and a little about pulling teeth. Among the items he sent home were eight blocks of marble (presumably for future sculptors) and a stuffed crocodile. No wonder Peter Mikhailov left a deep impression on those with whom he came in contact.

🔘 DOMESTIC REVOLTS AND FOREIGN WAR

Sophia and the *Streltsi,* who had bulked so large and fearsome in Peter's boyhood, continued to trouble him. A revolt among the *Streltsi* had delayed the departure of the Grand Embassy; another revolt cut short its tour. Peter had deprived the *Streltsi* of their special place and had sent them to garrison Azov and the Polish frontier. They mutinied in 1698 and began to return to Moscow, but broke and fled when confronted by Peter's regular army. Many were captured and jailed, some were executed. Peter, upon his return, ordered a new and more searching investigation of the insurrection. Some of the *Streltsi* claimed under torture that their mutiny had been plotted by Sophia. It pleased Peter to accept this dubious evidence and to use it as the basis for immuring Sophia in a convent. Upon the *Streltsi,* the tsar's hand fell with terrible heaviness. The organization was disbanded and some two thousand of its members were executed. Eudoxia, Peter's unloved wife, and her relatives were also the victims of this purge. Tsaritsa Eudoxia was packed off to a nunnery where, as the nun Helen, she lived for the next twenty years. Alexis, son of Peter and Eudoxia, was entrusted to the care of his aunts. The boy grew up hating his father and opposing all that his father sought to do. Years later Alexis became involved in a plot against Peter. He was tried and sentenced to death on evidence which is still disputed. The sentence was not carried out only because the tsarevich died, or was killed in prison. The official explanation was that Alexis died of apoplexy, but it seems more likely that he died under torture administered at Peter's orders if not, indeed, carried out by Peter himself.

It is not necessary to be an apologist for Peter to recognize that his ruthlessness, his vicious and vindictive cruelty are partially explicable in terms of his own youthful experiences as well as the nature of his times and the circumstances of his reign. Peter was at war against something or somebody throughout his whole career. We have already noted his war against the Turks, which, after the capture of Azov, dragged on until 1700 and was then renewed by the Turks in 1710. This second war ended badly for Peter, who was forced as a result of it to restore to the Turks Azov and its environs. But important as this struggle against the Ottoman Empire was, it was subsidiary to the "Great Northern War" of Russia against Sweden—a war which lasted from 1700 to 1721 and completely dominated Peter's reign. Almost everything that Peter did was in some way connected with this long conflict. It was the mainspring of most of his famous reforms.

It will be recalled that the Prussian king had suggested to Peter an alliance against Sweden. Augustus, Saxon king of Poland, whose candidacy Peter had supported, had made a similar proposal. There was nothing new to the Russians in the idea of attacking Sweden. Peter's immediate predecessors had been more concerned with the problems of Poland and Ukraine, which also involved conflict with the Turks, but the idea of continuing Russian expansion toward the Baltic was only temporarily pushed aside. Peter revived the policy. He did not originate it. The shooting war was preceded by diplomatic maneuvering which resulted in Russian alliances with Augustus of Poland and with the king of Denmark. The latter was somewhat more impatient for war than was Peter and argued that the accession to the Swedish throne of the young, untried, and apparently irresponsible Charles XII offered a unique opportunity. But Peter would not move until the conclusion of a peace with the Turks in 1700. Then he sent his armies toward the Baltic and besieged the Swedish fortress of Narva.

Charles XII astonished everybody by the skill and vigor with which he met this three-Power attack. He first sent his forces to attack Copenhagen and their successes compelled the Danes to make a separate peace. Then he turned upon the Russians at Narva and inflicted upon them a tremendous defeat in which he captured their artillery and their siege camp. This Battle of Narva (November, 1700) might have been decisive if Charles had followed up his victory over the routed and demoralized Russians. But Charles, instead, turned against the Poles. This gave Peter the time needed to gather a new army. The tsar got together a new and stronger force, replaced his artillery and even increased it, and made a fresh and tighter alliance with King Augustus. For the next several years the Russians fought on two fronts: in or near Poland, and in the Baltic lands. The Baltic army, commanded by Sheremetev, achieved a string of successes at the expense of Sweden. The Russians in 1702 captured the Swedish fortress which they renamed Schluesselburg, and in the following year took the Swedish stronghold of Nyenschanz at the confluence of the Okhta and Neva rivers. Near this place Peter at once built the fortress of SS. Peter and Paul, and beyond the fortress walls he began a settlement which grew into his name-city (St. Petersburg; later Petrograd; now Leningrad). The fortress of SS. Peter and Paul commanded an outlet to the Baltic Sea, and Peter immediately, applying some of the lessons he had learned, caused naval vessels to be built and launched. A little later he had a naval base built for this new Baltic fleet at Kronstadt. Narva, from which he had ignominiously been driven in 1700, was captured, along with Dorpat, in 1704. Peter now had a protected outlet to the Baltic.

While the Russian forces were winning their victories along the Baltic, Swedish troops under Charles were gaining successes in Poland. Early in 1707, King Augustus retired to his native Saxony and signed a peace which Charles dictated. The Swedish conqueror of Poland was now free to turn his whole force against Russia, at a time when domestic difficulties had seriously crippled Peter's ability to wage a foreign war.

🎏 MORE REBELLIONS AND MORE WAR

The causes of the domestic unrest were the direct result of the tremendous burdens which the war, and Peter's efforts to strengthen his country for war, had put upon the people. The people were required to pay taxes which were steadily increased to an unprecedented number and cost. They were also compelled to work directly or indirectly at the building of ships and the construction of towns and fortifications. Some five thousand peasants and serfs had been put at forced labor to build fortifications on the Sea of Azov (which Peter eventually lost to the Turks) and tens of thousands were forced to work constructing St. Petersburg. A great many more were taken into the army. These and other demands upon the people continuously provoked minor uprisings, and in 1705 were responsible for a large insurrection at Astrakhan. Two years later a very serious rebellion began among the Cossacks of the Don and spread rapidly. The immediate cause was Peter's attempt to place tax and other obligations upon the Don Cossacks just as he had upon the rest of his people. Back of this immediate cause, however, was a long-standing quarrel between the Cossacks and the government at Moscow. The lands, freedom, and opportunities of the Don region continued to attract large numbers of runaways from the rest of Russia. While the Cossacks did not welcome these immigrants, neither would they surrender them at the demand of the government. Peter, in 1707, sent an army into the regions of the Don—a direct violation of what the Cossacks regarded as their ancient rights—to find and to bring back these runaways, and to mobilize the wealth and manpower of the Cossacks themselves. The latter followed their "hetman," Bulavin, in a rebellion which was joined by the runaways and by many other malcontents, including those who had been forced to labor on a canal between the Don and the Volga. Bulavin's rebellion covered the vast region between the lower Don and the Volga, and it inspired other insurrections among the peasants and among non-Russian subject peoples such as the Tatars and the Bashkirs. Peter had to use a large force to suppress the uprising.

Meanwhile another complication had arisen in Ukraine. It centered on the Ukrainian hetman Ivan Mazepa, who had ruled that troubled land since 1687. He had managed skillfully to preserve Ukrainian autonomy, to keep the strife between the favored Cossacks and the other elements of the population within bounds, and still to maintain good relations with Moscow. Peter completely trusted Mazepa, and at first declined to believe reports that he was treasonously conspiring with Poland. An investigation whitewashed Mazepa who had, in fact, been guilty as charged, and who subsequently allied himself with Charles and the rapidly advancing Swedes. It was a Great Russian historian Platonov who neatly and fairly stated Mazepa's side of the case as follows:

> Everybody expected to see Moscow crushed, and the Cossack leader had to decide whether the Ukraine should remain loyal to Moscow, and share the hard lot of the vanquished, or make common cause with the Swedes and secure her independence. This is how and why Mazepa decided to enter into secret negotiations with the Poles and Swedes.

The campaign which Charles opened in 1708 was marked by Swedish victories which seemed to confirm the wisdom of Mazepa's choice. But Mazepa, his actions now revealed, was forced to take refuge with Charles, and a Russian army nearly annihilated the re-enforcements upon which the Swedes were counting. The winter of 1708–9 found the Swedish forces ringed around by Peter's troops—an encirclement which Charles was unable to break. In the spring Charles moved to besiege the frontier fortress of Poltava. The siege was held off by the garrison until, in June, 1709, a Russian army led by Peter himself arrived to relieve the garrison. The numerically superior Russian troops routed the Swedes, and captured or killed half the Swedish army. Charles escaped to Turkey, where he incited the sultan to reopen war with Peter. The Russian victory at Poltava proved to be the major turning point, despite the fact that the Great Northern War dragged on for another twelve years and that Peter was defeated by the Turks. As a direct result of Poltava, Denmark and Saxony joined against Sweden, Augustus was recalled to the Polish throne and Poland re-entered the war against the Swedes, and the Russian northern army captured many Swedish fortresses along the Baltic. After the Treaty of Pruth (1711), by which Peter was forced to surrender the Azov territory to the victorious Turks, the Russians were able to concentrate their efforts in the north.

Peter's successes awakened the fears of his Saxon and Danish allies, who had no desire to dislodge one Power from the Baltic only to have a stronger Power take its place. They accordingly cut down their operations, and this led Peter to make his second trip to western Europe in the hope of establishing an alliance with France. His mission was well received and royally entertained, but no alliance was made. Peter thereafter opened peace talks directly with Charles, but these were ended by the Swedish government following Charles's death in 1718. The Swedes made separate peace arrangements with Peter's allies but renewed the fight against Russia. Power had now entirely shifted, however, and Peter's armies invaded and devastated Sweden. Parleys were resumed in 1721 and culminated in the signature that year of the Treaty of Nystadt. This gave Russia Livonia, including Riga; Estonia; Ingria; and Karelia. These lands comprised almost the entire eastern coast of the Gulf of Riga, all the southern and eastern coasts of the Gulf of Finland, and the northern coast of that gulf almost to Helsingfors (Helsinki). The islands off Estonia also went to Russia—an important strategic gain, since they control the eastern Baltic. Peter had not only recovered the ancient Russian lands; he had also gained direct water access to the West. His triumph was in no way limited by the fact that the treaty required Russia to pay a large indemnity to Sweden. It is an interesting sidelight upon the diplomatic alliances and alignments of the time that Great Britain and Poland were both parties to the Treaty of Nystadt— Great Britain, on the side of Sweden; Poland, on the side of Russia. Spectacular celebrations marked the final achievement of this long-sought and hard-earned victory. The officers of his navy gave to Peter the title of admiral. The Senate went further and begged him to accept the titles "Father of his Country, Emperor of All the Russias, Peter the Great. . . ." He graciously agreed and henceforth styled himself Emperor and Autocrat of All the Russias. He also decreed that his country should henceforth be known not as "The Grand States of the Russian Tsardom" but as the "Empire of All the Russias."

🜚 PETER'S REFORMS: GENERAL

These changes were typical of many of Peter's celebrated reforms. They were the direct outgrowth of the war, they merely altered labels; or they were never fully operative. Military needs were always Peter's first concern; attempts to satisfy them, his major motivation. Frequently this created a sort of chain reaction that led him to meddle in many fields which may seem far removed from warfare. For example, his wars swallowed up tremendous sums of money. This necessitated tax reforms to increase the government's income. But to raise enough tax money it was necessary to improve the efficiency with which taxes were levied and collected. This led to a taking of a census which, in an effort to get every possible taxpayer on the rolls, changed the status of many people. It also necessitated an improvement in administration as well as an enlargement of the bureaucracy. Administrative reforms led to educational reforms in an effort to provide a supply of trained administrators. And the reforms were costly, though less so than the war, which necessitated further tax reforms. So it went, one reform leading to another, with most of them being hastily improvised under the immediate pressure of a current demand or interest, and with no long-range planning. Peter's reforms quite perfectly illustrate the old saying that no man travels as far as the one who doesn't know where he is going.

If there was any governing principle behind the reforms as a whole other than a desire to strengthen the state, it was Peter's conviction that the wealth and persons of all his subjects should be placed at the service of the state. He believed that every man, from the noble to the serf, should pay taxes and should serve the state by "labor of hand or brain: in some capacity." The tax decree of 1718, which replaced the tax on households by a poll tax, stated that the new tax was to be collected for all, "excepting no one from the aged to the very last babe." To achieve a further increase in tax revenue, Peter set up a special board whose duty it was to think up new taxes. Before the end of his reign taxes were levied on stamped paper for legal use; the wearing of beards; the sale of salt, cucumbers, and oak coffins; bathhouses; beekeeping; and many other things. These exactions raised a greater revenue, and the new poll tax increased the amount of land which was cultivated. The old tax on cultivated lands could be evaded, and was, by the obvious device of cultivating less land. The poll tax (which was levied only on males) set a fixed sum per head which could be met with something over by working more land. There was, however, another side to it.

⚓ EFFECTS ON PEOPLE

Peter's determination that no one should escape state service was implemented in many ways. Those "idle people"—manumitted serfs, non-taxpayers, hangers-on, and free men of various sorts—were required to enter the army or to take service with some landlord, or were put at forced labor. Moreover, and this was highly significant, the census of 1718 made no distinction between serfs and peasants. Originally, the two had been clearly distinguished in several ways. The serf had lived and worked in the manor house; the peasant, on the land. The peasant had paid taxes to the state as well as meeting obligations to his landlord, but the serf had paid no taxes. Sometime during the seventeenth century it had become a common practice for the owners to settle their serfs on the land and require them to cultivate it. By the end of the century, the state had begun to collect taxes from these serfs on the ground that they differed little from the peasants, even though they were not classed together. The 1718 census and the tax laws which were based upon it simply lumped these two groups together, making the male serf liable for the poll tax and transforming the peasant into the absolute subject of the landlord. The change was a degradation of the peasant rather than an elevation of the serf. Since the landlord was held responsible for the payment of the poll tax for all his people, he made no distinction among them either. A peasant writer of Peter's time wrote: "[The peasants] left their homes and ran away, some to the lowlands, some to the borderlands, others beyond the frontier, and so they settled foreign lands while leaving their own lands waste." Nobody knows how many peasants ran away to escape the tax collectors, the forced labor, the army service, and other obligations; but the number was extensive. According to a contemporary record, in one province half of a group of thirteen thousand peasants fled.

The lower classes were not the only ones who felt Peter's hard hand upon them. City people, who had been made a distinct legal class by the Code of 1649, were organized into associations or guilds, given a certain measure of self-government, freed from some obligations, but obliged to assume new and heavier ones. The old distinction among the nobility dating from Ivan Grozny's establishment of the Thousand was abolished. All were required to enlist in the service of the state for life, and only a limited number were allowed to choose the civil service. Sons of the nobility were required to enter service at the age of fifteen; before that it was demanded that they get at least a rudimentary education. Peter sought to establish the principle of equal opportunity in government service, and to that end he set up in 1722 a "Table of the Grades in All Ranks of Military, Civil, and Court Service." There were fourteen grades of classifications roughly equated for each service. Class I (the highest) included: in the navy, "General Admiral"; in the army, "Generalissimo, Field Marshal, General of the Artillery, General of the Cavalry"; in the civil service, "Chancellor or Regular Privy Councilor." The fourteenth class began with "Ensign or Cornet" in the army and "Collegiate Registrar" in the civil service. (There was no corresponding naval rank.) It was Peter's intention that everyone, noble or commoner, should start at the bottom and work his way up. The highest classifications conferred hereditary nobility upon their holders; lower classifications gave personal ennoblement. The nobles did not like these changes, nor did they like Peter's decrees which forbade them to divide their estates. He permitted them to name their own heir but insisted that the undivided estate go to the designated heir and to him only. Attempts at evasion of Peter's new rules were numerous, but the tsar tried to enforce them uniformly except that he permitted the sons of the highest nobility to do their military service in his favorite regiments, the Preobrazhenskoe and Semenovski. By the end of Peter's life the personnel of these two Guards regiments were almost entirely from the nobility, a fact which should be remembered in connection with the part subsequently played by the Guards in the numerous palace revolutions.

✪ ADMINISTRATIVE REFORMS

Whether Peter's various administrative reforms did more than change labels and add complications is somewhat controversial. Government under Peter was personal government—as it had been under his predecessors. Peter assumed that the will of the prince was law, and, although he consulted various advisers and counselors, it was he who made the decisions. The various officials derived their authority from their relation to the sovereign rather than from the office they happened to hold. Early in Peter's reign he made use of a body which still passed under the name of the Boyars' Councils but which actually bore little resemblance to that institution. Under Peter, it was no more than a small coterie of his own intimates. He sought to regularize this in 1711 by appointing nine men to serve as "the Governing Senate," more often called, simply, the Senate. Its powers and functions varied from time to time throughout Peter's reign, but its powers were always limited, since it was primarily a personal agency of the tsar. Finding it difficult to keep the Senate and his other administrators up to the mark—despite a steady stream of rules, regulations, scoldings, and punishments—Peter in 1722 created the office of procurator-general. This official was to supervise all government institutions, especially the Senate. The procurator was the direct agent of the sovereign and derived his power from that fact. In addition to this watchman, Peter also used a body of secret, political police whose task it was "to find out secretly, denounce, and expose" abuses by officials, and also to protect the regime from treason or threats of treason.

It has previously been explained that government business had long been carried on by a number of bureaus which had been created without plan or co-ordination. Kliuchevskii once compared the system to a set of farm buildings. The farmhouse represented the tsar and his advisers; the various smaller buildings—set higgledy-piggledy all about—were the various bureaus. There were some fifty of these bureaus by Peter's time, and their efficiency was greatly limited by overlapping jurisdictions and confused authority. Peter replaced them with twelve new departments known as "colleges." The name, like the institution, was borrowed from the West. Affairs which were not allocated to these new colleges—for example, many matters concerning the nobility—were given over to the Senate, which also had partial supervision over the colleges. The Senate was further given limited powers over the governors.

Back in 1708 Peter had ordered that the various districts of his country should be combined into provinces; the provinces, into governments (*gubernias*). Eight such governments were set up, each headed by a governor who was appointed by the tsar and who was held responsible for the raising of troops and for the collection of taxes in his *gubernia*. This reform was instituted to increase the effectiveness of the draft and of tax collection. Peter did not succeed in establishing uniformity of administration within the various *gubernias,* nor in making all of the governors equally responsive to the central authority. He did remove the cities from the control of the provincial administrators by subjecting them to a chief magistrate.

With some exceptions, these schemes all looked better on paper than they did in practice, since Peter had neither the time nor the patience nor the personnel to make them work well. Despite the various changes, the government remained basically what it was: a tsar operating through men who received their power from him but over whom he never exercised a control that was either absolute or perfect. There are few clearer illustrations that policy is more often made by administrators than by "policy makers." Peter could issue decrees, but he could not personally implement his orders nor always get others to do what he directed. That is one major reason why the results of his attempted administrative reforms were often disappointing.

ECONOMIC REFORMS

Peter's economic reforms also stemmed mainly from Russia's military needs. Recent studies have indicated that his accomplishments along economic lines were less than used to be supposed. He wanted to build a large-scale industry, which meant that he had to find more raw materials, obtain technicians, raise capital, and supply labor. The rich forest resources and varied agricultural products were readily available, but not the necessary mineral resources. Some prospecting had been done long before Peter's time. His distinction lies in the scale and vigor of his effort. His exploitation of the iron ore of the Urals was one of his most striking successes. We are so accustomed to think of Great Britain as the industrial pioneer that it is a little startling to find that Russia's mines and smelters were producing more pig iron in 1718 than the British produced in 1740. As for the technicians, Peter both sought out and employed aliens, and sent some of his own people to be trained in the West. His attempt to set up an educational system had as one of its aims the training of industrial technicians.

A large share of the capital necessary for Peter's industrial expansion was supplied directly by the state treasury, which initiated some enterprises and promoted others by subsidization. Most of the state revenue went for war needs, but some was devoted to industrialization in the expectation that this would eventually increase the country's military potential. But neither the funds in the treasury nor those acquired through taxation and through state monopolies on salt, tobacco, fish, oil, and oak coffins were sufficient to support the industrialization he wanted. Peter therefore sought to tap those stores of wealth which had been accumulated by the richer merchants and the larger landowners. Various inducements—such as monopoly rights, tax exemptions, and direct subsidies—were offered, and these were supplemented by an occasional use or threat of force. The need for an adequate supply of labor was met in several ways. One common device was to assign peasants living on state land to work in a designated mine, factory, or mill. A decree of 1721 permitted factory owners to buy peasants, who were thus transformed into landless serfs. Peasants thus assigned to industry became known as "possessional" or "ascribed," and they remained an important part of nonagricultural labor until the Emancipation. Forced labor was used widely. Some forced laborers were convicts, but very many of them were serfs or peasants who were simply abducted into this form of state service. And eleven years after Peter's death, a law deprived all who worked in factories, together with their families, of their freedom. A recent history of Russian economy states that "Russia's industrial proletariat, therefore, began as an unfree group, subject to the same disabilities as the serfs of the countryside from whose ranks most of these new proletarians were rudely taken by government fiat."

✿ CHURCH REFORM

Peter's most carefully planned reform, and the one which endured the longest, concerned the Church. The real or alleged foreign nature of Peter's behavior and of his reforms evoked a bitter opposition from most of the churchmen and many of the people. The schismatics (*Raskolniki* or Old Believers) were particularly vehement. They called Peter the Antichrist, and told the people that Peter was not the true tsar but a usurper and the bastard son of Patriarch Nikon. Many churchmen who had accepted the Nikonian position also found Peter's reforms increasingly distasteful. Even the Patriarch Ioakhim, who had been so closely associated with the government in the time of Peter's mother, strenuously objected to Peter's fondness for foreigners. The next patriarch, Adrian, also openly disapproved of many of the tsar's actions and was supported in his disapproval by other high churchmen. It was certainly partially due to this that Peter did not choose a new patriarch after Adrian died in 1700. The tasks of the office were given over to a Ukrainian—Iavorski, metropolitan of Riazin—a supposedly temporary arrangement that was continued until 1721.

Meanwhile, Peter had encroached upon ecclesiastical property and prerogatives. After his defeat at Narva (1700), the tsar, in desperate need of resources, turned to the handiest accumulation of wealth. He confiscated the bells of some three hundred churches, and used the metal for making cannon. He required the monasteries to hand over to him all except a small portion of the income from their lands, and then transferred the monastic lands—along with the peasants living thereon—to the control of a secular Bureau of Monasteries. He limited the jurisdiction of church courts by transferring many cases to secular courts, and also by infiltrating the church courts with state officials. To see these reforms in proper perspective, it is necessary to recall the tremendously favorable and privileged position of the higher ecclesiastics and the wealth of the monasteries. Monastic records show that the monasteries owned between nine hundred thousand and a million peasants. The Monastery of St. Sergius alone owned over ninety thousand. And precious little of this great wealth was used for the common good.

The crown of Peter's Church reform was the Spiritual Regulation of 1721. It set out in detail the nature and limits of the education of future clergy and of the examinations for admission to the priesthood. It also regulated the monasteries and the monastics. But its most significant provisions were those which abolished the patriarchate and created a special body, the Holy Synod, to manage Church affairs. The Synod had no power over any civil or governmental affairs and was itself subject to the control of a lay official appointed by the tsar, the high procurator, who was attached to it. In other words, the Russian Orthodox Church was made a department of the Russian State, and so it continued. Since 1943 the patriarchate has been restored, but to an extent even greater than ever before the Church under the new dispensation remains the servant of the State.

✤ MISCELLANEOUS REFORMS

Certain of Peter's miscellaneous reforms may serve as a measure of the catholicity of his interests and activities. He established various technical schools and academies which were chiefly patronized by the children of his lesser officials and other parvenus who saw learning as a road to advancement. Despite his efforts to force the nobility to acquire an education, it is recorded that less than 2 per cent of the pupils of his schools came from this class. The tsar also caused to be translated many Western books, chiefly but not exclusively of a technical nature, and even developed a new and simpler alphabet so that the translations might be more easily read. He was responsible for the publication of Russia's first newspaper, the *St. Petersburg Gazette* (1708). He created an Academy of Sciences, which developed into a major research center and compiled an impressive record of scholarship. Its greatest days came after Peter, but the original inspiration and foundation were his.

It is amusing to note that, among all his multifarious doings, the dynamic tsar somehow found time to meddle with the dress and with the social life of his courtiers. One of his earliest reforms (1698) obliged his subjects to shave off their beards or to pay a tax for the privilege of wearing one. The nobility at court had no option. Peter cut off the beards of several courtiers himself. He also required those about him to dress in the Western style. Among the translations which he ordered was one entitled *The Honorable Youth's Mirror, or The Rule of Worldly Manners*. And to give society a chance to practice what they learned in such books of etiquette, the tsar often arranged balls and other assemblies which they were required to attend. There were few things, indeed, to which Peter did not apply himself at some time or other, and about which he did not issue some order or regulation.

ESTIMATE OF PETER'S WORK

When Peter the Great, Father of his Country, Emperor of All the Russias, and so on, died near the end of his fifty-third year, no one under thirty years of age had personal memory of any other tsar, and no one under middle age could recall a time when Peter had not been tsar. What had he done? He had pushed his country's borders north and west to the shores of the Baltic and had built a new capital to symbolize his new empire. He had reached the warm waters of the south, though he had failed to keep his hold there. He had changed names and titles but not the essential form of the government. More important was his creation of a new nobility and officialdom which partly displaced the old. He had reduced organized religion to a department of the state, thus removing a potential rival and muting if not wholly silencing a formal voice of conscience. He had increased the amount of land in cultivation, the number of mines, mills, and factories in production, and the number of fugitives from his totalitarianism. He had introduced a few of his subjects to Western ways. He had built up a regular army of two hundred thousand troops and seventy-five thousand sailors. He had broken Swedish dominance and had freely interfered in Polish domestic affairs. And in his actions, he had regarded his subjects' lives and liberties as no less wholly expendable at his will than was their property. He raised one servant to a prince and a soldiers' doxy to an empress, but he made thousands of peasants into serfs and all men into slaves of the state, which he personified and directed.

Little that he did was wholly new. He began few things and finished less. There is more continuity than change in Peter's policies. The change was more in detail than in principle; more in the vigor of implementation than in the conceptions. Yet his traditional reputation is not wholly undeserved. One may reject as gross exaggeration the recent statement of a French scholar that Peter's work "determined the course of Russian life for two centuries," but nevertheless agree that the dynamic Peter, who "tried everything, and failed in much," stamped his mark upon his country and his people. The Petrine myths may have been determinants not less important than his actual deeds. Certainly Peter's shadow lies across the lives of his successors.

CHAPTER VIII

Guardsmen and Empresses

The death of Alexis Petrovich left only one male heir to the throne—the boy Peter Alexievich, grandson of Peter the Great. It may be assumed that Peter the Great intended to arrange the succession to his throne because in 1722 he had his Senate decree that the sovereign could name his own successor. But Peter delayed doing so probably much as many people postpone making a will, and he died intestate. When similar situations had arisen before, the prince-boyars or the patriarchs had taken the lead in selecting the ruler. Peter, however, had destroyed the patriarchate and had greatly reduced the power and prestige of the churchmen. He had also carried further the diminution of the boyars' powers. There were prince-boyars in Peter's service—notably, Golitsin, Dolgoruki, and Sheremetev—but there were also nobles such as Tolstoy, and others of Peter's own creation, such as Menshikov, Ostermann, and Catherine. When the scepter dropped from Peter's hand all these people scrambled to pick it up.

🐚 MENSHIKOV AND CATHERINE I (1725–27)

Menshikov allied himself with Catherine, Peter's widow, and with Tolstoy. He also—and this was decisive—enlisted the support of the Guards who, at his nod, demonstrated in Catherine's favor. The demonstration settled the matter. Catherine was made empress the night of Peter's death, and she reigned, under Menshikov's tutelage, until her own death in 1727. The Golitsin-Dolgoruki combination sought to curb Menshikov's power by forcing the creation of the Supreme Privy Council as the instrument of government. Menshikov was able to bring the council under his dominance. Ostermann, a Westphalian who had entered Russian service and risen to the post of vice-chancellor in Peter's reign, controlled Russian diplomacy. Menshikov began to scheme for his own continuance as the power behind the throne and, perhaps, as something more. He persuaded Catherine to name the young Peter Alexievich as her heir, arranged the betrothal of the heir to one of his daughters, and took the boy to live in his palace. But Menshikov's arrogance after Catherine died alienated the Guards and offended the boy-emperor. Peter II, under the influence of the Dolgorukis, took away Menshikov's power and titles, jilted the daughter, and exiled the family.

The real power now rested with the Dolgorukis and Golitsins, especially the former, who controlled the Supreme Privy Council. They left Vice-Chancellor Ostermann in control of foreign affairs, and permitted another German, General Münnich, greatly to increase his influence in the army. The Dolgorukis sought to secure their power by the same means that Menshikov had tried. They arranged a marriage between Peter II and one of the Dolgoruki princesses. Before the marriage took place, however, the boy-emperor (he was seventeen) died of smallpox. Like his grandfather, Peter II also died intestate. The Supreme Privy Council—which is to say the prince-boyars and notably the Dolgorukis—chose a successor.

🏵 ANNA OF COURLAND (1730–40)

They selected a middle-aged widow, Anna (or Anne) of Courland, to be their new empress. Anna was the niece of Peter I, the daughter of Peter's older half brother, Ivan V. The true reason for the selection of Anna, however, was that the council expected that they could control her. They offered her the crown only on condition that she accept certain drastic limitations on her power: "That the Empress Anna was to reign only in virtue of the resolves . . . of the Privy Council." Anna accepted the conditions only long enough to build up a party among the nonboyar nobility, chiefly the Guards. Then she literally confronted the council with some hundreds of nobles and armed guardsmen, upbraided Dolgoruki and his associates for their acts, and destroyed the limiting documents which she had been induced to sign. Shortly thereafter she abolished the Supreme Privy Council and exiled or executed many of the prince-boyars.

The Empress Anna did not herself exercise the autocratic power. Rather, she left it to her lover, Ernst Johann Bühren (or Biron) and to the other Germans who surrounded her. Ostermann remained as vice-chancellor and gained almost complete control of domestic civil affairs. The army was placed under Burkhard Münnich, who was made marshal and Minister of War. The upper bureaucracy, at least, was also largely taken over by Germans and Balts. Russian historians have almost unanimously condemned the decade of Anna's reign (1730–40) as a period of Germanic tyranny. Bühren is accused of caring nothing whatever for the Russian people, of using secret political police (including many spies and informers) to maintain his power and to protect himself, and of general cruelty. But since these were hardly novelties in Russia, one may wonder whether the real complaint was at tyranny as such, or at the efficiency of it, or at its exercise by non-Russians. There was grumbling enough about Bühren and his clique, but there was no serious challenge from the only class which counted politically, that is, the nobility.

Anna had no children whom she wished to acknowledge as heirs to the throne, so she designated as her successor her infant grandnephew. The baby's name (he was only five months old when his grandaunt died) was Ivan, and his mother's name was Anna. Bühren persuaded his dying mistress to name him as regent for Ivan, which meant that Bühren might be the real ruler of Russia for the next seventeen years. But he had already alienated the powerful Ostermann, and in the first weeks of his regency he angered the baby's mother and Marshal Münnich as well. They quickly took advantage of these blunders. Marshal Münnich, disappointed in his ambition to be made generalissimo, consulted with the emperor's mother, who was also in touch with Ostermann. Münnich, backed by the Preobrazhenskii Guards, arrested Bühren, divested him of his regency, and sent him into exile. The baby Ivan VI continued as emperor under the regency of his mother, Anna. Bühren's regency lasted three weeks; Anna's lasted a year.

THE EMPRESS ELIZABETH (1741–62)

By that time (1741) people had forgotten the cruelties and harshness of Peter the Great. His reign took on the flavor of "the good old days" before the Germans came. Some of this new feeling was extended to the handsome and dashing Elizabeth, daughter of Peter and Catherine I, and she became the focus of a plot which was sedulously fostered by the French ambassador, who wished to replace German influence over Russia with French power. When the coup came, it was carried off by Elizabeth and her favorites with the active support of the Preobrazhenskii Guards, who were joined by guardsmen from other regiments. The Regent Anna and the infant Ivan VI were kidnapped; Ostermann, Münnich, and some of their fellows were arrested;[1] and a manifesto was published to announce that Peter's daughter had assumed her rightful place as empress of Russia. The new empress had directed the whole affair, showing more resolution and vigor than at any other time in her indolent life.

During the reign of Elizabeth, domestic affairs were somewhat overshadowed by diplomacy and by the increasing involvement of Russia in

European affairs; and Elizabeth generally left the business of government in the hands of others. The chief agencies of state were the Senate, which she restored and enlarged by giving it legislative as well as administrative powers, and her several favorites. The most influential persons in her entourage were Prince Nikita Trubetskoi, who served as procurator-general and as president of the Senate; Prince Ushakov, head of the secret police (technically, the Secret Chancellery); Alexius Petrovich Bestuzhev-Riumin, who became Elizabeth's vice-chancellor and determined her foreign policy until 1756. Two Frenchmen were also important in the early years of the reign. They were Ambassador La Chetardie, who had helped formulate and finance Elizabeth's coup, and Lestocq, Elizabeth's private physician, whom she ennobled and made a privy councilor. They intrigued against Bestuzhev-Riumin with some success, but after he became Chancellor of the Empire, he expelled La Chetardie and exiled Lestocq. Michael Vorontsov, who had preceded Bestuzhev-Riumin as chancellor and who was again elevated to that post after Bestuzhev-Riumin's disgrace and exile, also belongs in this list.

DOMESTIC MATTERS

Nor can we omit those men whose service to the empress was personal rather than political, although some of them had political power. First probably in the heart of the empress was a young Cossack shepherd, Alexis Razumovsky. She rapidly promoted him to high honors after her accession, endowed him with great wealth, and reputedly married him in secret in the fall of 1742. His younger brother, Cyril, also enjoyed the generosity of Elizabeth. Neither of them played much part in politics. Another family which profited mightily by their associations with the empress were the Shuvalovs. Politically the most important was Peter, who eventually came to dominate domestic affairs. An older brother held high office in the secret police, and a nephew, Ivan, who became the empress's lover in 1749, distinguished himself by his patronage of arts and letters. The Shuvalov dominance over Elizabeth and her court dates from Ivan's elevation to the post of Gentleman of the Bedchamber.

Elizabeth's court was not distinguished for its strict morality. It was, however, remarkable for its lavish extravagance. Elizabeth loved clothes and indulged her passion without restraint. It is reported that the great fire in Moscow in 1747 destroyed four thousand of her gowns and that fifteen thousand more were found among her possessions after her death. She demanded that nobles of the first and second classes should have not less than ten servants to follow each of their carriages. It is recorded that one such carriage cost the equivalent of 35,000 dollars in the currency of that day. It is no wonder that finance was a problem both to Elizabeth's government and to her nobility.

Efforts to improve the financial situation included a coinage reform; a slight decrease in taxes but a major increase in the prices of such government monopolies as salt; the abolition of internal customs duties (1753); the establishment of state banks to loan funds to merchants and to the landowning nobility at a rate of 6 per cent, which was about a third that usually charged by private moneylenders; and various attempts to promote trade. The reign is also memorable for advances in arts and letters, which developed rapidly under the patronage of Ivan Shuvalov.

Schools were established for the nobility; a university was founded at St. Petersburg in 1747, and another in Moscow in 1755, which offered courses in jurisprudence, medicine, and philosophy. The Academy of Science, which Peter the Great had founded, was revitalized. It dispatched scientific expeditions into Siberia and Kamchatka. An Academy of Fine Arts was also established. Historical studies of the Russian past were begun by the imported German scholars Bauer and Müller, and by the Russian Tatishev. But the greatest single name was that of Michael Lomonosov, first of the great Russian scholars and founder of Russian science. The son of a peasant from Archangel, Lomonosov (1712–65) was a versatile genius. He founded Russia's first laboratory for the study of physical chemistry; was himself a chemist, physicist, and astronomer of note; a poet of more than ordinary talent; a learned linguist, and an expert grammarian. He was also a drunken and turbulent wastrel.

It was in Elizabeth's reign that the great Winter Palace was built by the Italian architect Rastrelli, whose work set a style widely copied in other government buildings and in the construction of nobles' palaces. Elizabeth is generally regarded as the founder of the first Russian theater. Most of the plays produced in her reign were translations from the French, but there were some of Russian authorship. By and large, this was a period of French hegemony in art, in letters, and in fashions. French modes and manners became *de rigueur* at court, where the French language virtually displaced the native Russian. The interest in things French, sometimes genuine but more often dilettante, extended to the writings of Vauban and St. Remy on military affairs, and to the works of the *philosophes* and Encyclopedists—most notably Voltaire, who had a very considerable vogue. French "cultural" leadership continued almost to the end of the reign of Catherine the Great.

🌐 FOREIGN AFFAIRS

It may therefore seem paradoxical that France was Russia's great diplomatic rival throughout much of this time. France was the leading European Power, although she was being very closely pressed by Great Britain in colonial and maritime development, and was further challenged both by Austria and by the rising power of Prussia. In the course of her long feud against Austria and because of her growing quarrel with Prussia, France sought to use the three easterly Powers of Sweden, Poland, and the Ottoman Empire very much as, after World War I, she tried to use the little Entente. Her oldest and most promising ally was Poland. During the sixteenth century there had been two Franco-Polish alliances, and at one time a Valois had been king of Poland. Richelieu and Louis XIV both vainly sought a firm alliance with the Poles. By the eighteenth century Poland was too weak to make a desirable ally, but France continued to have an active interest in Polish affairs.

It also happened that the three most pressing diplomatic problems of Russia in the seventeenth century also involved Sweden, Poland, and Turkey. The Swedish problem was largely solved by Peter the Great in the first quarter of the eighteenth century, although the Swedes at the incitement of France went to war against Russia in 1741. That war ended in 1742 with a Russian victory, which slightly increased Russian territories to the northeast of the Baltic. But the Polish and Turkish problems remained unsolved. In the case of Poland, the First Great Northern War (1654–67) had revealed such a complete weakness as to invite the intervention of other nations. Russia, Prussia, Austria, and Sweden even discussed the possibility of partitioning Poland. There was an ephemeral Polish recovery under King Jan Sobieski, but even during his reign foreign intrigues continued and Polish anarchy increased. The Saxon king, Augustus II, was placed on the throne by alien bribes and violence and was able to maintain himself there only by accepting foreign aid. His entrance into the Second Great Northern War (1700–1721) as an ally of Peter resulted in a successful Swedish invasion of Poland from which the Poles were freed only by Russian victories. It was an exchange of masters. Peter's troops roamed over Poland, his agents learned to exploit the Polish constitution and to play the nobility against each other and against the king. Polish sovereignty, in short, was most seriously impaired.

In 1725, France, Britain, and Prussia concluded an agreement aimed against the Hapsburgs of Austria and Spain. Since simultaneously there was a serious tension between Russia and Britain arising out of the Russian advance in the Baltic, Russia and Austria shared an enemy—

one of the most powerful of diplomatic cements. Ostermann concluded a treaty of alliance with Austria in 1726. The first test of these two alliance groups—Austria and Russia on the one side, Prussia, Britain, and France on the other—came at the death of the Polish king, Augustus II, in 1733. The triple alliance favored the election of Stanislas Leszczynski, while the dual alliance supported Augustus' son. The quarrel came to blows. Russian force prevailed and Augustus III was made the Polish king—a further encroachment upon Polish sovereignty. Meanwhile, as part of the diplomatic jockeying, Ostermann had made an alliance treaty with Persia, and the French had succeeded in instigating a Turkish attack on Russia. The resulting Russo-Turkish War lasted from 1733 to 1739. Despite the fact that Austria gave very little aid, and the Persians gave none, the Russian generals were successful in the field. The Russian diplomats were not. Thanks to the active support of France, Turkey escaped with a peace which restored the *status quo ante bellum*.

The dynastic confusion, frequent palace coups, and desperate need of many courtiers and officials for money to support their extravagances offered an opportunity for intervention in Russian affairs which was not neglected by the other Powers. In addition to La Chetardie of France, the Austrian and the British ambassadors financed intrigues. The Austrian allied himself with the French in an effort to oust Bestuzhev-Riumin; the Britisher plotted to make the Grand Duchess Catherine the immediate successor of Elizabeth.

In spite of the Austrian failure to give Russia adequate support during the Russo-Turk War, the two continued close relations. Russia sent twenty thousand troops to aid Austria in the War of the Polish Succession (1733–38). This was the first Russian army to make its appearance in western Europe. Bestuzhev-Riumin renewed the alliance with Austria, and, though Russia, slow to mobilize, made only a military demonstration in behalf of her ally during the War of the Austrian Succession (1740–48), this hastened the peace and enhanced the prestige of Russia. Meanwhile, in 1747, Bestuzhev reached a bargain with Britain by which, in return for subsidies, Russia undertook to supply troops for the defense of Hanover. Three years later, Britain joined the Russo-Austrian Alliance and subsequently extended the scope of the subsidy agreement. Bestuzhev-Riumin was, of course, seeking partly to counter French activities, but his primary objective was to balance the rise of Prussia, which he correctly interpreted as the most serious threat to Russia. His life was considerably complicated by the fact that his empress, who liked the French, did not like either the British or the Austrians. Bestuzhev-Riumin enjoyed her full confidence only in his anti-Prussian policy, since Elizabeth intensely disliked Frederick of Prussia.

Expansion 16ᵗʰ to 18ᵗʰ centuries
Dates of acquisition in parenthesis

Scale – 1" = 233 miles

BALTIC SEA

SWEDEN

Archangel

N. Dvina R.

(1721)

Pskov
(1510)

(Livonia)

(1772)

Tver

Moscow

(1795)

Smolensk
(1514)

Riazan
(1521)

Kazan
(1552)

Volga R.

(1793)

Kiev

(1667)

Astrakhan
(1556)

Bug R.

(1733)
("New Russia")

(1783)

Azov
(1783)

(1783)

BLACK SEA

The whole diplomatic alignment was suddenly altered in 1756 when France and Britain shifted sides (the Diplomatic Revolution). France forsook Prussia for Austria, while Great Britain abandoned her Russo-Austrian alliance to go to the side of Prussia. This sudden shift cost Bestuzhev-Riumin his power and prestige. The alliance with Britain was abrogated, and Russia joined France and Austria against Prussia. That was the alignment—Russia, France, and Austria versus Prussia and Britain—which fought out the Seven Years' War (1756–63). Elizabeth now took charge of her own foreign policy and prosecuted the war against Prussia with considerable vigor. When Apraxin, her commander-in-chief, failed to follow up his victories against Prussia, she promptly removed him from command and punished him. She did not, surprisingly enough, sever diplomatic relations with Great Britain, although the situation between them was often strained. The successes of the Russian armies had brought Frederick so close to disaster that he was ready to abdicate. At that very crucial moment Elizabeth died, and Prussia was saved from certain defeat.

⊕ PETER AND CATHERINE

Shortly after she became empress and before the development of her implacable hostility toward Prussia, Elizabeth caused to be brought to Russia her young grandnephew, Karl Peter Ulric of Holstein. She had him admitted into the Russian Orthodox Church, gave him a Russian name (Peter Fedorovich), and made him a grand duke of Russia. Then she announced that Peter, nee Karl, was her designated heir. He was then fourteen years old—frail, feeble, and distinctly wanting in common sense. Two years after Peter's elevation to tsarevich, there arrived in Russia a fifteen-year-old girl and her mother. Their visit had been brought about largely by the machinations of Frederick of Prussia, who was seeking to undo Bestuzhev-Riumin's policies. The girl's name was Sophia Augusta Fredericka. Her father, who was one of Frederick's generals, called her Fike. After a period of inspection, probation, and religious instruction, Fike was accepted by Elizabeth and by the Russian Church. Her new name was Catherine Alexievna. A month later (August, 1745) Catherine (Sophia) was married to the Grand Duke Peter (Karl). During the next sixteen years, he distinguished himself by his general lack of sense and by his passionate devotion to Frederick of Prussia.

Despite these characteristics—or perhaps because of them—a clique headed and directed by the almost moribund but still ambitious Peter Shuvalov, and including the aged Vorontsov and Trubetskoi, determined to place the crown on Peter's head. The Guards, directed by Trubetskoi, took their oath to support Peter. The new emperor was a sorry figure, but he was by no means the moronic monster, the horrendous tyrant, or the drunken debauchee that Catherine's protagonists later labeled him. He did, however, sacrifice Russia's expensive victories over Frederick, to whom he publicly referred as "the King my master." Four months after his accession to the throne, Peter III concluded a peace which restored to Prussia all the lands which Russia had conquered from her; and entered into a binding alliance with his idol.

He granted amnesties to various political exiles including Bühren and Münnich but, significantly, excluding the anti-Prussian Bestuzhev-Riumin. He granted full freedom of worship to the *Raskolniki* and permitted those who had fled before the persecutions of Elizabeth and Anna to return to Russia. He abolished the secret police and reduced the much-hated tax on salt. He sought to reform the army along the Prussian lines, and was interested in building up the navy. He also planned a codification of law on the Prussian model, but those to whom he assigned the task were incompetent to perform it. He transferred church property to a new government department, the College of Economy, and sought to change certain ecclesiastical habits and customs. He freed the nobility from their obligations to serve the state. He showed great partiality to his fellow Holsteiners and to Prussians, shoving aside Russian nobles to give places to the foreigners, and he not only replaced the Preobrazhenskii Guards with a regiment of Holsteiners, but also planned to break up all the Guards regiments. The idea was sound enough, but circumstances rendered it incredible folly and it cost Peter III his throne and his life. He might better have alienated almost any other group than to have offended the Guards.

CATHERINE'S PLOTS

Peter's most implacable and dangerous enemy was his wife, the Grand Duchess Catherine, architect of his downfall. Her plotting against Peter began while Elizabeth was still alive. A coup was planned to take place at the empress's death, but she surprised the conspirators by dying before they were ready. Catherine then took great pains to dissemble her intentions, at the same time taking advantage of Peter's many blunders. She enlisted confederates among the courtiers, particularly Nikita Panin, a favorite of Elizabeth, who had placed him in charge of Catherine's son, Paul. Panin was perhaps Catherine's chief adviser in the plot. Among her other associates at court were some of Peter's own men, as, for example, Glyebov, Peter's procurator-general, and Baron von Korff, head of the police. The Princess Dashkova—daughter of Vorontsov and sister of Peter's mistress—served as a liason between Catherine and the Guards. Gregory Orlov, Catherine's third lover, enlisted the support of his four brothers, and they, in turn, enlisted the support of other Guards officers with their men. The coup was precipitated by two events, Peter's involvement in a war against Denmark—in which he intended to use the Guards at the front—and the wholly accidental discovery of the whole plot and the arrest of one of the minor conspirators. It was imperative to carry out the schemes at once, and the plan was put in operation in the early morning of July 28, 1762. Catherine's own account of the day follows:

Alexis Orlov enters my room and says quite gently: 'It is time to get up; all is ready for your proclamation.' I demanded some details. 'Passek is arrested,' said he. I hesitated no longer. I dressed myself quickly without making my toilet and got into the carriage which he had brought with him. Another officer, dressed up as a valet, was at the carriage door, a third met us some versts from Peterhof.

Five versts from the town I met the elder Orlov with the younger Prince Bariatinsky. Orlov gave up his carriage to me, for my horses were done in, and we got out at the barracks of the Ismailovsky [Guards] Regiment. [At the gate] were only twelve men and a drummer who began sounding an alarm, when the soldiers came running out, kissing me, embracing my hands and feet and clothes, and calling me their deliverer. Then they began swearing allegiance to me. When this had been done, they begged me to get into the carriage, and the priest, cross in hand, walked on in front. We went to the Semenovsky [Guards] Regiment . . . [which] came marching out to meet us, crying, 'Vivat.' Then we went to the church of Kazan where I got out. Then the Preobrazhenski Regiment arrived, crying, 'Vivat'. . . .

I went to the new Winter Palace where the Synod and the Senate were assembled. A manifesto and a form of oath were hastily drawn up. Then I went down and received the troops on foot. There were more than fourteen thousand men. . . .

I sent Admiral Talisin [to secure the fortress of] Cronstadt. Then the Chancellor Vorontsov arrived . . . [and] they took him off to church to swear him in. Prince Trubetskoi and Count Shuvalov also arrived. . . . They were taken off to swear the oaths without [making] the least resistance.

After having sent off our couriers and taken every precaution, towards ten o'clock in the evening I put on a uniform of the Guards. Having been proclaimed [their] Colonel [traditional rank of the sovereign] with inexpressible acclamations, I took horse and we left only a very few of each regiment behind to protect my son, whom we left in town. I set out at the head of the troops, and we marched all night towards Peterhof [where Peter III was].

🔧 TRIUMPH OF THE NOBILITY

Poor Peter, by that time deserted by almost everyone of rank, abdicated in Catherine's favor. She sent him under close guard to his estate at Ropsha, where he was kept prisoner. A week after his arrival there, ex-Emperor Peter III was murdered. Catherine probably knew of the murder in advance. Thus ended the eighth palace revolution in eighteenth-century

Russia. The decisive fact in the accession of Catherine I, in the restoration of the autocratic power to Anna, in the removal of Bühren, in the elevation of Elizabeth, and in the triumph of Catherine II was the support of the guardsmen. For seventy-five years following the death of Peter I, the Russian crown was largely at the disposal of the guardsmen, who made and unmade sovereigns at their will. The Guards regiments were exclusively officered, and even to some degree manned, by the nobility. This was the class which became, in the eighteenth century, the real master of Russia.

Peter the Great had sought to wipe out the old distinctions among the nobility and had, by opening careers to talent, created a new nobility much as the Tudors did in England. He had also required that all noblemen spend their lives in the service of the state, which was in fact their *raison d'être*. The Empress Anna reduced the term of required service from life to twenty-five years and permitted retirement at the age of forty-five. She also exempted certain nobles from service of any kind. Peter had forbidden the nobles to divide their estates among several heirs. Anna allowed it. In Peter's time, several classes other than the hereditary nobility were allowed to own serfs. This right was taken from all except the hereditary nobility during the reigns of Anna and Elizabeth, until only these nobles could acquire or hold either land with serfs or serfs without land. The responsibility and the authority of the serf-owners over their human property were increased. The owner was made responsible for feeding his serfs in time of famine. He was also charged with collecting taxes from them, seeing that they behaved properly, and punishing them if they ran away. He was given the authority to punish runaways by any means he chose, and to punish other serious offenses by sending the offender into exile in Siberia or by setting him at punitive labor. As far as the serfs were concerned, their owners became, in effect, the only government they knew. The owners' authority was supplemented by the whole power of the state. A serf was forbidden to sue his owner or even to complain against him. Nor could a serf have any direct dealings with the government.

The triumph of the *dvorianstvo* (the land- and serf-owning, hereditary nobility) culminated in a law of Peter III which was later confirmed and extended by Catherine the Great. Peter's manifesto announcing this (1762) said: ". . . We have judged it to be no longer necessary to compel into [state] service . . . the nobility of Our Empire." Catherine's "Charter of the Nobility" of 1785 exempted the *dvorianstvo* from all obligation to serve the state, from the payment of personal taxes, and from suffering corporal punishment. Since Peter's "beard reform" had not been rescinded, the 1785 charter removed all obligations except that of shaving. It confirmed the *dvorianstvo* in the absolute possession of their estates and of everything on them, including the peasants, who were not distinguished from any other chattel. It also extended the patent of nobility to the wives and children of the noblemen. No wonder this period is referred to as "The Golden Age of the Nobility" and (by Soviet historians) as "the dictatorship of the nobility." They reached the apogee of power and privilege simultaneously with the removal of those obligations for service which alone could justify such a position. The reverse of the medal was the further extension of serfdom.

SERFS

Natural increase and highly successful political expansion in the eighteenth century—Russian power was extended over the northern Caucasus, over the Crimea and Azov region, over parts of Poland, and in the Baltic area—greatly increased the population of the empire. The total population in 1722 was about 13 million. This had increased to 29 million by 1799, to which must be added 7 million people resident in the annexed lands. Over 96 per cent of these 36 million people were country dwellers, and almost 56 per cent of them were serfs. Russian economy was obviously still predominantly agrarian and the system was essentially serf-based.

No figures are available to show the serf population before 1762 when it is estimated for Great Russia and Siberia at about 7.5 million out of a total of 17 million, or approximately 46 per cent. But Catherine transformed about eight hundred thousand state-owned peasants into privately owned serfs by giving away lands and the peasants who lived on them. Paul, by the same method, added another six hundred thousand serfs between 1796 and 1800. Mother and son, moreover, extended serfdom to the Ukraine, the Crimea, and the Caucasus. These actions brought the number of serfs to over 20 million in 1800. The distribution was not uniform. In the northern lands and in Siberia, less than 20 per cent were serfs. At the other extreme were the central provinces around and south of Moscow where over 80 per cent were serfs. Peasants in the forest-zone provinces had begun to turn to industry for employment. By the middle eighteenth century, between 20 and 33 per cent of the adult males in these provinces had shifted from agricultural to industrial work. *Barshchina* (labor on the master's land) serfdom in this area had largely given way to *obrok* serfdom (payment in money or kind), which was more profitable for the owners. Some of the serfs apparently also found it more profitable. The southern provinces, because of their more fertile soils and more favorable climate, increasingly specialized in agriculture. *Barshchina* remained the more common form of serfdom in these regions. But whatever its form, serfdom and serf economy were the major determinants of both agricultural and industrial development.

INDUSTRY

Industry on a scale greater and different from that of handicraft began to grow in the second half of the seventeenth century. The capital necessary for this development came from the landowners, the merchants, foreign investors, and the state treasury. Most enterprises during the reign of Peter I were assisted by the state, and the state was probably the largest consumer of the products of the growing industry. There were some free workers hired from among the artisans, and some skilled labor—mostly foreigners—but most of the workers were serfs. Peter had permitted factory owners to buy whole villages to meet their labor needs. Other peasants were arbitrarily assigned to certain owners or factories. These peasants were not technically serfs, but there was little practical difference between their status and that of the serfs who worked beside them. This system produced a competition for labor between the landowning nobility and the merchant-industrialists.

The word "factory" has certain connotations in our time which are not applicable to eighteenth-century Russia. Most of the enterprises depended largely if not wholly on manual labor using very crude tools and equipment. Many processes were carried out in scores or hundreds of separated units which resembled the cottage or home industries of western Europe. This was especially common in the textile and related industries.

State-owned and operated enterprises proved unproductive and were gradually transferred to individuals, who ran them under contract. A large share of the capital continued to be supplied by the government, which also continued to assign peasants and to permit the purchase of serfs for labor. The term "possessional" was applied to the purchased serfs, and the owners of possessional factories were given special favors such as freedom from compulsory state service, exemption from taxation, and tariff protection. Technically the labor supplied by the government was attached not to the owner but to the enterprise itself. This condition was not infrequently evaded—the owners using the labor in some other manner. In any case, it could have made little difference to most of the serfs, most of the time. The worker was bound to the factory, which sometimes gave him maintenance (room, board, and tax money) and sometimes paid wages. In the latter case, the worker had to pay his own taxes and often to provide for his own needs as well. Wages were extremely low. The workday varied from eleven to fifteen hours and was sometimes even longer. There was much child labor. Some possessional workers spent all their working time in the factory; others were transferred to farm work during part of the year. On the other hand, the owners and operators of the possessional factories were also subject to considerable restrictions. They could neither curtail production nor fire their workers. The type, volume, and quality of goods to be produced were set by the state, which also determined the sale price, the wage scales, and the general conditions of the operation.

Side by side with the state-owned and the possessional factories were the nobles' factories, which were usually situated on their estates. This was a development of the late eighteenth century. It coincided with the triumph of the nobility in other fields, and it increased the prosperity of the class as a whole. The profitableness of such enterprises, in spite of the generally low production of the serf labor, was due to three conditions: the ready availability of certain raw materials which could be produced on the estates themselves; the availability of a large pool of labor on the estates; and the existence of a comparatively certain market.

There were also some factories which were owned and run by serfs. The owners of the serfs sometimes encouraged enterprising men to build up their own industries. The serf entrepreneur paid a high *obrok* to his owner, which made it a very profitable venture from the owner's point of view.

The development of this sort of factory system by no means wiped out the handicrafts and cottage industries. These increased in number and importance. Peter I made a vain attempt to organize the handicraftsmen into guilds. Catherine II and Paul renewed the effort, but also met with little success. Catherine's industrial policy was largely determined by her relationship to the nobility. They demanded and got tariff protection and various other favors.

There are no adequate statistical measures of the quantitative growth of industry during the eighteenth century. Various estimates have been made, but the figures are widely at variance. Yet the fragmentary and contradictory records which have come down to us indicate that there was a respectable industrial growth during the century. There were certainly more factories and a very much larger industrial output in 1799 than in 1700, but the industrial techniques remained very backward, and labor productivity continued very low.

NORMS AND VALUES

By and large, the physical norms of everyday living continued relatively unchanged for the great majority of the Russian people. The wholesale adoption of European and especially of French fashions by the courtiers and upper classes produced a greater contrast between the privileged and the commoner than before. While the upper-class males shaved their faces, wore powdered wigs, and dressed in broadcloths, silks, and satins, men of the lower classes dressed much as their fathers and grandfathers had. They wore their hair long, did not shave their beards, and dressed in homespuns. Men of fashion wore knee breeches, colorful and elaborate coats and waistcoats, leather boots or decorated leather pumps. The peasants wore baggy trousers bound below the knee with wrappings of cloth; footcloths; bast shoes; and smocklike shirts, worn outside the trousers and tied at the waist with a sash or string. The ladies of the court affected the very elaborate hair-dos and dresses of Versailles, changing their styles to accord with changing modes in the West. The women of the lower classes dressed very much as their forebears had. Similar contrasts existed in housing. The peasants continued to live in small wooden hovels, sometimes of logs covered with rough boards but often of uncovered logs. The elaborate houses of the upper class were frequently built of stone or brick. Wooden houses were usually either covered with stucco or finished with dressed lumber.

The Westernization or Europeanization of Russia, which is so often spoken of, affected only the minority of privilege. Some of its effects did reach certain lower-class groups as, for example, the soldiers who were touched by the Prussophil reforms of Peter III or factory laborers who were placed under foreign masters. Many more people were indirectly affected by being forced to work harder and to give up more in order to provide their masters with European luxuries. But the masses were not immediately touched.

⚓ SERFDOM

For all practical purposes, "people" and "peasants" may be considered as virtually synonymous at this period. The social structure of the peasantry was extremely complicated because, although the majority were privately owned serfs (52 per cent of the peasant population in 1796) and state peasants (42 per cent of all peasants), there were numerous, small subgroups. The privately owned serfs were divided into domestic and field serfs. Domestic serfs, who were landless, were those in the immediate employ of the owner's household as house servants, craftsmen, and so on. The field serfs were provided with houses and the use of some land. They were subdivided into *barshchina* and *obrochny*. The state peasants were those who lived on the lands belonging to the state, which by the end of the eighteenth century included Church and monastic lands. Their obligations to the state were usually a little less than the obligations of the privately owned peasants to their masters. It was the state peasants, by the way, whom Catherine and Paul transformed into serfs by their gifts.

The *obrochny* paid a fixed amount (*obrok*) to the master. The assessment was usually based on the number of males in a family, but the payment was not direct. The family as a whole was responsible for paying the requisite amount to the village, which, in turn, was responsible for the payment of the total assessment. During the 1760's, the *obrok* was usually between one and two rubles per male. The amount was steadily increased: two to three rubles in the 1770's; four in the 1780's; five in the 1790's. Besides paying *obrok,* the *obrochny* were customarily required to furnish some agricultural produce and to supply cartage. But, on the whole, they were somewhat better off than the *barshchina* peasants. Custom fixed the *barshchina* at three days a week. That is, the serf worked three days for his master, three days for himself and did not work on Sundays or holidays. There were many variations of this practice, however, and an investigation made in 1765 showed that some owners worked the serfs more than three days or forced the serfs to complete the sowing or harvesting for the owner before doing their own work. Payments in cash or kind were sometimes demanded in addition to the *barshchina*. Contrariwise, some serfs escaped all or most of their nominal obligations.

The lot of the domestic serfs was in many ways the hardest, since they were wholly dependent upon their owners for food and shelter. They were also more closely watched. The occupational listings for domestic serfs covers a wide range of tasks and, among other things, indicates an effort to achieve self-sufficiency for each establishment. Domestic serfs were put at spinning, weaving, tailoring, shoemaking, carpentry and cabinet work, ordinary housework of all kinds, acting, singing, playing musical instruments, teaching and tutoring, and even poetasting. It was not infrequent, moreover, for owners to hire out their domestic serfs. Any serf could be sold, with or without his family, and with or without land. The essence of the matter was that serfs were regarded as chattels, not as human beings.

Catherine II ordered that serf-owners should be neither tyrannical nor cruel to their serfs. That such an order was thought necessary is in itself an indication that tyranny and cruelty were not uncommon. "Order" is perhaps the wrong word in this connection. It was more nearly an expression of a pious wish. During the whole of Catherine's reign there were only six court decisions dealing with abuse of serfs by owners. And there were more than six complaints registered, despite the fact that serfs were forbidden to complain to the state about their masters. There were undoubtedly decent and benevolent masters, but cruel and unusual punishments, brutal treatment, and abuse were quite common—as they are bound to be in any system which sets some men apart as subhuman and places them at the mercy of an elect. Fines, whippings, floggings, exile, and imprisonment were all customarily employed. Brandings, mutilations, and tortures were by no means unknown; and there are sordid records of crimes due to sexual abnormalities and manias. Existing in poverty at or only slightly above the subsistence level, worked like beasts of burden, often bred like livestock and treated like animals, the lives of the majority of the Russian serfs were nasty, dull, brutish, and short.

CHAPTER IX

Mistress of Men and of Politics: Catherine the Great

⊕ THE COURT VERSUS THE PEOPLE

And here is the characteristic trait of the epoch. The Winter Palace, with its military and administrative machinery, was a world of its own. Like a ship floating on the surface of the ocean, it had no real connection with the inhabitants of the deep, beyond that of eating them. It was the *State for the State.*

. . . .

One set gave or transmitted orders, the rest obeyed in silence.

. . . .

Behind the triple line of sentinels, in those heavily ornamented salons, there fermented a feverish life with its intrigues and its conflicts, its dramas and its tragedies. It was there that the destinies of Russia were woven.

. . . .

What interest, then, could the young German Princess take in that *magnum ignotum,* that people—muted, poor, semi-barbarous—which concealed itself in its villages, behind the snow, behind bad roads, and only appeared in the streets of St. Petersburg like a foreign outcast, with its persecuted beard and prohibited dress—tolerated only through contempt.

The writer of this shrewd analysis was Alexander Herzen, and it appeared in the preface to his edition of the *Memoirs of the Empress Catherine II Written by Herself.* The memoir, which covers the years 1744 to 1759, had existed only in a few manuscript copies, which had circulated surreptitiously among a few privileged persons. Tsar Nicholas I stopped even this circulation and the memoir was never published until Herzen brought it out in 1858. Herzen was the first great Russian socialist of the nineteenth century, which automatically made him the implacable enemy of the Russian government. Skepticism as to the accuracy of his editing has stood the tests of time and opposition, and his version of the memoir is generally accepted as authentic. As for the indictment quoted above, it is supported not only by the document he published but also by other fragmentary memoirs which were subsequently discovered and published in 1907 by the Russian Academy of Sciences.[1] In none of them does Catherine show any real concern for the Russian people. But in an epitaph which she composed for herself Catherine wrote:

> When she had ascended the throne of Russia, she wished to do good and tried to bring happiness, freedom, and prosperity to her subjects.

On the other hand, Catherine transformed some eight hundred thousand state peasants into privately owned serfs during the course of her forty-four-year reign. This is part of the manifesto which she issued on the occasion of a popular revolt led by Pugachev:

> In a word, there is not a man deserving of the Russian name, who does not hold in abomination the odious and insolent lie by which Pugachev fancies himself able to seduce and to deceive persons of a simple and credulous disposition by promising to free them from the bonds of submission and obedience to their sovereign, as if the Creator of the universe had established human societies in such a manner as that they can subsist without an intermediate authority between the sovereign and the people.

THE PARADOX OF CATHERINE'S "LIBERALISM"

Here is an apparent paradox. Was Catherine a liberal or were her liberal protestations nothing but shameful hypocrisy? She patronized arts and letters, and was herself the author of many works. She studied the works of Montesquieu, Beccaria, the Encyclopedists, and many other liberals of the day. She corresponded with Diderot, Buffon, and—most notably —with Voltaire. She called together a commission to codify the laws of Russia and set before them a long and detailed set of *Instructions,* which she herself had drafted. She had herself and her son inoculated against smallpox, then a highly daring and progressive action. But her commission, though it sat and worked persistently for seventeen months, never did codify the laws. And the condition of the serfs grew worse rather than better. It has appeared to many that Catherine's words were often liberal while her actions were not. She was not a liberal in our sense of that term, but neither were the other "Enlightened Despots" nor her philosophical mentors. The "Enlightened Despots" were those rulers who, it was held by themselves and by others, sought to practice the theories and teachings of rational philosophy. They were sovereigns of the Age of Reason, and they shared the optimism, the aspirations, and the limitations of that age. They believed what the rationalist thinkers had taught them, namely, that men and the universe were alike governed by natural laws; that men could discover and formulate these laws through the use of human reason; and that men could then reform society by making human institutions conform to the newly discovered laws of nature. In this way, they felt, progress could be made until a perfect society—orderly and well regulated—had been achieved.

When Catherine spoke of wanting "freedom" for her subjects, she meant freedom from "unnatural" and "irrational" bonds; that is, from laws, customs, and habits not based upon reason and natural law. She did not mean, as her manifesto on Pugachev made clear, freedom from authority or from a system.

When she described herself in her epitaph as one who had "republican sentiments" she meant that she favored an orderly and efficient government, founded and operated on "rational principles." The Russian sovereign, she wrote, is absolute, and necessarily so for "the Extent of the Dominion requires an absolute Power to be vested in that Person who rules over it. . . . Every other Form of Government whatsoever would not only have been prejudicial to Russia, but would have proved its entire Ruin." We are trained to think of liberalism and absolutism as antitheses, but Catherine did not so understand them and neither did her contemporaries.

The apparent paradox is therefore at least partially resolved when we stop judging Catherine by our standards and try to see her as her contemporaries did. To apply our meaning of liberal to Catherine is to judge her unfairly and to confuse ourselves. We must also take into account the circumstances of her accession. The French chargé d'affaires, reporting to his government soon after her coup, put it very bluntly:

> What a sight for the nation itself, a calm spectator of these events! On one side, the grandson of Peter I dethroned and put to death [Peter III]; on the other, the grandson of Tsar Ivan languishing in fetters [Ivan "VI"]; while a Princess of Anhalt [Catherine] usurps the throne of their ancestors, clearing her way to it by a regicide.

CIRCUMSTANCES AND CONSERVATISM

The chargé's report was more accurate than gracious. Catherine was a complete outsider with no legal right to be empress of Russia. The extralegal character of Catherine's position invited plots to replace her. The instability of her throne, as well as the manner of her taking of it, rendered Catherine peculiarly dependent upon the nobility, whose representatives had given her the crown. Whatever her personal will may have been, her government was necessarily committed to the promotion of class interests.

There was also another circumstance of her accession which helped to determine her policies. As Professor Kliuchevskii put it: ". . . inasmuch as the new Government's creation came of . . . opposition to . . . [its] predecessor, it had perforce to act in a direction . . . opposite to its predecessor. . . ." Peter III had always been more closely attached to his native Holstein and to his idolized Prussia than to his adopted Russia, and had been anti-Russian, at least in his foreign policy. Catherine had to be more Russian than the Russians. She was even more of a foreigner than Peter III. He was the grandson of Peter the Great. Her only connection with the Romanovs, aside from her marriage, was that her first cousin once removed had married a daughter of the first Peter. Catherine's own line of descent was German. Her position made it imperative for her to follow a strongly nationalistic policy.

Peter III had gravely offended the Russian Orthodox Church. His actions included the closing of the very numerous private chapels and the secularization of some Church lands and peasants. Peter III did no more than follow a policy earlier pursued by Peter I and subsequently carried to a much greater length by Catherine II. But Peter III made the unforgivable mistake of failing to treat the Russian Orthodox Church and its higher clergy with proper respect, and, further, of reducing somewhat the disabilities against the Old Believers. Catherine's skillful exploitation of the hostility which Peter's measures evoked can best be illustrated by the words of her accession manifesto:

All true sons of Russia have clearly seen the great danger to which the whole Russian empire has been actually exposed.

First, the foundations of our Orthodox religion have been shaken, and its traditions exposed to total destruction; so that there was absolutely reason to fear that the faith which has been established in Russia from the earliest times would be entirely changed, and foreign religion introduced.

In the second place, the glory which Russia has acquired at the expense of so much blood, and which was carried to the highest pitch by her victorious arms, has been trampled under foot by the peace lately concluded with its most dangerous enemy.

And lastly, the domestic regulations, which are the basis of the country's welfare, have been entirely overturned.

It is a sufficient commentary upon Catherine's opportunism that two years later she confiscated to the State the lands and peasants belonging to the Church, closed most of the convents and monasteries, and placed many of the higher clergy on the government payroll. Many of the lower clergy were alienated by these actions, and their discontent later led some of them to join in Pugachev's rebellion. But the higher clergy, with the single exception of the bishop of Rostov, made no protest. His challenge to the imperial orders cost him his life.

🏵 CATHERINE'S MEN

Catherine came to Russia just before her fifteenth birthday. Russia was her home for almost fifty-three years, and for more than thirty-four years she was empress. The first eighteen years she spent as the grand duchess, wife and consort of Peter. These years she described (with considerable but perhaps pardonable exaggeration) as a time of "tediousness and solitude which caused her to read many books." She read Voltaire and Montesquieu, Rabelais and Molière, and many others. She learned Russian and perfected her French. She wrote poems and plays and novels. It was a way of escape and an employment of a mind which was at least facile and able if not brilliant.

Peter was by no means the monster she described, but the two were totally incompatible, sharing only the misery created by their absolute dependence upon the Empress Elizabeth, who grew harsher with them as the years went by. Perhaps she was bitterly disillusioned with Peter, as many of Catherine's biographers suggest: certainly she was greatly disappointed that the couple long remained childless. And she made Catherine feel the pain of her displeasure. Most courtiers, of course, took their cue from the empress and vied in humiliating the grand duchess. Catherine took part in the life of the court, trailing around after the empress as she went on her peregrinations—attending formal functions, dancing at balls, taking part in masquerades—behaving in general with circumspection and apparent submissiveness. Riding and dancing were her favorite public amusements, but neither these diversions nor her studies filled that part of her life which her husband's incapacity left unsatisfied.

According to Catherine's version, it was at the urgent directive of Elizabeth that she accepted her first lover, in order to provide an heir to the throne. Whatever her motives and whatever the effects may have been Catherine took two lovers (Sergius Saltykov and Stanislaus Poniatowsky) between 1752 and 1758. During the next thirty-eight years, they had at least nineteen successors. Until she was made empress, Catherine conducted her affairs with some discretion, although they were open secrets at court. But after 1762, she paraded her lovers brazenly, flaunting them before her world much as the French kings displayed their mistresses. The current favorite was installed in apartments near those of Catherine, given the formal title of general aide-de-camp, and showered with gifts and honors. His expenses were paid by the state treasury and his generous mistress handed over to him money, jewels, decorations, lands, and peasants. In the case of her prime favorite, Gregory Potemkin, the empress fairly outdid herself. She made him, first a count; then a prince; gave him all the highest Russian decorations and then wangled foreign orders for him; gave him a regular allowance of twelve thousand rubles a month and special gifts on frequent occasions. If the gift was in money, the customary amount was one hundred thousand rubles, and such gifts were made several times a year. She paid the bills for his food and wine, and cheerfully paid his debts several times. She made him one of the richest land- and serf-owners in Russia and built for him a magnificent palace. With the others she was only slightly less lavish, and the cost of Catherine's kept men was fantastic. It was an expense which ultimately fell, of course, upon the people of the empire. It would be a little hard to say what benefits they got in return.

Only four of the twenty-one favorites have any claim to fame in their own right, and the claim of one of the four, that he fathered Catherine's son and successor, Paul, has been disputed. If Peter was the father of Paul, then the Romanov line was genetically unbroken, and the hereditary rights of Paul and his successors to the throne were unassailable. But if Paul was the son of Saltykov, then no Russian ruler after Peter III was, properly speaking, a Romanov. The Romanov family and the imperial government of course maintained that Paul was Peter's son and heir, and this has been generally accepted. But Herzen—on the basis of Catherine's memoirs—said flatly, "The avowal of Catherine on this point is very explicit—the father of the emperor Paul is Sergius Saltykov."

The second of the exceptional four was Poniatowsky, whom Catherine made king of Poland in 1764. The third was Gregory Orlov, who was one of the leading figures in the deposition and murder of Peter III. The fourth of this select group was Gregory Potemkin, who was remarkable on four counts: the wealth which Catherine lavished on him; the length of his tenure; the degree of his power and the success of his ventures; and, finally, the fact that he and Catherine were secretly married in 1774. Not the least amazing part of this almost incredible story is that Potemkin withdrew as favorite within two years. Until his death in 1791, he remained, however, the first man of the empire and the first in Catherine's heart.

He advised her and collaborated with her in the making of both domestic and foreign policies. He reformed the army (in which he served with distinction during both wars against Turkey, being commander-in-chief in the second war); colonized and fortified the southern frontier; conquered the Crimea, annexed it, and founded the still flourishing cities of Sevastopol, Ekaterinoslav (now Dnepropetrovsk) and Nikolyaev. Potemkin's influence even extended into the boudoir he had left. Of the sixteen lovers who followed him, Potemkin both appointed and dismissed at least four of them. Soldier and empire-builder, counselor and states-man, exhibitionist and wastrel, husband and panderer to his nympho-maniac empress—that was Gregory Potemkin.

Catherine also had less exotic and notorious advisers and assistants. In fact, one measure of her mind was her skill in finding and using tal-ented helpers—"Catherine's eagles," Pushkin termed them. Nikita Panin headed the Foreign Office (technically, the College of Foreign Af-fairs) for some time. He was succeeded there by Count Bezborodko, who was largely responsible at least for the details of Catherine's "Greek project." This was a most ambitious scheme which called for the partition of Turkey; the creation of a Greek Empire to be ruled by Catherine's grandson, Constantine, from its capital of Constantinople; and the erection of a buffer state between Russia and the new em-pire. It was never more than a project, but it continuously worried the Western Powers and sometimes embarrassed Russia. Many of Catherine's domestic reforms were carried out with the help of Count Sievers. Ivan Betski was her chief assistant in her attempts to improve education. On the military side there were the Marshals Rumiantsev and Suvorov, to name only the most famous. Rumiantsev, who com-manded in the first Turkish War (1769–74), also served as governor of Ukraine, which Catherine fully annexed. Alexander Suvorov was a brilliant general and a bizarre eccentric. The outstanding military figure in Russian history, Suvorov, who never lost a battle, ranks with the top military geniuses of all time. It is an interesting sidelight that his "Soldier's Catechism" (sometimes called his "Maxims") was widely publicized in the Red Army during World War II, and that his name was given to a new military decoration and to the select military academies which were established in 1943. The most famous naval leader was Alexis Orlov, one of the five brothers who made Catherine empress. At Catherine's death the Russian navy consisted of forty-eight ships of the line, thirty-one frigates, several hundred armed galleys, and numerous bomb ketches, gunboats, corvettes, and other small vessels. These were divided into three fleets (Baltic, Black, and Caspian) of which the Baltic was by far the largest. The regular army at that time numbered just over five hundred and forty thousand troops (in-cluding all branches), and the irregular forces were estimated at about an additional one hundred and fifty thousand.

🏷 GOVERNMENTAL REFORMS

The cumbersome machinery of government established by Peter the Great did not run well even when driven by his dynamic power. Catherine found that the Senate spent the first six weeks after her accession in hearing detailed reports about a disputed piece of meadowland in a small town. She also discovered that, although the Senate was charged with appointing the city governors, it did not know the number of cities in the empire. The Senate told her that the state revenues amounted annually to about 16 million rubles. She investigated and learned that the annual income was about 28 million rubles. Such disorder and incompetence were more than Catherine could abide. She sent an atlas of Russia to the Senate, so that they should learn some geography, and began a series of reforms designed to create an orderly state on a national basis.

The Senate was subdivided into six sections, each with its assigned functions and jurisdiction, and the whole was placed under a procurator-general, charged with keeping it in order. The business routine was streamlined in an effort to increase speed and efficiency. The various colleges (ministries) were also reordered in an effort to relieve the confusion and inefficiency. But the core of her domestic reforms centered on the Commission for Drafting a New Code of Laws. Reminiscing about this some thirty years after its appointment Catherine wrote:

> During the first three years of my reign, I discovered from the petitions handed me, from the acts of the Senate and of the various Colleges, from the dealings of the Senators and from conversations with many other persons that there were no fixed and uniform rules on any subject. The laws, too, which had been made at different times and in accordance with the conception of that time, seemed to be very contradictory. It was desired and requested that the laws should be put into a better form. From this I decided in my own mind that the general attitude and the civil law could only be improved by the adoption of useful rules, which would have to be written and ratified by me, for all the inhabitants of the Empire and for all circumstances. And to this end I began to read [study], and then to write the Instruction[s] for the law-making Commission. I read and wrote [for] two years. . . .

Catherine had forgotten, or did not choose to remember, that committees had been working more or less continuously at drafting a legal code since the time of Peter the Great. No practical reforms ever came from the work, but a committee was still busily redrafting and revising earlier redrafts and revisions when Catherine came to power. She did not, therefore, initiate the effort nor was she ever able to complete it.

The *Instructions* excited great interest when they were first published in 1767.[2] The Marxist historian Pokrovsky sneered at them as stupid plagiarisms. Platonov wrote that they embodied "the most advanced, liberal and humane ideas of her day." About four-fifths of the *Instructions* were directly derived from the writings of others, chiefly from the *Spirit of the Laws* by Montesquieu. Catherine also borrowed from Beccaria's *On Crime and Punishment,* from Bielfield's *Political Institutions,* and from the French *Encyclopedia.* But she never made any secret of her borrowings and never pretended that she created the whole work.

The range of the *Instructions* is so great that the work defies brief characterization, but a few sample chapter titles and a few sample aphorisms from it may give some idea of its nature. The twenty-two chapters (including the supplements) had such headings as "Of the Safety of the Institutions of Monarchy"; "Of Laws in particular"; "Of the Propagation of the human Species in a State"; "Of the Nobility" (but none of the peasants or of the serfs); "Of good Order, otherwise termed Police"; and "Of the Expences, Revenues, and publick Management of the Finances." A random sampling of the articles produced the following:

6. Russia is a European State.
34. The Equality of the Citizens consists in this; that they should all be subject to the same Laws.
48. Customs govern the Chinese.
178. Where the Laws are precise and clear, there the office of a Judge consists only in ascertaining the Fact.
322. Wherever there is Trade, there are Custom houses also.

Catherine submitted her first draft of the *Instructions* to some leading members of the nobility. "They crossed out more than half of what I had written," she reported later; and it was this emended version which was finally published and submitted to the commission "as rules on which to base an opinion, but not as a law." The Commission to Draft a New Code of Laws was convoked by Catherine in 1767. It contained representatives of the nobility, of the merchants and artisans from the cities, of state and of free peasants, and of the Holy Synod, but not of the lower clergy nor of the serfs. Altogether there were 564 members, who held some two hundred full sittings during a session which lasted a year and a half. Numerous committees were put to work on specific problems. And out of all these labors came what? Not a legal code because they never got around to drafting it. Not a revival of the old National Assembly (*Zemski Sobor*) because the deputies were dismissed and never recalled. Nevertheless, though the commission did not accomplish its set purpose, it was not a complete failure. The deputies, by Catherine's orders, had brought with them over 1400 *cahiers*. These set forth in detail the conditions, needs, and wishes of the various groups and thus supplied Catherine and her advisers with a great store of information upon which they drew in making later reforms.

Several of the more ambitious reforms remained mere projects. This was true of the plans to create a public school system and to establish municipal self-government. Catherine was more successful in reforming the provincial administration. An act of 1775 provided that for each three to four hundred thousand inhabitants in the empire there should be set up an administrative division known as a *gubernia*. This was to be subdivided into districts having from twenty to thirty thousand inhabitants each. At the close of her reign there were fifty *gubernias*. Each *gubernia* had an imperial governor; an Administrative Board which governed "in the name of the Imperial Majesty" and was presided over by the governor; a Crown Council, presided over by the imperial vice-governor, and charged with financial and economic affairs; a Criminal Court; a Civil Court; a "Court of Conscience" to handle cases involving juveniles, unintentional offenders, and the insane; and a Department of Social Welfare, which was entrusted with care of the public health and with the maintenance of public schools, hospitals, asylums, and prisons. The members of the courts and of the Welfare Department were elected.

Each district had a governing body which was equivalent to the Administrative Board and which was composed of a captain (*ispravnik*) and two members who were elected by the nobility. Towns were governed by an official appointed by the central government. Both *gubernias* and districts had separate, special courts for the nobility, the merchants, and the free and state peasants. The jurors for each of these were chosen by the class with which it dealt. The Reform of 1775, by granting new powers and laying new responsibilities upon the free classes, made it necessary to reorder the social structure. This was done in 1785 by the Charter of the Nobility and the Municipal Statute.

THE CHARTER OF THE NOBILITY

The Charter of the Nobility organized the nobles by *gubernia*. All the nobles in each *gubernia* formed a corporation presided over by a Marshal of the Nobility, who was elected by the nobles from among their own number. They also elected district marshals and, as noted above, chose their judges and jurors as well as the two members of the district's governing body. Elections were held and other business transacted at triennial assemblies. The corporations were given the right to petition the governor, the Senate, and the monarch at will. In other words, the charter transformed the nobility into a privileged class with great power and greater influence but with no responsibilities. They became, as a class, a parasitic, corporate body of privilege which bore no burden commensurate with its power; was separated both from the state and from the masses; and so was divorced from the real life of Russia.

That is a damning indictment and it focuses attention on one of the central facts of modern Russian history. The Russian state structure rested on two pillars: the obligation of state service laid upon the privileged; and the obligation laid upon the peasant serf. Catherine's charter knocked down one of these pillars. The other was not pushed over until the serfs were emancipated in the 1860's. With both supports gone, the state structure continued to exist and to command support largely because of the persistence of long habit. When the habit was broken, the structure fell.

Long before then—as far back as the middle of the eighteenth century—the serfs had somehow been aware of the duality of the obligation. They were not unconscious of the relationship between the landlords' obligation to serve the state and their obligation to serve the landlord. Pososhkov, their spokesman in the days of Peter I, taught that the real owner of the peasant (serf) was the tsar and that the landlord had only a temporary use of him. If the landlord should cease to serve the state, then the serf should cease to labor for the landlord.

THE SERF PROBLEM

There had been numerous and sizable serf mutinies before Peter's manifesto. Between the date of its issue (1762) and 1772, however, there were forty major uprisings in scattered sections which were put down only by the use of troops. The largest and, from the point of view of the government, the most dangerous of the peasant revolts was the one led by Emilian Pugachev between 1772 and 1774.

Pugachev himself was a Cossack who had fled from the Don to the Urals. The organized resistance of the Cossacks along the Don had been broken following Bulavin's Rebellion in 1707, but their persistent and violent opposition to the continuing encroachments of the government went on. They revolted in 1771 and were cruelly suppressed, but not annihilated. One of the aims of Pugachev was revenge for the treatment of his people by the government. He was supported and encouraged in his rising by Polish officers and money. Posing as Peter III, Pugachev raised the revolutionary standard about which there immediately flocked a heterogeneous group of malcontents, underprivileged, and opportunists. His force, which grew to 25,000, included Cossacks; Asiatic tribesmen such as the Tatars, Kalmuks, and Bashkirs; Orthodox clergy who resented Catherine's confiscation of Church lands and her Church reforms; Old Believers and other schismatics in rebellion against the harsh intolerance of Orthodoxy; possessional peasants; and serfs from field, mine, and factory.

Pugachev first led his rebellious rabble into the valley of the Volga, along which he successfully advanced. As those who followed him had been brutalized, so now, in their turn, they treated others with equal ferocity. The revolt reached such proportions that Catherine sent one of her best generals, A. I. Bibikov, to suppress it. Bibikov succeeded in driving Pugachev back to the Urals, but the general died before he could completely break the movement, and it flared up again in 1774. That spring, Pugachev reappeared with new forces; he failed to capture the fortress of Kazan, but burned the city; captured Saratov; and marched on Tsaritsyn. Catherine, thoroughly alarmed, recalled the great Suvorov from the Turkish war and set him the task of ending the revolt. Suvorov chased Pugachev back into the mountains. There the rebel leader was betrayed and captured. He was taken to Moscow and executed in 1775. This broke the revolt, although mopping-up operations and ruthless punitive measures went on for some time. Both Cossacks and serfs were drastically punished and temporarily quelled. There were only twenty more outbreaks in the remaining two decades of Catherine's reign, but peasant unrest was a banked and smoldering fire. In the short reign of Paul (1796–1801) there were 278 peasant disturbances.

It would be incorrect to imply that Catherine was ignorant of the problem of serfdom or that she failed to realize its gravity. Her *Instructions* make it clear that she did not favor any immediate or general emancipation, but she sought to promote discussion of such a possibility and took some steps—wholly ineffectual—to improve the condition of the serfs. She was totally unable to take any action which would have been unacceptable to the land- and serf-owning nobility.

FOREIGN POLICY

The successes of Catherine the Great in the field of foreign policy are attributable to three things: (1) her own skill in the arena of power politics; (2) the diplomatic talents of Panin and, later, of Potemkin; and (3) the distribution of power among the European nations. The most recent Soviet study speaks of Catherine as "an empress who personally decided all questions of foreign policy," and adds, "there was no serious problem in this field which escaped her attention, and no decision was taken without her personal intervention." This is an impressive tribute from that particular source. As for her advisers, Catherine herself once described Panin as "the ablest, most intelligent and most zealous man" at her court. She worked with him at diplomacy until late in 1780. His place in the Foreign Office was taken by Bezborodko; his place as chief adviser in diplomatic affairs, by Potemkin. Finally, the world situation in 1762 was peculiarly favorable to Russia. Her nearest western neighbors (Sweden, Poland, and Turkey) threw but faint shadows of their once great power. Turkey had been reduced to a second-rate nation; the others fell below that. Austrian strength had been whittled away by the expansion of Prussia, and Prussia was at a very low ebb as a result of the Seven Years' War. That same war cost France her maritime and colonial place, taken by Great Britain. There could scarcely have been a more opportune time for Catherine and Panin to reassert the independence of Russian policy which had been lost during the preceding reigns. They made the most of it.

They abandoned the alliance with Prussia which Peter III had made, but did not set aside the peace treaty and took no part in the last months of the general war. In 1764, Catherine concluded a defensive alliance with Frederick of Prussia. The secret clauses of this treaty provided for joint action toward Sweden and Poland, and for Prussian aid to Russia in case of a Turkish war against Russia. Two years later a commercial treaty was signed with Great Britain and an agreement was reached with her on the Polish question. Denmark was added to alignment shortly thereafter. It was Panin's hope that these several, separate agreements might be consolidated into a "Northern System" which would tie Russia, Prussia, Britain, and Denmark (as senior or active partners), Sweden and Poland (as satellites) into a grand alliance aimed against France and Austria. This proved impossible, largely because of Prussian coolness toward the scheme. Pivotal point in all these dealings was Poland, the major foreign interest of Catherine's reign.

THE PARTITIONS OF POLAND

The once great state of Poland was by the middle of the eighteenth century no longer an independent, sovereign state. It still claimed an area which ranked it third in size and a population which ranked it fourth in numbers among the Continental states. It still called itself the Republic of Poland. It still had a king, but he had long been chosen and maintained by foreign Powers; and it had a national assembly (the Diet) which was totally bereft of any real power. Its army, nominally twenty-four thousand, actually numbered less than twelve thousand. Its people were divided nationally, religiously, socially, and economically. Not over half of them were Polish; a third were Ukrainian or Bielorussian: the remainder included Lithuanians, Jews, Germans, Armenians, and Tatars. The Poles and Lithuanians were Roman

Catholic; the Ukrainians and Bielorussians, Orthodox Catholic; the Germans, Protestant. And in the eighteenth century Poland had a most unenviable record of intolerance and persecution against all non-Roman Catholics. Seventy-two per cent of all the people were peasants, 83 per cent of the peasants were serfs, and the lot of the serfs in Poland was the worst in all Europe. As one contemporary described them, "These people differ little from cattle, have no property, live from hand to mouth, and rot in filth and poverty. . . ." At the other end of the socio-economic scale were the seventeen "great" families, who had fabulous wealth and who behaved like sovereign princes. A little beneath them socially and far below them economically were the majority of the nobility, bedeviled no less by their great poverty than by their extreme and arrogant pride of caste. The late Father Lord once summed up the situation of Poland in the years before the partition in the following paragraph:

Without a government worthy of the name, without an army, without trade or manufactures, with misery universal in all classes save a small minority, rotting away under a system of 'liberty' which a sagacious Englishman described as 'merely a system of aristocratic licentiousness, where a few members of the community are above the control of law while the majority are excluded from its protection,' Poland had become in the opinion of foreign observers the weakest and unhappiest of nations.

The only modification of this description which might be suggested is that Poland was not really a nation but only an extremely loose agglomeration of some fifty to sixty independent states.

The policies of the Powers toward Poland have been sketched in the course of the narrative but it will be convenient to review them very briefly. The gross weakness of Poland was first demonstrated in the Great Northern War of 1654–67 and possible partition was discussed at that time. An ephemeral recovery under Sobieski soon gave way to increasing weakness and foreign intrigue which reached one high point with the enthronement by foreign interventionists of Augustus II. His entrance into the Russo-Swedish War (or Second Great Northern War, 1700–1721) resulted in the domination of Poland by Peter the Great. The death of Augustus II precipitated a war which ended in an Austro-Russian victory and the establishment of their candidate, Augustus III, on the throne. By and large, Poland's staunchest friend and ally was France, Russia's most dangerous enemy. The rise of Prussia temporarily led Austria to buy Russian friendship by supporting or co-operating with the Russian policy in Poland. This changed with the Diplomatic Revolution and Seven Years' War, so that when Catherine came to the throne Austria and France were co-operating against

Russia. In this, they enlisted the support of Turkey with consequences which will be discussed later.

The ancient and only truly implacable enemy of Poland was Prussia, to whom control of the coastal area at the mouth of the Vistula River was vital. It was not possible for a strong Prussia and a strong Poland to coexist. One could flourish only at the expense of the other. Besides, the Prussian Hohenzollerns coveted the Polish lands which separated the various Hohenzollern possessions. (Polish Prussia divided East Prussia from Silesia). The dream of dismembering Poland and adding these lands to Prussia had long attracted Prussian sovereigns. Frederick the Great probably hoped to get some Polish territories out of the Seven Years' War, but he was fortunate to escape without loss of his own lands. As long as Russo-Prussian relations were good, which they generally were except under the Empress Elizabeth, Prussia was willing to share Poland with Russia in order to exclude the Austrians and the French.

Tradition advances several Russian interests in regard to Poland. All of them had perhaps been important at some state of Russo-Polish relations, but by the eighteenth century they were excuses rather than causes. One was the claim that Russia needed to recover lands which had once been Russian. This had been important in the days of Ivan the Great and his immediate successors, but it was not significant after 1667. A second traditional claim was that Russia desired to "repatriate" those Russians who had been taken under Polish control. It must by now be apparent that Catherine was not seriously concerned with the well-being of the people nor with the rights of self-determination.

The Russian interests in Poland involved, on the one hand, security and self-defense; on the other, passage to Europe. The only major land road for the invasion of Russia from the West lies across Poland. By the reverse token, if Poland is Europe's gateway to Russia, it is also Russia's gateway to the West. Catherine wanted mastery of Poland for both reasons. She was convinced that Russian security demanded such control, and she was determined to play a major role in Europe—a project she could not accomplish without controlling Poland.

Her policy was typically opportunist—diplomatic interference and intrigue, backed up by occasional demonstrations of force. This was relatively safe, cheap, and easy. She also stood ready to annex Polish territories if such a chance arose. Probably she did not originally intend the annihilation of the Polish state, but she was not averse to it. The first victorious stroke of her policy was made in 1764 when she set her lover Poniatowsky upon the Polish throne. This was a thoroughly malicious choice, made because Poniatowsky was so weak that he could hold power only at her sufferance. Prussia was quiescent at this action because she was then allied with Russia, and Austria was unable to offer any effective opposition at the moment.

The second aspect of Catherine's policy was her active intervention in behalf of the Dissidents (non-Roman Catholics). She hoped to build up a pro-Russian, Orthodox party in Poland. But her efforts were too vigorous and the Poles united against her. Diplomacy having temporarily failed, in 1767 she sent her troops into Poland, suborned the Polish Diet, and concluded with the Diet and the puppet king a treaty which made her the guarantor of the Polish constitution. Full political and religious rights and tolerance were also granted to the Dissidents. The Polish nobility with characteristic gallantry and want of sense rose against Catherine and Poniatowsky. This resulted in four years of guerrilla war, which devastated Poland even further.

It was at the beginning of this civil war that France sought to divert Russia from Poland by stirring up troubles in the south. She was assisted in this by Austria. French and Austrian diplomats persuaded the Turkish government to incite the Crimean Tatars to attacks upon southern Russia. (It didn't take much prodding, since the Tatars had been doing it regularly for centuries.) When Russia retaliated, the French and Austrians supported the Turks in a war with Russia (1769–74). Russian victories so alarmed Austria that she allied herself with Turkey and threatened Russia with armed intervention. The situation was critical for Catherine despite the smashing successes of Roumiantsev and Suvorov. A general European war seemed likely. Out of this crisis came the First Partition of Poland (1772–73).

Austria unwittingly gave the signal for the First Partition by occupying some Polish lands, which gave Prussia a chance openly and vigorously to promote the scheme. It is, however, a mistake to suppose that the step was forced upon Catherine by Prussia. Her advisers had approved the principle of partition as early as 1763, and they only awaited a favorable opportunity to implement it. The final decision to dismember Poland was made by Catherine, and she apportioned the shares among the three predatory Powers. The Partition Treaties were signed at St. Petersburg in August, 1772, by Russia, Prussia, and Austria. Russia and Austria issued proclamations that chaos and lawlessness in Poland made the step necessary. Prussia, typically, issued a long, ponderous, and pedantic justification which raked up all sorts of ancient claims and documents in an effort to give an air of legality to the whole action. The three Powers forced the subservient Poniatowsky and the equally servile Diet to assent to the partitioning, which cost Poland about a third of her land and people. Russia took for her share the poor regions of Polotsk, Vitebsk, and Mogilev—the eastern section of Bielorussia.

Austria and Prussia were temporarily satisfied, and Catherine was left free to get on with her wars against the Turks and against Pugachev. She was dissatisfied, however, with the amount of support which her Prussian ally gave her, and there was a shifting of diplomatic alignments in the late 1770's. The Prussian alliance was dropped and replaced by an alliance with Austria, which had as its aim the partition of Turkey by the two Powers. This aroused a certain hostility on the part of Prussia. It also aroused the enmity of Great Britain, which was further increased by the wide publicity given to Catherine's "Greek project" and by her annexation of the Crimea in 1783. This annexation caused the Turks, who had British support, to go to war with Russia again in 1787. The war went badly for Russia at first, and her difficulties were increased when Sweden also declared war on her in 1788. Prussia pressed Austria to desert Russia and eventually succeeded. Austria made a separate peace with Turkey in 1790. Prussia attempted to undermine the Russian position in Poland. Then the tide turned. The Swedes were defeated and forced to accept a peace which returned matters to the *status quo ante bellum* (1790). Suvorov, in that same year, smashed the major Turkish fortress of Ismail, and peace negotiations began. They culminated in the Treaty of Jassy of 1791.

By her two victories over the sultan, Catherine greatly advanced Russian possessions and interests. Russia won control of the northern Black Sea coast from the River Bug almost to the Caucasus, and also acquired Crimea. These conquests, plus the subjugation of the Cossacks of the Don, opened these tremendously rich southern lands (often called "New Russia") to Russian exploitation and settlement. Catherine's victories, moreover, broke the Turkish monopoly over the Black Sea by forcing Turkey to open that sea and the Straits (the waterway between the Black and Mediterranean seas) to merchant vessels in peace times.

Meanwhile, in Poland King Stanislas (Poniatowsky) and the Diet finally succeeded in promulgating a new constitution in 1791. The Poles have always been very proud of this constitution, which was both progressive and liberal. Unfortunately, because of the irreconcilable opposition to it of the die-hard nobility, it was never really operative. It was, however, a deliberate challenge to Catherine, and she recognized it as such. Russian armies sent into Poland won quick and easy victories. Prussia repudiated her alliance with the Poles and joined Russia in the Second Partition (1793), which gave Russia most of Lithuania and of the western Ukraine. Poland was also forced to accept a Russian protectorate.

The progressive nobility and *bourgeoisie,* led by the heroic Thaddeus Kosciusko, rose in a gallant but hopeless revolt against the king and his foreign masters. This meant war against both Prussia and Russia. The result was the Third Partition of Poland (1795). Austria shared in this, thus redressing the balance which had been upset by the Second Partition. The Russian share was the remainder of Lithuania and Ukraine, and the Duchy of Courland. Poland did not reappear upon the map of Europe until 1919.

🔥 CATHERINE AND REVOLUTIONS ABROAD

Concern with these diplomatic matters led Catherine to set other matters aside. She was, for example, interested in Siberia and the Far East. She dispatched three exploring expeditions to the area, and caused bases to be prepared for a campaign to conquer the Amur region. Commitments in Europe prevented her from the following up of these preparations. Instead she gave a free hand to private merchants, making sure that she received her share of their profits, and it was private enterprise which established the Russian claim to the Kuriles, the Aleutians, and Alaska. The pioneers were Gregory Shelekhov and his partner, Ivan Golikov. Their company later merged with several competing groups to form the Russian American Company.

Nor was this Catherine's only contact with North America. The British government, in 1775, asked her for 20,000 soldiers to be sent to America to subdue the rebellious colonists. She was favorably inclined, but such action would have been displeasing to her ally Prussia, so she finally refused the British request. Three years later, after the conclusion of the Franco-American Alliance, she assured George III that she would not recognize the Americans as long as he regarded them as rebels. As a matter of fact, she never did recognize them. Her proclamation announcing the anti-British League of Armed Neutrality (1780) was very pointedly not sent to the American rebels, although they certainly had a strong interest in the matter. The Continental Congress voted American adherence to the league and sent Francis Dana as envoy to Catherine to ask for recognition and help. She refused even to receive him, and he returned home after a completely fruitless two-year wait.

Catherine's swing from Prussia to Austria in the 1780's led to her attempt (1788–89) to create a four-Power pact of France, Spain, Austria, and Russia against Prussia and Britain. This scheme was abruptly dropped after Catherine was badly frightened by the French Revolution and subsequent French expansion. She actively intrigued, before her death, to promote intervention against France, and sent Russian naval vessels to join the British fleet in its blockade of the Netherlands.

This change in attitude was also expressed in Catherine's letters, which after 1790 abound in vituperative abuse of France and all things French. It appeared also in two noteworthy acts of repression. One was the closing of Masonic lodges which had flourished among the nobility during her reign and the jailing of Novikov, the leading Mason of Moscow. Actually the Masons and the lodges were of all kinds—liberal, conservative, pleasure-bent, and socially minded. Novikov's lodge had established some schools and a publishing house. This would have delighted the young Catherine; it alarmed the old lady, who suspected the Masons not only of undue liberalism but also of supporting Paul. The other persecution was of A. N. Radishchev, a nobleman and government official who published in 1790 a book entitled *A Journey from St. Petersburg to Moscow*. It was a description of the evils and abuses of serfdom in almost the same terms that Catherine herself had once used. But power, age, Pugachev, and the French Revolution had wrought great changes. The book was suppressed and Radishchev was sent to Siberia. Which clearly demonstrates that Catherine the Great was never a "liberal" in the modern meaning of that term; she was a true daughter of the eighteenth-century Age of Order.

CHAPTER X

Alexander, Disciple of Order

✎ TSAR PAUL, 1796–1801

There is reason to suspect that Catherine the Great intended to disinherit her son, Paul, and to bequeath the imperial crown to Paul's son, her grandson, Alexander. There is somewhat less reason to credit the rumor, current following her death in November, 1796, and repeated by various historians since that time, that Paul destroyed Catherine's will which passed over him in favor of his son. Perhaps he did, but the story sounds suspiciously like many other gossipy reports which were widely circulated by Paul's enemies to discredit him. It is difficult to get an adequate and fair understanding of Paul for three reasons: first, Catherine and her apologists felt obliged to explain her treatment of him by repeated allegations of his total incompetence; second, the conspirators who overthrew Paul, including Alexander, who was an accessory before the fact to his father's deposition and to his father's murder, sought to justify their acts by blackening Paul's reputation; third, many of Paul's actions were so extremely erratic as to make charges of madness appear credible. This may be exemplified by a famous and persistent rumor before going on to an examination of the man himself.

A Guards regiment, so one version of the anecdote runs, was on parade before Paul. At his commands they successfully executed without fault a series of extremely complicated maneuvers. Paul congratulated them enthusiastically upon their skill and then shouted another order which, for some reason, was not heard and, of course, not obeyed. The emperor at once turned on the regiment in unbalanced fury and ordered that it march immediately to Siberia. Obediently it set off directly from the parade ground and was only recalled, thanks to the intercession of various people, after it had marched some fifty or sixty miles toward exile.

The entirely credible elements of the story are these. Paul delighted in parades and often took command. He was an unreasonable perfectionist in matters of discipline and frequently punished minor lapses with entirely disproportionate severity. He was capable of instantaneous changes of mood and of unrestrained fury. There are numerous and authentic records of his treatment of individuals in the manner the story alleges about the regiment. The story was credited because it did not seem out of character for Paul to act in that way. On the other hand, the rumor is also characteristic of the technique of character assassination so widely used by Paul's enemies. The incident might have happened. The story is plausible but unproven. Apocryphal or not, it dramatizes those aspects of Paul's character which were emphasized by his detractors. It also illustrates their methods.

Paul was only seven years old when his mother had accepted from her guardsmen the crown which some thought should have been the boy's. Until that time, Catherine had seen very little of her son and had had no control over his training, which was arranged by his great-aunt, the Empress Elizabeth. During the first years of her reign Catherine provided a series of tutors for Paul but paid only the most sporadic attention to him. Their relationship does not seem to have been unhappy, however, until two later events took place. The first was the discovery of a childish sort of plot against Catherine in which Paul was slightly involved. She did not punish him, but probably she began to regard him less as a son than as a potential rival who might be used by her enemies. At any rate, she never admitted him to any place of responsibility or authority in her administration. The second event followed the birth of Alexander. Catherine took the boy away from Paul—much as Paul had been taken from her—and took charge of Alexander's education. Then it began to be said that she intended to make Alexander her heir. It was also when the final break came between Paul and his mother.

As the long years dragged wearily by, Paul and his family lived in quasi-retirement and seclusion at Gatchina. He came to feel that his mother was depriving him of his rights, and the festering canker of frustration and hatred began to corrode his mind and his body. His days were spent in drilling his small body of troops and in planning what he should do when his chance should finally come. Meanwhile, the mother whom he had come to despise continued to live and to rule. When she finally died, Paul was already past his forty-second birthday. He was not mad, despite what his enemies said, but he was wholly wanting in judgment and in mental balance. His intentions were often good;

his implementation of them, execrable. But here one must distinguish carefully between Paul's relation to his people and his relation to the nobility.

The testimony of Prince Adam Czartoryski on this point is impressive. Czartoryski, sometime intimate friend and trusted counselor of Alexander, had enjoyed the somewhat uncertain favor of Paul. His social and political position aligned him with the Russian nobility, though his Polish nationality kept him a little apart from them. He was serving as Paul's ambassador to Sardinia at the time of the emperor's murder.

The conspiracy [wrote Czartoryski] had the sympathies of the higher classes and most of the officers; but not of the lower ranks of the army. The persons who suffered from Paul's insane fits of rage and severity were usually the higher military and civil officials; his caprices seldom affected men of the lower ranks, who, moreover, were continually receiving extra pay and rations of bread, wine, and brandy when they were on drill or on a parade. The punishments to which the officers were exposed did not produce any unpleasant impression on the common soldier; on the contrary, they were a sort of satisfaction to him for the blows and ill-treatment he constantly had to endure. . . . It amused and pleased the soldiers to see their Emperor dispensing endless punishments and severities among the officers, while he took every opportunity to afford to the men ample compensation for the work and trouble that was required of them.

THE PEOPLE AND THE PLOTTERS

This was a shrewd observation which might have been expanded to cover more than soldiers. The Russian people were not adversely affected by Paul's stoppage of foreign travel by his subjects, or by his prohibition against the importation of foreign luxuries, or by his enforcement of sumptuary rules, or by his strenuous efforts to shut out Western influences and ideas. These actions affected only the privileged few, and they were the ones hit by his attempted curtailment of the *barshchina* and by his efforts to make the obligations and responsibilities of the Guards officers match the favors and privileges which they had so long enjoyed. The personal and group security of the Russian people was threatened only very indirectly if at all, but the individual and class security of the nobility was in serious jeopardy. The Emperor Paul frightened and offended the only group in Russia whom no emperor could frighten and offend with impunity. His mother and his sons recognized the realities of their position and bowed to the nobility. Paul's greatest madness, if madness it was, lay in the fact that he did neither. He struck at the vested interests and the vested interests struck back.

There was, however, another side to Paul. He further confounded the existing confusion in administration by ill-considered efforts at reform, but he also straightened out the confusion about succession which had existed since the reign of Peter the Great. He ordered the price of salt (a government monopoly) reduced—a boon to the masses—and he directed that grain reserves should be everywhere established and maintained for the relief of popular distress in times of famine and scarcity. He sought to lighten the serfs' burden by ordering that *barshchina* should be limited to three days in a week, and by forbidding serf-owners to work their serfs on holy days and holidays. He also granted a slight increase in autonomy to the state serfs. Religious tolerance, including the right to have their own churches and their own clergy, was extended to the Old Believers; and efforts were made to improve the caliber, position, and morale of the Orthodox clergy, especially the parish priests. Paul tried to introduce preventive measures to reduce that scourge of the Russian towns and villages, fire. He limited the importation of luxury goods and sought to encourage domestic manufacturing. For these reasons, the Emperor Paul was by no means unpopular among the people. And the rising which dethroned him was in no sense a people's movement. It was a palace revolution carried out by men in high place.

Paul had recently moved himself and his family into his newly built, fortress-like palace of St. Michael. There, on the night of March 11/ 23, 1801, he retired early to his solitary bedchamber in accordance with his usual custom. Apparently he felt neither more nor less secure than usual. Some time earlier rumors of an intended plot had reached him and he had spoken of the matter to Count Pahlen who, as Governor of St. Petersburg, was responsible for security. Pahlen most disingenuously reassured his emperor with a partial truth, saying that such a conspiracy "cannot be formed unless I belong to it." Paul accepted the statement and, at Pahlen's subsequent suggestion, dismissed the usual guards about the imperial bedroom, keeping only his valets on duty. The palace, however, was heavily barricaded and, so Paul supposed, heavily guarded as usual.

Pahlen probably was correct in saying that no plot could exist without his complicity. What he did not tell his emperor, of course, was that he was one of the leaders of the plot. His closest associate was Count Panin, nephew of Paul's onetime tutor and, like Pahlen, a member of the Imperial Council. These two—Pahlen and Panin—had persuaded the Tsarevich Alexander to agree to accept the crown from their hands if his father should abdicate or be deposed. On that March night a company of some one hundred high-ranking officers—most of them drunk —entered the palace grounds under Pahlen's sponsorship. About half the company forced their way into Paul's bedroom and demanded his immediate abdication. When he protested the outrage instead of immediately complying with the demand, he was strangled. The conspirators then went to the apartments of Alexander (in the same palace), who had been impatiently awaiting the execution of the plot, and informed him that he was now tsar. Perhaps, as has been alleged, he did not intend the murder of his father. He was certainly in accord with the attempt at deposition. And it is significant that he never punished his father's murderers. Once again the guardsmen had unmade and made an emperor.

TSAR ALEXANDER I, 1801–25

The new emperor, whose manner and circumstance of accession resembled those of his grandmother, whom he greatly admired, was in his twenty-fourth year of life. According to "his great and good friend" (to borrow a modern euphemism) the Countess of Choiseul-Gouffier, his features were regular and delicate; his complexion, bright and fresh; his eyes, blue and expressive; his nose, well-shaped; his mouth, small and agreeable; and his hair, a golden blond. He was, by her account, which may be somewhat prejudiced, tall, noble, and majestic—perfectly formed though he carried himself with a slight stoop. His near-sightedness and the fact that he was deaf in one ear seemed to the countess only to enhance his charms. His portraits, undoubtedly flattering, indicate that he was certainly photogenic. He charmed many of his contemporaries besides the countess and other susceptible females. Napoleon spoke of Alexander's many intellectual abilities and of his "dazzling qualities which exercise a singular spell over those with whom he comes in contact." And Metternich, though he was contemptuous of what he called Alexander's "feminine weaknesses," nevertheless depicted the tsar as a high-minded, gifted, and likable person. Stroganov, one of Alexander's most loyal advisers, thought his imperial master was well-intentioned but incurably lazy.

The fact is that Alexander, like some other skillful and charming politicians, came pretty close to being all things to all men:

He had an infinity of shades of tone and manner [reported Countess de Choiseul-Gouffier]. When he addressed men of distinguished rank, it was with dignity and affability at the same time; to persons of his retinue, with an air of kindness almost familiar; to women of a certain age, with deference; and to young people, with an infinite grace, a refined and attractive manner, and a countenance full of expression.

The lady was speaking of Alexander's social graces, but her characterization was apparently applicable upon a much broader scale. Those who talked with him often seem to have come away with the impression that Alexander had agreed with them, while in reality he perhaps had not agreed at all or had done so only with important reservations. This may have been—indeed, often must have been—calculated duplicity. But if Stroganov was right about Alexander's laziness, it was often a case of evading argument by yielding in the face of determined opposition.

🎏 LIBERAL OR CONSERVATIVE?

This is perhaps one clue to a solution of the apparent contradiction between Alexander's "liberalism" and his "conservatism." The conventional solution is to say that he was liberal in his youth but was transformed into an extreme conservative by circumstances and by personal experiences. This interpretation has been sanctified by tradition and endorsed by many historians. Yet it seems to ignore one important series of facts.

The influence upon the youthful Alexander of his grandmother, Catherine, and of his Swiss tutor, Frederic-Cesar Laharpe, is usually cited as the source of his early liberalism. This influence was re-enforced by Alexander's associations with a select group of young noblemen whom he formed into an "Unofficial (or Secret) Committee" at the beginning of his reign, and was continued by his connection with the reformer Speransky. The tsar's early measures of reform; his interest in constitutions, and especially the constitutions which he granted to Finland and to Poland; and the recorded comments of the upper classes upon his accession are all cited as proofs of his liberalism. Proof of his conversion to conservatism is found in his change of advisers, in the establishment of a strong secret police and a rigid censorship, in his sabotage of his early educational efforts, and in his establishment of military colonies.

The first point—that of the influence of Catherine and Laharpe—may be granted at the outset, but only with an important provision. The nature of the liberalism expounded by them must be clearly understood. Laharpe, by all accounts, was an honest, sincere, and incorruptible believer in liberalism and republicanism. Since Catherine appointed him, it may be assumed that their ideas were not incompatible and we already know what liberalism meant to her. It did not appear to her to be inconsistent with despotism. The same may be said of the general eighteenth-century view, which she and Laharpe shared, of republicanism. "I give the name 'republic,'" said Rousseau, "to every state that is governed by laws: no matter what its form of administration may be." To say that the grandmother and the tutor influenced Alexander in favor of liberalism and republicanism is to say that they taught him to desire an ordered and orderly society. He also learned from them that this ideal society might be achieved through the promulgation of perfect regulations based upon and in accord with the "laws of nature." None of them expected these laws to be discovered, nor the rules to be issued "by the people, for the people." That was the responsibility and the power of the enlightened autocrat.

This was the liberalism and the republicanism which Alexander pledged himself to follow when, in his Accession Manifesto, he promised "to govern after the laws and heart" of his grandmother. Implicit in that promise, it may be noted parenthetically, was also a pledge to accept the paramountcy of the nobility—something that Catherine had done and Paul had refused to do. Once it is clearly understood that liberalism, republicanism, and constitutionalism did not mean to Alexander and his friends what they mean to us, many of the alleged contradictions disappear. This applies not only to the influences of Catherine and Laharpe, or to the prestige of the Unofficial Committee and of Speransky, but also to the whole of Alexander's reign. His character was complex and his actions were sometimes contradictory, but they were not incongruous with these concepts. Czartoryski once tartly observed that Alexander "would have willingly agreed that every man should be free, on the condition that he should voluntarily do only what the Emperor wished." And Alexander, who agreed with his sometime friend Karamzin that "Our tsars are not representatives of the peoples, but representatives of Him who rules empires," would have seen no reason why the imperial will should not have over-ridden all others.

The idea of an Unofficial Committee to work with the tsar was suggested by Paul Stroganov. Alexander adopted the idea and appointed Stroganov, N. N. Novosiltsev, Adam Czartoryski, and V. P. Kochubey. All were men of about the same age as the tsar, liberals and republicans in the Catherinean sense. The effective working period of the committee was only eight months (1801–2), and it never came to grips with the two great questions of serfdom and autocracy. Its main accomplishments were the reorganization of the Senate and the replacement of the old "colleges" by ministries on the Western model. Both were changes in technique rather than in principle, and neither in any way impaired the autocratic power. This was generally true of Alexander's other early reforms. The censorship was temporarily relaxed, but even during this period many books were suppressed and destroyed and their authors severely reprimanded. The discussion of certain subjects, notably serfdom, also remained taboo.

Alexander was concerned about serfdom and took some small steps toward reducing the abuses of the system. He revoked the right of the landlords to exile their serfs at hard labor, punished owners found guilty of abusing their serfs, and prohibited the sale of serfs on the open market. A decree of 1803 permitted owners to free their serfs, with or without compensation to the owners, but with the stipulation that land be allotted to the freed men. Less than one-half of one per cent of the total serf population was freed under this law. Alexander did not give away land and serfs as Catherine and Paul had done, but he did allow merchants and foreign investors to buy lands and serfs. And he restored the Charter of the Nobility, which Paul had revoked.

The tsar was also much interested during the early years of his reign in fostering education for the upper classes. A new Ministry of Public Instruction was created, and, for a few years, comparatively large sums of money were appropriated for its work. The plans called for the establishment of 405 district schools, 42 gymnasia, six universities, and several special institutes. Only a limited number of these were established before financial difficulties and other commitments virtually ended the scheme. There was obviously never any intention of establishing what we would recognize as a public school system. Nor, of course, was there any such intention in western Europe at that time.

The financial difficulties of Alexander's government were partly inherited from the preceding reigns and partly the result of Russia's foreign policy. Catherine had left the national finances in a bad way. She met her vastly increased financial needs by what were, in effect, forced domestic loans. This was done by issuing paper currency supposedly at par with the silver currency. But when paper issue followed paper issue, that is, when the government increased its indebtedness instead of retiring it, the paper currency depreciated. Expenditures mounted, deficits multiplied, and Catherine issued 157 million rubles of paper currency. Paul recalled and destroyed some 6 million rubles worth (face value) of paper. This was little enough numerically speaking, but coupled with his measures to stabilize silver currency, it did much to restore confidence, and the paper currency appreciated. Paul also stimulated trade by a tariff more liberal than that which Catherine had last imposed. There was a favorable balance of trade in the first years of Alexander's reign, and this bolstered the paper currency.

The government, in an expansive mood, spent extravagantly but made no serious effort to increase its income by tax reform. Deficits, which were incurred every year, and special needs were again met by the issue of more paper. By the beginning of 1805 some 300 million rubles of paper were outstanding. Confidence continued high, however, and their value stood higher than it had under Paul—until the war.

⊕ FOREIGN AFFAIRS UNDER PAUL

Catherine, it may be recalled, had sought to promote intervention against revolutionary France and had sent Russian ships to co-operate with the British in a blockade of the Netherlands, which were under French control. Paul recalled these ships, and refused to help Austria against a French attack. These actions benefited the French, but that was not Paul's motive. When the French occupied Malta and the Ionian Islands and created a Polish legion in Italy—events which threatened Russian interests—Paul acted differently. He broke off diplomatic relations with France, made an alliance with Great Britain, and then declared war against the French (1798). The Russian Black Sea fleet sailed through the Straits and, in co-operation with the Turkish fleet, captured the Ionian Islands from the French. The islands were then placed under a Turkish protectorate, but Russian troops occupied them until 1807. Meanwhile, one Russian army had been sent to fight at the side of the British against the French in the Netherlands; and a much larger Russian army, under the command of the great Suvorov, was dispatched to co-operate with the Austrians. (Paul also accepted a protectorate over Montenegro, thereby giving Russia a toehold for later use.)

The joint campaigns went very badly. The Russian and British armies were unable to co-operate effectively, and the French gave them a thorough trouncing. Suvorov won some truly spectacular victories in the Alps (which are overlooked by all who say that Russian troops have never been effective away from home), but the failure of Austria to do her part forced him to retreat. His withdrawal, though a brilliant success, was also a defeat in the broader sense. Paul, thoroughly and rather justifiably angry with his allies, now took Russia out of the coalition against France and began to build a new diplomatic structure. A defensive alliance was made with Sweden and a *rapprochement* opened with Prussia. These steps were followed by the renewal, at Russia's initiative, of the League of Armed Neutrality and by the formation of the "Northern Convention" of Russia, Prussia, Sweden, and Denmark. Napoleon, now the real ruler of France, was quick to take advantage of the changes. He and Paul talked of peace and of an alliance against Britain.

It was in this connection that Paul gave the orders which have so often been cited as conclusive proof of his madness. Without making adequate provisions for such an expedition, he commanded the Don Cossacks to march against the British in India. Perhaps all commanders who have ordered troops into action without sufficient preparation and without regard for logistics have been mad, but they have not always been so harshly judged. Anyway, the expedition was ordered and begun. The Cossacks had just crossed the Volga when the news was brought them that Paul was dead and that the new emperor had recalled them. Alexander's courier had, in fact, been dispatched on the very night of Paul's murder. Alexander also made haste to open negotiations with the British. Some concessions were made on both sides and a peace was signed between them in June of 1801.

🔥 ALEXANDER'S DIPLOMACY

Alexander wanted no trouble with Napoleon either. The peace treaty of which Paul had talked was drafted and signed in October, 1801. Simultaneously there was also signed a secret treaty which, in effect, made Alexander partner of Napoleon. This arrangement lasted until Russia broke it in 1804. One of the reasons for the break was probably Alexander's anger at Napoleon's murder of the Duke of Enghien, but matters of state interest were more important.

Alexander soon discovered that Russia was very much the junior in the partnership. The common action which the two had taken in the affairs of the Germanies had resulted in a growth of French rather than of Russian power. When Napoleon, renewing his war against the British, seized the British possession of Hanover, Alexander felt that his partner was moving east too far and too fast. The tsar now sent to Great Britain a mission headed by his friend Novosiltsev. It was a shrewd choice, since Novosiltsev had made many friends in England during an earlier visit there. Alexander's instructions to his envoy included both an immediate and a long-range plan. The immediate plan was to secure an alliance against Napoleon for the double purpose of freeing France from him and of freeing the conquered countries from the yoke which France had placed upon them. The long-range plan, set forth in secret instructions, included the following proposal which some historians regard as historical forerunner of the late League of Nations:

> When peace is made, a new treaty should be drawn up as a basis for the reciprocal relations of the European states. Such a treaty might secure the privileges of neutrality, bind the Powers who take part in it never to begin a war until after exhausting every means of mediation by a third Power, and lay down a sort of new code of international law which, being sanctioned by the greater part of the European states, would, if violated by any one of them, bind the others to turn against the offender and make good the evil he has committed.

The British were not receptive to this plan, but they concluded an alliance treaty by which they promised to pay Russia a subsidy to be based upon the number of troops she put in the field against Napoleon. (It worked out at a rate of approximately £1,200,000 subsidy for every 100,000 soldiers.) Prior to the signing of this treaty, Russia had made a secret alliance with Austria against Napoleon. These three Powers—Russia, Great Britain, and Austria—with the addition of Sweden formed the Third Coalition against the French. It was short-lived. Napoleon shattered it by defeating a combined Austro-Russian army at Austerlitz in 1805. Austria was forced out. Her place was taken in a Fourth Coalition by Prussia, who was brought in by British gold and by a secret treaty with Russia. Napoleon, however, could win at war if not at diplomacy. He routed the Prussian armies at Jena and Auerstadt (1806), occupied Berlin, and thus forced Prussia out of the war. His military might now fell upon Russia. The battle of Eylau was a bloody draw, but the battle of Friedland (1807) forced the Russian army to retreat.

Alexander's situation—and that of Russia, of course—had become precarious. None of his Continental allies could or would give him any effective help, and British aid was too little and too late. Moreover, Russia had become embroiled in two other wars: one against Persia; the other against Turkey. The war with Persia was a direct outgrowth of Russian expansion in the Caucasus area. In the late fifteenth and early sixteenth centuries the ancient, independent, Christian state of Georgia had been conquered by the Turks and Persians. On various occasions the Georgians besought the aid of Russia, but Russia was not strong enough successfully to challenge either Persia or Turkey until the reign of Catherine the Great. She established a Russian protectorate over Georgia, and Paul annexed that land to the Russian Empire. Persia did not take kindly to this. Her efforts to regain control of Georgia led to a war which began in 1805 and ended in a Russian victory in 1813. The other war—against Turkey—was largely brought on at that particular time by the machinations of Napoleon. It was a somewhat desultory affair which dragged along from 1806 to 1812. Russian troops eventually occupied Bessarabia and the Danubian provinces of Moldavia and Wallachia, and were moving forward across Bulgaria when peace parleys began. The peace treaty gave Bessarabia to Russia, but that is ahead of the story. In 1807, Alexander's troops were engaged on three fronts, against three enemies, and had just suffered a major defeat at the hands of their most formidable opponent. Moreover financial difficulties beset the government.

Under the circumstances, Alexander was constrained to make a deal with Napoleon. The two emperors met on a very large and elaborate floating structure (traditionally "a raft"—which at once evokes a misleading picture in American minds) anchored in the River Nieman. As a result of their conversations a peace and an alliance were arranged between France and Russia. Alexander agreed to join Napoleon's economic war (the Continental System) against the British, and bound himself to make military war against Britain if necessary. He also agreed to use force against Sweden if that country did not immediately make peace with Napoleon. Napoleon agreed, in the event of a Russo-Swedish war, that Russia might annex Finland. The two emperors also agreed in principle to a joint partitioning of European Turkey. Alexander was compelled to acquiesce, much against his will, in the creation of a Grand Duchy of Poland out of part of Prussian Poland. His opposition to this earned him the hostility of the Polish upper classes, who supported Napoleon. Alexander, for his part, could not help regarding the French-sponsored Grand Duchy as a potential spearhead aimed at Russia. This situation was one of the causes for the subsequent breaking of the alliance. The Tilsit agreements—the "raft" had been anchored at Tilsit—were confirmed in the following year (1808) by a second meeting of the two emperors, which took place at Erfurt. It is significant that Alexander, speaking to his sister about Napoleon after the Erfurt meeting, told her, "There isn't room enough in Europe for us both; sooner or later one of us will have to go." But temporarily Alexander had to be content with the alliance. At least, it gave him the necessary time to rebuild his strength and to attend to domestic affairs, which were not going very well.

🐝 DOMESTIC DEVELOPMENTS

One of the gravest and most pressing problems was that of finance. The Russian historian Kornilov calculated that the state income in 1808 was less than half its expenditures. The deficit was covered, as it had been for many years, by the issue of more paper currency. But the paper issue was steadily depreciating in value until by the end of 1809 it stood at half what it had been in 1805. Within the next twelve months the value was again reduced by nearly half and bankruptcy was imminent. The situation was partly the result of Russian adherence to the Continental System. About half Russia's export trade had been in the sale of flax and hemp to Great Britain. This was now almost stopped, although American vessels did carry some cargoes of hemp to the British. The export trade in grain was similarly affected. Wheat exports had stood at an annual average of 175,000 tons before Tilsit. After Tilsit the annual average dropped to 30,000 tons or less. Certain implications other than the obvious economic ones need to be drawn. It will be recalled that agriculture was Russia's chief source of wealth at this time, and that the agricultural products just named formed her major items of export. They were therefore the most important cash crops, and many land-owners depended on them for their profits. It was this fact particularly which turned the nobility (who were, of course, the landowners) and the wealthy merchants against France. They may have thought that the French alliance was a bad thing for Russia on national grounds. It is clear that this impersonal and nationally minded approach was greatly re-enforced by self-interest. Faced with this economic crisis and with the rising unpopularity of his foreign policy, Alexander leaned heavily upon his "brain-truster," Michael M. Speransky—a relationship usually interpreted as "proof" of the tsar's transient liberalism.

Speransky, like many another outstanding man in Russia and else-where, was the son of a village clergyman. His early life and his training took place in a church atmosphere and he always retained a strong in-terest in religion. This was one of his points of contact with Alexander. Speransky did not long remain in ecclesiastical circles. During Paul's reign he left his professorship of physics, mathematics, and rhetoric at a church seminary to become the private secretary of the procurator of the Senate. Soon after Alexander's accession, Speransky changed to the posi-tion of secretary to the Council of State, and from that post he moved into the service of Kochubey, newly appointed Minister of the Interior. This brought Speransky to Alexander's attention, and the emperor—favorably impressed by Speransky's ideas, intelligence, information, and industry—promptly pre-empted his services. Speransky became what our day has called a brain-truster—a position (then and now) the pres-tige of which is matched by its insecurity.

All went very well with Speransky for some years, to the intense an-noyance of many of the nobles, who resented the influence which this commoner had upon the tsar. Their grumblings and their intrigues were not immediately effective. Alexander took Speransky on a European journey in 1806, from which they returned with the shared conviction that Russia was potentially superior to Europe. "Our people," said Alex-ander, "may lack certain training, but no other people can match their innate gifts and native intelligence." The two men saw eye to eye on many other matters, also, including religious mysticism. They liked to speculate on the nature of man and to talk of man-made and natural laws. They shared the rationalists' faith in perfect law as the only path to full liberty and a perfect society, and they had great confidence in the efficacy of constitutions. Speransky prepared for their frequent discus-sions several drafts of constitutions for Russia. After Alexander and Speransky had returned from Erfurt, and after the tsar had concluded that some steps had to be taken to allay the rising discontent, he commissioned Speransky to work out a plan for the complete reorganization of the state.

🎗 CONSTITUTIONS

Speransky worked with typical diligence and even Alexander seemed unusually earnest about it. There were frequent and lengthy discussions of the proposal by the two men until Alexander approved the plan in principle, in the autumn of 1809. The essence of the plan was the streamlining of administrative machinery and the strengthening of centralized authority. Administrative functions were divided and allocated with doctrinaire orderliness, but the sovereign power remained with the emperor. The Council of State was reformed into a consultative body for the discussion and formulation of proposed major administrative measures and projected laws. Its decisions had no binding effect and the council was presided over by the emperor or his appointee. This was one of two fragments of the plan which Alexander put into effect. The other was the formation of heads of the ministries into a Committee of Ministers, who remained individually and jointly responsible directly and exclusively to the emperor. There was no prime minister, since the emperor himself served in that capacity. Both council and committee were created and existed only as agents of the imperial will, and neither impaired the power of the autocrat in any way. This was typical of the whole plan, which envisioned a monarch whose powers were limited by "natural law" but who was not answerable to any human agency. Such limited political powers as were granted to subjects were restricted wholly to the nobility. Clearly, this was not liberalism, republicanism, or constitutionalism as we understand them.

The same may also be said of the constitutions which Alexander subsequently granted to the Finns and the Poles. The former was a continuation, in substance, of the constitution Finland had during the Swedish regime. It was remarkable in that Finland was allowed to retain its native laws, courts, administration, and coinage. The government personnel was non-Russian, and no Russian was allowed to settle in Finland without Finnish permission. The major beneficiaries of this hands-off attitude were the Swedish aristocrats, who continued to be the real rulers of the Finnish people. The Polish constitution, largely drafted by Czartoryski, established a Polish Diet, a Polish army; provided that there should be Polish administrative personnel; guaranteed freedoms of speech, press, and association; and gave special protection and privilege to the Roman Catholic Church. But final power resided with the king of Poland, who was Alexander. He retained control of the budget and of the army; and maintained his brother, Constantine, and his friend,

Novosiltsev, as the actual governors of Poland. What this really meant was best explained by Alexander himself:

Alongside the liberal principles that a monarch believes he should adopt, he ought to establish the corresponding means of repression. I have given the Poles a constitution, but along with this I have created such organs of repression as will make the Poles understand that they must not go beyond a certain limit.

To return to Russia in 1809–10, Alexander's very limited application of Speransky's constitutional plan did not, of course, cope with the economic problem. So the tsar directed Speransky to solve that problem. Speransky produced a realistic and sound plan for financial reform. It called for the retirement and redemption of the paper issues (which were recognized as involuntary loans); the floating of an internal loan, properly secured; a sharp decrease in expenditures; and the increase of taxes to meet the needs of the government. It also suggested a revision of the tariff which, in effect, was a recommendation to withdraw from the Continental System. This last suggestion was followed in December of 1810 and contributed directly to the break with Napoleon. Kornilov holds that it was the only thing which saved Russia from complete ruin, but the nobility reacted hostilely to Speransky's plan. They naturally opposed the tax increase, but they also, and quite unfairly, blamed the financial crisis not on the men who had caused it but on Speransky, who had revealed it. When the new taxes, which were supposedly to retire the debt, were used for current expenses, and when the paper issues were increased instead of being reduced, the wrath of the articulate wealthy minority was understandably increased.

THE WAR WITH FRANCE

Meanwhile, not only had the French alliance become increasingly unpopular with many Russians; it was also being strained to the point of rupture. Neither had lived up to the letter or the spirit of the agreements. Napoleon had been at pains to strengthen the Grand Duchy of Warsaw by a substantial addition of land and people taken from Austria. He had also built up the Polish army—that is, the army of the Grand Duchy. This seemed to Russia to constitute a potential menace which might at any moment become an active threat, particularly because the steady advance of Napoleonic power into the central Germanies brought French support ever closer to the Poles. At the same time, Napoleon's persistent interest in the Levant seemed to foreshadow a Russo-French clash of interests there. This threat was markedly enhanced by Napoleon's marriage to Marie Louise of Austria and by the creation of an Austro-French alliance. As the likelihood of war with France increased,

Alexander made an alliance with Napoleon's enemy, Bernadotte of Sweden. And in March, 1812, he told Speransky in solemn audience:

The enemy approaches the frontiers of the Empire. In view of the situation in which we have been placed because of the suspicions aroused by your remarks and your conduct, it is extremely important that, in the event of a reverse, I should not appear in the eyes of my subjects to be responsible for this unhappiness. I certainly should so appear if I continued to extend my favor to you and allowed you to retain your present place. Conditions are such that I cannot advise you even to remain in St. Petersburg or its environs. Choose another residence where you can wait out the results of the coming events. We are embarking upon a great gamble—the greater it is, the more serious will be the danger to which you will be exposed in case of failure. This is because of the attitude of the people among whom you seem to inspire suspicion and hatred.

Speransky, in other words, was sent into exile not because, as his enemies maliciously alleged, he was an enemy of Russia or a confederate of Napoleon, but because Alexander hoped to regain the favor of the nobility. It ought to be recalled in extenuation of Alexander's conduct that his father had lost his throne and his life because he overrode the wishes of this group. It should also be remembered that Alexander, already at war with Turkey and Persia, was now facing a much greater challenge. It was expedient, if unprincipled, to do whatever he could to secure support at home from those groups whose backing he had to have for victory and for continuance in office. (Speransky was allowed to return to the capital after the defeat of Napoleon and was subsequently entrusted with several important assignments both by Alexander and by his successor, Nicholas, but he never regained the prestige he once had held.)

The Napoleonic invasion of Russia in June, 1812, unavoidably invites comparison with Hitler's invasion of the Soviet Union in June, 1941. Soviet historians have labeled the 1812 invasion as the opening of "The First Great Fatherland War" and the struggle against Nazi Germany "The Second Great Fatherland War." Superficially at least there seem to be many parallels. Alliances whose effective direction in both cases was against Great Britain were suddenly replaced by war (though the event was not wholly unforeseen in either century). In neither war did the Russian armies stand off the invaders, who drove rapidly forward. The Russians, fighting heroically in what amounted to rear-guard actions, were forced into continuous and speedy retreats. Both invaders were originally welcomed as liberators by many of the people, and both threw away this initial advantage by their cruelties. They had, in consequence, to face increasing guerilla harassments. The Russian peasants, once they became convinced that neither conqueror had any intention of liberating them from the system under which they were compelled to live, fought fiercely both as soldiers and as civilian irregulars. And in both wars it was, of course, the "little people" who suffered most grievously. Other similarities might be pointed out, but there were basic dissimilarities also. History does not repeat itself. The popular impression to the contrary takes account only of limited or surface features, ignoring the fact of change.

It would be inappropriate to attempt a detailed exploration of this theme here, but one or two illustrations drawn from the two invasions may be suggestive. The Napoleonic invasion and occupation of Russian lands lasted less than six months; the fighting then moved westward. The German invasion and occupation lasted for about four years. Napoleon captured Moscow, which Hitler was unable to do, but the more recent penetration was much deeper, more extensive, and also much more destructive. The number of troops involved was also very much less in the 1812 war. Napoleon launched his invasion with 420,000 troops (mostly non-French), to which he added about 150,000 later replacements. The Russians opposed him with forces somewhat more numerous—perhaps a million men in all were in the army during this period. Hitler began his invasion with 164 divisions against whom the Soviets opposed 119 divisions with 67 more in the immediate reserve. Both sides threw in very many more troops before the war was over. The international situation was also basically different, not only because of the rise of two new major Powers—one in America and one in Asia—but also because of the failure of European Powers to survive. Britain, Russia, and France were all first-class Powers in 1812; Austria and Prussia, though of somewhat lesser stature, were not far behind these leaders. In 1941 there were only three Great Powers in the Old World—Britain, Germany, and the Soviet Union. These examples are enough to warn against pushing the comparison between 1812 and 1941 too far.

ALEXANDER'S LEADERSHIP IN EUROPEAN AFFAIRS

The story of Napoleon's invasion and of his disastrous retreat (only about 100,000 of his troops got out of Russia) is spectacularly dramatic, but it has been too often told to need another repetition. This is also true of the foreign affairs which engaged Alexander's attention almost exclusively until after the Congress of Vienna (1815) and to a very considerable extent throughout the rest of his reign. It may be pointed out, however, that Alexander took the lead against Napoleon among the Continental Powers. Russia could never have beaten Napoleon alone, perhaps might even have fallen into disaster at home if it had not been for British subsidies, but the other Continental states would have faltered and possibly failed without Russian leadership. The treaties of Kalisch (Russia and Prussia, 1813) and Teplitz (Russia, Prussia, and Austria, 1813) formed the Continental alliance which, with the indispensable support of Britain, drove Napoleon westward across the Rhine. The alliance, renewed and greatly strengthened by the addition of Great Britain in the Treaties of Chaumont (1814), stormed on to take Paris, compel the abdication of Napoleon, and restore the Bourbons to the French throne. In all these measures, and in the Congress of Vienna, Alexander played a leading part.

A violent dispute over the disposition of Saxony and Poland almost broke up the congress and brought Russia and Prussia, on the one side, Britain and Austria, on the other, to the edge of war. Napoleon's melodramatic return from Elba and the spectacular Hundred Days (March to June, 1815) forced his opponents again to make common cause and an alliance against him. The congress then resumed and worked out a final settlement. Russia's gain was the Kingdom of Poland, which included most of the former Grand Duchy of Warsaw. Her less tangible, more subtle but nonetheless real gain was a Continental hegemony which endured—though not without some diminution—until the creation of the German Empire in 1871. The attention of the West has been so concentrated on Franco-German relations that it has generally failed to recognize that Russia and not France was the leading Continental Power after 1815. Consequently it was Russia rather than France which was unseated by Bismarck.

Immediately after the Congress of Vienna Alexander brought forward a proposal which promptly evoked the contempt of his fellow statesmen (Castlereagh called it "a piece of sublime mysticism and nonsense") and which has continued to draw ridicule upon itself and its author. It was a declaration which bound its signatories, who had to be monarchs, into a "Holy Alliance." Members pledged to abide by the precepts of Christianity in dealing with their subjects and with each other, to protect religion, to defend justice, to further the cause of peace, and to preserve the institution of monarchy. No one was very enthusiastic about it, but the Prussians and Austrians promptly signed in order not to offend Alexander, and eventually all the European monarchs except the king of England, the sultan of Turkey, and the pope also became members. (The sultan was not a Christian and therefore ineligible; the pope would have no dealings with a schismatic; and the British stayed out on a technical quibble.) It seems probable that this Holy Alliance was intended by Alexander as a preliminary to some sort of league of nations along the lines laid down in his instructions to Novosiltsev in 1804. If that were so, he never followed it through, perhaps because of the creation of the Quadruple Alliance and the establishment of a system of regular European conferences. The public promptly confused the Holy Alliance with the Quadruple Alliance and the confusion has persisted. The Quadruple Alliance was a working agreement, on the familiar model, which bound its signatories (Russia, Prussia, Britain, and Austria) to co-operative action if necessary to prevent a resurgence of Napoleon's power or of French aggression. They further agreed to hold periodic meetings (congresses) for joint discussion and action upon matters of common concern.

Four congresses were held under this agreement, Russia taking part in all of them. The second congress, held at Troppau in 1820, perverted the original purpose by arrogating to itself, Britain dissenting and abstaining, the right to interfere in the domestic affairs of European states for the purpose of suppressing revolutions. The initiative in this did not come from Russia, but she adhered to the principle—which is often taken as a mark of Alexander's "growing conservatism," and as a counterpart to his domestic activities during these years.

🔖 "CONSERVATISM"

The conventional interpretation of Alexander, given earlier in this chapter, noted the evidences which have commonly been cited to show his "conversion to conservatism." These included a change in advisers, the re-establishment of systems of political police and censorship, the sabotage of education, and the establishing of the so-called military colonies. During the war Alexander had left most of the business of government to the Committee of Ministers, and he never again paid more than sporadic attention to the domestic routine. Dissatisfied with the committee's conduct of the nation's business, the tsar made some changes in its personnel after the war, and, in effect, placed Count Arakchiev over it.

A. A. Arakchiev had been the loyal agent of Paul. He became the equally loyal agent of Alexander. It has been suggested that this appointment somehow gave Alexander a psychic recompense which soothed his persistent sense of bloodguilt at the murder of Paul. This is an interesting hypothesis, but it is both unprovable and unnecessary. Arakchiev was diligent in business, devotedly loyal to Alexander, and personally honest —a combination of qualities which the tsar found in few men. Kornilov, who very carefully examined the documents of the period, concluded that Arakchiev was essentially the agent and not the adviser of the tsar. As Alexander's agent, Arakchiev tried to carry out and even to anticipate the imperial wishes.

Professor Mazour has described Arakchiev as "tactless, bigoted, unsympathetic with suffering . . . hated by more people than any other statesman of his time." If Kornilov's interpretation is accurate, then the characteristics which Mazour ascribes to the man should properly be applied to the master. Kornilov, who studied all of Arakchiev's recommendations to Alexander, said that many of them were both just and humane. Is this further proof of Alexander's inconsistency (assuming Arakchiev to be his reflection)? It may be, but other explanations seem more plausible. It was easier for Alexander to overlook Arakchiev's illiberal actions than to try to find another agent who would be equally conscientious and honest. Indolence rather than conviction seems to have been the main determinant.

This seems to have been the case also in regard to the police and the censorship. Alexander created a Ministry of Police and allowed it a very wide scope. The censor, Magnitsky, was also given wide latitude. Magnitsky, together with Prince Golitsin, head of the Synod and later Minister of Education, seriously interfered with academic freedom. "The spirit of this reaction," wrote the statesman-scholar Masaryk, "is characterized by the fact that Magnicki [Magnitsky] had pathological specimens taken from museums and buried in church yards [cemeteries]." The tsar may not have known of this, but he must have known in general what Magnitsky and Golitsin were doing. Though he sometimes restrained their zeal, he did not stop them. On the other hand, Alexander knew in detail of secret societies (which will be described in the next chapter) for several years, and yet took no effective repressive measures against them. His one domestic interest was the military colonies.

These were established in order to maintain the military strength without plunging into bankruptcy. The financial situation had grown steadily worse. The national deficit, which had stood at 7 million rubles in 1801, reached 143 million rubles in 1809, and rose to 351 million rubles in 1822. The value of the ruble had declined by rather more than half during these years. The bulk of the national expenditure was military so the obvious remedy was to reduce the size of the army. Alexander was afraid to do this in view of the European situation. He proposed, as an alternative, to make soldiers into farmers and farmers into soldiers. When the former were not soldiering, they could be producing and thus make the army self-sufficient. When the latter were not farming, they could be soldiering and thus augment the country's defenses. And both could be settled in military colonies, which would at once defend and order the countryside.

The first attempt to establish such colonies, made in 1810, was aborted by the Napoleonic invasion. The plan was revived in 1816 and placed under the direction of Arakchiev. By the time of Alexander's death in 1825, there were some three-quarters of a million colonists. The new colonies, which the officials took care to show Alexander, presented a neat and orderly appearance. "Everything," wrote Mazour, "ran on schedule . . . [and] . . . Alexander usually left well pleased with the condition of the colonies." As a matter of fact, the colonies not only failed to achieve their objectives but were also extremely unpopular. It is an interesting commentary on the longevity of institutions that they were not abolished until 1857.

ALEXANDER RE-EVALUED

There is no doubt that Alexander was sometimes self-contradictory and inconsistent. It also appears that he was less confident in middle age than in youth of his ability to remake the world in the image of his dreams. Though his enthusiasms cooled, he remained, by and large, consistently loyal to liberalism and republicanism as he had understood them from Catherine, Laharpe, and Speransky. Perhaps it was this consistency which made him appear conservative in his later years. Catherine and the others belonged to an age whose dominant aspiration was the achievement of a rational order under national and international law. Alexander shared this aspiration. But times changed so that views which seemed new and liberal in 1800 were old-fashioned half a generation later. The change was not in Alexander but in the norms and values of Russian society. For many of these changes the wars with Napoleon were at least partially responsible.

CHAPTER XI

The Reign of Contrasts: Domestic Affairs, 1825-55

🏮 INFLUENCES OF THE WARS

The most immediately obvious impact of the Napoleonic wars was the effect of travel upon those Russians whose military or other duties took them to western Europe. There they came in contact with a set of norms and values which in many ways contrasted sharply with what they had known at home. Many of them became dissatisfied with the standard of living to which they had been accustomed, and upon their return to Russia sought to reproduce there what they had found abroad. Some were struck by the contrast between the apparently more advanced and efficient governments of the West (with which they could have had only a nodding acquaintance) and the administrative chaos and inefficiency of Russia (about which they knew more). Others had been attracted by the liberalism of Europe and some had joined liberal or quasi-liberal organizations. They came home burning with eagerness to continue in Russia what they had begun abroad.

A case in point is Freemasonry. Masonic lodges had flourished among the nobility of the capital during the "liberal" period of Catherine's reign, but Masonry had fallen under her displeasure in the later years and the movement suffered an eclipse. A small recovery was made under Paul and this grew into a revival under Alexander, particularly after the wars. There was an increase in the number of lodges and a considerable broadening of membership to include non-nobles as well as nobles. Of course neither all Masonic lodges nor all Masons were liberal. Some, in fact, were extremely conservative and even went so far as to denounce to the government the "radicalism" of their brothers. But Masonry had a strong liberal wing which included some men who were prominent in the government. It is noteworthy that most of the leaders of the "secret societies" and many of the leaders of the Decembrist Revolution of 1825 were Masons. It is also noteworthy that several of the latter had joined the Masonic order while they were stationed in Paris. Freemasonry, if it did not inspire these men with liberal ideas, at least brought them together, gave them opportunities for discussions, and furnished a model for the nonmasonic, secret, political organizations which they subsequently formed.

Other effects of the wars concerned the financial situation of the government, and the financial condition of the land- and serf-owners. Participation in the wars and continuing intervention in European affairs during the period of the congresses was a very expensive business. The foreign and domestic debts of the government mounted to what was for those days a staggeringly high figure, and the annual deficits rose by 245 per cent between 1809 and 1822. Some additional income was raised by increasing taxes, but there was a definite limit to the productivity of this device, since an impoverished peasantry could raise only so much tax money. Tax arrears were, in fact, very large. Despite the cancellation of some 80 million rubles in back taxes in 1826, the arrears stood at 178 million rubles three years later.

TAXES AND SERFDOM

The connection between the government's pressing need for tax money and the continuance of serfdom may profitably be recalled. Taxes were collected not from individual serfs but from the serf communities or mirs, which paid them to the landlord who, in turn, was responsible for payments to the government. Since it was manifestly easier for the government to collect taxes from some thousands of landlords than from some millions of serfs, the administration was naturally extremely reluctant to see any change in this part of the system. In fact, change seemed literally impossible. True, the existing system worked very badly, but the government had neither the personnel, nor the experience, nor the organization to set up a system of individual tax collections. This was a most powerful deterrent.

The desires of many of the landlords to live in a style to which they were determined to become accustomed was partly responsible for their increasingly unfavorable financial condition. It required a great deal of money to build or rebuild their houses in European fashion, and to clothe them and their families in the latest Western mode. A few sought to increase their incomes by improving the basic economy of their estates. More tried to do it by turning to manufacturing, and numerous "nobles' factories" were established. Despite an increasing importation of machinery for such enterprises, however, Russian industry found it ever harder to compete successfully against the more highly mechanized industries of Europe, and a good many nobles who had thought to repair their fortunes by turning industrialists found financial disaster rather than success.

Most of the landlords, however, neither sought to improve the productivity of their estates nor turned to industry. They took instead the apparently easier ways of exacting more from their serfs and of borrowing money. According to Professor Kornilov, over half the estates were heavily mortgaged by 1843. Figuring the annual, average value of a serf at one hundred rubles, Kornilov calculated the average indebtedness of the landlords was at the rate of sixty-nine rubles per serf at that time. As to the demands made upon the serfs, these had been steadily growing. *Barshchina* was still legally fixed at three days a week, but, in practice, four to seven days each week were often required during the summer. On some estates this was carried to the logical conclusion of transforming the serfs into economic slaves. In this case, the serf worked full time for his master and was paid a subsistence in kind instead of being given land to work for himself. *Obrok* was also constantly raised. The usual *obrok* in 1801 had been ten to twelve rubles for each adult serf a year. By 1825–26, it stood at thirty rubles an adult or higher. Other obligations, such as carting, were also increased. One effect was a growth in the number and violence of serf mutinies against their masters.

There are no complete records of these risings, and the official reports record only those of major seriousness. These reports show 148 serf uprisings between 1826 and 1834, 216 between 1835 and 1844, and 348 between 1845 and 1854. In at least two of the years, the mutinies were of sufficient scope properly to be described as mass movements. Mutinies and uprisings took place in twenty-six regions in 1826, and in 1832 all the central, black-soil provinces were affected. The most common cause for the risings was false rumors of emancipation, which frequently excited the serfs into taking matters into their own hands. Other causes, in decreasing order of importance, were the harshness of *barshchina,* famines on the estates, and the burdens of *obrok.*

🔥 CONTEMPORARY DESCRIPTION OF THE PEASANTS

An English scholar and traveler named Heber left a manuscript journal describing and analyzing the peasant situation as he saw it at the beginning of the nineteenth century. Some of his comments might even be applied to the current situation in Russia. With one or two exceptions (Heber makes no distinction between *barshchina* and *obrok,* for example), his description was accurate and his analysis was shrewd:

We observed a striking difference between the peasants of the crown and those of individuals. The former are almost all in comparatively easy circumstances. Their abrock [*obrok*] is fixed at five roubles a year, all charges included; and as they are sure it will never be raised, they are more industrious.

The peasants belonging to the nobles have their abrock regulated by their means of getting money; at an average throughout the empire of eight or ten roubles. . . . [Local variations may explain the discrepancy between these figures and those given above.] Each male peasant is obliged by law, to labour three days in each week for his proprietor. [This is *barshchina*.] The law takes effect on his arriving at the age of fifteen. [Recent studies hold that the obligation began for males at the age of seventeen and lasted until the age of fifty-five. For women, the obligation began at marriage and lasted until the age of fifty. But minors and older people were often registered for work on many estates. Local variations make accurate generalizations impossible.] If the proprietor chooses to employ him the other days, he may; as, for example, in a manufactory; but he then finds him in food and clothing. Mutual advantage, however, generally relaxes this law; and, excepting such as are selected for domestick servants; or, as above, are employed in manufactures, the slave [sic] pays a certain abrock, or rent, to be allowed to work all week on his own account. The master is bound to furnish him with a house and certain portion of land. The allotment of land is generally settled by the starosta (elder of the village) and a meeting of the peasants themselves. In the same manner, when a master wants an increase of rent, he sends to the starosta, who convenes the peasants; and by that assembly it is decided what proportion each must pay. If a slave exercises any trade which brings him in more money than agricultural labour, he pays a higher abrock.

If by journeys to Petersburgh, or other cities, he can still earn more, his master permits his absence, but his abrock is raised. The smallest earnings are subject to this oppression. The peasants employed as drivers, at the posthouses, pay an abrock out of the drink money [tips] they receive, for being permitted to drive; as, otherwise the master might employ them in less profitable labour on his own account.

The aged and infirm are provided with food and raiment, and lodging, at their owner's expense. Such as prefer casual charity to the miserable pittance they receive from their master, are frequently furnished with passports, and are allowed to seek their fortune [by begging] but they sometimes pay an abrock even for this permission to beg. . . .

No slave can quit his village, or his master's family, without a passport. Any person arriving in a town or village, must produce a passport to the starosta; and no one can harbour a stranger without one. If a person is found dead without a passport, his body is sent to the hospital for dissection. . . . The punishment of living runaways is imprisonment and hard labour in the government works; and a master may send to the publick workhouse any peasant he chooses. The prisons of Moscow and Kostroma were chiefly filled with such runaway slaves, who were for the most part in irons. On the frontier, they often escape; but in the interiour it is almost impossible; yet, during the summer, desertions are very common; and they sometimes lurk about for many months, living miserably in the woods. This particularly happens when there is a new levy of soldiers. The soldiers are levied, one from every certain number of peasants, at the same time all over the empire. But if a master is displeased with his slave, he may send him for a soldier at any time.

🔧 THE "SECRET SOCIETIES"

The existence of serfdom, with its gross inequalities, had begun to trouble some conscientious Russians long before the era of Alexander and Napoleon. One or two of them—notably Novikov and Radishchev—had spoken out boldly against the evils of the system during the reign of Catherine. They had been punished for their temerity (though in the case of Radishchev, at least, it was his strictures against autocracy rather than his attack upon serfdom which got him into trouble with the authorities), but their deeds and words continued to inspire a new generation of the liberally inclined—particularly those who were also affected by their experiences abroad.

Some of these men founded small, secret societies upon their return to Russia after the wars. All of them had rather vague aims and purposes, and wholly impractical methods and organization. But out of them grew the "secret societies" and the Decembrist Revolution of 1825.

Six young noblemen—all officers of the Guards, and four of them members of the Semenovski Regiment—formed themselves, in 1816, into "The Union of Salvation, or the Society of the True and Faithful Sons of the Fatherland." All of the six were sure that something had to be done, but none of them was sure what that something was nor how it should be accomplished. Force and direction (and trouble, it may be added) came into the movement when the six were joined by the brilliant and vigorous Pavel Pestel. Son of a governor-general of Siberia, young Pestel had been educated abroad and had served in the wars with distinction. He came back to St. Petersburg a convinced revolutionary, prepared literally to devote his life to the development and carrying out of a revolutionary program. His extremism was too much for some of the original members of the Union of Salvation, which soon split up and then reorganized.

The new organization took the name Union of Welfare, and adopted a code or constitution which was known as The Green Book. This was a very moderate affair, and it has been surmised on the basis of fragmentary evidence that it was either only a part of the intended project or a cover for more extreme plans. The real aims of the Union were to abolish the autocracy, to free the serfs, to end the hated military colonies, and to carry out some other reforms—objectives which could be accomplished only by revolution. Beyond deciding that the death of

Alexander and the accession of the new sovereign would furnish an opportune time, the conspirators reached no decision.

Pestel was transferred in 1818 from the capital to the south of Russia, where he promptly set up a southern branch of the Union of Welfare. This soon became the more active group. Then the establishment of a secret, political police by Alexander in 1821 and a consequent increase in restrictive measures resulted in a fake dissolution of the Union. This did not satisfy Pestel, who then created an organization of his own, The Southern Society. (A Northern Society was revived but the leadership remained with Pestel's group.) The Southern Society aimed at the destruction of the autocracy and the establishment of a republican form of government. Its program also included serf emancipation. Despite the audacity of this program and of Pestel, the societies might well have never gotten beyond the talking stage if it had not been for a curious mix-up over the succession to the throne.

❦ CHANGE IN SUCCESSION

The normal succession would have brought to the throne the Grand Duke Constantine, who was serving as commander-in-chief and governor in Poland. But Constantine, to the distress of his mother, the dowager-empress, had married a commoner. Alexander consented to this morganatic marriage on condition that Constantine accept a legal prohibition against the succession of any children of this union. It was partly this situation and partly a consciousness of his own limitations that led the grand duke to write as follows to his imperial brother in January, 1822:

> Not finding in myself the genius, the talents, nor the force necessary for the elevation to the Sovereign dignity to which I am entitled by right of birth, I beg your Imperial Majesty to transfer this right to whomever it should come after me. . . .

The tsar accepted Constantine's renunciation of the throne and, in a manifesto of August, 1823, decreed that:

> First, the voluntary act by which Our brother, the Tsarevich and Grand Duke Constantine, renounces his right to the throne of all the Russias shall be irrevocable. . . .
> Secondly, following the strict provision of the statute on the succession to the throne, be it known that Our successor shall be Our second brother, the Grand Duke Nicholas.

The mischief came because these provisions were not known. Alexander, for some reason never revealed, did not publish the manifesto. He placed it, instead, under seal; and its contents were known only to half a dozen persons or less. The people, of course, knew nothing whatever about it. Neither did most of the officials of the government. When Alexander died in November, 1825, the people naturally expected Constantine to be their next ruler. The Guards and the chief officials at once took an oath of allegiance to him. So, very curiously, did Nicholas, who must have known of the arrangement. Nicholas also wrote to Constantine, urging him to come at once to the capital, and saying: "I bow before my Sovereign after having pronounced . . . the oath which is due him. . . . In the name of Heaven, do not desert us, do not abandon us!" And he signed himself, "Your brother and faithful subject in life and in death." If this was a trick to test the sincerity of Constantine's intentions, Constantine passed the test. He replied promptly and sharply that his decision to renounce the throne was irrevocable, and that "unless everything is not arranged according to the will of our deceased Emperor" he would "leave Warsaw only to retire to some greater distance."

🞕 THE DECEMBRIST REVOLT

Still Nicholas hesitated, probably because he knew that many guardsmen were opposed to him. For three weeks Russia was an empire without an emperor. This interregnum was both an opportunity and an embarrassment to the members of the secret societies. It was an opportunity to carry out their planned revolution, but their plans were full of holes and their preparations were practically nil. Finally, after much hesitation, the leaders determined upon an open revolt. It was ill-conceived, abominably led, and amateurishly executed.

On December 13, 1825, some three thousand soldiers were persuaded by the leaders of the Northern Society to assemble in the Senate Square at St. Petersburg to demonstrate in favor of Constantine. That, except for one thing, was the only overt action taken; and there the soldiers stood all day long. (Wits bitterly called it, "the standing revolution.") Nicholas, out of caution or out of good will, made several attempts to open negotiations with the mutineers in order to bring the affair to a peaceful end. But the rebels shot at his emissaries, killing one of them. So, toward the end of the day, cannon were brought up and the mob was struck down by their fire. The revolution of the Northern Society was over.

The Southern Society, meanwhile, had been betrayed by traitors within its ranks, and Pestel had been arrested on December 13. Sergei Muraviev-Apostol undertook to lead some of the troops of the Chernigovsky Regiment in a revolt. The rebellion lasted several days before government troops caught up with the rebels and crushed them. The Decembrist Revolt ended, apparently, in ignominious failure. But, as often happens, the aftermath was more important than the event.

The affair, as Nicholas bitterly remarked, was "a pretty beginning for a reign." His part in the prosecution and persecution of the Decembrists did much to establish his evil reputation among liberals.[1] The affair undoubtedly confirmed Nicholas' aversion to innovations, especially to those of foreign origin. It also made him distrustful of the younger nobility and so led him to exclude that class from the government when possible. Their places were taken by a professional bureaucracy. On the other hand, the Decembrist Revolt forced Nicholas to take notice of the need for reforms and to undertake certain limited improvements.

It has long been the fashion to scorn and ridicule Nicholas for his fear of change and for the repressive measures by which he sought to forestall a recurrence of the movement which culminated in the revolt. But it should be admitted that his judgment of the probable aftereffects of this excursion into radicalism was borne out by events. Alexander Herzen, leader of the next generation of Russian revolutionists, once expressed his sense of obligation to the men of December in these words: "The heritage we received from the Decembrists was the awakened feeling of human dignity, the striving for independence, the hatred of slavery, the respect for Western Europe and for the Revolution, the faith in the possibility of an upheaval in Russia, and the passionate desire to take part in it. . . ." To which N. Lenin added: "The Decembrists awakened Herzen, and Herzen started the revolutionary agitation. The latter was taken up, widened, and strengthened. . . ." Who, in the face of this, can agree that the Decembrists failed, or blame Nicholas for his fears?

TSAR NICHOLAS

Nicholas was always the autocrat, and he became more and more despotic as time went on. His most influential friend and adviser during the first part of his reign was the historian N. M. Karamzin, whom Pushkin forever damned with the lines:

> In his *History,* simplicity and beauty
> Prove without prejudice
> The need for autocracy
> And the charm of the knout.

The poet's judgment was unduly harsh. Karamzin believed that autocracy was necessary for Russia and that citizens owed an absolute obedience to the monarch. He also believed that the monarch was under obligation to govern for the good of the state. And he thought that citizens had both the right and the duty to speak out when the monarch failed to fulfill this obligation.

Revolution was totally repugnant to Karamzin as it was to his imperial master, but neither of them denied the need for change, which they thought could best be carried out autocratically. This philosophy—conservative, certainly, but not necessarily reactionary—was not far removed from that held by Catherine and by Alexander, which again brings up the point that the change was less in the character of the Russian rulers than in the norms and values of the Russian upper classes. Nicholas was aware of the faults and weaknesses of the government and hoped to correct them, but he sought to do it within the existing framework—an impossible task, since the framework itself was faulty. His efforts at reform were, therefore, palliative at best.

It is not just a bow to convention to say that Nicholas ruled Russia for thirty years (1825–55). No other tsar except Peter I played so active a part in so many phases of government administration. In fact, personal government was one of the salient characteristics of Nicholas' reign. He handled many details himself and kept an eye on many more. Quite typical was his comment upon the dissolution of a commission for the codification of law, which had accomplished nothing during the twenty-odd years since its appointment by Alexander:

I have seen that the efforts applied to this subject for a great number of years have been frequently interrupted, and, for this reason, the aim has not been attained. Cordially wishing to secure the progressive completion of this work, I have judged it necessary to take it under my immediate inspection, and I have consequently commanded a special section to be assigned to it in my private chancery.

Most of the state's business came to be handled by this private chancery—"His Majesty's Own Chancery," as it was called. The heads of the sections or departments were men in whom Nicholas felt full confidence. They were given ministerial rank (though their title was Chief Director) and, what was more important, they had ready access to the tsar. Two chief directors and their sections need special mention: Speransky of the Second Section, and Benckendorff of the notorious Third.

Nicholas called upon Michael Speransky to help in the investigation and trial of the Decembrists—a task which he performed well enough to earn the tsar's approval and trust. He was then appointed chief director of the Second Section of His Majesty's Own Chancery and given the difficult and important task of codifying the laws of the empire. This involved the examination and editing of some forty thousand separate acts. Nicholas himself laid down the basis for the codification in a set of eight general instructions. All obsolete and repetitious laws were to be excluded. In the case of contradictory laws, the problem was to be resolved by accepting the most recent law on the ground that it nullified preceding legislation. Laws which dealt with the same thing were to be brought together into one section, and provision was to be made for adding new legislation, which was certain to be needed. The tsar also ordered his chief director to consult specialists to ensure the suitability of the laws which related to their work.

Speransky began his task in 1829 and completed it (or at least the first phase of it) in 1832. He then published a Legal Code together with a Digest of the Code. Both were kept up to date until Speransky's death in 1839. This was a genuine accomplishment even though some possible benefits were nullified by the continuance of "exceptional laws" and by the faults of the judicial system, which was not reformed until a generation later. But the code may properly be held a monument to Speransky and to Nicholas—a monument which would justify their pride in this work.

The other department and its work are bound to seem less creditable. The Third Department was a secret, political police charged with repressing everything which a suspicious mind could possibly interpret as being a threat to the security of the monarch or of the system. A partial listing of its duties and powers includes censorship; surveillance of foreigners and their actions; the gathering of information and the taking of action against dissenters, counterfeiters, and those under police surveillance; the exiling of harmful or suspected persons; and the supervision of all political prisons. The job was entrusted to General Benckendorff because of his actions against the Decembrists.

✿ THOUGHT CONTROL

Nicholas' efforts at thought control—efforts which seemed unrelievedly black to liberals of that day and later, but which appear amateurish, incomplete, and ineffective when compared with the system of Soviet thought control—included both a rigid censorship and a plan for "education." The censorship was enforced by punishments which were always heavy and often cruel, and its weight fell not only upon those who deviated from an increasingly narrow line but also upon those who were suspected of a desire to deviate. In time it became necessary to establish a special commission to censor the censors, and eventually to set up another special commission to watch over the first.

The "education" which Nicholas sought to establish was intended, like that of the Communist rulers of Russia today, to develop "desirable citizens, loyal and meek servants of the state." The tsar was particularly eager that education should not lead those who received it to wish or to strive for a station above that to which they were born. The basic philosophy was like that expressed in a famous and popular English hymn of that period which contained the lines:

> The rich man in his castle
> The poor man at its gate
> God made them, high and lowly,
> And ordered their estate.

In accordance with this general principle, Nicholas' orders on education provided that peasant children might attend only primary schools. Secondary schools and higher education were reserved for children of officials and of nobles. There were five universities in Russia at this time. The total university enrollment in 1836 was 2002; in 1848, 3998; and in 1850, 3018. It would be well to see how the situation appeared to a Russian liberal of the time. Herzen wrote in his *Memoirs:* "Down to 1848 the constitution of our universities was purely democratic. Their doors were open to anyone who could pass the examination provided that he was not a serf or a peasant detained by the village community." That a system which ruled out higher education for between 80 and 90 per cent of the people did not seem undemocratic to Herzen is one measure of the difference between his time and country and ours.

✿ THE SERF PROBLEM

The matter of most immediate and persistent concern to the government was not thought control but the ever-present serf problem. The basic difficulty was that the population continued to increase while the productivity of agriculture remained almost stationary. Between 1816 and 1835, the serf population increased by about a million. There was a definite limit to the number who could profitably be employed at agriculture under the prevailing system and methods, and that limit had been reached. Some of the excess serfs could be absorbed in industry, but not all of them; and industry was not universally profitable. The only place open to most of the serfs was domestic service, which was unproductive. Failure to solve this problem condemned the majority of the Russian people to poverty. It also condemned the government to low tax returns and deficit financing.

The fault lay not in any failure to recognize the problem nor even to understand its causes. The fault lay in the inability or unwillingness of those responsible to attempt to change the system. Nicholas once expressed his opinion on this matter as follows:

There is no doubt that serfdom in its present form is an evil, discernible and apparent to all. But to touch it would bring a still more ruinous evil. Tsar Alexander I intended at the beginning of his reign to free the serfs, but he afterwards gave up the idea as being premature and impossible of fulfillment. I will never venture to do it. Since the time is still far distant when it will be possible to take this step, any excitement about it now would be a criminal conspiracy against the peace and welfare of the state.

This may have been a reprehensible point of view, but it was at least a realistic one insofar as it urged against raising hopes which would be "impossible of fulfillment." Despite his feeling that it was dangerous to touch the problem, Nicholas for years not only had committees at work on it, but also issued numerous decrees designed to alleviate and rectify some of the evils and abuses of the system. The major laws—many of which proved unenforceable—may be briefly summarized.

One law forbade the sale of land without serfs, to prevent serfs from being deprived of their means of livelihood. Another decree prohibited the transfer of serfs to mines and forbade the rental of serfs to persons not legally qualified to own serfs. The Code of Laws limited the authority of the landlords over their serfs and also placed certain specific obligations upon the landlords (for example, to feed their serfs in times of crop failures and famines). Serf estates belonging to the clergy were taken over by the state—a move applauded by the serfs concerned, since the Church was a notoriously hard taskmaster. Another reform transferred state serfs from *barshchina* to *obrok*. This also apparently had serf approval, since the *obrok* was promptly paid and the state revenue was thereby increased. As a result of the work of the various committees and the laws enacted upon their recommendations, there were by 1847 four legal methods of serf emancipation. All of them were permissive, however, and not mandatory. That is to say, the landlords could free their serfs if they wished, but they were not obliged to do so. So few did that the institution of serfdom remained basically unchanged. One important thing was accomplished, however. The precedent of emancipation through government action was thoroughly established.

RUSSIA'S ECONOMIC GROWTH

The first half of the nineteenth century, covering the reigns of Alexander I and Nicholas I, was a period of considerable economic growth and change. Rapid development of a trading economy marked by production for market contrasted with the earlier production for consumption at home. The value of Russian exports increased three times over, and the value of imports almost quadrupled during the period. The growth of the export-import trade was more than matched by an increase in domestic trade. For example, the goods offered for sale at the famous Nizhni-Novgorod Fair of 1824 were valued at 40.5 million rubles. The value of the goods at the 1838 fair was over 129 million rubles. Fairs, which were very frequent and numerous, and peddlers were the major means of distribution and exchange of goods. Baron A. von Haxthausen, who made an extensive study trip through European Russia in 1843, described the relationship of one village to the fairs in the following words:

The village of Vizena is well built, and contains several stone houses. At the last Revision [census] there were 1820 souls in the village Commune. I have remarked that the majority of the inhabitants form an association of boot and shoe makers. There are also six glue and two wax-light [candle] manufactories, and eight large ones in which carpets and felt boots are prepared from horse and cow hair, a branch of industry carried on in many of the houses as a subsidiary occupation. At the Fair of Nizhni Novgorod a quantity of these, valued at 50,000 rubles are sold, and in smaller fairs in the vicinity an additional quantity amounting to 10,000 or 20,000 rubles. . . .

Two hundred of the inhabitants proceed every year to the Fair at Nizhni Novgorod, and remain there two months, working and selling the goods belonging to the villagers.

Elsewhere in his detailed and voluminous published study, Haxthausen described some typical local trade:

Ribinsk is 54 miles from Yaroslaf, and is the center of the internal trade of Russia. All the various products brought by the Volga and its tributary streams, and destined for St. Petersburg have here to be re-embarked in smaller vessels to be sent on the canals. These commodities arrive here in 1700 to 1800 large vessels, and are re-laden upon 6,000 barges and boats, and thus sent on to St. Petersburg; the value of the commodities is said to amount to forty or fifty million rubles. Before the formation [construction] of the canals which unite St. Petersburg with the Volga, Ribinsk was an insignificant township, whose inhabitants paid an obrok either in fish or money. When it rose to the rank of a city the obrok was remitted, and the inhabitants now pay only the usual poll-tax to the Crown, in addition to the town rates [taxes], which amount to 50,000 or 60,000 rubles. . . . The retail trade is carried on by the small burghers and by the Raznotchinstzi, a class between the burghers and the peasants. . . .

There is also considerable trade [in the Government of Yaroslav]. Corn, flour, and iron are brought from the south and east, and sent to the north and west; on the other hand, wine and colonial products come from St. Petersburg, and are sent to western Siberia. The great water and land highways cross each other here. The value of the whole trade is estimated at four million silver rubles. . . .

Haxthausen also took note of two other characteristics of Russian economy and of the reason for their existence. After pointing out that the annual peasant production in one of the districts of Yaroslav amounted to 556 pounds of bread per person, he went on to say:

The principal food of the Russian people consists of bread; potatoes are unknown in most districts; cabbage is the only vegetable which is much used. Animal food, milk, and butter are little eaten. In the army each soldier receives 2½ lbs. of bread a day. A healthy Russian peasant cannot subsist without three pounds; in the harvest he eats five pounds; and in White Russia even as much as seven pounds. If women, old people, and children are counted, one pound and a half must be reckoned for each individual of the population. A man and a woman, according to this calculation, require on an average 1094 pounds of bread in the year. There is always a deficit therefore of 538 pounds of bread for each couple . . . which can only be supplied by importations from other districts, and therefore only with the aid of auxiliary occupations and manufacturing profits, to enable the people to purchase these supplies.

In the northern districts . . . there is a tolerably dense population and little agriculture. The most important sources of production and employment are furnished by the forests . . . [and these] occupy the population during the winter and the short season of spring floods, but they have little to do in the summer. They therefore proceed in large numbers to the regions farther south and assist the inhabitants in field labour and the harvest for wages. Such migratory workers earn from sixty to eighty rubles for the four summer months.

The peasants themselves referred to those who left their native villages in search of work by the very expressive name of the "go-aways." Some "go-aways" worked on the farms, but many sought other kinds of employment. Frequently those with certain skills, as for example in carpentry, banded together to form a co-operative unit (the artel, a word beloved by crossword-puzzle makers). Projects were often financed by the village, which shared in the profits. Speaking of the village of Vizena, Haxthausen reported:

About 500 members of the Commune are always absent with passports; they wander about in search of work as far as Saratof, Astrakhan, Uralsk, and even into the interiour of Siberia. Some remain away ten or fifteen years, others establish themselves permanently in various towns, never returning to their homes; they do not however cease to belong to the Commune, but pay taxes here, and retain their houses, gardens, and communal rights, which they let out or deliver to some other person.

The "industry carried on in many of the houses," of which Haxthausen spoke (called *kustarnichestvo* or *kustarnyi* in Russian), had been a fixture of Russian life from earliest times. Textile production was the most common of these home or cottage industries, and it flourished particularly in the first half of the nineteenth century, competing successfully for many years with the growing factory system. For some time, in fact, the growth of mechanized textile mills stimulated the cottage industries. In the 1840's, the latter exceeded the former. For example, in the government of Vladimir there were eighty thousand looms in the "cottages" as compared to eighteen thousand in the factories. The factory system, however, was growing steadily and even spectacularly, as shown by Table 1, prepared by the Soviet historian Rashin.

TABLE 1

Year	No. of Factories	No. of Workers
1804	2,399	95,200
1811	2,421	137,800
1820	4,578	179,600
1830	5,453	253,900
1840	6,863	435,800
1850	9,843	501,600

The growth of industry was related to the fiscal and tariff policies of Count Kankrin, Minister of Finance from 1823 to 1844. He was a protectionist as far as tariff was concerned because he believed that without a protective tariff Russia would be unable to meet the competition of Western and, particularly, of English industry. He used the tariff, however, not only to protect Russian industry but also to prod it along by occasionally dropping the tariff barriers to stimulate Russian manufacturers to greater efforts by forcing them to meet foreign competition. His fiscal policies were equally shrewd and moderate.

The national treasury was almost empty when he took over, and loans could be made only on very unfavorable terms. By stringent economy, more careful tax collection, and the use of tariffs for revenues as well as for protection (he more than doubled the income from tariffs), he succeeded in improving the financial situation to the point where Russian credit stood fairly high. He also carried out a currency reform which gave Russia a metallic basis for its paper issues and which held the currency fairly stable until the Crimean War. Wars, in general, limited the success of Kankrin's measures. He was able to control the ordinary expenditures of the government, but he could not control the extraordinary expenditures for wars. The wars with Persia and Turkey and the punitive expedition against the Polish revolutionaries were all very expensive and necessitated heavy borrowing. Kankrin could not, therefore, decrease the debt, but he so managed matters as to keep Russian issues at par on the foreign exchanges.

During the late 1820's and 1830's Russian landowners, or at least the more progressive among them, had become very much interested in scientific farming as it was practiced in the West. The use of better implements and of machinery, the practice of crop rotation, the introduction of new products (especially sugar beets), and the development of large-scale farming or ranching were all enthusiastically tried. Experiments with sugar-beet production were the most successful, and the number of

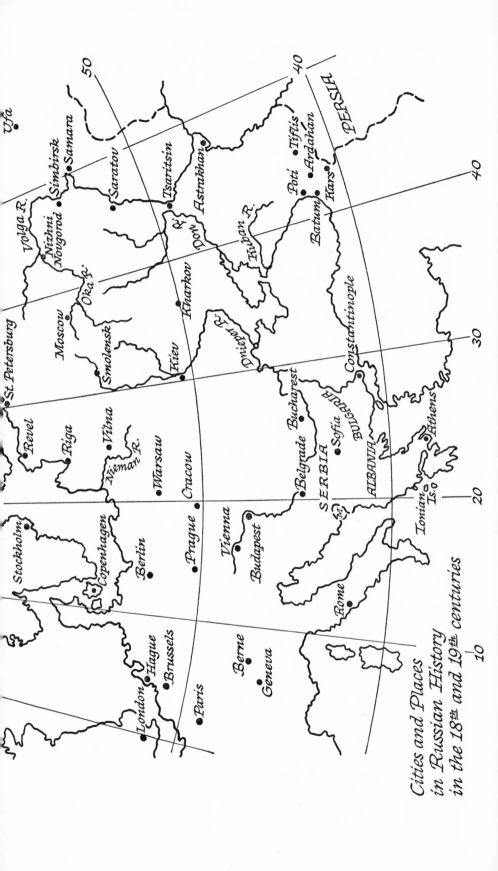

Cities and Places
in Russian History
in the 18ᵗʰ and 19ᵗʰ centuries

sugar-beet factories grew from seven in 1825 to 206 in 1844. But, in general, the practices which worked so well under the vastly different conditions of western Europe did not succeed in Russia, and were largely abandoned. Instead the landlords turned back to the older ways or concentrated on the production of grains. One result was that grain exports, which had amounted to only about 15 per cent of the total value of Russian exports from 1800 to 1844, jumped to over 30 per cent in the following decade and a half. The exports in the late 1830's and early 1840's were not over 454,000 tons a year. During the next ten years, the quantity exported went up to 918,000 tons a year. This was made possible only by putting more land into grain, since the yield per acre did not increase. It needs to be added that there were four very serious crop failures during Nicholas' reign.

"INNER LIBERATION"

The discussion of Russian foreign policy during Nicholas' administration is contained in the next chapter. But there is still another aspect of Russian history during these years. Russian historians used to speak of the tsardom of Nicholas as the "reign of contrasts—a period of outward repression and inner liberation." What they had in mind were the intellectual, artistic, literary, and philosophical movements of the period. There were two main lines of philosophical thought in the period, Slavophilism and Westernism—which underlay many of the other artistic and intellectual activities.

None of these were popular movements in the sense of mass participation. It is probable that less than ten out of every hundred Russian citizens were literate. "Literacy" is not, of course, the same thing as being "educated" or "intellectual." The intelligentsia was extremely small. It consisted of that minute, educated, articulate fraction of the population which was concerned with art, letters, criticism, philosophy, and abstract discussions of abstruse theories and principles. These were, with few exceptions, the Slavophils and the Westerners.

SLAVOPHILISM

There are still disputes over the genesis of Slavophilism. One Polish scholar traces it to Boleslaw in the eleventh century, and claims it as a Polish movement. Another theory credits it to a litterateur named Kollar of the late eighteenth and nineteenth century. It is more generally agreed that the idea was first expressed by a Croatian priest of the seventeenth century. His name, which is spelled in four or five different ways, was Yuri Krizhanich. It is also generally agreed that the movement owed a good deal to the influence of the German philosopher von Schelling,

that romantic denouncer of rationalism, that mystic, and transcendental-
ist who dreamed of subordinating the individual to a kind of world-
collectivism. Whatever its origins, Slavophil philosophy in Russia first
appeared in the literary circles of Moscow in the 1840's. The reason
for this rather odd place of origin is that literally no other forums were
available as a result of Nicholas' system of thought control. A few more
or less tame literati were allowed to speak, though their voices were
muted by censorship. Literary societies or "reading circles" were allowed
to exist, though they were regarded with suspicion and their members
suffered police surveillance and frequent punishment. But they did offer
an opportunity for discussions, so that literature became the medium of
political and social criticism, and the "reading circles" very frequently
dealt with nonliterary matters. In the case of Slavophilism, it was first
introduced as a quasi-literary, quasi-religious movement.

The man commonly thought of as the founder of Russian Slavophilism
(as distinct from other and earlier varieties) was Ivan Kireevski (1806–
56), the scion of a well-to-do family, who had been educated abroad and
who had come under the direct influence of both Hegel and von Schelling. Kireevski returned from Berlin with a Western orientation, but,
under the influence of his wife, he modified his position, although he
never became an indiscriminate enemy of the West as did some of his
disciples. He accepted a romanticized notion of the past glory and the
present mission of Russia.

Kireevski maintained that Russia and Europe were fundamentally different because of their religions. Russia, he said, was founded on and
guided by Eastern Orthodoxy. This made it the land of faith and of
divinely revealed truth. Europe had lost its faith because of the heresies
of Roman Catholicism and Protestantism. The remaining tenets of his
philosophy were equally fantastic from an historical point of view. He
held that the state in Russia had grown naturally out of the mir, whereas
the state in Europe had been built upon the subjugation and submission
of the people; that Russian law had grown organically out of popular conviction, but that European law had been imposed by conquerors; that
under the Russian mir the individual had value, while the practice of
private property in Europe made the individual merely subsidiary to the
soil. And, echoing the Theory of the Third Rome, Kireevski taught that
Russia had received true Christianity and with it, true civilization; that
she had cherished these gifts and preserved them unsullied. On these
bases, he concluded that Russia had a mission to carry the true faith to
the West and to develop a new civilization compounded of the best that
both Russia and the West had to offer.

Contemporary with Kireevski was Alexius Khomiakov (Homyakov), who was the great champion of Russian Orthodoxy against Roman Catholicism and Protestantism. His Slavophilism was much more nationalistic than was Kireevski's. A third Slavophil, born and bred in the same circumstances of wealth and privilege as the other two, was Constantine Aksakov (1817–60). He modified the philosophy by taking the position that Russia prior to Peter the Great had been free from vices, if not from sin; and that Peter had introduced slavery from the servile West. Russia, said Aksakov, was both a country and a state. The country was the organic fusion of communities into one. Its essence was the mir. The state represented coercive authority imported from abroad, made necessary because of human frailties. The history of Russia, according to Aksakov, was the story of the struggle between these two.

The link between Slavophilism and the movement known as Pan-Slavism was Ivan Aksakov (1823–86), brother of Constantine. His devotion to Slavdom sprang from his religious Orthodoxy. His thesis was that the Russian Slavs were the only possessors and defenders of Orthodoxy, which he regarded as the only pure form of Christianity and the *sine qua non* of civilization. The archenemy of Orthodoxy and therefore of Russia he held to be Roman Catholicism. He concluded that Russia had a divine mission to free her blood brothers by extending the Orthodox faith to them.

Essentially the Slavophils took the position that Russia and Europe each had a peculiar native character and genius, and therefore it was wrong to try to force Russia to follow a European pattern. They propounded an ideal of Orthodoxy and of a benevolent, patriarchal autocracy. In support of their views, they turned to revelation and tradition, denying rationalism and exalting emotionalism and faith. The later Slavophils were increasingly nationalistic. Whereas Kireevski had recognized and admitted Russia's failings and mistakes, the later Slavophils glossed over such things or ignored them. The early ones dreamed of an ideal Orthodoxy which had probably never existed; their later followers sometimes confused Orthodoxy with the state Church. The same thing happened with respect to the autocracy. For these reasons, the Slavophils came to be considered the reactionary defenders of the classic formula of Nicholas' reign—"Orthodoxy, Autocracy, Nationalism." This was inaccurate. Of course, the individual followers of Slavophilism differed on many points, but most of them favored a curtailment of bureaucratic powers, an increase in personal liberty, and the ending of serfdom. In these things they were no less "progressive" and "liberal" than their opponents, the Westerners.

WESTERNISM

Westernism was at first quite similar to Slavophilism but the two gradually diverged on certain issues. The Westerners prided themselves on being rationalistic, and, in terms of philosophical groupings, they were. But in practice they were as often divorced from reality as were their opponents. While the Slavophils were oriented toward Orthodoxy, the Westerners turned from that either to formalism or to agnosticism. The greatest difference between the two, however, was the Westerners' thesis that Russia and western Europe were not different in kind but only in degree. Russia, they said, was following the same line of development previously traced by the West, and the prime task of Russia was to catch up with Europe. The Westerners, in other words, denied that the Russian state, or the Russian country, or the Russian laws, or the Russian culture was unique in origin and nature. These things, the Westerners argued, had grown up along lines analogous to their development in the West. They wished to speed up the progress by adopting the best that Europe had to offer (a position not far from that of Kireevski). One institution which they much admired and wished to establish in Russia was constitutional government. In this, as in some other things, they were opposed by the Slavophils. But the two were in agreement in their patriotism, their opposition to the existing government, their idealization of the Russian peasant and of the institution of the mir, and their opposition to the bourgeois societies of western Europe.

CRITICS AND LITTERATEURS

These basic approaches were reflected in the intellectual, artistic, and literary works of the intelligentsia. Whereas Karamzin, a forerunner of the Slavophils, wrote a history of the monarchy, S. M. Soloviev, who held that Russian and European developments ran along parallel lines, wrote a history of the Russian people. Opposed to Kireevski's faith in Orthodoxy and his conviction that Russia would be great because of the purity of her faith was P. Chaadayev (1794–1856), who held that Orthodoxy had failed to provide spiritual leadership for Russia. In his *Philosophical Letters* (published in 1836), Chaadayev expressed doubts of Russia's past greatness and attacked her cultural backwardness. As punishment for this frankly expressed view, the tsar officially declared Chaadayev insane. Against the Aksakovs may be set Vissarion Belinsky (1811–48), probably the greatest of the Russian literary critics of the nineteenth century. Belinsky made literary criticism the vehicle for his political and social ideas, which were Western in their general orientation. Belinsky's faith was in reason and knowledge, not in theology and revelation. He agreed with the Slavophils that the individual was less important than the social group, but insisted that the group must allow individuals scope for the expression of their personalities.

Belinsky wrote to Gogol:

> You do not realize that Russia must see its salvation not in mysticism or pietism, but in the advance of civilization, education, and humanity—in awakening a feeling of dignity among people lost for so many centuries in dirt and ordure. . . . The most burning national questions now are the abolition of serfdom and of bodily punishment, together with a strict administration of existing laws.[2]

The outstanding intellectual development—partly by reason of the circumstance of censorship—was in the literary field. The giants were the poets Alexander Sergeevich Pushkin (1799–1837) and Michael Yurievich Lermontov (1814–41). They were primarily artists, but they were politically aware, as witness Lermontov's *Prophecy,* or these lines from Pushkin's *To Chaadayev:*

> Comrade, believe: joy's star will leap
> Upon our sight, a radiant token;
> Russia will rouse from her long sleep;
> And where autocracy lies broken,
> Our names shall yet be graven deep.

The first great genius of Russian prose was Gogol, whose work fell wholly within the reign of Nicholas. The tsar openly recognized the justice of Gogol's descriptions of the bureaucracy. Nicholas also extended his favor to the famous teller of fables Ivan Krylov (1768–1844), whose fables in verse wittily and satirically depicted the official world. One slightly lesser figure, Goncharov (1812–91), and three of the greatest figures in Russian literature—Turgenev, Dostoevsky, and Tolstoy—belong partly to Nicholas' reign also.

Goncharov's work *Oblomov* depicted a weak and charming man whose intentions were of the best but who somehow never accomplished what he intended. So telling was the picture, and so truly drawn the likeness, that the word "oblomovism" entered the language to describe good-natured indolence and well-intentioned ineffectualness. Ivan Turgenev (1818–83) is best known for his novel *Fathers and Sons,* in which he first applied the terms nihilist and nihilism to the leading intellectual movement of his time. His *Sportsman's Sketches,* however, is perhaps more interesting because of its brilliant pictures of Russian rural life. Some critics have held—with certain exaggeration—that this book had the same relation to serf emancipation as Mrs. Stowe's *Uncle Tom's Cabin* had to the freeing of the slaves in the United States.

Fedor Mikhailovich Dostoevsky (1821–81) is familiar in the West both for his novels (*Crime and Punishment, The Idiot,* and *The Brothers Karamazov*) and for his reputation as the great interpreter of "the Slavic soul." Count Lev Nikolaevich Tolstoy (1828–1910), novelist, mystic, and philosopher, has perhaps the widest reputation of the three. Many who never heard of Tolstoy and who certainly never read any of his works have seen the movie based upon his *Anna Karenina.* And who has not promised himself that he would some day finish the reading of *War and Peace?* The latter, by the way, is more a saga of family life than the great war story which it is popularly supposed to be.

When to these names are added those of the poet Zhukovsky, the historian Pogodin, the playwright Griboedov, and the poet Nekrasov—all of whom lived and worked in Nicholas' time—it is easy to see why this has been called the golden age of Russian literature. And when to the list of literati are added the name of Michael Ivanovich Glinka (1803–57), composer of *A Life for the Tsar,* and that of the greatest Russian romantic painter, Alexander Ivanov (1801–58), it becomes clear why Herzen called Nicholas' reign a period of inner liberation despite its outward slavery.

CHAPTER XII

The Outward Policies, 1825-55

The "Near Eastern Question," which was the central problem of Nicholas' foreign policy, was a complicated interplay of often conflicting national interests. The issues, the interests, and the crises were all more complex than this account will indicate because we shall concentrate on the Russian part of the story.

The power of the Ottoman Empire had been slowly decaying for generations, and it appeared to observers of that day that the final collapse of the Sublime Porte (the sultans' government) was an immediate prospect. As the sultans' grip upon their possessions seemed to grow more and more feeble, ambitious men and nations schemed to get a share. The problem was how to divide the Ottoman Empire without upsetting the balance of power and without causing a general European war. It was made more complicated because "the sick man of Europe," though obviously moribund, stubbornly refused to die. European diplomats hung around like ambulance-chasing shysters, or unscrupulous undertakers —scarcely able to wait until the patient expired. While they were waiting, they kept a wary eye on one another to see that no one hastened the demise.

🐝 NICHOLAS AND NESSELRODE

Nicholas was himself the chief agent of Russian foreign policy. The characterizations of Nicholas run all the way from pictures of a stupid, narrow-minded, black-hearted reactionary who wanted to stop progress everywhere, to fulsome eulogies reported to their sovereigns by foreign diplomats. Typical of the eulogies were the following comments made by Austrian and French agents during the early years of the reign:

His mind is perfectly organized [wrote one of the Austrians]. His ideas are clear, precise. He has a strong will which he knows how to control, and, moreover, he knows how to command obedience. . . .

It cannot be denied [said a French diplomat] that Nicholas has outstanding qualities and praiseworthy intentions. One sees in him a righteous heart, a noble and elevated soul. His love of justice and his faithfulness to his pledged word have become proverbial among the Russians. Young, active, enjoying good health, endowed with an attractive appearance . . . possessing that eloquence which moves crowds . . . the Emperor Nicholas is, in a word . . . the sort of person met only once in a century.

The truth seems to lie between the extremes of adulation and vilification. Nicholas was physically well favored. He looked like a king, which is an advantage if you are one. He was honest and straightforward— tactless on many occasions—and he had a strong sense of duty. His mind was rather slow and he was not prolific in ideas, but many of his ideas were quite sound, and what he knew, he knew thoroughly. Routine details attracted him, and he spent more time than a top authority should on petty matters. Pushkin once called him "an execrable sovereign, but a remarkable colonel." This was a demotion from Nicholas' own ranking of himself, since he had once remarked, "I am only a simple brigadier general." Superficially he resembled Wellington, England's famous Iron Duke—a great soldier but something less than a great statesman or diplomat.

Aside from Nicholas himself, the chief agent of his foreign policy was a professional diplomat who had served Alexander I. Count Karl Robert Nesselrode (immortalized in a culinary sort of way by the pudding which was named after him) was a Baltic German. That is to say, he was a descendant of one of the German families whose ancestral homes were in the Baltic regions which Russia had conquered. (There were always a large number of Balts in the service of the Russian government, particularly in the Foreign Office.) Nesselrode, though a Russian citizen, had been born in Lisbon, where his diplomat father was stationed, and had spent many years in western Europe. Educated in Germany, he had served briefly in the Russian army and navy before entering Alexander's diplomatic service. His first important diplomatic post was Paris, where he served in 1807–8. Returning to Russia, Nesselrode became in 1812 the chief professional diplomat, although he was not made foreign minister until 1816. He held that office for forty years, and also served Nicholas as vice-chancellor and then as chancellor of the Empire. Under Alexander and also—to a lesser extent—under Nicholas, Nesselrode was rather the mouthpiece of the emperor than the actual maker of policy. He has been described as a true courtier, which is not always a compliment. He was not a yes-man, though he always eventually bowed to the imperial will. He did not hesitate to disagree with his emperor nor to argue his case, but once the sovereign had ordered, Nesselrode obeyed.

Because he crushed the Polish Revolution of 1830, wished to act against the French revolutionaries of 1830 and 1848, did act against the Hungarian revolutionaries of the latter year, and intervened in the domestic affairs of Prussia, Nicholas has been ridiculed as the "gendarme of Europe." It is true that in the name of legitimacy he intervened in support of reactionary groups and it was his calmly arrogant assumption of the right to intervene which infuriated many Western politicians. Their resentment and the hostility of the "liberals" partially explain the opprobrious reputation which Nicholas has generally borne.

Russia had emerged from the Napoleonic wars as the most powerful nation of the Continent. This fact, generally resented by the West, is usually deliberately ignored or forgotten, and it is mistakenly assumed that France was still *the* Great Power of continental Europe.

🌐 RUSSIA'S POSITION

Russia's neighbors on the northwest were Norway and Sweden, both minor Powers. In Central Europe, Russia (which in fact if not in law included the Kingdom of Poland) was bounded by the Kingdom of Prussia and the Empire of Austria. Prussia was gaining in strength; Austria, declining; and neither was on a par with Russia. On the southern and southwestern borders of the Russian Empire was the decadent Ottoman Empire. In western Europe, France was still a first-class Power, but she no longer held the hegemony, although she usually acted as if she did. After all, despite the speed with which France resumed her place and her pretensions, she had been soundly beaten in the Napoleonic wars. The other Continental states—the Italies, the Netherlands, Spain, Portugal, and Switzerland—were comparatively insignificant. Only Great Britain, who was the dominant maritime, mercantile, industrial, and financial Power of the world equaled Russia. She and Russia were the Very Great Powers of Europe—the one, a whale; the other, an elephant. It was a fixed policy of the whale to see that the elephant did not become amphibious. Britain set herself, in other words, to see that the great land power of Russia did not attain a position from which to challenge British mastery of the seas. To Britain, this seemed a necessity of self-defense. To Russia, it seemed like willful obstruction of natural and justifiable Russian expansion. Anglo-Russian hostility was a constant of nineteenth-century diplomacy. In the Near East, British opposition to Russia began in 1799 when Pitt decided that Russian advance was a threat to British trade and to British political power. To limit the advance he supported the sultan, a policy which the British followed with only brief interruptions thenceforward.

A quick review of Russo-Turk relations in the seventeenth century will pull the threads together. The first major Russian victory over the Turks was Peter the Great's temporary conquest and occupation of Azov. This he lost when the Turks defeated him during his long struggle with Sweden. Anna won her war against the sultan, but lost the peace because of French support of Turkey. Russia gained some land, but was forced to destroy her military and naval establishments in the Black Sea region. Catherine was both stronger and more fortunate. She twice defeated the Turks and so won ownership of the Crimea and of the northern Black Sea coast from the River Bug almost to the Caucasus. She also forced the Turks to permit Russian merchant shipping on the Black Sea, thus breaking the ancient Turk monopoly. The Turks also promised Catherine that Russian merchant ships might pass through the Straits freely in times of peace, but they consistently dishonored this pledge until after their defeat by Nicholas in 1828–29. The Straits are formed by three distinct, continuous sections, each of which has a name. The short and narrow channel leading out of the Black Sea is the Bosporus. Constantinople (Istanbul) is situated on the European shore of the Bosporus near where it widens into the second section, the Sea of Marmora. From that sea another narrow body of water, the Dardanelles, leads to the Aegean. Neither the Dardanelles nor the Bosporus is more than a few miles across at its widest point, so they can be controlled by shore batteries or small fleets. These were maintained by the Turks, and as long as the Ottoman Empire was strong the Turks controlled the Straits. When the sultans' powers noticeably failed, Russia reached out for the Bosporus while France and Britain sought the Dardanelles. The competition gave rise to a series of crises and clashes which reached one climax in the Crimean War.

🖋 FIRST NEAR EASTERN CRISIS

Nicholas had inherited from Alexander the makings of the first Near Eastern crisis of his reign. In furtherance of a policy of weakening the Sublime Porte, Alexander had encouraged the development of separatist and revolutionary movements among the sultan's subjects. One such project was spear-headed by an ostensibly Greek organization called the *Hetairia Philike* (Friends of Antiquity). This group was led by a Russian army officer, Alexander Ipsilanti, and it had been founded in the Russian city of Odessa. In 1821, Ipsilanti started a revolution against the Turks. It failed, but it helped inspire another and more vigorous revolution in southern Greece, which was marked by brutalities on both sides. The murder of some Greek Christians by the Turks in retaliation for actions of the rebels led Alexander to send an ultimatum to Sultan Mahmud II. This was rejected by Mahmud, diplomatic relations were severed, and war seemed imminent.

Austria and Britain, however, were able to dissuade Alexander from going to war to support a revolution. What the Austrians and British really feared, of course, was unilateral Russian action which might have led to Russian gains. The position of all the European governments vis à vis the Greek war was peculiar. The governments were all inclined to support the "legitimate" authority of the sultan. But the heroic struggles of the Greeks caught the romantic fancies of the upper classes, who began to press the governments to aid the rebels. Religious prejudice was involved also, since the Turks were Moslems and the Greeks were Christians. The situation was further complicated when Mahmud enlisted the aid of his nominal vassal, the powerful and virtually independent Mehemet Ali, pasha of Egypt. Mehemet, who had already conquered Crete, now invaded southern Greece and defeated the rebels.

The Russian government was not, of course, moved by the pleas of Russian liberals—especially since most of them had been involved in the Decembrist movement—but Russia did not want to see a strong and revitalized Turko-Egyptian Power. Nicholas' government continued to toy with the idea of unilateral action. This prospect alarmed the British who sought to forestall it by promoting multilateral action. They sold Nicholas on a scheme for joint Russo-British co-operation against Mahmud and Mehemet (the Petersburg Agreement of 1826), and persuaded the French to join the arrangement (Treaty of London, 1827). In implementation of these agreements, a combined Russian, French, and British fleet was sent to watch over the Turko-Egyptian fleet. The two were anchored in Navarino Bay, when a set of curious mischances led to a battle between them. The Turko-Egyptian fleet was destroyed. The British and French were appalled at this weakening of Turkish power, which was the reverse of what they had intended, but the damage was done. Mahmud demanded reparations and threatened a "holy war" when the demands were refused. Nicholas thereupon seized the initiative and declared war on Turkey (April, 1828).

Exactly what Nicholas hoped to gain or intended to do is still not wholly clear. After Russian troops had conquered Adrianople and come very close to Constantinople (1829), the tsar offered peace terms to the sultan. Then Nicholas apparently began to prepare to capture Constantinople and the Dardanelles while coincidentally announcing that he did not wish to take either. Should one believe his words or his deeds? Europe didn't know. If his renunciation was sincere why did he prepare an attack? But if he really wanted Constantinople, why didn't he make the most of this very excellent opportunity to take it? The answer seems to lie in the military situation. The Russian army which had crossed the Balkan mountains and captured Adrianople was dangerously exposed at the end of long and uncertain lines of communication. Reserves were limited. Dibich, the army commander, reported that the Turkish forces confronting him were growing in strength and his position was precarious. Of course the Russians wanted to conceal this situation and preparations for continuing the advance were one way of doing it. Nicholas was bluffing in the hope of a finesse. Nicholas was probably relieved when he received word that Mahmud had capitulated.

The war was profitable for Russia in some ways. She got the eastern Black Sea coast almost to Batum, the Danube Delta, and an indemnity. The Danubian Principalities (Moldavia and Wallachia) were granted autonomy but kept under Turkish sovereignty, and Russia was allowed to keep an army of occupation in them until the indemnity was paid. This took five years and enabled Russia greatly to increase her influence in the principalities. Even if there had been other causes, this alone would have kept alive Europe's distrust of Russia.

The Vienna Settlement of 1815 had created a semiautonomous Kingdom of Poland which remained closely bound to Russia. This was a most unsatisfactory situation from the Polish point of view, and the Polish nationalists also bitterly resented the fact that the new Kingdom of Poland constituted only a fraction of what had been the Republic of Poland. For fifteen years the Polish nationalists dreamed and planned for a revolution which would throw off Russian control and restore the old Poland. Action was precipitated by news of the successful French Revolution of 1830, which encouraged the Poles, and by Nicholas' proposal to use a Polish army against the revolutionary governments of France and Belgium. The Polish rebels won some quick but very transient successes. They expelled the Russian garrison, declared that the Romanov dynasty over Poland was ended, and established a revolutionary government. Internal dissensions soon weakened the revolutionaries, however, and they were defeated during 1831 by a Russian army. Most of the Polish leaders fled to France, and the revolution collapsed. The Polish constitution was abolished, and Poland was left with only a slight degree of autonomy in administration. Its political rights were taken away, and a policy of attempted Russification was begun.

STRATEGIC ANALYSIS

There were three possible policies with regard to Turkey, all having historical precedents, which Nicholas could choose. One was to revive the

Greek project. This called for the destruction of the Ottoman Empire and its partition in some fashion. The second was to make an alliance with the Porte on such terms as would open the Straits to Russia while closing them to her enemies. The third was to see that Turkey was kept alive but weak. Nicholas appointed a special Committee of Seven in 1829 to consider these and other possible alternatives. Nesselrode, who was a member of the committee, argued that a weak Turkey, subject to revolts and unable to offer strong resistance to Russia, best accorded with Russian interests. Russia should try to keep Turkey alive while at the same time remaining constantly alert and ready to take the most energetic measures in case of a Turkish collapse. The committee accepted this view and further agreed that the expulsion of the Turks from Europe might lead to a Turkish renaissance and an all-Moslem union against Russia which would gravely threaten Russian interests in the Caucasus and Transcaucasia. As to the complete destruction and partition of the Ottoman Empire, the committee felt that it would be impossible to exclude the other Powers from participation. They warned that in this event Austria would take Bosnia, Albania, and Montenegro; France, Egypt; and Britain, Crete and the Aegean Islands. This would mean that Russia would be confronted by three strong neighbors instead of one weak one.

The committee also pointed out that the internationalization of the Straits would give Britain and France free access to the Black Sea. This was a matter of consequence in view of the relative naval strength of Russia, France, and Britain. Nicholas found when he took stock at his accession that the Russian navy had been neglected. He saw to it that the fleet was rehabilitated. An English naval officer who inspected the fleet at Kronstadt in 1828 reported that it was well equipped and in excellent condition. But it was never of a strength comparable to that of either France or Britain. When these two Powers combined, as they frequently did during these years, the disparity was further increased. This meant that if the Straits were open to all, the southern coasts of Russia would be exposed to superior naval forces. As long as the Turkish fortifications commanded the Straits and so long as Russia and Turkey were at peace, the Black Sea was relatively safe for Russian shipping. Against this advantage had to be weighed the inconvenience which closure of the Straits sometimes caused Russia. Successive Russian governments judged that the advantages were greater than the disadvantages, and this was a powerful motive in determining Russian policy toward Turkey and the Straits.

It was the unanimous conclusion and recommendation of the Committee of Seven that self-interest required Russia to try to prevent the destruction of the sultan's power. This meant self-denial as well as opposition to partition by any other Power. On the other hand, the committee also urged that Russia always be ready to forestall the other Powers in the event of a Turkish collapse. One preparation suggested was an international agreement for partition on future delivery, as it were. Nicholas accepted the committee's report and its ideas became a permanent fixture in his mind. Years later (in 1844) he told the British ministers, "I do not wish to establish myself in Constantinople, [but] I shall never consent to either England or France establishing herself there. . . ."

There were great risks inherent in the idea of future partition, not the least of which was caused by mutual suspicions. Russia was forever anticipating that some other Power would try to precipitate the collapse of the Porte, so preparedness became the standing order of procedure. Every Russian preparation immediately aroused the fears and distrust of the other Powers, who were sure that Russia was trying to get ahead of them. Their fears were enhanced and apparently justified by the activities of some lesser Russian officials who did not agree with the committee's recommendation and who wished to take the initiative against Turkey. Nicholas' orders for preparedness gave these people frequent opportunities to act contrary to the tsar's real policy. The other Powers suspected collusion between the tsar and his underlings and concluded that imperial protestations of good will toward the Porte were made in bad faith. Furthermore, the growth of Slavophilism, Pan-Slavism, and Russian nationalism created strong pressure groups who favored vigorous action against Turkey. The public pronouncements of these groups—and, even more, intelligence reports of their nonpublic doings and sayings—seemed to the West to confirm its worst suspicions. On the other hand, the attacks upon Nicholas by the refugee Russian liberals and Poles who had found asylum in the West, as well as the deeds and words of official and unofficial Frenchmen and Britishers, seemed very menacing to the Russians. The circle of fear tightened, pressures mounted within it, and more crises developed.

SECOND CRISIS

Mehemet Ali's demand that Mahmud award Syria to him in repayment for his aid against the Greeks produced the "Second Near Eastern Crisis." Mahmud refused, whereupon Mehemet revolted and sent his son, Ibrahim, to conquer Syria. Ibrahim soon defeated the Turkish forces and threatened the overthrow of the sultanate. Mahmud was in desperate need of aid, but he distrusted the French, and the British were temporarily unable to help him. The only remaining alternative was to accept Nicholas' proffered assistance. Mahmud was reluctant to do so because he shrewdly suspected that a bill would be presented. It was this or lose his throne, however, so he accepted the offer.

Russian troops promptly entered the Ottoman Empire and appeared along the shores of the Bosporus in February, 1833. The British and the French were aghast. The French tried to meet the situation by arranging a settlement between Mahmud and Mehemet. If this could be done, they thought, Russian aid would then be superfluous and the Russian troops could be sent home. They persuaded the sultan to offer some concessions, but not enough to satisfy the pasha, and, anyway, the Russians refused to leave. Then the French combined with the British to force both Mahmud and Mehemet into reaching a settlement which ended the revolt. Still the Russians stayed, and when a Franco-British fleet was sent to the Dardanelles (June, 1833) the situation became very tense indeed.

Nicholas' position was very strong—probably much stronger than that of Britain and France. Yet he did not take advantage of it either by overthrowing the sultan or making his occupation of the Bosporus permanent. This is convincing evidence of the sincerity with which he had adopted the policy recommended by the Committee of Seven. The tsar, however, exacted a price for his help to the Turks, just as Mahmud had expected. It has been suggested that this was also a price for withdrawal, but that is not certain. The terms were recorded in the Russo-Turk Treaty of Unkiar Skelessi (1833), which set up an eight-year defensive alliance between the two countries. The treaty also contained a secret clause which dealt with the closure of the Straits to warships. Guizot and Palmerston, the chief statesmen of France and Britain, believed that this clause closed the Straits to all except Russian war vessels. Neither Nicholas nor Nesselrode, however, placed this interpretation on it. Nesselrode, in fact, vetoed a suggestion that the Russian Baltic fleet be sent through the Straits into the Black Sea on the ground that this would be a violation of Unkiar Skelessi. Closure of the Straits was not Russia's real aim in this treaty. Her true purpose was to get an exclusive right of intervention in Turkey and, at the same time, to accustom the Turks to the idea that they were really Russia's vassals. This was part of the Russian preparation to seize the Bosporus in case the Ottoman Empire fell.

The European statesmen of that day were quite sincere in their belief that Russia had used the opportunity to get exclusive rights over the Straits. Guizot and Palmerston obviously had to act on the basis of what they thought and not on the basis of what we know to have been the real situation. They thought they had to break a Russian strangle hold on the Straits, and they spent their best efforts for several years in trying to do so. This naturally alarmed and angered the Russians, who therefore strengthened their Black Sea fleet, built up their Crimean fortifications, and kept large military forces virtually at combat strength and readiness in that area. These things naturally produced a reaction in the West, particularly because they coincided with a series of agreements among the sovereigns of Russia, Prussia, and Austria. Since the agreements were secret, the West was free to assume the worst, that the Holy Alliance of Alexander had been reactivated and given teeth.

🜚 THE AUSTRIAN, RUSSIAN, PRUSSIAN AGREEMENTS

Four treaties or agreements were made among Austria, Russia, and Prussia (the A.-R.-P. Powers) during 1833. The first provided common position on the Belgian and Dutch problems.[1] The second, known as the Munchengräetz Agreement, dealt with Turkey and Egypt. The third had to do with Poland, and the fourth, the so-called Berlin Agreement, bound the group to common action against revolutionaries. The initiative which led to these agreements came from Metternich and represented a reversal in Austrian policy. Austria had favored the Turks and opposed the Russians during the events of 1827 to 1829, but Metternich recognized that Russia and Austria shared a common interest in the maintenance of peace and order. Nicholas was understandably suspicious of Metternich's first overtures, but the latter's loyal co-operation with Nicholas against Louis Philippe of France removed his doubts. Both Austria and Russia subscribed wholeheartedly to the doctrine of intervention promulgated by the general European Congress at Troppau (1820).[2] They were of one mind on two points: their hatred of revolution and their hostility toward Britain. Metternich further wooed and won Nicholas by supporting the Russian actions against the Poles in 1830.

The most sweeping and most important of the four agreements was the fourth, the Berlin Agreement, which re-established the spirit if not the precise language of the Troppau Protocol. But the one which excited the most animosity and the greatest apprehension was the Munchengräetz Agreement. This dealt only with how to maintain the political and territorial integrity of the Ottoman Empire, and it actually contained a guarantee of the *status quo*. The British, and the French to a lesser extent, mistakenly believed that the Munchengräetz deal was precisely the reverse, namely, an arrangement for the partition of Turkey by Austria and Russia. The error was understandable, given the situation that existed, but it was certainly unfortunate. Munchengräetz did not revive the Holy Alliance, which the British also mistakenly supposed it did, but it led to a personal *rapprochement* among the sovereigns of the A.-R.-P. group, and to an understanding among them which was quite important. It also contributed to the general atmosphere of suspicion and tension which formed the background of the "Third Near Eastern Crisis."

🏛 THIRD CRISIS

This crisis involved British, Egyptian, French, and Turkish actions. The British had become interested in developing a new route to India across Asia Minor. This would have served the double purpose of providing an alternative route to the one across Egypt and of hampering possible French or Russian advances in Asia Minor. The sultan was complaisant, or relatively so, but Mehemet Ali did not relish increased British power and he therefore was opposed. Palmerston decided that British interests would best be served by supporting the sultan both against Mehemet and against Russia. The situation was complicated by French support of Mehemet in his anti-British and anti-Turkish activities.

In 1839 Mehemet and Ibrahim sent their forces against those of the newly enthroned boy sultan, Abdul Mejid, who was soon ready to yield. Britain and France temporarily submerged their differences over Mehemet in mutual concern lest Russia use the alliance of Unkiar Skelessi as an excuse to seize the Straits under the pretext of defending them against the Egyptians. A Franco-British fleet was sent to the Aegean with orders to prevent such Russian action. Russia made no move to take the Straits. Instead she joined the other Powers in collective actions and assured the British that she would not enter the Bosporus unless the British first entered the Dardanelles. The crisis now shifted from a Russo-British to a Franco-British conflict.

Palmerston demanded strong measures against Mehemet. Thiers of France firmly rejected Palmerston's demands and prepared to intervene alone. Britain then joined with the A.-R.-P. Powers to issue a quasi ultimatum to Mehemet who, sure of French support, rejected it. War again seemed imminent, but the French drew back and this crisis passed. The Near Eastern pot continued to boil over, however. Austria now began to plot with Great Britain against Russia. This was potentially extremely dangerous to Russian interests so she sought to counter it, and finally did, by getting the Powers to join in guaranteeing the Straits—a task which involved a great deal of complicated diplomacy. The Straits Convention of 1841, signed by the five Great Powers (Russia, Britain, France, Austria, and Prussia) was the instrument of agreement. Westerners who had been so unduly suspicious of the Unkiar Skelessi

The Black Sea Basin — mid-nineteenth century

Poti

BLACK SEA

SEA OF AZOV

Kuban R.

CRIMEA

Sevastopol

Dnieper R.

Bug R.

Odessa

Dniester R.

BESSARABIA

Pruth R.

MOLDAVIA

AUSTRIAN EMPIRE

WALLACHIA

Danube R.

OTTOMAN

EMPIRE

Bosporus

Constantinople

MARMORA

Dardanelles

AEGEAN SEA

Treaty regarded this convention as a reversal of that treaty and, therefore, as a major diplomatic defeat for Russia. This interpretation has been repeated by many Western historians as well as by Slavophils and Russian nationalists. The only possible justification for their thesis is that the convention formally replaced a unilateral guarantee with a multilateral one. But even this did not mean quite what it appeared to, because, two months after the signature of the treaty, Russia had admitted Austria as joint guarantor, through the medium of the Munchengräetz Agreement. The Straits Convention reduced the shares of both Russia and Austria. Since it also ended the Austro-British intrigue, Nesselrode felt that he had gained much and paid little. He regarded the convention as a diplomatic victory, which, if one looks at the substance rather than the formality, it was.

Nicholas explored the problem of Turkey with the British government in the course of a state visit which he paid Victoria in 1844. He was followed by Nesselrode, who went to Britain ostensibly for his health but actually to try to pin down the British to a formal agreement. He was not successful; the British refused to enter into a formal covenant. But both Nicholas and Nesselrode were firmly convinced that the British ministers had agreed to co-operate with Russia in protecting Turkish political integrity and in intervening if that proved necessary. A memorandum was drafted and an exchange of notes between Nesselrode and Aberdeen (the British foreign secretary) attested that the memorandum accurately expressed the understanding. The Russians thought that this was reaffirmed and accepted by successive British ministers. But, to run ahead of our main story a little, when Nicholas tried to cash what he thought was an honest check, the British government of that day (1852–54) refused to honor it. It is difficult to avoid the conclusion that the British acted in bad faith either in 1844–45 or in 1852–54. Until the very last moment, however, Nicholas clung to his faith in the supposed understanding, and this in spite of a sharp crisis in Russo-British relations in 1849.

The year of revolution, 1848, very greatly upset the tsar, who saw the system in which he placed his trust being swept away. His impulse for direct and personal intervention against the French revolutionaries had to be stifled because the state of the Russian treasury made action impossible. All that he could do in that case was to issue a bellicose manifesto whose only effect was to increase the disrepute in which he was already held by "liberal" Europe. But in the case of the Hungarian revolution the story was different. Nicholas munificently supported the fallen Hapsburgs by sending an army of 90,000 to engage the rebel forces. The Russian army was victorious after a hard campaign, and the revolution was crushed. Its leader, Louis Kossuth, and some of his immediate associates escaped the victorious Russians, however, and took refuge in the Ottoman Empire.

Nicholas joined Austria in demanding that the sultan hand over Kossuth and his friends to the Hapsburgs for punishment. The sultan refused, and the French and British supported him to the extent of sending a joint fleet to the Dardanelles. War again seemed very close, but the matter was amicably arranged and Nicholas somehow convinced himself that the affair signified no change in what he thought were his relations with Great Britain. He also deceived himself into thinking that the Hapsburgs would be too filled with gratitude toward him to oppose any Russian actions about the Straits. This was unrealistic, but it was not really unreasonable in view of the fact that Nicholas had also assisted the Hapsburgs against their rebellious Italian subjects and against Prussia when that nation sought to grab the leadership of the Germanies. As a matter of fact, when the Crimean War came Austria sided against Russia, but Prussia gave the Russians the support of a friendly neutrality.

THE CRIMEAN WAR: BASIC CAUSES

The eminent British historian Professor Harold Temperley once suggested that no Power really wanted or planned the Crimean War. Britain, he said, just drifted into it. Napoleon III bitterly regretted having raised the issue of the Holy Places which led to it. And Nicholas didn't really want it, although he followed a course which involved a calculated risk of war and actually precipitated the conflict. To speak of the Crimean War as "the war without causes or reasons" is to minimize or ignore the basic rivalries which existed. It will be more convenient if these are treated by country and by category, even though they really formed an interwoven and shifting complex pattern.

Catherine's acquisition of the Crimea and her subjugation of the Don Cossacks opened to Russian settlement and exploitation these very rich lands. "The New Russia," as these lands were often called at the time, proved to be a tremendously valuable asset. The quantity of grain, especially wheat, which was grown there and exported through the Black Sea ports rapidly increased. By the middle of the nineteenth century Odessa and Taganrog surpassed the Baltic ports in the value of farm products exported through them. By 1850 grain exports accounted for about a third of the total Russian exports. It is sometimes forgotten that the group which received most of the profits from this business was precisely the same one in whose interests and by whose support the Russian government was run. In other words, they were in a position greatly to influence if not to determine the course of Russian policy.

Trade competition was a factor which affected both Russo-Turkish and Russo-British relations. The Ottoman Empire was a major grain producer, and British buyers usually favored Turkish grain for both commercial and political reasons. Turkey was a free-trade country like Great Britain, and the British were glad to encourage free traders since their superior industrial and mercantile position enabled British traders to beat out their competitors in a free market. They were, in fact, commercially dominant in the Ottoman Empire—a position they naturally wished to maintain, while some Russians were naturally eager to upset it. Commercial-political rivalries were thus part of the story of Russo-British relations. So, also, were strategic and imperial rivalries.

Russia had been steadily expanding in Central Asia for three hundred years until she had reached the states of Persia (Iran) and Afghanistan, which border on India. Moreover, it seemed to Britain that Russian actions in general and her expansion in Caucasia and Transcaucasia in particular seriously threatened Turkey. Turkey nominally controlled all the British routes to India except the long sea road around Africa. Turkish failure might lead to Russian or French control of these routes and certainly would upset the power balance. Britain was determined that neither France nor Russia should become the new masters of these routes, which were so vital to British imperial power. On the other hand, Russia felt that the British were selfishly and wantonly blocking Russia's normal and justified expansion. Everywhere that Russia sought a sea egress, there stood Britain in the way. The North Sea, the Mediterranean, the Indian Ocean—all these and more were dominated by the redoubtable British navy. In the case of the Straits, these were not merely the sole all-year water route from Russia to the West but also the strategic key to the Black Sea and southern Russia. Mastery of the Straits by a strong and hostile Power would have created a constant threat-in-being which Russia would have found intolerable, and which she would have gone to almost any lengths to prevent.

The vicious circle of fear and suspicion should not be overlooked in summarizing the causes of Russo-British troubles. Several powerful and notable British statesmen—Pitt and Palmerston—to cite only two as examples—were Russophobic. Their distrust of Russia and the actions which they took because of this distrust created fears and suspicions in Russian circles. Nicholas, believing his interests threatened, made armed preparations in the Crimea and advanced into the Danubian

Principalities (as he did in 1853) in order to be ready to forestall any move against himself or against Turkey. These Russian actions confirmed the apprehensions of the Western statesmen, who therefore took countermeasures which produced further countermeasures by Russia, and so the circle tightened toward war.

Russo-French difficulties were partly due to a clash of personalities between the two emperors. Nicholas, who after eighteen years had reconciled himself to Louis Philippe, predecessor of Napoleon III, regarded the latter as a usurper and a parvenu and treated him accordingly. The Frenchman naturally resented this. Another difficulty was religious. Napoleon III, for reasons of domestic politics, championed Roman Catholicism. Nicholas, also for political reasons, stood as the defender of Orthodox Catholicism. Furthermore, French activities both singly and in combination with the British frequently injured or threatened Russian interests. The Russians, recalling the long tradition of French aggression in the Levant—a tradition given vigorous though unsuccessful expression by Napoleon I—were afraid that the "little Napoleon" might try to carry it on.

One reason for the always latent and sometimes open hostility between the Russian and the Austrian empires was the existence of a large Slav population in Austria. There was always a possibility that the subject-Slavs of Austria might make common cause with the Russian or other Slavs and bring about the downfall of the Hapsburg Empire. This, of course, was precisely what certain Russian Slavophils and Pan-Slavists hoped to accomplish. Nicholas did not make use of this sentiment until 1853, but many of his lesser officials were not so hesitant. They sometimes used their positions to further the Slavic cause (or what they considered to be the Slavic cause), so that the Hapsburgs had bona fide charges to lodge against Russia.

Another issue was the navigation of the Danube. Russia agreed to international, free navigation of the Danube by the Treaty of Adrianople in 1829. That same treaty, however, handed the Danube Delta over to the Russians. As long as the Delta (and the mouths of the river) were part of the Russian Empire there was always a possibility that the pledge would be violated and the river closed to non-Russian traffic. There was also the chance that Russia might use her position as the base from which to seek domination of the whole Danubian Basin. Russian promises to the contrary were not believed, partly, at least, because of the intrigues of the officials.

Personal clashes also were of some importance. Nicholas' manner toward the Emperor Franz Joseph was somewhat patronizing and domineering. The tsar felt, with ample reason, that Franz Joseph owed his throne and the continuance of his empire to Russian help in 1848–49. Nicholas expected gratitude in return for service. When war came Austria surprised Nicholas and the world with her "ingratitude." Personalities, national rivalries in the Balkans, and the Slav problem were all involved.

The Crimean War did not just happen. Every nation involved had its share of groups and individuals who thought that war would benefit their selfish aims and interests. Many of these persons undoubtedly were sincere in thinking that they were serving national rather than personal interests. Napoleon III, for example, believed that France had been very ill-served by the great Napoleon's wars against Britain. He therefore proposed that Britain co-operate with France, and he made use of the dispute over the Holy Places to bring this about.

✺ IMMEDIATE CAUSE

The immediate cause (or excuse) of the Crimean War was the dispute over the Holy Places in Palestine. These had come, during the course of years, under the domination of Orthodox Catholic monks who had the support of Russia. Napoleon III, partly because of pressures on him by French Roman Catholic groups, forced the sultan to grant certain privileges over these Holy Places to Roman Catholics. Russia then made counterdemands upon the Porte, including the demand for the recognition of a Russian protectorate over the Orthodox churches within the Ottoman Empire. The British had been supporting the Russians, but this demand for a protectorate went too far. They switched to support of the sultan and persuaded him to reject the Russian demand. All this took place in the late winter and early spring of 1853.

Shortly thereafter a Franco-British fleet appeared outside the Dardanelles, and in July Russian troops entered and occupied the Danubian Principalities. Further diplomatic dickering did nothing to solve the problem. A British fleet was then sent to Constantinople, and in October the Turks declared war upon Russia. French and British fleets sailed into the Black Sea in January, 1854, and Russia broke off diplomatic relations with the two Powers a month later. In March the French and British allied themselves with the Turks and shortly thereafter declared themselves at war with Russia. Austria and Prussia made a defensive alliance designed to prevent any Russian expansion at their expense, but except for that, Prussia took a position of benevolent neutrality. Austria allied herself with the Porte, forced the Russians out of the principalities and then occupied those lands herself. Later Austria also entered an alliance with France and Britain.

🐚 WAR AND PEACE

With the withdrawal of the Russian armies from the principalities, the theater of fighting shifted to the Crimea, which the allies invaded. Their goal was the Russian naval and military fortress of Sevastopol, which they besieged from October, 1854, to September, 1855, until the Russians were forced to abandon it. The siege was marked (for the West) by the allied victory at Balaclava, which inspired Tennyson's *Charge of the Light Brigade,* and by Florence Nightingale's efforts to relieve the intense sufferings of the troops. It was marked (for Russia) by the brilliant defensive work of Colonel Frants Todleben; the death (March, 1855) of Nicholas I and the accession of Alexander II; and, of course, by defeat. The rank and file of the armies, especially of the Russian army, fought heroically. But the superior officers, with a few exceptions, distinguished themselves only by the number and magnitude of their blunders. The Russian record was the superlative in this, also.

Military defeats, especially the loss of Sevastopol; the change in sovereign; and an Austrian ultimatum threatening active Austrian warfare against Russia led Alexander II to accept preliminary peace terms laid down by the victorious allies (February, 1856). The final settlement was made at the Congress of Paris (February–March) and recorded by the Treaty of Paris of 1856. Before summarizing the conditions of the treaty, it may be noted that a shift in the international alignment took place at that time. Britain began to draw closer to Austria as a counterweight to France, and the latter became receptive to Russian advances, thus beginning a brief *rapprochement.*

The war and the peace drastically cut down Russia's power in Europe. While the fighting was still going on, the British and French had published a guarantee of Sweden and Norway against possible Russian expansion at their expense. This was strengthened by a three-way treaty among Britain, France, and Sweden which pledged the two major Powers to come to the armed assistance of Sweden if Russia violated Swedish-Norwegian integrity. The Treaty of Paris carried this line of policy further by prohibiting Russia from having bases or fortifications on the Aland Islands (Ahvenanmaa) in the Gulf of Bothnia.

As to the Black Sea region, the Russian base at Sevastopol had been destroyed and her Black Sea fleet had been sunk or scuttled during the war. The treaty forbade the rebuilding of either the fleet or the fortress, although it did return Sevastopol to Russia. Russia was also deprived of Kars (in Asia Minor), southern Bessarabia, and the mouths of the Danube. That river was placed under an international commission to assure its free and safe navigation, and the Danubian Principalities were also put under joint guarantee. Russia was forced to give up her claim of a unilateral right to protect Christians in the Ottoman Empire. Finally, the Treaty of Paris closed the Straits to the warships of all nations, but a secret alliance of Turkey, Britain, Austria, and France virtually nullified this clause by providing that the Porte would open the Straits to her allies at need. Russia knew of this alliance.

The Russians abided by the injunctions against building a fleet and fortifying Sevastopol (which effectively neutralized the Black Sea) until 1870, when she unilaterally denounced these clauses of the treaty. The essence of the closure of the Straits and of the secret exception was renewed by the London Conference of 1871. After considerable diplomatic negotiations lasting from 1856 to 1858, the two Danubian Principalities were allowed to join as the United Principalities of Moldavia and Wallachia. Four years later they joined to form Romania. Its independence was recognized in 1878.

The Crimean defeat forced Russia into a secondary role in Europe and encouraged her to turn her eyes eastward. She did not reassume an active part in the Balkans for twenty years, but extended her control in Central and Eastern Asia.

🐦 RUSSIA MOVES EAST

Russia's conquests of the regions of the Caucasus and Transcaucasia began with Russian penetration of those areas in the tenth century. The motivation was mainly commercial: a desire to reach and tap the trade along the old silk road from India to the West. Explorers and pioneers were followed by Cossacks and by other military forces who built fortresses and maintained garrisons. Then came colonists and bureaucrats and the merging of the region into the empire. This process, which formed the standard pattern, was almost completed in the Caucasus and Transcaucasia by the middle of the nineteenth century. Roads and shipping lines (commercial steamship lines appeared on the Black Sea immediately after the Crimean War), and tariff systems tied the new lands into the imperial economy.

Penetration into Central Asia began somewhat later and went ahead rather more slowly than into Siberia. Military expeditions under Peter I had such limited success that a more tactful policy of divide and rule was then employed, and considerable advances were made during the remainder of the eighteenth century. During the reigns of Alexander I and Nicholas I, an aggressive policy—carried out under the guise of scientific expeditions—was begun with the building of the Siberian-Orenburg line of fortifications. There was also during Nicholas' time considerable growth in trade between Russia and Central Asia. According to Lyashchenko, the value of the trade approximately doubled between 1825 and 1855. Cotton, both fabricated and raw, was one of the most important items imported into Russia from the region.

The Russians were led eastward across Siberia by motives quite similar to those which led men across the continent of North America. Trade—especially fur trade—economic and other opportunities, the lure of the wide open spaces, and what American imperialists once proudly called "manifest destiny" were all involved. Trade had led the Novgorodian merchants across the Urals before Ivan IV had sent out exploring expeditions which reached the borders of China. Yermak Timofeevich, Cossack agent of the trading Stroganovs, had conquered the native town of Sibir and driven on to the Amur River by 1578. Other intrepid adventurers had followed all through the seventeenth century, seeking to trade Siberian furs for Chinese gold and silver, building bases (which the Chinese sometimes destroyed), and slowly building Russian power. The Treaty of Nerchinsk (1689) established the Russo-Chinese boundary along the Amur River and provided for trade and travel across the borders. This arrangement established the Russians more firmly.

Russian and Chinese interests did not coincide. What Russia wanted was trade. But she had few goods which the Chinese desired, so they were not much interested in trade. They wanted political dominance, especially over the native Kalmuks. Co-operation against the Kalmuks was often the price China exacted for trading and other concessions. But the Russians were persistent. The Treaty of Kiakhta (1727) gave them better trade concessions, a more favorable boundary, and the right to maintain a Russian church at Peking. This last grant gave Russia what amounted to a diplomatic and consular service at the Chinese capital and was of major benefit to her. Catherine the Great was interested in the Far East and thought of expanding there. She also permitted private traders to carry the Russian flag across the Bering Sea, and in 1781 a private company was formed to exploit the fur trade of Alaska. Little was accomplished by this company, however, until it merged with rival groups in 1797 to form the Russo-American Trading Company. This company, under the leadership of Nicholas Rezanov and Alexander Baranov, established Russian settlements in Alaska and California—Sitka and Fort Ross being the most important ones. In 1821 the Russian government limited Russian expansion to north of 51 degrees latitude, but declared the northern Pacific to be a Russian sea. The United States and Great Britain vigorously protested against this, and Russia withdrew the claim in 1824–25. Generally speaking, however, European affairs occupied the Russian governments to the virtual exclusion of Far Eastern expansion until the late 1840's.

The profits from whaling and the flourishing trade in furs gradually caused an increase in official Russian interest in Kamchatka and Alaska. When efforts to establish a land route across Kamchatka failed, attention was directed to a possible sea route. But Russia's only Pacific port, Okhotsk, was unsuitable, and covetous glances were cast upon the river and region of the Amur. The Russian government agency officially charged with policy and administration in the Far East was the Committee of the Ghiliaks. (The Ghiliaks were a native people.) Its policy was the cautious one of exploring the Amur region but not the river itself in order to avoid arousing the Chinese. The committee proposed to use the Russo-American Trading Company as a screen, by having it set up a trading post near the Amur, which the government could use both to dominate the Ghiliaks and to forestall the advances of any other Powers. But, as happened so often in Russian foreign relations, imperial action cut across the established lines of administration.

The gains of Great Britain as a result of the so-called Opium War against China—the British acquisition of Hongkong and advance in the Yangtze area—worried Nicholas. It was feared in St. Petersburg that the British intended to try to win control of the mouth of the Amur. Russian worry about the security of her Pacific interests was the counterpart of Britain's apprehensions about the security of India. Nicholas decided to meet what he thought was a British threat by sending a vigorous proconsul to look after Russian Far Eastern interests. He chose Count Nikolai Muraviev, who was serving as governor of Tula, and appointed him governor-general of Siberia. Muraviev's powers were almost unlimited, and, moreover, he received the strongest support from the tsar. This more than offset the authority and prestige of the committee.

Muraviev's policy was both risky and adventurous. Scorning the caution and sublety of the committee's plans, the new governor-general proposed to acquire the lands on the left bank of the Amur River and also to secure the right to navigate that stream. He began to implement this plan as soon as he arrived at his capital of Irkutsk in 1848. A small exploring expedition was at once sent out. It failed to return. He next arranged for a young naval officer named Nevelskoi to lead a water-borne exploration which resulted in the discovery that Sakhalin was not a peninsula, as the Russians had thought, but an island. He also found that the Amur was navigable by seagoing vessels. Muraviev, who had meanwhile transferred the Russian Pacific base from Okhotsk to Petropavlovsk, which he fortified heavily, was now called back to St. Petersburg to meet the opposition which his actions had aroused on the part of Nesselrode and the committee. The foreign minister was much concerned lest Muraviev's activities lead to Far Eastern entanglements just at a time when Russia's relations with Europe were moving toward war.

When the news reached St. Petersburg that Nevelskoi had exceeded his orders by founding a settlement (which he tactfully named Niko-laevsk in honor of the tsar) about twenty miles up the Amur, there were demands for the abandonment of Nikolaevsk and the punishment of Nevelskoi. Muraviev staunchly supported his man, and was, in turn, staunchly supported by the emperor. The opposition's face was saved by ostensibly handing Nikolaevsk over to the Russo-American Trading Company. This was a subterfuge, since control of what Nevelskoi rapidly converted into a very small city remained actually with the government. Muraviev and Nevelskoi continued their preparations to secure their regions from possible attack. Muraviev freed the serfs of the Nerchinsk district and made them into the Transbaikal Cossacks. Nevelskoi, de-spite Japanese opposition, announced the annexation of Sakhalin and carried on explorations and garrisoning of the mainland coast as far south as Korea. His garrisons, by the way, were unbelievably small— eight men at one place, six at another, and three at a third.

The foresight of Nicholas and Muraviev paid high returns during the Crimean War. Muraviev led a force of about eight hundred men down the Amur, stopping to found a settlement which he named Khabarovsk in memory of Khabarov, a seventeenth-century Russian empire builder. Muraviev's forces repulsed an Anglo-French landing attempt at Petro-pavlovsk, a victory which raised Russian prestige in the Far East to a new high. Muraviev, who won the suffix Amurski in recognition of his exploits, also sent some eight thousand settlers to colonize Russia's new lands. Long negotiations then ensued with China before that nation finally accepted the Russian *fait accompli.*

CHAPTER XIII

The State of the Nation
and Other Matters

The coincidence of the beginning of a new reign and the changes forced by the Crimean defeat mark a new chapter in the story of Russia. It also makes a convenient point to stop and look around, so to speak; to review in summary fashion a few items which may have been partially forgotten in following the details of the story; to pull together in one place bits of information which have appeared scatteringly; and to introduce aspects whose importance are more thematic than chronological. All these things, this chapter will try to do. By attention to a fixed point it will give a spot from which to measure the amount and direction of change. And by dealing with relatively timeless matters, it will avoid breaking the continuity of the narrative.

✹ THE RUSSIAN EMPIRE, 1855

The multinational, multilingual empire of which Alexander II became the emperor in 1855 had almost reached its full territorial growth, although its eastern and southern borders were still fluid. It was a stupendous expanse of territory on three continents. Russia's western border ran roughly from the mouth of the Nieman River on the Baltic to the mouths of the Danube on the Black Sea, with Russian Poland forming a bulge westward from this line. The southern border followed the Black Sea coast to Poti at the eastern end and then turned inland, east and southeast to the Aras River, which it followed to the Caspian Sea. The western and northern shores of the Caspian were Russian from the Aras to the Ural River, or thereabouts. (The line through Central Asia was not clearly delimited.) From there the boundary ran southeast past the southern ends of Lakes Aral and Balkash, thence easterly to the top of the great northerly loop of the Amur River. From there the line offi-

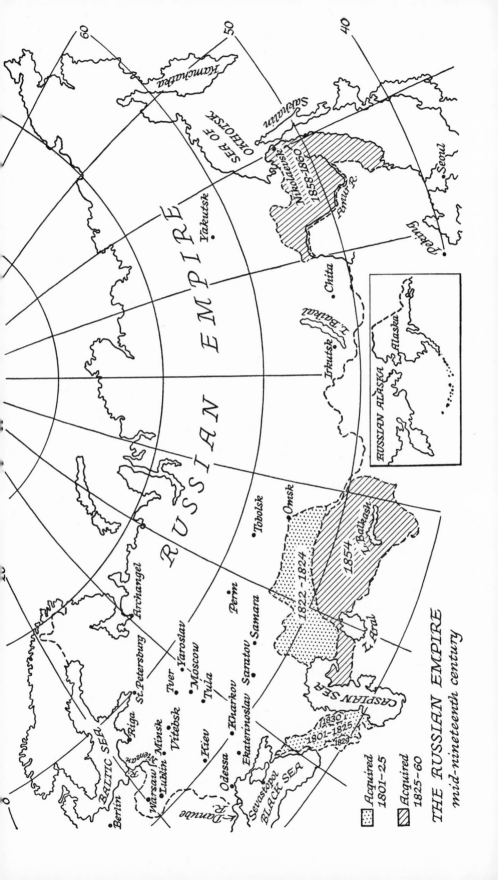

THE RUSSIAN EMPIRE
mid-nineteenth century

Acquired 1801-25

Acquired 1825-60

RUSSIAN EMPIRE

RUSSIAN ALASKA

Alaska

Kamchatka

SEA OF OKHOTSK

Sakhalin

Nikolaivsk
1858-1860

Amur R.

Seoul

Peking

Chita

L. Baikal

Irkutsk

Yakutsk

Omsk
1854

L. Balkash

1822-1824

Tobolsk

L. Aral

CASPIAN SEA

1830
1801-1825
1829

Perm

Samara

Saratov

Ekaterinoslav

Kharkov

Kiev

Tula

Moscow

Yaroslav

Tver

Vitebsk

Minsk

Lublin

Warsaw

Riga

St. Petersburg

Archangel

BALTIC SEA

Berlin

R. Niemen

Odessa

Sevastopol

BLACK SEA

R. Danube

60

50

40

cially ran in a northeasterly direction to the shores of the Sea of Okhotsk. But the lands between this official line and the Amur River were in the process of being acquired by Muraviev-Amurski and Nevelskoi. Technically, however, they had not yet been recognized as Russian territory. Sakhalin Island and the rest of Asia north and east of the mouth of the Amur were also Russian. The easternmost boundary of Alexander's empire lay on the continent of North America, since Alaska was still a Russian possession. From Kalish in western Poland to Sitka on the Alaskan panhandle was Russian territory!

Millions of square miles of this vast and sprawling empire were uninhabited and uninhabitable by men; and other millions of square miles were inhabited only by small groups of primitive people. The center of Russian life, and therefore of Russian history, lay west of the Urals. East of those mountains were few people of Russian origin and not very many of any other breed.

The number of the tsars' subjects steadily increased during the first half of the nineteenth century both through expansion and through natural growth. No one knows how many people there were in the Russian Empire prior to the census of 1897, and experts now question the accuracy and completeness of that count. The only guides we have prior to 1897 are the irregular, inaccurate, incomplete, and unsatisfactory "revisions" which were made from time to time for purposes of levying taxes and conscripts. The First Revision, made in 1719, was suppressed by Peter I as defective. The first of record was made in 1723 or 1724. Some revisions listed only males, and most writers have arbitrarily doubled this figure to get the total population. But the most recent study holds that that number of males should be multiplied by 2.6 instead of by 2. This seems a trifling difference until one begins to deal in millions; then its importance appears. Asiatic and frontier peoples were never accurately counted in the revisions. All population figures for Russia prior to 1897 are guesses which are subject to gross errors. The figures which follow must be taken as indicative rather than as precise.

The Fifth Revision in 1796 showed a total population of 36 million. The approximate increase was: 1815, 45 million; 1851, 67 million; 1859, 74 million. For comparison it may be noted that the population of the United States increased from 4 million in 1790 to over 31 million in 1860. Another contrast is also interesting and significant. In the 1790's both peoples had been country-dwellers in the approximate proportion of 95 to 5. By 1860, however, 20 per cent of the population of the United States was classed as urban, whereas in Russia only 5.7 per cent were so classed.

🔥 CLASSES AND LANDOWNERSHIP

Out of every hundred Russian subjects in 1858–59, 95 lived outside of towns and cities. In European Russia 92 out of every 100 were rural. Eighty-eight out of every 100 (in that part of the empire) were serfs; four were in military services; three were free commoners of some sort; two were merchants; two were nobles; and one was a clergyman. The subjects of Alexander II were divided into a minority of privilege and an overwhelming majority of peasants, most of whom were serfs. A measure of the disparity between the material conditions of the minority and the majority is found in the ownership of land. The state (in which are included the imperial family and the Church) owned nearly two-thirds of all the land. The nobility owned almost all of the remaining third, and less than 1 per cent was owned by the peasants. The serfs, of course, owned no land, at least in a legal sense.

Legalisms and statistics of ownership do not cover a unique and important feature. The peasants and serfs perforce acquiesced to the fact that the nobility controlled much of the land, but they never accepted the right of the nobility to landownership. The peasants, as Haxthausen observed in the early 1840's, believed that all the land originally belonged to God who gave it to His children as to a family. The land thus was the property of the national family of the Orthodox. (There seems to have been little doubt in the minds of the peasant-serfs that the members of the Russian Orthodox Church were the most important if not the only children of God. They often referred to themselves as "the Orthodox" and as "men of the Cross.") This may be one reason why the Russian peasants readily accepted as proper the prohibitions against ownership of land by Jews.

The tsar, according to the peasants, had the right of bestowing the land on his subjects because he was God's anointed, and the father of his people. The people had the right to share the land as long as they remained members of the tsar's (and God's) national family. Because the tsar could not dole out acres to each individual member of his family, he entrusted that task to the nobles. He shared the land and its disposition with the nobility who, in turn, were supposed to share their portions with those of lower rank. The tsar and the nobility, in other words, were regarded as trustees and not as owners of the land. The serfs, however, believed that the nobles might own them. Numerous Russian proverbs attest this common feeling that the minority might properly own men but did not own the land.

🔥 THE MIR

Another curious institution—curious, that is, to our way of thinking—
was the mir.[1] It was in one sense, not a physical institution but an
idea, namely: the concept of an entity like a modern corporation, which
has a legal personality, but no soul. A corporation owns property, em-
ploys persons, has rights and obligations, and is physically manifested
by its property and officers. So it was with the mir, which had an assembly; elected or appointed agents, the elders (*starosta*); obligations;
and rights. Land for the use of the villagers was assigned to the mir and
was then allocated by the mir to the individuals or families who made
up the community. In like manner, taxes and other obligations were laid
against the mir and were shared by the members. The mir was also responsible for the general behavior and well-being of the group.

The land, it will bear repeating, was owned jointly by the mir if it was
a community of free peasants; or, if it was a community of serfs, which
was more common, the lands set aside for serf use were assigned to the
mir for allocation to its members. This was a corporate or a collective
ownership or right of use. The members had the right of joint use of
woodlands, pastures, ponds, and streams on property belonging to or
assigned to the mir. Arable lands were divided on the authority of the
mir through the instrumentality of its assembly. Births, deaths, and removals constantly changed the ratio of arable acres to people, so the
arable lands were periodically distributed and redistributed. Natural differences in the fertility and location of land made equitable distribution
difficult. To meet this problem, it was the usual practice to divide the
whole into sections which were roughly equal as to advantages, and then
to subdivide the sections into strips which were assigned in some way to
the families who composed the village. Each family's strips were customarily scattered among the various sections. These strips were the
families' share of the joint property for use until the next redistribution.

On serf estates, a portion of the land was set aside for the master's
own use and the serfs were required to work it for their owner. The remaining land on the estate was assigned to the mirs (there might be
several or even many on one estate), which then allotted it as described.
Responsibility for working the master's portion and for the discharge
of other obligations rested with the mir, whose members decided in their
assembly what each family's share was to be. "Go-aways" had to have the
permission of the mir to leave and had to meet the share of the joint
obligation assessed against them by the assembly or elder. Free peasants, mostly in the north of Russia, sometimes rented or sharecropped
land. In these cases, also, the parties to the agreements customarily were

the landowner and the mir rather than the owner and an individual peasant. Joint ownership and joint responsibility were long-established customs. This is what the late Sir Bernard Pares referred to in his cryptic and often misunderstood comment: "If the Russian peasant is collectively minded, it is because he always was." This is not to say that collectivized agriculture under the Soviets is the same as the system of the mir. But the concepts of collective ownership, rights, and obligations were not introduced into Russia by the Communists.

🜨 *Narod*

The Russian word *narod,* which is now translated either as "people" or as "nation," had a more specialized meaning in the days of the empire. *Narod* was then used only in speaking of the vast majority of the population, the peasantry (both free and serf). The large number of legal classes among the population as a whole and also among the serfs and peasants may somewhat obscure the essential fact that the real division was twofold—those who were of the *narod* and the few who were not. In European Russia, counting the "go-aways" who made their permanent homes in the cities, the soldiers, who remained legally peasants, and a few other such groups, the total peasant population probably amounted to more than 95 per cent of the whole population. And almost the same percentage of peasants were serfs.[2]

The chief division among the serfs, and the only one with which we need to be concerned, was that between the state serfs and those who were privately owned. The former were all subject to the Ministry of State Property. All of them paid *obrok* and a poll tax and also had to meet certain other obligations. The landowners' serfs were divided in approximately the ratio of two to one between those who performed *barshchina* and those who paid *obrok.* Whether owned by the state or by persons, whether under *obrok* or *barshchina,* they were all *narod*—legally and factually a class apart.

The general conditions of the serfs steadily grew worse. Poverty and hunger were their everyday lot. Famine was their haunting specter. Laws required that a master feed his serfs in times of crop failures and famines. Some masters did, just as some of them treated their serfs with a sort of patriarchal benevolence. There were also Russian counterparts of Simon Legree. Legal limitations on a master's power were not always observed. But even under the most humane conditions, serfs had no right of personal freedom or individual liberty. They lived on sufferance. A serf could be bought or sold, given away or bequeathed, with or without his family, just as if he were a pig or a duck. He could be set at any task the master chose. He could be punished by fines, flogging, imprisonment, or exile. He could be deprived of any right to use the land for subsistence. (All domestic or household serfs were landless and therefore depended upon their masters' charity.)

The other side of the picture was that the serf, both by law and by custom, had some economic autonomy and a degree of economic security. As a member of the assembly of the mir, he had a voice in the allocation of land and in planning communal activities. But the mir acted only on sufferance or under duress, since both landlords and government agents could interfere with it. Whatever authority it possessed was always subject to the master, who was limited only by such restraints as custom, common sense, and self-interest may have laid on him. Against this power the serf had few defenses, evasiveness being the most common and the most important. The technique of appearing busy was one that the Russian serfs learned early and well. Calculated inefficiency, shrewd shirking, and sly sabotage reduced the burden of labor without incurring the penalties which fell upon any who openly refused to work. Of course there was some violent insubordination, and the number and seriousness of such mutinies were growing rapidly. The more frequent defense, however, was to slide away from a challenge which could not be faced. Evasiveness became and remains characteristic of the Russian peasantry. Very often the sliding away took the form of flight. Individuals, families, sometimes whole villages simply ran away.

❧ THE SERF FAMILY

The usual social unit of the peasant, free or serf, was the family. This was not the small family to which we are accustomed, but the old patriarchal family which included collateral relatives. Unmarried persons— brothers and sisters as well as children and grandchildren of the patriarch —were members of the family. Sons brought their brides home to the group. The old ties were somewhat looser in 1850 than they had been fifty or a hundred and fifty years earlier, but the large family was still the most common arrangement. Families ordinarily grouped themselves together in villages. There were wide local variations, but the usual village had a dozen or so houses which were set higgledy-piggledy along the only road. Haxthausen described the house of a prosperous peasant whom he visited in the early 1840's as follows:

The gable-end of the house faced the street. Next to it was a long narrow courtyard with a gate. This house had also an entrance from the street, which is not very usual; the door was situated on the left, with another small one on the right for the lower story of the house in which are the smaller animals. We ascended a staircase to the dwelling room which had no other furniture than a bench running around it. Opposite the door in the corner stood the image of the saint with a lamp burning under it; and on the walls were some shelves upon which were placed all kinds of vessels and utensils. Spinning wheels and hand looms testified to the widely disseminated linen manufacture in this district. An enormous stove, built up with bricks, filled one-third of the room; this in winter is a sleeping place; beside it a small staircase led down to the lower part of the house which serves as a store, and where the smaller animals, fowls and swine, take up their abode in the night; in winter the cows are also milked here. On the other side of the staircase are some closets, with very small windows, receptacles for all sorts of things such as boxes—one for each member of the family, containing clothes. In summer the family generally sleep here. The stove of the dwelling room serves for cooking, and is always heated, even in summer.

Half a century later an English traveler wrote the following description of a Russian peasant hut. Evidently there had been little change:

Ivan's is a one-roomed house—that is, there is but one room for general use. There is indeed a sort of black hole opposite, quite dark and very small, where Ivan keeps his poultry . . . and other articles out of place in a drawing room. The living room is a good size, perhaps fifteen feet by thirteen. It has two small windows with four panes in each. . . . Round two sides of the room runs a narrow bench, about a foot in width. In front of this, at the corner, is a table. In another corner of the room is the stove, a huge brick structure reaching almost to the ceiling, five feet in breadth and four feet deep, and having a lower portion jutting out from the side to a length of six feet or so. This branch establishment is used by the family to sleep upon, and a nice warm bed it makes.

Peasant life was truly hand to mouth. The peasant fed himself upon the products of his garden and fields. He clothed himself in woolens and linens homespun from sheep and flax he raised himself. He cooked his food and warmed his house with wood which he had cut, and he lighted his rooms by burning wooden chips. His small trade for salt, utensils, and other things he could neither make himself nor do without was usually by barter. If the harvest was good, the family hard-working and lucky, he might be able to earn enough in a year (over and above subsistence, taxes, and obligations) to get a new horse or cow. If it was a poor harvest or an unlucky year, the family went hungry. It was a life which, by our standards, was more like that of an animal than that of a man.

🪆 Dvorianstvo

At the opposite end of the scale of rights and privileges were the land- and serf-owning nobility, the *dvorianstvo*. Between them and the masses existed an unbridgeable chasm which was due only in part to their relative wealth and poverty. Not all of the *dvorianstvo* were wealthy; nobility was not synonymous with riches. Only about one in seven nobles was really wealthy. A considerably higher percentage lived very comfortably, but there were also many who were poor and many who were heavily in debt. It was remarked before that by 1843, over half of the nobles had mortgaged their property to the state. By 1860 almost two-thirds of the private estates were loaded with state mortgages, and there were an unknown number of very heavy private mortgages as well. It is a revealing commentary on the system that mortgage collateral was not land, nor buildings, but people. Serf-owning borrowers pledged their serfs as collateral.

Some of this extensive borrowing was to raise capital for the improvement of the estates and for investment in industry. Some of it is explicable as a natural accompaniment of the transfer then rapidly proceeding from an agrarian, barter economy to a trading, money economy. A great deal of it, however, seems to have been due mainly to the determination of the *dvorianstvo* to live more lavishly and more luxuriously. The wealthiest among them maintained tremendous establishments in several places. Those who could not afford the imperial capital had town houses in the provincial capitals. Others, less wealthy or less spendthrift, managed to spend the social season in the imperial or provincial centers. Only the least well-to-do or the eccentrics stayed in their own rural "nests"—a most descriptive name for their estates. The mansions and the manor houses differed greatly in size and luxuriousness, but in most of them European influences were apparent in the furnishings and furniture as well as in the modes and manners of the owners. The favored architectural style for country manor houses of this period was the Neo-classical or Empire. The finest of these were reminiscent of Mount Vernon or Monticello, to which they were not inferior. The houses ranged downward to ones which were scarcely distinguishable from those of the peasants. Most manor houses fell between the two extremes and would have been counted in our country as comfortable farm houses.

Contacts with Europe had early created a taste for European goods and manners among the upper classes. The imperial court, from the eighteenth century forward, had consistently adopted or imitated European norms and values ranging from modes of hairdressing to fashions in philosophy. And the *dvorianstvo* increasingly followed the lead of the court—an expensive luxury. The self-sufficiency of manors and villages which had seemed desirable to an earlier generation seemed less so to a generation which wanted new goods that could not be produced at home. This was one of the causes for the shift from an economy of production for home consumption to production for market. The physical labor which made this shift possible was supplied by the serfs. The profits from it went almost wholly to the owners.

In matters other than economic—that is, in social, cultural, intellectual, and political affairs—there was the same great disparity between the classes and the masses. The classes lived in a world of their own desiring and devising, a world apart from that of the masses, upon whom it rested. Social and official place belonged almost exclusively to the few. Education was their almost exclusive prerogative. What else could be expected when 103,400 persons literally owned about 25 million of their fellow men? The division between *narod* and *dvorianstvo* appeared also in the government.

THE AUTOCRACY

From a legal and theoretical point of view, the Russian emperor was an autocrat of unlimited power, the representative and servant not of men but of Almighty God. In the actual practice, however, the emperor was limited by many factors. He was primarily the agent of the *dvorianstvo,* without whose assent no imperial authority could long exist. The chief advisers of the emperor and the major executors of the imperial will were members of this class. So, also, was the court. On numerous occasions since the Romanov dynasty was established, tsars had been created and deposed by the *dvorianstvo*. Records of these *coups d'état,* some of which involved regicide, were part of the Romanov family history.

Tradition, custom, and protocol were also limitations upon what a Russian emperor might do. Certain acts were prescribed and others were proscribed. This was perhaps more limiting in small things than in great ones. More important was the fact that the tsar could order but could neither execute all his orders nor compel his bureaucracy to execute them. Bureaucratic apathy, inefficiency, resistance, and corruption were all brakes upon imperial action. It was quite possible, and not at all infrequent, for an order or a law to remain a dead letter simply because the officials who were supposed to carry it out couldn't or wouldn't do so.

AGENTS OF THE TSAR

Despite these limitations, the Russian government operated by and under the personal will of the emperor, who could override laws, reverse judicial or other decisions, short-circuit procedures, and generally interfere with administration. All government officials were empowered only as the direct or indirect agents of the tsar. They ordered and acted "in the tsar's name." It was, in short, a government of men and not of laws. The principal agents of the tsar at the highest levels are diagrammed below:

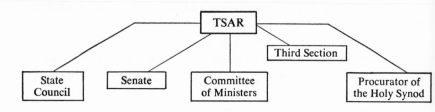

The Council of State, created in 1801 by Alexander I and revised as a result of Speransky's plan, was a consultative body. Its function was to discuss proposed laws, important administrative measures, and some judicial cases. It was divided into four departments: church and civil affairs, laws, war, and national economy; each department having its own chairman. Matters coming under its view were first discussed in the appropriate department and then by the council as a whole, the emperor or his appointee presiding. Decisions of the council had no legal force unless the emperor gave his formal approval. He was not bound in any way (legally) to accept their findings, although their prestige sometimes carried weight. The council had become so conservative—not to say obstructionist—by the middle of the nineteenth century that most major acts (except the great reforms of Alexander II) were passed without reference to it. In the case of the reforms, consultation of the council may have been partly a device for securing the support of the *dvorianstvo* (which, of course, it represented). In this, it resembled the early National Assemblies (*Zemski Sobors*).

The Senate had had a very up-and-down history since its establishment by Peter the Great. Sometimes it had been the actual ruler, and sometimes its power had been only a little less than that. Several times revised and remodeled, the Senate by 1850 was little more than an appellate court for certain special cases.

The Committee of Ministers had been set up under that title by Alexander I in 1802. There was a president, who presided when the emperor was absent, but who had no special powers. There was no prime minister in the Western sense of that office, since the emperor himself discharged those functions. Each minister was directly and personally responsible to the tsar and to the tsar alone. Joint responsibility in policy-making or in administration (such as exists in the British cabinet) was unknown. There were ten ministries at the beginning of Alexander II's reign.[3] Only two unusual features need be mentioned specially. The Ministry of the Interior had charge of the open police and by custom, though apparently not by law, supervised the provincial governments and governors. The Ministry of Justice included a special set of officials known as procurers. These acted as the emperor's special investigators, reporters, and agents. This rather curious institution was probably descended from the *ober-fiskals,* who performed these jobs for Peter the Great. It has been plausibly suggested that the procurers of old Russia were the precursors of the procurators of Soviet Russia.

The office of Procurator of the Holy Synod originated in the famous Spiritual Regulation of Peter I. The post was given ministerial status in 1824 and became a sort of Ministry of Church Affairs charged with the organization and administration of the Russian Orthodox Church and with the formal relations between Church and State. This ministry, too, operated in the name of the emperor, who had been designated as "head of the Church" by Paul's Law of Succession. This was interpreted to mean that the emperor was to be the "supreme protector and defender of the dogmas of Orthodoxy, guardian of the Orthodox faith and of orderliness in the Holy Church." No emperor presumed upon this status, however, to issue laws affecting either dogma or ritual or to promulgate creeds or litanies. The Church was no longer the extremely wealthy institution it once had been. Its estates—or most of them—had been secularized, and the sums it received from the government did not cover its costs. Ordinary parish priests were almost wholly dependent upon the fees which their parishioners paid them—a circumstance which sometimes led to abuses. Most of the lower clergy, incidentally, were of middle or lower-class origins. The place which the Russian Orthodox Church still held in the life of the nation throughout the nineteenth century was once admirably summarized by Professor Karpovich in the following paragraph:

To a large degree, it succeeded in retaining its hold over the soul of the nation. In spite of all its weaknesses and shortcomings, it remained a depository of spiritual forces deeply rooted in national consciousness and tradition. There was still a genuine Christian piety among the millions of Orthodox believers, and the Church still had worthy servitors in its ranks. Even during the synodal period of its history, the Russian Church possessed some important centers of religious learning and of earnest spiritual endeavor. And the rich heritage of Orthodox religious thought and art still could serve as a source of inspiration. Gogol, Dostoevsky, and Leskov, among the outstanding nineteenth-century writers, the thinkers of the Slavophil school, the philosophy of Vladimir Soloviev, the idealists and mystics of the early twentieth century—none of these cultural phenomena would have been possible outside the great Orthodox tradition.

To which it may be added that the outstanding exceptions to the generalization that education was the monopoly of the *dvorianstvo* were the sons of the clergy. The number of these among the intelligentsia was very high in proportion both to the size of the intelligentsia and to the number of clergymen's children. Since most of the Russian revolutionaries of the nineteenth and early twentieth centuries came from among the intelligentsia, it follows that the number of clergymen's children among the revolutionaries was also disproportionately large.

The Third Section, which is intentionally placed above the other institutions in the diagram, was instituted under that title and in that form by Nicholas I. This was the tsar's secret police, which was charged with the protection of the tsar and his officials and with the preservation of the *status quo*. All the institutions of government came under its surveillance. So did all classes of the Russian people.

⊕ IMPERIAL ADMINISTRATION

The empire was separated for administrative purposes into six regions: Russia, Finland, the Baltic States, Poland, the Caucasus, and Siberia. Each had a separate administration, deriving authority from the emperor. Russia—or Russia Proper, with which we are mostly concerned—had been divided into provinces (*gubernia*) by Catherine II. They had originally been set up on a basis of a province to every three or four hundred thousand registered inhabitants and subdivided into districts containing about thirty thousand each.[4] Population shifts and some other changes had occurred over the course of two generations, but the general pattern remained as Catherine had created it. There were forty-six provinces in Russia Proper at the end of Nicholas' reign.

A slightly simplified diagram will show the various administrative divisions and subdivisions, together wth the chief officers of the emperor at each level.

The ranking imperial officials in the provinces were the governors and vice-governors who were appointed by the emperor through the Minister of the Interior. According to the letter of the law, the governor and vice-governor were answerable only to the emperor and to the Senate. But in practice and by custom, they were usually controlled by the Minister of the Interior. Associated with the governors were the Corporations (Assemblies) of the Nobility (*dvorianstvo*) and those whom this elected. The latter included the Marshals of the Nobility, the assessors (judges), the district police officers (*ispravniki*), and a few others. Various imperial ministries had their agents in the provinces and sometimes at the district level, also. And, of course, the Third Section was ubiquitous.

The more exalted among the officials were physically and figuratively

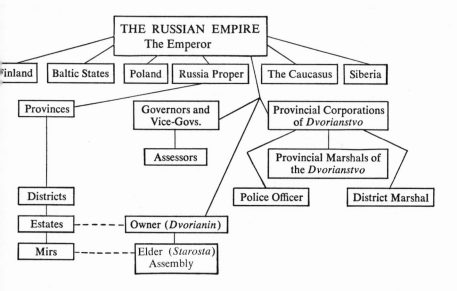

far removed from the masses of the people, most of whom knew the government only in the persons of their landlords and the lesser bureaucracy. Each landlord was, in effect, the agent of the tsar and governed his estate in the tsar's name. The landlord was responsible for maintaining order, and for seeing that the villages on his estate met their financial obligations to the government and supplied conscripts or recruits for the army.

Since municipal self-government did not in fact exist, despite imperial orders for its establishment, the only local self-government in Russia was in the village mirs. All adult villagers ordinarily took part in the village assemblies, which elected the elder and decided matters of common interest such as the allotment of land, the allocation of special rights or duties, and the apportionment of obligations. Local autonomy existed as a customary privilege rather than as a legal right and was subject to interference and curtailment by the landlords and by the government. Nevertheless, it did exist.

🏵 PEOPLE VERSUS GOVERNMENT

The bureaucracy, which of course actually ran the government machinery, was known in Russian as *chinovnik*. This name derived from the reform of Peter I which set up a table of rank or *chin*. A person who held rank (that is, had a *chin*) was a *chinovnik*, a man of rank. The rank determined the government position which its holder occupied. Members of the bureaucracy were popularly feared and hated and were often the targets of attack, both literary and physical. (Gogol's *Revisor* is a notable example of a literary attack.) A Russian revolutionary of a later generation, S. M. Kravchinski, who wrote under the name of Stepniak, left the following rather malicious description of a bureaucrat:

What is a *chinovnik?* It is a man convinced that were it not for his 'prescriptions,' 'instructions,' and 'enjoinments' the world would go all askew, and the people would suddenly begin to drink ink instead of water, to put their breeches on their heads instead of on their legs, and to commit all sorts of other incongruities.

As all his life is passed from his most tender youth upward in offices, amidst heaps of scribbled papers, in complete isolation from any touch with real life, the *chinovnik* understands nothing, has faith in nothing but these papers. . . . There is nothing in the world which can be relied upon but scribbled papers, and he is their votary.

Kravchinski's description may properly be suspect, since he was an avowed enemy of the tsar's government. But that same suspicion does not properly apply to the characterization of the Russian bureaucrats by the eminent British authority on Russia Sir Donald MacKenzie Wallace. Wallace, like Kravchinski, was writing in a period a little later than the time of this survey, but the breed of bureaucrats had not changed in the interval:

Looking for direction and approbation merely to their superiors, they have systematically treated those over whom they were placed, as a conquered or inferior race. . . . The genuine bureaucrat has a wholesome dread of formal responsibility and generally tries to avoid it by taking all matters out of the hands of his subordinates, and passing them on to the higher authorities.

Wallace caught the essence of the government's relation to its subjects when he accused the bureaucrats of treating the people like "a conquered or inferior race." The government habitually acted as if the Russian people were incompetent minors who were incapable of understanding their own interests and incompetent to advance those interests even if they had grasped them. In some ways, certainly, the government appeared both to fear and to despise its people. The people, for their part, distrusted and hated the government—except for the emperor himself. Him they regarded with an almost superstitious reverence and awe, clinging confidently to the myth that the troubles which bedeviled them were unknown to the emperor, who would have corrected the evils had he but known of them. Time and again the rumor spread among the peasants that the tsar had ordered this or that action (emancipation, for example) for their benefit but that the tsar's officials blocked the execution of the order.

Granted that the government treated its people as enemies or incompetents, what other courses were open to it? It was not possible after centuries of brutalization suddenly to try to rule the masses by reason and kindness alone. The average Russian peasant was rude, boorish, uncouth, evasive, and ignorant of any problems beyond those elemental ones with which he constantly had to grapple. If absolute power absolutely corrupts those who wield it, as Lord Acton thought, it does not leave unscathed those over whom it is exercised. You cannot hold a man in subjection for most of his life and then suddenly announce to him that henceforward he is a free and self-governing citizen who must at once accept both the obligations and responsibilities of that status. Without preparation to guide the newly free, to rescue them from the worst consequences of their blunders, and to protect them from the depredations of others, the result is likely to be chaos and disaster. It is possible for a strong nation to free a minority of its own people, though the period of tutelage and assimilation is long and difficult. It is quite impossible for a government to free a majority without signing its own death warrant. This, of course, was precisely what some of the intelligentsia wished it to do.

🔥 THE INTELLIGENTSIA

We can make some guess as to the maximum number of intelligentsia on the basis of literacy figures, since an illiterate obviously could not be a member of the intelligentsia. Among "colonial peoples" of the empire, illiteracy was almost 100 per cent. It was twice as high among women as among men, and a third again as high among the rural population as among the urban groups. It is not surprising that the total university enrollment was only 3000 or that the combined circulation of all the leading Russian periodicals was less than 12,000 copies. This meant not only that the intelligentsia was a tiny minority; it also meant that its audience was extremely limited. It follows that the men and women of the intelligentsia wrote, talked, discussed, and acted primarily for each other. This was not their intent. Their dreams were on a larger scale— of teaching the people and of acting for the people. But, with few exceptions, they could never bridge the chasm which separated them from the masses. What could an illiterate peasant have cared for a poem or play or novel or critique which he could not read? What interest had he in a learned literary or philosophical discussion which he could not follow? What could the illiterate, unskilled laborer (who worked for the equivalent of seventeen cents a day) have cared for abstract discussions of economics or academic expositions of abstruse socialisms? When 80 per cent of the bureaucracy were without any formal education what could you expect of the masses? What could they do? How could they participate?

The answer is, of course, that they did not take part. There were no mass movements in nineteenth-century Russia. There were only local, sporadic mutinies against local conditions which sometimes coincided and gave the impression of a general rising. The literary-philosophical circles of the 1850's and 1860's touched only a few hundreds at most. Even the famous "Populism" of the 1870's did not involve more than a few thousand active participants. The intelligentsia—or at least the revolutionaries among them—dreamed of doing things *for* the people and *to* the people. They were not in a position to do things *with* the people or *by* the people.

Yet three movements bore great fruit. Tiny, sometimes sadly confused, almost totally ineffective at the moment of their brief lives, nevertheless they eventually played a major part in changing Russia. For we are dealing here with ideas which are delayed explosives with greater potential destructiveness than atomic bombs. The Men of December perished on the scaffold or in muted Siberian exile. Their ideas, ideals, and dreams inspired the intelligentsia of the later nineteenth century. These perished, in their turn, or seemed to squander themselves in the great blackness. But Lenin learned from Herzen and from Chernishevsky, and Lenin helped Russia turn herself upside down.

ALEXANDER I. HERZEN

Alexander Ivanovich Herzen (1812–70) was the son of a wealthy landowner named Yakovlev and his German wife, Luise. Since the father and mother were married only by a civil ceremony and not by the rites of the Orthodox Church, young Alexander was regarded by some as an illegitimate child. This unwarranted stigma (which has become enshrined by printed repetitions) undoubtedly helped make the boy's childhood unhappy. Added to this was the fact that his father became an embittered eccentric so the family life was far from pleasant. Young Herzen sought a surrogate for companionship and affection in books. His father, who had been a disciple of Voltaire, had an extensive French library, which the boy read indiscriminately and thoroughly.

Alexander Ivanovich grew to young manhood idealizing the French Revolution and the Decembrists, and when he went to the university to study science he soon was attracted to one of the reading circles. This group was then particularly interested in the work of the French Utopian socialist Saint-Simon, and young Herzen was deeply and permanently influenced by him. In 1834 Herzen was first jailed and then exiled for being a member of the circle. When he returned to Moscow after his exile and his subsequent term of army service, he plunged into the study of Hegel, who was then the intellectual vogue. Among Herzen's confreres of this period were Chaadayev and Belinsky, whose political heir Herzen became. When his father died and Herzen inherited a large fortune, he promptly left Russia forever. His voluntary exile took him to Italy, France, and England, where he lived from 1852 to 1867. This was his most active period, and among his associates at that time were the Italian revolutionaries, Garibaldi and Mazzini.

Herzen was a most prolific writer and publisher. Among his works were a novel which among other themes attacked the institution of marriage, entitled *Who is to Blame?*; the *Memoirs of Catherine II* from which some passages have been quoted; *Past and Reflections,* his reminiscences; *Polyarna Zvezda* ("Pole Star"), a journal; *Kolokol* ("The Bell"), a periodical and his most influential work; and numerous stories. He also founded and supported the Free Russian Press which, in the safety of London, published underground literature to be smuggled into Russia. *Kolokol* was one of the items surreptitiously sent into Russia. Copies went to the imperial palace, and a persistent rumor listed Alexander II as one of the magazine's readers. Whether that was so or not, *Kolokol* was widely read and very influential among the intelligentsia for some time.

Herzen's major theme was the advocacy of a sort of socialism which he thought Russia could achieve through the agency of the mir, thus avoiding the intermediate states of bourgeois capitalism and democracy. He was also a staunch and ardent advocate of serf emancipation. After this had been granted he became the champion of self-government and of landownership in common. The most striking manifestation of his influence was the "movement to the people" (*V narod*). Here is the passage in which he first called for this crusade, evoked by the expulsion of a group of students from the University of St. Petersburg on charges (or suspicion) of revolutionary activities:

Where shall you go, youths from whom knowledge has been shut off? Shall I tell you where? Give ear, for even darkness does not prevent you from listening. From all corners of our enormous land, from the Don and the Ural, from the Volga and the Dnieper, a moan is growing, a grumbling is rising. This is the first roar of the sea billow which begins to rage, pregnant with storm after a long and tiresome calm. *V narod!* (To the people!) That is your place, Oh exiles from knowledge.

The peak of the movement to the people was reached in the middle 1870's.

🦋 MICHAEL BAKUNIN

Almost exactly contemporary with Herzen was Michael Bakunin (1814–76), a revolutionary of a very different stamp. Bakunin, like Herzen, was the child of wealth and privilege who became a revolutionary in his student days. He also spent years in jail, in Siberian exile, and in Europe. But those are almost the only points of likeness, except that both men were enemies of the system in Russia. Bakunin, educated in Russia and abroad, was outlawed by the Russian government when he refused to obey its order to return to Russia in 1840. Thenceforward he was a most active fighter for revolutions everywhere; literally a professional revolutionary. He fought on the barricades of Paris in 1848, went from there to fight in the revolutions at Dresden and Prague. Each of these latter actions caused the Prussian and Austrian governments to condemn him to death. The sentences were commuted to life imprisonment, but he served neither of them. Austria extradited him to Russia (which had a sort of a prior claim to him). Nicholas' government lodged Bakunin in the fortress prison of Petropavlovsk (SS. Peter and Paul) from 1851 to 1854, and then sent him to Siberia. He managed to escape from Siberia and returned to Europe via Japan and the United States, reaching the Continent just in time to take part in the Polish Revolution of 1863. Later he worked for revolution in Italy and France, became the bitter enemy of Karl Marx (their fight ruined the First International), and finally died in Switzerland. Bakunin's creed was anarchy. He was the archenemy of all existing institutions and the consistent apostle of destruction. His "brave new world," he believed, had to be created from scratch, and therefore all the old ways must first be destroyed. Russia, Bakunin thought, could lead the world to his goal. His influence on the Russian intelligentsia was considerable insofar as his creed fitted their conclusions that the existing institutions had to be wiped out before new and better ways could be developed. Among his disciples were Nechaiev and Breshko-Breshkovskaya, both of whom will come into the story later.

🦋 N. G. CHERNISHEVSKY

Of greater influence than Bakunin, and perhaps Herzen, was Nicholas Gavrilovich Chernishevsky (1829–89). He was the son of a distinguished Orthodox priest, and the descendant of a long line of clergymen. His father intended that the boy should follow the family profession, and young Chernishevsky made a brilliant record at the seminary in Saratov (his home town). From there he went to the University of St. Petersburg, where he studied history and philology. He graduated in 1850 and for the next three years taught literature in the gymnasium at Saratov. His thesis for the master's degree was, by all accounts, a brilliant piece of work. But it was rejected by the Minister of Education as being too radical.

Chernishevsky was, indeed, a student of revolution, or at least of writers whose ideas were bound to be revolutionary when applied to Russia. He knew the works of Hegel and other German philosophers; was familiar with the ideas of the French positivists and Utopians; was well acquainted with the studies of the English liberals; and won deserved repute for his translation and critical interpretation of Mill's *Political Economy*. He became a contributor to the magazine *Sovremenik* ("The Contemporary") with which were associated Belinsky and the poet Nekrasov. (Nekrasov is best known for his poem "Who Lives Happily in Russia?" a stinging attack upon the Russian system.) Later, Chernishevsky became the editor of this journal, when it enjoyed its greatest prestige. He was arrested in 1862, while editing *Sovremenik;* was kept in jail for two years and then sentenced to hard labor in Siberia. There he remained until 1883, when he was paroled to Astrakhan. Not until 1889, when he was deathly ill, was Chernishevsky allowed to return to his native Saratov.

During his two years (1862–64) in prison, he wrote a novel entitled *What Is To Be Done?* This strikes modern readers as intolerably long and verbose because it is really not a novel at all but a vehicle by which, literally under the eyes of his guards, Chernishevsky set forth his dream of a socialist Russia. His real faith was in the *narod,* and he believed that the Russian system could be improved only by improving the lot of the masses. The task of the intelligentsia, he said, was dual: to educate the people (*narod*), and to awaken in the rulers an awareness of the desperate need for serf emancipation and other reforms. He bitterly attacked the intelligentsia for their oblomovism, saying in his diary: "I do not like those gentlemen who say 'Liberty, Liberty,' but do not destroy a social order in which nine-tenths of the people are slaves and proletarians. The important thing is not whether there is a tsar, or whether there is a constitution, but that one class shall not suck the blood of another."

Nicholas Chernishevsky is a clear example of the linkage among succeeding generations of Russian revolutionary thinkers and champions. His ideas were derived partly from European thinkers, partly from Russian thinkers, and partly from the peculiar circumstances of his nation and time. He was to some extent the heir of Herzen, who had been the heir of Belinsky. And he was the spiritual ancestor of many in the next generation who knew him only by reputation. It is not insignificant that Lenin chose as the title for one of his most important works the one that Chernishevsky had used for his novel—*What Is To Be Done?*

CHAPTER XIV

Reforms and Revolutionaries

✪ ALEXANDER II, 1855–81

Alexander II ("Tsar of Freedom," Stephen Graham called him in his biography) was born in 1818, the son of Nicholas I and Alexandra Federovna. By blood and by cultural environment, the tsarevich was German. His mother (nee Princess Charlotte of Prussia), his grandmother, and his great grandmother were all Germans. So was his first tutor, Karl Moerder; and his second tutor, the Russian poet Basil Zhukovsky, owed his place at court and his appointment as tutor to his command of the German language. The atmosphere of the court and of the family circle were Western with a marked Germanic flavor. The tsarevich spoke German like a native, and when at the age of twenty-one he was taken on a European tour, Alexander felt more at home in the Germanies than elsewhere. On that trip, also, he fell in love with a German princess, Wilhelmina Maria of Hesse, whom he married in 1841.

Alexander's training was a curious combination of militarism, rigid discipline, and romanticism. Nicholas, strongly militaristic himself, hoped to mold his son in the same image. Even the wallpaper in Alexander's nursery carried out the theme—soldiers in uniform. As a youth, the tsarevich was made an officer of the Guards (which was not unusual for the heir to the throne), and, later, he was made a director of military affairs. Moerder, the tutor, was also a soldier and a strict disciplinarian. He taught his pupil that life was a school with God the headmaster—a Prussian concept which apparently did not take with Alexander. Moerder was also a deeply religious man and a staunch humanitarian.

Moerder's influence toward humanitarianism was strongly re-enforced by Zhukovsky, but even more strongly re-enforced was the romanticism of Alexander's mother. Zhukovsky's first emphasis in the training of his tutee was upon Russian history, which he taught from the works of that arch-absolutist, rigidly moralistic and moralizing, vigorously nationalistic historian, Karamzin. Karamzin stressed the obligations and duties of a monarch no less than the necessity for absolutism. Zhukovsky gave second place in his teaching to languages; and the third to European history. Alexander's education was thus broader and probably much better—despite gaps—than that given either to his predecessors or his successors. It included, in addition to the European tour, a journey through European Russia and a bit of western Siberia. Of course, this was all carefully stage-managed. Measures were taken to spare the tsarevich some sights—the least fortunate of the peasants were confined to their hovels by police orders—but he saw a good deal in spite of all precautions.

Alexander's training also included an apprenticeship in government. He was made a member of the State Council in 1841, officially replacing his father as its presiding officer. Six years later he was appointed to a commission to inquire into serfdom and was so shocked by its report that he formally petitioned his father to liberate the serfs. Nicholas replied that liberation would mean revolution (a perfectly sound judgment which was later borne out by events), and Alexander allowed the plan to drop. During the first years of the Crimean War he was (at least nominally) the military governor of St. Petersburg. Later he was put in command of the army which was posted on the Austrian front. Neither this army nor Alexander saw combat, but it was a responsible post, since the threat of Austrian intervention was real.

His personal life contained both happiness and tragedy. His marriage to Princess Wilhelmina (who became Tsaritsa Maria Alexandrova) was a love match. Despite several passing affairs on his part, the two lived a fairly simple and reasonably normal life (for persons of their position) for fifteen or twenty years. During that time, the tsaritsa bore eight children—six sons and two daughters. The first-born son, named Nicholas for his grandfather, seemed to Alexander to be becoming a sissy. So the tsar ordered strenuous physical training for the tsarevich. In the course of this, Nicholas was thrown from his horse, suffered a fractured spine and died of cerebral-spinal tuberculosis at the age of eighteen. The second son, Alexander, became the heir to the throne.

After the tragic death of Nicholas, the tsaritsa became increasingly pious to the point of insanity. Genuinely ill, she also became a hypochondriac. As a result, the tsar, after the death of his mother, sought other relationships. Chief among his women friends was the Princess Catherine Dolgoruki. At the time Alexander first met her, the Princess Catherine was a lovely ten-year-old child. Her family—a proud one of ancient heritage—had lost most of its wealth, and the tsar made the little girl his protégée. He sent her to school at the ultra-fashionable Smolny

Institute, which his own daughters attended, and kept loving watch over her. When she was seventeen she became his mistress and subsequently bore him several children. They carried the last name of Yurievski, but Alexander by a special law gave them princely titles and the right to use his name as their patronymic. All this was, of course, an open scandal, which did not decrease when, six weeks after his wife's death (1880), the tsar married Catherine and, by another special law, legitimatized their children. The imperial family was furious but powerless.

On this occasion the tsar stubbornly and with determined will defied the wishes and opinions of his family and of his court. He showed a like vigor and determination in the matter of reforms. Both these seem in contrast to his usual easy-going, friendly, good-naturedness. In fact, he was often charged with unbecoming indolence. He was long habituated to dependence upon someone—upon his father, upon Zhukovsky, upon his mother, upon Catherine (despite the great difference in their ages), and upon his advisers. In addition, he was plagued by asthma, insomnia, and digestive troubles—any one of them enough in itself to make him wish to relax. But when he was aroused by anger or conviction, Alexander showed a surprising strength of will and persistence. In the same way, he was usually a mild and gracious person, but he could be brutally severe and ruthless. He appeared to surge up and then subside like a half-angry sea at the end of a storm.

Alexander II was a believer in freedom and equality under law, and he demonstrated this belief by his emancipation of the serfs, by his judicial reforms, by his restoration of home rule to Finland, and by his actions toward the Jews. He was bucking not only conservatism, on the one side, but also irresponsible and often totally unrealistic demands on the other side. Only a year after the great serf reform, there was a plot to assassinate the man who had instituted it. This was foiled as was a second plot in 1863. A third attempt on the tsar's life was made in 1867 by a student named Karakozov. Karakozov's aim was poor and Alexander escaped. Karakozov did not. The tsar had also to face a revolution in Poland (1863) and the efforts of various revolutionary groups who were inspired by such leaders as Herzen, Bakunin, and Chernishevsky.

REVOLUTIONARIES

Revolution was made slightly easier in the first years of Alexander's reign by the relaxation (but not removal) of the censorship, and by the amnesties which he granted to political prisoners and many other offenders. Revolution was made much easier by the shock of the Crimean defeat, with its revelations of rottenness in the existing system, and by the deter-

mination of the tsar to overhaul that system thoroughly. When his measures did not prove panaceas, when he did not go as far or as fast as the
liberals and radicals wanted, the enthusiasm with which they had hailed
the reforms curdled. Here is another example of De Toqueville's famous
axiom that the most dangerous moment for a bad government is when
it begins to reform. The making of reforms is an open admission of the
need for them. People's hopes are aroused. Then, when the reforms do
not cure all evil, hope is followed by frustration, anger, and impatience.
This was certainly true in Alexander's day.

There was no mass base for the revolutionary movements. David
Footman in his informing study (*Red Prelude*) of Zhelyabov, one of
the principal revolutionaries, gives brief sketches of fifty-six of Zhelyabov's associates. Twenty-six of them were from the *dvorianstvo* class;
six from the clergy; five from the merchant class; six from the peasants;
ten were of varied classes; and the origins of three were unknown. Moreover, half of the fifty-six were students in universities or professional
schools. The exact proportions may not be accurate, but this, in general,
was the composition of the revolutionary groups.

The number of students in Footman's list is significant. Every Russian
revolutionary movement of the nineteenth century was university-
spawned. This was partly because it was at the universities that young
men and women came into contact with the ideas of liberalism, materialism, socialism, and other challenges to the existing norms and values.
This was where the influence of Western ideas and ideals was strongest.
And there are always many young people who are genuinely and sincerely
enthusiastic in their idealism. There are many who feel keenly the weight
of social responsibility, and who seriously desire to correct the wrongs
they see about them. The focus of these movements in the schools and
universities of nineteenth-century Russia also partially explains the
class character of them. Higher education was almost exclusively a class
privilege, and consequently it was the most vigorously "progressive,"
privileged youths who came under the influence of ideas and dreams.
This did not usually take place in their classrooms. It more often took
place in their reading circles and discussion groups. Dr. Bertram D.
Wolfe once painted a word picture of these young people in a manner
as brilliant and as flamboyant as the intelligentsia he was describing:

The cement which bound them together was a common alienation from
existing society, and a common belief in the sovereign efficacy of ideas as
shapers of life. They lived precariously suspended as in a void, between an
uncomprehending autocratic monarchy above and an uncomprehending unenlightened mass below. Their mission as independent thinkers was to be
critics of the world in which they had no place and prophets of a world

that had not yet come into being, and might have no place for them either. They were lawyers without practice, teachers without schools, graduate clerics without benefices and often without religion, chemists without laboratories, technicians, engineers, statisticians for whom industry had as yet no need, journalists without a public, politicians without parties, sociologists and statesmen rejected by the state and ignored by the people. They anticipated and oversupplied in advance the requirements of a world that was too slow in coming into being, and sought to serve a folk that had as yet no use for their services. . . .

Almost involuntarily they were forced into open enmity to the old order that had no use for them. Beginning as gentle dreamers, reformers, and humanitarians, they were constantly being punished for mere dreaming and forbidden to dream. In despite of themselves they were driven into open rebelliousness, a mood so general that the very word "student" would finally become synonymous with revolutionist.

🌀 NIHILISM

The intelligentsia were searching for values which would give their lives a meaning and a place. Discontented with the old ways, psychologically frustrated, their egos hopelessly dislocated by circumstances which they could not reorder, they felt a desperate need for change. Highly suggestible as people are in crisis, they often seized upon novelty only because it was novel. Chernishevsky had pointed out to them the poverty of the old approach. They were in reaction against the oppressiveness of the autocracy and the failures of romanticism. They sought a new basis for a new society. It was Turgenev's famous passage in *Fathers and Sons* which gave their movement a name:

"Nihilist," muttered Nicholas Petrovich. "That is from the Latin *nihil*, nothing, so far as I can judge; consequently that word designates a man— who acknowledges nothing?"

"Say, who respects nothing," Pavel Petrovich interrupted. . . .

"Who looks at everything from the critical point of view," remarked Arkadi.

"Is that not the same?"

"No, it is not the same. A nihilist is a man who bows to no authorities, who accepts not a single principle on faith no matter with what respect that principle is surrounded."

Very often this revolt against authority included rejection of all conventional behavior. Some Nihilists distinguished themselves, and gave the movement an unsavory reputation, by their eccentricities of dress, by their omission of all social courtesies, and by their amoralities or immoralities. Undoubtedly some of them seized upon and practiced only these superficialities. But the real devotees were desperately sincere, honest, and loyal to their cult. And it was a cult rather than a party or an organized movement. Its origins were a compound of Russian circumstances and Western influences—especially of the half-understood materialist philosophy which grew out of the new discoveries of science. Its nature was nonpolitical, and it was never popular since it was by that nature confined to the intelligentsia and pseudo-intelligentsia. It had, also, a rather wide lunatic fringe. And some of its adherents moved on from it into political activities.

The first definitely organized political party—a revolutionary party, of course—was known as Land and Liberty (*Zemlya i Volya*). It had its beginnings among the intelligentsia in 1861, and was formally organized in the following year. The Polish Revolution of 1863 split it into factions, and subsequent repressions drove it completely underground. Karakozov was probably connected with the left-wing, "immediate-action" splinter of Land and Liberty. His attempt to murder Alexander II, however, was apparently an entirely personal act and not a party affair. The party was blamed, nonetheless, and was crushed by arrests and persecution.

SERF EMANCIPATION

Of the reforms which failed to satisfy the revolutionists the first and greatest was, of course, the emancipation of the serfs. Measured by the number of persons affected, serf emancipation in Russia was the outstanding social reform of the nineteenth century. By any standard, it was an event of absolutely first-rate importance, and the course of its consequences has not yet been completely run. To call it a social reform is an understatement; it was much more. It was a revolution from the throne, and it could have been made only by an autocrat. No representative government, which would have had to take account of the wishes and needs of widely divergent constituents, could have put through legislation which so drastically affected so many. It was, to repeat, a revolution whether one speaks in terms of economics, of society, of law, of politics, or of all of them together. It brought in its train reforms and changes which were revolutionary in scope if not in the manner of their making. It led directly to three revolutions—one in 1905 and two in 1917, none of which could have happened without emancipation and its effects. Yet, contrariwise, the routine of the peasants' lives changed very slowly; on the whole, rather slightly; and in many ways, not at all. The peasant got personal freedom from slavery and serfdom at once, but he lost economic security thereby. He remained, moreover, a member of a class apart—still *narod,* still the underdog.

The reforms of landholding and of administration were essentially collective in nature and application. So were the freedoms which were granted. The reforms by deliberate intent continued and strengthened the old institutions of the household (or large family) and the mir. These were both collective social units, and continuance of them was the prolongation of a tradition which we have already noted. It was a tradition at great variance with ours—a point of great significance and one which is often ignored or suppressed by those who stress points of similarity between Russia and America. This difference was a major one.

🏵 CAUSES

Serf emancipation was an explosion, long foreseen, of forces long gathering. It had been considered by the Russian rulers and their counselors from the time of Catherine the Great. The palliative measures attempted by Paul, by Alexander I, and by Nicholas are all evidences of this continuing concern. They also furnished a useful historical precedent for Alexander II's more drastic action. The increasing serf discontent which was manifested by the growing number and seriousness of rebellions must have been indisputable evidence that change was overdue. It took a war, however, to precipitate it. As Pares often said, "The Crimean War rammed home to Alexander that the serf problem had to be settled by emancipation." There was no other way, and it is noteworthy that the manifesto which announced the Peace of Paris of 1856 to the Russian nation also promised internal reforms.

The hardest to measure of all the long-term causes was the change in intellectual climate produced by liberal intellectualism. This directly touched only a very few persons, but its indirect results were widespread. Taken by itself, intellectual liberalism would not have produced emancipation. On the other hand, emancipation as a possible solution for an economic and social problem would probably not have been thought of had it not been for prior intellectual changes. The revolutionaries—from Radischev and Novikov to Herzen and Chernishevsky —had challenged successfully some of the most important norms and values of old Russia. This, slowly and over a period of many years, had produced an atmosphere favorable to further changes.

Equally subtle, and perhaps more pervasive, was the influence of the traditional peasant assumption about landownership. Again, taken alone, this could not and did not cause emancipation. Moreover, the settlement did not conform to the peasant notion that the land properly belonged to those who worked it (provided, of course, that they were Orthodox and loyal children of the tsar). But the peasants' feelings created a tremendous and unrelenting pressure which was slower but no less effective for being inarticulate.

The economic causes of emancipation have been the most thoroughly explored. Emancipation came about, say the Marxists, because the serf system developed a fatal crisis in itself which resulted in a political crisis that forced action. It was done in such a way "as to leave the peasant in a position in which he could be exploited most harshly through economic compulsion." There is some justice in this charge, just as there is some truth in assigning economic causes to the event. Among such causes were the increase in population, especially in the black-soil provinces, which thus had a labor surplus impossible to absorb under the system of *barshchina* which prevailed there; the low productivity of serf labor both on the land and in the factories; and the steadily increasing financial difficulties of the landlord class. The shift to a trading, money economy was important both as a cause and as a symptom. None of these things, taken singly, brought about emancipation. Its causes, as even these few paragraphs show, were varied and complex. And it took a complicated series of maneuvers to bring the emancipation acts to completion.

NEGOTIATIONS

One of the reasons for the long-drawn-out and difficult negotiations which preceded the actual drafting of the law was the differences of opinion and the clash of interests among those who had a hand in making the reform. In the black-soil regions, where there were more serfs than could profitably be employed, it had already come about that land without serfs commanded a much higher price than land with serfs. The land, that is to say, was more valuable than the labor. The landlords in these regions favored an arrangement which would guarantee them full right of landownership while releasing them from any obligation to support an unproductive labor force. They wanted emancipation without land. The government was afraid that this would create a large number of landless unemployed who would menace the peace and security of the state. The government therefore favored emancipation with land. Some of the landowners of the black-soil regions desired that the serfs be given enough land to tie them to their villages, thus ensuring an adequate labor supply at hand. They also favored charging high fees for the land allotted to the serfs in order to provide themselves with more capital.

In the other regions, land with serfs was worth about thirty times as much as land without serfs. Landowners got most of their income from labor, so they demanded high compensation for the loss of their serfs but were not much interested in land allotments. In the areas where labor was in relatively short supply, or where the land was thought to hold great potential value, the owners sought an arrangement which would give the serfs just enough land to hold them as residents, but not enough to make them independent and therefore unwilling to work for wages. There was never any division among these groups as to the basic principle of ownership of the land. They all agreed that the land, whether in use by the serfs or by the landowners themselves, belonged to the landlords. No one suggested that the serf had any property rights, nor were the serfs in any way consulted about their own emancipation.

The first step was the appointment of a number of secret committees, charged with suggesting ways and means of emancipation. These worked through 1856. There was then appointed another committee which became the Main Committee. This dallied until the late summer of 1857, when the Lithuanian landowners, hoping to forestall government action, brought forth their own suggestion to liberate the serfs without land and without compensation. This galvanized Alexander into action, and he ordered Minister of the Interior Lanskoy to draft an order for the liberation of the Lithuanian serfs with land. The order was issued in November, 1857, and similar decrees later extended the reform to other sections. These actions committed the government to emancipation with land. Provincial committees of the nobility were now appointed (1858) to work out projects for submission to the Main Committee. Editorial work on the projects and the discussion of them took many months, and then the Main Committee again considered the results. Not until January, 1861, was the project submitted to the State Council, which gave its approval in early February. Alexander signed the Act on February 19, and published it March 5.

THE ACT OF THE NINETEENTH OF FEBRUARY

The Act of the Nineteenth of February, as it was called, was long and complicated and showed clearly the many compromises which had gone into its making. There were seventeen articles and several special rules, and each article had at least one hundred sections. It was obscure in some parts, confused in others, and even self-contradictory in places. But its first article was simple, precise, and definitive. It read: "The right of bondage over the peasants settled upon the landlords' estates, and over the courtyard people, is forever abolished." This sentence transformed the serfs belonging to private owners from chattel properties into human beings. It applied both to field workers and domestic serfs (the courtyard people). Later legislation freed the serfs belonging to the imperial family and to the state. Certain limited freedoms and personal liberties were granted immediately by the act; its other provisions did not become operative for two years. From the date of the act, the serfs (now peasants) were free to enter trade, take up a craft, marry without permission; but they were not free to choose their occupations. The landlords could no longer sell or otherwise dispose of the persons of their peasants, but they did keep the right of punishment and of maintaining order over them until special courts (called *volost* courts) were created. The peasants also had to pay certain obligations to the landlords (both *obrok* and *barshchina*) during the transition period, which in some cases was extended for twenty years.

The letter of the act provided that sufficient land should be allotted to the peasants "to guarantee their livelihood and the fulfillment of their obligations to the state and to the landlord." The allotments were made not to individual peasants or peasant families but to the mir, which was thus given control over its members. The general basis for land allotment was to give the peasant roughly the same area of land which he had worked for himself before emancipation. This meant approximately half the arable land. There were many local variations, some of them provided for by the act. In the black-soil regions, the allotments generally were a little smaller than the area used by the serfs before reform. The reverse was generally true in the other regions. By and large, this disparity evened itself out because of the difference in soil fertility. In both cases, the amount of land granted to the peasants was insufficient. The payments which the peasants had to make for these grants of land and liberties were also, generally, too high.

The price placed upon the allotments was called the redemption value and was calculated on the basis of a 6 per cent return upon capital. That is to say, an *obrok* of sixty rubles was arbitrarily held to represent a capital value of a thousand rubles. Since *obrok* was paid on activities other than the cultivation of the land, as well as upon that, the capitalization was inflated and the peasant obligation was unduly high. Thus the average selling price of an allotment in the black-soil regions before the act was 219 rubles. The redemption value placed on the same allotment was 342 rubles. The jump in the value of the allotments in the nonblack-soil regions was even greater; that in the western provinces, very much less. Because the newly free peasants could not possibly pay such sums at once, the government undertook to finance the procedure. If the peasants asked for the settlement, the government gave the landowner "redemption certificates" bearing 6 per cent interest for 80 per cent of the capitalized value. The remaining 20 per cent of the capitalized value had to be paid by the peasants directly to the landowners. In case the owners requested the settlement, they received only the 80 per cent in certificates. The government, which acted somewhat like a finance company in this transaction, then undertook to collect from the peasants the sum advanced to the landlord (including interest). These redemption payments, so-called, were spread over forty-nine years, and constituted a sort of installment plan for the purchase of land and limited freedom.

✿ CONSEQUENCES OF EMANCIPATION

These terms placed an undue burden upon the peasantry. They were recurrently and increasingly in default of their redemption payments to the government, so that these had to be reduced from time to time and, finally, written off altogether as bad debts. Before that was done, however, enormous sums had been paid—probably about two billion rubles. Moreover, the settlement made the peasants and the landlords economic enemies. The peasants, unable to live on their agricultural production from the lands allotted to them, had either to get more land by purchase or rental, or to increase their incomes by some sort of wage labor. Since the landlords derived most of their income from the rent or sale of their lands, they tried to get as high a price as possible for these things. They also sought to keep wages low. The peasants, of course, wanted just the reverse: high wages and low land-rentals and prices. The peasants suffered gravely. On the other hand, the place and power of the *dvorianstvo* had rested upon their ownership of land and serfs. They had now lost the basis of their strength. The result was that the *dvorianstvo* was a dying class from 1861 on. As a class, they lasted less than two generations after the Act of the Nineteenth of February, 1861.

The power of the aristocracy rested upon its absolute control over the most important natural resources of Russia; that is, upon its ownership of the land and the serfs. The power of the tsardom, in turn, rested upon the privileged aristocracy. The aristocrats (i.e., the *dvorianstvo*) headed the military and civil services; were the actual local rulers who collected taxes, supplied conscripts, administered law, dispensed justice, and, in short, ran the country. The power of the tsar was legally greater than that of the aristocracy. It was actually greater than that of any single aristocrat, but not greater than the power of the class as a whole. The tsars ruled with, by, for (and even to some degree at the sufferance of) the *dvorianstvo*. Emancipation broke the power of the *dvorianstvo* —not all at once, to be sure, but slowly. When their power went, the power of the government went with it. This was the greatest and most important long-term result of emancipation.

Of almost equal significance were the slow consequences of the grant of freedom to millions of men and women and their descendants. This freedom was severely restricted. The peasantry remained a class apart, subject to special obligations, special laws, and special courts. Their economic conditions were rather worse than better, at least for a long time. But the grant of freedom released a tremendous dynamic which, it may be ventured, is not yet exhausted, although presently it is terribly confined and channeled.

OTHER REFORMS: THE ZEMSTVA

Emancipation also had other results which were more immediate, more tangible, and much easier to describe. The "Great Reform" of Tsar-Liberator Alexander II made lesser reforms necessary. As the basis of the state and of the state's power was changed, it became imperative to alter the machinery of the state. New local governments had, first of all, to be created to take the place of the government-by-landlord which the Great Reform had destroyed. This was done by the law of 1864 which created zemstva assemblies and boards in provinces and districts.[1]

The man who conceived the general nature of the reform which established the zemstva was N. A. Miliutin, a liberal reformer and a most able statesman who had played a very important part in the Great Reform. Alexander appointed Miliutin as the head of the commission charged with drafting the law, but replaced him with a less liberal person before the draft was complete. The law was presumably somewhat less liberal than Miliutin had intended. It would have been even more conservative if the State Council had not rejected an effort to give the nobility complete pre-eminence in the zemstva assemblies and boards. These were established on paper for provinces and districts as of January 1, 1864, but they actually were introduced very slowly—at first in only thirty-three of the fifty provinces of Russia Proper. Before the zemstva were actually in operation a conservative reaction had already begun within the government so that the reform was not carried out as originally planned.

The district zemstva assemblies were elected by a three-class system of voting—a device not at all uncommon in Central and Eastern Europe. The peasants formed one class; the townspeople, a second; and the private landowners, a third. Each class elected its own representatives to the assemblies. Elections were indirect; that is, the voters chose electors, who then chose the assemblymen. For the peasant class, the system was as follows: The peasants' village assemblies, composed of the heads of families, appointed the members of the *volost* council. (The *volost* was a small administrative division made up of several neighboring villages.) The *volost* councils appointed an electoral assembly which then chose the delegates to the district zemstvo assembly. The arrangement for the other two classes was also indirect, but there were fewer stages between the electorate and the assembly. Suffrage was on a property basis for both townsmen and landowners. The amount of property necessary to qualify as a voter was very high for townsmen. For landowners the minimum was ownership of upwards of 500 acres, but it was possible for those who owned less than this to join together and to nominate as many electors as the sum total of their lands allowed. Thus four landlords whose total holdings came to 1600 acres could nominate three electors, and so on.

The provincial zemstva assemblies were elected by the district assemblies for a three-year term. Any member of a district assembly was eligible for election to the assembly of his province. But since very few peasants had the time or the money to allow their attendance at a provincial assembly, they usually left this to the landowners. Since the president of the provincial assembly was, by law, the Marshal of Nobility for the province, this meant that the provincial assemblies were almost exclusively composed of *dvorianstvo*. They met annually for a session not exceeding twenty days. Provincial zemstva boards, composed of paid employees, were chosen by the provincial assemblies. The boards were in continuous session throughout their three-year terms. The provincial assemblies and boards, in general, did on a provincial scale what the district assemblies and boards did on a smaller scale. (The district boards were also made up of paid employees. They were chosen by the district assembly and were also in permanent session. Assemblymen were not paid at either level.)

The zemstva were charged with the responsibility within their respective areas for building and maintaining primary schools, hospitals, asylums, roads, bridges, and other community projects. They also were supposed to provide medical services and charity, to promote agriculture, to improve animal husbandry, and so on. In order to finance these works, the zemstva were given the power to set local assessments and to levy local taxes. The conscientiousness with which the various zemstva accepted and discharged their powers and duties varied widely. Some were much more vigorous and efficient than others, and some accomplished truly remarkable feats. All of them suffered from increasing curtailment of their powers and their freedom of action during the generation following their establishment.

THE ZEMSTVA AND THE *Dvorianstvo*

Russian liberal historians and other liberal critics of the late nineteenth and early twentieth centuries generally charged the government with undue favoritism of the upper classes after the Great Reform. The distinguished historian and liberal politician Paul Miliukov said flatly that

". . . Russian noblemen were again taken under the protection of the government . . . [and] the government tried to make good the material losses of the nobility after emancipation. . . ." There is considerable evidence in support of this thesis. Elections to the district assemblies under the 1864 law returned a total of 13,024 members in thirty-three provinces. Nearly half of these (6204) were *dvorianstvo*. The peasants came next with 5171 and the townsmen were a poor third with 1649.[2] This gave one delegate to every eight private landowners or nobles; one to every 1800 male townsmen; and one to every 4300 peasant taxpayers. After the change in the zemstva elections by the law of 1890, the disparities were further increased. The *dvorianstvo* then elected 57 per cent of the members; the peasants, 30 per cent, and the townsmen 13 per cent.

The predominance of the upper classes obviously cannot be denied, but certain additional facts should also be pointed out. In the first place emancipation, by breaking down the existing system of local government, made it necessary to erect a substitute at once. In the second place, both tradition and current circumstances made it almost inevitable that the responsibility be entrusted to the *dvorianstvo* class. They had arisen originally on the basis of service, and the tradition of state service, stemming from Tatar times and greatly strengthened by Ivan Grozny and Peter the Great, had survived even the Charter of Catherine, though it had been weakened thereby. It was a natural following of precedent to continue to place responsibility for local government in the hands of this class. Besides, what other alternative was there? The newly freed peasants were scarcely competent to discharge this additional responsibility at once. These circumstances were changed and might have been changed further within the generation after the establishment of the zemstva. The government might have used those years to train the peasants in self-government. It didn't, and the laws of 1889 and of 1890 went precisely the other way. The law of 1890 further restricting suffrage has been mentioned. The law of 1889 established an official known as a "land captain" (*nachalnik*), who was made, as Vinogradoff put it, "the center of all administrative affairs of his district." The land captain was placed in charge of the peasantry; he served as judge in minor civil and criminal cases, had power over the village elders, and exerted authority over measures of public health, sanitation, poor relief, and so on. This clearly curtailed the work and authority of the zemstva. Yet observers generally agreed that peasants and nobles seemed to co-operate very well in the zemstva work. The nobles, with exceptions of course, did not ordinarily place the interests of their class above those of the group.

What the Zemstva Law of 1864 sought to do for the rural areas, the Municipal Act of 1870 sought to do for the towns. This act created town councils with powers and duties roughly comparable to those of the zemstva. All tax-paying town residents had the right of suffrage for elections to the town councils, but this apparent liberalism was nullified by a class system of voting. Taxpayers were divided into three groups on the basis of the amount of taxes paid. Those who paid the highest taxes elected one-third of the members of the council. The middle group of taxpayers elected the second third; and the majority of taxpayers also elected a third. What this meant can be seen most readily by the experience of St. Petersburg in 1873. There were 18,580 taxpayers out of the city's total population of about 800,000. Group I—those who paid the highest taxes—numbered only 224 people. They elected one-third of the council. Group II numbered 887. They also elected a third of the council. The remaining third was elected by Group III, which numbered 17,479. No comment is needed. Wallace said that the citizenry discharged their civic responsibilities so poorly that the imperial government was forced to reform the system. It did so in 1892, by restoring much of the authority and responsibility to the imperial bureaucracy.

🏛 JUDICIAL AND MILITARY REFORMS

The third of the lesser reforms was that affecting the judiciary. This was long overdue, because the court system was notoriously inefficient, corrupt, and unfair. Peter the Great's attempt to reform the judiciary on the Swedish model had only a very limited success. Catherine the Great's judicial reform resulted chiefly in complicating the system by greatly increasing the number of courts. The two generations between Catherine and Alexander II had seen no improvement, but, rather, the reverse. There were, to begin with, a multiplicity of courts: courts for every class, courts for arbitration, commercial courts, district courts, and so on. Second, judges and other court officers were often totally unprepared for their posts; many of them were illiterate or nearly so. Third, the venality of all court officials was literally proverbial. Bribery was the common practice—"No grease, no motion," as one of the proverbs expressed it. Finally, the rules of evidence were notoriously inequitable. For example, if the testimony of two witnesses differed, it was decreed by law that the testimony of a man be taken in preference to that of a woman; that of a noble, to that of a commoner; that of an educated man, to that of a man without education; and that of a clergyman, to that of a layman. As the crowning touch, the law also provided that when the evidence submitted was insufficient to support a verdict of "guilty" or "innocent," the person accused was not discharged but "left under suspicion." All these and other abuses the judicial reform of 1864 was intended to sweep away.

It was the purpose of the reformers to create a whole new judicial system based on the highest principles: equality before the law, absolute independence of the judiciary, open and public trials and charges, adequate defense of the accused, and trial by jury. But the "second thoughts of the autocracy" set in before the reform was drafted, and performance fell short of hopes. Instead of the equality before the law, which was promised, the reform left the peasants under the *volost* courts and the *volost* law, to which no other classes were subject. The newly established courts were for the nonpeasant minority only. However, there was equality before the law within these courts. In place of trial by jury, which was intended to be a guiding principle, certain cases—state treason, official misdemeanors, and freedom of the press—were removed from the competence of juries. Jury duty, moreover, remained the privilege of the well-to-do and did not become the duty and right of citizens. Jury lists were controlled by the government, which often barred from jury service any class or group which it did not trust. The reform came a little closer to establishing an independent judiciary, but even this was not fully achieved because the Minister of Justice retained the power of promoting and rewarding judges. Yet, in spite of all these concessions to conservatism and reaction, the judicial reform marked a tremendous improvement over previous conditions. At the very least, the reform established certain principles as working bases, even though these did not cover all the courts and were not always observed.

One other reform deserves attention, the military reform of 1874. This was the work of Dimitri Miliutin, brother of the Miliutin who began the work on the zemstva. The intent of the reform was a democratization of military conscription, which had hitherto fallen almost exclusively on the peasants. The reform of 1874 established a universal obligation for military service. Draft age was twenty, and draftees were required to serve six years of active duty, then nine years as reserves, followed by five years in the militia. Up to 1861, draftees had been required to serve twenty-five years of active duty, and the draft ages were from twenty to thirty-four. (The length of service was reduced to sixteen years in 1861.) Miliutin's reform provided for exemptions from the draft in hardship cases (only sons, sole support of family, and so on). So far the reform was democratic, but legal exceptions largely nullified its stated purpose. Instead of six years of active duty, university men were required to serve for only six months, or three if they volunteered instead of waiting to be drafted. Graduates of secondary schools had to serve only two years; those with middle education, three; and those with primary education, four. Only the uneducated—which meant, of course, the least privileged—were required to serve the full terms.

ANALYSIS OF THE REFORMS

This giving with the one hand while taking away with the other was characteristic of all of Alexander's reforms. This was normal enough, though it was frustrating in the extreme to hopeful liberals, impatient reformers, and revolutionary doctrinaires. The reforms, after all, were compromises between the norm and value patterns which had long existed and the new patterns which certain persons and groups wished to have established. Men generally cling tenaciously to old ways, stubbornly resisting and rejecting the new until its newness has been rubbed off. Vested interests offered coherent and at least semiorganized opposition which even an absolute tsar had to take into account. And, as always happens, there existed side by side those who felt that the changes had gone too far too fast, and those who felt that the changes had not gone far enough or fast enough. The extremists often felt driven to violence in defense of their positions. Violent action caused violent reaction. The attempt of Karakozov to murder Alexander called forth more stringent security measures which, in turn, evoked more reckless hostility to the government, which brought more vigorous repression, and so on.

It was this sort of conflict that produced the vacillation with which Alexander's government, after 1866, has often been charged. In the government were agents and champions of both reform and reaction. Now one, now the other was more influential. Karakozov's act and other evidences of violent discontent led Alexander to replace the liberal Minister of Education, Golovnin, with the reactionary Count D. A. Tolstoy; to replace the aging chief of the Secret Police with a vigorous young man, the antiliberal Shuvalov. The more liberal advisers—such as the Miliutins and Finance Minister Reitern—were temporarily eclipsed. But they were not ejected, and were sometimes able to carry their points.

REACTIONS TO THE REFORMS

Alexander's reforms were variously received. Not all the presumed beneficiaries were grateful by any means. The peasant reaction to the emancipation is an important case in point. Wallace points out that the peasants applied two tests to this reform and that the reform failed in both. One test was the peasants' concept of landownership. "We are yours, but the land is ours" was one of their ways of saying it. The Great Reform, as we have seen, did not give the land to the peasants.

The other test was whether the change was to the peasants' material advantage. It was not. The peasant reaction was described by Kravchinski in the following passage:

To begin with, they decline to believe in the authenticity of the Emancipation Act. To their candid, unsophisticated minds it seemed utterly incredible that their Tsars should have "wronged" them so bitterly as to the land. They obstinately repeated that their "freedom," i.e., the Emancipation Act, had been tampered with by the nobility, who had concealed the Tsar's real "freedom," which had been quite a different thing. The most emphatic declarations made before the peasants' deputies and elders by the Emperor's ministers and by the Emperor in person could not disabuse them. They persisted in believing against belief. There were hundreds of peasant rebellions in all parts of the empire, owing to this misunderstanding, especially during the first years which followed the Act of Emancipation.

The peasants certainly had adequate reason for complaint. Kornilov has estimated that a dozen years after the Great Reform the average peasant family was expected to pay an annual tax sum of about thirty rubles. "Such payments," concludes Kornilov, "were doubtless unbearable for the ordinary peasant." And in addition to taxes, there were also other heavy obligations which fell exclusively on the peasants. Moreover, the old bugbear of crop failures had not been removed, nor did the government take adequate measures for relief. Serious crop failures and famines occurred in 1867 and in 1870–73. The government at first refused to admit the existence of the 1867 famine and finally gave help to the starving only grudgingly and after long delay. It was such incidents, coupled with frustrated impatience at the incompleteness of the reforms and with reaction against the government's oppressive measures, that led some of the intelligentsia to open rebellion. It must in honesty be added that there was, on the part of some of the rebels at least, irresponsibility as well as a social conscience.

Among the irresponsibles was one Nechaiev, a disciple of Bakunin. He led a secret society formed from among university students, and his chief feat was to instigate the murder of one of the members of his group who opposed Nechaiev's extremism. The group was broken by arrests and exile after the murder. Equally extreme and melodramatic, and almost equally irresponsible, were two student groups: "Young Russia" and one of its successors, "Hell." Both were characterized by complete lack of restraint. "Kill the Tsar's party unsparingly. . . ." read one of the proclamations of Young Russia, "kill them on the squares . . . kill them in their homes . . . kill them in the narrow alleys of the towns, kill them on the broad streets of the capital, kill them in the villages." The proclamation went on to lay down the rule later adopted by Lenin and his successors. "Remember that whoever is not with us is against us; whoever is against us is our enemy and enemies must be exterminated by all means."

Much more important than these groups, which had extremely small followings, was "The Circle of Chaikovsky." This was also a small group in its beginnings—a handful of young men and women who gathered together originally for purposes of self-education, discussion, and philanthropy. They very soon discovered than none of their aims were attainable under the existing system, and they became "politicals" (that is, political opponents of the government) as a necessary first step. One of the members was the famous liberal-revolutionary Prince Kropotkin, who left a very sympathetic description of the Circle in his *Memoirs of a Revolutionist*. Another famous and important member of the Circle was the woman known in the West as Catherine Breshkovsky. She was a remarkable person and of the essence of the revolutionary movements with which we are dealing.

✈ BRESHKOVSKAYA AND THE *Narodniki*

Ekaterina Konstantinova Breshko-Breshkovskaya was the daughter of a wealthy and aristocratic Polish landowner. Her mother was a member of the Russian aristocracy. Madame Breshkovskaya grew up in wealth and comfort, with her material well-being and social position assured. Since her father was liberal, in a mild sort of way, he permitted his daughter to go to St. Petersburg when she was in her late teens. She promptly became associated with the liberal and revolutionary groups which centered at the university and was one of The Circle of Chaikovsky. Her own convictions, re-enforced by these associations, led her to become a follower of Bakunin for a time and, later, of the *Narodniki*.[3]

Leaving her husband and their son, Madame Breshkovskaya plunged into work among the peasants. Betrayed by some of those whom she sought to help—a very common misfortune of the *Narodniki*—she was arrested and jailed. Four years later she was tried and sentenced to hard labor in Siberia. An attempted escape which failed led to prolongation of her sentence. After serving the "hard" part of her punishment, she was kept in Siberia until 1896. Then, twenty-two years after her first arrest, she returned to European Russia.

Immediately she set about organizing the Social Revolutionary Party, which she helped to found. A brief period of voluntary exile, part of it spent in the United States, was followed by a return to Russia and a resumption of her underground work. She was again arrested, in 1908, and again exiled to Siberia, where she stayed until the Revolution of February/March, 1917, brought her release. By that time the revolution had outsped this "grandmother of the Russian Revolution," as her admirers called her. Madame Breshkovskaya went again into exile abroad after the Bolshevik victory. She died in Prague in 1934 (at the age of ninety), a vigorous opponent of the Communists.

Most of her associates among the *Narodniki* shared neither Breshkovskaya's longevity nor her flaming courage, which survived so many ordeals. The movement was clearly failing and would probably have died altogether if the government had not fallen into a panic of wholesale arrests and strict suppressions. According to a count made by the secret police in 1874, there were only 770 members in all the revolutionary groups together. Two hundred and sixty-five of them were already in jail, 452 were under police surveillance, and only fifty-three were unknown to the authorities. Yet the government acted as if tens of thousands of armed revolutionaries were on the march. Its actions, especially the "Trial of the 193," crystallized a new sort of desperate opposition—terrorism. The signal for its outbreak was a tragic and rather curious incident.

ZASULICH AND *Narodnaya Volya*

Trepov, chief of police in St. Petersburg, had a flogging administered to a young student who was held as a political prisoner. In revenge for this, a young woman named Vera Zasulich (afterwards an associate of George Plekhanov, Russia's first Marxist) shot Trepov with the intention of killing him. Arrested and brought to trial, Zasulich did not deny the charge, but the jury acquitted her just the same. The crowd, which heard the verdict with glee, prevented the secret police from rearresting Zasulich, and she subsequently escaped to the West. This event, in 1878, marked the beginning of terrorism. Its chief exponents were the members of a revolutionary group who called themselves *Narodnaya Volya* ("The Will of the People").

The forerunner of *Narodnaya Volya* was a small group in the city of Kiev which tried in 1877 to assassinate the procurator. The attempt was a failure, but the group—which signed itself "The Executive Committee," though it had no real organization—published its program by posting placards about the city. The leaders in this movement subsequently joined forces with other young revolutionaries. Some of the larger group wished to continue the old *V narod* program and went their own way until after 1881, when they were broken up by the government. The others—plus some further additions—organized the *Narodnaya Volya* party in June, 1879. Their program, published as a manifesto, began:

By fundamental conviction we are socialists and men of the people. We are sure that only through socialistic principles can the human race acquire liberty, equality, and fraternity; secure the full and harmonious development of the individual as well as the material prosperity of all; and thus make progress. We are convinced that all social forms must rest upon the will of the people themselves, and that popular development is permanent only when it proceeds freely and independently, and when every idea that is to be embodied in the people's life has first passed through the people's consciousness and has been acted upon by the people's will. The welfare of the people and the will of the people are our two most sacred and most inseparable principles.

The manifesto went on to say that the Russian people lived in a "state of absolute slavery" and that, therefore, the first task of *Narodnaya Volya* was "to remove the crushing burden of the existing system . . . and to make a political revolution with the object of giving power into the hands of the people." The instrument of popular will and power was to be a freely elected constituent assembly. But the group recognized that the people were not yet ready to take on such great responsibilities, and it was proposed to undertake a gradual program of education prior to the revolution. The specific points to be achieved were gradual popular representation; local autonomy; replacement of the standing army with a militia; complete freedom of speech, press, assembly, and elections; ownership of mines and factories by the workers; and the ownership of land by the people (*narod*).

The group proposed to move toward these goals (which could be fully realized only after the revolution) by four main routes: (1) infiltration into the army, the administration, and popular groups; (2) the organization and centralization of secret societies; (3) "propaganda and agitation"; and (4) "destructive and terroristic activity." "Towards the government as an enemy," the manifesto declared, "the end justifies the means; we regard as permissible every means leading towards the end." Readers will be struck by the resemblance between the program of *Narodnaya Volya* and that of the later revolutionary groups led by Lenin. The only part of their program which the members of *Narodnaya Volya* actively carried out was terrorism. Their target was the Tsar-Liberator himself. Their first attempts miscarried, but in March, 1881, as the emperor's carriage, escorted by Cossacks, rolled along the Catherine Canal, one of the terrorists tossed his bomb under the horses' hooves. The horses were killed and some of the Cossacks were wounded. Alexander, in complete disregard for his own safety, went to the aid of the injured. A second conspirator threw his bomb directly at the feet of the emperor. Alexander, horribly mangled, died after a few hours of agony. With him died the era of the reforms.

CHAPTER XV

Expansion and Foreign Policies from Crimea to Korea

The story of foreign affairs during the reign of Alexander II is almost as full as the story of domestic developments. There were two major wars (the Crimean and the Russo-Turk War of 1877–78); successful expansion of the empire in Central Asia and the Far East, and contraction of it by the sale of Alaska; a revolt in Poland which had important diplomatic ramifications; and a Russo-Prussian diplomatic friendship which lasted for about twenty years. This was also the heyday of Pan-Slavism, its efforts culminating in war. We shall deal with these things thematically, beginning with the Far East, where Russia harvested the results of Muraviev-Amurski's work.

THE FAR EAST: CHINA

It will be recalled that Muraviev had sent three expeditions down the Amur River between 1854 and 1856. Each had been a little larger than the preceding one, and each had left settlements behind. The Chinese resented this violation of what they considered to be their property, but they were unable to do more than protest, since the T'ai P'ing Rebellion, which lasted from 1850 to 1864 and a series of wars between China and the French and British (1856–60) had all but crippled the Chinese government. Russia was able to turn China's embarrassment to her own advantage.

As early as 1853, Muraviev-Amurski had opened negotiations with China for the purpose of getting legal recognition, by treaty, of his conquests and annexations. The Chinese were naturally loathe to acquiesce in their own despoilment, and the conversations dragged on without issue until 1858. Then Muraviev-Amurski demanded the cession of the left bank of the Amur River and the whole of the so-called Maritime

Provinces. Yi-chan, the Chinese envoy, refused these demands, where-upon Muraviev threatened war. China yielded, or appeared to, and signed the Treaty of Aigun (1858), which provided for joint navigational rights on the Amur, Ussuri, and Sungari rivers; joint occupation of the Ussuri area; and freedom of frontier trade. China never intended to live up to this agreement. She refused to ratify it, and disavowed Yi-chan, who had signed it. Only under the continuing and combined pressures of the rebellion and foreign interventions did she finally recognize the treaty as binding.

Meanwhile, the Russian government had sent one Putiatin to protect Russian interests and to act as an observer during the three-way negotia-tions among the British, the French, and the Chinese. (The United States also sent an observer.) Putiatin's instructions were to get for Russia whatever new or additional advantages might be given the French or the British. Putiatin joined with the American, the Frenchman, and the Britisher to force China to negotiate and compel her to sign the Treaty of Tientsin. Putiatin conducted himself with adroitness and managed to serve as mediator between the Chinese and the others. His reward was the very favorable treaty, which was signed in 1858 and ratified a year later. This treaty gave Russia rights to a permanent em-bassy at Peking, consulates at the open ports, the benefits of extraterri-toriality, and unlimited land trade with China. It also established regular diplomatic relations on the Western model and promised that Russia would never be treated less well than the nation most favored by China in subsequent agreements. The Treaty of Tientsin, complemented by the Treaty of Peking (1860), formed the main legal basis of Russian re-lations with China down to 1917.

The Treaty of Peking was the direct result of the Ignatiev mission to China. Nicholas Pavlovich Ignatiev, one of the most brilliant and daring of the Russian diplomats of the nineteenth century, was sent out to China in 1859 to follow up the work of Putiatin. Ignatiev was directed to get more favorable trade agreements, better boundaries, and the cession of the Ussuri region. He was also to implement the agreement made by Putiatin, under which Russia was to supply China with guns and military instructors. (Ignatiev's mission was, in fact, a military one.) But the Chinese suddenly got tough. They refused to accept the military mission; refused to ratify the Treaty of Aigun—but then yielded and did so—refused to ratify the Franco-British Treaty of Tientsin, but ratified the Russian treaty; and climaxed it all by capturing the French and British missions in Peking. The two Western Powers promptly re-opened their war against China, but it was almost a year before they could bring their power to bear and during that interval the Chinese refused

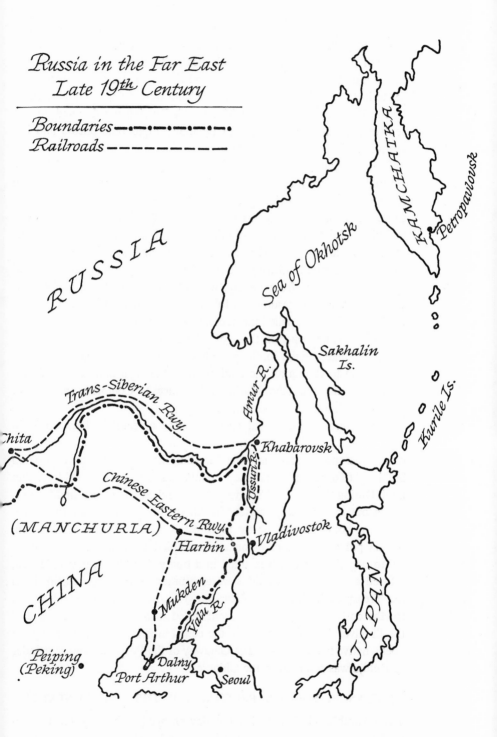

Russia in the Far East
Late 19th Century

Boundaries —·—·—·—·—·—·
Railroads ——————————

RUSSIA

KAMCHATKA

Petropavlovsk

Sea of Okhotsk

Sakhalin Is.

Trans-Siberian Rwy.

Amur R.

Kurile Is.

Chita

Khabarovsk

Ussuri R.

Chinese Eastern Rwy.

(MANCHURIA)

Vladivostok

CHINA

Harbin

Mukden

Yalu R.

JAPAN

Peiping
(Peking)

Dalny
Port Arthur

Seoul

all negotiations with Ignatiev. When the superior power of the West began to change defeat into victory for the French and British, the Russian policy showed a profitable flexibility. Ignatiev was ordered to act as a middleman between China and the West. He was instructed to see to it that the Manchu emperors of China were saved from destruction by the West, but not from punishment. A Russian naval squadron was sent out to add military force to Ignatiev's diplomatic finesse and immorality.

Ignatiev then double-crossed the Chinese and the French and British. He told the Western Powers that Russia had stopped her military mission for fear that the Russian guns would be used against Anglo-French troops. This of course was a lie, since it was China and not Russia who had blocked the mission. He told the French that the fall of the Manchus would cripple trade, which was at least debatable. And he suggested to the French and British that it would facilitate negotiations if they removed their troops from Peking, which they had captured in October, 1860. When this suggestion was followed, Ignatiev then told the Chinese that Russia had compelled the Western Powers to withdraw. So successfully did Ignatiev operate that both the French and the Chinese asked him to mediate. He did so, the price to China being the Treaty of Peking, which gave to Russia all the land between the right bank of the Ussuri River and the sea (the Maritime Provinces). Complete freedom of frontier trade was also established.

There were six additional Russo-Chinese agreements between 1860 and 1896. Most of them were modifications of previous treaties, but one needs special mention. The Manchus had at one time conquered Sinkiang (Turkestan), and they maintained a precarious hold on that land. During the late 1860's, a very serious rebellion against the Manchus broke out in the Kuldja region (northern Sinkiang). Partly to protect her own holdings, and partly to forestall and counter British action, Russia put down the rebellion and occupied Kuldja. Chinese protests led to negotiations which resulted in a treaty that China, having signed, refused to honor. Negotiations were resumed and culminated finally in the Treaty of Ili (or of St. Petersburg) in 1881. China repaid Russia for the costs of the occupation, and ceded to her the strategic gorge of the Ili River. The significance of the ceded area is well expressed by the poetic native name for it—"The Gateway of the Peoples." The remainder of Kuldja was returned to the Chinese.

✪ FRANCE, POLAND, PRUSSIA, AND THE UNITED STATES

The favorable relations which Ignatiev enjoyed with the French in regard to China were one aspect of a general diplomatic *rapprochement* between Moscow and Paris. This was largely the work, on the Russian side, of Prince Alexander M. Gorchakov (1798–1883), who was once called by his famous schoolfellow Pushkin, "Fortune's favored son." After extensive diplomatic service under Nesselrode, Gorchakov succeeded him as foreign minister in 1856 and, later, as Chancellor of the Empire. Gorchakov had initiated the move for better relations with France before the Treaty of Paris, which ended the Crimean War, and the negotiations were continued during the conference which made that treaty. In 1857 Alexander II and Napoleon III, who wanted Russian support for his Italian policy, met at Stuttgart. The outcome of their meeting was a secret Russo-French treaty in which Russia promised benevolent neutrality in the event of an Austro-French war. Gorchakov also sought to influence the German states against Austria. The Austrian answer was unofficial and clandestine support of the anti-Russian, Polish nationalist movement.

Poland was one of Alexander II's more difficult problems. The 1830 revolt had resulted in Poland's loss of political rights and in a policy of strict repression by the Russian governors. Alexander relaxed some of the more restrictive measures and granted amnesties to Polish political prisoners. The result was neither gratitude nor peace and contentment, but demands for more concessions. The situation became so tense that street demonstrations in Warsaw grew to riotous proportions in 1861. Russia then created a State Council for the Tsardom of Poland, giving the Poles a limited autonomy. This was not what the Polish upper classes wanted. They wanted the lands taken by Russia in the Partitions and the restoration of Polish independence, or, at the very least, complete autonomy. Russia was willing to go a long way, but not this far and not so fast as the more impatient Polish nationalists desired. Polish extremists engaged in acts of terrorism which were answered by drastic measures. In 1863 a handful of Poles revolted against the might of Russia. (The Polish peasants, who formed the overwhelming majority of the population, were either indifferent to the revolt or hostile to it.) The fighting—mostly on a guerrilla scale—went on for slightly more than a year, but the final outcome was never in doubt except when there was the possibility of foreign intervention on behalf of the Poles.

Bismarck, in Prussia, saw a chance to break the Russo-French combination, which greatly worried him, and possibly to embroil the Polonophil Napoleon III with Alexander. Within a fortnight after the revolt began, Prussia concluded a treaty with Russia promising all aid in suppressing the revolt and particularly in preventing the Prussian Poles from aiding their kinsmen. This support was very much appreciated by Russia, especially in view of the contrary actions taken by the other

Powers, and resulted in a pro-Prussian orientation of Russian policy. (Russia was benevolently neutral toward Prussia both during the Austro-Prussian War and the Franco-Prussian War.) As for Britain, France, and Austria, public opinion was pro-Polish or anti-Russian but not strongly enough to outweigh other considerations. Austria was still somewhat weakened by the Italian War of 1859, and was also rather apprehensive lest a successful Polish revolt against Russia arouse her Polish subjects to try the same thing. Napoleon was seriously entangled in his Mexican venture and was also mindful of how difficult it had been to fight Russia in Russia during the Crimean War. Palmerston of Great Britain was not at all inclined to go to war for Poland. The three Powers, nevertheless, made two formal diplomatic protests on behalf of the Polish rebels. Gorchakov flatly rejected the protests, correctly judging that none of the protestants would take action. He and Alexander did, however, take the precaution of removing the Baltic and Black Sea fleets from the possibility of blockade. This led to an incident of special interest to Americans.

During the fall of 1863, while the Polish situation was at its tensest point, a fleet of six Russian warships visited New York and another fleet of five visited San Francisco. The ships stayed about two months and the visitors were very hospitably welcomed. Presumably the North was glad of a chance to make the visits appear to the world as manifestations of Russian sympathy for the Northern cause. But neither officials nor the press had any illusions about the real reason for the incident. Secretary of the Navy Welles and Senator Sumner of Massachusetts, for example, both noted privately their opinion that the tsar intended to prevent any possible bottling up of his ships by ice or hostile fleets. The press from Maine to California pointed this out and added that Russia intended to use these ships as commerce raiders in the event of war with Britain or France. These were indeed the purposes of the visit, as the secret orders of the Russians' commanders showed. The often repeated assertions either that the visit was a friendly gesture or that it was so interpreted at the time are both incorrect. The action, like the subsequent sale of Alaska to the United States, was dictated solely by Russian interests. This was quite thoroughly understood in the United States at the time. In the case of the Alaska purchase (1867), Russia felt that she was getting rid of a possession from which the ready wealth had been taken and which she could not hope to defend in case of war. She felt that she was making a profitable sale. (The Russo-American Trading Company was on the verge of bankruptcy.) Some Americans felt the United States was getting a great bargain—as we were.

But to return to Poland, three events in 1864 deprived the revolutionaries of what little support they had. Austria finally blocked their use of Galicia, which had been their only source of supplies; the revolutionary leaders were betrayed to the Russians, captured, and hanged; and extensive Russian-sponsored peasant reforms turned more of the Polish people against the revolutionaries. Though these reforms were, as one English authority once put it, "carried out in the worst possible spirit," they nonetheless gave land to the Polish peasants. The Edict of 1864 granted to the peasants perpetual ownership of the lands which they cultivated and extended the right of the peasants to gather wood and use pasturage on the landowners' estates. The amount of land given to each peasant was inadequate, and the method of compensating the landlords was such as to make the peasants and the estate owners mutually hostile. But it is significant that the majority of the Polish peasants were not sympathetic with the violent anti-Russianism evoked among the upper- and middle-class Poles by the Russification policies which followed the suppression of the revolt.

EXPANSION IN CENTRAL ASIA

Meanwhile, Russia had been slowly and steadily expanding in Central Asia. This consistent drive in the general direction of Persia, India, and China may be regarded as the Russian equivalent of the overseas expansion of western Europe during the second half of the nineteenth century. Like that expansion, the Russian advance added many, many square miles of territory and millions and millions of non-European peoples to the empire. It also was the cause of international friction.

A combination of motives lay behind Russia's overland expansion. One series was economic; another, defensive and strategic; a third, the force of tradition; and so on. There was some sense of "a civilizing mission"—the equivalent of the French *mission civiliatrice* and of the British "white man's burden"—and some religious proselytizing. There were Russians—as there were Britishers, Frenchmen, Italians, Germans, and Americans—who sought gold or glory or adventure or, more simply, employment in expansion. The point is that the Russian movement was neither more nor less mysterious, nor nefarious, nor beneficent than the overseas imperialisms of the West. The Russians had as much or as little right to Turkestan, for example, as the United States had to Texas or California; or as the British had to India, or the French to Morocco, or the Germans to East Africa.

The economic motives for expansion included the relatively uncomplicated desire for trade, and the somewhat more complicated desire to profit from cotton-raising in Turkestan. (The American Civil War, incidentally, gave a tremendous boost to the cotton industry in Turkestan. The price of Turkestan cotton jumped 500 to 600 per cent between 1861 and 1864.) The building of railroads in Central Asia during the 1880's simultaneously enhanced the economic importance of that area, made it more readily defensible, and also increased the need for controlling it. The marauding tribes of the steppes interfered with the trade and, naturally, opposed the Russian occupation of their lands much as the American Indians did in the United States. This necessitated the maintenance of garrisons in force, and offered an excuse if not a reason for punitive and conquering expeditions. These, in turn, provoked fresh resistance which called for further "security" measures, which called forth new disturbances and so on, with the frontier being pushed farther south and east all the time. This expansion of Russia in Central Asia aroused the fears, the hostility, and—it may be added—the jealousies of Europe and especially of Great Britain.

At every point along her southern and eastern frontiers—the Ottoman Empire, Arabia, Persia, Afghanistan, Tibet, China—Russia found herself face to face with British power and pretensions. Time and again Russian advances called forth British fears and hostility, while British measures in turn aroused the Russians. Sometimes there was, or was thought to be, bad faith on both sides. The Russians, for example, once assured the British that an expedition against Khiva was for punitive purposes only and would be limited to 4200 men. But in reality a force of 14,000 was sent, and it proceeded to conquer and virtually to annex the region. On a later occasion, the Russians believed that the British had incited the Afghans to attack Russian forces and accused British officers of having led the attack. There was a temporary agreement, made in 1873, which established a boundary between Afghanistan and the Russian protectorate of Bokhara. But British support of the Turks at the time of the Russo-Turk War of 1877–78 and at the subsequent Congress of Berlin brought the two Powers very close to war. A British fleet steamed into the Dardanelles, and Russian forces in Turkestan began preparations for a campaign against India. The threatened war was averted, but the fears and enmity remained.

The British managed to turn Afghanistan into a subsidiary—which, of course, worried the Russians. The Russians, after several setbacks, conquered the fierce Tekke Turkomans and a little later added the important city of Merv to their possessions. This city is only 250 miles from Herat, "Gateway to India." The Russian government decided, at the end of 1884, that they would push to within about seventy miles of Herat (which would give them the Pendjeh district and Zulfikar Pass) but would go no further. The British did not believe reiterated Russian assurances. The crisis came in 1885. There was bold talk, but action was avoided and the danger passed. It may be added that the confidential reports of the Russian general staff for this period do not reveal any Russian projects for invading India. However, the Russians did use the threat of possible invasion as a club to bludgeon Britain into becoming "more accommodating" in Europe, especially in the Balkans. This brings us to the subject of Pan-Slavism, and of Russia's westward advances.

⍟ PAN-SLAVISM

Russian Pan-Slavism [1] was a romantic movement among the privileged upper-class minority. It was partly an outgrowth of Slavophilism, though it was also akin to various romantic and nationalistic movements of the West—an interpretation which the Slavophils would probably have decried. At any rate, it was the transition between Slavophilism and full-fledged Great Russian nationalism. Actually the three coexisted. The Russian prohibition of Morachevski's Ukrainian translation of the Gospels and of Lithuanian books in the Latin alphabet in 1863 were clear examples of nationalism and came before the publication of the most important Pan-Slav books. Ivan Aksakov was one of the early Pan-Slavists. More closely identified with the development of Pan-Slavism were N. I. Danilevsky (1822–85), R. A. Fadayev (1824–83), and N. P. Ignatiev (1832–1908). This is the man who was so active in Russo-Chinese relations.

Nicholas I. Danilevsky published in 1869 a long and ponderous tome entitled *Russia and Europe*. Its length and verbosity discouraged prospective readers until enthusiastic converts to Pan-Slavism found it a rich mine of arguments in their behalf. God, wrote Danilevsky, created separate, unchanging "national types" which cannot help being different and which cannot be transmuted any more than fish can suddenly develop lungs. Russia cannot develop Western institutions since these are incompatible with the Russian "national type." There is a glorious future for Slav civilization, especially for Russian civilization, if the Slavs are politically emancipated from western Europe. This can be accomplished only by war, which will also solve the "Eastern Question." Russia will win this war, and the fruit of victory will be a Russian-dominated, Slavic federation with Constantinople as its capital. These—plus the thesis that force was the dominating factor in international relations— were Danilevsky's main themes. He also set forth a project which has a startlingly modern sound.

Russia was to annex to herself Galicia, Bukovinia, and Carpatho-Romania. The next step was the formation of a Kingdom of Serbs, Croats, and Slovenes, which was to include Trieste and Montenegro. The third step was the formation of a Kingdom of the Czechs and Slovaks. Finally, these kingdoms were to be combined—plus Greece; plus Bulgaria, including Macedonia and parts of Romania; plus the province of Constantinople—into a Slavic federation under Russian dominance.

No less ambitious were the plans which Rotislav A. Fadayev set forth in his *Opinion on the Eastern Question*. The West regarded this book, published in 1869, as the epitome of Pan-Slavism. It was certainly provocative. It was also influential. Russia, declared Fadayev, must either extend her frontiers to the Adriatic or else withdraw to the Dnieper. She can win the full support of her fellow Slavs by setting up independent Slav states, and then combining them into a federation under her control. The most serious obstacle to the realization of this plan would be Austria, who would have the backing of Prussia. Therefore, said Fadayev, knock out Austria, seize Eastern Galicia and Bukovinia, and Turkey will fall. The way for successful Russo-Slav expansion will then be open and easy. The schemes of these men seem almost like prototypes of the Soviet plan and actions during and after World War II. The dynamics, however, were quite different—so different, in fact, that this may not be regarded as "history repeating itself."

Danilevsky and Fadayev, though certainly not without influence, were theorists and publicists. Ignatiev was a different sort. The West thought of him as the leading Pan-Slavist, but he was a Pan-Slavist only in the sense that he made use of their theories, excuses, and support in carrying out his own plans. His interests and aims were political and practical, not theoretical and mystic. A believer in and champion of Slavdom, but not of Orthodoxy, Ignatiev promoted common Slav action under Russian leadership. He believed that Russia had to attain mastery of Constantinople and the Straits either by diplomacy or by force, and he set himself to do this. He held, moreover, that the problem of the Straits was exclusively a Russian problem, and he rejected collective European action. More specifically, he sought (successfully) to revise the 1856 Treaty of Paris and (unsuccessfully) to end the collective guarantee of the Porte.

Ignatiev was a link between unofficial Pan-Slavism and its official and quasi-official aspects. He headed the Asiatic Department of the Foreign Office for a time; served as head of the legation (later raised to an embassy) at Constantinople from 1864 to 1877; and later (1881–82) served as Minister of the Interior. He was, throughout most of his career, a bitter rival of Gorchakov, who was, of course, his superior in the Foreign Office. The relations of the Foreign Office to its Asiatic Department were rather peculiar. Theoretically the department was the subordinate branch of the Foreign Office which handled affairs dealing with

Asia and European Turkey. The department, however, controlled most of the consular and diplomatic posts in the Near and Middle East, and it filled these places with men loyal to it. (Most of its staff were Balkan or Great Russian nationals, as contrasted to the Balts who predominated in the Foreign Office.) Gorchakov may have announced the policies, but Ignatiev and his men executed them or didn't execute them as the case might be. Pan-Slavs from the Asiatic Department were strong in the Russian embassy at Vienna, also, and they intrigued throughout the Balkans in connection with the so-called Slavonic Benevolent Committees and Societies.

These had been founded in 1858 with the approval of Alexander II for the original purpose of aiding in the development of national institutions among the Serbs, Croats, and Slovenes (or Yugoslavs). The program included bringing young Yugoslavs and young Bulgars to Russia for their educations. (The Soviet rulers have made extensive and successful use of this same technique.) Various branches of the committees and societies were developed both inside and outside of Russia. They enjoyed the strong support of the Orthodox Church and of the Asiatic Department during Ignatiev's term there. Their membership remained small and not very influential, however, until 1875, when the societies, with the blessings of some persons close to the throne, became very active in collecting funds for the Balkan rebels. There is clear evidence that this and other Russian actions were what kept alive these Balkan revolts of 1875–76. Monies were raised and sent—the Russian Church being very active in this—recruiting offices for the rebel armies were opened in Moscow, of course with the permission of the Russian government; Russian army officers were permitted to resign their commissions in order to enlist in the Servian army, with the right of later reinstatement to rank in their own army; and the government also facilitated the issue of passports and visas and even supplied special trains to transport the volunteers.

The position of Alexander II in all this was somewhat contradictory. He gave some backing to the Benevolent Committees, and showed marked favor to the Asiatic Department, especially under Ignatiev. That department was allowed to establish far more consulates in Serbia than was warranted by any legitimate need—a method of infiltration which the Soviets have also used. Alexander also allowed the department, the Holy Synod, and the Ministry of Education to co-operate in training Balkan Slavs, especially Bulgars, as Russian collaborators. Yet Alexander's support of the Pan-Slavs was neither unlimited nor consistent, and he does not seem to have become one of them, although both his wife and one of his daughters-in-law, the wife of the Tsarevich Alexander, were much influenced by Pan-Slavism. The emperor yielded to Pan-Slav pressures in 1875–76, however, and in an important public announcement he linked Russian Orthodoxy with the Slavic cause and spoke of a Russian mission in terms which would not have displeased Danilevsky. This came at a period of international crisis whose rise must now be treated.

✿ CRISES AND WAR

Back in 1871, following the Franco-Prussian War and the establishment of the German Empire, Austria had begun a *rapprochement* with Germany. This worried the Russian Foreign Office, which feared that an Austro-German combination might be set up against Russia. (The emergence of the new Germany drastically altered the balance of power in Europe to Russia's disadvantage.) When a meeting was in prospect between the German and Austrian emperors, Russian anxiety mounted so high that Alexander invited himself to attend. The three emperors reached a mutual understanding and made a verbal agreement to maintain the *status quo*. This was implemented early in 1873 by a Russo-German Military Convention, which bound each signatory to send 200,000 troops to the aid of the other in the event of an attack by a European Power. A month later (in June) the Schönbrunn Convention was signed between Russia and Austria. This was only a generalized agreement binding the two to consultations and eventual co-operation in the event of an attack on either of them. Germany also adhered to this agreement, thus forming the loose and indefinite Three Emperors' League (Dreikaiserbund), 1873–78. The weakest tie was between Russia and Austria, because their interests in the Balkans were basically opposed, but the first open friction among the partners developed between Russia and Germany.

In the spring of 1875 the French, resurgent after their defeat by the Prussians, increased the size of their army. This alarmed Bismarck, who realistically expected the French to undertake a war of revenge against him. He was determined to forestall this, and even more determined to prevent any Russo-French combination, which would threaten him on two fronts. He sent a special mission to Russia to keep his relations with that country in good repair if possible. On the other side, he caused to be published in the German press a provocative article entitled "Is War in Sight?" This almost precipitated another Franco-German conflict. The Russian Minister and Chancellor Gorchakov hated and mistrusted Bismarck, and primarily for that reason gave France his moral support in the crisis. Europe escaped the war, but Russo-German relations were seriously strained and the Three Emperors' League was very greatly weakened.

The year 1875 was a lively one diplomatically. In addition to the Russo-German squabble and the Franco-German crisis, there were serious Russo-British clashes in Central Asia and troubles in the Balkans and the Ottoman Empire. Crop failures throughout the Balkans in 1874 had created hardship conditions which, coupled with an increase in taxation by the sultan and with growing persecution of Balkan, Christian peasants by their Moslem landlords, produced revolts among the subject peoples. First the Herzegovinians, then the Bosnians, and then the Bulgars revolted against the Turks (1875). The revolutionaries had the support of Serbia, and behind Serbia stood the Russian Pan-Slavs and the Russian Empire. Austria also supported the revolts because she wanted an excuse for intervention. The sultan, hoping to end the revolts and to forestall European intervention which loomed ahead, ordered a whole series of reforms throughout his empire. The Powers were agreeable, but the insurgents were not and so the situation went on into 1876.

Then the members of the Three Emperors' League drafted a memorandum calling for an armistice and for certain reforms. This was accepted by France and Italy, but rejected by Britain chiefly because she resented the failure of the A.-R.-P. group to consult her in making the agreement. A British fleet was sent to Turkish waters to protect British interests and to demonstrate British power. Then a palace revolution in Constantinople resulted in a new sultan, a process that was repeated three months later. Just at the beginning of the summer of 1876, Serbia declared war on Turkey. The Serbs were soon joined by Montenegro, and they had the strong support of the Russians. Despite this, the war went against them. At this juncture, Russia and Austria sought to arrange the future. By the Reichstadt Agreement of July, 1876, they sought to provide for three possibilities: In the likely event of a Serbian defeat, they agreed to insist upon the restoration of the situation which had existed prior to the war, except for demanding that certain reforms be made in Bosnia and Herzegovina. If Serbia won, the two agreed that Russia was to take Bessarabia while Austria was to have the larger parts of the two provinces of Bosnia and Herzegovina. And in case the Ottoman Empire collapsed, Constantinople was to be made a free city; Bulgaria and Rumelia were to be given independence or autonomy; and Greece was to acquire some territory.

The Serbs were defeated in September, and promptly besought the intervention of the Powers. When a Russian suggestion for collective action was not immediately followed, Ignatiev presented an ultimatum to the sultan demanding that Turkey conclude an armistice with Serbia. This was done, but Russia continued to prepare for war against the Turks. (This was the time when Alexander spoke of the Russian mission, but it was also the time when he told the British that he had no intention of making any annexations in case he had to go to war with the Porte.) Attempted agreements among the Powers failed, largely because of Russo-British hostility, but Russia succeeded in enlarging the area of her agreement with Austria. Austria promised neutrality in case of a Russo-Turkish war, and received in return the promise that Russia would not oppose the Austrian annexation of Bosnia and Herzegovina. (Austria did not choose to annex these provinces until thirty years later, and it precipitated another very serious crisis when she did.) Russia also subsequently promised not to erect any large state, Slavic or otherwise, in the Balkans. During these months, Russia also sought to enlist Bismarck's full support. He was continually evasive but finally said that he would not permit either Russia or Austria to destroy the other.

Russia finally went to war against the Turks in April, 1877. Russian troops suffered several reverses until Romania allied herself with Russia in August. Then the allies moved swiftly forward both against the Turks in Asia Minor and in Europe. They captured Kars (in Asia Minor) and reached a point just outside of Constantinople. Meanwhile, the British, though vacillating on the means to use, had stuck to the policy of backing the Turks and of keeping the Russians out of Constantinople and away from the Straits. There was acute tension between London and St. Petersburg which was not reduced when Britain, at Turkey's request, sought to mediate a peace. Russia rejected mediation but signed an armistice with the Porte. While Russian troops stood just outside of Constantinople, war fever mounted in Britain. Finally, in February, 1878, a British fleet entered the Dardanelles, and there it stayed for over a year. Russia and Turkey signed and ratified the Treaty of San Stefano in March. This treaty granted independence to Serbia, Montenegro, and Romania; promised reforms in Bosnia and Herzegovina; gave Kars, Ardahan, and Batum to Russia; and created the large, autonomous state of Bulgaria, which was to have a Russian garrison for two years, and which reached to the Aegean Sea. Austria charged Russia with violating the Reichstadt and subsequent agreements, and demanded a revision of the treaty. Britain took even stronger action; she called up her reserves and garrisoned some eastern Mediterranean stations. Russia countered by creating a Cossack brigade in Persia, thus threatening India, and war again loomed. But it was once more avoided. By a secret agreement with Britain, Russia reduced the size of Bulgaria—pushing it back

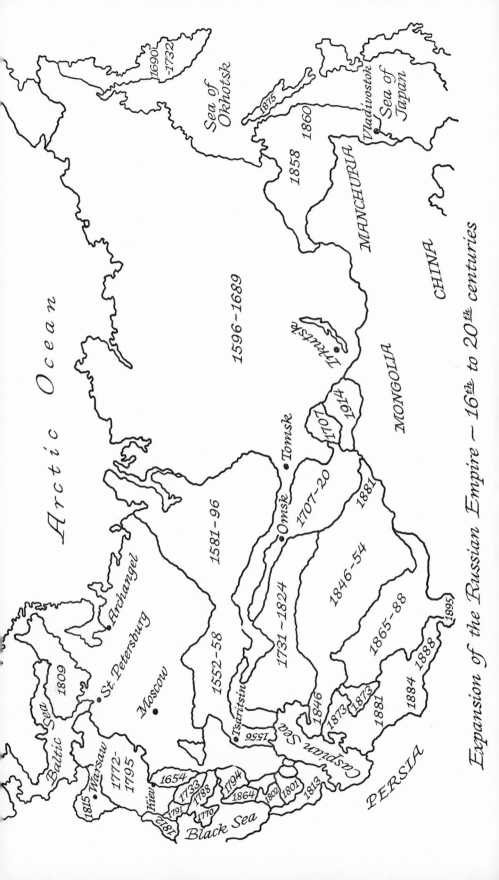

Expansion of the Russian Empire — 16th to 20th centuries

from the Aegean—and divided it into the autonomous principalities of Bulgaria and Eastern Rumelia. Macedonia was returned to Turkey.

 RUSSO-GERMAN RELATIONS

When these and other agreements had been made among the Powers, the British acquiesced in an earlier Russian suggestion that the whole matter be submitted to a general European conference. The Berlin Congress of 1878 opened in June under Bismarck's auspices. Agreements previously made were ratified, and the congress adjourned after a month. From the Russian viewpoint, its outstanding effect was to reduce Russian influence in the Balkans. Later, but not at the time of the congress, Russian nationalists and Pan-Slavs bitterly criticized Bismarck, whom they accused of having favored Austria at Russian expense. The Russian Foreign Office was less concerned with this than with the continuing row with Great Britain which flared out in Afghanistan. The Three Emperors' League did not survive these events, and Bismarck, though he later renewed his understanding with Russia, chose Austria as Germany's real partner. The Russians tried to block this alliance but failed, and the Dual Alliance of Germany and Austria was made in 1879. It remained the pivot of European diplomacy until 1918.

Russo-German relations were not, however, allowed to deteriorate seriously. Bismarck continued "to keep the wire to St. Petersburg open," and the Russians were receptive. This story will take us through the reign of Alexander III, which has not yet been described. But it will make a more coherent account to deal with foreign affairs before treating domestic developments.

When Alexander III became emperor, he formally announced to the Powers his intention to pursue a pacific foreign policy and to concentrate upon the material and moral development of Russia. This change in policy, reflected in the retirement of Gorchakov from the Foreign Office, cleared the way for the conclusion of a second Three Emperors' League. This was established in June, 1881, for a three-year term and was then renewed for another three years. It was a secret agreement which was not wholly satisfactory to the Russians, who would have preferred a bilateral agreement with Germany. Bismarck, however, insisted that his ally Austria be included. The essential terms were a mutual promise of neutrality in case any of the signatories went to war; a mutual promise to make no changes in the territorial *status quo* of Turkey without a previous agreement; the recognition of a special Russian sphere of interest in Bulgaria, and of an Austrian sphere in Serbia, Bosnia, and Herzegovina; and a promise to support Russia against Britain in the Near East. The agreement was partially nullified by a secret Austro-Serb treaty of 1881, which virtually made Serbia an Austrian protectorate, and by a very secret Austro-German-Romanian alliance in 1883. This last was so secret that its existence was not even suspected for many years. Essentially it was a defensive alliance against Russia, signed first by Austria and Romania, with Germany at once adhering.

Two other impinging events must also be noted. In 1882 the Triple Alliance was formed of Austria, Germany, and Italy—an agreement which continued in force, with some modifications, down to World War I. In its original form it was a defensive alliance. The second event was the serious Russo-British clash, already described, over Merv and Afghanistan in 1884–85. In 1885 a revolt broke out in Eastern Rumelia, which sought to unite with Bulgaria. This immediately involved both Russia, who wanted to maintain her control over Bulgaria, and Austria. Tension increased throughout 1885 and 1886. Russia because of this clash refused to renew the Three Emperors' League in 1887. Austria had the support of Britain, but Bismarck restrained the Austrians by warning them that the Dual Alliance did not cover their expansion in the Balkans. Germany also bid successfully for Russian friendship by loaning large sums of money and by announcing that she would be neutral if the Russo-British quarrel in Central Asia developed into war. Both crises passed without war, but the Eastern Rumelian crisis had important aftermaths.

THE RUSSO-FRENCH ALLIANCE

Once again it is necessary to mention impinging events in the general field of European relations. The first was a series of Mediterranean agreements engineered by Bismarck which effectively guaranteed against French or Russian advances in that region. The second was the renewal and modification of the Triple Alliance; and the third was an effective Russo-French co-operation against the British in Egypt. All these events, which took place in 1887, affected Russian foreign policies. In that same year a secret Russo-German "Reinsurance Treaty" was signed. This was a security pact guarding Germany against a two-front war and guarding Russia against a British attack. Germany recognized Russia's special interests in Bulgaria and promised to support Russian aims in the Black Sea and the Straits. The negotiations which led to this agreement had been difficult. Bismarck, in order to put pressure upon Russia, had caused the German money markets to be closed to further Russian borrowings. This was the greatest diplomatic blunder of his career. The French at once let the Russians know that francs were available, and two large French loans to Russia were floated in 1887 and in 1888. These were the first of many between that time and 1918, and they were extremely significant. Much of the money which Russia borrowed from France was promptly spent for French arms and military equipment. Russian military purchasing missions went to France to supervise the transactions, and it was a matter of ordinary courtesy for the French military men to entertain their Russian colleagues. It was also a matter of high politics. Out of these entertainments grew military and political conversations which finally led to the making of an alliance. An outline of the steps by which this came about follows.

Early in 1890 Bismarck was dismissed from office by his new emperor, William II. William II also threw out Bismarck's policy toward Russia. When the Russians sought to renew the Reinsurance Treaty, William brusquely rebuffed them. Partly because of this and partly because of Russian economic developments, a Russo-German tariff war raged for three years. Meanwhile, Russian financial relations with France continued to be excellent, and there were suggestions that the co-operation be extended to other fields. In July, 1891, a French fleet paid a courtesy visit at the Russian naval base of Kronstadt. The next month there was signed a watered-down agreement providing for future consultations. The Russians were the reluctant parties. The Foreign Office continued its preference for dealings with Germany, and Alexander III was loath to associate too closely with French republicanism. The eventual decision in favor of a French alliance, however, was the tsar's, who placed national interest above personal choice.

The French offered a military agreement in 1892. After some talk Russia accepted in principle, which meant absolutely nothing, since the very essence of a military agreement is precision. Negotiations were retarded at this point by a serious famine in Russia and by the Panama scandals in France. But forces were operating to bring the two Powers closer together. The German army was increasing, which worried both the French and the Russians. A short but very severe Anglo-French crisis over Siam revealed French isolation. And commercial and tariff disputes between Russia and Germany reached an acute stage with the Russian rejection of a proposed German trade treaty. The Russian fleet, somewhat belatedly, repaid the 1891 visit of the French ships; and further conversations were held. These resulted in an exchange of notes (December, 1893, and January, 1894), by which the two Powers accepted in detail the convention agreed to in principle in 1892. In order to avoid the necessity of submitting the agreement to the French Chamber and thus publicizing it to the world, the convention was called a military one. Actually, it was more political than military. It exchanged three promises. First, Russia promised to support France in case the latter should be attacked by Italy or Germany. Second, France promised to support Russia in case she was attacked by Austria or Germany. Third, both Powers promised to mobilize their forces at once if the Triple Alliance mobilized. One of the curiosities of this Franco-Russian Alliance was that, although Britain was nowhere mentioned in it and Germany was, it was anti-British rather than anti-German. It is noteworthy, in this regard, that Russia promptly ended its tariff war with Germany by making a commercial treaty in February, 1894. The political purpose of this was to reassure the Germans. The first test of the Russo-French Alliance was against Great Britain in the Far East.

Russian interests there, aside from her relations with China, centered on Korea. That nation was gradually emerging from vassalage to China, though the Chinese government from time to time still claimed sovereignty over it. A Russo-Korean treaty of friendship was signed in 1884, but was kept secret until two years later. Late in 1888 a secret Russo-Korean treaty named Russia as the protector of her small neighbor.

This was not pleasing to Japan, who had opened Korea to Japanese trade and gotten the right to maintain a Japanese representative at Seoul in 1876. But the Japanese, who had traded the southern half of Sakhalin Island to Russia in return for the Kurile Islands in 1875, were not in a position openly to challenge the Russian advance in Korea. This was the situation in 1894 when a war broke out between China and Japan over intervention in Korea. The ramifications of this war will be treated later.

CHAPTER XVI

"Pregnant with Meaning"

The reign of Alexander III (1881–94), despite the attention which has been paid to certain aspects of it, is, on the whole, one of the neglected periods of Russian history. Often it is cavalierly dismissed as a time of black reaction during which nothing of importance took place because all initiative was stifled by the government. The general tone of this interpretation may be exemplified by the report on Russia which the Danish critic and historian Georg Brandes made in the late 1880's:

> Russia is primarily and in its very essence a patriarchal state, a state where the father has the authority and the children are in a condition of equality with one another. . . . Russia has become a bureaucratic state, where official power has destroyed all spontaneous and natural growth in the relations of public life. . . . The form of government in Russia is not now of the kind to give free scope for any sort of originality . . . independent thought in political affairs is not allowed any outlet, and is almost equally debarred from full and free expression in literature on account of the censor. . . .

The ideas of the West, partially molded and partially reflected by literary critics such as Brandes, were further influenced by the bitter criticisms which Russian exiles like Kropotkin and Kravchinski hurled at their government, by the writings of Russian novelists and playwrights (Chekhov, for example) made available in translation, and by the hair-raising accounts of the system of administrative arrest and Siberian exile. The most important reports on Siberia, at least in America, were those of George Kennan.

Mr. Kennan had made his first visit to Russia, and wrote his first book about it, in connection with the abortive scheme to run a telegraph line from the United States to Europe via Alaska and Siberia. He returned to Russia in 1885 with a commission from a magazine to report on the system of political prisons and punishment. His accounts, based upon extensive firsthand observation, were first published as a magazine series and later as a book entitled *Siberia and the Exile System*. This book—replete with eyewitness reports, accounts of interviews with political prisoners (Kennan incidentally was the man who first introduced Madame Breshkovskaya to American readers), reprints of revolutionary documents and official reports—had a great vogue among Western liberals. Most of what Mr. Kennan wrote was true, and most of the criticisms made by the political exiles were justifiable; there was reaction; there was rank disregard for the individual; there were grievous injustices. But there were other aspects of life in Russia in the time of Alexander III. It was not a period in which nothing happened. On the contrary, it was a time of many beginnings and some accomplishments. The story of its foreign policy has already shown this, and the story of internal developments will bear it out.

🔯 TSAR ALEXANDER III, 1881–94

Alexander Alexandrovich was the second son of Alexander II. He was elevated to the position of heir at the death of his older brother in 1865. His education was entrusted to tutors, among them the very able liberal historian Soloviev and the brilliant conservative Pobedonostsev. But both as a student and as a man, Alexander III was rather dull-witted. Physical activity was more in his line. He was a man of tremendous stature and strength, who loved to bend horseshoes with his bare hands. Physically and mentally he was closer to the peasants, whom he loved, than to the intelligentsia, who made him uneasy and fearful. He gloried in his nickname of "The Peasant Tsar," for to him the peasants were the whole of Russia. Alexander was also a man of great physical and moral courage who lived all his life in fear of assassination. As Kravchinski wryly put it, ". . . [Alexander III] without any craving for distinction, made himself a wretched prisoner for life in order to maintain a show of power which he did not enjoy and could not use." The implication is that he was a fool for not giving up the place he had inherited. But obstinate devotion to routine was another of Alexander's characteristics. If he had inherited a constitutional monarchy instead of an autocracy, he would have played the game according to those rules with equal straightforwardness and loyalty. Since he inherited an autocracy, he behaved autocratically. Even in his family circle he was something of a tyrant, and his children feared him. But it should be said in his favor that he retained and loyally supported his ministers, even when he did not understand or wholly approve of their actions. This was in marked contrast to his son and successor, upon whom no one could depend.

🔥 REFORMS—PROPOSED AND ACTUAL

A case in point was Loris-Melikov, whom Alexander had, so to speak, inherited from his father. General Loris-Melikov had distinguished himself as a soldier and as an administrator during the later years of Alexander II's reign. Following the unsuccessful attempt upon the latter's life in 1880, Loris-Melikov was placed at the head of a Supreme Commission charged with meeting the crisis in government. Loris-Melikov was not a believer in democracy or in constitutions; perhaps he was not a liberal. Professor Karpovich has characterized him as a compromiser who wished to draw the teeth of the revolutionaries by granting concessions. Pares believed that Loris-Melikov meant to complete the work of reform which had been started in the reign of Alexander II. Whatever his motives, Loris-Melikov carried out certain changes and planned others. He abolished the Third Section, putting the political police under the control of the Ministry of the Interior, and replaced some of the more reactionary ministers. He also relaxed the press censorship, proposed to reform the systems of taxation and justice as these applied to the peasants, and sought the aid of the zemstva for the reform of peasant administration. It is revealing that his efforts, and his sincerity, had the endorsement of the Zemstvo of Tver, the most liberal and progressive of all the zemstva.

As newly appointed Minister of the Interior, Loris-Melikov presented a plan which called for the convocation of consultative commissions of zemstva men, professors, and journalists to assist the government in administration and legislation. Alexander II, on the morning of his murder, had ordered the discussion of this scheme at the next meeting of the Council of Ministers. One of the first acts of Alexander III was to order the publication of the Loris-Melikov plan, but he rescinded the order before it could be executed. He carried out his father's wish, however, by having the council discuss the plan. They approved it by a vote of seven to five, but among the five opponents were Pobedonostsev, then Procurator of the Holy Synod, and the Slavophil Ivan Aksakov. These two men had great influence upon Alexander III, and they persuaded him to issue a manifesto which reaffirmed the autocracy and killed the plan. The seven ministers who had favored the plan were given no warning of the manifesto. Three of them—Loris-Melikov himself, Dimitri Miliutin, and Abaza (Minister of Finance)—immediately resigned. The emperor accepted their resignations, but he may have been influenced by them just the same. At any rate, the same manifesto which killed the plan also promised to continue the reforms. This promise was published and emphasized by N. P. Ignatiev, whom Alexander III named to replace

Loris-Melikov as Minister of the Interior. Ignatiev also promised that peasant rights and liberties would be guaranteed, that their taxes and other burdens would be reduced, and that adjustments would be made in the land settlement. Shortly thereafter he summoned some zemstva men and others to discuss the lowering of redemption payments, the problem of peasant migration, and the regulation of the sale of liquor. This was not far removed from what Loris-Melikov had planned.

According to a sketch of Alexander III which appeared in a Parisian journal during his reign, the emperor had in mind a six-point scheme of reform. The authenticity of this is not established by documents, but it is borne out by the record. The points were these: (1) reduction of the redemption payments; (2) radical change in the tax system, which bore too heavily on the peasants; (3) abolition of the poll tax; (4) facilitation of peasant migration to less crowded lands; (5) reform of the passport system to give the peasants greater freedom of movement; and (6) the establishment of peasant banks. Kravchinski observed that "most of these reforms have been more or less realized in a queer way," and so they were.

N. K. Bunge, Alexander's Minister of Finance from 1881 to 1887, was the man chiefly responsible for carrying out the reforms. He lowered the redemption payments, and enforced obligatory redemption for the 1.4 million peasants who had remained under the so-called "temporary obligations." He removed the poll tax, which had affected peasants, artisans, and the lower-middle class; and instituted in its stead an inheritance tax and a tax on bonds. It may be noted, relevant to the *dvorianstvo* and the zemstva, that they favored the introduction of a graduated income tax. Since such a tax would have fallen most heavily upon the *dvorianstvo,* and since this class controlled all the provincial and about two hundred of the district zemstva, here is proof that the zemstva did not represent class interests. It may also be noted that the zemstva were largely responsible for the abolition of the hated salt tax, and that they prevented the reintroduction of this tax in 1893. Bunge also instituted a corps of tax inspectors who were charged with regularizing and improving the collection of taxes. It was evidence of his alertness as well as of Russia's changing economy that Bunge introduced a series of regulatory labor laws.

These were not the first labor laws in Russia. Contrary to the general impression, tsarist Russia was a pioneer in labor legislation. A whole battery of regulations, made in 1741, dealt with hours, wages, and working conditions. A law of 1785 established a six-day work week and a ten-hour workday. These laws were not generally observed, but they remained on the statute books and furnished a precedent. The 1882 law forbade the employment in factories of children under twelve, limited the workday to eight hours for children between the ages of twelve and fifteen, and prohibited night work for them. This last prohibition was extended in 1885 to boys and girls under seventeen. A law in 1886 sought to regularize the payment of workers by their employers and to reduce the fines which were customarily leveled for infractions of discipline (or for alleged infractions). A corps of factory inspectors—never sufficient in number, but generally conscientious—was appointed to enforce these labor laws. Some parts of the laws were never observed, and other sections were often evaded, but Bunge's attempts at labor regulation may nevertheless be regarded as having been both advanced and generally effective within their stated limits. They did not, of course, end the exploitation of labor, but they did check some of the worst abuses.

Further to Bunge's credit was the creation in 1884 of the Peasant Land Bank for the purpose of financing the purchase of land by peasant groups. (The peasants, of course, were still bound to the mir.) This bank was financed by the government, which gave it 500,000 rubles of state credit and permitted it to issue $5\frac{1}{2}$ per cent bonds, guaranteed by the government up to 5 million rubles a year. During the first year of operation the bank financed the purchase of 567,000 acres of land. The figures for 1885 and 1886 were, respectively, 858,600 and 796,500 acres. The total purchase price for the three years was 41 million rubles, of which the bank supplied 34.5 million rubles and the peasants the remainder. The interest rates were fair, and the scheme worked out about as Bunge had planned—as long as he and his appointees were in control. After he resigned, however, the situation changed. The bank then advanced only from one-quarter to one-half of the purchase price, and was quick in foreclosing delinquencies. The result was that, while some of the richer peasants benefited, the needy did not. The whole affair seems picayune when compared to the activities of the Nobles' Land Bank (established in 1888), which advanced to *dvorianstvo* on mortgages more than three times the amount advanced to the peasants for land purchases. *Narod* was still the underdog.

🎯 ECONOMIC POLICIES

It will be remembered that in the period just after the Crimean War the fiscal reforms carried through by Kankrin had established Russian finances on a reasonably sound basis which was, however, destroyed by the expenses of the war and of the reforms. The situation was made worse by a large unfavorable balance of trade soon after the war. In 1862 Alexander II appointed M. K. Reitern Minister of Finance, a post he continued to hold until 1878. He tried at first to raise the value of paper money, but his methods were faulty and he failed. Then he turned to an effort to increase Russia's productive capacity, principally by building railroads. The first railroad built in Russia was a short line from St. Petersburg to Tsarskoye Selo, constructed in 1837. Then followed the Warsaw-Vienna line (1851), the St. Petersburg-Moscow (or Nicolayevskaya) line (1851), and the St. Petersburg-Warsaw line (1859). This last was built by the Main Company of Russian Railroads, which was formed in 1857 for the purpose of connecting the grain-growing regions with the seaports by rail lines. The government guaranteed a 5 per cent return on the company's stock, and the agreement vested ownership of the roads in the company for ninety-nine years. The company was inefficiently and dishonestly run so that construction costs were unduly high, and the first lines built were not profitable so that the government had to make good its guarantee of stock dividends. A new arrangement was made with the company, and Reitern sought other private capital—both Russian and foreign—for the construction of more roads. The successful construction of the profitable Riazan-Kozlov-Moscow line in 1866 encouraged investments, and there was a flurry of building. Lyashchenko has summarized the results in the following paragraph:

After the railway fever of 1870–75—a five year period during which railway trackage was increased by 4,971 miles—construction proceeded at a slower pace from 1876 to 1890. But from 1891 to 1895, new railway construction added 4,148 miles of new trackage, while the next five year period (1896–1900) added 10,036 miles, and the total trackage was increased to 37,209 miles in 1901. . . . It should be noted that . . . the European part of Russia had 9.7 kilometers of railway trackage per thousand square kilometers of territory; England had 106 kilometers and Germany had 80 kilometers for the same unit. . . . At the beginning of the 20th century, the total capital invested in railroads throughout the whole country amounted to 4.7 billion rubles, 3.5 billion rubles of which belonged to the government.

It may be emphasized that by 1900 the Russian government owned almost 75 per cent of the railroads. Long experience and habit of state ownership and control in this and other things facilitated the acceptance of nationalization after the Bolshevik Revolution. It may also be added that railroad building in Russia was marked by the same extravagant frauds and scandalous dishonesty which characterized it in other countries.

In addition to railroad building, Reitern was interested in increasing private credit facilities. The Imperial Bank, which opened in 1860, two years before his appointment, had given Russia its first, organized private credit. Reitern exploited this and also sought to encourage the formation of private banks. As to his tariff policies, he switched in 1877 from a virtual "free trade" tariff (which he had instituted in 1868) to an increasingly protectionist policy. By forcing the payment of customs dues on a gold basis, the dues were jumped by 40 to 50 per cent. Higher tariffs were simultaneously placed upon many items. His original purpose may have been to gain an increase in revenues, but the effect was more and more protectionist, reaching full flower by 1891. The 1890's are generally regarded as having been—either in spite of protectionism or because of it, depending upon the point of view—the decade of Russia's industrialization. Table 2 shows, however, that this development was not a sudden or rootless phenomenon. There had been great industrial advances in the preceding generation.

TABLE 2

Production in Selected Industries
(*in tons*)

Year	Coal	Oil	Iron	Pig Iron	Iron and Steel
1860	329,400			352,800	223,200
1870	763,200	32,400	825,750	372,600	261,000
1880	3,610,800	612,200	1,083,600	469,800	635,400
1890	5,049,600	4,348,000	1,913,400	993,600	871,200

Some part of the credit for this industrialization belongs to Reitern, some to Bunge, and some to his successor as Minister of Finance, Vyshnegradsky. No one man, of course, was wholly responsible. In the broad sense, these developments were among those which followed serf emancipation. They were continuations of the changing character of Russian economy to which attention has previously been called.

⚙ AKSAKOV AND POBEDONOSTSEV

Two men wielded tremendous influence over Alexander III, and through him, over Russian affairs. One was the Slavophil Pan-Slavist Ivan Aksakov, whom the tsar once described as "truly Russian, with a pure soul, and, although a maniac on certain questions, everywhere and always a defender of Russian interests." Alexander, while still tsarevich, had had some contacts with Aksakov through the latter's wife, Anna Tiutcheva, who was for a time a governess in the imperial household. Shortly after Alexander's succession, Ivan Aksakov presented to the tsar a memorandum which had been drafted for Alexander II by Constantine Aksakov, Ivan's brother. The main points of this memorandum may be summarized by enumeration:

1. The Russian people have no desire to govern themselves, and have assigned unlimited power to their government, reserving only liberty of life and conscience.
2. The government must be an absolute monarchy.
3. The people may offer opinions to the government which may accept or reject them as it sees fit.
4. If the people resort to force, or if the government restricts liberty of life or conscience, nothing but evil will result. This has already happened, and only the government can cure the trouble.
5. The government must re-establish the principles of its own freedom of action and legislation, and of the people's freedom to express their opinions through a *Zemsky Sobor,* and of the people's liberty of conscience.

The tsar's enemies have charged that Alexander III understood only the second point—that an absolute monarchy was essential to Russia—a thesis which recalls Catherine the Great's *Instructions.* It is true that Alexander in commenting on Aksakov's memorandum wrote, "I will never allow any limitation of autocratic power which I consider necessary and useful for Russia." This was also the view of Aksakov's schoolmate, Pobedonostsev, Alexander's most trusted adviser.

Konstantine Petrovich Pobedonostsev (1827–1907) first came into contact with the Romanov family in 1861, when he was appointed lecturer on legal subjects to the grand dukes. Originally concerned mainly with the Tsarevich Nicholas, after the latter's death in 1865 Pobedonostsev's major attention and affection were transferred to Alexander, whom he served as tutor and adviser. Aside from these duties, Pobedonostsev was professor of civil law at the University of Moscow and also served on the commission which prepared the judicial reform of 1864. He counted himself a member of the Moscow group of Slavophils and continued his contacts with them long after he came to hold important posts in the government. In fact he often served as the liaison between Alexander and Aksakov. Pobedonostsev's rise to power was steady rather than spectacular. He was appointed to the Senate in 1868, to the State Council in 1872, and made Procurator of the Holy Synod in 1880. He held this post until 1905–6—a year before his death. His influence over Alexander III and over Nicholas II, whom he also served as tutor and counselor, was tremendous. Many of the conservative and reactionary measures taken by these two tsars were directly traceable to him. So were some of the Pan-Slav (or Pan-Russian) machinations in Austria.

He was, because of his views and his power, cordially detested by all Russian liberals. Some unnamed wit composed a clever and biting little jingle about him based upon the fact that in Russian *pobedonostsev* means conquer, *obedonostsev* means seneschal, *bedonostsev* means impoverisher, and *donostsev* means tale-bearer:

(*Pobedonostsev*)	Conqueror of the Synod
(*Obedonostsev*)	Servant to the court
(*Bedonostsev*)	Impoverisher of the people
(*Donostsev*)	And stool pigeon to the tsar.

Pobedonostsev was, however, a very able man, a competent scholar, and an outstanding philosopher. He was more than a reactionary; he was also a philosopher of reaction who arrived at his view through a combination of religious mysticism and rational thought. Believing that the power of the state rested upon faith, he rejected the principle of a free church in a free state as leading to the certain destruction of both. Regarding parliamentarianism as "the great political lie which dominates our age," he found it "sad to think that even in Russia there are men who aspire to the establishment of this falsehood," and he set himself against any such development. A free press he held to be only the tool of powerful, irresponsible, and selfish proprietors. It must therefore be avoided:

To live without power (the depository of truth), is impossible. . . . The first necessity of power is faith in itself and in its mission. Happy is power when this faith is combined with a recognition of duty and/or moral responsibility. Unhappy is it when it lacks this consciousness and leans upon itself alone. Then begins the decay which leads to loss of faith, and in the end to disintegration and destruction.

These, in brief sample, were the ideas which governed one of the most influential men in the last generation of old Russia. With his name are properly associated the curtailment of academic freedom, the restriction of the zemstva and of the mirs, and the persecution of religious and national minorities.

✿ RESTRICTIONS AND BURDENS

During the reform era of Alexander II, several marked advances had been made in public education. The first high school for girls was opened in 1858, and all primary schools were given a state subsidy beginning in 1864. During the reign of Alexander III the number of pupils in schools and colleges increased. Professor Timasheff has calculated the figures for elementary schools enrollments as follows: 1880, 1,141,000 pupils; 1891, 2,559,000 pupils; and 1894, 3,275,000 pupils. This was more than a doubling both absolutely and relative to the total population. Figures from other sources show 198 secondary schools with 50,000 pupils in 1876; 1010 secondary schools with 230,000 pupils in 1886. There were eight universities in European Russia in 1877, with a total enrollment of 6208. This had grown to 14,207 ten years later. Although it is clear that education remained a privilege of the minority, a system of public education was slowly developing. On the other hand, there were serious setbacks and repressions. All primary schools for peasant children were placed under Church control in 1884, thus practically ensuring their backwardness. And the universities were deprived of their autonomy and of their academic freedom in the same year. Three years later the secondary schools were closed to children of artisans, shopkeepers, servants, and tradesmen. Admission quotas were also established for Jews.

The quotas were part of a "Russia for the Russians" program which is generally blamed on Pobedonostsev. He certainly followed it, but it antedated him. It was Ignatiev who was responsible for the laws of 1882 which forbade Jews to buy or to rent land or to live outside the cities and towns within the Pale. (The Pale was an area in Poland and southern Russia to which Jews had been confined by Alexander I.) Under Pobedonostsev's influence, however, the Pale was reduced in size in 1887, and in 1890 the laws of 1882 were suddenly retroactively enforced. This greatly increased both the hardships and the injustice, since many Jews, assuming the laws of 1882 to be dead letters, had acquired lands of which they were now deprived. They were the hardest hit by the Russification policies of Pobedonostsev, but they were not unique in being persecuted. Poles, Kalmuks, Uniates, Stundists, and all other religious and ethnic minorities felt the heavy hand of the government.

The curtailment of the rights and powers of the zemstva and mirs may be quickly reviewed. Decrees of 1889 and 1890 established the office of land captain (*nachalnik*). This official, who had to belong to the *dvorianstvo* class, was nominated by the provincial administration and appointed by the Minister of the Interior. He had power only over the *narod* (i.e., the peasants) but his authority included the right to veto any action by the mir; the right to bar the discussion of any subject by a peasant assembly; the right to fine or to imprison a peasant without trial; the right, as rural magistrate in control of the *volost* courts, to inflict corporal punishment or to condemn to exile; and the right to convene and to preside over peasant meetings called to nominate candidates for the zemstva. Since voting in these meetings was viva voce, this gave great power to the land captain, who was in a position to take severe reprisals against any peasant who crossed him. The Zemstvo Law of 1890 removed the peasant right of election and substituted for it the right of nominating candidates for each vacancy. The provincial governor, with the advice of the land captain, then elected one of the nominees. The same law made Marshals of the Nobility ex-officio members of the zemstva, and also gave the government the right to appoint one member for every five zemstva members who were elected by the usual groups.

It is amazing that so many of the zemstva not only continued to function with increasing effectiveness but also continued to be the spokesmen of liberal political opposition. As the eminent Russian jurist and historian Paul Vinogradoff once put it:

> In all cases when force was required to put by-laws into execution, to collect rates [taxes] to seize goods, etc., the Zemstva could not act by themselves but had to apply for help to the general police, which was often very remiss in assisting the new organizations and in any case regarded their requirements as of secondary importance. Lastly, the acts of the Zemstva, both as to decrees or by-laws and as to appointments of all kinds, were subjected to constant and suspicious supervision by governors and other agents of the Central Authority; when the trend of general policy pointed towards reaction, as it often did, the Zemstva were hampered and harassed under the slightest pretexts. . . . The wonder is not that they were hampered and distracted, but that they achieved so much. It is not an exaggeration to say that a new age was initiated by their activity in Russia.

The zemstva's greatest opportunity for service came with the famine of 1891–92, which swept the Volga region and the southern provinces. The government sought at first to deny and conceal the existence of this disaster. Then it sought to hamper the work of relief undertaken by private organizations, among which the zemstva were very prominent. Only belatedly and grudgingly did the government undertake any relief measures. But the services which the zemstva men rendered during the famine did much to overcome the lingering peasant resistance to zemstva leadership. Zemstva prestige dates from this time. As to the famine itself, it was an acute attack of a chronic disease caused by very low productivity and very heavy obligations on the peasants.

The peasants paid 95 per cent of the total taxes levied on agriculture, and over half the peasants' yearly income was taken by taxes. Miliukov says that between 1883 and 1892 the population increased by 16 per cent; the taxes, by 29 per cent. But taxes owed and taxes paid are two quite different things. The amount of tax arrears—largely uncollectible—which the peasants owed the state increased steadily. If this had been spread out evenly, every acre owned by peasants during the years 1871–80 would have owed seven cents in tax arrears. The per acre tax debt for the years 1881–90 would have been nine cents, and for the years 1891–1900, twenty cents. In some provinces tax arrears ran as high as 210 per cent by 1890; in others they were only 35 per cent of the assessments. There were equally wide differences among villages. The increasing depression and impoverishment of the peasants were also reflected by the jump in the cost of relief given by the government, from 10 million rubles during 1881–90 to 191 million rubles during the following decade. This figure must be interpreted with caution, however, since it is impossible to say how much of the increase represented a greater need, and how much was demonstration of a keener social conscience. But of mass peasant poverty there can be no doubt. It had existed for centuries before the emancipation of the serfs, and it was not wiped out in the generation which followed.

CHANGES IN LANDOWNERSHIP

Yet there were significant changes going on in Russia, even among the peasantry. One was in the patterns of landownership. The land census of 1877 showed that (in European Russia) the peasants owned about 34 per cent of the land; the nobles, about 24 per cent; and the state, about 39 per cent. Stated in terms of the total amount of land which was privately owned, this meant that the peasants owned 7 per cent of this land; the nobles, 79 per cent. Ten years later, in 1887, the respective percentages were 13 and 68. As a further measure and as a forecast, it may be said that these respective percentages for 1905 were 24 and 53; and that the total acreage held by the peasants had increased from 301 million acres in 1861 to almost 500 million in 1917. Marxist analysts, including Lenin, have insistently pointed out that this change did not benefit all peasants equally, and of course it didn't. Some were luckier or abler or harder working, and prospered far more than others. About a third of the rural population (according to Lenin) belonged to the well-to-do group. These were the ones who, for the most part, bought or rented additional lands. They were also the ones who used most effectively the lands they held. (The poorer peasants planted only a fifth to a third of their land; the more prosperous planted from a third to over half of theirs.) These differentiations among peasant groups became marked during the reign of Alexander III.

Even more important changes, but of an entirely different nature, were taking place among the intelligentsia. Consideration of them will require a somewhat lengthy digression involving two men—neither of them Russian—Karl Marx and Friedrich Engels.

MARX AND ENGELS

There can be no doubt that the theories propounded by Marx and Engels were of first-rate importance, nor that their ideas profoundly influenced the lives of hundreds of millions of people. One may readily admit all this, and admit also the value to society of some aspects of their work without, however, accepting the myth that they created a "science of society" or that they tapped the only wellspring of truth. No student of society can reasonably deny that the work of Marx and Engels greatly enriched the study of society. But he may well agree with Max Bober that Marxism is a key which opens many locks but few doors.

Karl Heinrich Marx was born in the then recently Prussianized city of Trier (or Treves), which, shortly before his birth, had become a part of the Kingdom of Prussia. He received a Ph.D. from the University of Jena. Legend has it that Marx wanted to teach but that he was denied the opportunity because he refused to conform to the pattern of re-actionism which was required. This is incorrect. The fact is that one of Marx's friends had recently been appointed to the faculty of the University of Bonn and had brashly promised to get Marx a job there. The friend forfeited his own job through fantastic indiscretion and so was unable to help Marx. Some other friends then came to his aid. They had been running a small newspaper called the *Rhenish Gazette* and had gotten into trouble with the censor because of their enthusiastic espousal of Utopian socialism. Marx at that time, was, both in public and in private, violently opposed to all socialism. So they hired him to put out a paper which would not offend the censor. Marx promptly fired his old associates who had given him the job and proceeded to edit the paper for three months. Then he wrote an article in praise of atheism which the censor found most offensive. The *Gazette* lost its license to publish, and Marx lost his job. He promptly announced that he had been silenced because of his democratic radicalism and socialism.

Soon after his dismissal for atheism, Karl Marx discovered communism. (That label was first used in 1827, and not by Marx.) The introduction was performed by the gentle, humanitarian, and rather vague rabbi Moses Hess. Hess told Marx that the old system was dying, and that society had to be rebuilt without the evils of money, property, and profit. Marx found these ideas appealing, and they germinated in his mind during the months of unemployment while he lived on the generosity of his wife's mother. Then another friend of his Berlin days put up the money to publish a magazine called the *Franco-German Yearbook,* and gave Marx the job of editing it. The Marxes moved to Paris, where the first and only number of the magazine was published in 1844. It was an immediate failure, but it contained two prophetically significant articles by Marx. One was scurrilously anti-Semitic; [1] the other contained four formulae which Marx and Engels spent their lives in elaborating and in trying to prove. It is significant (and, of course, wholly contrary to the legend) that Marx—according to the evidence of his own letters—knew nothing whatever of economics or of economic history when he wrote this article. He simply postulated certain hypotheses without reference to facts, and subsequently insisted that these were "the laws of human development."

The first formula was the doctrine of inevitability. "The system of trade and money-making, of property and the exploitation of human beings," wrote Marx in the *Yearbook,* "leads to a breach in extant society which the old system is powerless to heal." This, of course, is not provable either way. Marx and his followers, however, consistently have asserted it (and still assert it) not as a guess or a hypothesis but as a proven fact. The second formula was the doctrine of violent revolution. "Material power," said Marx, "must be overthrown by material power." The third formula had to do with the proletariat. Marx wrote that they were the only unspoiled class in society, and that they lived in "fundamental chains," bowed down by "universal sufferings" and "total injustice." From these chains they must free themselves, since they can expect no help from the rest of society, to whom they owe only antagonism. But, the fourth formula concluded, this army of the proletariat must be led by the "science" (the general staff) for which Marx was begetting the laws. Here was the genesis of what Marx, stealing the label from Proudhon, later called "scientific socialism."

Marx lost his job when the *Yearbook* failed. He decided to make socialism his profession, and began for the first time to read and study the writings of economists. He visited meetings of French and German workers; came to know William Weitling, the pioneer German proletarian communist, and associated himself with the "League of the Just." He also met and talked with the Russian anarchist Bakunin, and with the Frenchman Proudhon. Most important, he made a second and lasting contact with Engels. The two men, as their collaboration continued, grew to think so much alike, to speak and to write so much alike that they became intellectually one unit. The writings and theories which are conventionally called Marxian or Marxist ought properly to bear the names of both Marx and Engels. Either without the other would have been much less than he was.

Marx in 1845 left Paris for Brussels, where Engels joined him, and it was in Brussels that they worked out what they first modestly called "our theory." It was also at Brussels (which was Marx's headquarters until 1848) that it ceased to be a theory in the minds and writings of its originators and became a "science," "laws," "universal laws," "absolute laws," and "infallible laws." Once during this period Marx and Engels visited England to talk with English workers and their leaders. What these people told them did not square with the Marx-Engels "science," so Marx announced that English workers simply did not understand their own country, or their own class, or even themselves. Back in Brussels, Marx and Engels founded the Communist Party. Fifteen others joined, including three proletarians. Very soon there were disagreements and the first purges. The first to be expelled by Marx-Engels was an obscure person named Kriege. The next was Weitling, whom Marx had hailed two years before as the embodiment of all proletarian virtues. Then it was the turn of Hess, who had converted both Marx and Engels to communism. The pattern was set very early—accept unquestioningly the dictation of the leaders or suffer expulsion.

Marx-Engels in 1847 accepted the invitation of the London branch of the League of the Just to merge the London, Paris, and Brussels branches into a Communist League, which would adopt the Marx-Engels "laws." The invitation was accepted, and out of it came the famous *Communist Manifesto*—remarkable for its inaccuracies, inconsistencies, and self-contradictions, but far more remarkable for the hold it has won upon the imaginations of billions of people. Without any doubt, the *Manifesto* is the most significant single statement of socialist ideas which has ever been published. It also holds the essence of the doctrines which Marx-Engels later elaborated in their longer works.

During the revolutions of 1848, Marx was required to leave Brussels. He returned to Paris briefly and then went to Cologne, where he set up the headquarters of his Communist Party (no longer called a league). He summoned to him his three hundred followers and deployed them in tactics now familiar—infiltration, "front" organizations, the disruption of reforms, the sabotage of elections, attempts to override the will of the majority, and so on. His efforts to organize a revolt in Cologne failed, but his techniques have lived on—largely through Lenin, who learned as much from Marx's activities as from his words. Leaving Cologne in 1849, Marx found sanctuary in London, where he lived until his death in 1883. These were years of poverty. Marx held only one job, as a poorly paid correspondent for Greeley's *New York Tribune*. He and his family lived on the charity of Engels and others, eked out by a few small legacies until Engels gave his partner an annual subsidy of £350. Meanwhile, Marx studied and wrote voluminously—pamphlets, broadsides, reviews, articles, and letters. He turned out a *Critique of Political Economy* (1859); *Capital* (Vol. I, 1867; second ed., 1873); and the *Critique of the Gotha Program* (1875). The last was in some ways the most significant, but his major effort was *Capital,* which, still incomplete at Marx's death, was finished by Engels. (Engels lived until 1895.) Marx also was active in the Workingman's International Association (The First International), which was founded in London in

1864. He was so active that he could truthfully write Engels in 1868, "I am in fact the head of the whole works." The nominal heads were two Englishmen; Marx worked behind the scenes. Conflicts soon developed within the organization, especially between Marx and Bakunin. Marx won every fight, and killed the First International in doing so. This, too, set a pattern which his disciples have followed.

🔊 AN ANALYSIS OF THE MARX-ENGELS THEORIES

But how does all this fit into the Russian story? The Marx-Engels analyses were sound at some points, but most important they contained a promise—neither clearly defined, nor well-described—that was enormously appealing. It is the promise that an inevitable revolution will bring a day of gladness when men shall be freed from evils and ills. It is a vision of a better world to be; a dream which has entranced and sustained men from time immemorial; a hope which has been shared by billions of men and women who never heard of Marx-Engels or who, having heard, reject most of their teachings. It is a glimpse of the ideal society of Plato, of Isaiah ("beat their swords into plowshares, and their spears into pruning hooks"), of Jesus, of Thomas More (*Utopia*), of Saint-Simon, of Robert Owen, and of "many who humble and nameless, the strait, hard pathway plod." It was all this, and something else besides.

Marx-Engels claimed to have discovered the secret, as the authoritative Soviet journal *Bolshevik* put it in 1945, ". . . of foreseeing the course of events, of understanding . . . current developments; and of recognizing not only how and in what ways events are now developing, but also how and in what ways they must develop in the future." This is enough to intrigue almost anyone. Imagine being able to unravel the story of the past, to understand the present, to foresee and predict the future, all with absolutely guaranteed accuracy. It sounds slightly absurd when put in this way, but it is not regarded as such by the faithful. The quotation from *Bolshevik,* which might be duplicated from literally hundreds if not thousands of other Marxist sources, is evidence that they take it seriously. What were the major claims of this "guide to action," as the Communists call it?

Marx-Engels claimed that manual labor was the sole source of value, and that the worth of any product was determined solely by the number of hours of socially necessary labor required to make it. Value includes profits, and profits are created in this way. John Doe, worker, can with thirty minutes' labor produce an item having an exchange value of two dollars. He can make two such items, with a total value of four dollars, in an hour. But John is paid only two dollars an hour by his employers.

The first thirty minutes of each hour is an even swap—two dollars of exchange are created and two dollars are paid to the creator of the value, John Doe. The value created in the second half hour, however, is surplus value which is kept by the employer as his profit on John's labor. This is robbery of the worker by the employer (or capitalist) and is the essence of the capitalist system, according to Marx-Engels. The capitalists keep on stealing the surplus value and therefore get richer and richer. The richer they get, the more rapacious they get, so that they compete among themselves and the big ones eat up the substance of the small and middle-sized. These now join the dispossessed, the "have-nots"—that is, they are depressed to the status of labor. And the status of labor gets worse and worse.

The capitalists (the "haves") use some of their profits to buy machines to make goods. Marx-Engels noted that this was a curious contradiction because machines cannot create wealth or value, for that is the exclusive function of labor. Presumably the capitalist invests in machinery in order to increase his production and his profits, but Marx-Engels insisted that the machinery produced no profit. All it did was to make it possible for the employer-capitalist to exploit labor more ruthlessly and thus to squeeze more wealth out of the creators of wealth. This goes on and on. Workers are forced to work longer and longer hours, for lower and lower pay, under worse and worse conditions, until eventually things are so miserable that the workers rise in violent revolution and overthrow the system. This thesis, it ought to be clearly understood, is not that wrongs and injustices exist, but they grow continually worse. It is a thesis of increasing misery which ends in revolution.[2]

Socialism (not communism) then takes its place. This is a transition stage in which powers belong to the "revolutionary dictatorship of the proletariat." "He who comes forward against the dictatorship of the proletariat and against the armed, violent overthrow of the capitalist class," thundered a Soviet textbook of 1935, "is against the teachings of Marx, and is a traitor . . . and an enemy of the proletariat."

It is not to be supposed that these few paragraphs have adequately summarized the complicated Marx-Engels system, which included a general philosophy ("Dialectical materialism is the world outlook of the Marxist-Leninist Party"); an interpretation of history ("The history of all hitherto existing societies is the history of the class struggle. . . . the determining element in history is ultimately production . . ."); a criticism of capitalism ("What the *bourgeoisie* produces above all are its own grave diggers"); and a vague, indefinite, and undeveloped forecast of the utopia to come. Perhaps enough has been said to show why this beautifully precise though unproven and unprovable system fascinated many intellectuals and pseudo intellectuals. Among those who were attracted to it was the Russian exile then living in Switzerland. He was George Plekhanov, who, as Lenin once acknowledged, managed to "bring up a whole generation of Russian Marxists."

⊕ PLEKHANOV AND ULYANOV

The fires of reform and revolution which had flared up in the humanitarianism of the *Narodniki* in the 1870's and in the terrorism of *Narodnaya Volya* in the early 1880's had been reduced to smoldering embers. Nevertheless they persisted—some in Russia itself and some among Russian exiles abroad. The brightest glow among the latter came from a small handful of exiles who lived in Switzerland. Their leader was George Valentinovich Plekhanov (1850–1917), onetime member of the group which developed into the *Narodnaya Volya*. Associated with him were Vera Zasulich (the woman who had sought to kill Trepov), Paul Axelrod, and Leo Deutsch. In 1883, the year of Marx's death, these people created in Switzerland the first Russian Marxist organization. They called it "The Liberation of Labor"—a grandiose title for a group of struggling exiles who were cut off from their native land and had no support in their adopted one. But they had Plekhanov, with his brilliant mind and ready pen, from which flowed, as the Bolshevik historian Pokrovsky phrased it, "practically all the basic ideas which formed the stock-in-trade of Russian Marxism up to the end of the century." The particular target of Plekhanov was the ideas of the *Narodniki:* that the Russian peasant was the hope of the revolution, that Russia might by-pass the capitalist stage and go on directly to peasant socialism, and that terrorism was the most effective weapon possible. These notions he subjected to a "Marxian analysis" which, he and his disciples felt, demolished them. They may have been demolished intellectually, but they continued to be held by many Russians. However, Plekhanov's ideas and those of Marx began to catch the imagination of some young Russian liberals and radicals, largely because the growing industrialization of Russia and its accompaniments were beginning to affect the intelligentsia.

The gross exploitation of the Russian workers, which went on in spite of attempts by the government to regulate wages, hours, and conditions of labor, produced during the decades of the 1870's and 1880's a series of strikes and the organization of the first Russian labor unions. The earliest of these was the South Russian Workers' Union, organized at Odessa in 1875. The second was the Northern Union of Russian Workers, formed at St. Petersburg in 1878. Political demonstrations and the first large strikes occurred during these years. The movement developed more rapidly in the 1880's. Between 1881 and 1886 there were forty-eight strikes which involved approximately 80,000 workers. The largest of these was the Morozov strike in 1885, which affected some 8000 workers, and which the government finally quelled by using troops. When the strike leaders were brought to trial, the evidence revealed such exploitation of workers that the defendants were acquitted, and the government undertook some of the reforms which have been mentioned. These relieved but did not cure some of the worst abuses, and the difficulties of labor increased as its numbers grew. Strikes increased in the 1890's, and so did the efforts of the radical intelligentsia to organize this spontaneous labor movement along their own lines. More and more, these were the lines of Marx as interpreted by Plekhanov. But the *Narodniki* persisted, and so did their ideas and some of their tactics, which the Marxists now adopted. One of the tactics was a continuation of the formation of "reading circles" among the people. To the Marxists the "people" were not the peasants. They were the urban proletariat. There were several such reading circles in St. Petersburg and elsewhere in the early 1890's. To one of the Petersburg groups there came late in 1893 a young man from the Volga. His name was Vladimir Ilyich Ulyanov, and the pseudonym which he adopted in 1901 was N. Lenin.

Vladimir Ilyich Ulyanov was born in 1870 at the provincial capital of Simbirsk on the Volga. His father, who had been a teacher, had been appointed inspector of schools in the province of Simbirsk in 1869. Reliable, respectable, and able, the elder Ulyanov climbed the bureaucratic ladder of state service to the rung of hereditary nobility. In 1874, young Vladimir, born a commoner, became a nobleman at the age of three. The life of the Ulyanov family was comfortable, cultured, quiet, and happy until the death of the father in 1886 and the execution in 1887 of the oldest son, Vladimir's brother Alexander, as a revolutionary. Alexander, then a student in St. Petersburg, had associated himself with a wholly idealistic but half-baked student group immediately after his father's death. This group took for its name the title of "The Terrorist Section of the *Narodnaya Volya*"—though there were no other "sections" and the old organization was dead. It numbered seven young men, including Alexander Ilyich Ulyanov. He was not its leader, nor did he organize the attempt which the group sought to make upon the life of the tsar. The plot was discovered, the conspirators tried, and five were sentenced to hang. Alexander was one of the five. This tragedy, which came when Vladimir was in his middle teens, had a profound effect upon his life. Dr. Bertram Wolfe has summarized it excellently:

It loaded young Vladimir with a man's responsibility; it put iron into his soul; it barred his path to respectability; it opened an unbridgeable gulf between him and the regime that had taken his brother's life. And it inoculated

him with a profound contempt for the "liberal society" which had abandoned the Ulyanov family in its time of trouble. That contempt found far
more frequent and eloquent expression in his writings than did his opposition to the Tsar. It drew the line of distinction between him and most of his
associates in the socialist movement.[3]

A month after the hanging of Alexander, Vladimir graduated at the
top of his class from the gymnasium at Simbirsk. It is one of history's
curious ironies that the director of this school, the man who wrote the
recommendation that got young Ulyanov into a university despite his
brother's crime, was Feodor Kerensky. His son, Alexander Kerensky,
was Lenin's chief opponent in 1917. Vladimir entered the University of
Kazan, from which he was expelled by police order—not because of his
behavior but because he was the brother of a convicted "traitor"—after
three months. Repeated requests for readmission to the university were
denied, but finally, in 1890, he was authorized to take the Petersburg
examinations in law whenever he was ready. In just over a year Vladimir
covered the four-year course in jurisprudence and passed the final
examinations with highest honors in 1891. He was now, in the language
of his time and country, an "external graduate" of the university, and was
admitted to the practice of law. He spent a dreary eighteen months at
his profession as a junior lawyer in Samara, losing ten cases and winning
one. Much more important was his discovery of the works of Plekhanov
and his consequent study of Marxism. In 1893 Vladimir Ulyanov wrote
his first Marxist work intended for publication. Shortly thereafter he
went to St. Petersburg.

⚙ BRONSTEIN AND DZHUGASHVILI

The two chief associates of Vladimir Ilyich's later career were both born
late in the year 1879. The elder by some six weeks was the son of a
hard-working and prosperous Jewish farmer who lived in the village of
Yanovka in Ukraine. The family name was Bronstein, and the son was
called Lev or Lyova, meaning in Russian "lion." Life in the Bronstein
family was simple, uncultured, and full of hard work. Little Lev, however, managed to learn to read and write before he was nine, when he
was sent to live with some cousins in Odessa. There he was educated.
There, too, he made his first acquaintance with revolutionary thought
and groups. His first impulse led him toward the ideas of the *Narodniki*.
Only in the mid-1890's did he become a Marxist. By then he was a skilled
disputant and pamphleteer. For a time he wrote under the pseudonym of
"The Pen." But the name by which he is best known is Trotsky.

The younger associate was born in the little town of Gori, Georgia, on
December 21, 1879. His father, Vissarion Dzhugashvili, was a hereditary

peasant who earned his living as a cobbler. He died when the son, whose given name was Joseph, was eleven years old. Two years before that the boy who became Stalin entered a parochial school, where he remained until 1894. Then he entered the theological seminary at Tiflis. He was expelled in 1898.

🐚 S. I. WITTE

It was at Tiflis, where Stalin attended the seminary, that a third man had been born almost half a century earlier. His name was Sergius Iulevich Witte. His father was a minor civil servant and his mother was a descendant of the famous Dolgoruki family. It was her father and mother who gave the Wittes a home and supervised the bringing up of the Witte children. Sergius Witte boasts in his autobiography of the family's place in society and of the scale on which they lived. He was educated by tutors and then, following a playboy period in the gymnasium, graduated from the University of Odessa. Under family pressure, and with this grandfather's influence strongly behind him, young Witte served briefly in the government of Odessa and then entered the service of the Odessa Government Railroad. He soon became its traffic director and was responsible for the moving of troops at the time of the Russo-Turkish War of 1877–78. Partly because of the skill with which he performed this task he was appointed the director of the Southwestern Railroads. He held that job until he was appointed the director of the Department of Railroad Affairs in the imperial government in 1888. Four years later he was made Minister of Ways of Communication, a position he occupied only for six months before being named by Alexander III to the post of Minister of Finance. He held that place until 1903.

The financial situation of the Russian government when Witte became finance minister in 1892 was very poor, despite the work of his predecessors, Bunge and Vyshnegradsky. The effects of the 1891–92 famine were still being felt, and the treasury was literally so empty that Witte was able to meet his first government payroll only by postponing payday until he could have several millions of paper rubles printed. The ruble was extremely unstable. Between 1888 and 1890 its exchange value had fluctuated from about 38 cents to about 62 cents, and speculation in rubles was rife. One of Witte's first measures was to stop the speculation in paper rubles (1893). In the next year he established a "credit ruble," and in 1897 succeeded in placing the Russian currency upon a gold standard. This was his most important financial reform, but like most of his other major activities it belongs to the story of the next reign.

The outstanding impression which one gathers from reading the memoirs of Sergius Witte is of his enormous conceit. He never admits to having made a mistake in judgment or in action. Failures and errors are always attributed to someone else. But he was by all odds the outstanding Russian statesman of his day. Able—even brilliant—very hard working, and aggressively ambitious, Witte made few friends and many enemies. His enemies have called him wholly unscrupulous and totally lacking in principle. He certainly was a coldly calculating opportunist who thirsted for power and intrigued incessantly to get it. His relations with Alexander III, whom he liked and admired, were good. His relationships with Alexander's successors, whom he neither liked nor trusted, were poor.

CHAPTER XVII

The Distaff Scepter

🔹 ZEMSTVA AND TSAR

Your Majesty: In the solemn days of the beginning of your service to the Russian people, the Zemstvo of Tver greets you with the greeting of faithful subjects. . . . Together with the whole of Russia we have listened to the significant words by which Your Majesty has announced your accession to the Russian throne. We are filled with gratitude with your resolution to devote yourself to the happiness of your people, and we hope for the success of the great task you have set yourself. We trust that the voice of the people's needs will always be heard on the height of the throne. We trust that our prosperity will grow, together with an unflinching obedience to law both on the part of the people and of the Administration; because the law, expressing in Russia the will of the monarch, must stand above the changeable views of individual agents of that supreme authority.

We earnestly hope that the rights of individual citizens, as well as of corporations [classes], will be protected. We expect, Sire, that public bodies [e.g., the zemstva] and corporations will have the opportunity and the right to express their opinions upon questions concerning them, so that the monarch may be able to hear the views and the desires not only of the Administration, but also of the Russian people. We believe that through closer relationship with the representatives of all classes of the Russian people, who are equally devoted to the throne and to the nation, Your Majesty's authority will find a new source of strength and a pledge of success for your generous intentions.

Your Majesty [ran the address to the throne of the Zemstvo of Tula]: As men standing very close to the people, we strongly believe that local needs can be satisfied only through representation of local interests, and we beg our Tsar to have confidence in us. . . . We beg for a free access to the throne for the spokesmen of the Zemstva.

To these sincere and modest requests His Imperial Majesty Nicholas II, Emperor of All the Russias, replied:

I rejoice to see gathered here representatives of all the classes of the realm who have come to give expression to their sentiments of loyal allegiance. I believe in the sincerity of these feelings which have been those of every Russian from time immemorial.

But it has come to my knowledge that lately, in some meetings of the zemstva, voices have made themselves heard from people who have allowed themselves to be carried away by foolish fancies about the participation of representatives of the zemstva in the general administration of the internal affairs of the state.

Let every man know that I will devote all of my strength to the good of my people, but that I will uphold the principle of autocracy as firmly and as unflinchingly as did my ever-lamented father.

There—greatly oversimplified, of course—is the essence of the difficulties into which the last of the Romanovs fell. The zemstva men were suggesting the road of moderate reform, of evolutionary development toward representative, parliamentary democracy. "The path we point out to you," the great liberal zemstvo leader Ivan Petrunkevich told the tsar on a later occasion, "is a path of peace. It is to lead the country to a new order of things without convulsions, without bloodshed, without thousands of unnecessary victims." The road which Nicholas chose was one which he hoped would lead Russia back to the times of his namesake—to the Orthodoxy, autocracy, and nationalism of Nicholas I. It is interesting but futile to debate whether Nicholas II could have chosen otherwise than he did. A "liberal autocrat" is a contradiction in terms, and the number of autocrats who have voluntarily surrendered their autocracy is extremely limited. Perhaps—given the Romanov family tradition, including a sense of trusteeship over family property; given also the restraints of protocol and the pressures of vested interests, especially of the court and the *dvorianstvo*—no tsar could have brought himself to surrender his powers or parts thereof. Perhaps a man of different mold—a man of strength and vigor—an unselfish man—a man of vision and of courage might have done it. No one can say. Nicholas II was not of the temperament and character to try. To his personality and to that of his wife, the Tsaritsa Alexandra, must be laid part of the responsibility for the fall of the Russian monarchy. How great or how little a share is assigned to men, and how much to "forces," depends upon whether one holds with Emerson that "there is properly no history, only biography," or with Marx and Stalin that "in acquiring new productive forces men change their mode of production, in changing the way of earning their living, they change all social conditions." Of course one may reject both these extremes in favor of a sort of middle way which denies neither the importance of men nor of "forces" as makers of history, and assumes, further, that the relative importance of each is variable. This is the approach which this book seeks to follow.

🔥 TSAR AND TSARITSA

We know a great deal about the personalities, thoughts, and actions of the last tsar and tsaritsa through the publication of many letters, diaries, reports, and memoirs. We know that Alexandra dominated her husband almost from the beginning, that she was much the stronger of the two. It is conventional to say that Nicholas' outstanding characteristics were gentleness and charm. It is also charitable. It seems more accurate to describe him as primarily selfish—the kind of a person who for the sake of his own ease of mind and comfort will never openly disagree with another and who will yield (or appear to) rather than make the effort to stand up for his own convictions. His almost perfectly consistent surrendering to Alexandra's wishes may have been a measure of his devotion to his wife. It may also have been that he found it more comfortable to acquiesce than to disagree. He was not a liar in the crude sense, but no one could count on him for long. He appeared to agree while disagreeing; to be convinced, while lacking conviction. As Baron Rosen very tactfully put it, Nicholas "possessed in a supreme degree the art of agreeing with his interlocutor in such a way as to make him believe that he had been much impressed and quite convinced by what he had been told—a most delicate kind of flattery." As a result, his ministers could never depend upon Nicholas. Time and again he let them down. He was, as has been diplomatically remarked, singularly open to reasonable argument, which is a very polite way of saying that whoever saw him last made up the tsar's mind. Of course this was not invariably true. Nicholas was not unintelligent. He had a most retentive memory, and, like most weaklings, he was capable of obdurate stubbornness. But he was usually stubborn about the wrong things. So was Alexandra.

Alexandra Federovna was the Russian name with which the Princess Alix of Hesse-Darmstadt had been rechristened when she accepted Russian Orthodoxy in order to marry Nicholas. She was a granddaughter of Queen Victoria of England, and one of her difficulties in Russia was that she was entirely a proper Victorian. She fell in love with Nicholas at their first meeting (she was then fourteen), and quietly but with that steadfast persistence which characterized all her actions determined to marry him. The way was not easy. Alexander III, showing greater perspicacity than he is usually credited with having, was strongly opposed to the marriage. It took the intercession of Victoria herself to smooth away the obstacles. Alix and Nicholas were engaged in April, 1894. Then, in the fall, came Alexander's illness, which proved fatal. The dying tsar summoned the Princess Alix, and her formal betrothal took place in his sickroom; the wedding was celebrated by a mourning court after his death. It was a sadly prophetic beginning of a reign, but the marriage, in spite of all tragedies, was a most happy one. "Nicky" was as devoted to his "Sunny" as she was to him, and both were devoted to the five children who were born to them during the first decade of their marriage. The youngest child, and the one w..o was dynastically and historically the most important, was a son who was named Alexius. No parent can fail to understand what the feelings of the imperial couple must have been when it was discovered that their only son, the heir to the throne, was a hemophiliac. It was stark tragedy for the family, for Russia, and perhaps for the world. We shall trace its historical consequences later; now we shall relate it only to Alexandra.

Alexandra had been deeply, almost abnormally religious from her youth. It was extremely hard for her to give up her own church for Russian Orthodoxy. (This was, on her side, the one obstacle to the marriage.) When she accepted Orthodoxy, she did so wholeheartedly. Neither can there be any doubt of the extreme attraction which religious mysticism, often in its most debased and fraudulent forms, held for her. The most famous and important instance is, of course, that of Rasputin (who will be discussed later), but he was by no means the first to trade successfully upon Alexandra's superstitious mysticism. Alexandra was quite unhappy in the Russian court and she thoroughly disapproved, with Victorian primness, of much of Russian Society (with a capital S). She played the public role required of an empress, but increasingly she turned to her family and to her religion for her real life. Finally, she realized that hemophilia was not only hereditary but was transmitted by the female line.

The distress which any parent would feel was exacerbated in Alexandra's case by a sense of guilt and failure—guilt because the illness had been her wholly involuntary and unintended legacy to her son; failure because little Alexius was not just a baby boy, he was the tsarevich and if he died the male line of the dynasty died too. Alexandra set her heart upon two things, namely, to see to it that Alexius survived to inherit the throne; and that the powers of the throne should be in no whit diminished. She was determined that Alexius should be the autocrat of Russia. To the pursuit of these goals she eventually surrendered her reason. To them, also, she bent her will and that of her weaker husband. Fanatic, bigoted, and of limited intelligence, Empress Alexandra Federovna pursued her fated way like the chief character in a Greek tragedy, and she carried her family—and many others—with her.

🔥 THE TSAR'S ADVISERS

Though he was diligent enough in routine, Nicholas was inclined during the first years of his reign to leave most of the business of government to his ministers and advisers. Chief of these were Pobedonostsev, Witte, and Plehve. Pobedonostsev was the author of the accession manifesto in which the zemstva were rebuked for their "senseless dreams" of representative government. Later Pobedonostsev reported to Nicholas:

> As a result of this speech there has risen an undercurrent of complaint particularly among officials and intelligentsia. What is more deplorable is that this complaint is heard among the superiors who have power. That is why it is particularly imperative now, more than at any other time, to assert the ruling will in all issues.

The procurator did his best to see that the "ruling will" was forcefully exerted. The policies of Russification were continued and extended, especially against Finland, whose rights had been untouched even by Nicholas I and Alexander III. (On the other hand, Nicholas somewhat relaxed the persecution of Germanic, Lutheran Balts, whose special privileges had been attacked by Pobedonostsev and Alexander III.) The persecution of the non-Orthodox, particularly of the Jews, whom Nicholas hated, was intensified. Pobedonostsev further had a decisive hand in some important ministerial appointments, notably that of I. L. Goremykin as Minister of the Interior in 1895.[1]

Witte sometimes collaborated with Pobedonostsev, as he did in the case of this appointment. More often Witte went his own way, as he did in 1900, when he got Nicholas to replace Goremykin with D. S. Sipyagin, a thoroughly reactionary person who had been Goremykin's assistant. The post of Minister of the Interior was tremendously important, since it carried with it control over the police (both open and secret). It also had certain occupational hazards. Sipyagin was murdered by a Social Revolutionary terrorist in 1902, and his successor, Plehve, was murdered by another Social Revolutionary terrorist in 1904.

Vyacheslav K. Plehve (1846–1904) was a thorough-going reactionary of the worst sort and a professional bureaucrat. He went to work for the government after graduation from the St. Petersburg Law School and rose rapidly in police work, becoming director of the State Police in 1881. (He was also a carry-over—as were Witte and Pobedonostsev—from the reign of Alexander III.) Later he was made assistant minister and a member of the Imperial Council. He distinguished himself by arranging the confiscation by the state of the lands and wealth of the Armenian-Gregorian Church, by the diligence and ruthlessness with which he followed the Russification policy in Poland and in Finland,

and by his notorious anti-Semitism. (The charge that he directly incited the horrible massacres of the Jews in Kishinev does not appear to be supported by adequate evidence.) Plehve is also noted for his bitter feud with Witte, which was primarily a struggle for power. It might have been with Plehve in mind that Witte remarks in his memoirs that the terrorists quite often picked the proper persons to attack. It was Plehve who told General Kuropatkin on the eve of the conflict with Japan that what Russia needed was "a small victorious war." These were the sort of men who governed Russia in the tsar's name during the first dozen years of little Nicholas' reign. Now we turn from individuals to masses by reviewing the norms and values of the Russian people at the turn of the century.

✪ REVIEW OF RUSSIA IN 1900

There were, as a starter, a great many Russian subjects. Dr. Frank Lorimer, basing his work on the 1897 census, sets the total population of the Russian Empire in 1897 at 125,640,000, of whom 94,331,000 (or over 75 per cent) were what he terms "Russians," that is, Great Russians, Ukrainians, and Bielorussians. This represents an increase of over 200 per cent in the total population and of about 160 per cent in the Russian population during the generation after Emancipation. At least 85 per cent of the population were peasants. Lorimer has calculated that this was an increase of 68 per cent in the peasant population (or 56 per cent if those peasants who moved to urban areas are omitted). A different set of statistics gives the total population in 1903 as about 139 million with 111 million, more or less, listed as peasants. Roughly 100 million peasants were engaged in agriculture, but approximately two-thirds of them were unable to produce enough on their own lands to support themselves. They had to eke out their income by other employment or by government relief. All of these statistics indicate the large number of peasants both absolutely and in relation to the total population, and the economic insecurity of the majority of them.

The typical peasant answer to this problem was to seek more land. The preceding chapter mentioned the increase in peasant lands—Lorimer says that these increased 40 per cent between 1861 and 1905. But the number of peasants increased more rapidly than their landownership. This meant that the per capita average ownership declined. This is an arbitrary and unreal figure because not all peasants shared equally in the increased landownership. Finally, the persistence of peasant poverty, despite the gradual taking over of the land by the peasants (they owned about 80 per cent of all the arable land in Russia in 1916, and leased much of the remainder), shows that lack of land was certainly not the only cause of the peasants' troubles. What else was wrong? Taxes were, for one thing.

Bunge had decreased the direct taxes on the peasants by approximately a third, but his successors, Vyshnegradsky and Witte, more than counterbalanced this decrease by increasing indirect taxation. The result was harmful for the government and for the peasants. It was reliably reported to an official commission of inquiry in 1903 that the tax arrears for nine provinces totaled more than 15 per cent of the amount assessed in the preceding decade. It was further reported to the same group that the government had been forced to spend so much for the relief of hunger in these same provinces that its real loss was 44 per cent of the assessment. "It is evident," said the report, "that the population was actually unable to pay more than it really did." What it paid, even though totally insufficient for the government, contributed to its own impoverishment. Professor Paul Miliukov, lecturing in 1903–4, suggested still another cause for peasant distress:

Prior to the emancipation of the peasants . . . economic life in Russia still preserved its mediaeval character. It was based on home production for home consumption—at least so far as peasant life was concerned. The outlay for food, lodging, clothing, fuel and light—in short, for all the chief items of the family budget—was practically naught. A man paid nothing for his own hovel; he fed on the products of his own field and garden; he was amply supplied with homespun clothing made from the wool of his own sheep and of the fiber of his own flax; he did not spare the wood to keep hot the old-fashioned oven which filled a quarter of the house, and which during the long winter months turned it into a bathhouse; nor did he spare his eyes, for he lit the interior of the hut with thin chips constantly renewed in a stand of prehistoric shape, during the long winter evenings while the women spun threads on their distaffs and spindles.

Now, however, all this has changed. Wooden chips have given way to a kerosene "smoker"; homespun linen has been superseded by calicos, while woolen stuffs have disappeared without a substitute; fuel has become very scarce and expensive. Food—which consists of vegetable products alone—is insufficiently supplied; too often it has to be bought by the grain-producers themselves. . . .

. . . The fact is that the peasant now is too poor to utilize his and his family's work for himself; and, at the same time, he has no more raw material for his home industry. He can no longer have his clothes prepared by the women of his own family, because he has no more wool or linen to spare. His new expenses for the factory calico are certainly not inspired by any taste for factory articles, but by mere necessity; and his purchases are generally cheap and of inferior quality. He can hardly be accused of lavishness on the ground that he has to buy some food in the market, since the fact is that on an average his yearly consumption is still below the necessary minimum. . . . [He] does not eat wheat, which he produces for sale only, but rye or, more frequently, potatoes . . . on the average he eats meat only four times a year.

One must discount somewhat Miliukov's too glowing picture of pre-reform sufficiencies, since, as has already been seen, poverty, hunger, and famines were common before the Emancipation. But his general picture is not inaccurate, and his description of peasant living standards is not overdrawn. What Miliukov said vividly may be restated more prosaically and accurately. The old way of life was not geared to the growing money economy of Russia. As to the living standards, one who was a boy in a small Russian village at the time of which Miliukov spoke recalls the life as "having very little of the world's goods or comforts, living very close to a primitive existence." The average peasant home in his village was a one-room, earth-floored, log cabin which the peasant family often shared with a pig or a goat. Clothing was of the poorest kind. Moccasin-like shoes, woven of dried reeds, were the common footwear. Only the more prosperous had leather shoes, which they wore only for best. This man remembers, also, the isolation and parochialism of the village. His first sight of a railroad train was when he was on his way to the United States. With this lack of contact and want of education (over 75 per cent of the rural population of Russia over ten years old were illiterate in 1897), it is not surprising that most peasants were concerned only with their immediate, personal problems. What is surprising, on the contrary, is that so many of them soon began to take an interest in other affairs.

By 1900 the aggregate output of Russian industry, which did not occupy more than 10 per cent of the population, exceeded in value the output of agriculture, which engaged at least eight times as many persons. The average per acre production of wheat and oats in Russia was less than half that of the United States. The average per capita production of small grains in Russia was a quarter that of Canada; less than half that of Romania. There were many reasons for this poor productivity. One was the persistence of the mir, with its periodic redistributions of land. No farmer wanted to break his back improving land which might go to another at the next redistribution. Moreover, the growth of population had forced so many subdivisions that each household's "strips" were much too small for productive cultivation. The strips, as explained earlier, were scattered over the whole area controlled by the mir, so that much time was lost just in coming and going. The persistence of the two- and three-field systems, with a half or a third of the arable land lying idle at each planting, was also a contributing factor. So was the lack of adequate animal or artificial fertilizers, and of adequate implements. The poverty of the peasant also perpetuated itself. He could not afford fertilizers or better implements or more productive seed or more livestock. Pulling oneself up by one's own bootstraps is proverbially difficult. The Marxist contention that the peasants' troubles were caused by the contradictions and conflicts inherent in the system does not explain the period of agricultural prosperity which occurred prior to World War I, partially as a result of actions taken after the 1905 Revolution.

✤ INDUSTRIAL GROWTH

The first decade of Nicholas' reign was a time of spectacularly rapid growth. Production increased 100 per cent. There were almost 6000 more industrial enterprises in 1900 than in 1890, and close to a million more workers. According to official data, the total value of industrial production for the years 1878–87 was 26.1 million rubles a year; for the years 1888–92, 41.6 million rubles a year; and for the years 1892–97, 161.2 million rubles a year. The textile industries increased fastest, but speedy advances were also made in the heavy industries, such as mining and metallurgy. The tonnage of coal mined almost doubled between 1890 and 1895 and again between 1895 and 1900. During the 1890's, the tonnage of oil and of iron and steel produced almost tripled; the amount of iron mined and of pig iron smelted more than tripled. Most of this increase was in large-scale production. Big industries employed half of the total industrial workers in 1900; the figure for 1880 had been one-third. As one would expect, the amount of capital invested in industries also increased tremendously—from 580.1 million rubles for all industries in 1890 to 1,742.3 million rubles in 1900. The highest percentage increase was in the metallurgical industries (826 per cent); the lowest, in the food industry (75 per cent).

The Marxist economic historian Peter I. Lyashchenko [2] has summarized these developments as follows:

> Thus, in the course of the years 1890 to 1899, industrial capitalism—overcoming low productivity, stereotyped techniques, and backward social conditions—rapidly moved Russian industry far ahead. The volume of production in certain industries, to be sure, still lagged far behind the advanced countries of that period. Nonetheless, Russian industry advanced very significantly in those ten years, achieving a rate of concentration much higher than in the outstanding capitalist countries, and outstripping nearly all other countries in the speed of development.

Table 3 will show at a glance the evidence upon which Lyashchenko based these conclusions.

TABLE 3

Increases in Production, 1890–99
(*Percentages*)

	Russia	Germany	England	U.S.
Pig iron smelted	190	72	18	50
Iron produced	116	78	8	63
Coal mined	131	52	22	61
Cotton spindles	76	—	4	26

The rate of growth of Russian industry continued high down to World War I. It was not quite so spectacular in the first decade of the twentieth century as in the last ten years of the nineteenth, due to a financial crisis which reached its lowest point in 1902. The Russo-Japanese War and the Revolution of 1905 also slowed the advance. The total value of goods produced, for example, increased by only 73 per cent between 1897 and 1908, as compared to an increase of 113 per cent between 1887 and 1897. But there was a recovery, and the speed of expansion in certain areas again reached the spectacular. The production of farm machinery in 1912 was 136 per cent greater than it had been in 1908, 392 per cent greater than in 1900, and 570 per cent greater than in 1897. This was not out of line with the 152 per cent jump in pig iron and steel between 1910 and 1913. Rate of growth can be very misleading, since it is obviously easier to quadruple a low output than materially to increase one which is already high. The Russian coal industry produced 145 per cent more in 1913 than in 1910, but the Russian total in 1913 was only 36 million tons, while that of the United States was over 517 million tons. The output of electrical power in Russia in 1913 was at the per capita rate of 14 kilowatt hours; the per capita rate in the United States was then 176 kilowatt hours. Such comparisons help to keep a reasonable perspective, but they should not obscure the economic progress of tsarist Russia. Russia was advancing, not standing still or going backward, at the time of the 1905 and 1917 revolutions.

Two other factors had an important bearing upon domestic and foreign policies. One was that Russian industry remained deficient or totally lacking in certain key areas. The manufacture of precision instruments, machine tools, and electrical equipment were significant cases in point. These goods—and others—Russia had to import, which affected not only her trade and credit balances, specifically, but also her international relations in general. And these lacks proved disastrous in World War I. The other factor was the investment of foreign capital in Russia. France was the heaviest foreign investor in Russian banks and industrial corporations and in loans to the Russian government. Great Britain led in investments in Russian securities (followed by the United States); was second in industrial investments, and third in banks. Germany ranked third among the foreign investments in industrial corporations; second, in banks. It is apparent that foreign capital was increasingly important, though its total volume remained lower than that of Russian capital. Certain enterprises were particularly dependent upon foreign investment. Half the total capital in Russian joint-stock companies was foreign by 1900; by 1917, 90 per cent of the capital in mining and 42 per cent of the capital in metallurgical enterprises was non-Russian. As to the Russian state debt, one estimate holds that it almost quadrupled between 1894 and 1914, with France holding about 80 per cent of it and Great Britain, 14 per cent. Germany made its most effective bid in the field of trade. Almost half of Russia's imports in 1913 (which were approximately double what they had been fifteen years earlier) came from Germany.

🔥 THE FOREIGN OFFICE

Russia had three foreign ministers during the first dozen years of Nicholas' reign. Lobanov-Rostovsky was appointed in 1895 following the death of De Giers, who had held the office throughout the reign of Alexander III. Lobanov also died in office and was followed, in 1897, by Michael Muraviev. He, too, died in office. His replacement was V. N. Lamsdorff (1900–1906), generally regarded as Witte's man. None of these three left any strong personal mark on the policy, partly because of the shortness of their terms and partly because foreign policies were often determined by someone other than the minister. Witte, in particular, often interfered, especially in Far Eastern affairs. His policy there was one of peaceful penetration by means of railroads and trade. In 1890 the Chinese statesman-politician Li Hung Chang planned the building of a railroad from west to east across Manchuria, but it had not gotten beyond the preliminary stages before war with Japan halted it. Meanwhile, Russia had learned of Li's scheme and in 1891 had begun the construction of the great Trans-Siberian railway. Work on this project was in process in the Amur region by 1894, and plans were already afoot for a trans-Manchurian cutoff to save the long haul around that province. Witte, who had been in charge of railroad affairs when the Trans-Siberian railroad was started, continued to maintain a very lively interest in it after he moved to the Ministry of Finance. His more ambitious plans were opposed by China and Great Britain, with whom Russia was having other troubles.

Some of these had to do with the long-standing Russo-British clash over Afghanistan and over Russian expansion in the Pamirs. (These were temporarily settled by agreements in 1895.) More serious was a row involving Turkey. An Armenian rebellion against the sultan was crushed by the Turks in 1894. At the suggestion of the British, a joint Russian-French-British commission investigated the massacre and drew up a program of reforms which the three Powers asked the sultan to apply (1895). But Russia balked at a further British suggestion that they join in a working agreement against the Porte, and when the British proposed to intervene after a second series of Armenian massacres, a serious crisis developed. A British fleet was sent to the Aegean and stood on and off the Dardanelles. The Russian ambassador to Constantinople, Nelidov, urged the little Nicholas to send an expeditionary force to seize Constantinople. The plan was seriously considered, but—according to Witte—Pobedonostsev opposed it. So did Witte himself for reasons which he explained to the Procurator: ". . . at the present time and under present conditions, to occupy the heights of the Bosporus without an understanding with the Great Powers, would be, in my opinion, dangerous and ruinous for Russia." Probably what Witte had in mind was, first, that the French were opposed to any such action on the part of their ally, and, second, that Russia was not prepared to risk the consequences of it. The plan was dropped only to be revived again two years later and once more abandoned for the same reasons. The crises passed, but added to the tenseness in Russia's relations with Britain. The two had tangled again, meanwhile, in the Far East.

✿ THE FAR EAST

Russia, who had refused a British suggestion for Russo-British intervention against Japan in 1894, was nevertheless determined somehow to check the Japanese advance in Korea. Russian interests there were mainly strategic. Korea dominates Vladivostok and the Russian Maritime Provinces. It has, also, open harbors which the Russians covet. (Russia tried to get one of these—Port Lazareff—in 1885, but Britain forced the cancellation of the arrangement.) Unilateral intervention during the Sino-Japanese War was not feasible, but after Japan had defeated China and forced her to yield the Liaotung Peninsula, Russia acted. Russia suggested to Germany and France that they join her in forcing Japan to give back the peninsula to China and to take an indemnity in place of it. The suggestion was carried out.

China, of course, had no money with which to pay the indemnity, so the French and the Russians promptly loaned a large sum to China. The money was supplied by France; the diplomatic leadership, by Russia. This was the first test and the first proof of the Russo-French Alliance, and it resulted in a major diplomatic victory for the allies at the expense of the British. The victors were jubilant and gleefully went forward with the next stage of their plan to force the British out of China. (The plan was for Russia to advance from the north to meet the French, who were to advance from their bases in the south.) The next move was to exact concessions from China in payment for their "help." While China had been engaged with Japan, Witte had caused a survey to be made for a railroad across Manchuria. He had also persuaded the French to invest heavily in the Russo-Chinese Bank, which he founded[3] and which had made the loan to China. In 1896 Li Hung Chang visited St. Petersburg and there concluded the Li-Lobanov Treaty. This was so secret that, although several more or less apocryphal versions appeared from 1896 on, the full text was not published until 1931. The treaty set up a Russo-Chinese defensive alliance against Japan. In return, China gave the Russo-Chinese Bank a contract for the building of the Chinese-Eastern Railroad across Manchuria. The contract gave the bank not only the right of way for the line, but also full administrative and police powers and all mineral rights in the designated zone. The Chinese government helped to pay for the building of the line (which was completed in 1903) and reserved the right to buy it after thirty-six years. The actual construction and operation was entrusted to the Chinese-Eastern Railway Company, which was under the presidency of a Chinese. But the railroad itself was built to the Russian gauge; and the Russo-Chinese Bank, which created and controlled the company, was dominated by the Russian Ministry of Finance.

The year 1896 was also significant in Russo-Japanese relations involving Korea. Russian troops occupied the Korean capital, Seoul, in February. Japanese protests led to conversations and negotiations which culminated in the Lobanov-Yamagata Treaty, which set Korean finance as the Russian sphere; Korean trade and industry as the Japanese sphere. Witte and Lobanov promptly implemented this by establishing a Russo-Korean Bank (with French capital) and by arranging for the appointment of a Russian as controller of Korean Customs and master of the Korean treasury. His vigorous actions produced a crisis in the Korean government and more protests from Japan. The upshot of the matter was the Rosen-Nishii Agreement, by which both nations agreed to refrain from interfering in Korean politics. Russia also promised not to interfere in Korean industry and trade. This was in 1898—a very busy year in other respects, also.

Late in 1897 German forces occupied the Chinese territory around Kiauchau Bay. Russia was agreeable because Kaiser William had previously warned Nicholas and had promised to support the acquisition by Russia of a base in China. The Russians followed Germany by sending a fleet to occupy Port Arthur and by offering another loan to China. The price for the proposed loan was the replacement of the Britisher who was serving as inspector-general of the Chinese Customs by a Russian, and the granting to Russia of a monopoly upon all railway concessions to be granted in northern China and Manchuria. The "reluctant Dragon" sought aid from the British, who promptly offered a loan. Russian opposition was so violent that Britain, who was having serious troubles elsewhere, tried to find some compromise formula. Very complex negotiations finally resulted in the cancellation of both loan proposals and the exaction of concessions from China by both Russia and Great Britain. The Russian concession was a ninety-nine year lease of Port Arthur (which was made into a Russian naval base) and Talienwan (which was renamed Dalny and developed into a commercial port). Then a Russo-French group, acting under the cover of a Belgian syndicate, got a concession for a railroad which cut directly across the British sphere. Once more there were very complicated negotiations which ended in an Anglo-Russian agreement, assigning Manchuria as the Russian sphere. Russia was rather unscrupulous about abiding either by this agreement or by the Rosen-Nishii Agreement with Japan.

THE JAPANESE WAR

The Boxer Uprising (1900–1901) gave Russia an excuse to occupy several sections of Manchuria, including Mukden. A Russian resident who took charge of important Manchurian affairs was sent to Mukden. After the settlement of the Boxer troubles, Russia promised to withdraw from Manchuria but delayed the fulfillment of the promise. She left Mukden once, but soon came back. Meanwhile the Japanese, beginning in 1900, had simultaneously sought an alliance in London and in St. Petersburg. Though the Russians were not receptive, the British were, and the result was the Anglo-Japanese Alliance of 1902. From the moment this was signed, Japan prepared for action against Russia. Russia—partly because of differences of opinion and clashes of authority within the government—adopted an utterly fatuous attitude. She refused to make any new agreements with Japan and did not live up to those which had been made. On the other hand, she did not prepare to defend herself or her interests in the Far East. At this juncture, an utterly unscrupulous and irresponsible group, headed by Bezobrazov, gained influence over the little Nicholas. They formed the East Asiatic Company for Exploitation of Timber in Korea and Manchuria, and sold the tsar upon their proposal to exploit the resources of the Yalu River district between Korea and Manchuria. Witte was very much opposed to the actions of this group and the general Russian policy toward Japan. He would at all costs have avoided a war with Japan. But Witte was suffering a temporary eclipse. He was transferred from the Finance Ministry to the chairmanship of the Committee of Ministers, a post which sounded important but wasn't.

The Korean adventure went on. The company started lumbering operations on the Korean side of the Yalu River, and in January, 1904, Russian soldiers were sent to guard the company's operations. Japan severed diplomatic relations with Russia on February 6, attacked and bottled up the Russian fleet in Port Arthur on February 8, and declared war on February 10. Japanese troops promptly occupied Korea, with whom their government first made an alliance and over whom they then set up a protectorate.

The Russian record was one of repeated defeats relieved only by individual acts of heroism. Her supplies and forces were inadequate. It is enough to know that the fighting took place some 6000 miles from the center of Russia; and that the best Russian troops were kept at home "more or less to sit on the heads of the Russian people," as Pares once phrased it. Leadership was in the hands of three men: Alexeiev, Stössel, and Kropatkin. Alexeiev, a bastard son of Alexander III, had been appointed viceroy of the region through the influence of Bezobrazov. But Alexeiev was a complete booby, who finally had to be removed in disgrace. Stössel, commander at Port Arthur, was a traitor who, after standing a long siege, sold out the fortress to Japan for one million rubles. General Kropatkin, who had enjoyed a brilliant reputation as Chief of Staff, distinguished himself as commander-in-chief in the Far East only by his skillful conduct of retreats. Finally, the government was fighting without the support of the people.

The year 1905 found the Russian government without a fleet, driven from her advanced Far Eastern bases, and facing extremely serious trouble at home. Nicholas was ready to talk of peace despite the assurance of his new commanders that the army had been reorganized and was ready to attack. The Japanese were also willing to talk of peace. Their rapid advance had strained their resources. They could hardly hope to carry the war to the heart of Russia. And the British bankers who had been financing Japan were worried about their investments. A tactful British suggestion to President Theodore Roosevelt resulted in an American offer of mediation, which was accepted by both combatants. Nicholas, in this crisis, turned again to Witte, whom he appointed as head of the Russian delegation. Witte made the best of a bad situation. He withstood the Japanese demand for an indemnity, but he could not withstand their demand for the southern half of Sakhalin Island, which they were, in fact, occupying. The Treaty of Portsmouth (September, 1905) ceded to Japan southern Sakhalin; Port

Arthur and Dalny (Talienwan, Dairen); and the Chinese-Eastern Railway from Port Arthur to Chang-chun, with all its accompanying rights. Subsequent agreements in 1907 and 1910 marked out Korea as a Japanese area, reserving northern Manchuria to Russia.

Another item which must be mentioned here is the Hague Peace Conference (1898–99). The Hague Conference was suggested and sponsored by Russia for less idealistic reasons than many hoped. Russia was finding it financially and industrially impossible to arm as rapidly as Austria. It occurred to the tsar, or some of his advisers, that any arms holiday would give Russia a chance to build up an arsenal equal to Austria's. The conference, however, was unable to agree on disarmament or on armament limitations, though it did set up a permanent court of arbitration.

🌑 GROWTH OF POLITICAL OPPOSITION

There had been developing in Russia during the first ten years of Nicholas' reign three different types of political opposition. One was Marxian socialist in principle; the second, basically agrarian socialism, was a sort of revival and extension of the *V narod* and *Narodnaya Volya* movements; and the third and last to form was a liberal, constitutional movement. The center of the movements in the early 1890's were the literacy committees, which were continuing the efforts of the *Narodniki* to educate the masses. The Literacy Committee of St. Petersburg had about a thousand members; that of Moscow about four hundred. They contained all variants of liberal, democratic, and radical opinions; and included both Marxists and non-Marxists. It was to the Marxist faction of the St. Petersburg Committee that Ulyanov adhered when he went to the capital to live, and he soon plunged into the violent controversy between the Marxists and the *Narodniki*. Doctrinaire loyalties and bitterness forever kept these two groups at swords' points, though they were more complementary than antithetical. Both believed in socialism —the *Narodniki* in an indigenous, humanitarian, and agrarian variety which put its faith in the extension of the mir; the others in a Russian version (especially a Leninist version) of Marx-Engels, a version which insisted that the peasant was a bourgeois and put its faith in the urban proletariat. Parenthetically it may be noted that neither Marx nor Engels could be persuaded to favor the one movement above the other, holding that both had a proper place in Russia. Both groups were critical of capitalism and of the Russian system. The *Narodniki* hoped that Russia could be improved without going through the capitalist stage. The Marxists insisted that Russia was already in the capitalist stage, from which she could be rescued only by a socialist revolution. The *Narodniki* underestimated the significance of Russia's growing industrialization and the importance of the urban workers. Their Marxist opponents underestimated the persistence of the traditional norms and values, particularly the mir.

🌀 MARXISM-LENINISM

Lenin's [4] first contribution to the polemical warfare between the two was the hand-written and clandestinely circulated "Little Yellow Books" which he put out in 1894. That same year another young Marxist named Peter Struve asked the censors for permission to publish his treatise against the *Narodniki*. The censors and the police (practically the same thing) were happy to help promote conflict between the groups. To the great surprise of Struve and many others, permission to publish was given. This began the rather curious movement known as legal Marxism. The dropping of the barrier let loose a spate of Marxist books, pamphlets, and journals. Characteristically, Lenin used this channel for all it was worth while at the same time he continued to write and circulate secretly leaflets which could not get by the censor. In 1895 Lenin was allowed to go abroad for his health. After brief stays in Germany and France, he sought out "the old revolutionaries"—Plekhanov, Zasulich, and Axelrod—in Geneva. Upon his return to Russia he began to organize Russian branches of their Union for the Liberation of Labor, but he was arrested, jailed, and, in 1897, sent into exile for three years. He did not waste them. His chief theoretical work, *The Development of Capitalism in Russia,* was written during this period (and one of its chapters was published in the legal Marxist journal which the police financed). So was his pamphlet *The Problem of the Russian Social Democrats,* which may be said to have represented him in a famous conference held at Minsk in 1898.

This meeting was the third attempt to organize the various Marxist political groups into a single party. Nine delegates, representing six groups, met for a hurried three-day session. They adopted a platform, Marxist of course; issued a manifesto written by Peter Struve, which insisted that the world revolution must be led by the workers of Russia; and set up a three-man Central Committee, with strictly limited powers, to guide the work. Eight of the nine delegates, including two of the three committeemen, were arrested as they left the meeting place, and so unification and organization remained a dream. It was also while Lenin was in exile that the majority of the Marxian socialists accepted the thesis that the workers should concentrate on strengthening the labor unions and fighting for economic gains such as higher wages. Political opposition was to be left to the middle-class liberals. Lenin thought that this turning taken by "The Economists," as they were called, ran into a blind alley; and he waged unrelenting polemical warfare against them. This was the first of many times when conviction of his own rightness made him contemptuous of the will of the majority.

His exile over, Lenin in 1900 was again allowed to go abroad. When he made contact with "the old revolutionaries" he found not only that the fight with the Economists was going on among the *émigrés,* but also that he had grown apart from Plekhanov and the others. They quarreled bitterly, but then sought to compose their differences in order to organize their movement by means of a revolutionary newspaper. This was Lenin's idea. He chose its name *Iskra* ("The Spark"); borrowed its masthead device from Pushkin ("Out of the spark shall spring the flame"); and wrote the first leading editorial, "The Urgent Tasks of Our Movement." It was a statement of the program of the party he wished to create, and it laid down many themes which he later expanded and reiterated:

> Our principal and fundamental task is to assist the political organization and political development of the working class . . . to organize for a determined struggle against the autocratic government and against the whole of capitalist society. . . . We must train people who will devote not only their spare evenings, but the whole of their lives to revolution . . . they should accept all methods of fighting. . . .

THE SOCIALIST REVOLUTIONARIES

The industrial and commercial boom of the late 1890's produced a rash of strikes—118 in 1896, 145 in 1897, and 215 in 1898. Their aims were economic rather than political, although political motivations inevitably entered into them. The crisis which began in 1899 reduced the number of strikes—189 in 1899, 125 in 1900—but not the discontent and unrest. (The figures for strikes are incomplete, since they show only industries under government factory inspection.) One manifestation of the unrest was a wave of fruitless demonstrations; another was the formation of the Social Revolutionary Party. Propaganda among the peasants had gone on intermittently but persistently since the days of Herzen. Now, at the turn of the century, various local groups (the Union of Socialist Revolutionaries and the Agrarian Socialist League, for example) had been formed to carry on this work. These gradually amalgamated, issuing their first joint manifesto in 1900, and completing their organization as the Peasant Union of the Party of Socialist Revolutionaries in 1901. This long title was soon shortened by usage to the Social Revolutionary Party or, more simply, to Essars (S.R.s). Their program, as laid down in a manifesto of 1902, called for "a deliberate and measured advance" toward the "accomplishment of the socialist ideal in its fullness"; for the socialization of land; and for ". . . the development among the peasantry of different forms of social union [and] economic co-operation for the dual purpose of liberating the peasants from . . . capitalism and of preparing [them] for the forthcoming collective agricultural production." Their attitude toward the peasants as compared to the city workers was summed up in the following sentences:

But is it wise to set ablaze a revolutionary fire among hundreds of thousands or even millions of proletarians, when tens of millions of peasantry may come like ice-water to extinguish the fire? For this to happen, it would not even be necessary for the peasantry to act against the proletariat, it would be enough if they only remained neutral.

The Essars, therefore, placed peaceful propaganda among the peasants as their first task—emphasizing the political aspects, as they said, and using economic arguments mainly for purposes of agitation. Their weapons included terrorism against the bureaucracy, and they set up a "Fighting Organization" to carry it on. Their murders of the Grand Duke Sergius, Plehve, Sipyagin, and others were so spectacular as to obscure the other parts of their program, and they came to be thought of mainly or even exclusively as terrorists. They were not. Many of them were notable humanitarians. Despite their lack of rigid discipline and tight organization—or perhaps it was because they did not insist upon these things—the Essars became the largest of the revolutionary parties.

⬦ ZEMSTVA LIBERALS

The third line of political opposition, that of the middle-class liberals, was an outgrowth of the zemstva. The interference which the zemstva suffered at the hands of conservative and reactionary government officials [5] compelled the zemstva men to become the political opponents of the government in order to carry out their assigned functions. Many became convinced that their jobs could never be properly done until the government had been thoroughly reformed. What they sought, however, was reform and not revolution, and many of them supported the government against the terrorists and other extremists while, at the same time, demanding the grant of extensive reforms. Co-operation among the various zemstva groups began in 1894 with the summoning by Dimitri N. Shipov, head of the Moscow Zemstvo, of a private, regional conference of zemstva leaders. The first session dealt with farming. Later sessions studied such common problems as "the decay of home industries," "fire fighting and prevention," fire insurance, and so on. Inevitably, politics came into the discussions, particularly after a serious repression of the zemstva in 1901 provoked a group of the younger zemstva men into direct political opposition. A year later this group, known as the Zemstva Constitutionalists, established a newspaper which served to rally supporters and to direct the work for their group. The paper, which was published at Stuttgart, was titled *Osvobozhdenie* ("Liberation") and the movement for which it spoke became known as "The Liberation Movement." Its first editor was the same P. B. Struve who had written the Minsk manifesto of the Marxists in 1898. Among the contributors to it were the veteran liberal Petrunkevich, who had suffered long exile for his outspoken championship of individual rights; the brilliant lawyer Fedor Rodichev, author of the famous 1894 address to the throne of the Tver Zemstvo (for which he had been disfranchised and banished from the capital); Prince Dolgorukov, who had also been punished for his work in the zemstva; the liberal professors Miliukov and Vinogradoff; and several others, including Shipov. It was a mixed group—of mixed social origins and class, of many professions and vocations, and of different political convictions. There were socialists, liberal conservatives, and conservative liberals. There were Slavophils and Westerners. But all of them were staunch believers in the worth and dignity of the individual, and championed individual rights and freedoms. Their standard was political freedom, and around it they rallied in 1903 a "Union of Liberation," which was less a political party than an association of more or less like-minded men.

🌐 BOLSHEVIK AND MENSHEVIK

Nineteen hundred and three was also the year of an important conference of forty-three Russian Marxists in London. The meeting had opened in Brussels, but the Belgian police had ordered the delegates to leave so the session was transferred to London. The most contentious delegates continued their wrangling all the way—even seasickness while they crossed the Channel induced only momentary pauses. There was plenty to argue about. The meeting had been called because of the increasingly bitter friction between Lenin and the others of *Iskra's* editorial board. Lenin's preparations had been thorough and detailed. He had published in March, 1902, a book which not only served as the point of departure for the debates at the 1903 meeting, but also remains to this day the basic handbook of Communist tactics and strategy. Its title is *What is to Be Done? Burning Questions of Our Movement.* One of the "burning questions" was the composition and size of the party which the conferees hoped to found. The "old revolutionaries," Zasulich and Axelrod; Lenin's contemporary, Martov; and the young recruit to

Marxism, Trotsky, all favored a party open to all who would accept its program and work under its leadership. Lenin took the position that they were building not a mass party but a revolutionary party, and that ". . . the organizations of revolutionists must be comprised first and foremost of people whose profession is that of revolutionists . . . . not too extensive and as secret as possible." He also demanded a strongly centralized organization with rigid discipline and absolute obedience to its leaders.

The opposition won the first vote on the programs, 28 to 22; but by manipulation and political trickery Lenin got the matter reconsidered after seven or eight delegates had withdrawn or been expelled from the meeting. This time he won by a very slender majority, and with a keen sense of publicity, he took for his group the title *Bolsheviki,* meaning those belonging to the majority. His opponents were left with the less desirable *Mensheviki,* those of the minority. But the actual votes on two key issues hardly bore out the claim of Lenin's title. The tabulation was: for Lenin, 22; not voting, 20; blank ballots, 2; delegates withdrawn or expelled, 7. According to the Party histories, this 1903 London Congress created the Russian Social Democratic Workers' Party. The theory that this was one party with two factions, Bolsheviks and Mensheviks, was maintained for years. It would be closer to fact to say that the London meeting resulted in the formation of two Social Democratic parties, Lenin's Bolsheviks and Martov's Mensheviks. Neither of them played an important part in the 1905 Revolution, although they claimed a joint membership at that time of five million—the highest membership figure attained until the close of World War II. Incidentally, Lenin lost control of *Iskra* and established in its place the Bolshevik newspaper which he called *Vpered* ("Forward"). This lasted until April, 1905, when it was replaced by *Proletaii* (the "Proletarian") which, in turn, was replaced in Russia by *Pravda* and at Lenin's headquarters by the *Social Democrat*. With newspapers as with followers, Lenin continued to associate only with the ones he could control. The others were cast off.

🗟 GOVERNMENT ACTIONS

The government tried several devices to squelch the growing opposition. One was the familiar police repression, with its administrative arrest and punishment supplementing, in fact almost supplanting, open action. Between 1894 and 1903, according to Masaryk, there were legal (open court) proceedings against 20,684 persons; administrative proceedings against 16,230. And there were 64,000 police arrests in 1903. Another device was legal Marxism, already mentioned, and still another was the so-called Zubatov Plan. S. V. Zubatov, of dubious repute, was the head of the Political Police in Moscow when he conceived of the idea of having the police sponsor labor unions in order to guide them away from "dangerous" lines of action. Plehve approved, and the plan was first tried in 1901 at St. Petersburg with temporary success. An attempt to extend the plan to Odessa failed and the scheme gradually died out. But the police, through stool pigeons and *agents provocateurs*, continued to keep a close watch on union activities as well as upon those of the revolutionary parties.[6] Plehve was responsible for two other schemes. One was his request for "a small victorious war," and the other was his use of the Jews and other minorities as scapegoats. It was probably this last policy which led Azev to plot his murder in 1904. Plehve's successor as Minister of the Interior was Svyatopolk-Mirsky, whose sympathies were with the liberals and who permitted the zemstva men to hold a general conference—a request which Plehve had denied.

THE ZEMSTVA PROGRAM

The conference met in November, 1904, under the leadership of Shipov, who served as its president. Shipov was himself a rather conservative liberal, and the majority of the delegates were prepared to go much further in their demands than he was. But he was a genuine liberal despite his reservations, and, though he exercised a restraining influence on the delegates, he nevertheless led them loyally and wisely. It was, in the main, Shipov's program which the Zemstvo Conference adopted. It called for freedom of conscience, religion, press, speech, and assembly; equality before the law for all citizens and equal civil and political rights for all; guarantees against arbitrary arrest and punishment; and the extension of local self-government. It also recommended ". . . that the supreme power [the emperor] summon freely elected representatives of the people in order, with their co-operation, to bring our country onto a new path of Imperial development in the spirit of the principles of justice and of harmony between the Imperial power and the people."

Within a matter of weeks this Zemstva Program was adopted by many professional groups. Russian law permitted professional men—engineers, doctors, lawyers, journalists, clerks, and so on—to form societies and to hold meetings for the discussion of matters pertaining to their professions. Many such meetings were now held, and, in case after case, the meetings adopted and endorsed the Zemstva Program as their own. The town councils, led by that of Moscow, joined the movement—an important addition since the councils spoke mainly for the powerful merchant class. Even the Marshals of the Nobility announced their adherence to the program. This was particularly infuriating to Nicholas, but he had to make a show of yielding to the opinion of so many responsible citizens. On the other hand, he was determined to give away none of the autocratic power—a determination which was perhaps largely planted and sustained by Alexandra and Pobedonostsev. Characteristically, the tsar tried to please both sides. He issued an edict which promised limited reforms—to be carried out by the very persons and agencies which most needed reforming. Then he formally and publicly rebuked Shipov and the other leaders for "trying to bring confusion into the life of society and of the State" and for "working not for their country, but for its enemies." He also told the zemstva men and councilors to mind their own business, which, he said, did not include political reforms. So, on this wholly inconclusive and totally unsatisfactory note, ended the year 1904.

CHAPTER XVIII

Deviation from Autocracy

THE WORKERS AND THE GOVERNMENT

Sire: We, workers and dwellers in St. Petersburg, have come to Thee, Sire, with our wives, our children and our helpless old parents to seek truth and protection. We have become beggars; we have been oppressed; we are weighted down with unbearable toil; we have suffered humiliations. . . . The awful moment has come when we should rather die than continue to bear these intolerable sufferings. We have stopped working and we have told our masters that we will not work again until they grant our demands . . . reduce the working day to eight hours . . . minimum pay of a ruble a day . . . no more overtime. . . .

The officials have brought the country to complete ruination, and have involved it in a detestable war. . . . We workers have had no voice in the spending of the huge sums taken from us in taxes. . . .

These things beset us, Sire, and have brought us before the walls of your palace. We seek . . . salvation. Do not refuse to help your people. Give their destiny into their own hands. Free them from the intolerable oppression of officials. Break down the wall between Yourself and your people, and, together with Yourself, let them rule the country . . . order the calling of a National Assembly at once . . . order elections . . . to be carried on by universal, equal, and secret voting. . . .

The document, paraphrased in part above, was a strange and curious petition which some 200,000 men, women, and children sought to present to their emperor on January 9/22, 1905. Unarmed and peaceful, carrying icons as was most fitting for a Sunday morning, singing over and over again "God Save Our Noble Tsar," these people streamed into the city from the factory suburbs. What did they want, these subjects of the tsar in holiday dress moving slowly but inexorably toward the Winter Palace? Perhaps they were not sure in detail. Their petition was a hodgepodge of catch phrases from the Zemstva Program and slogans from the strikes (especially from the one at the huge Putilov works). But their main purpose was clear. It was to vault the wall between themselves and the tsar, "Father of the Russian People."

One of the most deeply rooted social values of the Russian masses was their patient, persistent, almost pathetic faith in their tsars. Abuses and oppressions, most of them were convinced, were their lot despite the will of "The Little Father" and not because of it. His officials fooled him, lied to him, failed to carry out his orders. He did not know how his people were being treated. If he knew, he would act. So ran the popular myth. These thousands of people were marching toward the Winter Palace on that Sunday morning because the striking workers from the Putilov plant, whose representatives had been fired upon by agents of the management, insisted that they would tell their troubles to their "Dear Father Tsar" so that he might set things straight. They walked the road to tragedy and to revolution.

The leader of this curious demonstration—if anything so formless can really be said to have a leader—was not a member of any of the revolutionary parties or groups nor of the zemstva professional organizations. He was a Ukrainian priest named George Apollonovich Gapon, an honest, sincere humanitarian. He was also almost incredibly naive or stupid, or both; and since 1902 he had been in the employ of Zubatov, Plehve, and the secret police. Zubatov had been discredited, Plehve had been murdered, but Gapon continued to lead his Union of Russian Factory Workers—which had been endorsed by Plehve, and which was supported by police funds. By the end of 1904 the workers of St. Petersburg—who were glad of any opportunities to meet under any sponsorship—had rushed to join it. Gapon's eloquence swayed the great mass meetings which gathered to hear him; to sing the praises of the tsar who, in his loving wisdom, had replaced the oppression of police with the sympathetic leadership of the priest; and to talk about their troubles. Soon it was the masses who were leading Gapon. (It must be remembered that ninety-four of every hundred workers were peasants, almost half of them newly come from farm and village. And it was among the peasants that faith in the essential good will of "The Little Father" was strongest.)

Now what of the other side? What were "The Little Father" and his advisers doing besides financing Gapon. The memoirs of Kokovtsov, who had replaced Witte as Minister of Finance, are very revealing, though, of course, one-sided:

One must bear in mind that at that time there was no co-ordination among the ministers. Each ministry was a closed, self-contained entity, managing all by itself the business within its competence. . . . There was never any preliminary discussion except when friendly relations existed between separate ministries. . . . Thus no one knew for sure what was being prepared in the secrecy of this or that ministry. . . . Let me repeat that at this time there were no general conferences of representatives of different ministries. All ministers acted independently, each in his own province. . . .[1]

The Minister of the Interior, whom Kokovtsov regards as having been entirely Witte's man, was Svyatopolk-Mirsky. Kokovtsov speaks of him as having been both ineffectual and as having asked Witte's advice "literally at every turn." But it must be remembered that Kokovtsov was Witte's political enemy and also was very much put out at not being consulted about labor problems, which he thought properly belonged in his jurisdiction. Besides, as Kokovtsov himself points out, the initiative passed from Svyatopolk-Mirsky to D. F. Trepov, who was made Assistant Minister of the Interior early in 1905. Trepov, says Kokovtsov, "followed the directions of his minister only outwardly." His policies were a combination of the Zubatov methods with strict repression. He and various other officials were at a conference to which Kokovtsov was summoned by Svyatopolk-Mirsky on the evening of January 8/21. There, Kokovtsov says, he learned for the first time that Gapon had planned a demonstration for the next day, that the police had been ordered to prevent it, that the tsar had moved from the Winter Palace to nearby Gatchina on Friday. Kokovtsov accuses Witte of being behind all this, an accusation which Witte publicly denied. Responsibility may be in doubt, but what happened on January 9/22—Bloody Sunday— is wholly clear.

✥ BLOODY SUNDAY AND A SPREADING REBELLION

The marching masses were met, both en route and at the square before the palace, by almost point-blank fire. Even "little boys who had climbed the trees to watch what was going on were shot down like birds." No one knows the number of casualties. A later investigation reported 150 killed and 200 wounded. Bolshevik histories say that a thousand were killed and two thousand wounded. Other sources which were closer to the movement give the respective figures as 500 and 3000.[2] "In any case," as Wolfe put it, "enough blood was shed to baptize the day as Bloody Sunday." And the shock to public opinion was terrific. "Five years ago," a peasant told Pares in 1905, "there was belief and fear. Now the belief is all gone, and only the fear remains." It was an excellent summation. The events of January 9/22 disabused the people of their cherished notion that the tsar was their salvation. It was horribly apparent now how "The Little Father" felt. And because Trepov, who was made head of the police, promptly exiled from the capital all who had taken prominent parts in the demonstration, firsthand reports were spread all over the empire.

The effect was comparable to the scattering of delayed-action incendiary bombs. There were strikes of all kinds—in single factories, among whole trades, among white-collar workers, among students, among domestic servants. There were isolated, spontaneous acts of terrorism —incidents of arson and of murder. There were separatist risings among the subject nationalities. The government still controlled the police and the armed forces and held the means of communication. But a kind of creeping paralysis attacked the whole system, as, for example, when Urussov resigned the governorship of Tver rather than to serve under Trepov, or when the zemstva in various regions adjourned their annual meetings on the ground that nothing could be done under existing conditions. And highly articulate agitation continued.

The professional men became more outspoken at their meetings, and many changed their professional societies into professional unions. The engineers and technicians were the first to organize, closely followed by professors and students, who formed the Academic Union. Then came unions of bookkeepers and clerks, primary school workers and teachers, doctors, lawyers, writers, secondary school teachers, railway employees, and others. The Railway Union included workers as well as professional men and intellectuals and was, for that reason, especially important.[3] Professor Paul Miliukov, one of the leaders in the Liberation Movement, was largely responsible for the combining of most of these into a loose "Union of Unions," which kept up a steady and telling pressure on the government all during the summer of 1905. It then faded out, but from it there developed Miliukov's party, the Constitutional Democrats or Kadets. (Its formal title was "The Party of the Peoples' Liberty," but few called it that.)

Politics and finance and foreign relations also got tangled up as a direct result of Bloody Sunday. Kokovtsov was carrying on loan negotiations with German and French groups when Gapon led his demonstrators toward the Winter Palace. The incident had no effect on the Germans, who readily concluded the loan agreement. But more money was needed, and the French became skittish. Kokovtsov and Witte arranged for the head of the French banking group (who was also an unofficial agent of the French government) to have an audience with the tsar. The Frenchman spoke bluntly of the need for better relations between the Russian people and the Russian government as a guarantee against further disorders. Nicholas, as was his wont, said what the Frenchman wanted to hear, and the latter departed quite reassured and ready to go ahead with the loan negotiations.

Then, suddenly, the tsar issued an order to Bulygin, who had replaced Svyatopolk-Mirsky as Minister of the Interior, demanding that the full force of the government be thrown against its opponents. There was no word of faith in the people nor of reforms. Witte and Kokovtsov both remonstrated with the tsar and warned of the probably chilling effects of this action on the French. "The Tsar," reports Kokovtsov, "gave no direct answer, but promised to think it over." Soon Bulygin was ordered to prepare a plan "for drawing the population into 'an active and constant participation in the work of legislation.' "—as Kokovtsov put it. This was the beginning of the acts which led to the establishment of the Duma.

Both domestic and foreign pressures continued. On the domestic side there were continuing demonstrations, disorders, strikes, and demands. The most effective of the demands were those formulated by the zemstva men, especially by the Zemstva Constitutionalists, and by the town councils. Strikes were still epidemic, and the strikers numbered hundreds of thousands. The famous strike at Ivanovo-Voznesensk, for example, lasted almost three months and involved about 70,000 strikers. The disorders culminated in a successful mutiny on board the battleship "Potemkin"—the first major defection in the armed forces. These domestic events were partially the reflections of foreign affairs, which were going very badly for Russia. Port Arthur surrendered to the Japanese in January; Mukden fell in March; and in May the Baltic fleet, which under Admiral Rozhestvensky had made the long trip around Africa, was met and sunk in the Battle of Tsushima Straits with a loss of almost 5000 officers and men. En route to its destruction, some units of this fleet had fired on and sunk some British fishing trawlers off the Dogger Bank, thus producing another crisis in the always explosive relations with Britain. Prodded reluctantly forward by these events, Nicholas reaffirmed his promise to grant a national assembly (Duma), and invited public discussion of the project. The minority of the articulate liberals joyously accepted the invitation, the zemstva again being especially active. They asked for a legislative assembly instead of merely a consultative one. They had their answer in August when the "Bulygin Duma" was announced. It was to be a consultative body only, and, moreover, was to be elected on the basis of a very restricted suffrage.

✈ THE 1905 REVOLUTION AND THE SOVIETS

This was not enough by far. A Peasant Union, which claimed some 200,000 members, was formed during the summer and joined the Union of Unions, to which it gave added prestige. Disorders continued and so did the strikes, which reached a climax with the great General Strike of October. This strike was precipitated when the government arrested delegates to the conference of the Railway Union. Their colleagues promptly refused to operate the trains. The strike spread like oil on water. The streetcars stopped, the mails were not delivered, the banks closed, the Imperial Ballet would not dance. For several days the whole of the country was virtually at a standstill. It was the most successful general strike on record, and it was the climax of the revolution. Characteristically, it was at first quite unorganized. Only when the spontaneous strike had been in process for several days did leadership appear and seek to organize it.

It is not possible to say with assurance from whence the initiative came, but the Mensheviks were prominent in it, and the first organizer seems to have been Khrustalyev-Nosar. This man escaped from his guards as he was being removed from the prison-fortress of SS. Peter and Paul and went first to Moscow where he organized an association of workers. From there he went to the capital where he directed the formation of the Council of Workmen Deputies. This was the first of the famous soviets (the Russian word *soviet* means "council"). As Khrustalyev-Nosar himself told it later:

> . . . we began working to create another such autonomous organization [like the one in Moscow] in St. Petersburg. Our appeal met with an enthusiastic reception among the workmen. In spite of all the objectionable efforts of the Social Democrats, the foundation-stone was laid, and in October took place the first sitting of the new working men's organization in the quarters of the Technological Institute. [The exact date was October 13/26. The general strike had begun on October 9/22.] At the start it did not possess either a precise title or strictly defined functions. The workmen of the factories and works chose one deputy for every 500 workmen. Small enterprises and the lesser workshops met together and sent a common delegate. Neither political nor religious nor national differences played any part in the matter. Thus the whole mass of workmen scattered over St. Petersburg, who had no access to professional unions or to political parties, was cemented and drawn into the common work.
>
> . . . the Council of Workmen Deputies was a most democratic 'working men's parliament,' and its discussions and resolutions were the equivalent of the views and feelings of the agitated working classes in Russia during the revolutionary epoch. They were obeyed *imperio rationis, sed non ratione imperii* [by order of reason, but not by reason of orders] as the Council of Workmen Deputies had no means of compelling obedience. But at the word of the Council the workmen struck work, and by the resolution of the Council they resumed it. . . .

Khrustalyev-Nosar, who was the president of the St. Petersburg Soviet, went on to say that the power and functions of the group grew at a fantastic rate. Soviets were organized, either on local initiative or by sponsorship of the St. Petersburg Soviet, in many places. There were peasants' soviets and military soviets and student soviets and village soviets and city soviets "from St. Petersburg to Tiflis, and from Warsaw to Vladivostok." The Union of Unions and The Peasant's Union recognized the leadership of the Soviets. "Officials and the employees of banks, offices, railways, post, telegraph, and telephone sent their representatives to the council, and submitted to its decisions." Even Witte had to enlist the help of the soviet to send a government telegram. For somewhat less than the fifty days of its actual existence, the Soviet was as much the government of Russia as was the official administration headed by Witte. "Will Witte assassinate Khrustalyev or will Khrustalyev assassinate Witte?" was the way the matter was stated in common conversation. The conservative newspaper *Novoe Vremya* acknowledged the existence of "two governments, the government of Count Witte and the government of Khrustalyev." (The paper might have added the name of Trotsky to that of Khrustalyev. Trotsky, then "in his Menshevik phase," returned from exile after the St. Petersburg Soviet had begun to function. He became its vice-president.)

Meanwhile, the emperor had been forced by the General Strike to take action. He turned once again to Witte, who told him that there were only two alternatives—either the establishment of a military dictatorship or the grant of a legislative, national assembly. Witte and Nicholas both believed that the second alternative involved the granting of a constitution. The decisive influence was apparently that of the Grand Duke Nicholas, who presumably would have been the dictator if the first alternative had been adopted. He threw his weight entirely behind the second alternative—for which the empress never forgave him. So, on October 17/30, 1905, the Emperor Nicholas II, very much against his will ("It makes me sick," he wrote his mother), issued a manifesto promising civil rights and liberties and the creation of an elected, national, legislative assembly. The suffrage arrangements proposed by the *October Manifesto,* much more generous than those proposed by Bulygin, were further broadened by Witte's law of December, which established virtually a manhood suffrage. The extreme conservatives and the radicals were equally dissatisfied, but for opposite reasons, of course. Both did what they could to discredit and to hinder this development. The middle-of-the-roaders—which included most of the people as well as those identifiable as conservative liberals and liberal conservatives—were happy and hopeful. Their country was, they thought, about to receive a constitution and to begin upon a liberal, parliamentary era. As for the government—the tsar and his bureaucracy—their attitude may be illustrated by Sir Bernard Pares' report of an interview accorded him by Witte.

"Are we right in regarding you as author of the October Manifesto?" [Pares asked Witte]. "Certainly," he said. "Then we may regard you as author of the Constitution?" "Certainly," he said. "And what do you think of the Constitution now?" "I have a constitution in my head," he said, "but as to my heart, I spit on it!" and he spat on the floor in front of me.

The attitude of the man who had been made prime minister [4] for the purpose of implementing the promises of October was shared by the majority of his associates and, of course, by the tsar and the tsarina. They at once set about reneging on their promises, an action that was greatly facilitated by the deepening split which at once appeared in the ranks of the opposition. The Essars and the Social Democrats continued to press for socialistic measures. The Essars demanded land for the peasants and organized peasant disorders against the landowners in many parts of the empire. These usually took the form of burning down the manor house, and often included physical violence to the owners. The soviets of the cities kept calling strikes, which failed, and in December attempted an armed uprising in Moscow, which was a fiasco and completely discredited the movement. Violence and terror horrified the timid and gave justification to those who were willing to use any measures to undo even the mildest of the reforms. The most notorious of these rightists were the "Black Hundreds," who operated under the more formal and better-sounding labels of the Union of the Russian People, the Union of the Russian Land, and the Russian Orthodox Committee. These proto-storm-troopers had the active moral and financial support of P. N. Durnovo, who became Minister of the Interior in Witte's Council of Ministers, and of Trepov, who, removed from office by Witte, had become the tsar's close and trusted adviser. ("Durnovo," wrote Nicholas to his mother, "is doing splendid work. Trepov is absolutely indispensable to me.") This precious pair undermined both Witte and the constitutional reform. They also arranged pogroms and attacks upon national minorities as devices to divide the people and thus recover power for the government.

🏴 THE DUMAS

Elections to the Duma were arranged, the government often interfering to exclude individuals. Miliukov, for example, was excluded from candidacy by a police trick. The people watched with interest which was buoyed by hope but tempered with great doubts. Despite the boycotts against the election announced by the Essars and Social Democrats, the majority of the people exercised their new rights of suffrage to choose their best men. The general participation of the peasants in the elections to the first two Dumas is contrary proof to the often-heard claim that the Russian people never had any interest in governing themselves. When they had any chance at self-government—as in the zemstva and these two Dumas, and, again in the Constituent Assembly of 1917–18—they showed a lively and intelligent interest. To return to the First Duma, just four days before it was scheduled to open the imperial government announced not the constitution which had been expected but a revision of the Fundamental Laws of the Empire, which contained in its first section the two following sentences: "The supreme autocratic power belongs to the Emperor of All the Russias. Acceptance of his authority is dictated not alone by fear and conscience, but also by God Himself."

The Fundamental Laws abided by the letter but not the spirit of Nicholas' promises by creating an elective, legislative assembly (the Duma). The Duma was made the lower house of a bicameral body whose upper house was a State Council, half of whose members were appointed by the tsar. Legislative power was shared by both houses and the emperor, who could summon, adjourn, or dissolve the Duma. In case of dissolution, the decree had to provide for a subsequent session. No change was to be made in the Fundamental Laws without the concurrence of the Duma and Council, but the Duma could not initiate such changes. Ministers remained responsible only to the emperor, although the Duma was given the right to interpellate them. Military matters and about half the budget (beside some other matters) were placed beyond the Duma's power, and its financial powers were also further limited. These were severe restrictions, but the Duma had some authority and it gradually acquired more powers than the strict letter of the law allowed. Russia remained an autocracy, but the autocrat could no longer legislate by his authority alone. Laws had to have the consent of the Duma and Council.

THE FIRST DUMA

The First Duma was formally opened on April 27/May 6, 1906, with 497 members. The largest single group were the 191 peasants who comprised 39 per cent of the membership. The next largest group were the 123 members of the *dvorianstvo*. There were 20 workers and three "industrialists." Classified by occupations, the largest group were, again, the peasant-farmers. There were 64 professional men and 13 clergy, mostly of the Russian Orthodox Church. One man called himself "a colonist," and another said only that his occupation was being "a candidate for the zemstvo board." The development of parliamentary political parties was one of the accompaniments of the Dumas. The only one which was really organized at the time of the First Duma was the Constitutional Democratic Party (Kadets), which claimed 184 members in the Duma. Generally speaking, the Kadets were more interested in political than in social reforms, although they were neither unaware of the need for the latter nor hostile to the idea. They wanted to make the Duma into something resembling the British House of Commons, and the views of Miliukov, their leader, were essentially those of the British Liberal Party of that day. The First Duma was allowed to hold only forty sittings (spread over 73 days) before it was dissolved by Nicholas' order, so that other parties had too little time to organize and discipline themselves. Precision as to party strength and memberships is impossible, but careful estimates give working figures, and, through them, a measure of the temper of the electorate.

There were only seven extreme rightists and 38 moderate rightists, as against 17 Essars and two Social Democrats at the far left. One hundred and five others belonged to the left of the Kadets, but the range of their "leftism" was considerable. Over one hundred members of the First Duma, mostly peasants, refused to join any party, adopting a wait-and-see policy. In spite of party labels and differences, there was remarkable unanimity on certain points. One was the general "Address to the Throne," originally drafted by Vladimir Nabokov, and accepted after a long sentence-by-sentence debate by all except ten of the members. The tsar finally sent old Goremykin, who had replaced Witte as prime minister, to deliver a reply. This was a scolding, plus a complete rejection of the Duma's proposal for giving more land to the peasants. The Duma then passed a vote of censure against the ministers—and nothing happened. The ministers did not resign, and the Duma, after some indecision, went on to discuss certain specific bills. The simple fact was that neither side knew what to do. Nicholas himself wanted to dissolve the Duma and Goremykin supported him. But Trepov suggested a deal with the liberals, and there was even some talk—probably not in good faith—of asking Miliukov to head a Kadet Ministry. Kokovtsov, who was back again in the Ministry of Finance after having been forced out by Witte, opposed this, and so did Stolypin, who must shortly be introduced at greater length. The Duma, for its part, developed differences within itself; debated at length and with vigor; passed bills which the government rejected; and finally sought to appeal to the people. We need follow the details no further. The government suddenly dissolved the Duma and ordered new elections; the majority of the Duma members, led by Miliukov and his Kadets, promptly organized a rump session at nearby Viborg in Finland. This group then issued the so-called Viborg Appeal, demanding the recall of the Duma and urging the people to refuse to pay taxes or to accept conscription until this was done. The appeal, which was wholly illegal, fell absolutely flat. Its only result, almost, was that those who signed it were barred from election to the next Duma. The dissolution of the First Duma, the election of the second, and the promulgation of a major agrarian reform in between the two were the work of Peter Stolypin, who took Goremykin's place as prime minister.

🌀 P. A. STOLYPIN

Peter Arkadevich Stolypin was not long past his forty-fourth birthday when he became president of the Council of Ministers, but literally half his life had been spent in the service of the state. The son of a wealthy landowner who also spent his life in official posts, Peter Stolypin graduated from St. Petersburg University and went directly into the bureaucracy. After five years in minor jobs he was made a Marshal of the Nobility, first for the district and then for the Province of Kovno. These offices he held until 1902 when he was appointed acting governor of Grodno. The following year he was given the governorship of Saratov Province, where he stayed until 1906. His province was troubled, like all the others, by the disorders and uprisings of 1904–5. But Stolypin, unlike most of the other governors, distinguished himself by the firmness, fairness, and tact with which he met the situation. He was harsh in his punishments of rioters and revolutionaries, but, as he said later, he tried to distinguish the harmless from the mischievous elements and to act accordingly. On one occasion he protected the revolutionaries—who had only talked revolution—from an unfriendly mob. He was called from Saratov, at Witte's dismissal, to become Minister of the Interior, stepping from that office to the prime ministership, as previously noted. He was murdered in 1911 by an agent of the government's own secret police.

Physically, Peter Stolypin was a tremendously big man—"a regular Russian bear of a man," one of his acquaintances recalled him. His courage and his will matched his size. Intellectually he was not brilliant, but his judgments were often as shrewd as his expressions of them were pithy. One of his talents, and one of his gravest faults, was oversimplification. His answer to the charge that the government broke its own laws is illustrative of this characteristic. It is also indicative of his shrewd realism and of his forthright honesty:

In countries where no definite standard has yet been fixed the center of gravity, the center of power, lies not in institutions, but in men. It is natural for men to make mistakes, to be tempted, to abuse their power. Let these abuses be exposed, let them be examined and condemned. But the government must take a different view of attacks made on itself when they aim at creating an atmosphere of feeling hostile to its own continuance; such attacks are calculated to cause in the government, in the holders of office, a paralysis of will and thought. All such attacks can be summarized in two words addressed to the official world: 'Hands up.' To these two words, gentlemen, a government conscious of its own integrity, without any alarm, can only reply: 'We are not afraid of you.'

Two other short quotations revealing the quality and mind of this man may be added. The first was a portion of his explanation of why he dissolved the First Duma. The second concerns his program of action for the Second Duma:

There were two ways out. A ministry might be taken from the majority of the Duma. This solution was seriously discussed. But in the Duma there were not enough men with experience in governing; and as the Duma was revolutionary in character, I mean it was always encroaching, the new ministers would not have ruled the Duma but been ruled by it. In a single day they would have disarmed themselves, surrendering all the resources of power; and, as revolution is very strong now . . . the issue would have been fatal. Another way out was sheer reaction, which of course I would never have consented to support.

There was a third way, a middle course, which was my own; to keep the power of the government intact . . . to have new elections and a new Duma . . . to take the initiative . . . and to carry through reforms where they are required. But as revolution is so strong, my position must be one with two fronts: that is, I must carry effective measures of reform and at the same time I must face revolution, resist it and stop it.

[In the interval between the First and Second Dumas] the government must itself bring forward new measures. . . . The mistake has been that the government [ministry] had no policy and consequently all the new bills came from the Duma. . . . All the bills, all the definite proposals came from the opposition. This was an impossible position.

Stolypin's two-front program won him enemies on both sides. His punishment of revolutionaries and suspected revolutionaries was swift and ruthless. He set up "field courts martial" (or drum-head courts martial) to deal with acts of terrorism. According to Masaryk, these courts martial executed 676 persons between August, 1906, and April, 1907. Such actions seem to justify the depictation of Stolypin as a cruel and black-hearted reactionary. (Stolypin was automatically suspect to certain minds because of his wealth. He owned over 5000 acres of land, plus other property, and his wife owned 14,500 acres of land.) His arbitrary and illegal change in the electoral law, which will be described shortly, appears to justify labeling him a reactionary, but an accurate characterization of him is not so simple. For one thing he made an honest and whole-hearted effort to clear out the rogues from the government. ("This is a debt of conscience," he said; "Russia must have her house clean.") Among those whom he attacked was Rasputin—for which the empress never forgave him.

The fact seems to be that Stolypin was frequently a conservative in the best sense of the word. That is, he neither opposed change because it was new nor clung to the past because it was old. But he felt that change was not always or necessarily progress, and he believed that some things were worth conserving. Stolypin in his lesser moments was, however, a good deal less than a good conservative. He yielded to Great Russian nationalism in depriving Finland of a large part of her self-government (1910) and in measures aimed at extending the system of the zemstva to the western portions of the empire; he discriminated against the Jews and the Poles. His tactics were often so brutally direct as to amount to riding roughshod over both the spirit and the letter of the laws. There were times, also, when his motives might properly have been suspect. Both cavalier action and disingenuous motivation were demonstrated in his very important agrarian reforms.

STOLYPIN'S LAND REFORM

Stolypin took office in 1906 convinced of three things: (1) that the government must take the initiative; (2) that the best way to fight the revolutionaries was to enlist the support of the peasants; and (3) that the most desirable lure which the government could offer the peasants was to free them from the mir and enable them to acquire private property. These were the motives which led him to drive through his greatest reform. His tactic was to use Section 87 of the Fundamental Laws, which permitted the government, on its own and sole authority, to issue laws when the Duma was not sitting. Such "emergency legislation" had to be presented to the Duma for confirmation—which was never withheld. By using this device, Stolypin was able to order the reform in time, he hoped, for his action to affect the elections to the new Duma. The essence of Stolypin's first land law was that it permitted individual peasants to claim their share in the land held by their mir, and to receive that share all in one piece.

This first law was defective in that it left the mirs with legal ways and means of evading or frustrating a peasant's request for title to his share of the land. The Third Duma, on Stolypin's initiative, remedied this defect and also extended the scope of the reform. The revised laws provided that a final distribution of land had to be carried out whenever a two-thirds majority of the members of the mir so demanded. A family consisting of a husband and wife and their offspring were given an individual title to their share. In the case of a household which included grandparents, uncles, in-laws, and so forth, the title showed a joint ownership. Whether the titles were individual or joint, the owners could have all their lands on one plot instead of having them scattered all over the community. This was a change of the greatest significance, but its potentialities were never fully realized because of World War I and the 1917 revolutions. Nevertheless, between 1906 and the end of 1914 almost six million of the total twelve million peasant families in the 47 agricultural provinces of European Russia petitioned to receive their shares—a clear indication of the peasant desire for private ownership, or at least for family ownership. (Slightly less than half the applicants sought individual titles.) Despite the aid which the government gave to the petitioners (by making loans, arranging surveys, and so on), the division was a lengthy process. Roughly four million of the six million petitions had not been carried through to completion by 1915. Over a million individual farms and almost as many family farms had been set up, however. During the same period (1906–14), the government had also set up some three million individual, independent farmers in Siberia. These changes helped to bring about a period of prosperity.

Communist Party histories, which call the years from 1906 to 1915 "the Stolypin reaction," now scorn this agrarian reform as an evil plot to help the rich peasants at the expense of the poor. But Lenin, in 1908, made an entirely different appraisal of it. It was, said Lenin, a step toward the creation of a middle-class monarchy which might very well succeed. "If this should continue for very long periods of time . . . it might force us [the Bolsheviks] to renounce any agrarian program at all. . . . If Stolypin's policy is continued . . . then the agrarian structure of Russia will become completely bourgeois. . . ." Lenin agreed with Stolypin's remark that "the small owner is the nucleus on which rests all stable order in the state" and, as Dr. Wolfe observed, "saw the matter as a race with time between Stolypin's reforms, and the next upheaval." No shrewder analysis of the real meaning of Stolypin's reforms has yet been made. It introduced the element of change—from communal to private landownership in this case—which, along with continuity, forms the essence of history. To see Stalin's collectivized agriculture as simply an extension of the communal system of old Russia is to ignore the very important events just described.

🦅 THE SECOND DUMA AND STOLYPIN'S COUP

The alert reader, noticing that the Stolypin agrarian reforms were finally enacted by the Third Duma, may have wondered what happened to the second—the one whose election Stolypin hoped to sway by his original land act. Its brief story may be very quickly told. The Second Duma was convened on February 20/March 5, 1907, and held only 53 sittings before it was dissolved on June 2/15 of that year. No significant work was done, but the character of its membership reflected the temper of the country. Partly because the government's action excluded the signers

of the Viborg Appeal, and partly because the peasants often chose professional revolutionaries to represent them, the Second Duma was composed almost entirely of new men. (Only 31 persons were members of
both the First and Second Dumas.) It was also, for these same reasons
plus the fact that the leftist parties dropped their boycotts, far to the
left of the First Duma. There were 216 who were clearly left of the
Kadets, and only 52 were clearly right of them. The Social Revolutionaries (Essars) claimed 34 members and three "associates"; the Social
Democrats had 66 members in the Duma; the Labor group—a loose
coalition—had 98; and the Kadets had 99. Less than 10 per cent of the
Second Duma's 520 members could be accurately labeled reactionaries.
A third of the members listed themselves as farmers; and just over a
fifth, as landlords. There were 33 workers. Barely more than half the
members (51 per cent) were property owners. As in the First Duma,
some unusual occupations were represented, the most extraordinary
being "sultan" and "poet and satirist." Sixty-two per cent of the members
were Great Russians, but, altogether, 28 different national groups were
represented, including 15 Asiatic groups. These figures will give a point
from which to measure the effects of Stolypin's electoral coup.

Between the handful of articulate, determined (and police-supported)
reactionaries on the one side and the larger group of articulate and
equally determined revolutionaries on the other, the Second Duma was
quickly torn apart. Neither of these groups wanted the Duma to succeed,
and their tactics played into the hands of Stolypin, who found in them
confirmation and justification for his own lack of faith in parliaments.
("I am a constitutionalist, not a parliamentarianist," he said. "If you
took an assembly which represented the majority of the population, sane
ideas would not prevail in it.") So the Second Duma was dismissed on
the manufactured charge that some of its members were conspiring
against the government. Before the Third Duma was elected, Stolypin
greatly altered the electoral laws in direct violation of the Fundamental
Laws, which stated that no such change should be made except with the
concurrence of the Duma. The Duma had no chance to concur. It was not
consulted, and the people were faced with a *fait accompli.*

THIRD AND FOURTH DUMAS

Stolypin's new electoral law favored the large landowners and the wealthy
gentry at the expense of the other classes; favored the country districts
at the expense of the cities; and favored the Great Russians at the expense of the non-Great Russians. The results were plainly apparent in
the Third and Fourth Dumas, which were elected under this law. Almost half the members of these Dumas were landowners, as compared

with less than a quarter of the members in the Second Duma. Ninety-eight per cent of the Third and 93 per cent of the members of the Fourth Duma were property owners, in contrast to the 51 per cent of the Second Duma. Thirty-nine per cent of the members of the First Duma had been peasants. The figure for the second was 36 per cent; for the third and fourth, 19 per cent. The percentage of gentry had gone from 25 in the first to 28 in the second, jumped to 44 in the third, and reached an absolute majority of 51 per cent in the fourth. There were only 20 national groups in the Third Duma, and the number of their deputies was less. Only five Asiatic groups sent deputies to the Fourth Duma, as contrasted to 15 in the second. The number of extreme rightists went from ten in the second to about 50 in the third and about 60 in the Fourth Duma. The Kadets lost half their strength; the Labor group, 85 per cent of its strength; the Social Democrats, more than two-thirds; and the Essars disappeared altogether (at least as a party). The largest single party group in both the Third and Fourth Dumas was the "Union of the seventeenth of October," whose members were usually called Octobrists. They were also the wealthiest group. They split into left and right wings in the Fourth Duma. The right, and smaller, wing was thoroughly conservative; the left wing was quite liberal. It sought advanced labor legislation, equalization of the tax burden, juridical and civil equality for the peasants, and economic aid to the peasants.

None of the Dumas were truly representative of the Russian people. The approximate ratio of representation is shown in Table 4.

TABLE 4

	1st Duma	2d Duma	3d Duma	4th Duma
Peasants	1: 800,000	1: 900,000	1: 1,700,000	1: 1,700,000
Gentry/nobility	1: 28,000	1: 25,000	1: 17,000	1: 15,000
Urban workers	1: 150,000	1: 91,000	1: 600,000	1: 1,000,000

The representation of the gentry/nobility was, in other words, almost doubled; that of the peasants was halved; that of the urban workers was reduced by 85 per cent between the Second and the Fourth Dumas. This would have been less significant except for the fact that the Provisional Government of 1917 was established by the members of the Fourth Duma, and was, therefore, as little representative of the people as that Duma had been. Elections to the Dumas were multistaged and indirect; that is, the voters chose electors who chose the deputies. This was so arranged, before Stolypin's electoral coup in 1907, that some 70 million peasants chose 1168 electors; 12 million workers, 112 electors; 8 million middle class, 590 electors; 500,000 wealthy men 788 electors; and

200,000 landed gentry, 2594 electors. The electoral law so changed matters that the two favored classes, totaling about 700,000 persons, chose as many electors as all the other groups put together.

The letter of the law remained restrictive of the Duma's powers, but, in practice, these restrictions became increasingly less. Military matters and matters of Church administraton, for example, which legally were "out of bounds" did not remain so. The rebuilding of the Russian armed forces after the debacle of the Japanese War was largely the work of the Duma, and particularly of Alexander Guchkov, leader of the Octobrists. This was accomplished through the Duma's power over the budget—a power strictly limited but one which the Duma leaders learned to use with increasing effectiveness—and through the right to question ministers. Although the Duma never got to the point where it could appoint ministers (that is, there was never established an administration completely responsible to the Duma), it did dismiss ministers (or, more accurately, compel their dismissal). The Duma was particularly effective in encouraging agricultural improvements and land settlement under the Stolypin system. The Third Duma alone increased the expenditures for land settlement more than six times over; and for improvements nearly three times over. The Duma also did a great deal to advance education. State expenditures for public education more than doubled between 1907 and 1912, largely as a result of activity of the Duma. Illiteracy was being steadily, if slowly, reduced. The literacy figure for the whole empire for 1897 was 28 per cent; by 1914 it had risen to 43 per cent. The percentage of children of school age receiving elementary education had also approximately doubled during these same years. The Duma's aim, which was not reached before war and revolution ended the institution, was the establishment of universal, free, elementary education.

OKHRANA PROCEDURES

There were, however, important segments of the government and of government action over which the Duma had very little or absolutely no control. One such area—and a very broad one it was—was covered by what the Russians called *"okhrana* procedures." The *okhrana* was both the secret police and the state of "reinforced protection" under which both the secret police and the ordinary administrators were given wide latitude "to preserve public peace and order." Exile without trial, punishment without a hearing, the rankest violation of the rights of the individual were all instances of *okhrana* procedure. So widely was this procedure employed that an official reported in 1905 that a whole generation had grown up which knew the law only from books and from *okhrana* practice. The *okhrana* procedure, though classified merely as an administrative ordinance, had really been the law since 1881. This law, under which all Russia was at least partially governed, practically nullified the Duma's control over administration and suspended the civil rights which Nicholas had repeatedly promised. It gave to local and imperial officials the right of search; the right to imprison any suspect for two weeks—the two weeks might be indefinitely extended by order of the Minister of the Interior; the right to exile a suspect for five years without a trial or without bringing charges; the right to forbid residence in a given area for an indefinite period; the right to suppress meetings, even those for which official permission had been given; the right to dismiss employees of the zemstva and town councils; and the right to hand civilians over to military courts martial. Even this list is not exhaustive. The present police apparatus in the Soviet Union is much larger,[5] more efficient, and more ruthless. But a police state is neither a new phenomenon nor a Communist innovation in Russia. The Duma frequently criticized bitterly the excesses and abuses of the *okhrana* procedure and sometimes attempted to limit it by legislation. Both the criticisms and the efforts were futile.

"DARK FORCES": RASPUTIN

The inability of the Duma to control ministerial and administrative appointments was another of its very great weaknesses. With some exceptions (Kokovtsov was president of the Council of Ministers from Stolypin's death in 1911 until 1914), the top administrators became increasingly reactionary. What was much worse, to borrow a sentence from Samuel N. Harper, who was one of America's top authorities on Russia, "they were definitely controlled by 'those dark forces laying rough hands on the machinery of state,' to use the circumlocution which all understood to mean Rasputin." For this state of affairs, the Empress Alexandra was to a considerable degree responsible.

Gregory Efimovich Novykh was one of the "Dark Ones," which is to say that he was uneducated and barely literate. His home village of Pokrovskoe, in Siberia, knew him for two things: his skill in handling animals and his utterly dissolute behavior. The skill made him useful around his father's stables. His debauches won him a nickname so apt that it became, to all intents and purposes, his surname. The nickname was Rasputin, and it meant "the rip" or, less colloquially, "the licentious." In 1903 or 1904 Rasputin abandoned his family and set out upon his travels, which he said were required of him by God. He became associated with one of Russia's most exotic sects, the *Khlysty* ("Flagellants"). Whether he was actually a member of the sect is not proven, but he behaved like one—alternating orgies of sex and drink with orgies of religious fervor. He traveled all over Russia, visited the Balkans, went twice to Jerusalem on pilgrimages, and spent some time in various monasteries. He was not, however, either a monk or a priest. Rasputin belonged to that rather large company of "holy wanderers" (*stranniki*) —always eccentric and usually ascetic religious fanatics who, from time immemorial, had wandered over Russia like the holy beggars of India.

Probably in 1904, Rasputin became acquainted with S. M. Trufanov, who became the monk Iliodor and a popular preacher and who was finally unfrocked by the Synod. Through Trufanov-Iliodor, Rasputin was introduced to Hermogen, bishop of Saratov; and to Bishop Theophan (or Feofan), Inspector of the St. Petersburg Ecclesiastical Academy and sometime confessor to the empress. These men later repudiated Rasputin, but originally they accepted him with that excess of naive good will which seems often to mark the attitude of the clergy to unworthy persons and causes. Rasputin also acquired other backing. He became a protégé of the grand duchesses Militsa and Anastasia, two Montenegrin princesses to whom the wits referred as "the Dark Ones"—superficially because of their coloring but also in sly reference to their superstitious ignorance and their susceptibility to charlatans. Through them, and through the empress's quasi-confidante, quasi-client Anna Vyrubova, Rasputin was introduced into the imperial household. How that household always persisted in regarding this man whose recorded behaviors were so vile that the records may not be printed for general circulation is indicated by the following entry in the tsar's diary for November 1/14, 1905: "We have got to know a man of God— Gregory—from the Tobolsk province."

The explanation for this almost incredible and apparently incomprehensible attitude is, in reality, quite simple. It goes back to the hemophiliac tsarevich, Alexius. The best medical help which the parents could command—and they had literally untold wealth at their disposal— could not cure the little boy. (No medical cure for hemophilia is yet certain, although the disease can be arrested and somewhat relieved.) Then appeared this man with a reputation as a healer, and he brought relief to the boy and to his parents. How this was done no man can say. That it was done is amply attested. Rasputin himself once told his close associate Aaron Simanovich that he sometimes used drugs, sometimes pretended to use drugs, and sometimes "trusted entirely to his willpower." It has been plausibly suggested that Alexius' hemophilia was psychosomatic in origin, which would, of course, explain much that now appears inexplicable. This is only a guess and is wholly unproven. At any rate and by whatever means, Rasputin got the boy through several serious attacks, and the gratitude of the parents almost literally knew no bounds. Nicholas once remarked, "He [Rasputin] is just a good, religious, simple-minded Russian. When in trouble or assailed by doubts I like to have a talk with him, and invariably feel at peace with myself afterwards." When Stolypin's children were seriously wounded in an attempt upon their father's life in 1906, the tsar offered to send Rasputin to heal them.

Alexandra was, characteristically, even less restrained. As Pierre Gilliard, tutor to the imperial children from 1905 and an intimate of the family, explains:

> The mother clung to the hope he [Rasputin] gave her as a drowning man seizes an outstretched hand. She believed in him with all the strength that was in her. As a matter of fact, she had been convinced for a long time that the saviour of Russia and the dynasty would come from the people, and she thought that this humble *moujik* had been sent by God to save him who was the hope of the nation [that is, the tsarevich]. The intensity of her faith did the rest. . . .

The empress, in her letters, customarily spoke of Rasputin as "Our Friend." Once she referred to him as Christ returned to earth. There can be no doubt either of her fanatic sincerity or of her growing mental unbalance. She became, where Rasputin was concerned, at least, as mad as a March hare.

✤ EFFECTS ON POLITICS

How this affected the political life of Russia may be shown by a brief, simple, and incomplete catalogue. Stolypin, who had no illusions whatever about Rasputin's character, gave the emperor a full report, and early in 1911 ordered Rasputin out of St. Petersburg. The emperor, however, sent Rasputin to interview Alexius Hvostov with a view to appointing Hvostov as Minister of the Interior in Stolypin's place. Hvostov made the mistake of grossly underestimating Rasputin's influence and so displeased the emperor's emissary that the appointment was withheld. The circumstances of Stolypin's murder gave rise to strong suspicions of collusion between the murderer, who was one of those strange combinations of revolutionary and police agent, and the police, who were certainly aware of the hatred felt for Stolypin by the empress and her husband. Bishop Theophan protested to the empress about Rasputin. Theophan was removed as her confessor and sent from the capital. Iliodor and Hermogen sought to get rid of Rasputin. They were sent to remote monasteries. A. A. Makarov, appointed Minister of the Interior after Stolypin, raised the question of Rasputin with the tsar and was dismissed. The same thing happened to the devotedly loyal Kokovtsov, who early in 1912 tried to persuade Rasputin to leave St. Petersburg. Rasputin left, but shortly returned; and when Kokovtsov next saw the empress, who had been most cordial to him, she turned her back on him. Such examples could be multiplied at great length. The plain fact was that Rasputin, who had first gotten control of the Church—he blocked the efforts to reform it and in 1912 got his man, Sabler, appointed to the post of Procurator of the Synod—was gradually gaining control of the government. The situation eventually reached the point where no man could hold a place for long if he lacked Rasputin's endorsement, and few decent men could bring themselves to seek the favor of a debauched rake. The resulting deterioration of the bureaucracy can be imagined. One by one most (but not all) of the better men were forced out; one by one they were replaced by ambitious adventurers, unscrupulous self-seekers, and outright criminals.

The climax came during World War I, when, in September, 1915, ". . . the Russian Emperor was compelled by his wife to flout all thinking Russia, his Ministers, the Duma, the organs of local government and the general public, and go off to the front to win the war without them, leaving her to manage the rear for him." [6] It was done, as the Grand Duke Alexander later observed with approval in his autobiography, on the same basis as when the lord of a manor, off to the wars, handed over the management of the estate to his wife. That, in truth, was the way the Romanovs regarded Russia—as a family estate. It meant that the fate of the Russian Empire was placed in the hands of a mentally unbalanced woman and of an ignorant, indecent, power-mad peasant. This precious pair literally ruled Russia from that date until Rasputin's murder in December, 1916. One illustration is enough to show the nature of their rule. In 1916 the posts of Prime Minister, Minister of the Interior, and Minister of Foreign Affairs were entrusted to a man named Boris V. Stürmer. Perhaps the least damning comment which can be made on Stürmer was that he was a common criminal. To this degradation had the Russian government been brought.

🈯 RASPUTIN'S MURDER

Rasputin's murder, though chronologically it belongs to the story of the 1914–18 war, may be given here in barest outline. The story is as extravagant and bizarre as his career. The chief conspirators were neither revolutionaries, nor liberals, nor men of the people. They were, on the contrary, men of wealth, place, and privilege, and two of them were connected with the tsar's family. One was V. M. Purishkevich—brilliant, eccentric (he wore bracelets which he jangled as he spoke), probably not quite sane—member of the Duma, founder of the Union of the Russian People (the Black Hundreds)—the chief anti-Semite in Russia.

The second was Felix Yusupov—member of the Imperial Corps of Pages, one of the richest men in Russia, husband of a niece of the tsar, and well known to Rasputin, who called him "the Little One." The third conspirator, who played a lesser role, was the Grand Duke Dimitry, cousin of the emperor. Two others—an officer and a doctor (Lazavert)—were active in the plot, and the liberal Duma leader Basil Maklakov was also privy to it. So, in fact, were many others, for on the eve of the affair Purishkevich gave the full story of the plot to newspapermen attached to the Duma, and Yusupov also talked quite freely.

Yusupov invited Rasputin to his home to meet the Princess Yusupova (who was, in fact, in the Crimea at that time). Rasputin accepted and Yusupov himself went at midnight to fetch him. The conspirators had prepared a room in the cellars—complete with an icon and with poisoned food and wine. Rasputin ate and drank enormously, demanded that Yusupov sing to him (which he did), but the poison apparently had no effect. Finally—the conspirators being now in a state of hysterical panic—Yusupov borrowed the grand duke's revolver and shot Rasputin. Still he did not die. Roaring with pain and fury, Rasputin crawled on all fours up the stairs and out into the courtyard. Purishkevich dashed out after him and fired four shots into Rasputin's body, then ran to the soldiers who were on guard at the front of the house. "I have killed Grishka Rasputin," he told them; and they helped him drag the severely wounded man into the house. For Rasputin still lived and continued to live while Yusupov beat him with the proverbial "blunt instrument." Finally, Purishkevich summoned a policeman and more soldiers to whom he again described how he had killed Rasputin. Together they managed to bundle the still-living Rasputin into Dimitry's car, drive to a bridge over the Neva River, and throw the dying man into the water. Then they discovered that in their panicky haste they had forgotten to attach the weights which they had prepared so that the body would sink. They threw the weights in anyway, along with Rasputin's coat (which they had also forgotten) and one of his boots. (The other was overlooked. They had to burn it later.) When the body was recovered a few days later, the police reported that Rasputin had been killed not by the poison, not by the bullets (though two of the wounds would have eventually been fatal), but by drowning. "Our Friend" was buried in the palace park, mourned by the imperial family. His murderers received only the lightest punishment, house arrest followed by exile to a not unpleasant place.

CHAPTER XIX

The First Ride of the Four Horsemen

⚙ ALTERNATIVE ALIGNMENTS

Two international alignments were possible for Russia in the years from 1904 to 1914; with France and Great Britain, or with Germany and Austria. There were very powerful pulls in both directions. Russia was of course allied with France, and the bonds of gold were strong, even though those of sympathy were uncertain. On the other hand, France in 1904 established a working partnership with Great Britain which became increasingly close and effective. Great Britain had been Russia's chief antagonist for a century. Against that tradition must be set the growth of British investments in Russia, and the sympathetic admiration of the Russian liberals for the British system of life and government. The welcome accorded by the Russian liberals to any ties with France and Britain was doubly significant, for, what the liberals favored, the government usually opposed.

There was no alliance between Russia and Germany, but there were economic ties which the Germans were at great pains to strengthen. German money was loaned to Russia, and, much more important, Germany captured the larger share of Russia's trade. Certain goods which were vitally important to Russian industry—chemicals and machine tools and electrical equipment, to name only three—were chiefly supplied by Germany. Germany's aim was nothing less than to make of Russia an economic colony, and she was making marked progress toward achieving that aim. Trade and finance were weapons of diplomacy as well as economic affairs; and matters of high policy were often involved in what seemed to be commercial or financial transactions. To counterbalance the traditional Russian hostility toward France's partner, Great Britain, there was the traditional enmity between Russia and Germany's partner, Austria. When Russia transferred her interests to the Balkans after the setback in the Far East in 1905, the Austrian hostility loomed increasingly large—and the quarrels with Britain seemed correspondingly less immediate. Just as Russian liberals welcomed ties with the democracies, so the Russian conservatives welcomed ties with the autocracies. There was between these groups a sort of sympathetic understanding, a sense of a commonality of interests and problems. Foreign affairs clearly affected Russian domestic politics and vice versa.

The two alternatives were almost in balance, and this was reflected by the difference of opinion in the Russian Council of Ministers in 1914. Half the ministers were pro-Britain and France; half were pro-Germany and Austria. Among the pro-Germans was V. A. Sukhomlinov, Minister of War from 1909 to 1915, who was finally dismissed from office and jailed on charges of treasonable negligence. Through the intercessions of Rasputin and the empress he escaped trial until the Provisional Government took up his case in 1917. Then he was convicted and sentenced to hard labor for life, but the Bolsheviks released him in 1918 and he found asylum in Germany. Another who favored Germany was the very able but thoroughly reactionary P. N. Durnovo (the same one whom Nicholas had called indispensable). He was no longer a minister, but he had influence still, both in the court and in the government. In 1914 he presented to the emperor a most cogent brief in support of his pro-German views.

✦ FLIRTATIONS WITH GERMANY

There was, as has been previously reported, a tradition of Russo-German co-operation which had been broken but not discarded in the early 1890's. The Russo-French Alliance had been followed by a Russo-German commercial treaty, and by Russian assurances to the kaiser that the alliance was not really aimed at him. These assurances had been borne out by the use of the alliance against Great Britain in the Far East, and by frequent Russo-German co-operation there. Russian difficulties with Japan's ally Britain during the Russo-Japanese War—especially the incident of Dogger Bank and British financial support of Japan—operated to promote closer relations with Germany. Russo-German diplomatic negotiations in October–November, 1904, led to the acceptance by Nicholas II of a draft treaty which bound each Power to aid the other in the event of an attack anywhere by another European Power. The Russian Foreign Office quite properly took the view that this treaty conflicted with the obligations under the Russo-French Alliance, and refused to put it in final form without first clearing the matter with the French. This was a hurdle which could not be vaulted, and the matter was allowed to drop temporarily.

But the flirtations continued. German bankers made a large loan to

Russia despite the disorders of the 1905 Revolution, while French bankers used these same disorders as an excuse to postpone a loan and, as it appeared to some Russian officials, to interfere in Russian domestic affairs. Conversations between Kaiser William II and Tsar Nicholas II in July, 1905, resulted in their initialing of the Björkö Treaty. This was similiar to the draft treaty of the preceding October, except that it was limited to affairs in Europe and was not to become operative until after the war with Japan had ended. The Russian Foreign Office was not enthusiastic about the tsar's essay into diplomacy, but the professional diplomats did consult the French with a view to getting French adherence to the treaty. France flatly refused to adhere, and, furthermore, insisted that Russia drop the whole matter. Russia did so—to the fury of the German kaiser, who accused his cousin, the tsar, of breaking his pledged word. This caused a temporary rift, but did not end the efforts to reach some sort of agreement. Nicholas, meeting the kaiser on the very eve of the completion of an agreement with Great Britain (1907), was at pains to assure him that the new arrangement was not directed against Germany.

RAPPROCHEMENT WITH BRITAIN

The discussions which resulted in the Russian understanding with Britain began in December, 1905. There was very marked reluctance on both sides—due perhaps more to habit than to any immediate clashes. The French, who were tied to Russia by an alliance and to Great Britain by their understanding of 1904, exerted pressure on both Powers. More important was the fact, on the Russian side, that Germany had largely taken over the Austrian "drive to the East" (i.e., through the Balkans), which created a basic conflict with Russian interests; and the fact, on the British side, that Germany had indicated her intention of challenging British naval supremacy. Of course, the balance of power had a role. The German Empire had replaced the Russian Empire as the leading land power, and Great Britain was determined to keep her from the seas. These things operated to overcome the opposition of the pro-German groups at the Russian court and the fears of Alexander Izvolski (foreign minister, 1906–10).

The agreement—less extensive than that between Britain and France and of an entirely different order from that between France and Russia —dealt with Persia, Afghanistan, Tibet, and the Straits. Persia, which was then the major focus of Russo-British competition, was divided into three spheres: a Russian sphere in the north (where the oil is); a neutral, buffer sphere in the center; and a British sphere in the south (of more value to a naval Power). Russia accepted British hegemony over Afghanistan in return for the British promise to make no changes in the status of that nation. Both Powers recognized Chinese overlordship of Tibet and both promised to keep hands off that region. Finally, Russia accepted British dominance over the Persian Gulf region, while Britain indicated that she would favor Russian interests in the regions of the Straits. This last exchange was the subject of a later dispute. Izvolski maintained that the British had promised him that they would support a Russian request to open the Straits to Russian warships. The British denied making the promise. Subsequently they agreed to the opening on the condition that Turkey give her permission. The Turks refused. Anglo-Russian relations, despite this 1907 agreement and despite the efforts of groups in both countries, were never intimate or wholly easy. But they were infinitely better than they had been, which opened the way for a new Russian drive toward the Straits and the Balkans, and this proved the decisive factor in the power alignments of Europe.

THE CRISIS OF 1908

Russia's minimum aim in regard to the Straits was the establishment of international control with free passage for all vessels. Her maximum aim was the establishment of her own unilateral control. To get free passage through the Straits for Russian warships became almost an obsession with Izvolski. His desire for an aggressive policy was staunchly opposed both by Stolypin and by Kokovtsov, who feared that overly vigorous action would lead to war and who saw clearly that another war would destroy the Russia they served. Izvolski had to trim his sails somewhat, but he did manage to get promises from Italy and from Germany that they would support his request for the free passage of Russian warships. The Dual Monarchy of Austria-Hungary, which really held the key to the matter, was noncommittal. The Austro-Hungarian foreign minister at this time was Baron Aehrenthal, like Izvolski an ambitious career diplomat with aggressive plans. The moves of the two men brought them into collision and led to their meeting at a castle near Buchlau. What actually was agreed between the two at this so-called Buchlau Conference is still a mystery, despite repeated and careful researches by many scholars. What is known, however, makes a curious and intriguing story.

Izvolski and Aehrenthal quickly reached a general agreement to the effect that Russia would adopt a benevolent and friendly attitude when the Dual Monarchy finally should decide to use the right she had acquired thirty years earlier of annexing Bosnia and Herzegovina; and that Austria-Hungary should adopt a like attitude toward the Russian attempt to open the Straits to Russian warships. The disagreement came over the timing of the annexation and the submittal of the whole affair to a general European conference. It appears that Aehrenthal tricked Izvolski on both points by annexing the provinces before the Russian expected such action and before the conference could be arranged.[1] This touched off a crisis of major proportions which brought Europe very close to war in 1908–9. Serbia, who wanted Bosnia and Herzegovina for herself and who had the support of Izvolski, began to prepare for war with Austria. Turkey, who was nominally the owner of the two provinces, accepted the *fait accompli* of Austrian annexation; and Germany suggested with some force that Russia drop her support of the Serbs. (The German suggestion was not an ultimatum, as Izvolski claimed. He was little if any more straightforward in this business than Aehrenthal.) Since Russia was still trying to rebuild her armed forces and was in no condition to push the matter further, and since Stolypin was opposed to any further adventures, Izvolski was glad to accept the German suggestion. The crisis ended, but the aftermath was most important. This affair was one of the incidents which convinced the leading Russian ministers that Russia could achieve her maximum goal in the Straits only in the event of a general European war. It also deepened and widened the chasm between Russia and Austria, and, since Germany loyally backed her ally, between Russia and Germany as well.

✤ THE BALKAN WARS

Attempts to bridge this chasm were made by a Russo-Austrian agreement to maintain the *status quo* in the Balkans (February, 1910)—a move dictated on Russia's part by fear of another Austrian coup, and by an attempted Russo-German deal over the Near East (the Potsdam Agreement of November, 1910). The Potsdam Agreement relieved the Russo-German tension temporarily, at the cost of coolness in Russo-British relations. The Austrian agreement was little more than a formality, empty of real meaning. Tensions continued to tighten as crises brewed, broke, and subsided, only to be followed by new crises. Russo-British relations were badly strained by the Russian occupation of their sphere in northern Persia in 1911, but fear of Germany prevented an open break. A Russian-sponsored Serbo-Bulgarian alliance (March, 1911), which Russia regarded as a defensive measure against Austria, grew into a Balkan League which went to war against Turkey in October, 1912. Russian support of Serbia during and after this war (which ended in May, 1913) brought acute friction with the Dual Monarchy. This reached the stage of war preparations on both sides, and was relieved only because Russia, still unready for war, dropped her support of Serbian demands and stopped her own mobilization. Poincaré, premier of France, had meanwhile made use of the crisis to tighten the Franco-Russian Alliance by a naval agreement and other means.

Then came the second Balkan War (summer, 1913), Bulgar-provoked, in which Serbia, Romania, and Greece fought beside Turkey against Bulgaria. Bulgaria was defeated, and Serbia—perhaps counting too much on Russian aid—set out to conquer Albania. But Russia, still not ready for war, could not risk a headlong collision with Austria; and the Serbs had to yield to an Austrian ultimatum to withdraw from Albania. At the end of the year 1913 occurred still another crisis when the Turkish government appointed a German general to command the Turkish forces in Constantinople and gave him other extensive powers. Russia, supported staunchly by France and very mildly by Britain, who was still smarting over the business of Potsdam and Persia, protested so vigorously that the German's powers were reduced. The incident, however, led the Russian ministers to discuss the possibility of war with Germany. Sazonov (foreign minister from 1910 to 1916) and Kokovtsov (who was soon after dismissed in most cowardly fashion by Nicholas) were strongly opposed to war, and the majority agreed with them.

⊕ PREPARATIONS

Three events of 1913–14 are part of the background of the crisis which led to war. One was the lengthening of the term of military service for those entering the Russian army. This had the effect of increasing the size of the army, so that as of January, 1914, Russia had about 1.8 million men under arms. The rebuilding and reorganization of the army and navy, both of which had been shattered against Japan, had been the particular concern of Stolypin and Kokovtsov, among the ministers, and of Alexander I. Guchkov, among the Duma leaders. Guchkov, grandson of a serf, was a flamboyant and able man—devoted to his country and her welfare—"a conservative at bottom." Pares, who knew both men well, frequently remarked that Guchkov was the Churchill of Russia. Guchkov was the founder and leader of the Octobrist Party in the Third and Fourth Dumas. Unfortunately for Russia, Sukhomlinov, Minister of War, was almost completely incompetent and inefficient. But he alone was not to blame for the failure to equip and train the army adequately nor honestly and effectively to expend the huge sums which the Duma provided. The Department of Artillery, headed by the Grand Duke Sergius Mikhailovich, was almost completely independent of the War Ministry. Sergius was incompetent and probably corrupt; his immediate associates were certainly dishonest. That is why Russia entered the war with only 60 batteries of heavy artillery as contrasted with Germany's

381, and why the German infantry divisions had twice as many batteries of artillery as did the Russian infantry. It is also the reason for the acute shortage of ammunition which soon crippled the Russian armies. (By 1916 the annual need of the Russian armies was 42 million rounds of ammunition; the annual production of Russian munition factories was 600,000 rounds.)

The second event was a very large loan which Kokovtsov arranged with French bankers to finance the building of strategic railways to facilitate Russian mobilization. Various figures have been given as to the size of the loan, but Kokovtsov himself says that the agreement he made in January, 1914, called for 500 million francs a year for five years. Most of this sum, of course, had not been received, let alone spent, when the war began. The railways, which had been urgently requested by the French military, were not built.

The third event was an effort to arrange an Anglo-Russian naval convention in order to strengthen the ties of the Entente (Russia, France, and Great Britain). Extended discussions were held, but opposition pressures in the British parliament forced the dropping of the project. It is apparent from Russia's behavior that she was preparing for a war which seemed certain to come.

THE 1914 CRISIS AND RUSSIAN AIMS

The incident which set it off was the murder of the Austrian Archduke Franz Ferdinand at the Bosnian town of Sarajevo on June 28, 1914. By July 21 Foreign Minister Sazonov had decided that Russia would not permit Austria to attack, or threaten to attack, Serbia, whom Austria held responsible for the murder. In this attitude, publicly announced on July 24, Sazonov had the full endorsement of Poincaré, then in Russia for a brief visit. On that same day Sazonov suggested partial mobilization to protect Serbia. The Russian army chiefs refused because they were sure that war with Austria would automatically mean war with Germany also, and they did not wish to commit their forces prematurely. Hoping to bluff Austria, Sazonov on July 25 agreed to preliminary, general mobilization. The necessary first orders went out on the twenty-sixth, and, on the morning of the twenty-ninth, Nicholas signed the final orders for full mobilization. These were rescinded that afternoon in response to an urgent request from Kaiser William for time to make one more effort to solve the crisis without war. Partial mobilization against Austria was substituted, but the military correctly insisted that this was dangerously unwise, and their views prevailed. Full mobilization was again ordered on July 30, and went on despite an ultimatum from Germany (July 31) demanding that military preparations on the Russo-German frontier be stopped. And on August 1, 1914, Germany ordered her general mobilization at 4:00 P.M.; declared war on Russia at 7:00 P.M.

Russian diplomacy during the war had three objectives: (1) to maintain her alliance with France and Britain, and secure new allies; (2) to safeguard her Far Eastern possessions and interests; and (3) to plan with her allies for the division of the spoils. Sazonov co-operated with his French and British colleagues in bidding for Italian and Romanian adherence to the Entente. This success was a diplomatic victory and a military liability. Romania was overrun and beaten soon after joining the Entente. Russia then had to stretch her forces to cover the new front. Russia concluded a secret convention with Japan (1916) which pledged the maintenance of the *status quo* and arranged for joint action in the Far East to protect Russian and Japanese interests against encroachments by a third Power (which may have meant Germany, but could equally well have meant the United States). By secret treaties with France and Britain in 1915 and 1916 it was agreed that Russia might annex the Straits, including Constantinople, and the northeastern part of Asia Minor.

This sketch of the history of Russian foreign policy after 1914 has attempted to answer the question: how did it happen that Russia entered World War I on the side of the Entente?

THE STATE OF THE NATION, 1914

Russia was an autocracy, slightly modified by increasing political opposition, but still a rule of men rather than of laws. Industrial expansion was still proceeding though at a slightly slower rate. Between four and one-half and five million persons were engaged in transport, manufacturing, mining, and construction by 1914. The growth of labor unrest kept pace with the enlargement of the labor force and the increase in industrial enterprises. There were over 2000 strikes each year in 1912, 1913, and 1914, involving roughly a fifth of the nonagricultural labor force. At least as many persons—and perhaps half again as many more —were occupied in whole or part-time home industry as in the occupations listed above. Working as individuals or in small groups, these home-workers supplied a large share of the wood products, leather goods, and household utensils used by the peasants. Periodic fairs, town and city markets (permanent fairs, so to speak) were an important part of the system of distribution, but most peasants still did business with traveling peddlers and village merchants.

The general status of agriculture improved markedly between 1905 and 1914, although, of course, the increased prosperity was not evenly shared. The majority of the Russian peasants remained very poor, but their position as a group was improved. This was due partly to a series of unusually good harvests, partly to the improvements in transportation which increased the market, and, in part, it reflected the government's policies. The Stolypin reforms should be given a major share of the credit. An important contributor to the improvement was the opening of Siberia to peasant migration (about three million people emigrated from the crowded land of the west to the open spaces of Siberia during these years). The rapid growth of the peasant co-operative movement, which was particularly strong in Siberia, ought also to be singled out. There were approximately 33,000 co-operatives in 1914, with a total membership of 12 million. In 1901 there had been only 700,000 members in about 2000 co-operative associations.

Statistics and formal descriptions have an indispensable place in the story of Russia, but they do not convey the sense of the time so well as less formal reports. There is fortunately available, among many others, a most penetrating and understanding description of Russia as it was in 1914, written by Harold Williams.[2] Here are a few of his comments on the civil servants, the men who actually were engaged in governing their fellow subjects of the last tsar:

> Governors, senators, clerks of court, tax-collectors, school-inspectors, telegraph clerks, customs officials, wardens of the peasants, heads of consistories, all are engaged in the business of the Empire, all are formally in the service of the Tsar. It is a State in uniform. The very schoolboys wear uniforms, and even high-school girls have to wear brown dresses and brown aprons. Ministers wear uniforms, not in the routine work in St. Petersburg, but on State occasions and when they travel about the country. Judges wear uniforms, and so do Government engineers and land-surveyors, and a host of other people whose salary filters down through many channels from the St. Petersburg Treasury. Brass buttons and peaked caps, peaked caps and brass buttons, uniforms with blue, red, or white facings meet the eye with a wearisome monotony from end to end of the Empire, from the Pacific to the Danube. . . .
>
> All the Government officials . . . stand in a definite *chin,* or rank. . . . Once a man is drawn into the subtle mechanism of the Table of Ranks he may go on from grade to grade with hardly an effort on his part, by the mere fact of existing and growing wrinkled and grey-haired.

Dr. Williams goes on to describe some of the ranks, pointing out that the titles, which have no meaning except to indicate the grade, sound more imposing when retranslated into their original German. Thus, *staatsky sovietnik* becomes *Staatsrath,* or Councilor of State. The rank of Real State Councilor conferred nobility upon its holder and his heirs. It also carried the rank of General and the right of being addressed as "Excellency." (This was the *chin* attained by Lenin's father.) He continues:

From the big dreary-looking yellow or brown buildings in St. Petersburg, in which the Ministries are housed, currents of authority, or directive energy go forth to all ends of the great Empire in the form of telegrams or occasional oral messages by special couriers, but above all in the form of endless "papers." Pens scratch, typewriters click, clerks lay blue covers full of papers before the "head of the table"; the "head of the table" sends them to the "head of the department," "the head of the department" sends them to the Assistant Minister, if need be, and in the more important cases, the Assistant Minister sends them to the Minister. Then back go the papers again with signatures appended, down through the various grades for despatch to a judge, to another department, to a Governor, to a *chinovnik* [official, literally, "holder of a *chin*"] on special service, or to some petitioner from the world without. Incoming and outgoing papers are the systole and diastole of the Chancelleries.

There is something hauntingly familiar about Dr. Williams' description of the bureaucracy as he knew it. It sounds little different from the comments quoted from Kravchinski and Wallace in Chapter XIII. The bureaucracy had apparently changed little in over a generation. Russian government was an autocracy tempered by a big bureaucracy and a small (but articulate and persistent) political opposition. One phase of that opposition needs further consideration. This was the opposition led by Lenin and his associates.

⚙ LENIN AND STALIN

"The years 1908–12," reads the official *History of the Communist Party of the Soviet Union (Bolshevik)*, "were a most difficult period for revolutionary work." This is an interesting admission, even though it is also a rather inaccurate understatement. For one thing, the difficulties began earlier—at least as early as 1906—and continued much longer. For another thing, despite an uneasy "unification" of Bolsheviks and Mensheviks, which nominally lasted from 1906 to 1912, the movement lost much of its strength. (Lenin, though he professed to favor and to abide by the unification, actually maintained his own faction throughout the period.) Party membership—not as important an index in the case of revolutionary conspiracies as it is in the case of regular parties, but still one measure of influence—dropped markedly. The two Social Democratic groups combined claimed five million members in 1905; one million in 1906; 750,000 in 1907; 174,000 in 1908; and 46,000 in 1910. This decline continued until at the beginning of 1917 the Bolsheviks numbered only some twenty-odd thousand out of a population of about 140 million. But Lenin's group was never (and the Communist parties are not now) a political party in the sense that the Kadets, for example, were. Lenin's followers were what he intended them to be, namely, a small, tightly disciplined band of professional revolutionaries who devoted the whole of their lives to their crusade for power.

Lenin, who spent most of these years in exile, slowly and inexorably tightened his control over his faction. His leadership was neither unchallenged nor always victorious. His tactics were as flexible and opportunistic as his goal was rigid. That goal was mastery of his own conspiratorial band; through it, mastery of Russia; and, ultimately, of the whole world. To achieve this end, Lenin was ready to use any persons and all means. He told his followers, "we must take part in the elections" to the Dumas because "the masses, in one way or another, learn about politics" at election time and, therefore, are more suggestible to Bolshevik propaganda and manipulation. He sanctioned the formation of a Bolshevik "party" in the second session of the Fourth Duma under the name of the "Russian Social Democratic Worker's Party"—a label chosen to emphasize the split with the Mensheviks which Lenin engineered in 1912. When relaxation of the censorship made it possible, Lenin ordered the foundation of the legal Bolshevik newspaper *Pravda* (originally to further the Bolshevik election campaign for the Fourth Duma). He had some troubles with the censor—the paper was suppressed eight times between 1912 and 1914, but immediately reappeared in slightly different guise until the eighth suppression, which put it out of business until February/March, 1917. But he had more trouble keeping his editors in line. They continually made common cause with the Mensheviks. *Pravda* was a limited outlet, even when Lenin was able to run it his way, so he continued to make extensive use of an underground press and of clandestine activities. Among the most spectacular of the latter were a series of robberies engineered primarily to provide the Lenin faction with money. The most celebrated of these "expropriations" was the robbery of 341,000 rubles from the State Bank of Tiflis in 1907. The active leader in the actual banditry was an Armenian—named Ter-Petrossian, and nicknamed Kamo—who was the leading guerrilla chief in Georgia. The liaison man (and perhaps the overall planner) was a revolutionary known to the police as an "intellectual, has connections with railwaymen"; and known to his revolutionary associates as "Koba." His part in this robbery, plus the fact that he was a Georgian, who, unlike most of his fellow nationals among the Social Democratic revolutionaries, leaned toward the Bolsheviks, commended him to Lenin. In 1912 Lenin added this man to his Central Committee. We know him as Stalin.

Just what Dzhugashvili-Koba-Stalin did in the years after his removal from the Tiflis Ecclesiastical College is a matter of obscurity and controversy. It is obscure partly because his revolutionary work was, of course, illegal and was therefore kept as secret as possible; and partly because the records were violated in the process of building up the Stalin legend. It is controversial because Stalin's detractors do their best to minimize his importance and his partisans do their best to exaggerate it. Even those who are on the same side do not always agree with each other. Truth, at the moment, comes off a poor second to fable.

The British "Marxist" Jack Murphy, in his biography of Stalin, dates Stalin's apprenticeship as a revolutionary from 1894 and refers to him as a professional revolutionary beginning in 1898. The currently official Soviet account says, "His activity as a professional revolutionary dates from 1901." Apparently that is the date of his first police record as a "political." At any rate, he supported himself by part-time janitorial work in the Tiflis Observatory and was active as a labor organizer in the railway shops at Tiflis. When the police made Tiflis too hot for him, Stalin transferred his agitation to the industrial centers of Baku and Batum. He was arrested at Batum in 1902 for participating in a strike, and after eighteen months in jail was exiled to Siberia, but he escaped within a month. It appears that between 1902 and 1917 Stalin was arrested eight times, jailed and exiled seven times; he escaped five times from exile, served out one term in exile, and was amnestied from his exile to Turukhansk (1913) by the Provisional Government. The origins and the nature of Stalin's relations with Lenin are much in dispute. He first met Lenin in 1905, but close collaboration seems to have begun in 1913, when Lenin summoned Stalin to help him prepare an article on the Bolshevik attitude toward the national minorities. To this long polemic, entitled "Marxism and the National Question," was signed the pen name K. (for Koba) Stalin.

Lenin took an uncompromising position against World War I, thus further splitting the Social Democratic movement. It was, wrote Lenin in his newspaper the *Social Democrat,* a war designed by the *bourgeoisie* to fool the working people and to wipe out the vanguard of the revolutionary movement. "The only correct proletarian slogan is the transformation of the present imperialist war into a civil war . . . . [and] the lesser evil for the Russian Social-Democrats would be the defeat of the tsarist monarchy." So ordered Lenin, and the Bolshevik leaders in Russia obeyed his orders to oppose the war and to sabotage the Russian war effort. The Russian government, naturally regarding this as treason, arrested the leaders and sent them into exile. What remained of the Bolshevik movement in Russia went underground until after the February/March Revolution.

THE RUSSIAN PEOPLE AND THE WAR

The attitude of the rest of the tsar's subjects ranged, with exceptions, from ardent support to resigned acceptance. ". . . let domestic strife be forgotten," pleaded Nicholas in announcing the war to his people. "Let the union between the Tsar and His people be stronger than ever. . . ." The Duma responded in kind. Its one-day session pledged full support, and (the socialists abstaining) voted the necessary appropriations. A resolution adopted unanimously (with the socialists again abstaining) read in part:

> . . . the Duma expresses its unshakable conviction that in this grave hour of trial, in the face of the approaching war storm, all nationalities of Russia, united in the common sentiment of love for their native land, and firmly believing in the righteousness of their cause, are prepared, at the summons of their Sovereign, to stand up in defense of their country, its honor, and its possessions.

The national minorities, with exceptions, did rally to the support of the tsar. (Major concessions were promised the Poles in return for their support.) The liberal middle class and the liberal intelligentsia welcomed with eagerness this chance to co-operate more closely with the democracies whom they rather extravagantly admired. If they did not welcome the war—which "experts" generally predicted would be over in a matter of months—they gave vigorous and patriotic support at the outset. Labor was not so enthusiastic, but the strike records show that it was not obstructionist.

There had been 2404 strikes involving 887,096 strikers in 1913. Almost half the strikes were political, that is, in opposition to the government. From January to July, 1914, there were 4098 strikes involving 1,449,284 strikers, 1,035,312 of whom struck for political reasons (2538 of the strikes were political). But there were only seven political strikes (2845 political strikers) out of a total of 68 strikes (and 34,752 strikers) between August and December, 1914.

PEASANT NORMS AND VALUES

The peasants were a different matter. "But," as Dr. Harold Williams warned, "there are so many types of peasants, there is such a variety of character and custom that it is difficult to make general statements that will be absolutely true of all. 'Not a village but has ways of its own,' is a Russian saying." He then went on to describe the social norms and values of the Russian people. He chose as his sample Vladimirovo, a village of thirty-five houses situated on the Volkhov River. The houses were two-storied, built of unpainted wood. The upper story contained the living quarters—furnished and furbished much as those previously described—of "one, two, or three rooms, according to the wealth of the owner and the size of his family." Though the living rooms and stables were "practically under one roof," the houses were "as a rule, remarkably clean." Vladimirovo had a small store, a tiny chapel, and a two-storied "unusually large and well-equipped" school which taught domestic science and manual training as well as the three R's:

The staple food is home-made rye bread, which is called black . . . but is dark brown. This bread [is] pleasant to the taste and very nourishing, but to assimilate it a long training is necessary. . . . The peasant eats meat rarely. . . . But every day there is a meatless soup of some kind . . . in which preserved cabbage or sauerkraut is the chief ingredient. Potatoes are eaten as a kind of sauce or condiment to bread. . . . Barley and buckwheat porridge is frequently eaten. . . . On their simple but monotonous diet the peasants seem to thrive fairly well, although digestive complaints are not infrequent.

To drink there is plain water and tea . . . [which] is drunk very weak and very pale, without milk. . . . But there is another beverage to which the Russian peasant is greatly addicted, and that is *vodka,* a spirituous liquor as innocent-looking as water, but a most potent kind of brandy.

Dr. Williams went on to say that the Russian peasants do not drink as heavily as usually supposed. Sundays and holidays are the days for peasant drinking—moderately on ordinary holidays and Sundays, very heavily on special holidays such as the festival of a village's patron saint. He added "the nearer peasants are to the cities or to manufacturing districts the more they drink."

The effects of industrialization were reflected in the peasants' clothing. Men's shirts and blouses, and the clothing of women and children, were still home-made, but no longer home-spun or home-woven. The fabrics were factory-made and were sold to the peasants by peddlers. Traveling tailors and feltmakers went from village to village, making suits and overcoats and felt boots for winter wear. The women of Vladimirovo wore cotton shirts and blouses and tied kerchiefs on their heads. The men wore the so-called Russian shirt, and tucked their trousers into high boots. Town fashions in clothes, as in other habits, were infiltrating the villages.

The village governed itself, within rather narrow limits, by its own assembly (the *skhod,* composed of all adult males) and its annually elected elder (*starosta*), assisted by a village policeman. The elder collected the taxes and was the liaison between the village and the *volost,* which was the next higher administrative unit. The *volost* had its own assembly, and elder (*starshina*), and court. The *volost* courts operated under the customary laws of the district. The courts were so notoriously corrupt that it was a standard joke to say "a bottle of beer to the *starshina* and a ruble to the *pisar* [secretary] is sufficient to secure judgment in the desired direction." The government policeman (as distinct from the village police) lived in the *volost* town. These various officials and the *volost* itself were concerned only with the peasants. This was an administration only for peasants; no others were under its jurisdiction. (The peasants, in other words, were still a class apart.) Also at the *volost* level was the special overseer or warden of the peasants, the land captain, whom the peasants regarded as the chief authority in their district. He was, for them, the personification of the government. It was not to be expected that the peasants would welcome the war with any enthusiasm. They accepted it as they accepted other unpleasant facts of life—to be grumbled about, but to be borne, since there seemed to be no way to escape from it.

🔥 WAR AND REVOLUTIONS

The war did not cause the revolutions of 1917 since, in the broadest sense, their causes were inherent in the political and social system of the empire. But the war certainly precipitated the revolutions. For Russia, the war was not a climax but the prelude to a climax. The fundamental causes of the revolutions were those conditions which the last several chapters have been devoted to describing. The immediate causes were apparently minor events, relatively speaking.

Russia from 1914 until the beginning of 1917 was, on the whole, a very good ally to the French and the British. This is not to deny the Russian faults and failures, the criminally stupid mistakes and miscalculations which were made, nor the incredible inefficiency and astonishing corruption of many of their leaders. But the military reputation in the West of tsarist Russia has never recovered from the fact that Russia was knocked out of the war, and this at a time when the Western allies were desperately hard-pressed. Nor has it generally been recognized that the Russian defection was to a considerable extent brought about by the selfish and almost unlimited demands which those same allies made upon her. The British ambassador, Sir George Buchanan, was one of the very few who recognized clearly the unwisdom and injustice of what was done. "I wish," he said, "that we did not ask them to do too much." The military chiefs of the West were obsessed with the idea of the "Russian steam roller." This may seem wholly incomprehensible since mention has been made so far only of weaknesses in the Russian armies. There were also elements of actual and potential strength, one, of course, was Russia's tremendous manpower. The

Russian military forces mobilized at their full, initial strength some 3.5 million men in 114.5 divisions, 70 of them being of first-line rank. (Before the end of the war Russia mobilized about 15.5 million men—approximately a third of her total manpower of working age.) The Russian General Staff was on a par with those of her allies and her enemies —as good as or at least no worse than the others. Her officer corps was also of high caliber. One of Russia's greatest weaknesses, however, was her almost complete lack of adequate replacements for commissioned and noncommissioned officers. She could make good the losses in rank and file, but not in leadership. And these losses were staggering from the very beginning.

🏵 CAMPAIGNS

The Russians did not dig in as the French and British did, on the western front, partly, at least, because of the incessant demands from the West that steady pressures be maintained on the eastern front. This began at once when the Russians prematurely undertook an invasion of East Prussia in response to piteous pleas from France. It was a gallant action—though marred by crass stupidities (such as sending wireless orders uncoded and thus keeping the Germans fully informed of Russian plans), by personal jealousies among generals, and by a total lack of co-ordination. It saved Paris by forcing the Germans to send two army corps to the east on the eve of the first Battle of the Marne. It was the Russian peasant soldier, as well as the famous taxicab army of Gallieni and Joffre, who kept the Germans out of the French capital. But the cost to Russia was terrific, for this was the Battle of Tannenberg in which Russia's estimated losses were 170,000. This was in late August, 1914, and within three weeks the Russians suffered another terrific loss in East Prussia. Along the southern end of their front, however, Russian forces were outfighting those of Austria. In the early spring of 1915 the Russians smashed the Austrian position at Przemysl and threatened to overrun northern Hungary.

Germany now joined her ally to turn back this threat, and together they mounted a tremendous offensive in Galicia. The Russian troops, literally without munitions and arms, fought with incredible courage and horrific losses. Sir Bernard Pares, on His Britannic Majesty's service, had wangled an appointment with the armies in Galicia and was with the Third Caucasian Corps during what he always referred to as "the Galician smash." Here are his figures (which he sent to the British War Office) of what their gallantry cost in men. The company with which he was associated was reduced from 250 men to 5; their regiment, from 4000 to 41; their division, from 15,000 to 500; and the corps, from

40,000 to 4000. Through Guchkov and his associates, who took this rather desperate way to by-pass Sukhomlinov and the Russian War Office, Pares was given the figures on Russian losses and lists of Russia's munition needs to take to Lloyd George. The losses for the first ten months were 3,800,000 men. (Russia's total casualties, 1914–17, will never be known because the records are forever incomplete. Pares thought it ran as high as 9,250,000 men. This, obviously, was a major, immediate effect of the war on the Russian people.)

A second great Austro-German offensive in 1915 cost the Russians all of Poland, Courland, and Lithuania. It was at this stage that the tsar relieved the Grand Duke Nicholas of supreme command and went to the front leaving Alexandra and Rasputin to rule the rear. The year of the battles of Verdun and the Somme and of the Austrian offensive against the Trentino, 1916, was, in Russia, the year of Brusilov's first great drive against Austria. Like that of Rennenkampf and Samsonov into East Prussia in 1914, it was prematurely begun in order to give as much help as possible to the Italians and the French. Brusilov whipped the Austrians readily, but was stopped by some 15 German divisions sent for that purpose. The operation cost Russia at least a million men. A year later, after the first (February/March) revolution, Brusilov tried again. The story was a repetition with variations. Victories and rapid advances against the Austrians (who were virtually knocked out of the war), defeats and checkmate and, finally, rout by the Germans, who were rushed in to save their ally. This was Russia's last great military effort.

BANKRUPTCY OF THE GOVERNMENT

As to the government, the war revealed its bankruptcy. Imperial prestige had never recovered from the effects of Bloody Sunday. The apparent unanimity evoked by the outbreak of war was superficial and fleeting. Perhaps it might have been built into something real and enduring. Instead there was the scandal of Rasputin, which finally revolted even the reactionaries. There were also Alexandra's attempts to turn back the clock, which alienated even conservatives. After Rasputin's murder, the empress lost both will and purpose, and her husband's government lost the little force it had possessed. The tsar, from the beginning, had turned his back upon the bureaucracy, which was his agent. Without his favor, and despised as corrupt, inefficient, and officious by the majority, the bureaucracy lost whatever small virtue and prestige it had possessed. This was not entirely the fault of the bureaucrats. A law of August, 1914, transformed most of western Russia (including St. Petersburg) into a military district, subject to martial law and to the control of the military officials. Between them and the civilian officials there at once began a constant feud with all imaginable consequent confusions and contradictions of authority. Each hampered the other, and each blamed the other for its failures.

There was left of the national government, the Duma and the ministers. The baleful influence of Rasputin over the ministers has already been described but may be supplemented by mention of two other ministers: A. N. Khvostov and A. D. Protopopov. Both held the most powerful post in Russia, that of Minister of the Interior; the former from October, 1915, to March, 1916; the latter from September, 1916, to the end of the autocracy in 1917. Both were intriguers and time-servers. Both were associated with Rasputin, Protopopov more intimately than Khvostov. Protopopov was, also, an unbalanced neurotic. The Duma was very gravely hindered by the implacable opposition and deliberate attacks of the empress; by its own initial enthusiasm which had led it to give virtual carte blanche to the administration; and by the fact that it could not and did not speak for the people.

The Duma, despite all this, remained the strongest element in the government. Some of its leaders and members proved themselves industrious, honest, capable, and effective, particularly in the work of the several civilian war committees. This was a rather strange phenomenon, which was both an indication of the weakness of "duly constituted authority" and also a contributing factor to the growth of that weakness. Soon after the beginning of the war, the zemstva men organized a Zemstva Union and the city (and town) councils organized a Union of Cities, which plunged wholeheartedly and effectively into Red Cross work. This was most urgently needed since the army's medical services were almost nonexistent. The Zemstva Union supplied hospital trains, doctors, nurses, 175,000 hospital beds, drugs, and so forth. After the "Galician smash" the directing boards ("Main Committees") of the two unions consulted and co-operated in supplying food, clothing, and munitions to the army. The Zemgor Committees (*zem* from *zemstva, gor* from *gorodskaya* [town or city]) did valuable work. But, of course, they collided with both the civilian and military services and helped to undermine them. Later the tsar created five special councils (national defense, food, fuels, transportation, and refugees) to handle and to co-ordinate some of this work. The main result was to increase jealousies, frictions, and confusions. The Duma was closely connected with the Zemgor Committees because of interlocking membership, and backed the committees against the administration. An army which has to rely upon the spontaneous humanitarianism of civilians for its medical service and a government which leaves the regulation of supply in the hands of extralegal groups are both in a parlous state.

⊕ EFFECTS OF THE WAR ON THE ECONOMY

The effects of the war upon the general economy of the Russian Empire have often been misunderstood and misinterpreted. Thus it has repeatedly been said that industrial production seriously declined due largely to labor shortages. But the value of the gross industrial output in 1916 was 6,831,000,000 rubles as compared to 5,621,000,000 rubles in 1913. There were 2,094,000 workers in 1916; 1,927,000 in 1913. In like fashion, it is reported that there was a serious decline in grain production (which there was), but it is not always pointed out that the stoppage of grain exports meant that there was more grain available in Russia than ever before. Part of the solution of these apparent paradoxes lies in the variation among industries, part lies in the enormously increased demand caused by the war, and part lies in the failure of the distribution system, which created shortages. The cotton industry illustrates the first two points. It was not one of the military industries (although by 1916 the military took 80 per cent of fabrics produced) so that it did not enjoy special favor. Moreover, it depended heavily upon foreign cotton, which could no longer be imported, and this alone forced the shutdown of many looms with a consequent drop in output. A price increase of 200 per cent reflected the short supply and the demands of the military.

The sudden stoppage of Russia's land trade with the West, plus the sea blockades which shut off the Baltic and (with Turkey's entrance into the war on the side of Germany) the Black Sea as well, was disastrous. Russian imports dropped from 1,470,000,000 rubles (January, 1913–June, 1914) to 297,000,000 rubles (July–December, 1914). They subsequently recovered and surpassed the earlier figure, as Russia's allies began to send great quantities of supplies via Archangel and Vladivostok. But these were military supplies in the main. Exports declined even more sharply, and these did not recover. The effects of the blockade were, of course, military as well as economic and were of major significance in Russia's defeat.

Army living standards were not high, judged by those of the West, but they were higher than the level at which many of the poor and middle-class peasants subsisted at home. This meant an increased consumption and demand, and contributed toward the creation of shortages. Shortages developed early and grew steadily worse so that life was an ordeal in Russian towns and cities by 1916. The villages, more nearly self-sufficient, were somewhat better off. That familiar trio of shortages, enlarged demands, and the increased buying power of certain groups helped build up inflationary pressures. The government, which had stopped the sale of vodka at the outset of the war as a measure of internal security, had thereby deprived itself of a very significant part of its revenue. (Witte had made the sale of vodka a government monopoly in 1897.) At the same time, of course, expenditures had increased enormously. Over 38 per cent of this increase was covered by printing paper rubles, which soon depreciated. This showed up, among other places, in the cost of living. The general price index went up from 100 (prewar) to 156 (December, 1915); then to 196 (June, 1916); and to 222 in the following month. By then (i.e., July, 1916) the rises in the prices of specific commodities (taking 100 as the prewar base) were: meat, 332; butter, 220; flour, 265; potatoes, 144; and salt, 585. Nominal wages had increased (the average annual wage in the Moscow area had gone up 185 rubles between 1914 and 1916), but real wages had declined. Life was hard in Russia as the war went into its third year—not equally hard for all, and not nearly so hard as it was shortly to become, but hard, nonetheless.

✪ LACK OF LEADERSHIP

One of the hardest things about it—and one of the most subtle and difficult to pin down—was the absence of any effective or trustworthy leadership. Given a leadership which they can trust, the powers of persistence of a people are truly amazing, as World War II amply demonstrated. Crushing casualties, humiliating and dangerous defeats and failures can be borne if the people have confidence and hope in their leadership. Without that confidence and hope, there is a sense of being "lost." This was what was happening to the people of Russia.

Morale was highest in the fighting lines, but it fell rapidly as one went to the rear. The garrison troops—scrapings of the manpower barrel—were mutinously discontented. Ill-housed, ill-fed, and ill-led, they were the foci of rebellion. Among the civilians was a spreading war-weariness and a growing distrust of the leaders. This was greatly enhanced by the steadily mounting volume of criticism directed against the government by the liberal intellectuals. The censure was both quantitatively larger and qualitatively more bitter. But the tone was also more hopeful of improvement if certain changes could be made. And the most powerful voice was that of the Duma.

During the third sitting of the last Duma there was formed a coalition of almost three-quarters of the members under the name of the "Progressive Bloc." In August and September, 1915, this bloc presented to

Nicholas and his ministers a declaration which contained the following phrases in its preamble:

> The undersigned representatives of parties and groups in the State Council [Upper House] and the Duma, with the conviction that only a strong, active, and firm government can lead the nation to victory, and that such a government can only be based on the confidence of the public and so be capable of organizing the active co-operation of all citizens. . . .

After lengthy discussions among the ministers, "Prime Minister" Goremykin consulted Nicholas. He returned to tell his colleagues, ". . . I have His Majesty's Command to close the Duma not later than . . . [tomorrow], which I shall do. . . . His Majesty's orders are not to be criticized in the Ministerial Council." The squelching of its demand for a "Ministry of Confidence" did not end the bloc. When the Duma next reassembled, the plans of the bloc called for the establishment of a genuine constitutional monarchy. The leaders of the Duma —from Miliukov of the Kadets to the notorious rightist (and murderer of Rasputin) Purishkevich—spoke out with shocking bluntness.

Notably absent from this chorus were the voices of Lenin's Bolsheviks, though they have not hesitated to claim credit for making the revolution possible. They were active in agitation and sabotage both on the home front and in the armed forces. Among the soldiers they preached fraternization with the enemy and the defeat of Russia. It is not possible to measure the effectiveness of their work, though it certainly was not as important as their historians claim. There is no doubt that the activities of the Bolsheviks, the Mensheviks, and the Social Revolutionaries contributed toward creating an atmosphere which favored change. But the February/March Revolution was in no sense a Bolshevik or Marxist movement in causation, organization, or direction. It was a chaotic happening.

CHAPTER XX

The Year 1917

The Russian monarchy was not overthrown by the planned actions of any organized group or party. The February/March Revolution was a series of spontaneous, unrehearsed, and jumbled events which no one controlled. Things just happened—now here, now there—with one action leading to others. Its essence was a lack of order. Though the story can be reduced to a neat and simple timetable, both neatness and simplicity were foreign to the events which are thus set down.

✪ DISCONTENT AND COUNTERACTIONS

Throughout the month of January, 1917, there was a steadily increasing number of demonstrations, strikes, and disorders which involved more and more people, and appeared in more and more places. Disaffection ranged from the grand dukes, who talked of "annihilating" the empress; through highly placed generals who plotted to remove the empress and to force the abdication of the emperor; through the Progressive Bloc which, under the lead of Miliukov and Guchkov, laid plans for a forced abdication and a regency; to the workers, who expressed their unrest by strikes. We have noted that there were only 68 strikes from August to December, 1914. The number jumped to 928 in 1915, and rose to 1284 (involving nearly a million workers) in 1916. During the two months of January and February, 1917, there were 1330 strikes (676,300 strikers). Economic demands were paramount, but the number of political strikes was very rapidly increasing. Petrograd (as St. Petersburg had been renamed during the war) and Moscow were the most important but not the only strike centers. Nicholas' best solutions to the mounting problems were to support the neurotic Protopopov, and to suspend the meetings of the Duma from January 6/19 to February 14/27.

During these days, the government, chiefly under the direction of

Minister of the Interior Protopopov, took steps to quell a possible uprising in the capital. Both the leaders of the government and their critics
clearly realized the increasing gravity of the situation and tried to bring
the tsar to an understanding of it. The Grand Duke Alexander wrote
to the tsar in January, urging upon him the establishment of an administration in which the people could have confidence. ". . . it must
be remembered that the Tsar alone cannot govern a country like
Russia," the letter read, ". . . it is absolutely indispensable that the
ministries and the legislative chambers shall work together." The
grand duke explicitly disclaimed any desire for a responsible ministry,
but said bluntly that the ministry must "be chosen from persons who
enjoy the confidence of the country." The Minister of Education, Count
Paul Ignatiev, who had long been close to the tsar, resigned his office
rather than to continue ". . . to be an accomplice of these persons
whose acts I regard as ruinous to the throne and to the state." And
Michael V. Rodzianko, president of the Third and Fourth Dumas,
spoke out with blunt courage in an audience with the tsar on January 7/20:

From my second report, Your Majesty may have seen that I regard the
situation as worse than ever. The frame of mind of the country is such that
very serious outbreaks may be expected. Political divisions no longer exist,
but Russia, as one, demands a change in Government and the appointment
of a responsible Prime Minister who has the confidence of the country. . . .
It is believed by the people that you have removed all the Ministers who had
the confidence of the Duma and public organizations [the zemstva and the
town councils], and replaced them by incapable and untrustworthy persons.
. . . There is not one honest man in your entourage; all decent people have
either been sent away or have left. . . . In order to save your family, Your
Majesty must find a way to remove the Empress from politics.

. . . .

On February 10/23 I had an audience with the Tsar. I was received very
coldly. . . . The Tsar listened not only with indifference, but with a kind
of ill-will. . . . When I spoke of Protopopov, he became irritated. . . .
When I called his attention to the threatening situation in the country and
the possibility of a revolution, he broke in again by saying: 'The information
I have is quite contrary to yours which can hardly have been the truth, [and
as to the Duma], I should like to say that if it permits itself such harsh
speeches as last time, it will be dissolved.'

On February 6/19, the capital city was removed from the jurisdiction of the Western Military District and placed under the command of
General Khabalov, who was directly answerable to the tsar. Heavy batteries of artillery and machine guns were brought into the city and em-
placed in what the authorities hoped would prove strategic locations.
The Chief of Staff sent three crews of sailors to aid in maintaining or-

der. It was a curious choice since disaffection was at least as great, if not greater, among the sailors than it was among the troops. The men at the naval base of Kronstadt were particularly discontented, and revolutionary agitators found ready hearing among them.

Then, on February 23/March 8, the little tsar disregarded all his counselors and left his threatened capital for army headquarters. It was at a moment when strikes in Petrograd were spreading, and when the Duma, once again in session, was castigating the government for its food policies. (There was food in stock, but failures in distribution produced local shortages in the cities.) On Friday (February 24/March 9) there were about 200,000 strikers in Petrograd alone. Their demonstrations forced the cessation of streetcar service in the city. Large crowds gathered on the Nevski Prospekt (one of the city's most important streets). They found the troops and the Cossacks friendly, although there was some firing against the people later in the day. General Khabalov issued a proclamation ordering people to stay indoors for the next three days. No one paid the slightest attention to the order.

The situation was markedly more tense on Saturday. Clashes with the police were more numerous and more violent, and the crowds thronged the Nevski Prospekt and spilled over into the other main streets. All the bridges were guarded by troops. Reports spread throughout the city that armed bands of strikers were being organized in the factory districts. On that day, Nicholas wired General Khabalov, "I command that the disorders in the capital shall be stopped tomorrow, as they are inadmissible in this serious time of war with Germany and Austria." Here is the clearest proof that the emperor simply did not understand what was happening.

🐚 RIOTS, MUTINIES, AND REVOLUTION

People in general slept late, or went to church, or at least stayed home on Sunday morning (February 26/March 11), but the crowds were out again in the afternoon and evening. There were police guards all over the city and they were re-enforced by Cossacks and other troops. The crowds, which had been rather good-natured, began on this day their chant of "Bread! Bread!" and as the chanting swelled in volume and continued the geniality decreased. There was some firing—over the heads of the crowds, mostly, but sometimes into them. That day also, the Pavlovsky Regiment, which was garrisoned in Petrograd, mutinied and refused to carry out the orders to disperse the crowds. The example of this regiment was followed on Monday by the Preobrazhenskii (which had begun its mutiny on Sunday afternoon), and by other troops. As the Soviet's later proclamation of revolution put it, "But the soldiers would not go against the people, and turned against the government. Together with the people, they seized arms, arsenals, and important government buildings."

While these disorders were going on, the prime minister—the aging Golitsin—appeared before the Duma to order its dissolution. (The order had been issued by the tsar on Saturday, February 25/March 10, but it was not countersigned and presented by Golitsin until Monday.) Outside the Tauride Palace, where the Duma was assembled, the disorders became more violent. There was a good deal of shooting. Fires broke out, and the mobs often kept the firemen from fighting the blaze. By afternoon, the police had disappeared from the streets. Some had taken off their uniforms and joined the mobs, or run away. Others had retired to the police stations, where they were besieged. More and more soldiers went over to the people, taking arms and munitions with them. By evening, Petrograd was out of control. In fact, the government had simply vanished from the national capital. The fortress-prison of SS. Peter and Paul had been captured by the mob, and political and criminal prisoners had been turned loose on the city. Minister Protopopov resigned and went into hiding.

DUMA AND SOVIET

Back in the Tauride Palace, the Duma listened to the order for its dissolution. Under the direction of its Senior Council (composed of the leaders of the major political parties), the Duma accepted the order but did not disperse. Its members continued to sit "as private persons." An "Executive Committee of the Duma"—thirteen men, under the presidency of Rodzianko—was then created. The Duma members authorized the formation of a "Provisional Committee" of twelve members who were appointed by the Senior Council. This committee took upon itself the task of trying to re-establish some order simply because there was no one else to make the attempt. But on this same day—Monday, February 27/March 12—another governing body set itself up. The incident was typical of the revolution.

Since the Tauride Palace seemed to be the center of whatever authority remained in the capital of Russia, the political prisoners released from the fortress-prison made their way there. So did thousands of others. The leaders and would-be leaders among them assembled in the palace. In its corridors there met an entirely self-appointed, chance-chosen group of socialist politicians, workers, and soldiers. These men —then and there, by their own action—constituted themselves "The Provisional Executive Committee of the Soviet of Workers' Deputies." This was a deliberate reversion to the pattern of 1905. The word "soldiers" was omitted from the title, and their membership as a special group was not apparently planned. But many soldiers came and had to be included. The Provisional Executive Committee of the Soviet summoned people to a meeting of the Soviet to be held that Monday evening. This stormy mass meeting was the first session of the Petrograd Soviet. It set up an Executive Committee, composed mostly of Essars and Mensheviks. The Bolsheviks were subsequently represented on it by Scriabin (Molotov) and Stalin, along with lesser-known persons. On Tuesday morning (February 28/March 13) armored cars cruised the city scattering a hastily printed "newspaper" with the long title, *Izvestia of the Petrograd Soviet of Workers' Deputies*. One side of its single sheet carried the following proclamation:

TO THE PEOPLE OF PETROGRAD AND RUSSIA FROM THE SOVIET OF WORKERS' DEPUTIES

The old government brought the country to ruin and the people to starvation. It could be borne no longer. The people of Petrograd went into the streets to give voice to their dissatisfaction. Volleys [of rifle fire] met them. Instead of bread, the tsar's ministers gave the people lead.

But the soldiers would not go against the people, and turned against the government. Together with the people, they seized arms, arsenals, and important government buildings.

The struggle is not over; it must continue to the end. The old government must be completely crushed and way made for government by the people. In this will be Russia's salvation.

To succeed in this struggle for the establishment of democracy, the people must build their own organs of government.

Yesterday, February 27, there was created in the capital a Soviet of Workers' Deputies, chosen from the representatives of the mills, factories, revolutionary military units, and from among the democratic and socialist parties and groups.

The Soviet of Workers' Deputies, meeting in the Duma, has taken for its chief duty the co-ordination of popular forces and the fight for the complete realization of political freedom and popular government in Russia.

The Soviet has appointed ward commissars for the establishment of the people's government in the wards of Petrograd.

We ask all people of the capital immediately to join forces with the Soviet, to create local committees in the wards, and to take into their own hands the management of all local affairs.

All together, we shall fight to wipe out completely the old government, and to summon a Constituent Assembly chosen on the basis of universal, equal, secret, and direct suffrage.

🝖 A PROVISIONAL REGIME

Even while the proclamation was being distributed, troops began to arrive at the Tauride Palace. They swore allegiance not to the Soviet but to the Duma's Provisional Committee. The building swarmed with people, and there was wild confusion. On the streets of the city there was considerable shooting. The fighting was mostly between the soldiers and their officers. The officers set up their headquarters at the Hotel Astoria and were besieged there. On Wednesday, the rebels captured the Admiralty, where the remnants of the old government had sought to make their final stand. Protopopov surrendered, and was protected —most melodramatically—by Alexander Kerensky. The other ministers fled or surrendered. There were spontaneous, popular jubilee parades throughout the city. The banks and the stores reopened for business. Sugar, meat, butter, and other items which had long been unobtainable were brought out of the government warehouses. There was a rush to buy them. And the Soviet issued its famous "Order Number One" which virtually shattered whatever discipline remained among the troops. This was not its intent.

"At the front, and in the performance of military duties," the order read, "soldiers must obey the strictest military discipline. . . ." It also directed that all weapons, equipment, and munitions be put under the control of committees which were to be established by the rank and file. It further ordered, "In all their political activities, the fighting units shall be directed by the Soviet of Workers' and Soldiers' Deputies and their committees. The orders of the War Commission of the Duma shall be carried out *unless they contradict the orders and resolutions of the Soviet of Workers' and Soldiers' Deputies.* [My italics.]" This alone was enough to confound confusion further, but there was much more to come.

Nicholas had left army headquarters on February 28/March 13 with the intention either of returning to Petrograd or of going to Tsarskoe Selo, where his family was. But the revolution had run along the railway tracks, as it were, and the tsar's trains were shunted away from the capital. Finally, on March 1/14 (Wednesday), he arrived at Pskov. Meanwhile the Duma leaders—Rodzianko, Shulgin, and Miliukov— came to the conclusion that the only way to save the institution of the monarchy was to get rid of the present monarch. They were supported by the unanimous opinion of the military leaders. Nicholas, to whom all these things were constantly reported, acquiesced and abdicated in favor of his son, Alexius, with the Grand Duke Michael as regent. The document was signed on March 2/15, but before Guchkov and Shulgin, who had been sent to receive it, had reached Pskov, Nicholas changed his mind. He changed the order of succession (and the words of his abdication) to hand the throne directly to the Grand Duke Michael. Guchkov and Shulgin accepted, but the grand duke—after some consideration—refused the offer. The Russian monarchy had ended. The Soviet was pleased, and ordered the arrest of "the dynasty of the Romanovs." The Provisional Government reluctantly acceded and issued its order for the arrest on March 7/20.

This Provisional Government had been established by the Duma's Executive Committee with the quasi blessing of the Petrograd Soviet. It was composed of ten members, under the leadership of Prince Lvov, who had headed the Zemstva Red Cross. Two of the ten were Octobrists (Guchkov being one of the two); one was a moderate rightist; six were Kadets (led by Miliukov, who became foreign minister); and one was an Essar. This lone socialist, the only one of the Provisional Government connected with the Soviet, was Kerensky, whose formal introduction cannot be longer delayed.

A. F. KERENSKY

Alexander Fedorovich Kerensky was the son of that schoolmaster of Simbirsk who had tried to help the young Vladimir Ilyich Ulyanov. As a young lawyer, Kerensky had won his spurs by acting as counsel for the defense in political trials. It was a course of action which required great moral courage. Membership in the Third and Fourth Dumas gave him immunity from arrest, which protected him while he traveled through the country as a political organizer and revolutionary worker. The police were frantic but helpless because he was the head of the Labor Group in the Duma, and the temper of the country prohibited police action against a man in that position. (The Duma records, by the way, always listed Kerensky as a member only of this Labor Group. It is generally asserted that he was secretly a member of the Social Revolutionary Party to which he later openly adhered.) During the war he co-operated with the Duma leaders, and Rodzianko has testified to the sincerity of Kerensky's support. His criticisms of the government immediately before the revolution had become extremely bold, and had won him considerable prestige. He was a member of the Duma's Executive Committee and of its Provisional Committee; as well as being a vice-president of the Soviet and Minister of Justice in the first Provisional Government. Later he became Minister of War and Navy, and, finally, the head of the government.

His career was spectacular. Duma member and party leader at thirty-one, prime minister of Russia at thirty-six, permanent exile from his native land at thirty-six—his taste of power was brief. His flair for the melodramatic—there was much of the actor in Kerensky—and his super-charged emotionalism have led some to dismiss him as a shallow, flamboyant demagogue. His failure to do the impossible caused others to brand him a mountebank. His inability or unwillingness to come to grips with certain realities has been alleged as the cause for his failure to transform Russia into a lasting democracy within half a year. There was something of the demagogue in Kerensky, and something of the poseur. His judgment of men and events was not always sure or well founded. He sometimes relied on his talents as "persuader-in-chief" to please the crowd with words when something more was required. But he was faced by opponents who were both vicious and unscrupulous, and he was confronted by a situation which could not be resolved by any man in a few months.

THE PROVISIONAL GOVERNMENT VERSUS THE SOVIET

The February/March Revolution, with its abdication, resignations, and flights, had swept away in the course of a few days the tsardom, which included the whole hierarchy of the *chinoviki* as well as the emperor and the imperial office; the Council of Ministers; and the State Council (the upper house of the legislature). The Duma never met, in the strictly legal sense, after the imperial dissolution of it. But the members of the Duma carried on the business of government (or tried to) for eight months. The first Provisional Government was the creation of the Duma, and it represented the same groups and classes which had dominated the Dumas after Stolypin's electoral coup. It is ironic that the changes by which Stolypin sought to meet the challenge of radicalism in 1907 made the government less able to cope with the challenge in 1917. The men of the Provisional Government—if one judges by their actions— generally believed that the revolution was caused by dissatisfaction over the conduct of the war. Failing to recognize other causes, failing to understand the new forces at work, they sought to carry on in their old, semi-liberal tradition. They felt in honor bound to continue to fight as an ally of France and Britain. They wished to postpone all final settlements of the problems of government and property until these could be settled by a popularly chosen Constituent Assembly.

The Petrograd Soviet was, by its size and manner of creation, closer to the man in the street—at least of the capital. There were originally three thousand members of the Soviet, more than two-thirds of them being soldiers. A stricter verification of credentials soon cut these numbers in half. There were several factions in it, and they were divided not only against each other but often among themselves. Both the Essars and the Social Democrats gave it support at the start. Its original leaders were Kerensky and the Mensheviks Chkeidze and Skobelev. Even the Bolsheviks co-operated with it and usually followed the lead of the Soviet until after the arrival of Lenin. The Bolsheviks did not gain a majority in the Petrograd Soviet until September. In October, Trotsky became its president.

There immediately developed between the Provisional Government and the Soviet a competition for power, and a clash of interests. The great advantage of the Soviet was that it came nearer to understanding the mood of the people and therefore was better able to enlist popular support. The basic and irreparable weakness of the liberals, who dominated the Provisional Government in its beginnings and remained influential in it until the end, was that they were so far removed from the people. The liberals wanted parliamentary constitutionalism. Some of them wanted a constitutional monarchy. The people, more accurately the peasants, were vitally interested in political questions, as their voting record in the election of the Constituent Assembly proved. But they were not interested in political forms and not at all in political theory, whereas the liberals were greatly concerned with both. Moreover, the liberalism of the Kadets was of a moderate and limited type. It was conservative liberalism. The liberalism of the peasants was radical liberalism. They were not sure what brand of radicalism they wanted—Marxist or non-Marxist; Bolshevik or Menshevik or Social Revolutionary—but they were sure that they did not want conservative answers to their problems. The liberals wanted mild social reforms, carried out in orderly fashion by due legal process. The masses neither knew nor cared about due legal processes. They wanted, above all else, land; and they wanted it at once. The peasant-workers and the peasant-soldiers (which meant most of each group) were not less eager for land than were the village peasants. The peasant-workers and the peasant-soldiers were in frantic haste to get home to their villages before their brothers had grabbed all the good land.

This is another way of saying that the masses did not want to fight any longer. They wanted peace at once. And the peasant-soldiers (as well as the worker-soldiers and others) took the most direct and simplest method of getting their way. They stopped fighting. As Lenin once described it, "The soldiers voted for peace with their feet," which was to say that they deserted in ever-increasing numbers. The liberals (chiefly but not exclusively the Kadets) wanted to continue the war. Their motives were mixed. There was that sense of solidarity (or hope for solidarity) with the Western democracies. This was increased by the entry of the United States into the war. There was a feeling of obligation to live up to Russia's pledges both as a matter of honor and as a tactic of practical politics. And there was more than a tinge of national selfishness. Said Miliukov after his forced resignation from the post of foreign minister: "I admit quite frankly, and stand firmly by it, that the main thread of my policy was to get the Straits for Russia." It was this insistence upon continuing the war which, more than any other single thing, destroyed the Provisional Government. The mood of the Russian people was overwhelmingly for peace. The masses of Russia were unutterably war-weary, and no government which proposed to keep on fighting could continue governing.

It needs to be emphasized that the Provisional Government never had any effective coercive authority. The police power of the state, using that phrase in the broad sense of the government's authority and ability to maintain order and compel action, did not survive the February/March Revolution. The Provisional Government could only try to persuade people to follow it. It could not command popular support, and it could not win popular support because of the gulf between it and the masses. On the other side, it was too radical for the conservatives, so it could not gain support from them either. It was too bold for the timid, and too timid for the bold. So it repeatedly lost to the Soviet, which at least partially understood the will of the people, although its factions differed among themselves as to how this will should be satisfied.

The first issue to be faced was abdication. The Provisional Government was willing to accept a change in tsar. The Soviet said that there should be no tsar. The Soviet won. The Provisional Government sought to establish a dual responsibility with the Soviet. That is to say, the government took the position that the inclusion in it of Kerensky bound the Soviet to support its actions. The Soviet was unwilling to accept this, and held that it would back the government's program only when that program was socialistic. Since the Provisional Government could not force the Soviet to support it, the Soviet won this fight also. The Provisional Government stood for continuing the war. The Soviet held that the war was for the benefit of the capitalists and injurious to the people. It therefore stood for peace. On this point, the Provisional Government enjoyed (or was injured by) the support of her allies who —up to July—were desperately afraid that Russia would make a separate peace. (After the debacle of the July Offensive, the allies were afraid that Russia wouldn't get out of the war and that they would have to defend her.) The allies—up to July—high-pressured the Provisional Government to go on fighting, which was entirely agreeable to Guchkov, Miliukov, and most of their associates. The Soviet counter-pressured for peace, and appealed to the workers of all countries to unite in stopping the war. The Soviet pressure did have one major effect. In May, it forced the resignation of Guchkov and Miliukov and the formation of a second Provisional Government. The new administration included two Social Democrats—Skobelev and Tseretelli—both Mensheviks, and two Essars—Kerensky and Chernov.

Two other points at issue were the matter of army discipline and the elections to the Constituent Assembly. The Provisional Government hoped to restore discipline in the armies and to maintain them as fighting units. The Soviet, unintentionally perhaps, undermined discipline by its Order Number One. Later it sought to explain this and to minimize its effects by an Order Number Two, which had about the same effect as a newspaper's retraction which is buried among the last pages of the paper. As to the election, the Duma group originally favored a delay for fear that the event might divert attention from prosecution of the war. The Soviet was in favor of speeding the election. Speed, however, proved to be impossible due to the size of Russia, the necessity for creating unfamiliar machinery from the foundations up, the general chaos, and the specific machinations of certain groups. Repeated delays—mostly unavoidable—gave the Bolsheviks openings for attack, and they used the opportunities very effectively. The story of the Bolshevik action during these months pivots on Lenin's return to Russia on April 2/16.

🦋 BOLSHEVIK ACTION: LENIN

The Bolsheviks were as astounded and as unready for the February/ March Revolution as was everybody else. Lenin was in Switzerland; the lesser leaders were either in exile or operating a rather ineffective underground. Lenin tried to guide his followers by his "Letters from Afar," but this proved unsatisfactory. When the Provisional Government— most unwisely but true to its liberal values—decreed an amnesty for political prisoners and exiles, Lenin decided to get back to Russia if he could. But the allies controlled the ocean routes and they correctly believed that Lenin's presence in Russia would aid the German cause. They therefore refused to allow him passage. It was the Menshevik leader Martov who first suggested that German permission be sought to enable Lenin to return to Russia overland. The German High Command agreed with their enemies that Lenin would aid the German cause, and gave permission. Lenin and his party crossed Germany by train, then took a ship to Sweden, and from there entered Russia through Finland. Until Lenin's arrival in Petrograd, the Bolsheviks had more or less followed the lead of the Soviet. They had no positive program beyond obstructionism. Lenin lost no time in presenting a specific ten-point program, his "April Theses," on April 3/17; and, within a month, had overcome the opposition to it of a majority of the Bolshevik's Central Executive Committee. The points of his program may be summarily enumerated:

1. '. . . it is impossible to end the war . . . without the overthrow of capitalism.' Spread this propaganda among the troops.
2. The Party must be flexible as to tactics during this transition stage.
3. Give no support to the Provisional Government.
4. We are a very small minority and so long as this is true we must seek to build up the power of the soviets while also building our own power within the soviets.
5. There must be no parliamentary republic. The army, the police and the bureaucracy must be abolished.
6. All landowners' estates must be confiscated, and all land nationalized.
7. All banks must be merged in a single national bank under soviet control.
8. Help the soviets extend their control over production and distribution.
9. Call a Party Congress. Change the Party program to meet the new situation. Change the Party name to Communist.
10. Take the lead in creating a new revolutionary international organization.

What Lenin did in these months was nothing less than to change the course of the revolution and of history. He set the objectives, planned the strategies, organized the tactics, drilled—and almost created—his forces. No one else so accurately gauged the temper of the Russian people. No one elso so effectively made use of this popular mood. The most burning question of all—the land problem—is an excellent illustration of this.

THE LAND PROBLEM

The Kadet program for land reform was a case of too little and too late. Miliukov saw clearly that what the Russian peasant wanted was not liberty but land. His diagnosis was accurate, but his prescription was inadequate. He was willing that the peasants should have the land of the nobility—of the great landowners—but he could not see his way to handing over, also, the lands belonging to the middle class, which he represented. What the peasants demanded (and proceeded to take) was all the land at once. He and his party therefore accepted the program of the more moderate socialists, namely that final land reform must wait for the meeting of the Constituent Assembly. This seems to have been Kerensky's idea, also. His associate Chernov, who became Minister of Agriculture in May, originally was in favor of letting the peasants have the land immediately and without compensation to the owners. He was unable to promote this program as a member of the administration, but he did so by encouraging the "All-Russian Congress of Peasant Deputies" (which the Essars organized in April and May) to demand the immediate "transfer, without compensation, of all lands now belonging to the state, monasteries, churches, and private persons into the possession of the nation, for equitable and free use by agricultural workers." The intent was to face the Constituent Assembly with a *fait accompli*. But, during the summer, Chernov reversed his position and tried, by legislation, to stop the taking of land by the peasants. It had the same effect as it would to declare by law that there should be no more common colds. The peasants simply went ahead and took the land.

This, of course, was lawlessness. But it is easy to understand. The peasants regarded the land as rightfully theirs to use. The Emancipation Settlement (and subsequent additions to it) had given them part of the land, but they were excluded from the remainder by a fence. This fence was the government's police power. The fence went down in February/March and the peasants just swarmed across the debris and took the land for themselves. Lenin and his Party encouraged them to do so. But, despite all Communist claims to the contrary, the Bolsheviks did not give the land to the peasants. The Bolsheviks did not have it to give because the peasants had already taken it. But Lenin's apparent, though deceptive, championship of what the peasants were doing won his party considerable support in the villages. Meanwhile, confusion, competition, and a steady shift to the left continued in the national administration.

THE PROVISIONAL GOVERNMENT WEAKENS

The First All-Russian Congress of Soviets opened in June and was promptly made the theater of warfare between the Mensheviks and Essars on the one side and Lenin and his Bolsheviks on the other. A major issue was support of the Provisional Government. Lenin refused any support and was joined in this by some of the more radical Mensheviks and Essars. The majority favored limited support, however, so Lenin lost the first round, but the fight went on. Then, with Chernov's switch on the land program—plus some other happenings—the Executive Committees of the Congresses of Peasant Deputies and of the Soviets combined to work against both the Provisional Government and the Bolsheviks. July was a crucial month. The collapse of Brusilov's offensive (which had been sparked by Kerensky) thoroughly discredited the Provisional Government and greatly increased Bolshevik influence in the army. The Ukrainian separatists broke away from "Muscovy" and this precipitated the resignation of the remaining Kadet ministers in the Provisional Government. These events caused new turmoil in the capital, and a group of irresponsibles (including a number of Bolsheviks) attempted an insurrection against the administration. Lenin, whose preparations were not yet complete and who judged the movement premature, sought to stop it. He couldn't and so, with that flexibility which always characterized his tactics, he ordered his men to join the insurrection in the hope of thus gaining control of it. (The alternative —continued abstention—would have cost the Bolsheviks irreplaceable prestige.) The rebellion flared for three days and then died out. Lenin and some of his colleagues had to leave the capital for hiding places in nearby Finland, but he continued to control his party. A new Provisional Government was formed with Kerensky as Prime Minister and Minister of War and Navy. The socialists were now in control of the Provisional Government and they sought the support of the *bourgeoisie* just as the Kadets had early sought their backing.

Late in August there was summoned to Moscow by the administration some 2500 persons representing the members of the four Dumas, the peasants, the soviets, the Zemgor combinations, the armed forces, the co-operatives, and many others. The purpose, as Kerensky phrased it, was "to appeal and demand that it [the Provisional Government] be supported in its great work of saving the country and saving the revolution." All that the Moscow State Conference actually did was give a thorough demonstration of the complete disunity of the groups who participated. The socialists—except, of course the Bolsheviks—accepted Kerensky as their champion; the more conservative groups put forward as their hero the new commander-in-chief of the army, General Kornilov. The beneficiaries of the rivalry which fast grew between these men (and of the lack of unity displayed at the Moscow State Conference) were the Bolsheviks.

Kornilov, who had distinguished himself as an adventuresome commander on the southwestern front, was an honest and patriotic but politically naive person. His ability to restore and maintain discipline in the army commended him to Kerensky, who was responsible for Kornilov's rapid advancement. But Kornilov became the tool of a reactionary financier named Zavoyko, who tried to use the general as a front for a reactionary movement. Upon the advice of Zavoyko, whom Kornilov accepted as his political adviser, the general began to demand more powers. Finally, through an intermediary who seems to have taken it on himself to interpret rather than merely to repeat the messages, Kornilov demanded (as Kerensky understood the garbled message) dictatorial authority to set up a new administration. Kornilov was to be its head; and Zavoyko its Minister of Finance. This demand Kerensky understandably refused, and ordered Kornilov to give up his office. The general sought to lead his troops against the capital, but the rank and file refused to follow and his bubble burst. The Kornilov affair cost Kerensky support on both sides. The beneficiaries, again, were the Bolsheviks.

THE BOLSHEVIK COUP

After this event—really before its outcome was certain—Kerensky shifted from a Provisional Government to a Directory of Five and proclaimed the establishment of a republic. In a vain effort to rally some support for this he summoned (September/October) a "Democratic Conference" which had no effective consequences. Equally full of talk and equally futile was the Council of the Republic (or, Pre-Parliament), which met late in October. Kerensky's power was fast running out. He had moved away from the Soviet without, however, approaching the Duma group. Now he stood almost alone. The national administration had virtually ceased to exist. Local administration had vanished in February/March. The fall of the tsar carried down with it the provincial governors, who held power from the tsar and acted as his agents. They were deposed or fled. The district police chiefs, who held power from the governors, were deposed or killed or forced to run away. So it went down the line. The wheels of the bureaucracy continued to turn, but the gears no longer meshed. In every locality there sprang up soviets, "citizens' committees," or local "strong men." There was no clear delegation of authority or responsibility. On the contrary, there was rivalry, overlapping, contradiction, and confusion. Disorder and lawlessness were the characteristics of the time. This was the situation for which the patient and crafty Lenin had been waiting. On the evening of October 24/November 6, he wrote to his Party's Central Committee:

> The situation is critical in the extreme. It is absolutely clear that to delay the insurrection now would be truly fatal.
>
> I exhort my comrades with all my strength to realize that . . . we are being confronted by problems which cannot be solved by conferences or congresses (even Congresses of Soviets) but exclusively by peoples, by masses, by the struggle of armed masses. . . . We must at all costs, this very evening, this very night, arrest the government. . . .
>
> We must not wait! We may lose everything! . . .
>
> The government is wavering. It must be given the finishing blow at all costs. To delay action will be fatal.

On the next morning, there appeared on the streets of Petrograd a poster which began:

From the Revolutionary Military Committee of the Petrograd Soviet of Workers' and Soldiers' Deputies

To the Citizens of Russia

The Provisional Government has been overthrown. Governing power has passed into the hands of the agent of the Petrograd Soviet . . . the Revolutionary Military Committee. . . .

The Petrograd Soviet was now headed by Lenin's closest collaborator and first lieutenant, Trotsky, and the Revolutionary Military Committee was the agent of Lenin's Bolsheviks. The October/November Revolution had begun. As Professor Pitirim Sorokin recalled it:

> The Council of the Republic convened, and a proposal to protest against the criminal attack on the rights of the people and of the Government was made and debated. But the discussion did not last very long, for suddenly the Hall was invaded by a troop of soldiers who announced: 'According to a decree of the new Government the Council of the Republic is dispersed. Leave here immediately or submit to arrest.'
>   . . . The resolution [of protest] was carried. Then the chairman said: 'Under pressure of violence the Council of the Republic is temporarily interrupted.' Such was the end of the first Republic. . . .

 ANALYSIS

The Bolsheviks have always stressed the apparent speed and ease with which they seized power, since this enables them to claim that they had popular support. But there are other explanations of the ease with which they gained control.

There was no nationally accepted government or administration in existence by the end of October, 1917. The Provisional Government had, in fact, been replaced by Kerensky's administration, and Kerensky was unable to command support, even in Petrograd. The former leaders were discredited; the temporary leaders had not established themselves. Moreover, the Bolsheviks in winning Petrograd had not won Russia, because there was no centralized administration for them to win. Each region, each district, each city, even each village had become autonomous. Events in them could be and were greatly influenced by events in Petrograd and Moscow, but it was a matter of influence and not of control. The Petrograd revolt affected only that region directly; the Moscow revolt changed the government only in Moscow and its environs. Each area, region, district, city, and village had to be won over separately. This took years, literally. The Bolshevik Revolution was not just one quick convulsion. It was a series of continuing convulsions which went on at least until 1921. What is traditionally called "the Civil War" was simply a prolongation of the revolution. It was neither quick nor easy. The speed of the Bolshevik advance varied greatly in different regions. Where the soviets were strong, and where the Bolsheviks managed to capture the soviets before October, it was rapid. This was true in Petrograd and Moscow. It was also true of many of the railroads. Soviets were particularly strong among railroad men, and the Bolsheviks had long concentrated much of their agitation and organizational work among them. Virtually the only Bolsheviks across the great stretches of Siberia prior to 1918–19 were employees of the Trans-Siberian Railway. The extent of Bolshevik power among railroad men explains why Trotsky was able to control transportation from north to south across western Russia by November or December, and to control it across Russia from east to west by November, 1918. This tactic of gaining control of transportation and communication lines was a most important and successful one. But it would have been of no lasting value to a group less tightly organized or less rigidly disciplined. Lenin's years of effort paid rich dividends.

When major changes come so thick and fast that people cannot keep up with them, the majority become highly suggestible. Eagerly seeking help and guidance, trying desperately to place themselves in relation to the new circumstances, most men will readily listen to and follow any man or group who speaks with what sounds like a voice of authority. There were many, many voices in Russia in 1917. Some were discredited by the past and some were pitched too high, as it were, to be audible to the masses. This was true of the voices of the Duma group and of the "liberals" in general. Many voices were indistinguishable by their very babbling. The similarity of much of what they said was as confusing as the stridency with which each decried the other. This was the case of the left Essars, the right Essars, the Mensheviks, the Popular Socialists, and so on. Moreover, these groups were so busy being against something that they had little time or voice left to enunciate positive programs. And, of course, they dissipated their strength against each other instead of concentrating against the Bolsheviks. In all this welter of confusion, only the Bolsheviks spoke with one voice, and even among them there were overtones of differences, although these were insignificant by comparison with other groups. And the Bolshevik leaders took pains to listen to the murmurings of the people and to have their followers repeat—along with certain specific Bolshevik elements—what the people wanted to hear. ("All power to the soviets"; "Peace, Bread, and Land.")

🦞 BOLSHEVIK OPPORTUNISM AND AMORALITY

Furthermore, there existed by October no effective alternative to the Bolsheviks. Conservatism, even very moderate conservatism, had few followers among the people of Russia. When the elections to the Constituent Assembly were finally held in late November, the fight was between the Bolsheviks and the Essars. The Kadets were virtually out of the running. (Many people who were not ready to follow either the Bolsheviks or the Kadets were not prepared to accept the Essars. Their attitude was one of disgust, and in the election to the Second Congress of the Soviets, many didn't bother to vote at all.) The Essars were divided among themselves, partly because their organization had always been loose and their program vague, and partly because the Bolsheviks skillfully employed the tactics of divide and rule. They bid high for popular support, undeterred by any questions of morals and ethics. They promised what they had no power to give and what they had no intention of actually giving if they should win power. This is a harsh indictment which calls for concrete evidence in its support. Here are three items of proof.

The peasants had already taken most of the land. On October 25/November 7, the Bolsheviks put through the Second Congress of Soviets (which they dominated) a Land Decree which authorized the peasants to take the land at once. This was nothing more than a recognition of an accomplished fact and an effort to outbid the Essars, whose vacillation on the land question had cost them some popularity. In February, 1918, after the Constituent Assembly had been elected and dismissed so that campaign promises were no longer needed, the Bolsheviks decreed the "socialization" of the land. A year later (February, 1919), the land was nationalized. It is an entirely different thing to say, "The land belongs to the state" than to say, "The land belongs to the peasants who occupy it."

On November 15/28, the Bolsheviks passed a decree sanctioning workers' control over the factories. Factories by that time fell mainly into two classes: (1) those which were continued under the same ownership and management as before the revolutions—these amounted to about 20 per cent; and (2) factories which had been taken over by local committees of workers—the remaining 80 per cent. This is what the Bolsheviks gave temporary legal sanction to by their factory law. Later, when they felt more secure, they nationalized first the larger factories and then the smaller ones. That, again, is not at all the same as giving the factories to the workers.

The mood of the country was overwhelmingly for peace. Effective war against Germany had ended before the Bolshevik Revolution, although Russian soldiers were still in the field. On October 25/November 7, the Bolshevik-dominated Congress of Soviets passed its "Peace Decree" which announced that it was ready to end the war on a basis of no annexations and no indemnities. (The formula had been devised by

the Petrograd Soviet very shortly after the February/March Revolution.) When the Bolsheviks' attempts to negotiate a peace with Germany failed, in February, 1918, they sought frantically to rally the
Russian people to another campaign. They failed even more signally
than had Kerensky. Only then did the Bolsheviks accept a peace (Treaty
of Brest-Litovsk) which they did not intend to keep.

⚙ INTERPRETATIONS

There is no doubt that such promises and concessions won many persons to the support of the Bolsheviks. (Since that time, and in many
countries, the Communists [1] have repeatedly demonstrated their ability
to enlist the sympathies and support of many sincere but gullible persons.) There is also no doubt that the utter poverty of the split opposition and the disgust of many voters with the whole business won a
greater majority for the Bolsheviks. They elected 390 out of the total
of 650 delegates to the Second Congress of Soviets. This Congress was
no more truly representative of the people of Russia than the Third
and Fourth Dumas had been. The Dumas represented one segment of
the population; the congress, another. The Bolshevik majority in it,
strengthened by an alliance with the left Essars, elected an all-Bolshevik
Council of People's Commissars (SOVNARKOM). The chief members
were Lenin, chairman; Rykov, Commissar of the Interior; and Trotsky,
Commissar of Foreign Affairs. Stalin was named Chairman of Nationalities. It was this group which promulgated the land, peace, and factory
decrees which have already been mentioned. It also decreed the confiscation of all private homes, with local soviets being given authority
to expel the owners and install workers in their places. This was not the
same thing as nationalization, which came later.

The Bolsheviks immediately instituted a censorship of the press,
speech, and assembly far more rigorous than that against which they
had so bitterly and vehemently protested in the days before they came
to power. All the middle-class political parties were at once outlawed,
and this outlawry was soon extended to include all the socialist groups
except the left Essars who, in the words of the official Communist Party
History, entered a "united front" with the Bolsheviks. "However," the
History continues, "this agreement lasted only until the signing of the
Peace of Brest-Litovsk and the formation of the Committees of the
Poor Peasants. . . ." Then, though the *History* does not so express it,
the party of the left Essars was liquidated as the other political parties
had been before it. Since that time, there has been only one political
party in Russia—the Communist Party; and since that time, also, there
has never been freedom of speech, press, or assembly. The year 1917

also saw (in December) the setting up of the first secret, political police —an institution without which the Communist regime in Russia has never operated. The title of new police was "The All-Russian Commission for the Suppression of Counterrevolution, Sabotage, and Speculation." It is spoken of in Western accounts as the "Cheka"; in Party accounts as *Vcheka*. By any other name it would also stink of tyranny.

The cold factual reasons behind the establishment of the tyranny and despotism, behind the suppression of free speech and of all opposition, can be very simply stated. This was the only way by which the Bolsheviks, having seized power, could retain it. The story of the elections to the Constituent Assembly and of the fate of this assembly gives firm support to this interpretation. The plain fact was that "Three weeks after the October Revolution, the Bolsheviks had signally failed to secure popular sanction for their seizure of power and had mustered only one-fourth of the electorate behind their banner." [2]

Out of the approximately 41.5 million votes which were cast, the Bolsheviks received about 10 million; the Essars, about 16 million. Roughly 12 million voters supported other socialist groups, and only 3.5 million voted a conservative ticket. (The Kadets got the largest share of these—not quite 2 million.) In terms of delegates, the Essars elected 380 out of the total of 703; the Bolsheviks, 168; the Mensheviks, 18; the left Essars, 39; the Kadets, only 15, and there were 83 others. Nationally speaking, the struggle was between the spiritual descendants (so to speak) of the *Narodniki* and of Marx-Engels. Only in the two great cities of Moscow and Petrograd did the Kadets do well, and there they were well ahead of the Essars but a poor second to the Bolsheviks.

The Bolshevik strength was greatest in the urban, industrial areas, in the army garrisons, and in those portions of the front-line armies which were closest to the metropolitan centers. They also did well in those rural regions from which large numbers of peasants regularly went to the cities to work. (Novgorod Province was an outstanding example.) In regions where, as Radkey puts it, "peasants really were peasants" and not "half-proletarian, half-peasant" the Essars were strongest. Their centers were Siberia, the Volga valley, and the black-earth belt except where, in Ukraine, a strong nationalist movement cut across other lines. The election returns show, incidentally, that this Ukrainian nationalist movement was a genuine grass-roots affair, but they do not prove it to have been a separatist movement. Three other points stand out: the strong influence of the Bolsheviks upon the troops, the strong influence of returning soldiers upon the elections; the fact that "the vast majority of electorate freely exercised the right of suffrage"; and that the peasants, who showed much more interest and confidence in this effort at self-government than did most of the urban people, were "an easy prey to demagogues who carefully concealed what lay in store for them during the period of militant communism and the era of the five-year plans."

🔹 LENIN AND HIS PARTY OPPONENTS

The story of the year 1917 may be concluded by noting that Lenin did not have the unqualified support of all Bolsheviks. He faced (and overcame) opposition from within his party as well as from outside it. The Bolsheviks Zinoviev and Kamenev opposed the uprising on October 24–25/November 6–7 and resigned from the Party's Central Committee soon afterwards. They were joined in this action by Rykov and Miliutin. Eight of the members of the newly appointed SOVNARKOM (Council of People's Commissars) also resigned from that body at the same time. Lenin, though very flexible and opportunistic as to tactics, had totally inflexible ultimate goals. One of his close associates, Lunacharsky, once described his leader in the following words:

Lenin does his work imperiously, not because power is sweet to him, but because he is sure he is right, and cannot endure to have anybody spoil his work. His love of power grows out of his tremendous self-confidence . . . and, if you please, out of an inability . . . to see from the point of view of his opponents.

N. Lenin was one of those rare individuals who derive their estimate of themselves from their own standards and not from the standards of others. The judgment of society did not count with Lenin because he measured himself by what he thought and not by what others thought of him. For this reason, he was incorruptible and untouchable. Neither pressure nor pleasure could swerve him from his purpose. It follows, also, that he had complete confidence in himself, in the correctness of his goals, in the rightness of his judgments, and in the propriety of his actions. He could be gracious to his colleagues, could and did defer (or appear to defer) to others' opinions; but time and again he demonstrated that in his opinion Lenin was always a majority of one. Lenin was a man who knew what he wanted. He wanted power and he worked all his life to get it. How he got it and how he kept it were of little concern to him. To resort when necessary "to all sorts of stratagems, manoeuvres, illegal methods, to evasions and subterfuges" was one of his recommendations to his Party. It is our duty, he told his associates, to adapt our tactics to every change. "If you are not able to adapt yourself, if you are not inclined to crawl in the mud on your belly, you are not a revolutionary but a chatterbox. . . ." Lenin, with great skill and no scruples, secure in his profound assurance that he was right and his cause was righteous, was a perfect exemplification of his own teachings.

CHAPTER XXI

The Second Ride of the Four Horsemen: Opposition to Revolution

⊕ PERSISTENCE OF NORMS

When one stops to think of it, perhaps the most astounding thing about a revolution is that everyday life goes on. This is so commonplace and so taken for granted that it usually doesn't seem noteworthy. Attention is fixed on the spectacular and the dramatic, on what is destroyed and on what is created, that is, upon change. We forget to remark that amid hunger, violence, disease, hardships, sufferings, and almost complete insecurity, men continue to live as best they can. There is continuity even in the midst of the most sweeping changes because no matter how drastically revolutionaries alter certain patterns of their societies, they do not and cannot change them all. They do not, of course, change men's basic physiological and psychological nature and needs. The greatest long-term problem of Lenin and his successors was the persistence of popular habits. Oblomovism and evasiveness, to mention only two, did not vanish with the Romanovs.

The whole of Soviet history is a story of wars of various kinds. Lenin and those who followed him have always had to fight simultaneously on many fronts. They have had to contend with anti-Bolshevik, Russian armies and groups; with foreign invaders; with indifference, ignorance, and laziness as well as with planned opposition; with accumulated filth, endemic diseases, recurrent famines, and other accompaniments or consequences of habitual and continuing poverty. They have also had to fight against nature—against cold, and drought, and distance. Never in the Soviet period have their people known the ease, peace, security, and comfort which we habitually assume to be our proper due. They have had to struggle mightily for every advance, and their sacrifices—whether voluntary or forced upon them—have been terrific. Some of them have been sustained by ambition; some, by dreams come true; some, by dreams yet to be fulfilled. There is no doubt that the revolution and the Soviet regime have meant unprecedented opportunities for millions of men and women. A very large number of persons have been given chances to better themselves—chances which their ancestors did not have. This has been the great dynamic released by the Communists, and it is the greatest single source of Soviet strength. But very many of their people have been borne up only by the habit of living and by human reluctance to surrender life even when life seems miserable. And very many—the very young, the very old, the strong who attempted too much, and the weak or slothful who attempted too little, the unlucky, and the least adaptable—have fallen by the way.

The fact of continuity in the middle of change needs to be kept in mind as one seeks to follow the Soviet story. There was no longer a single political and administrative unit in what had been the Russian Empire. There was no nationally accepted executive authority; no national army or navy; and no national judiciary or legal system. After Lenin forcibly dissolved the Constituent Assembly before its first session was through, there was no legislature which could claim to be national.

🐝 BOLSHEVIK AND ANTI-BOLSHEVIK CENTERS, 1917–18

The Bolsheviks were dominant (though certainly it was not an unchallenged dominance) in the central and the northwestern part of what the first chapter called the Russian "wedge." They held the two main cities—Petrograd, which they renamed Leningrad, and Moscow, to which they transferred their capital. They were strong in the industrial centers, in those parts of the armed forces which were stationed closest to Leningrad and Moscow, among the peasantry of the forest zone, and among the railway men. This was strategically the strongest position, but it lacked the industrial and mercantile centers along the western line and within the southern and southwestern portions of the wedge. It also lacked the fertile, black-soil belt. Anti-Bolsheviks of various sorts—the Whites—held the Archangel region and were soon supported by French, British, and American troops. Finland had declared its independence of Russia. So had the Lithuanians. Latvia and Estonia, along with Poland, were under German control.

The situation in Ukraine was complicated. There were Bolsheviks in control in Kharkov, where they set up a "Provisional Ukrainian Soviet Government," which lasted about three months. Kiev, the capital of Ukraine, the country districts, and the Crimea were not in Bolshevik hands in early 1918. The Bolsheviks had a precarious hold on the region of the Don, however, but lost it during the late spring and early summer. Nationalisms were stronger than any other "isms" in the Caucasian area, although the Mensheviks, whose movement interlocked with Georgian nationalism, were strong there. This was the only place, incidentally, where the Mensheviks continued to be a major factor.

The Cossack lands along the southern part of the wedge were the strongest centers of antibolshevism. There was created the Volunteer Army—led first by General Kaledin and General Kornilov, later by Generals Denikin and Wrangel. There, also, was the Don Cossack group led by General Krasnov and supported throughout most of 1918 by the Germans. There were other anti-Bolshevik groups in the Volga and Volga-Urals region, and in Siberia. The most significant thing about these numerous White groups was their lack of unity. They were separated not only by distance but also by differences of aim and by personal dissension among their leaders. Denikin, for example, found it impossible to co-operate with Krasnov. A few of the Whites were fighting to bring back the Romanovs and the entire old system. A few more were hoping to bring back some of the old, but not all of it, and not the Romanovs. Others wanted a constitutional democracy, and some favored a military dictatorship. There were among them Rightists, Octobrists, Kadets, Social Revolutionaries, Popular Socialists, and various other splinter groups. There were nobles and commoners, landlords and peasants, intellectuals and workers, soldiers and civilians, socialists and capitalists, and anarchists. But there was little unity or coherence or co-operation, and precious little understanding of the masses. All the major White forces had the aid and support of foreign Powers—of Germany (until the end of 1918), of Britain, France, the United States, and Japan. Although this made possible some temporary successes, it was a long-run liability for two reasons. First, the aid was never sufficient in quantity nor opportune enough in point of time to be decisive. Second, it made credible the Bolshevik exaggeration that the Whites were only the hirelings of the foreign Powers, and were fighting against the Russian people, rather than in their behalf.

INTERVENTIONS

In the summer of 1918 there were no less than 30 governments in existence in what had been the Russian Empire. Most of these had some relations both with the Bolsheviks and with foreign Powers.

Without first defining what is meant by "interventions," it is hard to say when they began. They certainly came long before the Bolsheviks. The British and the French intervened quite directly in Russian affairs from 1914 on, and one might even call the French insistence on the building of strategic railways in 1912–13 a form of intervention. The part Sir Bernard Pares played in by-passing Sukhomlinov and the War Ministry was a kind of intervention. There were British and French civilian and military agents and missions in Russia throughout the war, and there were also some very small Allied forces there. After the February/March Revolution, the nature of the intervention changed and the amount of it increased. An American Railway Mission was sent to reorganize the Russian railroads, and an American propaganda office was established to try to stiffen Russia's will to fight. The United States recognized the Provisional Government within three days of its establishment—which was before anyone could know its actual status. Between May and October, the United States offered credits of 325 million dollars to this government and actually advanced more than half this sum.

Pares tells in his autobiography [1] how he joined a group of Mensheviks in a self-appointed, self-designated "League of Personal Example" which traveled around Russia in a special train provided by the War Office. The group spoke in favor of going on with the war, but, Pares reported, "our success was only at face value; everyone cheered us, and then went away hoping the war would soon be over." Later Sir Bernard was the only foreign member of the All-Russian Central Committee of the Volunteer Revolutionary Army. "All we English in Russia," he noted, ". . . were thinking all the while how many lives we should lose on the Western Front if Russia dropped out. . . ." That last sentence contains the most important key to the interventions. Their purpose was to keep Russia fighting on the Allied side, and the interventionists were ready to do business with any person or group to that end. Nor were the Bolsheviks excluded because they were radicals. The British dealt with them clandestinely (largely through Bruce Lockhart), and the United States dealt with them unofficially (largely through Raymond Robbins).

The Bolsheviks had repeatedly spoken of the desirability of a Russian defeat; they were known to have connections with the Germans and to have accepted German help—a fact which made credible the rumor that they were German agents. Whatever their intentions, the Bolsheviks materially assisted the Germans at a time when the Allied cause looked very bleak. Much of the feeling against the Bolsheviks was due to these actions, but there were also other reasons for fear and hostility. By far the most important was the fact that the first and major aim of Bolshevik foreign policy was the promotion of world revolution.

🖉 PROMOTION OF WORLD REVOLUTION BY BOLSHEVIKS

The very first act of Lenin's group in the field of international relations was the proclamation of the Peace Decree, which called upon "all combatant peoples and their governments to begin immediate negotiations for an honest democratic peace." It was a shrewd appeal which touched many men of good will who did not know, and did not trouble to find out, what the Bolsheviks meant by an "honest democratic peace." And it was the first use of a tactic which the succeeding rulers of Russia have found most valuable in gaining a sympathetic hearing. After setting forth what was meant by an "honest democratic peace," the decree concluded with the following appeal:

. . . the Provisional Workers' and Peoples' Government of Russia also appeals especially to the class-conscious workers of . . . England, France, and Germany . . . the workers of the above-mentioned countries understand the problems which now fall on them—of liberating humanity from the horrors of war and its consequences . . . these workers by their decisive and devotedly energetic activity will help us successfully to bring to fruition the cause of peace and, along with this, the cause of freeing the toiling and exploited masses of the population from slavery and exploitation of every kind.

This was no less than an invitation to the workers of the West to revolt against their governments, and it was so understood by those governments. It suited the tactics and strategy of the German High Command to profess agreement to starting peace talks on bases set forth in the decree. The Bolsheviks probably knew or at least suspected that the Germans were acting in perfect bad faith (which they were), but it served Lenin's ends to take the German reply at face value. Agents of the two met on November 20/December 3, 1917, and concluded an armistice after two days of talks. Their peace conference, held at Brest-Litovsk, opened fifteen days later. Meanwhile, the Bolshevik propaganda machine was exploiting the situation for all it was worth. The Bolsheviks invited the peoples of all warring nations to join in the peace. "Such a peace can be made," the Bolsheviks declared, "only as a result of a direct and brave struggle of the revolutionary masses against all the plans and usurping aspirations of the imperialists." "Imperialists" was a Leninist synonym for "capitalists" so that this was also an incitement to revolution. It was quickly followed by an appeal "To All the Toiling Moslems of Russia and the East" which declared:

The rule of the robbers, who have enslaved the peoples of the world, is falling. . . . A new world is being born, a world of workers and of freed people. At the head of this revolution stand . . . the Council of Peoples' Commissars.

. . . Russia is not alone in this sacred cause. The great watchword of liberation, proclaimed by the Russian Revolution, is caught up by all the workers of the West and East. The peoples of Europe, exhausted by the war, are already stretching out their hands to us and creating peace. The workers and soldiers of the West are already gathering under the banner of socialism, storming the ramparts of imperialism. And faraway India . . . has already raised the banner of insurrection, organizing its Soviets . . . calling the peoples of the East to struggle and liberation.

The reign of capitalist pillage and violence is crumbling. . . .

Three days later came a direct injunction to the working classes of Germany, Austria-Hungary, Bulgaria, and Turkey "to set against the imperialistic program of their ruling classes their own revolutionary program. . . ." The proclamation called "the workers of all lands" to the "struggle against all the imperialists." "There is," it said, "no other way." Nor did the Bolsheviks confine themselves to proclamations. Late in December, 1917, the Commissars, holding "it necessary to come to the aid of the Left, Internationalist wing of the workingclass movement of all countries, with all possible resources, including money, quite irrespective of whether these countries are at war or in alliance with Russia, or whether they occupy a neutral position" decided "to place at the disposal of the foreign representatives of the Commissariat for Foreign Affairs two million rubles for the needs of the revolutionary Internationalist movement."

Volumes more of evidence could be produced along this same line, but there is no need to follow the matter further. Lenin and his colleagues, without any exceptions, were convinced all through the first years of their rule in Russia that the Russian Revolution was only a beginning. Lenin, when he first entered Petrograd in April, 1917, had hailed not the revolution in Russia, but "the world socialist revolution," and he continued to think along those lines. The Bolshevik leaders believed that a socialist revolution would sweep Europe almost at once and extend over the entire world soon afterwards. They regarded their Russian successes only as the first steps toward greater victories, and they originally valued the Russian gains only because these enabled them to go forward with more ambitious plans. Time and again they showed themselves ready to sacrifice Russian interests to promote their brand of internationalism. The appropriation of two million rubles for revolutionary work abroad at a time of great stringency in Russia was a case in point. This was partly a tribute to their confidence in the "revelations" of Marx-Engels-Lenin, and partly a reflection of events which seemed to be bearing out those expectations. The world—not just Europe—was filled with discontent and disorders. Strikes, demonstrations, riots were everywhere common. There were insurrections in some countries and full-scale, temporarily successful, socialist revolutions in Germany and Hungary. There was more than a modicum of justification both for the Bolsheviks' confidence and for the apprehensions of their opponents. There were many people besides Lenin and his colleagues who hoped or feared that there was (in Lenin's words) "a new epoch, the epoch of victorious socialism which is now beginning for Germany and for the whole world."

It would be unnecessary to labor this point if these facts had not been so often forgotten or suppressed. It was the Marxists who, in 1848, had defined themselves as the irreconcilable enemies of capitalism. And it was Lenin's party which formally and publicly began the hostilities in 1917. The Bolshevik "peace appeals" were not really appeals for peace. They were declarations of war against the capitalist states. The international relations of the period—including the Brest-Litovsk conference and peace, and the interventions and the refusal of the Allies to admit the Bolsheviks to the Versailles Conference, and the Allied blockade of Bolshevik Russia (which went on until 1920)—need to be studied with this background in mind. It is not reasonable to expect any government to aid those who are openly inciting its people to revolution. That is precisely what the Bolsheviks were doing. They repeatedly declared in so many words, and repeatedly backed up their words by actions, that they were the implacable enemies of any and all non-Bolshevik groups.

🎲 POWERLESS POLITICS

Before returning to the story of Brest-Litovsk, there is another background fact which must be set down. It is one which those who regard "power politics" as the sole root of international tensions and troubles might do well to ponder. When the Bolsheviks first took over in Petrograd and Moscow, and for some time thereafter, they didn't play "power politics" for the sufficient reason that they had no power. Russian military and naval force had vanished into the villages and cities to which the servicemen had returned. Russian industrial strength, though it had not yet reached its nadir, was rapidly diminishing. The Bolsheviks were not masters in Russia. They had neither lands nor resources with which to bargain with other Powers, nor forces with which to compel other Powers. They could offer neither effective resistance nor attractive inducements. The two things in their favor were the mutual preoccupations of the Great Powers with the war, and the state of mind and body which that long struggle of attrition had produced in the peoples of the world. And the Bolsheviks held ideological and propaganda weapons which they hoped and which the Western Powers feared might be effective against the war-weary masses. Words and ideas constituted their arsenal;

opportunism, their tactics. This was politics without power, but neither tensions nor troubles were abolished thereby. How words and ideas and unscrupulous opportunism were combined may be quickly exemplified.

One of the constantly repeated Bolshevik themes was the right of self-determination of nations and groups. They "categorically" proclaimed that "free self-determination" was one of "the inalienable rights of the Russian nationalities." One of their resolutions phrased it this way: "All nations in Russia must have the right of free separation therefrom and the rights of free and independent states." Presumably this applied to the Lithuanians and the Finns, both of whom declared their independence of Russia in 1917; and also to the Latvians, the Estonians, the Ukrainians, the Georgians, certain Siberian groups, and others who declared their "separation therefrom" and their establishment as "free and independent states" in 1918. But Bolshevik actions belied Bolshevik resolutions. The Bolsheviks sent armed bands into each of these new states and did their best to nullify separation and self-determination. What they couldn't cure they endured—temporarily. They gave formal recognition to the independence of Estonia, Latvia, and Georgia in 1918; to Lithuania and Finland in 1920; to Ukraine and Bielorussia in 1921. But Bolshevik troops conquered Georgia and put an end to its independence in 1921. Bielorussia, Ukraine, and Siberia were brought under Bolshevik control and incorporated in the new Union of Soviet Socialist Republics when that was established in 1922. Estonia, Latvia, and Lithuania existed somewhat longer. They were not absorbed by the U.S.S.R. until 1940. By then, politics without power had become politics of great power. But we must go back to the beginnings of "powerless politics"—back to Brest-Litovsk.

🐝 BREST-LITOVSK

Both the Bolsheviks and the Germans genuinely wanted a settlement, but their reasons were entirely different. The German High Command was planning a gigantic spring offensive in the hope of knocking the French and British out of the war before United States troops could make their presence felt. The German military therefore wanted to secure their eastern front. Germany also wanted free access to the rich resources of the Ukraine, and their long-range plans called for the transformation of Russia into a series of small German protectorates which could serve as bases for future conquests in Asia. The German Foreign Office wanted territorial gains which might later be used in bargaining with the Allies. There was some friction between the diplomats and the soldiers, but the soldiers held the whip hand and their wish prevailed. Peace—"a victor's peace to crown a victor's war"—was desirable to the Germans. Peace at any price was an absolute imperative to the Bolsheviks. Lenin was very realistic about the situation. He was determined that his revolution and his power should be preserved as a basis for his world revolution. He recognized that he could not defend his regime against German troops and he judged that the entry of German forces into the Bolshevik portion of the wedge would mean a quick ending to his dreams. The only chance, as he saw it, was to make peace with Germany on whatever terms he could get and then to gamble that the Allies would win the war

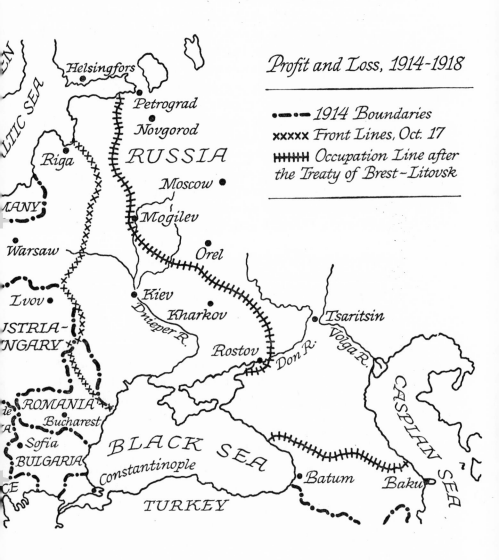

Profit and Loss, 1914–1918

•—•—• *1914 Boundaries*
xxxxx *Front Lines, Oct. 17*
ᚻᚻᚻᚻ *Occupation Line after the Treaty of Brest–Litovsk*

and wipe out the Bolshevik-German peace. Said Lenin in answer to those who opposed his policy, "Germany is still only pregnant with revolution; and a quite healthy child has been born to us—a socialist republic which we may kill if we begin war."

Trotsky, who foresaw that the Brest-Litovsk conference would be fully reported to the world, saw the peace negotiations as an unparalleled chance to present the Bolshevik case to a huge audience. As the chief Bolshevik negotiator, he made the most of his opportunities for spreading propaganda. One of his publicity tricks, brought out when the negotiations broke down in February, was the declaration, "no war, no peace." ("We withdraw from the war, but we are obliged to refuse to sign the peace treaty. . . .") This, however, did not satisfy the Germans, who promptly began an offensive which was virtually unopposed. The day after it started, Lenin and Trotsky wired Berlin that they would sign a peace. The Germans, when they replied, set up new terms and gave the Bolsheviks forty-eight hours to accept them, three days to sign the peace, and two weeks to ratify it. The terms were harsh (although the semi-official German press described them as establishing a "peace of understanding and conciliation"), and some of Lenin's associates were opposed to them. There was a bitter fight in the Party's Central Committee which ended only when Lenin threatened his complete withdrawal if the German offer were rejected. The committee finally voted as follows: to accept, 7; to reject, 4; not voting, 4. The treaty was signed on March 3, 1918, and the Fourth Congress of Soviets ratified it.

If the Treaty of Brest-Litovsk and a subsequent treaty which the Germans exacted in August had been carried out, Russia would have lost 34 per cent of her population, 32 per cent of her agricultural land, 54 per cent of her industries, 89 per cent of her coal mines, and 98 per cent of her oil fields. But the treaty was never fully executed, so that Lenin bought the survival of his regime at a great bargain. Eight months after Brest-Litovsk, Germany signed the Armistice and her treaty with the Bolsheviks was wiped out. So was the German occupation of Ukraine and so were her other interventions. Her place was taken by the victorious Allies and interventions continued as did the Bolshevik Revolution. The most complicated story is that of Ukraine.

GENESIS AND GROWTH OF UKRAINIAN NATIONALISM

We have not dealt separately with Ukraine since its incorporation into the Russian Empire in the reign of Catherine II. It will be recalled that Catherine extended the institution of serfdom into the region, and, further, that this "New Russia" became economically very important. But for all that it was legally a part of the empire, Ukraine remained a borderland where Ukrainians jostled Great Russians (and vice versa) and where both jostled Poles and Jews. Sometimes the jostling was literal and physical, more often it was intellectual and figurative. The new Ukrainian nobility created by Catherine and her successors became quite generally and thoroughly Polonized. They, along with some intellectuals, had romantic dreams of a Polish restoration. Such dreams, however, took no account either of the realities of power or of the gulf which separated the dreamers from the people. Equally removed from the people was a literary nationalism which grew and flourished among some Ukrainian intellectuals in the middle of the nineteenth century. Its center was the small, secret "Brotherhood of Saint Cyril and Saint Methodius," one of whose members, the serf-born painter and poet Shevchenko enjoyed a considerable vogue in Moscow and St. Petersburg as well as in Kiev. The interest of this group in the songs and stories of the peasants—the folk-history of the Ukrainian past—led to a development of the study of Ukrainian national history and to the appearance of Ukrainian nationalist historians. Some of these people were scholars, but more were political agitators who used their versions of the past as means of getting power. When one of the genuine historians, Kulish, administered scholarly rebukes for their exaggerations of "the Ukrainian national idea," they turned upon him and succeeded in discrediting him.

The Austrian government, which suffered from the machinations of the Russian Pan-Slavs among the Slavs within the Hapsburg lands, was quick to use this opportunity of embarrassing her opponent. A new center of Ukrainian nationalists was created in Lvov under Austrian auspices. It soon was linked to Ukrainian politician-scholars of the universities of Kiev and Kharkov. Perhaps nothing much would have come of this if the government of Alexander II had not made the irreparable blunder of trying to Russify the Ukrainians. Repression begat opposition, and the Austrians skillfully exploited the situation by fostering Ukrainian separatism. It did not catch hold even among the politician-scholars for some time. Dragomanov, who dominated the Ukrainian nationalist movement during the 1880's, had strongly opposed separation from Russia. "All talk of separatism," he once said, "is simply to be laughed at." His influence lasted into the 1890's. Then the Austrians found a scholar-politician who would work with them. His name was Michael Hrushevsky, and they gave him the Chair of East European History at the University of Lvov. Mr. W. E. D. Allen succinctly stated Hrushevsky's record in the following paragraphs:

His magnificent *History* [of Ukraine-Rus] was to build a sound foundation for Ukrainian separatism. He succeeded in representing 'Ukraine-Rus' as something entirely different from 'Moscovia.' According to this thesis Kievan

Russia was the cradle of 'Ukraine-Rus,' but the Russian state which was later constituted round Novgorod . . . and Moscow, was in no way the true successor of Kiev. . . .

All the work of Hrushevsky, both historical and linguistic, formed the basis for the activities of the Lvov politicians who . . . had declared themselves adherents of 'political separatism.' [2]

The greater freedom of the Duma period made it possible for Hrushevsky to move to Kiev and carry on his work there. His nationalist theme found rather extensive response, but the separatist theme was less popular and the Ukrainians generally were loyal to Russia during World War I. There were some troubles between the anti-Russian and pro-Russian groups of Ukrainian nationalists, and during Russia's early successes on the southwestern front the pro-Russian groups sometimes took vengeance against the anti-Russians. This was reversed when the Germans came into Ukraine, but in general the Germans did not have much success in stirring up or utilizing anti-Russianism. Matters stood in a rather uneasy balance at the time of the February/March Revolution, but the vigorous leaders of the Ukrainian separatist movement—Hrushevsky, Vinnichenko, and Petliura—soon changed that. They organized a "Ukrainian Conference" which selected a "Ukrainian Rada." Late in June, 1917, the Rada proclaimed the establishment of the "Autonomous Ukrainian Republic." The Provisional Government in Petrograd could only protest and then acquiesce. But the Rada, as Vinnichenko himself freely admitted, did not really represent the Ukrainian people and did not have their support. It had, in Vinnichenko's words, imposed itself upon the people in the hope of getting the help of foreign Powers to maintain the old social order. The Bolsheviks, who were backed by German money and who promised the people land and property, began to build up a following in the cities. They were not ready to challenge the Rada in October/November, 1917, but they did so soon after. They took Kharkov and set up there a Provisional Ukrainian Soviet Government. Both this "government" and the Rada sent agents to the Brest-Litovsk meetings.

The Germans chose to deal with the Rada. They signed agreements with the Rada, forced the Bolsheviks to withdraw their forces from Ukraine, and sent in an Austro-German army of occupation. The Rada was kept as the nominal government until it was clear that it could not deliver the foodstuffs and minerals which it had promised to the Germans. Then the Rada was most unceremoniously dismissed, and the Germans installed their puppet, Skoropadsky, as "dictator." Both the Rada and the general ruled only on German sufferance and "only with the support of German bayonets." When the Germans were forced to evacuate Ukraine after the 1918 armistice, their puppets disappeared with them. Even before the Germans had left, the Bolsheviks had come back in force. Rich, unhappy Ukraine became a land of anarchy, and a battleground contended over by Reds, Whites, Poles, and various other groups including plain brigands. Vinnichenko, Petliura, and some others announced the formation of the "Ukrainian People's Republic" under the rule of a Directory which, naturally, included themselves. Their forces captured Kiev in December, 1918. Two months later the Bolsheviks took Kiev away from them and held it until September, when they lost it to Denikin's Volunteer Army. Then back came the Bolsheviks for the third time. Altogether, Kiev changed hands a dozen times between 1917 and 1921. The situation in the rest of Ukraine was hardly less confused. The "Petliurians" fought the Bolsheviks and the Volunteer Army and almost anybody else who happened to be around. All the participants in these wars—Reds, Whites, Poles, Petliurians, local chieftains—were guilty of constant attacks on Jews during the year 1919. Repeated pogroms culminated in what Allen describes as "probably the greatest pogrom of all time" at the town of Proskurov. Jewish sources estimate that upwards of 31,000 Jews perished in Ukraine during 1919.

THE WHITES

Another center of conflict was in the south, which became the base for several anti-Bolshevik groups. To it gravitated Whites of all kinds, with much dissension among them. The Cossack Krasnov set up an independent "Republic of the Don" over which, with German help, he maintained a precarious hold. Generals Alexeyev, Kaledin, and Kornilov also set up in this area a Volunteer Army. This force had the support of the French and the British—the former largely concentrating in Odessa and the Crimea; the latter, in the northern Caucasus. It came under the command of General Denikin in April, 1918. His announced aim was the "restoring of a united sovereign Russia," and he claimed for himself "supreme authority" in the regions occupied by the Volunteer Army. At one time this included all of southern Russia, but the Volunteer Army never had the support of the peasant majority so that it was like a house built on sand. Denikin's successor, General Wrangel, continued to fight—being driven ever farther west—until the closing months of 1920. The war was fought on both sides with the utmost viciousness and brutality. There were Red terrors and White terrors, and the people suffered terribly at the hands of both.

Much activity centered in the regions of the Volga and the vast expanse of Siberia. The various White groups in these areas were even more disunified, and the situation was even more complicated by foreign interventions than in Ukraine. By the summer of 1918, there were a dozen separate "governments" in this area, and antibolshevism was virtually the only thing they had in common. The most unified of all the groups—really the only effective fighting force—was the Czechoslovak Legion. Its story is curious. Most of its members had originally been conscripts in the Austrian army. During the war, sometimes singly but often in large groups, they had gone over to the Russians. The tsar's government would not permit them to form a separate unit, but this permission was given by the Provisional Government. There were about 45,000 such soldiers in Ukraine when the Bolsheviks signed the armistice with the Germans. It was agreed between the French government and the Czech political leaders that the legion should be transferred intact to the western front. Since Archangel was closed by ice, it was necessary to transport them all across Siberia to Vladivostok. Permission was sought from the Bolshevik authorities and was granted. The Czechs began their long trek eastward. But the permission was twice withdrawn, twice reissued, then modified, and finally, in May, 1918, withdrawn entirely. Trotsky ordered that every armed Czechoslovak be shot on sight. This led to open war between the Czechs and the Bolsheviks, and the Czechs were successful in forcing their way along the Trans-Siberian Railroad, over which they established control. Capture of towns and stations by the Czechs was followed by the establishment of self-appointed "governments" in these places. The Essars in Samara set up a "Committee of Members of the Constituent Assembly." It lasted through the summer. The capture of Omsk and Tomsk was followed by the establishment of "The Provisional Government of Western Siberia" under rather radical Essars. This was soon replaced by a strongly conservative "Siberian Provisional Government," which declared Siberian independence. These groups, not without considerable difficulty, formed an all-Russian government (The Ufa Directory) in September, 1918. Meanwhile the Czechs had reached Vladivostok, and kicked out the Soviet government of the city. Various claimants for power appeared, including the ultraconservative Horvath; the Japanese-supported Semenov; and the British-sponsored Admiral Kolchak.

The man who was responsible for the British decision to back Kolchak once told me that his purpose was "to establish a new eastern front against the Germans in Siberia." To that end the British gave Kolchak support when, in November, 1918, he overthrew the completely disunited and powerless Ufa Directory and established himself as the "Supreme Ruler." For some months, the British investment seemed about to pay dividends. Kolchak rallied a sizable army and, against very weak Bolshevik opposition, advanced westward almost to the Volga. Things looked very black for the Bolsheviks. Allied troops were supporting the White "Provisional Administration of the North" in the Archangel region. General Yudenich, with British naval support in the Baltic, advanced to the edges of Petrograd. Denikin, in control of south Russia, almost reached the Volga from that side. But there was no co-ordination of efforts. Kolchak did not push on to join the White forces at Archangel, which he might have done. The Allied troops were shoved out of that area and so did not help Yudenich. Denikin went his own way in the south. So, by the weakness and division of their enemies, and by their own almost superhuman efforts, the Reds beat back the threats one by one.

When the tide turned, it ebbed very fast indeed. The basic reason for the Red triumph was that the White forces were all essentially conservative and the peasants were all essentially radical. Both Kolchak and Denikin favored the restoration of the landlords, for example. The governments of the Whites demonstrated an astounding lack of understanding and consideration of the people. It was not only the reactionaries and the conservatives who were guilty of this. The liberal and radical groups were almost as bad. Kolchak's last Minister of Justice once told me that their cabinet meetings were given over to theoretical discussions and to petty jealousies and squabbles. He added that neither he nor any of his colleagues ever made any serious effort to discover what the people wanted or to satisfy those desires. But this was wisdom long after the event. The facts of Allied support and influence also counted against the Whites, and the Bolsheviks made shrewd use of this. One version of a propaganda ditty which was popular after Kolchak's fall at the end of 1919 will illustrate this point:

> The uniform is British,
> The epaulettes, from France.
> Japan sends tobacco.
> Kolchak leads the dance.

> The uniforms are tattered.
> The epaulettes are gone.
> So is the tobacco, and
> Kolchak's day is done.

The day of the White armies was soon done, too. By the beginning of 1920, Yudenich had been defeated; the Donets coal basin had been reoccupied by the Reds; and Denikin was in full retreat. During the spring, the Red forces won the Baku-Grozny oil fields; and, in the fall, Wrangel was driven from the Crimea. But the story of the Bolsheviks' troubles in the first years of their regime has hardly been begun.

🐌 THE POLISH INTERVENTION, 1918–20

The collapse of the Russian, German, and Austrian empires gave the Poles the opportunity for which they had been waiting for almost a century and a half. A Polish Republic was proclaimed at Warsaw on November 3, 1918. Two days before that, the Poles had begun a war against Ukraine for the recovery of Galicia and such other lands as they could get. This was characteristic of the republic's first government (headed by Pilsudski), which took as its first task the recovery of lands taken from Poland in the partitions of the eighteenth century. It was Pilsudski's intention to unite Lithuania, Bielorussia, and Ukraine in a federation under Polish leadership. To achieve this end, he had to fight the Lithuanians, the Bielorussians, the Ukrainians, and the Bolsheviks. He began by conquering Vilna in the spring of 1919, and then swung his forces against Galicia and Volhynia. A year later, having reached a working agreement with Petliura, the Poles marched eastward into Ukraine, taking Kiev in May. The Bolsheviks gathered their forces and their army, commanded by Tukhachevski, reconquered Kiev and Vilna, and drove westward almost to Warsaw. The Poles then sought, and, on a promise of renouncing future conquests, got the support of the French and British. With munitions from the West, with the expert advice of Marshal Weygand of France, and with gallant efforts by his Poles, Pilsudski drove the Bolsheviks eastward beyond the "Curzon Line" which the Western Powers had suggested as the proper eastern boundary of Poland. This was, perhaps, the lowest point of Bolshevik power, and Lenin felt constrained to accept the peace terms which Poland imposed. The preliminary treaty was signed at Riga in October, 1920; the final treaty, in March, 1921.

This was the last great diplomatic reversal which the Bolsheviks suffered, although they were excluded from the Washington Conference (1921–22), as they had been from the Versailles Conference in 1919. Despite their continuing efforts to promote world revolution, the diplomatic barriers began to go down. An Anglo-Soviet Trade Pact was concluded in 1921, and during the years 1921–22 nineteen treaties of peace or of friendship were concluded between the new Soviet state and its neighbors. Soviet Russia and Weimar Germany—the two pariah nations—were invited to the Genoa Conference of 1922. When it failed, the two signed an agreement of their own—the Treaty of Rapallo. This was an economic agreement, not an alliance, as many suspected at the time, but it established a Soviet-German entente which flourished for about a dozen years.

THE DRIVE FOR WORLD REVOLUTION

Lenin and his Bolsheviks had continued to press for world revolution throughout these first years of their regime. They had given all aid they possibly could to the German Communists when these groups revolted in 1918–19, and they also supported the Communist revolt of Bela Kun in Hungary (1919). This support was more than verbal. "The All-Russian Central Executive Committee," read a decree of October, 1918, "has therefore resolved to levy on the propertied classes in cities and villages a lump-sum tax of ten billion rubles . . ." for the support of the revolution in Russia and abroad. And to quote from the official *History of the Communist Party of the Soviet Union* (*Bolshevik*) (1939 edition):

In March 1919, on the initiative of the Bolsheviks, headed by Lenin, the First Congress of the Communist Parties of various countries, held in Moscow, founded the [Third] Communist International. Although many of the delegates were prevented by the blockade and imperialist persecution from arriving in Moscow, the most important countries of Europe and America were represented at this First Congress. The work of the congress was guided by Lenin.

. . . The congress adopted a manifesto to the proletariat of all countries, calling upon them to wage a determined struggle for the dictatorship of the proletariat and for the triumph of Soviets all over the world. . . . Thus was founded an international revolutionary proletarian organization of a new type—the Communist International [Comintern]—the Marxist-Leninist International.

This was certainly an open avowal of purpose and a frank statement of Russian leadership in the revolutionary movement. Corroboration, if any was needed, was furnished by the installation of Communist regimes under Russian sponsorship in Armenia, Azerbaijan, Georgia, and in Central Asia. Further evidence of intent was provided by the revolutionary "Congress of the Peoples of the East" summoned in 1920 by the Russians for the purpose of stirring up and using Asiatic nationalisms. In 1922, Soviet Russia annexed the allegedly independent "Far Eastern Republic" which had been established subsequent to the fall of Kolchak and the withdrawal of Western troops. And also, by 1922, the Russian Communist Party [3] had begun its active support and attempted direction of the Chinese Communists.

The Soviet government maintained consistently that there was no necessary connection between it and the activities of Communist Parties outside of Russia, or between it and the Comintern. This was a transparent fiction which fooled only those who wished to believe it. There was, however, a real difference between the bases of the formal Soviet foreign policy and the Comintern's promotion of world revolution. National policies including those of Soviet Russia, depend for their success upon the power-in-being of the nation. Power-in-being includes armed strength, economic strength, the attitude of the people, and the relative power position of the nation compared to that of other nations. Comintern policies called for the exploitation of existing conflicts and weaknesses, and depended more upon the opponent's weakness than upon the attacker's strength. They were policies of finesse rather than of force and could be executed by a very small body of trained, disciplined, unscrupulous revolutionaries who operated under the same type of leadership. The Political Bureau (Politburo) of the Soviet Communist Party supplied the leadership. The Communist Parties of all nations have supplied the drilled and obedient followers. This should not be interpreted as meaning that the obedience was letter-perfect from the beginning, nor that the leadership assumed by Lenin and his successors has never been challenged. The struggles of the Bolsheviks within their section of the wedge during the first years amply demonstrate the opposition they faced.

✪ OPPOSITION WITHIN THE RED ZONE

The opposition forces were as diverse within this area as they were outside of it. They ranged from extreme Rightists through Kadets and Moderate Socialists (as well as Essars and Mensheviks) to Anarchists. They included workers and peasants, as well as intellectuals; men of wealth, and members of the middle classes. They also included the uncoordinated actions of individuals who had no special party affiliations. Many of the professional bureaucrats, for example, grimly fought rearguard, harassing actions by refusing to hand over funds, keys, documents, files, and so on to their Bolshevik-appointed successors. The Bolsheviks called this sabotage and counterrevolution (which it was) and dealt with it by means of the Cheka and the Red Guards (later, the Red Army) and by special "committees." There were protests and criticisms and mutinies and insurrections by peasants and workers and Red Army men and others:

We workers of the Bogatyr factory . . . call the attention of the People's Commissars, who claim that they were elected by us and that they defend our interests, to the fact that we protest most energetically against their acts in relation to us as workers. We protest against the shooting of workers who asked for bread. . . . We protest against the civil war which the commissars have started all over Russia. We protest against the food policy. . . . We protest against the policy . . . which has delivered us to . . . the Germans.

[Saratov] A group of Red Army soldiers, numbering according to official figures about six hundred and according to unofficial estimates about three thousand, revolted against the Soviet authorities, demanding the reelection of the Soviet and free trade in flour and other food products. . . .

[Perm] . . . Enraged by the enforcement of the bread monopoly, the peasants of Shlykovsky Volost killed a member of the Gubernia Executive Committee, four Red soldiers, and a grain accountant.

During the early part of this month [November, 1918] in Riazin, Kaluga and . . . Tula gubernias, counterrevolutionary elements and local kulaks revolted against the Soviet Government. The rebels, organized in bands, overthrew local Soviet authorities . . . broke up committees of the poor. . . .[4]

In Moscow itself there were formed the Moscow Center of the Right, a highly conservative group which sought German aid; the Union for the Defense of the Fatherland and Freedom, composed mostly of Kadets; the Union for the Regeneration of Russia, made up of left-wing liberals and socialists; and the Socialist-Revolutionaries of the Right, which included many Mensheviks as well as Essars. These last three groups asked aid from the Allies. Their activities led Lenin to declare martial law in Moscow in May, 1918; and, a little later, to order the expulsion of the "Right Socialists" from the soviets. The Bolsheviks were also attacked, mostly for signing the Brest-Litovsk Treaty, by the left Essars. Since they were members of the Central Executive Committee of the Soviet and of other governing bodies, the left Essars carried on their fight from within. In July, 1918, they attempted an uprising against the Bolsheviks but were routed both in Moscow and in Petrograd. They were then expelled from the Fifth All-Russian Congress of Soviets and from other governing bodies, which now became wholly Bolshevik.

ⓖ TERROR AND THE CLASS WAR

The Bolsheviks answered this internal opposition with terror. Said Dzerzhinsky, first head of the Cheka, "We stand for organized terror—this should be frankly admitted. Terror is an absolute necessity during times of revolution. Our aim is to fight against the enemies of the Soviet Government and of the new order of life. . . . To these [enemies] we show no mercy." [5] Among the thousands whom the Cheka killed were Nicholas, Alexandra, and all their children. This action was approved by the Central Executive Committee of the Soviet. (Incidentally, and contrary to the rumors which were widely circulated at one time, no member of the the tsar's immediate family survived this massacre.) What went on before an attempt was made on Lenin's life on August 30, 1918, was as nothing to what went on thereafter. A systematic Red terror was begun. The Council of People's Commissars authorized the "shooting of all persons associated with White Guard organizations, plots, and conspiracies." As Bunyan noted, "Arrests and executions spread rapidly throughout the country and continued on a wholesale scale for several weeks." How guilt was determined was explained by one of the heads of the Cheka: "Do not ask for incriminating evidence to prove that a person opposed the Soviet either by arms or by word. Your first duty is to ask him what class he belongs to, what were his origin, education and occupation. These questions should decide the fate of the prisoner." This may come as a shock to those who have been taught that such methods and such standards were innovations of the Stalinist regime. But it was Lenin who once asked rhetorically, "How can you make a revolution without shooting?" It was also Lenin who sent the following telegram to Zadonsk Soviet: "Take most vigorous action against the kulaks and their allies, the left Socialist-Revolutionary swine. Issue an appeal to the poor peasants. Organize them. . . . The Kulak blood-suckers must be unmercifully suppressed. . . ."

Lenin's reference to the kulaks and to the poor peasants introduces another technique used extensively by the Bolsheviks. This was the promotion of "the class war" in the villages. Peasants were arbitrarily classified by Soviet authorities into rich (*kulaks*), middle (*seredniaks*), and poor (*bedniaks*), and the last-named were encouraged to attack and to despoil the others. In May, 1918, the Central Executive Committee of the Soviet resolved:

. . . it is imperative to point out the urgent necessity of uniting the toiling peasantry against the village *bourgeoisie*. Local soviets must undertake immediately the task of explaining to the poor that their interests are opposed to those of the kulaks, and of arming the poor with the purpose of establishing their dictatorship in the village.

And Lenin in a fighting speech a month later said:

We are engaged in building up a dictatorship, a regime of violence against the exploiters; whoever does not grasp this simple truth we cast away from us. . . . We need . . . to arouse the poor against the rich . . . to lead in the food war against the kulaks. The fight against the kulaks is taking the form of uniting the poor against them . . . and this we have already done.

The Committees of the Poor were organized the next week. They cooperated with "Workers' Food Requisitioning Squads" and with "The Food Army" (both of which were set up a little later) to carry out "food crusades." This simply meant that armed groups of workers and soldiers, acting with the full sanction of the government, roamed the countryside seeking and taking food. The Committees of the Poor acted as spotters or to point out their fellows who might be concealing grain or other foodstuffs. Few could resist the opportunity to pay off old scores. This, too, had been calculated by the Bolsheviks who intended to give free rein to old hatreds and ancient grudges as a part of their technique of dividing and ruling. Even more important was the garnering of food, which will be dealt with in the next chapter. The beginnings of two other instruments of government need to be noted here: the Red Army and the 1918 Constitution.

THE RED ARMY

The Bolsheviks began to build the Workers' and Peasants' Red Army in January, 1918. Its forerunner had been the Red Guards, who had been organized under the direction of the Military Revolutionary Committee. The Red Army (and the Red Navy) were at first volunteer organizations and were quite democratic. Power rested in the soldiers' (and sailors') committees, which elected the officers. This proved too loose and inefficient for the demands which the continuing revolution placed upon the armed forces. A decree of the Central Executive Committee at the end of May stated that "the All-Russian Central Executive Committee of Soviets finds that present conditions in the country necessitate our changing from voluntary enlistment in the army to a general conscription of workers and peasants." The *bourgeoisie* were later conscripted into "reserve regiments to do the menial work of the army." Immediate control of the army and navy was vested in a Revolutionary War Council, headed by Trotsky; overall control of the "mobilization of the forces and resources of the country" for defense was given to the Council of Workers' and Peasants' Defense, which was created in November, 1918. Lenin was named president of this council; Trotsky and Stalin were both members of it.

The change to a conscript army was accompanied by the reintroduction of strict military discipline on the old basis. To overcome the almost complete lack of trained Bolshevik or worker leadership, Trotsky invited and coerced officers of the tsarist army into serving the Red Army. More than 22,000 tsarist officers joined the Red Army in 1918. Their good behavior was insured by holding their families as hostages and by subordinating them to "Political Commissars." These were either Party members or, rarely, what might be called "trusties" and they had a dual responsibility. Their first task was security—to watch over the officers. Their second job was to propagandize for bolshevism. The army numbered about half a million in 1918, and went up to a high of approximately four and a half million in 1921, dropping to just over half a million in 1923.

❧ THE 1918 CONSTITUTION

The Third All-Russian Congress of Soviets promulgated in January, 1918, the "Declaration of the Rights of the Toiling and Exploited People." This was a general statement of principles which called for all power to the soviets; the nationalization of land, resources, banks, and factories; the formation of a workers' and peasants' army; and the establishment of universal, compulsory labor. It was made a part of the Fundamental Law of the R.S.F.S.R. which was adopted by the Fifth Congress of Soviets in July, 1918. This first Soviet constitution was based upon the *Communist Manifesto, Capital,* and the experiences of the Paris Commune of 1871 (which the Communists with complete disregard for historical accuracy claim as their first revolution). There were, of course, some modifications due to circumstances and to Lenin's interpretations, but the line of descent is clear in the document. The *Manifesto* had called for the welding of the workers into a class-conscious group which could overthrow the *bourgeoisie* and take over power. The 1918 Constitution declared, "Power must belong completely and exclusively to the toiling masses"; and it disfranchised the *bourgeoisie* and gave disproportionately large representation to the urban workers. The Commune had popularized the slogan "Expropriate the expropriators," which was an abbreviated way of expressing the Marx-Engels theory that capitalism was the robbery of the worker and that this should be reversed. The 1918 Constitution decreed the confiscation by the state of land, resources of the land, mines, banks, and factories.

The 1918 Constitution was a class document and didn't pretend to be anything else. It did not establish either a democracy or majority rule (the peasants were still the majority in Russia, but they were subordinated to the urban minority). The constitution was intended to make possible a government by an elite, and that is what it did. The elite, of course, was the Communist Party.

CHAPTER XXII

Some Economic and Other Experiments

That the preceding chapter dealt mainly with foreign relations while this chapter deals chiefly with domestic affairs should not lead anyone to suppose that the two were unrelated. On the contrary, domestic developments and foreign affairs reacted and interacted upon each other in many ways.

ECONOMIC CONDITIONS, 1917

A resolution passed by one of the government bodies in 1918 called attention to this relationship. "The conditions of Russia's economic development are determined, on the one hand, by the change in its boundaries in consequence of the Brest-Litovsk Treaty, and, on the other hand, by the change in its mode of production." [1] This was a considerable oversimplification, which ignored many points. Two and a half years of war followed by two revolutions had also wrought great changes in Russia's economic development. What those great events had done to the Russian economy was very ably described by the late Sir John Maynard. Here is his brief summation of the situation at the end of 1917:

Some of the economic conditions at the November Revolution were these. The cultivated area had been reduced by the war by a sixth, the number of horses available for agriculture by nearly a third, the cereal harvest was down by 14 per cent. A very imperfectly industrialised country had been deprived of its access to foreign manufactures, except through the north and the far east. The produce of industry was a little more than three-fourths of what it had been in 1913. The railway system had suffered severely from the strain of war. Most of it led towards the most highly industrialised regions, and these had passed out of Russia's hands. Some of the surviving factories catered for luxuries, for which the Revolution had stopped the demand. The money in circulation was twelve times as much as in July, 1914. In the country the paper rouble was worth from a tenth to an eighth of the pre-war rouble, though the foreign exchange was rather better than this, doubt-less because a virtual blockade had for three years stopped imports, except of war material, as well as exports.

It was not yet economic exhaustion. The country was to endure another three years of war and blockade, with the temporary loss of large portions of its territories, including those which provided its surplus food, its cotton, and its principal fuels and metals, before that stage was reached.[2]

Sir John did not mention what the resolution had called "the change in its mode of production," but this was also a major factor. The resolution had declared in its opening paragraph:

> Our economic policy, the basic aim of which is to overthrow the bourgeois and landowning classes and to transfer power to the proletariat, is at present directed toward the establishment of a socialist order in Russia and the struggle against the aggression of international imperialism. All our meas-ures in transition to socialism are influenced by the bitter fight which we must wage against the *bourgeoisie* inside and outside of Russia.[3]

The necessities of the "bitter fight" were real enough, but they were not the whole story. One may reasonably suspect that the temptation to use these necessities to excuse unpopular actions and to explain faults and failures was often too great to be withstood. William Henry Cham-berlin, whose reputation is not pro-Soviet and whose two-volume history, *The Russian Revolution* (1935), is still the best single account of the years 1917 to 1921, thought that economic developments might have taken "a much more moderate turn" if there had been "no civil war and no foreign intervention." Less cautious writers than Mr. Chamberlin have often flatly asserted this to be the case. However, the thesis that the expansion of the revolution and the foreign wars were the decisive determinants seems dubious. The Bolsheviks were committed by their doctrines both to war against the capitalists and to the attempt to build a new economic and social order. The conditions under which they fought and built were certainly not wholly of their own devising, but the choice to try to build and to fight under those conditions was theirs. Events forced stratagems and tactical compromises. The Bolsheviks did not have any exclusive control over events, but they had some control and prided themselves on being sufficiently flexible to accommodate to whatever they could not control. Flexibility was, in fact, the keynote of their policies throughout these years.

"MILITANT COMMUNISM"

"War Communism" (or "Militant Communism"), which is the label Soviet historians give to this first period, was characterized by shifts, compromises, improvisations, opportunism, and harshness. Contrary to a rather widespread impression, the Bolsheviks did not, generally speaking, attempt to force all Russian life into a doctrinaire strait jacket. For the most part, it was an extraordinarily hand-to-mouth, day-by-day sort of business. The Bolsheviks were not omniscient and they made mistakes (which Lenin was wise enough to recognize and try to correct), and their doctrines were not, after all, detailed, precise instructions. They had an overall plan in the Marx-Engels-Lenin theories and they had many lesser plans, but these only indicated general principles and broad directions. Lenin's April Theses, for example, had called for the transfer of land and other properties from private to state ownership. This was no problem in the case of those very large areas of the economy which had been owned by the imperial family or in the case of the industries which had remained in private hands. But most of the privately owned lands and factories had already been taken away from their original owners. Were the factories to be taken away from the workers who had seized them and the lands from the peasants who had taken them? Yes, these lands and factories were to be taken, but not at once. (We have already seen how this was done.) Circumstances forced a temporary "tactical retreat" from the doctrines in these and other instances.

It should also be noted that decrees, orders, regulations, and instructions were not always either enforceable or enforced. It would be a mistake to assume, for example, that "the lives, health, and work of all persons engaged in any form of economic activity" were immediately safeguarded because a decree of May, 1918, established "labor inspection." There was a whole battery of laws decreeing the extension of social insurance and social assistance before 1917 and 1921, but as a Soviet study flatly states, "This whole body of laws was never effectively applied. . . . The assistance given was entirely unsatisfactory . . . ." and the whole record of these attempts is "only of historical interest." It was one thing to order, but quite another thing to make the order effective; and many orders were no more than expressions of intentions or sops to public opinion.

CONDITIONS WORSEN, 1917–21

There is not enough data available to permit a complete or detailed description of the economic state of Russia from 1917 to 1921, but there is enough to show clearly that conditions deteriorated during those years. The overall industrial production, which had stood at roughly three-fourths of the 1913 level in 1917, plunged to about one-sixth of that level by 1920. Coal production in 1917 was down to 82 per cent of the 1913 output; it dropped to 33 per cent of that figure in 1918. The 1920 production of pig iron was about 3 per cent of the prewar output, and so it went all along the line. According to Soviet historians, the gross output of large-scale industry in 1920 was just over one-seventh of the prewar amount, and the gross agricultural output was roughly half what it had been before the war. However, it may be more meaningful to cite a few facts about conditions in Odessa, which was a fair, average sample of Russian cities and towns. Fuel became so short in Odessa that the electric power station was closed, the water supply was shut off, the streetcar service was stopped, the municipal bathhouses were shut, and to get a little oil for cooking, one had to stand in line for forty-eight hours.

Two things stand out. The year 1917 was not the worst by any means. Matters got a whole lot worse before they grew any better. Second, the trouble in 1917 was less with supply than with distribution. There were foodstuffs in the country. There was fuel in stock. But the facilities for getting these things to urban areas were totally inadequate. This is what had forced the Provisional Government to attempt rationing. It had compelled the reduction in the bread from a pound a person a day (March, 1917) to three-quarters of a pound, then to half a pound, and, after the Bolshevik Revolution began, to one-eighth of a pound. Bread was literally the staff of life in Russia, and this was a starvation ration. How did the people manage to survive these years of acute hunger and hardship?

The glib and conventional answer is either that their survival is proof of the toughness of the Russians, or that only the tough survived. This is partly true, but it is far from a full answer to the question. For one thing, most of the people lived in country villages. One of the characteristics of the period of War Communism was the flight to the villages of many city dwellers. The population of Leningrad (Petrograd), for example, dropped from 2,300,000 in 1917 to 700,000 in 1919. All other Russian cities except Kuibyshev (Samara) also declined very sharply in population. Life in the villages was not easy. There were famine conditions in the grain-consuming (as opposed to the grain-producing) provinces by the spring of 1918. Following the droughts of 1920 and 1921, there were terrible famines (to some degree, man-made) which affected some 33 million persons, of whom more than half faced death by starvation. Ukraine was particularly hard hit. In spite of these things, it was easier to get food, fuel, and shelter in the country than in town.

One needs to bear in mind the obvious fact that Russia is a huge country and that conditions were not everywhere uniform. Even in the horrible famine years of 1921–22 in Ukraine, where three provinces had only 5 per cent (or less) of their normal crops, one province had a better than usual harvest. Russia, in other words, had a sort of economic defense in depth. Her reserves were not piled in one or ten or a hundred large depots, but in millions of tiny depots, which added up to a tremendous total. Another factor was the relative simplicity of the economic life of most of Russia's millions. A very high proportion of the people were not dependent either upon industry or upon an extensive trade. Most of their needs could be supplied locally and many could, in a pinch, be self-supplied. Long habituation to poverty and hardship was also of some importance. All of which is not to say that the hardy do not suffer from privation, but only that they are better able to take it. As for the cities, life there was worse, and men were reduced to all sorts of methods of trying to sustain themselves. Bootlegging, black market, and direct barter with the peasants for food and fuel were normal. A combination of circumstances and theory made things difficult for the rulers and the ruled.

The circumstances revolved around the continuing revolution and war. The theory called for the establishment of a barter economy between the food-raisers and the industrial workers, with the state acting as a sort of middleman. According to this scheme, the peasants would grow grains, raise livestock, and produce other food. The amounts needed for their own use and for seed or breeding would be left to them. Everything above this set amount was to be deposited with the government. Workers in factories, mines, and mills were to go on producing, and the surplus above their immediate needs was also to be deposited with the government. Then the government was to appraise the foodstuffs and the goods, work out some formula of equal values, and distribute the goods to the peasants, the food to the workers. This theory was, in part, a bow toward the doctrine of a moneyless economy—the same doctrine which led the Bolsheviks to decree that exchanges among nationalized industries should be by barter, and which led also to payment of wages in kind and to the effort to make money worthless. It was also, however, partly a bowing to certain economic realities. Farmers raise surpluses in order to earn money for taxes, rents, mortgage payments (and other charges of this sort) and also to provide the wherewithal for the purchase of necessities and luxuries. If these compulsions disappear—if rents and mortgages need not be paid, if commodities are not purchasable, or if the farmer's labor does not earn a normal return—then, as Maynard vividly expressed it, ". . . the driving-belt of the conveyor slips from its place, and the wheels which convey the grain to the hungry cease to function."

This is precisely what happened in Russia in the years of Militant Communism. The factories and shops could not, or did not, produce enough commodities to make possible any equitable exchange of goods and foods. The destruction, in accord with the doctrine of "expropriating the expropriators," of the peddlers and small merchants wiped out what had been the major system of distribution and exchange.[4] There were other difficulties in the way of the fulfillment of this barter scheme (for example, how does one decide how much the peasant needs for his own use and for his continuation in the business of growing things), but the inability to supply manufactured goods in exchange for food was the basic problem. The peasants simply declined to do business on those terms. They sold their surpluses to individuals or consumed them themselves. But they did not deposit the foodstuffs with the state—at least not willingly.

Food was an absolute necessity for the regime. It was the cities which were hungry, and it was on the cities that the Bolsheviks had to count for support. Unless the urban workers could be fed and clothed and warmed, the regime was sure to be overthrown. It was this necessity which led to the establishment of the Food Requisitioning Squads and the other coercive machinery which were described in the preceding chapter. "The class principle" was applied also to food rationing. Theoretically, no food could be had without ration cards, and "nonworkers" could have no ration cards unless they had "labor books" which certified that they had done their share of "assigned public work." The Food Decree of December, 1918, provided only for soldiers, sailors, state employees, and workers in mines, factories, shops, and transportation. (The Moscow and Petrograd bread ration for "nonworkers" was then at the rate of one-sixteenth of a pound of bread a day—"to insure," remarked Zinoviev, "that the *bourgeoisie* do not forget the smell of bread.")

✺ THE GOVERNMENT VERSUS THE PEASANTS

The Bolshevik regime in its early years was unable to arrange the production of sufficient goods or food to supply the people. It lived, as one Party leader frankly put it, on its inheritance from the old regime. That is to say, it lived on the reserves stored in the millions of tiny depots. The government coaxed and coerced these reserves out of hiding in sufficient amounts to keep going, and they called forth terrific opposition to themselves in the process. The peasants, harassed and plundered and generally put upon, fought back with the only weapons they possessed. They evaded rules and orders and laws; bribed, fooled, and fought off enforcement agencies; concealed supplies and refused to grow foodstuffs. Large stocks escaped the dragnets which the government repeatedly cast. The peasants, in effect, went on strike. They stopped raising those crops which were subject to requisition, and when new crops were added to the list they stopped growing them, too. Lenin's efforts to counter this by vigorous encouragement of "communal farms" were even less successful than his other methods. (The coercive food-collecting agencies took roughly 125 per cent more foodstuffs from the peasants in 1919–20 than in the preceding year.) The peasants also killed and ate much of their livestock rather than see the animals confiscated for the benefit of someone else. These were the "man-made causes" of the 1921–22 famine. The extent of that disaster may be measured by the fact that starvation caused some three million deaths, and another six million died from related causes, such as disease and exhaustion.

The Bolsheviks very early discovered that men will not work merely for the joy of working. When wages will not buy necessities, let alone luxuries, and when other customary compulsions fail, new compulsions have to be introduced or new inducements have to be offered. The Bolsheviks used both compulsions and inducements. Strikes and work stoppages were declared "betrayals of the proletarian cause" (July, 1918); the (July) 1918 Constitution of the R.S.F.S.R. declared that work "was the duty of every citizen of the Republic and proclaims [proclaimed] the slogan: 'He who does not work, shall not eat.' "; and a decree of October, 1918, laid it down that "All citizens of the R.S.F.S.R. . . . are subject to compulsory labor." Other instruments of compulsion have been mentioned previously, as have, also, the laws dealing with social insurance. The latter were intended as part of the inducements. Money wages were increased, but raging inflation made paper money meaningless. ("For the purpose of balancing the accounts of the People's Bank [created by merging all private banks, and charged with handling the finances of the national economy]" ran a decree of October, 1918, "the Soviet of People's Commissars hereby authorizes the Bank to issue additional banknotes to the amount of 35.5 billion rubles.") Payment in kind was therefore resorted to so that people worked directly for food and goods.

RESULTS

The result was summed up by Lenin in his report to the Tenth Party Congress, "The poverty of the working class was never so vast and acute as in the period of its dictatorship. The enfeeblement of workers and peasants is close to the point of complete incapacitation of work."

Very few of the experiments and improvisations were turning out as planned. The nationalization of foreign trade (June, 1918); the attempts to capture or else destroy the co-operative movement (1918); the attempts to transfer trade from private to state control, to establish a moneyless economy, and to collect extraordinary taxes and taxes in kind (October, 1918); the abolition of inheritance (April, 1918) and of private ownership of real estate (August, 1918) all had failed to achieve the desired objectives. So had the government's attempt to regulate labor and wages (October, 1918). The Supreme Economic Council, which had originally been intended as a policy-planning organization with very broad supervisory powers, became during the summer of 1918 the chief central organ for controlling industrial production (or, at least, trying to control it). But here the various commissariats— Trade, Finance, Industry, and so on—overlapped the SEC with a consequent confusion and conflict.

It was Lenin's conviction when the Supreme Economic Council was created that it would be the sole survivor of the "withering away of the state," and it was therefore very highly regarded by all concerned. At the head of it was Alexis Rykov, very close to Lenin in those days but purged as a "traitor" in 1937. His associates on the SEC were other state officials (all Party members), technical experts (most of whom were not Communists, but who were there because the Communists needed them), and agents of the trade unions. The unions in these very early days were practically the masters of industry, such as it was, and their men could not be kept out of the SEC. A running fight went on between the SEC and the unions for some time, until the unions were finally defeated. The original scheme had been for each branch of industry to be run by a committee composed of representatives of the unions in that branch. Each of these committees was to be represented on the SEC, which was to act as the co-ordinating agency for all industry together. The plan did not work well, partly because the government could not compel the local branches to obey orders.

It certainly was never the intention of Lenin and his men to produce the situation which he described in his report to the Party, nor was it altogether of their making. But they were the rulers of Russia and were therefore held responsible. Discontent, often manifesting itself in violent outbreaks, had occurred throughout these first years. Now the outbreaks increased in violence and in frequency, and, moreover, became clearly anti-Communist. Government food reserves and other stock piles were looted. Food and supplies in transit were highjacked, and there was a mounting wave of crime. The peasants were among the most rebellious, although active discontent was not confined to them. Professor Timasheff has noted that during 1920–21 there were peasant revolts in

21 out of the 50 provinces of European Russia. One was so successful that the whole province was out of Moscow's control for over a year. The climax came a week before the meeting of the Tenth Party Congress, when the sailors at the Kronstadt naval base rose under the slogan "Soviets without Communists." Bolshevik histories blame this uprising upon "White Guards, in complicity with Socialist-Revolutionaries, Mensheviks, and representatives of foreign states." All these may have been involved, but the causes were neither as simple nor as malicious as that account would imply. Discontent was bona fide and justifiable. The revolt was serious enough in itself, and it also carried symbolic overtones. Kronstadt had been one of Bolshevism's strongholds in 1917, and men from there had taken an extremely important part in the Petrograd coup. Now men from the same base were in open revolt against the regime which sailors from Kronstadt had helped to create. Their revolt was suppressed and the revolutionaries were annihilated, but the widespread discontent did not diminish. Suppression of force by force was not enough. As the official *History* disingenuously puts it, "The Party was confronted with the necessity of working out a new line of policy on all questions affecting the economic life of the country, a line that would meet the new situation. And the Party proceeded to work out such a line of policy on questions of economic development."

THE NEW ECONOMIC POLICY

The decision was not as easy as this account makes it sound. Some of the Party leaders ascribed the faults and failures to too little War Communism. These leaders proposed to stand uncompromisingly in the way they had begun and to increase, rather than to relax, their controls. The other group held that the failures had been caused by too much control and not too little. They therefore demanded a "tactical retreat," that is, a compromise of immediacies but not of the ultimate goal. Since Lenin led this second group, and since he ruthlessly cracked the whip on his followers, its way prevailed. The Tenth Party Congress ordered the adoption of a New Economic Policy. The NEP, as this was customarily known, was in force from 1921 to 1928.

The resumption of private trade and small private industries and certain other capitalistic forms in the domestic economy of Russia misled many observers into supposing that Lenin had put Russia on the road back to capitalism. The NEP was hailed as proof (which it was) that the system introduced in 1917–18 had failed, and also as proof (which it was not) that Russia was about to "return to normalcy." The Communist leaders, in contrast, spoke of the NEP as the road to communism. Unless it is supposed that they meant their own brand of communism this must also be considered an erroneous interpretation. The official explanation of the change used to be that undue enthusiasm had led to a major error. It had been forgotten that, according to the Party's gospels, socialism was a necessary intermediate stage. It was not possible, said the doctrine, to jump directly from capitalism to communism. That, however, is precisely what had been attempted and, ran the official explanation, it was necessary to make a fresh beginning by frankly going back to the intermediate stage. Later Communist explanations have said that the NEP was not really a return to anything because what Russia had had between 1917 and 1921 was not real communism anyway. It was merely a situation created, as the Party history now puts it, by the war and the blockade. This new explanation relieves the leaders of the onus of having made a bad blunder which they had to correct. Lenin was more honest.

Probably all these interpretations contain some part of the truth, but none of them is wholly correct. The NEP was not one thing, but many things. There was certainly a restriction in the scope of the controls. The Committees of the Poor and the Food Requisitioning Squads were disbanded. The class war in the villages was stopped, and the confiscation of foods was ended. The peasants were now required to give only a part of their produce to the state, and were allowed to keep or sell the rest. They were, however, required to pay a tax which was somewhat higher than it had been in the tsarist period. The middle peasants (*seredniaks*) were now favored instead of the poor peasants (*bedniaks*). Gifts or loans of seed and implements and new laws on landownership and use were employed to encourage the middle peasants. Private trading in the domestic market was permitted under a licensing system, and private traders (who were called Nepmen) were encouraged to do business. They did so with great enthusiasm. About three-quarters of the retail trade in 1922–23 was carried on by private merchants. Small industrial concerns—those employing less than 20 workers—were released to co-operatives or to individual private ownership. But here one of the other aspects of the NEP becomes apparent.

Between 91 and 92 per cent of all the industrial concerns in Russia were given over to co-operative or private or combined state and private control. But the 8.5 per cent of the industries which continued to belong to the government employed almost 85 per cent of all industrial workers. The government, in other words, kept the larger share. It also tightened rather than loosened its controls. All banking and credit facilities, all transportation, all foreign trade, most large-scale domestic trade, and all large-scale industry remained in the hands of Lenin's organization. So did the machinery of government. These things were held more tightly than ever before. The Supreme Economic Council was made responsible for large industry, and was given authority commensurate with the responsibility. Each segment of industry was placed under the direct management of a trust which was run by a committee somewhat like a board of directors. The number of such trusts finally reached 486. Each trust was required to submit plans and reports to the SEC for approval, and 50 per cent of the profits of every trust were assigned to the state. Legally, however, each trust was an independent enterprise which was to be operated for profit, and which was free to buy or sell to state organizations (including other trusts) or to private business-men. The trusts soon engaged in vigorous competition for funds, sup-plies, labor, and sometimes for markets. Super-trusts, or syndicates, were then created to regulate prices, competition, the distribution of goods, and the allocation of raw materials. It was a complex and com-plicated system, which was not very efficient, but which worked, after a fashion.

The NEP was a gamble in which the stake was the continuance of Lenin's regime. Lenin hoped to quiet the country by appeasing the peasantry, and to use private enterprise to rebuild the shattered economy. It was a shrewd and daring gamble. One aspect of the NEP was, there-fore, the removal or reduction of state control over some activities. The other aspect was the simultaneous tightening of the remaining controls. This is borne out by the Party's actions during the NEP in noneconomic fields.

✺ ORGANIZED RELIGION IN RUSSIA SINCE 1918

One case in point was the Bolshevik policies and actions in regard to or-ganized religious groups. The decree of February, 1918, had legally separated Church from State and Church from education. Under this and other decrees, all church property—real estate, vestments, icons, treasure of various sorts to the value of one and one-half billion dol-lars—was confiscated by the state. The laws permitted the leasing of church buildings for religious use by individual congregations, but those who did so were always subjected to harassments and often to perse-cutions. (For example, those who were collecting the monies or goods with which to pay the rent on the property were sometimes arrested on charges of hoarding.) Many church buildings were destroyed or allowed to decay or taken over for secular uses. The Soviet press re-ported in 1937 that only 25 out of the pre-1917 454 churches in Moscow were being used for religious purposes. Approximately two-thirds of the monasteries were liquidated. Clergymen and their families were dispossessed and disfranchised and so left with no resources. They were discriminated against in the rationing of food, clothing, fuel, and shelter; and in opportunities for jobs and for education. Some hundreds were killed outright, although this was a less common happening than is often supposed. The most notorious legal actions were the arrest and trial of several leading churchmen in 1922 and 1923. This, it will be noted, was after the start of the NEP, which was marked by a general increase of the antichurch activities. One such action was the creation of the "Living Church" by a schism from the Russian Orthodox Church:

> The Living Church Schismatic group succeeded in spreading their influence and organization widely because of government aid in placing their candidates as bishops, deans and rectors in most of the great cities, and even towns, of the Soviet Union. The Soviet authorities gave support to the Living Church by removing or even exiling to the North or to Siberia those incumbents who refused to accept the schism. . . . The Living Church Movement was stronger in its apparatus than in its popular support. . . .[5]

Another action which began in the period of the NEP was the creation in 1925 of an association called "The Friends of the Godless," which was built up around an antireligious magazine the *Godless*. The association was transformed in 1926 into the "League of the Godless," and then into "The League (or Union) of the Militant Godless." Under its leader, Emil Yaroslavsky, the Militant Godless published antichurch magazines and papers; arranged antireligious museums, exhibits, parades, and demonstrations; and, in general, spear-headed the antireligious drive. The league announced its own five-year plan in 1929 which called, among other things, for a membership of 17 million by 1932. Its own records show that it fell far short of this goal, but it reached the 5.5 million, which was a considerable number. The league was ostensibly dropped during World War II (in 1942), but its work was subsequently taken over by the "Society for Political and Scientific Research" which, in the early fall of 1950, announced the launching of an intensive crusade against the "medieval Christian outlook." "The fight against the gospel and the Christian legend," said the leader of the society, "must be conducted ruthlessly and with all the means at the disposal of Communists." Five years later Soviet schoolteachers were being told by their leaders: ". . . the Soviet school must fill its pupils with an implacable attitude toward religion, [with] a realization of the need to fight against it, and [with] a desire to take an active part in the fight. . . . The basic theoretical foundation of Communist education is Marxism, which is irreconcilably hostile to religion." Even Yaroslavsky (who died in 1943) could not have asked for much more.

The legal position of religious groups in Russia has varied somewhat under the different constitutions. The first constitution had read: "Freedom for religion and antireligion is granted to every citizen." This was very significantly modified in 1929 to read: "There is freedom for religious confession and antireligious propaganda." Yaroslavsky's magazine (the *Godless*) explained that this meant, "Now any activity of propaganda or agitational character on the part of any religious or church people cannot and must not be looked upon as activity permitted by the laws, but on the contrary as activity extending beyond the limits of the freedom of confession guaranteed by the law, and falling under the action of criminal and civil laws."

The laws to which this passage referred were passed in 1929 and were subsequently extended by the Criminal Code. They restrict and modify by definition the pledge of the 1936 Constitution that "Freedom for the conduct of religious worship . . . is recognized for all citizens." The laws restrict the churches literally and exclusively to "the conduct of religious worship" by which is meant formal services and instructions only. No church or religious groups may set up co-operatives, mutual-aid funds, or "use the property at their disposal for any other purpose than the satisfying of religious needs"; give material aid to their members; "organize either special meetings for children, youth, women, for prayer or other purposes, or general meetings, groups, circles, departments, biblical, literary, handworking, labor, religious study, etc."; or maintain libraries, reading rooms or medical aid. The matter of religious education was covered in the 1918 law, which decreed, "Instruction in religious doctrine is not permitted in any governmental or common school, nor in private educational institutions where general subjects are taught. Citizens may give or receive instructions in a private manner." Private instruction was later defined to mean groups of not more than three children. In addition to the legal restrictions, of which those listed are only a sample, there were often illegal or extralegal persecutions on a local scale. One of the most damaging devices, from the point of view of the churches, was the establishment of a six-day work week which brought the one holiday on Sunday only once every six weeks. Since absenteeism from work was very severely punished, church attendance dropped. Other harassments included prohibiting the sale of Christmas trees and Easter cakes, and the ringing of church bells. These and many other prohibitions were dropped during World War II, when the Russian Orthodox Church was officially restored and the election of its patriarch was officially permitted and recognized. There is reason to believe, however, that concessions made during those years represented only a temporary deviation from the antireligious policies of the Soviet regime. However, as the then Minister of Education,

Lunacharsky, remarked in 1928, "Religion is like a nail; the harder you hit it, the deeper it goes into the wood." There is no doubt that a very large number of Soviet citizens have retained their religious faith in spite of all that has been done to eradicate it. In this and in their efforts to break down the family, the Communists have come up against extremely persistent norms and values.

Early Communist decrees abolished religious marriage ceremonies by providing that only civil marriages would be recognized. This became simply a matter of notifying the proper office either in person or by mail that a marriage had been arranged. Divorce was made equally easy and informal. It was the probable intention of these changes, at least in part, to help create an equality of sexes by abolishing the strict tsarist laws covering marriage and divorce. This interpretation is borne out by the emphasis which was placed upon the establishment of legal, juridical, political, and economic equality between men and women, but emphasis was also placed upon giving the state precedence over the family, and this was another of the purposes of the reforms. The attack on the family was vigorously continued throughout the NEP in spite of a passive and unorganized, but strong, popular resistance. A new Family Code was adopted in 1927 which made unregistered marriages legally equal to registered marriages. Abortions were approved in law and in practice so long as they were performed under legally endorsed auspices. Communal nurseries and child-care centers were established either to free women to work or to weaken the family, or both. These experiments received considerable acclaim among certain Western observers. So did the Soviet experiments with education.

✍ EDUCATIONAL EXPERIMENTS

Lenin and his men were quick to see that "education" could be made an invaluable weapon for the use of the Party and Communist cause. The NEP marked a time both of wild experimentation and of quantitative advances in popular education. The experimentation was due partly to desire and partly to necessity. A revolutionary society ought, obviously, to have a revolutionary system of education. But the Communists had no "revolutionary" educational theories of their own, so they were forced to borrow the "most advanced" educational theories and practices of the West. This meant, for the most part, "progressive education" as it was preached or practiced at the time. The Soviets adopted it wholesale, taking some things which were good and many things which were not so good. Discipline, order, and orderliness gave way to "democracy" (which often meant mob rule by the students). Training in fundamentals was dropped in favor of "projects" designed to cater to the students' "interests."

The quantitative advance—measured in terms of the number of school buildings, pupils, and teachers, and by the reduction of illiteracy— was considerable. In 1920 there were 9,207,000 pupils in Soviet elementary schools (that is, in the first four grades). This enrollment dropped to under 7 million in 1923, but climbed almost to 10.5 million by 1928–29. Four years later the enrollment in elementary schools exceeded 18 million. The number of pupils in intermediate and secondary schools (that is, in grades five through ten) jumped from a low of 600,000 in 1922–23 to 3.6 million in 1923–33. It does not detract from the real Soviet accomplishment to point out that the rate of school growth before the revolution was approximately the same.

Size is not, or should not be, the sole criterion of educational progress. Standards and qualitative measures are fully as important as quantitative yardsticks, and here the Soviet record was less impressive. Buildings and teaching staffs did not keep pace with the growth in the number of pupils. While the enrollment of school children more than quintupled between 1923 and 1933, the number of school buildings increased by only 60,000. Overcrowding was an extremely serious problem, and an obstacle to effective teaching. Moreover, the demand for teachers so far exceeded the supply that many teachers were not adequately prepared for their jobs. Soviet figures showed that only half of the elementary-school teachers and less than two-thirds of the secondary-school teachers had been properly trained. These facts are enough to warrant some doubts as to the quality of the work. The reduction of illiteracy, which has been the subject of much prideful boasting, was a great achievement; but it also needs to be placed in perspective, particularly in view of the iterated claim that only a Soviet society could have done it. The percentage of illiteracy among Soviet peoples in 1940 was only slightly higher than the percentage of illiterates among the least-favored ethnic group in the United States, the Negroes, in that same year.

Although the full story of the transformation of education into Party indoctrination properly comes a little later, it is appropriate to note here that Party control of education was vigorously carried forward during the NEP. Russian universities, which had enjoyed a most unusual autonomy after 1905, lost their autonomy completely in 1922, when control over them was taken by the Communist Party. Both faculties and student bodies were purged of all whom the Party did not trust, and the purgees included some of the ablest and most distinguished scholars and teachers of Russia. The practice of giving preferment to students solely on the bases of their class origin and their Party contacts had some great and obvious faults. On the other hand, it had the merit of tapping talents among groups who had often been ignored. This was one of the greatest sources of Soviet strength, and it was also one of the ways of enlisting popular support for the regime.

🜚 GOVERNMENT: THEORY VERSUS FACT

It may be again repeated that in speaking of the regime it is necessary to differentiate between what may be called "the ruler-in-law" and the "ruler-in-fact." The latter has been, since 1917, the Communist Party. The ruler-in-law, which was introduced by the previous discussion of the 1918 Constitution, has undergone many changes. Its story provides an interesting demonstration of what happens in the Soviet Union when facts collide with theories. The Marx-Engels theory confidently predicted the withering away of the state (or government), but the state set up by Lenin did not wither away. On the contrary, it expanded in structure, in functions, and in space. The story of the latter—the territorial expansion of Bolshevik power—has already been told and need not be repeated. By 1922 the territory under Lenin's control had become so extensive that a new ruler-in-law had to be created. There was accordingly set up the Union of Soviet Socialist Republics, which consisted of four "union" or "member" republics. The four were Russia proper (the Russian Socialist Federative Soviet Republic), the Ukrainian S.S.R., the Bielorussian S.S.R., and the Transcaucasian S.S.R. By 1935 the Transcaucasian S.S.R. had been split into the Georgian, the Armenian, and Azerbaizhanian republics; and three entirely new republics— Uzbekistan, Turkmenistan, and Tadzhikistan—had also been added to the U.S.S.R. The administrative subdivisions of the various member republics had also increased in number. For example, there were 11 "autonomous republics" within the R.S.F.S.R. in 1924; 15, in 1935.

The machinery of the ruler-in-law also increased in size and in complexity. The 1918 Constitution (which was concerned only with the R.S.F.S.R.) set up a relatively simple machine. It established an All-Russian Congress of Soviets, an All-Russian Central Executive Committee, a Council of People's Commissars (SOVNARKOM), and 18 commissariats. The 1924 Constitution provided for all these (but on an All-Union instead of an All-Russian scale), and also added other institutions of government. Among the additions were a Presidium of the Central Executive Committee, a Council of Labor and Defense, a Supreme Court, and a Procurator of the Supreme Court. Moreover, the Council of People's Commissars and the Central Executive Committee were both divided into two bodies. There was also another agency added by the 1924 Constitution. Known first as the State Political Department (GPU or Gay-Pay-Oo), and later as the Unified State Political Department (OGPU), this was the political police. Its predecessor had been the Cheka and its successors were the NKVD and the MVD. The three main governmental institutions set up in 1918 had thus increased to eight in 1924, and the other governmental machinery also became more extensive and more complicated. This fact was the reverse of the theory of the withering away of the state.

Fortunately for the Party theoreticians who had to reconcile fact and theory, a basis for changing the emphasis of the doctrine (if not, indeed, the doctrine itself) could be found among Lenin's voluminous and variegated writings. It was discovered (or rediscovered) that Lenin had once said, ". . . the complete abolition of the government . . . will be possible when every trace of exploitation has been abolished, i.e., in a socialist society." This enabled the theoreticians to explain the continuing existence of a government on the ground that a socialist society had not yet been achieved. But this ground was cut out from under them later by Stalin's ex cathedra pronouncement that socialism had been achieved in the U.S.S.R. It became necessary to alter the doctrine again, and so Stalin announced that the state would remain in being until "capitalist encirclement is liquidated." This presumably meant that the Soviet people need not expect to see their government vanish until such time as a World Soviet Socialist State is established. This quick and sidelong glance at Leninist-Stalinist theory illustrates its flexibility, but neither this illustration nor any amount of description of the ruler-in-law gets to the heart of the problem of how the Soviets are governed. That can be done only by studying the ruler-in-fact—a task which will be taken up in the next chapter. But the ruler-in-law was (and is) a part of the fact of government in the U.S.S.R., and this account of the 1920's would be incomplete without some further description of the machinery set up by the 1924 Constitution.

This constitution gave the right of suffrage to all productive workers, housekeepers for productive workers, soldiers, and sailors. The voting age was eighteen years. Soldiers, sailors, collective farmers, and workers in large enterprises were termed "organized voters," and voted at their place of employment. Housekeepers, Nepmen, craftsmen, and so on— the "unorganized voters"—voted in their villages, towns, or wards, that is, by geographic units. Village voters elected deputies to the village soviet on the basis of one deputy for every hundred voters. The village soviets elected the deputies to the district soviets which, in turn, elected deputies to the regional congresses of soviets. These last elected the deputies to the All-Union Congress of Soviets on the basis of one deputy for every 125,000 voters. City voters got double representation. They elected delegates to the regional congresses, and they also elected directly to the All-Union body on the basis of one deputy for every 25,000 urban voters. The favoritism shown to the urban minority is apparent. All voting was by show of hands, which made it very easy to see who voted for whom.

The All-Union Congress of Soviets was theoretically the highest organ of government, but in practice it was not. Its sessions were infrequent, and between sessions its powers were supposedly vested in the Central Executive Committee. But this body also met only at intervals, and the interim power was handed on to the Presidium. The Presidium was a long way removed from the majority of the voters, but it was very close to what Stalin once called "the helm of the state"—that is, the Communist Party.

⚙ ECONOMIC PLANNING

Long-range economic planning on a national scale did not go into effect in the Soviet Union until 1928, but its beginnings predate the NEP. Some authorities trace the origins of large-scale planning to a Russian engineer named Grinevetsky. Grinevetsky, who incidentally was anti-Bolshevik, published in 1919 a suggestion for the planned development of heavy industry. Other writers trace the origins to Lenin's dream of rural electrification. This was one of his pet projects. "Communism," Lenin told the Eighth Party Congress, "is the Soviet government plus the electrification of the whole country." Later he wrote the then chairman of the State Planning Commission,[6] "We must make propaganda for electricity. How? . . . [by] popularizing it. For this purpose a plan must be worked out at once for the installation of electric light in every house in the R.S.F.S.R. That will be a long business. . . . Nevertheless, we need a plan at once. . . ." Lenin then went on to suggest a plan which was crude in the extreme because of his ignorance of the technical difficulties involved. But the plan prodded the experts into action, which was what he wanted. A special body, called the State Commission for Electrification (GOELRO), was created and given the task of producing the plan Lenin demanded. This plan was later used by the State Planning Commission. That commission in 1925–26 published its first set of "control figures," which established approximate goals for the main branches of the economy. Control figures were also prepared for 1926–27 and for 1927–28. The Supreme Economic Council presented its own draft plan in January, 1927.

Meanwhile, Lenin and his successors were using private enterprise under the NEP. Gradually the national economy recovered. By 1926 the national income was slightly above the 1913 level, which meant that it had increased tremendously over both the 1921 and the 1917 figures. (The increase between 1921 and 1926 was 13 billion rubles.) The gross output of all industry had reached the prewar level by 1926, and agricultural production had increased beyond the prewar records. It has been generally assumed that this recovery was due to Lenin's New Economic Policy. Perhaps it was. It may have been the cumulative result of the efforts of millions and millions of people who worked very hard for many years. At any rate, there was a recovery, the regime was saved, and it became possible to resume the attack upon private enterprise.

The Party simultaneously encouraged state-run and co-operative-run trade and industry, and discouraged private trade by discriminatory taxes and restrictions. Little by little, the private traders were driven out—after they had served the Party's purposes. Private traders handled 75 per cent of the retail trade in 1922–23. They had only 23 per cent of it in 1928; 6 per cent in 1930; and none thereafter. Private industry showed a like decline. It accounted for 20 per cent of the total industrial production in 1925–26, and for only 6 per cent of it in 1930.

CHAPTER XXIII

Party Feuds and
the First Five-Year Plan

🏛 PARTY HISTORY

The intimate relationship of politics to economics is one of the characteristics of the Soviet scene for the simple reason that the same group which controls the political life of the U.S.S.R. also controls its economy. That group, of course, is the Communist Party of the Soviet Union— the ruler-in-fact, as it was termed in the preceding chapter.

"Ruler-in-fact" and "ruler-in-law" are two of the labels which have been devised to describe and to explain the political situation of the Communist Party in the Soviet Union, where it is the real seat of power and authority. There is nothing illegal or extralegal or informal about the Party's position. The Party's power is legal and its organization is formal. The Party has its own governing bodies, its own statutes, and its own agencies. Its place is formally guaranteed in the 1936 Constitution, which declares the Party to be "the leading core of all organizations . . . both public and state."

Political scientists, especially within the last ten or fifteen years, have often described the Party as "monolithic," meaning that it appears to be of one pattern, solidly uniform without any flaws of dissent or opposition. But it has not always been so. It was spawned in contention. The London Congress (1903) created what amounted to two rival parties, the Mensheviks and the Bolsheviks. A fiction of unity between the two was maintained until 1912, when Lenin formally set up his group as a separate organization, but certainly there was no monolithism during that decade or the next.

Many Bolsheviks originally opposed Lenin's April Theses in 1917. He converted most of these "oppositionists" to his views, but there was still no uniformity. Instead, at the time of the "July Uprising," there was open defiance of Lenin's leadership. On the very eve of the coup in Petrograd, Zinoviev and Kamenev headed a very serious opposition to Lenin's demand for an immediate revolution. These same men, together with Rykov and others, continued to oppose Lenin even after the coup had succeeded. The Brest-Litovsk Treaty also called forth very violent protests from the so-called Left Communists, led by Bukharin. Lenin won that struggle only by threatening to withdraw completely if he could not have his way. Disagreements among the leaders continued even through stresses and strains of the civil war. A minority group of the top leaders opposed the creation of a Red Army. When it was organized in spite of them, they then fought against the employment in it of officers from the imperial army. A group known as the "Democratic Centralists" opposed other policies of Lenin's, including his encouragement of monolithism in the Party; and another group, "The Labor Opposition," also struggled against him.

Gradually it appeared that there was one Party boss who was more often out of step with the Leninist majority than were any of the others. This habitual nonconformist was Trotsky. But it would be a mistake to associate opposition and dissension exclusively with him. He was not the first, nor the last, nor the only leader of opposition within the Party. He became, however, the most important such leader and his fight with Stalin was a major climax of intra-Party struggles. Some of the issues fought out by Stalin and Trotsky are understandable only when viewed against the general pattern of the Party's development after 1917.

There were two major themes in this pattern. One was the growth in the number of Party members. It is impossible to say precisely how big the Party was at any given time. Authorities, including the official Party records, contradict one another. Moreover, changes have been continuous and sometimes very rapid. The number of members in 1917 varied from about 23,000 (January) to almost 250,000 (August). However approximate the membership figures are, the long-term trend has been a great increase in the number of Party members (from 23,000 in January of 1917, to 7,200,000 in January of 1957), and, though there have been brief reversals of the trend, its general direction has been upward.[1]

The second theme of the general pattern was the monopolistic centralization of authority within the Party. It is most clearly visible in the history of the Party "organs" (as the Party calls its various institutional bodies). According to the rules of the Party, the highest Party organ is the Party Congress, elected by Party members on a basis of one voting delegate for each 1000 members and a nonvoting delegate for each 2000 members. There was originally some basis for describing the Party Congress as the highest Party organ, but that basis disappeared over the years. During the first part of Lenin's regime, Party congresses were elected and convoked annually, and the delegates took an active part in the formulation of major policies. As the Party grew in size, so did the congresses. There were, for example, 2000 delegates to the 1934 Congress as contrasted to the 104 delegates to the 1918 Congress. This tremendous growth was allegedly one reason for changing the place of the congress in the Party's operations on the ground that the congresses had become too unwieldly to function as originally planned. At any rate, what happened to the congresses, which were supposed to meet at least once every three years, is a matter of record.

There were annual Party congresses until 1925. Then a year was skipped and a congress met in 1927. The next convocation of a congress was in 1930 and then no congress met until 1935. The last congress before World War II was held in 1939. Then there was an interval of thirteen and a half years before the Nineteenth Party Congress met in 1952.[2] Moreover, as each congress convened from 1925 to 1952 it found its powers lessened. The delegates discovered that they had been convoked not to make policies but to hear about policies which had already been made. The congresses had become "consent-building sessions."

The Party rules also provided for a Central Committee, elected by the Party Congress and charged with "directing" the work of the Party when the congress was not in session. It actually so functioned only during the first few years of its existence. By 1920, the real power had been shifted from the Central Committee to its subcommittee "for political work"—the Political Bureau or, as it was more commonly called, the Politburo. The authority for the statement about the shift in power is Lenin, who said, in 1920, that "the Politburo decides all questions of international and internal policy." Evidence recently published for the first time suggests that Lenin might have begun to regret this shift and to plan for an enlargement and rehabilitation of the Central Committee. The plans were not carried out, and the 1925 Congress was told flatly, "The Politburo is the highest Party organ in the country." In other words, the Party Congress had become inferior to what was technically its subordinate, the Central Committee; and that committee had become inferior to what was technically its subordinate, the Politburo. Power had been effectively centralized in the Politburo by 1925.

Moreover, although the Politburo grew somewhat in size over the years, its growth did not keep pace with that of the Central Committee or of the Party congresses or of the Party. The original Politburo (1917) consisted of five members and two alternates—a ratio of roughly one to every 35,700 members of the Party. There were ten members and five alternates on the Politburo in 1934 when Party membership stood at 2,800,000—a ratio of approximately 1 : 187,000. (The ratio in 1957 varied between one member or alternate of the Presidium, successor to the Politburo, to every 654,500 Party members before July and 1 : 480,000 after July.) The Central Committee, just to round out this part of the record, grew from 25 members in 1919 to 84 members and 95 alternates in 1939; 124 members and 110 alternates in mid-March of 1953; and 133 members and 125 alternates in 1956.

The Party, to sum it up quickly, has grown tremendously in size but it remains a tiny minority of the total population (about 3.7 per cent in 1957). Power within the Party, having been shifted from the congresses to the Central Committee and then from the committee to the Politburo (now the Presidium), has been concentrated in the hands of a dozen men or less. Back in 1903 Trotsky, in the course of one of his arguments with Lenin, said, "The organization of the Party takes the place of the Party itself; the Central Committee takes the place of the organization; and finally the dictator takes the place of the Central Committee." What happened to the Party was probably not precisely what Trotsky had in mind, but his words proved an accurate prophecy.

✇ LENIN, TROTSKY, AND STALIN

Mention of Trotsky leads to a consideration of the Communist Party of the Soviet Union as an association of men. Persons and personalities have played a very large role in the history of the Party and in the history of the lands and peoples which have come under the Party's rule. The ways in which Lenin affected the course of developments in 1917 and thereafter have already been stressed. (Even Communist historians have modified their economic determinism enough to admit that Lenin changed the course of history.) The imprint of Lenin's ideas, of his personality, and of his will was deep and lasting. Striking proof of this was the claim of those who sought to follow Lenin to be his only true disciples. Stalin and his confederates sedulously fostered the doctrine that Stalin had been Lenin's closest associate, his best pupil, his chosen heir, the devotedly loyal continuer and developer of Lenin's policies. Stalin's opponents were equally diligent in spreading specific and blanket denials of these claims. Both groups ignored and distorted truth to serve their own ends. Whether Stalinism was "Leninism brought up to date" or "a perversion of Leninism and a betrayal of its principles" is a matter best left to the rival polemicists. There is enough complexity in what happened without complicating the story further with opinions as to what should have (or should not have) taken place.

It was one of the marks of Lenin's greatness that he so often was able to reconcile strong individualists to his leadership. As long as Lenin's physical and mental strength was unimpaired, he was able either to hold disagreements within safe limits or, failing that, to repair their effects. (There were splits in the Party, and resignations and removals from high places in Lenin's time.) In view of what happened when Lenin's health failed, it is reasonable to think that Lenin's greatest exploit was to keep Stalin and Trotsky on the same team. Certainly their personalities and their talents were widely disparate, and their ambitions clashed violently.

Stalin began his revolutionary work near the turn of the century. From 1901 to 1917, he was a "political," an outlaw, a revolutionary conspirator, an organizer of "expropriations," a jailbird, an exile, and an escapee. His collaboration with Lenin apparently began in 1913 and was then interrupted by war and exile. Stalin returned to Petrograd before either Lenin or Trotsky, and, until Lenin arrived, Stalin more or less co-operated with the Soviet. He accepted Lenin's April Theses soon after their enunciation, and seems to have been close to Lenin during the summer and fall of 1917. He was one of Lenin's links with the Party in Petrograd after the July fiasco forced Lenin to hide in Finland. (Stalin had been added to the membership of the Central Committee in 1912, and had retained that post.) In May, 1917, when the Politburo was informally created, he became a member of that subcommittee. He was retained as a member when the Politburo was formally set up later, and apparently he was put on the Orgburo (Organization Bureau) and the Secburo (Secretariat) at the same time. He was also one of the delegates to the founding Congress of the Third International (Comintern), which was held that same year—1919.

When Lenin set up his first government (October/November, 1917), Stalin was appointed Chairman of Nationalities in the Council of People's Commissars (SOVNARKOM). He held this appointment until 1923 but could not give it much time. During 1918 he was a member of the Council of Defense and of the Executive Committee of the Council of Commissars. His special responsibilities included the supplying of Moscow and Petrograd with food from southern Russia, and the defense of Tsaritsyn (Stalingrad). The next year, 1919, Stalin was named Commissar for Workers' and Peasants' Inspection—a Party post of considerable power, since it had the authority to check the efficiency, loyalty, and actions of state employees. Stalin held this job until 1922, when he was named General Secretary of the Communist Party. Meanwhile, he had been added to the Revolutionary War Council in 1920, and had won distinction by conquering his native Georgia (thus reversing the Party's earlier encouragement of national self-determination and the formal recognition of Georgian independence).

It is clear that, although Stalin was not widely known outside of Russia or even outside of the Party, he held a place of importance among the Party's leaders. The positions and responsibilities which were entrusted to him are evidence of this. The food supply for the Bolshevik centers of Petrograd and Moscow, for example, was absolutely vital to the Party's continuing existence. Moreover, the Party posts not only were important but also gave unparalleled opportunities to an ambitious man. Stalin made the most of them. Quietly and with skilled persistence, he built up a personal political machine. It was his greatest single asset.

Trotsky differed from Stalin in background, abilities, personality, and in almost every other way except in ambition. Trotsky was an intellectual. Stalin was not. Stalin was an organization man. Trotsky was not, although he did acquire a strong and loyal following. Trotsky was a brilliant writer and orator. Stalin's writings and speeches were quite ordinary. Trotsky was mercurial, impetuous, quarrelsome. Stalin was patient, persistent, rather ponderous. Trotsky differed openly and often with Lenin. Stalin did not. This offset the fact that Trotsky's associations with Lenin antedated Stalin's by many years. Trotsky had opposed Lenin at London in 1903 and had more or less lined up with the Mensheviks thereafter. (It has been said of him, with some justice, that whether he wore the label of Menshevik or of Bolshevik, Trotsky was first and foremost a Trotskyite.) He had just arrived in New York at the time of the first revolution in 1917, and he returned to Russia as fast as he could. Detention by British and Canadian authorities delayed him, and he did not arrive home until May. Not until July did he align himself with Lenin and the Bolsheviks, but he soon earned a top place among Lenin's closest collaborators in the Politburo.

He was a member of Lenin's first government, holding a much more important and prominent place than Stalin. As Commissar for Foreign Affairs, Trotsky gained international notoriety (if not fame), especially for his work and his frequent pyrotechnics at Brest-Litovsk. Trotsky was always good copy, which Stalin was not, and his words and deeds were widely reported in the world's press. It is no wonder that to the world "Lenin and Trotsky" symbolized and personified Bolshevik leadership. Nor was this an entirely erroneous impression. Trotsky was one of the Party's major leaders. As Commissar for War, he was chiefly responsible for creating and organizing the Red Army. He was prominent in the Comintern. As a member of the Politburo and of the Central

Committee, he was one of the policy-making elite. But he early began to disagree. In 1920 Trotsky differed sharply with Lenin and others on the methods to be used in rebuilding the national economy. Trotsky favored an extension of the use of "labor armies." This name was first applied to Red Army units who were transferred from military duties to the tasks of mining coal, digging peat, cutting wood, and so on. Trotsky's proposal, essentially, was to combine this device with the compulsory-labor decrees. The proposal was rejected by the Party leaders. Later Trotsky called for "the nationalization of the trade unions," by which he meant that the unions should participate directly in the management of the nation's economy and in the administration of the state. This was also turned down, as was Trotsky's five-year plan for the metallurgical industry, which was brought forward in 1923. (A general five-year plan which he advocated later was also rejected.)

✇ STALIN VERSUS TROTSKY

These affairs—except for the long-range plans—all took place while Lenin was still alive and still fully vigorous. He kept Trotsky with him despite their disagreements. A cerebral hemorrhage partially incapacitated Lenin in 1922, and a second one in 1923 left him almost completely invalided. His condition forced the other Party leaders to appoint a three-man Executive Committee in December, 1922. Lenin continued to write articles, directives, and memoranda, but he was unable to attend the Twelfth Party Congress in April, 1923—"The first Communist Party Congress without Lenin," the Party histories sadly call it. The Executive Committee, which functioned in Lenin's stead, was a rather odd assortment. It was composed of Stalin; Zinoviev, head of the Comintern and boss of the Party in Leningrad; and Kamenev, Trotsky's brother-in-law. Zinoviev and Kamenev will be remembered as having opposed Lenin in 1917. In 1923 they—along with Stalin—opposed Trotsky, who did not gather enough associates to attack the three until October. Then he publicly accused them of suppressing democracy within the Party; of making the most grievous and dangerous errors in both foreign and domestic policies; and of leading the Party to degeneration and ruin. Particularly did he strike at them for attempting "to build socialism in one country." This, declared Trotsky, was an impossibility—socialism could be built only in the condition of continuing revolution abroad. The conflict was thus very much out in the open before Lenin died in January, 1924. It continued with increasing vigor.

Trotsky was unable to command a majority in support of his views, but he continued to attack those in power. They retaliated, rather mildly considering the fury of his onslaught, by ousting him from his posts as War Commissar and Chairman of the Revolutionary Military Committee. This was in January, 1925. Zinoviev and Kamenev, meanwhile, had begun to move away from Stalin. The break came in April when Zinoviev and Kamenev announced their conviction that socialism could not be built in one country alone. When the Fourteenth Party Congress met (December, 1925) these two stood forth as the leaders of "The New Opposition." The majority sided with Stalin, and voted against the New Opposition just as they had voted against Trotsky at the preceding congress. Neither Trotsky nor Zinoviev and Kamenev were willing to accept the majority decisions as valid and binding upon them. They continued to agitate in behalf of their own proposals, and, in the late spring of 1926, formed an opposition bloc. The Trotsky-Zinoviev-Kamenev bloc then proceeded to challenge the Stalinist faction by both open and secret means. Again Stalin triumphed. Zinoviev was fired from the Politburo and from his Comintern post in July. Three months later, Trotsky and Kamenev were expelled from the Politburo for violating their pledges not to engage in further "factional opposition."

The fight flared out again. Trotsky and his associates attacked Stalin and the Stalinist policies in fiery articles and in vehement speeches and demanded drastic changes in the Party's leadership. When the Central Committee threatened them with expulsion, Trotsky and Zinoviev made a gesture of recanting. But they continued to oppose Stalin with might and main and for that reason they were removed from the Central Committee in October, 1927. Then they attempted to appeal to the people (as distinct from the Party) by organizing anti-Stalin demonstrations on the occasion of the celebration of the tenth anniversary of the revolution. The demonstrations, which were branded as "open revolution" by the Stalinists, were broken up and the demonstrators were punished. Kamenev was dropped from the Central Committee; Trotsky and Zinoviev were expelled from the Party. The Fifteenth Party Congress, held in December, 1927, was all Stalin's. "The Opposition," as Trotsky ruefully remarked, "was completely routed." Kamenev and 74 other "oppositionists" (as the congress labeled them) were purged from the Party. As for Trotsky, he suffered in increasing measure the penalties of defeat in a struggle for the control of a "monolithic party." He was exiled to Central Asia in 1928, expelled from the U.S.S.R. in 1929, and killed in Mexico City in 1940. By 1929 Stalin had emerged as the most powerful individual in the Communist Party of the Soviet Union. His leadership, however, was not unchallenged.

The key figures in the new opposition (often called the "Right Opposition" to distinguish it from Trotsky's so-called "Left Opposition") were all men of stature within the Party. Bukharin was the editor of

Izvestia, the government's newspaper, and secretary of the Comintern. Tomsky was the head of the Council of Trade Unions, and Rykov was the chairman of the Supreme Economic Council. These three men, together with their followers (for it is not to be supposed that only Stalin had support), were highly critical of Stalin's increasing centralization of power within the Party and of the speed with which he was forcing industrialization and the collectivization of agriculture. They also opposed his purging of non-Stalinist elements from the Comintern. There was some thought of creating a possible bloc by combining the Right Opposition with the remnants of the Left Opposition, and Bukharin made overtures to Kamenev in 1928. Within the Central Committee, the three opposition leaders fought Stalin by refusing to carry out Party orders and by threatening to resign and so further to disrupt the Party. Stalin struck back by removing Bukharin and Tomsky from their positions in April, 1929. Stalin's next move was to depose all three from the Politburo. They recanted and apologized at the Sixteenth Party Congress (1930), but none of them recovered his former high place and none survived the "Great Purge" of the late 1930's. Although that purge is conclusive evidence that opposition continued to exist, the expulsion of the Right and Left Oppositionists may be said to mark the beginnings of the "monolithic Party."

✿ ANALYSIS AND ESTIMATE

The disagreements which caused the Party feuds, especially the struggle between Stalin and Trotsky, are fiercely controversial. Final and definitive interpretations of these disputes are not yet possible, but certain matters are clearer now than they were in the 1930's and even in the 1940's.

First, the differences between Stalin and his opponents were over tactics and means, not over aims and final goals. The fight, in other words, was not over their destination, but over the route to follow and the time to allow for various stages of the journey. The ultimate goal which they all sought was world revolution and the establishment of a World Soviet Socialist Republic. Stalin—to cite one famous point— favored temporary concentration on Russia in order to build a secure and powerful base from which to launch a later campaign for world dominion. Trotsky thought that the domestic and foreign campaigns had to go on simultaneously. It is not possible, however, to separate genuine differences of opinion over tactics from the clashes of personal ambition. The two things were inextricably confused. Did Stalin oppose Trotsky's proposals for long-range economic planning because he thought the proposals were inopportune or because he was unwilling to have such plans go forward under Trotsky's sponsorship? Did Stalin reject the Right Opposition's demand for a less drastic policy against the prosperous peasants because he really believed the policy to be unsound, or did he reject it because the Opposition proposed it? The Party congress which declared Trotsky a heretic and all his works heresies also ordered the preparation of a large-scale economic plan not unlike the plans which Trotsky had advocated. And less than two years after he had handcuffed the Right Opposition, Stalin ordered a slower tempo for collectivization. These facts have been held to prove that his opposition was personal rather than on the basis of merit. But it is also a fact that circumstances had changed between the time of the first proposals and the date of their adoption by Stalin.

No definitive answer can be made to the question of the importance of personal rivalries in this struggle. Despite the voluminous arguments which have been advanced on both sides, the case is not proved. One similarity between Trotsky and Stalin may be noted, however. Neither man in any way rejected Lenin's dogma that leadership must be by an elite. Both may have intended to govern "for the people." Neither had the slightest intention of creating a government "of the people" or "by the people."

THE FIRST FIVE-YEAR PLAN

Long-range planning in the Soviet Union is not and has not been exclusively a matter of economics. Where production and distribution are the business of the state, politics and economics are indissolubly linked. "Planned economy" was, to the Soviet rulers, a means to an end—the triumph of communism all over the world—but there were also intermediate goals which varied from time to time. With Stalin's victory within the Party, the main (but not the sole) intermediate goal became "the building of socialism in one state." Two points may be emphasized. First, this intermediate goal was looked upon as a necessary first step toward the final objective. Second, "building socialism" meant not just the construction of an economic system, not just the planning of production, but the building of a whole way of life. This can be very readily demonstrated by a glance at the organization of the planning agencies. The State Planning Commission was divided into eleven sections, each having jurisdiction over a specified area. Seven sections dealt with economic areas such as transport and communications, power, industry, agriculture, and so on. One section was concerned with statistics, and one with organization. Two divisions were devoted to matters which were certainly not primarily economic: science—covering research in all fields—and "culture"—a term which covered schools and all other educational institutions and devices.

The broadly stated economic goal was to transform the U.S.S.R. from an agrarian to an industrial economy. This was broken down into subgoals which included the introduction of modern technology; the construction of heavy machinery for industry, transport, and agriculture; the "squeezing out utterly [of] the capitalist elements" in industry and trade; and the strengthening of the national's defensive capacity. The Fifteenth Congress, which had ordered the preparation of the plan, had also resolved to transform "the petty individual farms into large-scale collective farms." These subgoals had also to be broken down into specific targets, most of which were very ambitious. "Class A" or basic industries—coal, iron, steel, oil, machine-building, and so on—were to triple their output. "Class B" or consumer-goods industries were to double their output. The total value of production was to be more than doubled. The goals set for individual industries were also ambitious. The output of pig iron was to be increased three times over; that of electric power, four times over; and that of the chemical industry, twenty-three times over. The value of the total agricultural production was to be increased from 16 billion to 26 billion rubles. The planted area was to be extended by 22 per cent and so on.

Such grandiose planning could be implemented only by almost superhuman efforts, particularly because the tremendous amount of capital necessary had to be found at home. Terrific sacrifices were demanded of the Soviet people both in terms of labor effort and in putting up with desperate shortages in consumer goods, housing, and personal comforts. Concentration of investment and effort on the capital-goods industries was decreed with the full knowledge that this meant deprivation for the people. Hardships were justified on the ground that it was the part of wisdom to subordinate present comfort to future luxury. Harshness to individuals was condoned on the basis that the welfare of the individual was of no consequence compared with the future welfare of the group. This was, in fact, tantamount to an all-out war, and the matter was so presented to the Soviet people. They were organized into "brigades" and "shock troops." They were exhorted "to win the battle of the steel front" (or the "coal front" or the "fuel front" or whatever had to be pushed). They were coaxed and flattered, conscripted and mobilized into service. Workers were assigned to jobs and shifted all over the country. Many persons were induced or forced to leave their native farms for industry. Women were put to industrial tasks. All in all, the number of persons employed in nonagricultural labor almost doubled between 1928 and 1932. The Soviet's richest resources—both actual and potential—were their people. Men and women were plentiful, self-replacing, and therefore expendable. Rich in natural resources and in labor supply, but short on capital, on experience and "know-how," on basic industries and equipment, the Soviets spent lavishly what they had in the greatest abundance—people.

It is customary to measure the success of the First Five-Year Plan (and of the subsequent plans as well) in statistical terms of so much coal mined, so many steel mills built, so many illiterates taught to read. Such measures have their important uses, but it is possible to so group and emphasize them that they can appear to prove almost anything. Thus it can be argued that the First Five-Year Plan succeeded because accomplishments exceeded plans. For example, oil production was 107 per cent of the plan; machine-building, 157 per cent; and railway loadings, 128 per cent. On the other hand, it can be claimed that the plan failed because railway trackage increased only by 88 per cent of the planned amount; consumer-goods production missed its goal by 26 per cent; ferrous-metal production fell short by 32 per cent, and so on. Another test is to measure accomplishments against officially announced objectives. By this test only one objective was fully attained—the virtual elimination of private capital and private capitalists from trade and industry. Professor Harry Schwartz, in his authoritative study *Russia's Soviet Economy,* has summed the matter up as follows:

. . . the First Five Year Plan may have been fulfilled if one defines fulfillment narrowly in terms of some overall indicator which balanced failures in one area with unexpectedly good performance in another. In retrospect, however, there can be no claim that the Five Year Plan, as approved in 1929, was anything but a bad forecast of what actually did happen after its adoption, except in the most general sense that the plan did call for a heavy program of capital investment, increased population, and greater socialization in all major areas of the economy.[3]

THE PEOPLE UNDER THE PLAN

There is still another way of looking at the First Five-Year Plan, and that is to try to estimate what it meant to the Soviet people. Since there was no full and free expression of public opinion possible to the people, this involves guesswork on the basis of fragmentary evidence. It would seem that the plan must have meant personal insecurity—both material and psychological—for very many people. To be uprooted from a familiar routine and plunged abruptly into a new way of life is very upsetting, and this is precisely what happened to millions of Soviet citizens. Whether they were attracted into industry or forced to seek work in factories, the unsettling effects must have been much the same. They had to learn a new norm and value pattern. They were compelled to accommodate themselves to a new way of life. This is hard enough under the most favorable conditions, and the conditions under which it took place in the Soviet Union were, for the most part, highly unfavorable. One case in point (which will shortly be considered more fully) was the forced collectivization of agriculture. Another was the transfer of labor not only to new occupations but also to strange and distant sections of the country. A third instance was the shortage of what we would consider the necessities of everyday life—food, clothing, living quarters, fuel, medical care, and so on. Hardship and suffering were the common lot of the Soviet people, partly because of their government's deliberate choice of emphasis upon capital-goods production, partly because of the inefficiency of the plan and of its execution, and partly because of the immensity of the task which was undertaken. Yet there is another side which ought not to be forgotten.

The First Five-Year Plan (and the subsequent plans, also) offered new advantages and new opportunities to many people. To leave one's native village for urban employment, either from choice or from economic necessity, had been a common pattern of peasant behavior for centuries. (Recall the "go-aways" of old Russia.) With the five-year plans, the stringencies may have been greater but the opportunities were greater, too. There were more than enough jobs to go around, and during the first and second five-year plans it was possible and common (though illegal and sometimes dangerous) for workers to move from job to job and from place to place in search of better returns. This situation represented an unprecedented opportunity for some Soviet citizens. The area of opportunity was extended by the availability of training which opened the way to more desirable jobs and to a higher social and economic position. Such advantages were not equally available to all. On the contrary, very many persons were specifically excluded from such opportunities. Nor was the training generally of high quality. It was markedly incomplete and imperfect. But it was more than had been previously available to the groups who received it, and this is a very significant point which is sometimes overlooked.

The point is not that there were no opportunities in old Russia, nor—as has so often been alleged—that the Communist rulers introduced opportunities for the common man. Neither of these claims is true. Alexander Guchkov, for example, was the grandson of a serf, and Lenin's father had climbed the hierarchical and social ladder. These were not isolated cases. The point is that the shift in power resulted in the creation of opportunities for different people. There is in the Soviet Union a very definite elite which corresponds quite closely numerically to the elite of tsarist times. The personnel of the elite, however, has changed almost completely. Here is one of the great—if not the greatest— dynamics of the Soviet power. The Bolshevik Revolution tapped new sources of power and strength. It released a new or, at least, a different dynamic.

COLLECTIVIZATION OF AGRICULTURE

Several references have been made to that part of the First Five-Year Plan which called for the collectivization of agriculture. This affected, directly or indirectly, every Soviet citizen. By 1917 almost 80 per cent of all the arable lands in European Russia were peasant-owned, and an additional 10 per cent were peasant-rented. Peasant-owned and peasant-rented did not, however, usually mean individual ownership or rental. While it is true that about half of the peasant households in European Russia had applied for private ownership under the Stolypin reforms, it is also true that less than 10 per cent of the peasant households had acquired it before 1917. Peasant land tenure, in other words, was preponderantly communal. Then came the February/March Revolution with its attendant confusions. The Provisional Government took no effective action on the land question. The Social Revolutionaries favored a "socialization" of land, by which they meant that it should become the public domain with distribution for use controlled by the peasant communes. The Bolsheviks had no definite land policy, although they were opposed to "socialization." As for the peasants, they simply took the land. According to the Russian scholar Dubrowski, the peasants forcibly confiscated almost six thousand large estates before October.[4] The Bolsheviks, as previously noted, first gave formal recognition to this *fait accompli* and then later reversed themselves by decreeing the nationalization of the land. (There was also an intermediary stage in which Lenin temporarily acquiesced in an Essar socialization decree.)

The Bolsheviks experimented with several systems of landowning and use during the years of War Communism, although their primary concern was the immediate necessity of getting food to the cities. One of the experiments was with state farms—"factories in the fields," they were sometimes called. These were large farms operated by the government, and those who worked them were state employees just as were workers in large-scale industry. Another experiment was an attempt to develop collective farms of some sort. Neither experiment was very successful. Despite these efforts and despite the decree nationalizing the land, from 1918 to 1921 almost 96 per cent of the arable land in European Russia was owned and farmed by individual peasants or peasant households.

The NEP was marked both by considerable relaxation of pressures and controls, on the one side, and by continued encouragement of collectivization, on the other. Title to the land remained with the state, but right of use was granted to collectives, co-operatives, and peasant households (though not to individuals). The leasing of land and the employment of hired hands were also permitted under certain conditions. The statistics on the 1926–27 harvest gave a measure of the relative importance of the different types of farming. The state farms produced less than 2 per cent of the total grain crop, and the production by collectives was also fractional. Over 85 per cent of the total grain production came from the poor and middle peasants, and approximately 13 per cent from the "rich" peasants. During the next year the number of collective farms was doubled, but their combined acreage (1927–28) was less than 2 per cent of the total, and their combined membership was only about half a million peasant households. The number of peasant households outside the collectives at that time has been estimated at between 24 million and 26 million.

The rulers, who still had to see to it that industrial and city workers were fed, and who were faced with a tremendous projected increase in this obligation because of the Five-Year Plan, had to be concerned not only with the amount of grain produced but even more with the amount sold to the state. Experience showed that state farms and collectives could be counted on to provide much more grain to the state than did private farmers—in proportion to the amount produced, that is. The poor and middle private farmers grew over four-fifths of the grain produced, but they consumed almost 90 per cent of what they produced. The crux of the problem was not only that the Communists were a tiny minority, but also that they were an urban minority whose strength depended upon industrial and urban workers. If grain and other foodstuffs could not be provided for these workers, the planned industrialization would be impossible and the power of the Party would almost surely vanish. But so long as the peasant majority (and the village population in 1926 was about 82 per cent of the whole) remained even quasi-independent, the Party could get the vitally necessary grain only on the peasants' terms. These terms centered on a demand for consumer goods, but if industry was set to producing consumer goods in sufficient quantity to meet this demand, the whole essence of the five-year plans (concentration on heavy industry) would have to be abandoned. The only way out, as the Party bosses saw it, was to deprive the peasants of their freedom of action by inducing or forcing them to give up private farming for collective farming which the Party could control. From the Party's point of view, a hungry and discontented countryside might be deplorable but it was far less dangerous than a hungry and discontented city. To collectivize some 20 million peasant households was a terrific undertaking, but was regarded as an absolute necessity—a gamble for the highest stakes, namely, continuance in power. Only "the director of production and the master of produce," to borrow a phrase from Gsovski, could hope to continue as the ruler of Russia.

Doctrinal sanction was found in Lenin's pronouncement that the peasants formed the last capitalist class, and Stalin explained that as long as the peasants carried on small-scale commodity production, they were bound to produce capitalists among them. The poor peasant, said Stalin in 1929, is a supporter of the workers; the middle peasant is their ally; but the rich peasant (kulak) is the enemy of the workers. "The expropriation of the kulaks," he went on, "is an integral part of setting up and developing collective farms." And he announced that the policy had changed from "restricting" the kulaks to "liquidating the kulaks as a class." The 1939 edition of the Party's own *History* gives the following summary of what happened:

Prior to 1929, the Soviet Government had pursued a policy of restricting the kulaks. It had imposed higher taxes on the kulak, and had required him to sell grain to the state at fixed prices; by the law on the renting of land it had to a certain extent restricted the amount of land he could use; by the law on the employment of hired labor on private farms it had limited the scope of his farm. . . .

At the end of 1929 . . . the Soviet Government turned sharply . . . to the policy of eliminating the kulaks. . . . It repealed the laws on the renting of land and the hiring of labour, thus depriving the kulaks both of land and of hired labourers. It lifted the ban on the expropriation of the kulaks. It permitted the peasants to confiscate cattle, machines and other farm property from the kulaks for the benefit of the collective farms. The kulaks were expropriated. They were expropriated just as the capitalists had been expropriated in the sphere of industry in 1918. . . .

This account is, typically, accurate in most details and misleading in general. It tells only part of the story.

The drive for collectivization was complicated by the necessity of meeting an immediate food crisis by confiscating grain stocks on a large scale. Simultaneously, these hard times were turned to account because they made offers of subsidies particularly attractive. By giving credits, machinery, seed, and other aids to newly formed collectives, the government was able to attract many peasants to them. By June, 1929, there were 57,000 collective farms composed of more than a million peasant households. This was enough to demonstrate conclusively that the government could, as it had anticipated, force the collective farmers to supply to the state a much larger percentage of their crop than the free farmers would. But it was not enough actually to supply all the grain needed. As industrialization proceeded, transferring millions of farm workers to cities, the grain crisis became increasingly acute. The Party decided to go all out in its efforts to force rapid collectivization. A law of February, 1930, decreed wholesale collectivization for the chief grain-producing area. Village communes were broken up, and all forms of land tenure except the collective were forbidden. Local authorities were empowered to confiscate all property belonging to kulaks and also to send all kulaks into exile. The confiscated property, which included personal belongings, was turned over to the collectives. To speed the process of collectivization, the Party sent some 25,000 picked workers to the farms and villages to see that the law was fully applied. The results were quantitatively spectacular. Within a matter of weeks, the number of collective farms was increased from 59,400 to 110,200; and the number of collective-farm households, from 4,400,000 to 14,-300,000, or more than half of all the peasant households in the Soviet Union.

These results were obtained by the application of force without stint or scruple. Objections were figuratively, and objectors literally, beaten down. It was a veritable reign of terror and it evoked a tremendous peasant resistance. The peasants destroyed or ate their grain reserves and their livestock, broke up machinery and implements, and burned their buildings rather than see these things taken over by the collectives. They killed some 4 million horses, almost 5 million head of cattle, and over 30 million sheep and goats. So violent was the peasant reaction that a disastrous crisis loomed immediately ahead. It looked for a time as if the 1930 crops would not even be planted, let alone harvested. Faced with this resistance, the Politburo promptly reversed its field. "Who profits by these distortions, by this bureaucratic decreeing of collectivization, by these unseemly threats against the peasants?" demanded Stalin. "Nobody," he answered himself, "nobody but our enemies." The pressures were promptly removed, the blame, of course, being shifted from the Party, who had ordered the pressures applied, to the rank and file who had carried out the order. Again within a matter of weeks there was a highly spectacular result. The number of collective farms dropped from 110,200 to approximately 82,000; and 8.5 million peasant families (about 30 million persons) promptly left the collectives.

This, however, was only a retreat. It was not a rout. The long-run advantages were all on the side of the ruling Party, and it used them cunningly. Collective farms and farmers were given tax exemptions, more generous credit on easier terms, tractors and other machinery, seeds, and other assistance. Life for the individual peasant family, on the other hand, was made as hard as possible. Most of those who withdrew from the collectives were given back only a fraction of what they had been forced to contribute on joining, and many got nothing back at all. The attacks upon the kulaks continued. They were discriminated against by law and by administrative procedures. They legally could be punished for deeds which were not regarded as offenses if performed by nonkulaks, and punishments inflicted upon kulaks were more severe than those visited upon other classes. They continued to be deprived of property, liberty, and life. For their part, the kulaks continued their resistance.

By the time that the ending of the First Five-Year Plan was announced (December 31, 1932), another 10 million horses, another 9 million cattle, and an additional 27 million sheep and goats had been destroyed. The gross output of agriculture had dropped almost a billion rubles since 1930. But, on the other hand, the process of collectivization had gone steadily forward. By 1933, almost two-thirds of all the peasant households in the U.S.S.R. belonged to collective farms, and these farms cultivated almost 85 per cent of the total sown area. One dreadful aspect of all this was a terrible famine which struck Ukraine in 1932–33, partly as a result of the destruction of crops and livestock by the peasants and partly as a result of the deliberate starvation of its opponents by the Communist regime. At least three myths have been fostered about this famine. Party apologists have claimed that threatened Japanese aggression forced the government to deprive its people of food in order to build up supplies for the army; and that only the "enemies of the people," that is, the kulaks, suffered. Enemies of the regime have claimed that this was the greatest famine in all Russian history and one of the greatest in world history. This last claim has been denied by Sir John Maynard, whose professional competence and personal integrity were beyond reasonable challenge. The Party explanations do not accord with evidence which has accumulated. There can be no doubt, however, that this was a terrible scourge which was largely man-made.

As for the kulaks, Party spokesmen have glibly explained (and proudly announced) that "the kulaks have been liquidated as a class." This smooth phraseology attempts to conceal some brutal facts. According to the official Soviet reports on agriculture in the U.S.S.R., there were, in 1928, 5,618,000 kulaks. The same source gives the number for January 1, 1934, as 149,000. What happened to the more than 5 million kulaks who thus disappeared from the records? They were deprived of their homes, their possessions, their families, and their freedom. The overwhelming majority were sent as slave laborers to mines, mills, construction jobs, and lumbering operations in the far north and in Siberia. Some survived and were "rehabilitated." For most of them, however, it was slow death. Their lives were part of the price of collectivization and of the First Five-Year Plan.

CHAPTER XXIV

Collectives, Plans, and the "Ruler-in-Law"

The vigor and the persistence of the drive to collectivize agriculture can be most vividly summarized by a few statistics. When the First Five-Year Plan began in 1928 less than 2 per cent of all peasant households and just over 2 per cent of all sown lands had been collectivized. By 1932, when the first plan was triumphantly announced as completed ahead of schedule, these percentages had risen to 61.5 and 77.7, respectively. When the Second Five-Year Plan was declared ended in 1937 (also ahead of schedule) 93 per cent of the peasant households and 99.1 per cent of the sown land were in collectives. The process was resumed after the interruption caused by World War II. Less than 17 per cent of the peasant households and .03 of the sown land remained outside of collectives in 1953.[1] Collectivization was not, however, as easy or peaceful a process as these statistics might seem to imply. Nor has the system been as perfect in operation as the figures might lead one to infer. On the contrary, the almost steady stream of laws, orders, directives, and instructions which have been issued by the Party and the government during the past quarter of the century indicate that the Soviet leaders still find much to be desired.

✪ THE COLLECTIVE-FARM CODE

The basic law on collectives was issued in 1932. This was supplanted in 1935 by a new Standard Charter of an Agricultural Artel, more commonly referred to either as the Collective-Farm Code or as the Standard Charter. By the terms of the charter (as well as by the 1936 Constitution, which will be discussed later) the use of its land was secured to each collective farm "for an indefinite period, that is to say, forever." The charter also provided that each household on a collective farm should have the use of a dwelling and of a plot of land not to exceed 2.47 acres. This land might be used as the household chose—to grow vegetables or other produce, to support an unlimited number of poultry or a limited number of livestock. The produce, the poultry, and the livestock were the private property of the household and might be sold or consumed as the household chose. But the prime purpose of the charter was neither to secure the land tenure of the collective nor the personal property of the peasant household. It was to ensure that the collectives should "fulfill their obligations to the state" by supplying the required amounts of agricultural produce and by paying taxes and other charges. The law also made it clear that private farming was to come second to work on the collective. This proved extremely difficult to enforce. The 1939 Party Congress was told that in some regions collective farming had become secondary to private farming and that the income from the latter exceeded amounts earned by labor for the collective.

Collective-farm property—crops, seeds, buildings, livestock, tools, equipment, supplies, and so on—was defined by the code as "socialist property," thus putting it on a par with government property. This concept was re-enforced and extended by subsequent legislation, judicial interpretations, orders, and practices, so that practically any action which the rulers chose to define as adversely affecting the operation of a collective came under this law. Fraudulent or careless bookkeeping, reporting, or accounting; destruction of machinery by carelessness or intent; larceny; embezzlement; "subversive" reduction of sowing standards; and misappropriations of funds are a few of the many offenses which have been punished under this legislation. Punishments have ranged from reprimands and fines to confinement at "correctional labor" for terms up to 25 years. And the laws have been applied against nonmembers as well as against members of the collectives.

When a person joins a collective (these provisions of the code are still in effect at the time of this writing) he pays a small entrance fee and contributes whatever stock or farm property he possesses. From a quarter to a half of what he contributes goes into the "share capital" of the collective; the remainder becomes a part of the "indivisible capital" which may not be reduced or distributed in any way. If a member leaves or is expelled from the collective he gets only the cash value of his portion of the "share capital." The actual property he contributed, the part of it assigned to "indivisible capital," and the house and garden plot assigned to the member remain with the collective. The first charge on the collective income is delivery of produce as demanded by the government. The payment of taxes and insurance premiums (as set by the government), the repayment of loans and advances, payment in produce for the use of large machinery, and the building up (as decreed by the government) of reserves for seed and for emergencies come next. Only after all these charges have been met may the remainder of the income be divided among the members on a basis of the number of "workdays" accredited to each.

The number of workdays is determined not only by the amount of work done but also by the type of work performed. Seven general types have been defined by the government ranging from chairmen and tractor drivers at the top to chore-hands at the bottom. Top people may get as much as ten times more pay than those at the bottom. Rewards are given for over-fulfillments and penalties for failure to meet the standards. Computing the number and value of workdays is a complicated and intricate process. Dishonesty in computing workdays and in crediting them to individuals has been common if one may judge from measures taken to correct such abuses. The same type of evidence has indicated that some members of collective farms shirked collective jobs almost entirely in order to work on their own plots. It was, for example, officially reported in 1939 that some collective farmers accumulated only 20 workdays in a year while some of their colleagues earned credit for 600. Minimum requirements were then established so that every member of a collective had to earn a set number of workday credits within each calendar period or face expulsion and further punishment. These minimums were subsequently increased.

🐀 PARTY CONTROL AND THE M.T.S.

Stalin announced in 1933 that the Party had to take over the control of the collectives, but this order was difficult to carry out because most Party members were not farmers. Only 12,000 of the 243,000 collective farms which existed in 1939 had primary Party organs—the basic and smallest Party unit. The proportion of peasants in the Party membership has been consistently low. Molotov commented in 1922 that it was "primarily a city party, not a village one," and this has continued to be true. Throughout the late 1920's peasants comprised less than 25 per cent of the Party membership, and this dropped to about 20 per cent in 1930. A special recruiting drive in the villages brought it up to almost 29 per cent in 1934, but it had fallen to 19 per cent in 1941. There weren't enough peasant Communists to go around, so the Party hit on the device of the Machine Tractor Station.

This institution grew out of a plan to set up joint-stock companies to own heavy farm machinery such as tractors, combines, harvesters, and threshers. At least a quarter of the necessary capital was to be supplied by the peasants, and it was hoped that such companies might be cooperatively owned and operated by several collective farms working together. It later occurred to the Party that such machine-owning companies were in a position to exercise effective controls over all farms which used or wanted to use the machinery. This new function was assigned by a law of 1933 which decreed that the Machine Tractor Stations (M.T.S.) should be political centers as well as technical centers. The Party set up special political sections in the stations with instructions to be "the eyes and control of the Communist Party in all spheres of life and work of the M.T.S. . . . and the collective farms served by the M.T.S." The primary task of the political sections was to see that the collective farms met all their obligations to the government promptly and in full. Seventeen thousand picked Party members were assigned to the new political sections to carry out these orders. Annual contracts are made between the collective farms and the Machine Tractor Stations. This sounds like local autonomy. The contracts, however, are drawn by the government and they vest complete control of the farming operations of the collective in the M.T.S. No alterations in the terms of the contracts are allowed on the ground that the contract has the force of law and "is a means of execution of the policy of the Communist Party." The contracts specify the services to be performed by the M.T.S. —mainly the supplying of machinery. The amount, time, and method of payment by the collective for these services are also specified. So are the penalties to be enforced against the collectives for failure to meet their obligations to the government. Collective farms which do not have contracts with Machine Tractor Stations are required to deliver more produce in kind to the government than are farms which have contracts. The Party reported in 1947 that farms with M.T.S. contracts supplied half again as much produce to the government as did the noncontract farms. The device, in other words, has worked.

There is much more to the story of collectivization and of collective farms than what has been told here. It is a vitally important part of Soviet history, not only in testing the power of the Communist Party but also in affecting the everyday lives of the ordinary people of the Soviet Union. Collectivization, though not generally popular, has not been an unmitigated curse for all peasants. Rural electrification, machinery, better seeds, improved techniques and implements have benefited some of Russia's millions and millions of peasants. So have opportunities for education and other "cultural advances." This is not to say that some other system might not have produced equal or better results. But no other system existed, and poverty in Russia was not created either by collectivization or by the Communist Party. The description of the Standard Charter as it has operated has served as a vehicle for depicting a part of the conditions under which most Soviet citizens lived during the 1930's and later. Other parts include the successive five-year plans.

Table 5 sets these plans in chronological sequence.

TABLE 5

The Five-Year Plans

Plan	Date of Adoption	Scheduled Period of Operation	Actual Period of Operation
First	Dec., 1927	Sept., 1928–Sept., 1933	1928–Dec., 1932
Second	Jan., 1934	Jan., 1933–Dec., 1937	1933–Mar., 1937
Third	Mar., 1939	Apr., 1937–Mar., 1942	1937–June, 1941
Fourth	Mar., 1946	Jan., 1946–Dec., 1950	1946–Dec., 1950
Fifth	Aug., 1952	Jan., 1951–Dec., 1955	1951–Dec., 1955
Sixth	Feb., 1956	Jan., 1956–Dec., 1960	1956– ?

The plans did not operate as scheduled until after World War II. The first two plans, as previously noted, were announced as having been completed before the scheduled date. The third plan was interrupted by the war. It was replaced by a series of "war economic plans" which operated from 1941 through 1945. The Fifth Five-Year Plan was very drastically altered in 1953, almost to the extent of creating a new plan. However, there was no change in title or number. The early plans aimed at forcing the maximum possible growth in the shortest possible time rather than at a balanced, on-schedule development. As Dr. Harry Schwartz pointed out in his study of Soviet economy, the Soviet five-year plans were not comparable to a railway timetable. A train that runs ahead of its schedule is regarded as just as much a violator of the timetable as a train that runs late. Under the Soviet plans, an industry which ran ahead of schedule was rewarded. Only those which ran late were punished.

Once a plan has been decreed by the Party (and given rubber-stamp approval by the government) it is held to have the force of law and is supposed to be carried out exactly as ordered. But the Party can set aside plans as well as laws. If a part of a plan backfires, as did the collectivization scheme in 1930; or if circumstances render the entire plan unfeasible, as they did in 1941 and 1953; the Party will modify or discard the plan. Stalin once said, "For us . . . the Five-Year Plan is not something given once and for all and finished. For us, a Five-Year Plan is like any other plan—accepted only as an initial approximation which must be altered, made more precise, and completed on the basis of experience." The plans, in other words, are means and not ends. They are important, but not sacrosanct. Alteration and extension on the basis of experience were apparent in some of the contrasts between the first two five-year plans.

✺ CONTRAST OF FIRST AND SECOND PLANS

For one thing, the second was much more complicated and much wider in scope. The first had dealt with agriculture, finances, and about fifty industries. The second dealt with collectivization, specific crops, construction, and about 120 industries. The first plan had stressed quantity of production and had largely ignored quality. Experience demonstrated, however, that it was better to build 100 units which worked than to rush through 150 only to find that 75 had to be scrapped. So the second plan emphasized quality and efficiency in production. The first plan had stressed "industrial construction on a gigantic scale"—"big automobile plants," "giant tractor plants," and "mammoth agricultural machinery plants," as the Party campaign literature described them. When it was discovered that the biggest was not necessarily the best, this emphasis was derided as "giant-mania." The second plan provided for more decentralization. The first plan had grossly overestimated attainable rates of growth. For example, it had called for the production in 1932 of 17 million tons of pig iron—a record which had not been achieved even by 1940. The second plan was, at least by comparison, more realistic. It also paid more attention to the production of consumer goods, although these were still secondary to capital goods.

Pressure upon all workers and managers for increased production was unremitting, and this led to the formal abandonment of the old Marx-Engels formula, "From each according to his ability, to each according to his need." In its place was put a new formula, "From each according to his ability, to each according to his production." This change had been clearly foreshadowed in 1931, when Stalin announced that differential wages were an integral of part of Soviet industry. Thereafter it was repeatedly, officially, and elaborately explained that Soviet socialism did not mean equality. "Equality," thundered Stalin in 1934, ". . . is reactionary, petty bourgeois nonsense. . . ." And the Labor Code was amended in that year to provide that, "If an employee . . . fails through his own fault to reach the standard of production proscribed for him, he shall be paid according to the quality and quantity of his work, but he shall not be guaranteed any minimum wage."

In accordance with these directives an ever-growing number of workers were put on a piecework basis, not only at jobs where piecework is customary, but also at jobs where piecework seems almost impossible. The "proscribed standard of production" (the norm) was set for job after job, and frequently raised. If a worker fulfilled his norm in quality and quantity, he was paid the base wage for his job. If he failed to turn out the required quantity and quality, he was docked. On the other hand, if he "over-fulfilled" his norm, he was paid a bonus which mounted rapidly as he increased his output. Numerous awards and honors, some of them carrying substantial material rewards as well as glory, provided additional incentives to over-fulfill the norms. "Socialist competition," so called, was everywhere encouraged among individual workers and among groups of workers. On collective farms, for example, much of the work was assigned to "brigades." If one brigade outproduced the others, the members of the winning brigade were credited with extra workdays; but if a brigade fell below the average, it was penalized by a reduction of workday credits. Competition within a brigade was maintained by dividing the brigade into squads whch tried to outdo each other. The use of military terminology is revealing. Life in the Soviet Union partakes of the nature of war. "Brigades fight the battle of hog-raising" on the collective-farm front. "Shock troops (or shock-workers—*udarniki*)" are hastily thrown into the "battle" to bolster weak spots and "to capture objectives." This is more than a propagandist's trick. It is indicative of a state of mind which is important.

STAKHANOVISM AND THE LABOR CODE

Growing use was made throughout the second plan (and thereafter, also) of the "speed-up," which was glorified and made glamorous after the middle 1930's under the label of Stakhanovism. During the summer of 1935, a young coal miner named Alexei Stakhanov hit upon a technique which had long been standard in capitalist-owned mines. Instead of dividing his time among various tasks, such as looking after his own tools, clearing away rock falls, timbering, preparing the "face" for drilling, and so on, young Stakhanov assigned those jobs to members of his gang. He was then able to concentrate on the actual breaking out of the coal, and he promptly surpassed all previous Soviet production records. The story of his exploit reached the top Party bosses, who quickly saw in it an opportunity to speed up production. The tremendous power of the whole propaganda machine was thrown behind the promotion of Stakhanovism. Stakhanov himself was lionized and showered with honors so that he became one of the nation's heroes. The highly glamorized story of his deeds and of those who imitated him was used to stimulate other workers. Those who made record over-fulfillments of the norms—whether by topping more sugar beets than anybody else or by establishing a record run with a freight train—were given the title of Stakhanovites and were held up as models to all the others. Stakhanovites were given higher wage rates, preferential treatment in food and housing, and other perquisites— all of which added highly material inducements to the trumpets of glory.

The use of inducements combined with coercions has been a mark of

Soviet life. "We must," said Lenin in 1917, "either overtake and out-strip the advanced countries technically and economically or perish." And his successors have paid the most careful heed to these words. It will be remembered that the 1918 Constitution had made all able-bodied persons between the ages of fifteen and fifty-one liable for compulsory labor. This law was replaced during the NEP by a Labor Code which abolished general compulsory labor except in emergencies. Under the Labor Code, which became applicable to every person as soon as he took a job, workers were forbidden to leave their employment without the specific consent of the head of the enterprise. The extraordinary demand for labor made this unenforceable. It became a regular practice, in defiance of the law, for workers to shop around for the highest wages and the best living conditions. Labor turnover reached great heights in many industries, management and labor alike ignoring the law. Tardiness and absenteeism also became very serious problems which the Party and the government sought to overcome by a decree of 1932 ordering, "that even in the case of one day's absence from work without sufficient reason, the worker shall be dismissed from the services of the factory or enterprise, and shall be deprived of the ration cards issued to him . . . and shall also be deprived of the use of the lodgings which were allotted to him. . . ." The Soviet courts, at least until 1939, held that this law covered tardinesses as well as absences. A tardiness of more than twenty minutes "without sufficient reason" was held to be tantamount to a day's absence and was punishable, therefore, by dismissal. Failure to enforce this law uniformly made it even more of a threat to a worker. This 1932 law was supplemented in 1938 by a decree which required all workers and employees in "all state and co-operative institutions and enterprises" to have workbooks, or, as they have sometimes been called, "labor passports." The text of the decree is self-explanatory:

Workbooks are to contain the following information about the owner of the book: surname, name, and patronymic; age; education; profession; information about his work and about his movement from one enterprise to another, the causes of such shifts, and also [a record] of encouragements and rewards received. . . .

Workers and employees must produce their workbooks for inspection by the managing board when signing up [for a job]. Managing boards may employ only workers and employees who present workbooks. . . .

The workbook is to be kept by the management . . . and returned to the worker or employee on his dismissal.

Such stringent restrictions upon the free movement and employment of workers and peasants as those described here are paradoxical in a nation whose constitution proclaims it to be a "socialist state of workers and peasants." Solution of the paradox is supplied by the authoritative Soviet pronouncement that "the dictatorship of the proletariat is a power not limited by any laws." The application of this principle to labor law has been that the law was not for the protection of labor but for the purpose of increasing production. Dr. Gsovski has noted that ". . . the legislation enacted since socialism has been declared achieved in the Soviet Union has tightened labor discipline and increased the powers of management at the expense of the rights of labor." [2]

GENERAL ACCOMPLISHMENTS OF THE SECOND AND THIRD FIVE-YEAR PLANS

The declaration of achievement was officially made in the first article of the 1936 Constitution. The national income, according to Soviet claims, was increased from 35 billion rubles in 1930 to 128 billion rubles in 1940. Within the same period, gross industrial production was boosted from just under 32 billion rubles to over 138 billion rubles. Most of this increase was in the value of capital goods produced. That figure went up from 23 billion rubles in 1932 (the 1930 figure is not available) to almost 85 billion rubles in 1940. The figures for the value of consumer goods produced in those years were, respectively, a little over 20 billion rubles and a little under 54 billion rubles. Emphasis was still on the making of producer goods. Production of these was raised by almost 370 per cent; production of consumer goods, by 270 per cent.

It is impossible for many reasons to say with certainty what these developments meant in terms of the general welfare and the living standards of the Soviet people. After 1930 the Soviets did not publish those statistics necessary (national income, price indices, and so on) for an accurate, adequate statistical measurement. Statistical measures can be very misleading even when honestly drawn on the basis of full information. They are sure to be misleading when they have an incomplete basis of fact. Eyewitness reports have been completely contradictory—partly because of prejudices, partly because of ignorance, and partly because of Soviet restrictions and camouflage. Many tourists in the summer of 1937 who saw only new cars on the streets of Moscow did not know that an official decree in April, 1937, had banished all old automobiles from the capital to the provinces. Many observers forgot the obvious truism that Leningrad and Moscow are the Soviet's showcases. The existence of tremendous variations of living standards not only among the population as a whole but even within special groups or occupations makes accurate generalization impossible. A member of one of the few millionaire collectives, for instance, had a far higher living standard than a member of an ordinary or of a marginal collective. Yet both were collective farmers. "Industrial worker" might have meant an unskilled laborer whose average monthly wage in 1935 (according to Soviet figures) was 118 rubles or an engineer whose average monthly wage was 436 rubles. A "buck private" in the Red Army received 10.5 rubles a month; a Red Army colonel, 2400 rubles; and so on. Since the ruble had no real connection with any foreign currency it is impossible even to translate these figures into dollars. The best that can be offered is a general approximation.

Prosperity and austerity are relative terms which have no fixed meaning. It needs to be remembered, in speaking of living standards, that the Russian people have never enjoyed as good living as have the people of the United States. It ought also to be noted that as of 1935–36 46 per cent of the Soviet people (according to Soviet figures) had been born after 1917, so that they had no non-Soviet basis for comparison. Stalin's declarations in 1936 that "Life is better. Life is more cheerful," seemed to many of his people to be no more than simple statements of fact. Those middle years of the second plan were the peak of Soviet prosperity between 1918 and 1955. There had been a substantial recovery from the extreme hardships which attended the first plan. Nominal wages kept going up, and the supply of consumer goods kept increasing despite certain flaws in distribution. It was reported in 1935 that 50 million Soviet citizens owned state bonds. Rationing was abolished in 1935–36. In 1937 collective farmers were "forgiven" their arrears in grain collections, and their fees to the M.T.S. were reduced. Workers and their dependents benefited from the cancellation of all arrears on their tax and insurance payments before 1936. And in 1938 it was reported that the total savings deposits of Soviet citizens had reached a new high of over 4 billion rubles. On the other hand, it has been calculated that the average employed Soviet citizen did not live as well at the peak of his prosperity as did the average unemployed citizen of the United States at the depth of the depression of the early 1930's. There were also other contradictions.

Nominal wages went up, but real wages did not increase until after 1935, and then they did not keep pace with prices. In Moscow, the price of rye bread had risen from .08 rubles per kilogram in 1928 to .85 rubles a kilogram in 1936; rice, from .48 to 8.00; potatoes, from .11 to .30; sugar, from .62 to 4.10; and beef, from .87 to 8.00. This was inflation and it reflected the fact that, though there were many more goods on the market, there were also many more would-be buyers. Price reductions between 1936 and 1939 eased this situation, and—along with the end of rationing—showed an increased volume of foodstuffs and goods. The increases were, however, very uneven. According to Soviet figures, the amounts of meat, milk, and fats (calculated on a per capita basis) were less in 1938 than in 1928. But there were twice as many potatoes, and twice as much sugar, and three times as much soap. Total production of such items as shoes, cottons, and woolens had greatly increased, but the increase had not kept pace with the population growth. So, on a per capita basis, there was not very much difference between 1928 and 1937 as far as availability of these items was concerned. Here was another apparent paradox. Russia in 1912 had had about a million retail trade outlets. There were about 645,000 of them in 1927; 285,000 in 1933; and 354,000 in 1938. This meant about one retail outlet for every 600 rural consumers, and one for about every 320 urban consumers. But the general impression was that there were more goods—shoes, sheets, yard goods, silk stockings, suits, books, magazines, phonographs, phonograph records, cosmetics, and so on—in these years than many Soviet citizens had ever seen.

Beauty shops and specialty shops were opened in the larger cities. Real food—in variety and in quantity—replaced the wooden and plaster models which had filled store windows during the hungry years. There still was not enough to go around, partly because more people demanded goods than before. Some items were always hard to get and were snapped up as soon as they were put on sale. There was no equality in distribution or in buying power. It has been estimated that about a third of the national income (exclusive of what the government kept for itself) was paid to government workers, who comprised only an eighth of the working population. A second third went to the nonagricultural, nongovernment workers, who numbered between a third and a fourth of the working population. The peasants, who made up considerably more than half of the working force, received less than a third of the national income.

Housing was another very serious and unsolved problem despite strenuous construction efforts. Almost half of the nonfarm dwellings in use in 1941 had been built by the Soviets, but the urban population had more than tripled in the same period. Acute shortages and appalling overcrowding therefore continued. Rents, however, were kept very low. One authority has asserted that the average rent charge was not more than 5 per cent of the family income. This may be misleading, however, unless it is noticed that the figure is for the total family income. Most Soviet families have more than one wage earner.

A new marriage and family law was promulgated in 1936. This made it much harder and much more costly to get a divorce. In fact, a sort of sliding scale was established so that a second divorce cost much more than a first; a third, much more than a second, and so on. The amount of alimony was also increased. The new law prohibited abortions (which had been legal) and then went to the other extreme of giving state aid to large families. Bachelors had to pay a special tax. The effects of this new law may be illustrated by two items from the Soviet press. The first was a report in July, 1936, that divorces in Moscow had dropped from 2214 in June to 215 in July. The second was a report in November, 1937, that divorces in Leningrad had declined from 10,313 (January–June, 1936) to 3860 (January–June, 1937) and that the birth rate had greatly increased.

"SOCIAL SECURITY" AND TAXES

It has sometimes been asserted that deficiencies in wages, housing, and possibilities for real home life have been more than offset by the Soviet advances in social security and social services. One typical account, after speaking of deficiencies in housing, said:

> Of decisive importance in making crowded conditions more bearable has been the development of community facilities which have freed the dwelling from many functions. Hospitals and maternity hospitals take care of the sick and of young mothers; nursery schools, kindergartens, and junior clubs are the daytime homes of many children. Many meals are taken in dining halls and restaurants. . . . A good deal of social life goes on in clubs. . . .

This is a statement of fact—as far as it goes. The Soviet government has established day nurseries and nursery schools in connection with factories, collective farms, and other enterprises. These are not universal, but they are general. Whether one interprets this as, "The Soviet mother is free to work, since she may leave her baby in the factory nursery (or farm nursery) visiting the infant to give it suck or to play with it," or as, "The Soviet mother is forced by economic necessity to work, and must leave her baby in the nursery," may perhaps be a matter of opinion. Instances proving either case could be cited, but the weight of evidence seems to indicate that it is more often a matter of necessity than of choice. Pupils, from nursery schools to universities, ordinarily have at least one meal a day at school. Workers eat at their places of employment and their wives, if they are not themselves employed, usually are allowed to eat there too. Is it choice or necessity? Is it more desirable for a family to have its social life in clubs and in "parks of culture and rest" or in the home? The reader must answer for himself. The fact is that such clubs and parks were built in increasing number throughout the 1930's and later. They ranged from show places in Moscow to literal "holes-in-the-wall" and barren dumps, and they were used by an increasing number of people.

As for social security and social services, these, too, were increased through the 1930's. Social security covered all factory and office workers, and included sickness, disability, old age benefits; care in rest homes;

sports facilities; and children's institutions. Collective-farm workers were not under social security, the collective farms being required to set up funds for their own benefit. Precise measurements of the amount of money spent by the government on social security are lacking, because published figures lumped social security, housing, education, and other items together. The total for 1937 was approximately at the rate of 157 rubles per person per year. It was higher in 1938. Social services include medical and other health services, educational and recreational facilities. The improvement in medical and health services may be quantitatively measured. The number of physicians was increased from 63,100 in 1928 to 112,400 in 1938. (The figures have been rounded off.) Other increases in the same period were: hospital beds, from 217,700 to 603,-800; maternity hospital beds, from 27,300 to 134,800; urban medical centers, from 5600 to 12,600; and rural medical centers, from 7500 to 11,500. These are notable gains, but demand exceeded supply here as in consumer goods. The well-publicized rest homes where workers may spend their vacations increased their capacity some five times over between 1928 to 1938, but still accommodated only about 10 per cent of the workers. The peasant majority were the least favored; industrial workers were somewhat better off; and government employees, especially Party members, were the most favored. Political affiliations, type and place of employment determined the benefits received more often than did need. Favoritism—intentional or due to circumstances—was also to be found in education.

All the tremendous growth in production, social services, and defense measures had to be paid for by some means. The official Soviet reports claimed that the First Five-Year Plan required a capital investment of 52.5 billion rubles; the second, 115 billion rubles. The third (which had to be broken off), even more. Where did all this money come from? Some was raised by domestic loans; some, by direct taxation on property, income, and inheritance; and some was provided by profits from industry. But since 1930, when it was first introduced, the greatest part of the state's revenue has come from a "turnover tax." This tax, calculated on the retail selling price, is assessed against every item produced or handled by state-owned agencies. (The present tense is used here because the turnover tax is still so calculated and collected.) This covers not only the output of mines, factories, mills, oil wells, lumbering, and other industrial or processing enterprises, but also the handling of foodstuffs and other agricultural produce. It will be recalled that the first charge against a collective farm is to provide the government with a share of the produce at a price set by the government. (The size of the share is also established by the government.) This produce pays a turnover tax. Throughout the Second Five-Year Plan, this tax on foodstuffs amounted to roughly two-thirds of the total turnover tax, or about a half of the total state revenue. The turnover tax, in the same period, supplied approximately three-quarters of the total state revenue. What this meant in terms of an individual may be surmised from the following example. The state-fixed price for 2.2 lbs. (1 kilogram) of sugar in 1936 (after the end of rationing) was 4.2 rubles. Eighty-five per cent of this (3.57 rubles) was the turnover tax. During 1937 the turnover taxes ranged as follows: on flour and bread, 70–80 per cent; on salt, 66–83 per cent; on cigarettes, 75–90 per cent; on soap, 34–59 per cent; and on cotton goods, 44–65 per cent. (The percentages, to repeat, are percentages of the retail prices.) The answer to the question of where the money came from for industrialization, reforms, and other government expenditures is that most of it was raised by the very heavy, indirect taxation of the Soviet masses.

⊕ FORCED LABOR

One other aspect of the forced industrialization of the U.S.S.R. under the five-year plans cannot be ignored without doing very serious violence to the truth. This is the use of forced labor—more graphically termed slave labor—on projects vital to the development of the Soviet economy. There are legitimate doubts and disputes over details, but the general fact of the existence of forced labor as an integral part of the Soviet economic system (at least between 1930 and 1954) is undeniable. Immediately after Lenin's coup in 1917, Bolshevik authorities began sentencing offenders to "corrective labor." A year later concentration camps were established for "counterrevolutionary *bourgeoisie*." The two were, in effect, combined in 1923 with the setting up of correctional labor camps in the north. These were controlled by the OGPU (Unified State Political Police—the secret police) from the start, and by 1929 there were seven such camps in that region with a total camp population of above half a million. Inmates were chiefly employed at lumbering and fishing; and the exports of lumber which they prepared helped in the building up of Soviet credits abroad. Then came the five-year plans with their tremendous demands for masses of workers to construct new industrial centers; to build railroads, canals, and highways; and to supply raw materials. Since labor could not be induced in sufficient quantity to do these vitally necessary jobs, compulsion became necessary. The victims—mainly but not exclusively—were the "rich" peasants whom the Party had determined to liquidate as part of the process of collectivization.

Confinement to a jail as punishment was largely replaced by sentences to corrective labor camps (for terms of three years and longer) and to corrective labor colonies (for shorter terms). Short-term sentences almost disappeared. They had accounted for about a third of all sentences imposed in 1927; in 1930 they amounted to less than a fiftieth. Sentences to hard labor more than tripled during the same period. But the great growth in forced labor came after the publication of laws, in 1932, for the protection of state property. Minimum punishment was ten years at forced labor. Whether so intended or not, this guaranteed an adequate labor force for the construction of the Baltic Sea–White Sea Canal. The job was assigned to the OGPU in November, 1931, and was completed in June, 1933. The canal—triumphantly named after Stalin—was 141.05 miles long, and had 19 locks, 15 dams, and 32 subsidiary canals. Its total cost was relatively low because the work was done by forced labor. The total number of workers has never been revealed, but there were almost 300,000 employed toward the end of the job. Seventy-two thousand were released as "rehabilitated" at the end of the task. The OGPU also built the Moscow–Volga Canal (1933–37) using some 200,000 forced laborers on the project. While this was in process, the OGPU was abolished and its functions were handed over to the People's Commissariat of Internal Affairs, the NKVD. The new agency was empowered to send persons into exile or into forced labor for periods up to five years without a trial. The labor supply thus ensured, a special department—the Chief Administration of Corrective Labor Camps and Settlements (GULAG)—was set up to handle it, and the construction of all highways was entrusted to the NKVD.

No figures have been released, but it is apparent that the OGPU-NKVD was the largest single employer of labor in the U.S.S.R. during the 1930's. Its activities increased in scope, number, and variety throughout the next decade. Forced labor was regularly employed on the construction and maintenance of roads, railroads, canals, harbor works, air fields, and fortifications; the construction of factories and industrial settlements; lumbering, fishing, quarrying, mining of all kinds; agriculture; and certain industries. A conservative estimate, based on calculations from published Soviet data, placed the number of forced laborers in the U.S.S.R. in 1940 at over 13 million. This is a guess which in the absence of the necessary data cannot be conclusively proved or disproved. There is, however, enough evidence to demonstrate beyond any reasonable doubt that the forced laborers in the Soviet Union must have numbered not hundred of thousands but millions. These victims of the system contributed directly and indirectly to Soviet productivity. Moreover, since their housing, food, clothing, and all other perquisites were substandard, even for the Soviet Union, they helped to improve the living standards of their more fortunate compatriots. Shortages and inadequacies of all kinds would obviously have been very much greater if supplies and facilities had had to be stretched to cover an additional 13 million shares. Forced labor was not merely a by-product of the five-year plans. It was an indispensable and integral part of them.

⚙ THE 1936 CONSTITUTION

This fact—together with others which have been presented about collectivization, labor laws, and political power—will explain to the reader why consideration of the 1936 Constitution has been delayed until now. No amount of study of this document or of the circumstances of its promulgation will reveal the realities of political power or of life in the Soviet Union. "Here in the Soviet Union, in the land of the dictatorship of the proletariat," Stalin proclaimed, "the fact that not a single important political or organizational question is decided by our Soviet [i.e., "state"] and other mass organizations without directions from the Party must be regarded as the highest expression of the leading role of the Party." It is also pertinent to recall in connection with the "Fundamental Law of the Union of Soviet Socialist Republics" (which is what Soviet jurists always call the constitution) the authoritative statement, previously quoted, that "the dictatorship of the proletariat is a power not limited by any laws." Stalin in presenting the 1936 Constitution said, it ". . . preserves the regime of the dictatorship of the proletariat just as it also preserves without change the leading position of the Communist Party of the U.S.S.R." The argument sometimes advanced that the 1936 Constitution represented an ideal toward which the regime was striving was flatly and repeatedly refuted by the Party bosses themselves. The constitution, they declared, was "a summary of gains already achieved"; a description of an existing reality, not of a desired, future Utopia. This was so manifestly untrue, as the reader may see for himself by comparing the constitution with the record so far presented, that some may wonder why any attention at all should be given to the Fundamental Law. The answer is twofold. The promulgation of the Fundamental Law was a part of the Soviet story, and the formal state machinery which it established is a very real part of Soviet life. It would be just as misleading to ignore it as to depend upon it exclusively for information.

The decision to create a new constitution was first made by the Party bosses. Orders to implement this decision reached the Eighth Congress of Soviets in February, 1935. A Drafting Commission of 31 members under the presidency of Stalin set to work, and about a year and a half later it produced a draft constitution. The document was given the widest possible circulation. Newspapers published the text in full, and (reputedly) 60 million copies were circulated all over the U.S.S.R. Hundreds of thousands of groups, under Party direction and orders, discussed the proposal; and it was reported that they suggested 154,000 changes. This was mass participation on a grandiose scale. Measured by the actual terms of the document as finally adopted, it didn't mean much. Only 43 of the 154,000 suggestions finally found their way into the new constitution. But the fact that they were consulted at all—even as a gesture—undoubtedly gratified and satisfied many persons. At any rate, the revised draft was presented by Stalin to an extraordinary session of the Eighth Congress of Soviets with his assurance that it was "the only thoroughly democratic constitution in the world." Either the congress was satisfied with it or didn't dare to dissent, because the Stalin Constitution was adopted unanimously with only a few editorial and no substantive revisions on December 5, 1936, a date which has since been celebrated as a Soviet holiday.

The first of its thirteen chapters describes the "Social Structure" of the U.S.S.R., which is defined as "a socialist state of workers and peasants." Its "political foundation" is the system of Soviets of Workers' Deputies. Its "economic foundations rest on the socialist system of economy and the socialist ownership of the tools and resources of production." All property is designated either as "socialist property" or as "personal property." There is no private property in the sense in which it exists in the United States. Socialist property may exist "either in the form of state property [belonging to the whole people] or in the form of co-operative and collective-farm property." To the category of state property belong the land, all natural resources, mills, mines, factories, banks, municipal enterprises, most dwellings in urban and industrial areas, all transportation and communication systems, and so on. Co-operative and collective-farm property includes collective-farm buildings, livestock, equipment, and tools; and (as previously noted) the land occupied by collective farms. Personal property includes savings, income from labor, dwelling houses, house furnishings and furniture, and, in general, what may be described as "articles of personal use and convenience." The right of inheritance of personal property is guaranteed. But no property may be used "for the exploitation of the labor of others," and none may be used in any manner deemed by the authorities to be opposed to the interests of socialist economy. Mismanagement of personal property may result in its forfeiture to the state—which, through its agencies, decides whether there has been mismanagement. Personal property, in short, may not be used at its owner's discretion.

🔹 "RULER-IN-LAW"

Jurists and international lawyers have sometimes disagreed as to whether the Stalin Constitution established a federal union or a federation or a confederacy. At the risk of technical inaccuracy, the U.S.S.R. will be spoken of here as a federal union, and its major constituent parts will be called member republics. There were eleven of these when the constitution was adopted. Five more were added in 1940, one of the latter dropping out again in 1956. The constitution declares them all to be equal, but they range in size from the Armenian Soviet Socialist Republic—about 1,600,000 people (1956) and 11,568 square miles—to the vast Russian Soviet Federative Socialist Republic—over 113,200,000 people (1956) and more than 6,360,000 square miles. The R.S.F.S.R. contains well over a half of the total population and more than three-quarters of the whole area of the U.S.S.R. Its laws obtain within the Kirghiz, and the Kazak S.S.R.'s. The R.S.F.S.R. is actually the dominant member of the union.

The federal constitution and laws are superior to those of the member republics, and authority over most important matters is centralized in the federal government. Specified rights are reserved to the member republics, but the constitution vested in the federal union control over all economic planning and implementation thereof; all taxes and revenues—federal, republican, and local—all industrial, mercantile, and financial enterprises of more than local scope; and the monetary and credit system. Education, public health, labor legislation, national security—including control of the armed forces and the police powers—are all in the hands of the federal government. So is the power to make war and peace. The local and republican government agencies and officials, furthermore, also serve the federal government, to which they are subordinate. The governmental machinery set up by the Stalin Constitution is, in other words, highly centralized.

The pattern, which was set during the discussion of the constitution, of mass participation in at least the outward forms of government was carried on and extended by the provisions in regard to suffrage and the soviets. All Soviet citizens of sound mind who are eighteen years of age or older and who have not been specifically deprived of suffrage by court action have the right to vote in local, republican, and federal elections. Voting is by secret ballot, and the elections are direct. This marked a decided departure from the previous practice, which had featured limited suffrage, open voting, and indirect elections. Almost every possible inducement and pressure has been used by the Party and the government to see to it that the citizenry exercised their rights of suffrage. The results, as officially announced, have been spectacular, at least in the case of the federal elections. In the election of the first Supreme Soviet in 1937, 96 per cent of all those qualified to vote did so. The official records for the second federal election (1946) claimed a 99.7 per cent vote; for the third federal election (1950), a 99.8 per cent turnout, and for the fourth (1954), 99.98 per cent.

It should also be noted that in addition to the federal Supreme Soviet there are six other levels of soviets ranging from the supreme soviets of the member republics to the village soviets. (At the time of the local elections in 1947–48 there were more than 66,000 soviets altogether, and their total membership was about 1,400,000.) All these deputies are elected on the basis of universal citizen suffrage. Lower soviets, unlike the federal Supreme Soviet, which only ratifies actions taken by others, frequently make decisions (always subject, of course, to reversal from above). Moreover, these lower soviets meet frequently—once a month in villages and cities, every other month in districts and areas, and every third month in regions and territories. They serve three important purposes in the Soviet scheme of things. First, they form a complex series of ubiquitous gauges of public opinion. Second, they create the feeling among the citizenry of being a part of the state system. Even if this feeling were entirely an illusion, which it is not, it would still be important as a tie binding Soviet people to their regime. Third, the soviets form the bony structure, the muscles, and the flesh of the body politic, whose brain and nerve nets are the Party. There is no split between government and Party in the U.S.S.R. The government is the creature and the agent of the Party, as may be illustrated by the method of nominating candidates for public office.

The Stalin Constitution makes the following provision for the nomination of candidates: "Candidates are nominated by election districts. The right to nominate candidates is secured to public organizations and societies of the working people: Communist Party organizations, trade unions, co-operatives, youth organizations, and cultural societies." An authorized explanation of this provision stated that each group was bound to try to choose as candidate a person who would be equally acceptable to Party members and to non-Party people. So far as is known, no one to whom the Party was opposed has ever been nominated. This does not mean that all nominees have been Party members. Some have been Party followers (non-Party Bolsheviks is what they are called in the Soviet Union) or, at least, fellow travelers. Nomination is synonymous with election since only one candidate may be put up for each post. Approximately one out of every four deputies elected to the Supreme Soviet in 1937 was not a Party member. (The figures for the

1946 and 1954 elections were, roughly, one out of five.) The percentage of non-Party people in the lower soviets has been, on an average, somewhat higher.

The federal Supreme Soviet, which has been repeatedly mentioned, was declared by the 1936 Constitution to be "the highest organ of state power" with exclusive right of legislation for the U.S.S.R. It is a bicameral body with coequal chambers: the Soviet of the Union and the Soviet of Nationalities. The former, elected on the basis of one deputy for every 300,000 persons in the U.S.S.R., is supposed to consider all matters before it from the viewpoint of the whole federal union. The Soviet of Nationalities, elected on a basis of a set number of deputies for each type of unit, is charged with considering matters from the viewpoints of the groups represented. A Supreme Soviet is elected for a four-year term,[3] and has two regular sessions a year. The length of the sessions (the two chambers meet simultaneously and often sit jointly) has varied somewhat, but it has usually been less than a week. The size of the Supreme Soviet (1143 deputies in the first, 1339 in the second, 1317 in the third, and 1347 in the fourth) and the brevity of its sessions have guaranteed that it should not be a deliberative body. The experience of the second session of the first Supreme Soviet (which met in August, 1938) may be taken as an illustration.

There were eight items on the agenda proposed, and these were unanimously adopted by both chambers without question or discussion literally in a matter of minutes. Among the subjects were such important and complicated matters as "the unified state budget," the creation of an entire judicial system, the election of a Supreme Court, and the consideration of several major interim acts and appointments. All these were dealt with in eight working days. The story of the adoption of the budget—up to then, the largest in Soviet history—is as follows. The federal Commissar of Finance presented a report of some 14,000 words to a joint sitting of the two houses. The joint sitting was then immediately adjourned, and the budget was considered separately by each chamber, which heard a further report of some 7000 words from the chairmen of their Budget Commissions. Each soviet then devoted three sittings to "debates" on the budget. Fifteen deputies (out of 569) and two administrators spoke in the Soviet of the Union; fifteen deputies (out of 574) and one administrator, in the Soviet of Nationalities. The budget chairmen and the Finance Commissar then "replied to the debate" and both chambers proceeded to adopt the budget, first, section by section, and then as a whole, without one single dissent or abstention. This was not an atypical event.[4]

Appointments and elections by the Supreme Soviet include the members of the Presidium, the members of the Council of People's Commissars,[5] the members of the federal Supreme Court and special courts, and the procurator-general. The latter is charged by the constitution with "supreme supervisory power to ensure the strict observance of the law" by all officials and all citizens. He is appointed for a seven-year term. The Supreme Court of the U.S.S.R. is "the highest judicial organ" and is charged with the supervision of all other judicial bodies. Its members are elected for terms of five years. The Council of People's Commissars is "the highest executive and administrative organ of the state power." Its decisions and decrees are binding throughout the U.S.S.R., and it is superior to the Council of Commissars of the member republics. It is answerable to the Supreme Soviet or to the Presidium. The Presidium was given very extensive powers by the 1936 Constitution and these have since been increased. When the Supreme Soviet is not in session—which is most of the time—the Presidium has full power to issue decrees, appoint or dismiss commissars and top military officers, order mobilization, declare a war, ratify treaties, and proclaim martial law. This listing is not exhaustive. The Presidium also has the sole authority to convene and dissolve the Supreme Soviet, and to arrange the elections to that body. And it can interpret legislation even when the Supreme Soviet is in session. Of course, the constitution provides that "The Presidium . . . is accountable to the Supreme Soviet for all its acts," but so far no action taken by a Presidium has ever been challenged, much less reversed.

✆ CIVIL RIGHTS AND DUTIES

One other chapter of the 1936 Constitution must be briefly discussed. This is "Chapter X: Fundamental Rights and Duties of Citizens." The constitution is explicit on the matter of freedoms, rights, and duties. The specified rights include the right to work, the right to rest and leisure, the right to maintenance in old age and in case of illness or disability, the right to education, and the right to unite in public organizations. Equality of these rights without regard to "race or nationality" is guaranteed. The specifically listed freedoms are freedom of conscience, freedom of religious worship and of antireligious propaganda, freedom of speech, freedom of the press, freedom of assembly, and freedom for street demonstrations. The equality of sexes, the inviolability of persons and homes, and the privacy of correspondence are all also guaranteed. The citizen is duty-bound to work; to abide by the constitution; to observe the laws; to maintain labor discipline; "to safeguard and protect public, socialist property as the sacred and inviolable foundation of the Soviet system." Military service is also decreed a universal obligation, and defense of the country is defined as "the sacred duty of every citizen of the U.S.S.R."

The bitterest of arguments have raged ever since the adoption of this constitution over the question of whether these provisions of rights and freedoms have been operative. The constitution—aside from the official statement that it represented an accurate description of existing realities—said flatly that these rights and freedoms existed. The operative words were all in the present and not in a conditional tense. The articles read "have the right," "are guaranteed," "are protected," and so on. One additional, special point may be made. Stalin in offering the draft constitution in 1936 said, among many other things, that "there is no room within the U.S.S.R. for the existence of several [political] parties or for freedom for those parties. There is room in the U.S.S.R. only for one party, the Communist Party." And the article which states the right of citizens to unite "in public organizations" also says that the Communist Party is "the vanguard of the working people" and "the leading core of all organizations." This one-party monopoly can be reconciled with freedoms and democracy only by accepting the Communist view that a political party represents a class and that there can be several parties only when there are several opposing classes. The first article of the Stalin Constitution recognized the existence of only two classes in the U.S.S.R., workers and peasants. Stalin announced that these two "far from being mutually hostile are, on the contrary, friendly." Hence, so the Communist argument runs, there can be only one party. It may also be pointed out that all public disputes over the existence of civil liberties and personal freedoms within the Soviet Union have taken place beyond the Soviet borders. Either all Soviet citizens have been in perfect accord on this point or the promised freedoms have not covered an expression of disagreement. The record of what happened within the Party during the middle and later 1930's would seem to indicate that the second alternative was the correct one.

THE GREAT PURGES

Party purges or cleansings had long been used to weed out the unfit and weak. They had also been marked (in varying degrees) with the patterns set by Marx when he expelled from his infant Communist Party Weitling and Hess and everyone else who did not accept Marx's leadership. Lenin had done the same thing during his years of exile, but when in power he found room—even at top levels—for men who disagreed with him. There is no room for dissidents in a monolithic party, however, as the purges of the 1930's proved. A purge in 1933–34 cut the Party's membership by about a third, and purgings which were equally drastic but less extensive numerically went on steadily until 1938. The murder (in December, 1934) of Stalin's closest associate, Sergei Kirov, set off a purge which reached a series of climaxes in five spectacular trials.

Zinoviev, Kamenev, and several other onetime Party luminaries were brought to trial on charges of treason in January, 1935. They were convicted and sentenced to imprisonment. About a year and a half later, Zinoviev and Kamenev were again brought to trial along with some of their followers. This time they were charged with conspiring, under the leadership of Trotsky, to overthrow the regime with the aid of foreign states. The accused men confessed to the charges. Sixteen of them were convicted and executed. In January, 1937 Radek, Pyatakov, and other "old Bolsheviks" were tried and convicted. Thirteen of the group were executed. Six months later, eight army officers of very high rank—including Marshal Tukhachevski, who had been regarded as the top man in the Red Army—were convicted of treason by a secret court-martial and shot. The commander-in-chief of the Red Navy (Orlov) was shot as a traitor in February, 1938. The final climax came with the highly publicized trial in March, 1938, of twenty-one persons. Among them were Rykov, once head of the Supreme Economic Council and close associate of Lenin; Yagoda, who had been head of the NKVD; and Bukharin, former editor of *Izvestia*. The twenty-one were charged with "having on the instructions of the intelligence services of foreign states hostile to the Soviet Union formed a conspiratorial group named the 'Bloc of Rights and Trotskyites' with the object of espionage . . . wrecking, diversionist and terrorist activities, undermining the military power of the U.S.S.R. . . . dismembering of the U.S.S.R. . . . and, lastly, with the object of overthrowing the socialist . . . system existing in the U.S.S.R. and of restoring capitalism. . . ." The prosecuting attorney was Vishinsky, who later won notoriety in other fields. The accused all confessed their guilt in open court, and were duly convicted and sentenced. The trial and especially the confessions were stunningly sensational. Here were men—long-time Party members—who had held positions of great trust and responsibility (Rykov, for example, had succeeded Lenin as chairman of the Council of People's Commissars) and who had hitherto been identified only as Party stalwarts, now abjectly confessing the most heinous crimes against the regime of which they had been distinguished agents.

Almost inevitably certain questions rise to mind. Were the charges true? If so, how can one explain the betrayal of a cause by men whose whole lives had been devoted to its furtherance? Were the charges false? If so, how can one explain a cause which will betray its servants? If the accused were really traitors, what could have happened to make them plot the destruction of a system which they themselves had labored to build? If they were not traitors, what had happened to their Party colleagues that they were willing to sacrifice their comrades? There are no answers which fit all the known facts, but there is enough evidence to support certain generalizations.

That there were purges and trials on a very extensive scale is an obvious fact which may serve as a starting point. The victims included an unknown number of "little people" as well as the more famous persons. (About a fifth of all the Party members were expelled, many were exiled and many were killed.) The feeling of helplessness in the face of an unholy and apparently insatiable terror was universal. Observers of the most varied sympathies reported that the people as a whole were haunted by a horrible insecurity. No one knew where next the blows might fall. These are simple facts. Less simple, but no less well attested and therefore no less factual, was the existence of a number of opponents of the powers-that-were. Some of these operated as individuals, some as members of various kinds of associations which ranged from loose, informal groups to tightly knit, conspiratorial bands. Among such "oppositionists" were some who accepted the leadership of Trotsky, and some who were ready to deal with anybody who could or would serve their purpose of changing the personnel of the regime. There is evidence—not that presented by the government at the trial or elsewhere—which proves that there were deliberate acts of sabotage and "wrecking." There is also evidence which proves that not all who were purged and punished were guilty of sabotage or wrecking or treason or anything else. Old grudges were paid off, and ambitious individuals removed those who blocked their advancement. Many fell victims to a hysteria which fed upon itself. There is one further general and obvious fact. Those Party leaders who had opposed Stalin before the Party became monolithic either did not survive the Great Purge, or, if they survived, they no longer were leaders. Those who had not crossed Stalin fared better.

CHAPTER XXV

Conspiracy and Diplomacy

REVIEW OF FOREIGN POLICIES

The primary, overall aim of Lenin's foreign policies was the promotion of world revolution. He wrote in 1917 (in his "Tasks of the Proletariat"), "There is one and only one kind of internationalism in deed: working wholeheartedly for the development of the revolutionary movement and the revolutionary struggle in one's own country, and supporting—by propaganda, sympathy and material aid—such, and only such struggle and such line in every country without exception." In another directive, Lenin said that it was the obligation of the country where the revolution was first victorious to do "the utmost possible in one country for the development, support and awakening of the revolution in all countries." It was to further these ends that Lenin established, in March, 1919, the Third Communist International (or Comintern). He told its second congress, "The principal task of the Communist Parties at present is to unite the scattered Communist forces, to form in every country a united Communist Party (or to reinforce or revive already existing Parties) in order to increase tenfold the work of preparing the proletariat for the conquest of political power, the conquest of power precisely in the form of the dictatorship of the proletariat." And that congress (held in 1920) adopted and published the following description of itself, "The Communist International is the concentrated will of the world revolutionary proletariat. Its mission is to organize the working class of the whole world for the overthrow of the capitalist order and the establishment of communism." Stalin, immediately after Lenin's death, declared that:

Lenin never regarded the Republic of the Soviets as an end in itself. To him it was always a link needed to strengthen the chain of the revolutionary movement in the countries of the West and East, a link needed to facilitate the victory of the working people of the whole world over capitalism. . . .

Departing from us, Comrade Lenin adjured us to remain faithful to the prin-- ciples of the Communist International. We vow to you, Comrade Lenin, that we will not spare our lives to strengthen and extend the union of the toilers of the whole world—the Communist International.

As far as the Communists themselves have been concerned, there has never been any conflict between the twin aims of extending Soviet power and bringing about world revolution. It is the task of all Communist parties, explained Stalin in 1925, "to support Soviet power and foil the interventionist machinations of the imperialists against the Soviet Union . . . mainstay of the revolutionary movement in all countries. . . ." He went on to say ". . . the maintenance and strengthening of the U.S.S.R. means the speediest victory of the working class over the *bourgeoisie.*" This was afterwards more elegantly, but not more authoritatively, stated before the Comintern's executives, "The U.S.S.R. has no interests which are at variance with the interests of world revolution, and the international proletariat naturally has no interests which are at variance with those of the Soviet Union."

The "peace offensives," the "appeals to the toiling and exploited masses," and the appropriations of funds which were made by Lenin and his group in the years of War Communism were concrete efforts toward world revolution. This was the period of politics-without-power. The Bolsheviks, it is true, were able to muster power enough to defeat the divided Whites and to nullify the inadequate and indecisive interventions of the Allied and associated nations. They were also able to intervene directly and indirectly in the domestic affairs of Hungary, Germany, India, China, and elsewhere. They did not send troops or quantities of material into these countries, but they did send leaders, money, and propaganda.

The Comintern underwent several important changes during the years of its existence. During the first five years—probably its most active period—the Comintern was under the dominant influence but not the exclusive control of the Russian Communist Party. It began active support of the Chinese Communists in 1922, and sought to foment a revolution in Germany in 1923—an effort which missed fire badly. Partly because of this failure (and others), but mostly because the Comintern came more and more under Soviet control and therefore was involved in the intra-Party fights of the Soviet group, there was a gradual shift in policies. The move was toward support of Stalin's thesis that the proper tactic was "to consolidate the dictatorship of the proletariat in one country, using it as a base for the overthrow of imperialism in all countries. . . ." The move was gradual, however, which presumably reflected both a division of opinion among the Comintern leaders and the fact that the Stalinists had not yet captured full control. The 1928 Comintern Congress (its sixth) marked the ending of a phase. There was still some free discussion at this congress, and the delegates still made some decisions, but the congress adopted the Soviet thesis: "The U.S.S.R. inevitably becomes the base of the world movement of all oppressed classes, the center of international revolution, the greatest factor in world history."

Thereafter, the Comintern became exclusively the tool of the Soviet Communist Party. The disgruntled who were forced out of the movement (or chose to leave it) regarded this as a perversion and referred derisively to the post-1928 Comintern as the "Stalintern." It would seem to an outsider, however, that this development had been clearly forecast by Lenin. In either case, it is a matter of record that no Comintern congress was summoned between 1928 and 1935. The 1935 meeting, which was the seventh and last congress, found that it had been summoned to hear announcements and orders about new policies which had already been decreed and even, in the case of some, implemented by the Soviet Communist Party. The essence of the new policy was an order for a "united front."

The Soviet government always insisted that it was not responsible for the acts of the Comintern and its agents. Against that insistence may be set, first, the unchallenged fact of Stalin's mastery of the Soviet Communist Party and, through it, of the Soviet ruler-in-theory; and, second, the following statement by Dimitri Manuilsky, who was a member both of the Comintern's Executive Committee and the Soviet Politburo. He said, "Not a document of importance, possessing major international significance, was issued from the Communist International without the most active participation of Stalin in its formulation."

The making of the foreign policies of any nation is a very complex and complicated business. Policy makers have to take account not only of changing circumstances at home and abroad, but also of many interests which are not always compatible with each other. Often there are conflicts between immediate needs and long-range projects, which can only be resolved by temporarily sacrificing the one to the other. This has been just as true in the Soviet Union as anywhere else. The promotion of their particular brand of revolution has never once ceased to be the main objective of Soviet policy makers, but they have not always been able to move directly toward that end. Often they have sought to solve this dilemma by using two instruments of policy simultaneously. The "open" diplomacy of their Foreign Office has appeared to follow one line while the clandestine actions of the Comintern, its adjuncts, and successors have followed another. While Trotsky, who was Lenin's first Commissar of Foreign Affairs, talked peace with the Germans at Brest-Litovsk, for example, Bolshevik agents were busily trying to promote mutinies and rebellions in Germany. Chicherin—a brilliant neurotic who took over the Commissariat of Foreign Affairs when Trotsky resigned that post in 1918, and who held the job until 1930—was presumably bound by the formal recognition of independence which his office had extended to Georgia in 1918. But Soviet troops conquered Georgia in 1921. While Chicherin's office was busy negotiating the Anglo-Soviet Trade Agreement of 1921 and the many treaties of peace and friendship which the Soviet government signed in 1921–22, the Comintern was equally busy fomenting revolution. The signature by the Foreign Commissariat of the Soviet-German Treaty of Rapallo in 1922 did not prevent the Soviets from trying to promote a Communist revolution in Germany the following year. The NEP, to cite one further example, required capital, technicians, and other aid from abroad. Since it could not be expected that these were likely to be forthcoming to a government which was openly at war with the capitalists that aspect of "open" diplomacy was dropped. The new line had been forecast by Chicherin in a comment evoked in 1920 by the American rebuffal of a Soviet bid for recognition:

> Seeing that in America and in many other countries the workers have not conquered the powers of the government and are not even convinced of the necessity of their conquest, the Russian government deems it necessary to establish and faithfully to maintain peaceful and friendly relations with the existing governments of those countries. That the elementary economic needs of the peoples of Russia and of other countries demand normal relations and an exchange of goods between them is quite clear to the Russian government, and the first condition of such relations is mutual good faith and nonintervention on both parts.

One might safely conclude from this statement that Chicherin was perhaps rather quicker than some of his colleagues to recognize that the day of world revolution was not immediately at hand. But the record shows clearly that anyone who took Chicherin's remark about mutual good faith and nonintervention at face value was rather naive. It has been standard practice for Soviet and Communist spokesmen to put on a show of outraged innocence and to pretend complete inability to understand why anyone should hesitate to take such fair words as definitive definitions of Soviet policy. At the very least, such doubters have been accused of troublemaking and war-mongering. Facts, however, are stubborn, and one of the facts was that the Soviet Foreign Commissariat and the Comintern were not two separate institutions, but two arms to one body, the Communist Party of the Soviet Union. Another fact is that good faith has been noticeably absent from Soviet foreign policies. This does not imply that other nations always or even usually act in good faith in their international relations. Sometimes they do, but there is little morality in international affairs. As for the Soviets, their agreements, alliances, and dealings with capitalist nations are—by Communist definition—no more than provisional understandings made necessary by immediate circumstances and having no real binding power. Despite this known fact, most capitalist states entered into formal diplomatic relations with the Soviets. The United States was the outstanding exception.

RUSSO-AMERICAN RELATIONS

Tsarist Russia and the United States had relatively few contacts of any importance—which is probably why the general impression developed that the two Powers were friendly. The Russians were neither anti–United States nor pro–United States; and the United States was neither pro-Russian nor anti-Russian, though both countries were willing to enlist each other's support against a third nation. During much of the time the policies of both Russia and the United States were generally anti-British. But when Russian and American interests were in competition, friendship played no part. This was certainly true in the case of Catherine the Great's refusal to recognize (let alone aid) the rebellious American colonies or the new American nation. It was equally true during the early nineteenth century when Alexander I wished the United States to aid him with her shipping and by becoming a part of his counterbalance against the British. But the first treaty of commerce between the two nations in 1832 was followed by acrimonious disputes which lasted as long as Russian interest in the northwestern part of North America. The visit of the Russian fleets and the sale of Alaska to the United States were motivated by Russian interests and not by friendship. The United States had several bitter clashes with the Russians when interests collided in Manchuria, Korea, and China, and there was a vituperative press war between the two—due in considerable measure to American protests against the pogroms and the policies of Russification—which culminated in the abrogation (in 1911) of the trade treaty. Americans who wrote or talked on the subject generally disliked the tsars, and held that the Russian people would be fine people if only they would get rid of their "brutal—tyrannical—bigoted—corrupt—autocratic" government (to quote a few of the adjectives regularly employed).

Nevertheless, there developed among Americans a tradition of Russo-American friendship, despite its lack of basis in fact. Relations between the countries from 1911 to 1917 were of slight consequence, but trade between them grew steadily though slowly until World War I. Then Russian purchases in the United States boomed while American imports from Russia very sharply declined. In 1911, Russia had imported from the United States goods worth approximately 25.5 million dollars. This had climbed to almost 28 million dollars by 1914, and had zoomed to 470.5 million dollars in 1916. (Russian exports to the United States in those same years were [in round figures]: 1911, 16 million dollars; 1914, 14.5 million dollars—a drop of 10 million dollars from the preceding year; and 1916, 8.5 million dollars.)

Just as Russian liberals hailed the entry of democratic America into World War I, so did American liberals give enthusiastic greeting to the Provisional Government. The United States extended diplomatic recognition to the Provisional Government with unseemly haste and promptly granted extensive credits to it. Boris Bakhmeteff was received as the ambassador of the Provisional Government and he continued to be recognized until June, 1922, while Ludwig Martens, whom the Bolsheviks appointed as their ambassador to the United States in 1919, was deported from this country in 1920. There was no doubt that the United States did not like the Bolsheviks—at first, mostly because Americans believed them to be German agents, and, later, on other grounds. (President Wilson's famous Fourteen Points were enunciated largely in an effort to counteract Bolshevik peace propaganda.) Somewhat reluctantly, the United States took part in the interventions, and American troops remained on Russian soil until 1920. Technically the United States did not participate in the Franco-British blockade of Russia, but actually achieved the same effect by placing all trade with Russia under license and then refusing to issue any licenses. These restrictions were not removed until 1920.

🎹 NONRECOGNITION AND TRADE

The years from 1920 to 1933 in Russian-American relations have been described as "the period of nonrecognition." Two attempts by the Soviet government to obtain diplomatic recognition were sharply rebuffed by the United States. Trade relations were both sporadic and erratic. Soviet imports ranged, roughly, from a low of 8.9 million dollars to a high of 114 million dollars. Soviet exports to the United States varied from under one million dollars to over 24 million dollars. Both exports and imports generally matched or surpassed those of the 1911–13 period, but Soviet imports did not reach the 1914–17 levels. To handle its business interests in the United States, the Soviet government set up several agencies, among which were the Products Exchange Corporation, Arcos-America, the All-Russian Textile Syndicate, and others concerned with special types of goods such as agricultural products and consumer items. These were eventually all brought together in a single agency, known as Amtorg, which was established in 1924 to handle both export and import business. During the late 1920's, American concerns and American engineers and technicians began to go to Soviet Russia in considerable numbers. The list of American companies who dealt with the Soviets in these years is long and includes such concerns as Ford, Dupont, General Electric, American Asbestos, and the Radio Corporation of America. The Hugh L. Cooper Company took the contract for the building of the great dam and hydroelectric power station of the Dnieper—a construction job of which the Soviets have been very proud. The dam, completed in 1932, was built by Soviet labor and engineers under the supervision of American engineers and technicians. Other major construction and engineering jobs were carried out by Stuart, James and Cooke (the Donbas mines); A. G. McKee and Company, United Engineering and Foundry Company, and Freyn Engineering Company (the steel mills of the Urals); and Albert Kahn and Associates (architects). Many American engineers took employment under Soviet contracts and helped in the industrial developments under the first two five-year plans. A number of American workers also went to the U.S.S.R. to share in the work. So, also, did many German, British, French, and other workers and technicians. Later, most of them were dismissed by the Soviets.

Besides doing business with the United States the Soviets also gratefully accepted American aid (to the amount of some 66 or 67 million dollars) for the relief of the 1921–23 famine. The two Powers also found themselves in accord (though for different reasons) in disliking the League of Nations, in favoring disarmament, and in making formal, and hopeful, pronouncements against war. But as late as May, 1933, the United States Department of State was not willing to go beyond the following, formal statement: "The Department of State is cognizant of the fact that the Soviet regime is exercising power and control in the territory of the former Russian Empire." Before jumping to the conclusion that this attitude was utterly unreasonable, one ought to note also the following statements. The first is from the 1921 Statute of the Comintern; the second from the constitution and rules of the Comintern which were adopted in 1928:

The new International Association of workers is established for the purpose of organizing common activity by the workers of various countries who are striving towards a single aim: the overthrow of capitalism, the establishment of the dictatorship of the proletariat and of the International Soviet Republic, for the complete abolition of classes and the realization of social-ism—the first step to Communist society.

The Communist International . . . is a World Communist Party. As the leader and organizer of the world revolutionary movement . . . the Communist International . . . fights for the establishment of the world dictator-ship of the proletariat, for the establishment of a World Union of Soviet Socialist Republics, for the complete abolition of classes and for the achieve-ment of Socialism—the first stage of Communist society.

Previous comments on the relationship of the Soviet rulers to the Comin-tern need not be repeated, but to them may be added Manuilsky's state-ment, made in 1939, that the Comintern "was following the path of Lenin and Stalin."

A series of happenings combined to bring about a change in Soviet-American relations. The Japanese had begun their temporarily success-ful adventures in Manchuria and northern China. Hitler and his National Socialist Workers' Party had risen to power in Germany. (Both these matters will be referred to later at some length.) A world-wide de-pression, which some Soviet leaders thought forecast the anticipated collapse of capitalism, and whose effects the U.S.S.R. did not wholly escape, had begun in 1929. One of its results in the United States was a growing concern over the decline of Soviet-American trade. Measured in dollars, this decline sounded very startling. Soviet imports from the United States had fallen from 24.3 million dollars to 9.7 million dollars in the same period. Measured in percentages of total trade, the figures sound less impressive. The goods which the Soviet Union took from the United States in 1930 amounted to only 3 per cent of the total Amer-ican export trade for that year. By 1932, this was down to 0.8 per cent. They were, on the other hand, much more significant to the Soviets, ac-counting for 25 per cent of all Soviet imports in 1930 and for only 4.5 per cent in 1932. Soviet sales to the United States in 1930 were almost 4 per cent of their total foreign sales; 3 per cent in 1932. Despite the relatively small total amounts involved, however, sales to Amtorg were quite important to certain firms, notably those which produced machine tools and oil-well machinery. Some of these concerns added their in-fluence to groups favoring recognition, on the ground that it would be good for business. A study of the case histories of a selected number of American firms who did business with Russia showed that this anticipa-tion was not fulfilled even in the case of one company whose trade with Amtorg in 1928 and 1929 had amounted to 10 per cent of the company's total export business. That, however, is knowledge after the event. There were Americans who favored recognition because they expected trade increases.

On the Soviet side, the matter of trade was somewhat different but not unimportant. All foreign trade of the Soviets has been a government monopoly since 1918, and it has been used as a political weapon as well as a matter of economics. The British government in 1927 had raided the quarters of Arcos Limited and of the Soviet Trade Delegation. Soviet protests that this was a violation of diplomatic immunity guaranteed to the delegation by the agreement of 1921 were met with a British countercharge that the Soviet agents had been engaging in espionage and in anti-British propaganda. The British then ended the trade agreement and broke off diplomatic relations. The Soviet government ordered that trade should be conducted only with those nations with whom they had normal diplomatic relations. This order was not applied to the United States, but it illustrated a political use of the trade monopoly. Another use of the monopoly may be demonstrated from the record of Soviet-American trade.

Soviet imports from the United States were of two general kinds: finished goods and raw materials which were brought in only now and then to meet special conditions, and fabricated articles which were imported steadily. The fabricated articles consisted mainly of machinery, iron and steel products, motor vehicles and parts, and precision tools. From 1928 through 1931, goods of this type accounted for 83 per cent of all Amtorg purchases in the United States. The proportion of this type to the whole declined somewhat thereafter but remained high. The other class of goods included agricultural machinery, cotton, wool, hides, dyestuffs, and similar products. These imports were geared to immediate economic needs. One authority, for example, has remarked that Soviet agriculture would probably have failed completely had it not been for the importation of tractors to take the place of the draft animals which were destroyed in the struggle over collectivization. Imports of this class —for example, cotton—declined as Soviet production increased. Foreign trade, and specifically trade with the United States, was therefore important to the Soviets as a source of certain goods. Whether they expected this flow to be increased by formal diplomatic recognition may be doubted, however, since they had found that they could buy whatever goods they wanted, as long as they could pay for them, without regard to the formalities of diplomacy.

It was also important to the Soviets to obtain certain technical assistance either by direct contract or in connection with purchases. Numerous American companies sent their men to the U.S.S.R. to install machinery and plants purchased by the Soviets and to train Soviet technicians in the use and maintenance of the equipment. (About two-thirds of all such arrangements for technical help up to 1935 were made with American or German firms.) This need decreased as the number of trained Soviet engineers and technicians increased, but it still existed in 1933. The Soviet government may well have thought that diplomatic recognition by the United States might facilitate not only the sending of Americans to Russia, but also—and this was probably much more important in their minds—the sending of Soviet citizens to the United States for training. Nor is it likely that technical training as such was the only objective of such persons. Espionage both in general and concerning specifics was a further Soviet objective. The establishment of formal diplomatic relations made possible the setting up of various consular and diplomatic agencies, all of which could be and were used as centers for intelligence work. This included contacts with members and sympathizers of the American Communist Party—a body which the Attorney-General of the United States charged (in November, 1950) "has been and is substantially dominated and controlled by the Government and Communist party of the Soviet Union and by the foreign organization controlling the world Communist movement. . . ." [1] These contacts were facilitated and extended in numerous ways as a result of the establishment of "normal diplomatic relations" between the United States and the Soviet Union. It may safely be presumed that this was one of the results which Stalin and his associates expected to flow from recognition.

❦ RECOGNITION, TRADE AND DEBTS

The initiative came from the then newly elected President of the United States, Franklin D. Roosevelt, who addressed a preliminary inquiry to Michael Kalinin, Chairman of the Central Executive Committee of the U.S.S.R. Kalinin's prompt and favorable reply was followed by the dispatch to Washington of Commissar Litvinov. Conversations among Litvinov, Roosevelt, and Secretary of State Hull led to an exchange of notes on November 16, 1933, by which formal diplomatic relations were established. On the American side, the move was accomplished by executive agreement in which Congress played no part until the Senate was asked to approve the appointment of Mr. William C. Bullitt as ambassador to the U.S.S.R. and the Congress was asked to supply the necessary monies. On the Soviet side, the decision was made by the Politburo (of which Kalinin had been a member since 1925) and then by the Central Executive Committee. This was also action by executive order.

One of the problems which had delayed recognition had been the debts allegedly owed to America and Americans by Russia and Russians. (One of the early acts of the Bolsheviks had been the formal repudiation of all debts contracted prior to their coup.) This question had been left to future negotiations by Litvinov and Roosevelt. Bullitt raised the issue soon after he arrived in Moscow. Against his claims, which totaled about half a billion dollars, the Soviets promptly presented counter-claims for an unspecified amount of damages alleged to have been caused by the American intervention at Archangel. Litvinov and Bullitt finally reached a compromise which scaled down the Soviet debt to the United States to one hundred million dollars. There matters deadlocked. The Soviets refused to make this a binding agreement unless the United States would grant new loans to the U.S.S.R. Litvinov insisted that it had been understood during his talks in Washington that new loans would be made in return for an agreement to pay the old debts. Hull flatly denied that there had been any such understanding, and virtually called Litvinov a liar. Then the United States passed the Johnson Act which forbade loans to any nations who had defaulted on payments of earlier debts, and this made a new loan to Russia impossible. The United States offered to circumvent its own law by arranging long-term loans through the Export-Import Credit Bank, the interest charges to be high enough to repay the old debts. The Soviets refused this offer, and repeated their claim that the matter had been settled in Washington in 1933. The negotiations on this problem broke down completely in January, 1935, and the breakdown was followed by mutual recriminations in diplomatic notes and in the press of both countries.

Despite this falling out, a Soviet-American Commercial Pact was signed in July, 1935. The pact bound the Soviets to purchase during the next years American goods to the value of 30 million dollars. It was renewed for one year in July, 1936. The amount to be purchased was raised to 40 million dollars in August, 1937, and the new arrangement was regularly renewed until it was replaced by lend-lease agreements in 1941. Under the pacts, Soviet purchases from the United States rose to over 69.6 million dollars in 1938; dropped slightly in 1939; and then rose sharply in 1940. These figures by themselves may be misleading. The dollar volume of Soviet imports from the United States increased almost eight times over between 1932 and 1938. As a proportion of total United States exports, however, this was an increase—from .5 per cent to 2.3 per cent—which is not very impressive. However, the imports from America accounted for over 28 per cent of all Soviet imports in 1938. Soviet exports rose from about 16 million dollars in 1932 to almost 31 million dollars in 1937, and then leveled off at about 25 million dollars. These figures represent 3 per cent of the total Soviet exports in 1932; 7.8 per cent in 1937; and slightly less thereafter.

THE COMINTERN AND THE "UNITED FRONT"

The signature of the first American-Soviet Commercial Pact in 1935 almost coincided with the Seventh (and last) Congress of the Comintern. While Ambassador Bullitt and his staff were completing the details of the formal "open" diplomatic agreement, Messrs. Browder, Foster, Darcy, and other delegates from the American Communist Party were preparing to report to and to receive orders from the Comintern Congress, now under the complete control of Moscow. The American Communists reported boastfully of how they had expanded their Party and movement and of how they had fomented strikes and other disorders. As a matter of fact, they somewhat exaggerated their claims and were unduly sanguine as to their plans. But both their reports and their plans were accepted and endorsed by the congress. Communism in the United States was not, however, the chief business nor the main interest of the Seventh Congress. Its primary purpose was to inform all Communists of the dual policy of the united front. This is usually presented as "a united front against fascism," which is only a part of the truth. The Bulgarian Communist George Dimitrov, who was then high in the Kremlin's favor and held the post of the General Secretary of the Comintern, defined it more accurately (but still not completely) when he addressed the congress. "For a successful struggle against the offensive of capital, against the reactionary measures of the *bourgeoisie,* against fascism . . . it is imperative that unity of action be established between all sections of the working class . . . even before the majority . . . unites . . . for the overthrow of capitalism and the victory of the proletarian revolution."

This call for unity against capitalism and fascism reflected the view of Soviet theoreticians that fascism and capitalism are kin. They considered fascism inherent in capitalism and unable to dissociate from it; it was "a manifestation of capitalism in its imperialistic phase." Only from mid-1941 to mid-1945 did Communist spokesmen draw a distinction between "capitalist democracies" and "Fascist aggressors." Before and after those dates, the two were treated as one. So what Dimitrov had demanded was a united front against three aspects of one system (capitalism, reactionary *bourgeoisie,* and fascism). But this was not all that was meant by a united front. The official *Outline History of the Communist International,* published in 1934, had offered the following, additional definition of it.

United front tactics, the chief object of which in the opinion of the Comintern is the establishment of the unity of all workers in their struggle against capitalism, the unity of their militant action, are the tactics of irreconcilable struggle against the main obstacle in that struggle, viz., Social-Democracy. In adopting these tactics the Communists reserve to themselves the unlimited right to expose the Social-Democrats even at the time of joint action; and they carry out these tactics primarily in the form of a United Front from below.

Following this dual directive, the Communists sought to form a "united front" with any working-class organizations which could be inveigled into such a program—and this included Social Democratic parties and groups. At the same time, however, the Communists were busily wrecking Social Democratic parties and liquidating their leaders whenever possible. This is the explanation for the unholy alliance so often formed in Germany between the Nazis and the Communists. The two totalitarian groups frequently ganged up against Social Democrats and trade-unionists, and successfully defeated them. Under the same directive, the Communists everywhere tried to form "popular fronts," that is, general coalitions which were not limited to workers' groups but which sought to take in all comers, especially, liberal intellectuals. Many were completely taken in by this tactic. Simultaneously, the Communists were doing their best to injure genuine liberal movements and to discredit all liberalism and all liberals.

These were clearly self-contradictory tactics. The Communists were riding two horses at once. Under Moscow's leadership, they were saying one thing openly while secretly doing something quite different. (This applies also to their efforts in championing "collective security," which will be discussed later.) This was very puzzling to lay observers, as it was meant to be. It must also have involved endless frustrations for the rank and file, who repeatedly found their efforts blocked and double-crossed by the actions of some of their associates. But there was basically no confusion in the matter. The key principle was the advancement of the power and security of the Communist Party of the Soviet Union. As Dimitrov put it:

The historical dividing line between the forces of fascism, war, and capitalism, on the one hand; and the forces of peace, democracy, and socialism, on the other hand, is coming to be, in fact, the attitude toward the Soviet Union—not the formal attitude toward Soviet socialism and Soviet power in general, but the attitude toward the Soviet Union which has been in existence for twenty years under the leadership of the Party of Lenin and Stalin.

This was not a new theme when Dimitrov enunciated it in 1937. Communist spokesmen had time and again insisted on "the historical dividing line." "Either the Soviet governments triumph . . . or the most reactionary imperialism triumphs" Lenin had declared in 1918; and two years later he had said, ". . . a funeral dirge will be sung over the Soviet Republic or over world capitalism." Even before their regime was secure, Soviet Communists had held that the primary obligation of all Communists was to help Russia, and this theme was given increasing emphasis. Stalin in 1925, for example, placed "defense of the Soviet power" high on the list of the tasks of the non-Soviet Communist parties. Two years later he declared, "A revolutionary is he who without arguments, unconditionally, openly and honestly . . . is ready to defend the U.S.S.R." And the Comintern's executives were informed in 1933 that, "He who does not devote all his strength to the defense of the U.S.S.R. is no revolutionary; he is a counterrevolutionary. . . ."

It was, at the time of the 1935 congress, the other Powers which first protested the actions of their national Communists. The United States took no action until mounting pressures from certain labor and religious groups virtually forced the government to act. Then an extremely forceful protest was filed, which the Soviet government blandly rejected on the ground that it was not responsible for the Comintern. The protest was pointedly repeated and just as pointedly rejected. The Soviets could not accept and act upon the legitimate American protests without thereby ceasing to be the leader of world communism. The result was a deadlock with no action except that Mr. Bullitt, who had pushed the matter so hard as to become *persona non grata* to the Soviets, was replaced as ambassador by Mr. Joseph E. Davies.

Soviet-American relations did not change materially thereafter until the Russian attack on Finland late in 1939. Though the Soviet-Nazi Pact of 1939 and the subsequent Soviet invasion of Poland threw many American fellow travelers, Party followers, and even Party members into confusion, there was little formal reaction except the freezing of Polish funds in the United States, and this was as much anti-Nazi as anti-Soviet. The attack on Finland, however, was a different matter. President Roosevelt sought to avert the Russian attack by a personal appeal to Stalin. Kalinin responded (on the legal fiction that he, rather than Stalin, was the head of the Soviet state) with a flat guarantee of Finnish independence. But Molotov, who had succeeded Litvinov in 1939 as Commissar of Foreign Affairs, then censured American "intervention" and warned that the war in Europe would be greatly protracted if the American Congress repealed the arms embargo. President Roosevelt charged the Soviets with bad faith, and there was a demand in Congress that Ambassador Steinhardt (who had replaced Davies) be recalled. The

Soviet military attack on the Finns, launched on November 30, 1939, prompted Roosevelt to denounce vigorously the aggression and to call for a moral embargo upon the sale and shipment of planes and other war supplies. The American Congress seriously considered breaking off diplomatic relations with Russia, and in March, 1940, extended credits to Finland. The Soviet advances into the Baltic states evoked more protests from the United States and caused the freezing of Baltic funds here. In January, 1941, however, the United States very cautiously began to give some economic aid to the Soviets, but this was cut off at news of the Soviet pact with Japan in April. That is where matters stood at the time of the German invasion of the U.S.S.R.

DISARMAMENT, THE LEAGUE AND "NONAGGRESSION"

The developments within the Comintern affected all of Soviet relations abroad, not just those with the United States.

Because they were starting from scratch, the Soviets were extremely busy with the establishment of routine diplomatic agreements of the kind which seldom make headlines. Between 1920 and 1937 they entered into almost three hundred agreements, most of them made after 1924. Roughly four-fifths of these were bilateral, and one-fifth were multilateral agreements of all kinds. Of the bilateral agreements, a hundred dealt with specific points such as boundaries, consular relations, and postal arrangements. The remainder were concerned with trade and economic matters, neutrality and nonaggression, and diplomatic recognition of the U.S.S.R. During the next four years (1937–41), the Soviet Union made over seventy diplomatic agreements (including renewals of existing ones) of all sorts. Most of these post-1937 agreements were in some way concerned with the war and with Soviet expansion.

One line of Soviet diplomatic activity which succeeded at least in a public-relations sense was the professed championship of disarmament. Chicherin, in protesting against the exclusion of his government from the Washington Conference of 1921–22, stated that the Soviets "would be happy to welcome any disarmament." The Soviet delegation at Genoa proposed both a general disarmament and a specific barring of gas and aerial warfare, but their motion was not discussed. Later that same year the Soviets suggested reciprocal arms reduction to Estonia, Finland, and Poland, along with a proposal for nonaggression and the arbitration of disputes. These were rejected. A year later (1924) Chicherin flatly rejected a League of Nations draft treaty which treated disarmament as part of the whole problem of security. The Soviets, he said, favored the limitation of armaments, but they would have nothing to do with any international agreement or organization which would "imply a possibility of measures of constraint being exercised by any international authority whatsoever against any particular state."

The U.S.S.R. then proposed a special conference to arrange agreements to limit the amounts of military budgets and the size of armed forces. This led to an invitation to take part in the preliminary (and later in the general) disarmament conference at Geneva. The Soviets promptly accepted the invitation, but their quarrel with Switzerland over the acquittal by Swiss courts of the assassin of the chief Soviet delegate to the Lausanne Conference (1923) delayed matters. The Soviet representative, Maxim Litvinov, did not join the preliminary sessions until October, 1927. Then he at once caught the world's attention by proposing "the complete abolition of all armed forces on land, on the sea, and in the air." Neither this proposal nor any of the subsequent repetitions and extensions of it had any success so far as adoption by the conference. It did succeed, however, in influencing people. Disagreement both as to the sincerity of the Soviets in making the proposals and as to the sincerity of the conferees in refusing to accept them has been very bitter. No conclusive proof has been presented by either side, so all that can be said with certainty is that the proposals were made; were rejected, openly or by default; and that no nation disarmed because of them. Along this same line was the Kellogg-Briand Pact "outlawing war." The Soviets not only adhered to it but extended it by the Litvinov Protocols, which put the pact into effect (February–July, 1929) in the U.S.S.R., Poland, Estonia, Latvia, Lithuania, Romania, Turkey, Iran, and Danzig. Later the Soviets forswore this pledge, but so did most of the other signatories of the pact and the protocols.

A random sampling of the Soviet press through the later 1930's gives a different picture of Soviet policies in regard to armaments. The 1936 military budget was 175 per cent above that of the preceding year, and the army was increased by 200,000 men. This was the year of the alliance with France, and joint Russo-French military plans were prepared. Litvinov and others continued to propagandize for "collective security," but the draft age was dropped from twenty-one to nineteen, and a big naval building program was undertaken. A Commissariat of Naval Affairs was established in the following year; a defense loan of four billion rubles was oversubscribed, and the military budget continued to rise. In 1937 the Soviet's per capita defense expenditures stood at $23.34—the highest in the world. At the beginning of 1938 Marshal Voroshilov announced that Soviet coastal defenses had been strengthened during the preceding five years, and that the Red Navy, though still not first-rate, was adequate for coastal defense. He added that the other armed services were as good or better than those of the other countries. (This was regarded as vainglorious boasting by those foreign commentators who held that the purges and punishments of the top army and navy commanders had ruined Soviet armed strength.) There was also another four billion ruble loan in 1938, divided between military and industrial projects. As a matter of fact, much of the industrial growth was dictated by military considerations. Plans were drawn for the building of new plants in regions removed from the frontiers and for the removal of some existing plants to those safer areas. Some of these plans were implemented. The training of civilians not only for air raids but also in marksmanship, skiing, riding, gliding, and parachute jumping was also greatly increased in these years. (The civilian training programs had been started as early as 1920 and were augmented after 1927. They were financed chiefly by lotteries.) Stalin in 1938 listed the "Society for Assistance in Defense and in Aviation-Chemical Construction" (OSOAVIAKHIM) as one of the major defense arms of the U.S.S.R. The Soviets wisely did not rely on conspiracy and diplomacy alone.

Many persons were bitterly critical because Soviet Russia was not invited to join the League of Nations until 1934. In view of the publicly expressed Soviet attitude toward the League from 1919 to 1934, it is a little difficult to believe that any such invitation would have been accepted if it had been offered. The Communist Party program of 1919 (which, by the way, was still technically in force in 1957) described the League as "an international organization of capitalists for the systematic exploitation of all the peoples of the earth." The formal Soviet note of March, 1923, which accepted the League's invitation to attend a conference on naval disarmament, also stated, "The Soviet Government's attitude to the so-called League of Nations remains unaltered." The note went on:

It [the Soviet government] regards it [the League] as a coalition of certain States, endeavouring to usurp the power over other States and masking their attempts on the rights and independence of other nations by a false appearance of groundless legality. . . . The Soviet Government maintains its conviction that this pseudo-international body really serves as a mere mask to conceal from the broad masses the aggressive aims of the imperialist policy of certain Great Powers or their vassals.

Almost the same charge was repeated by Chicherin's Commissariat in 1926. It came as something of a shock, therefore, when Litvinov and Molotov suddenly spoke well of the League in December, 1933. The League, said Molotov, had "exerted a certain restraining influence upon those forces which are preparing for war." Litvinov conceded that "the tendencies which are interested in the preservation of peace would seem to be gaining the upper hand in the League." When the invitation to membership was finally forthcoming, the Soviets accepted it. For the next five years the Soviet representatives at Geneva were the highly articulate supporters of peace, disarmament, and collective security—all, of course, on Soviet terms. There was reason to doubt their good faith, but there was equal reason to question the good faith of other League members. Japan had not been expelled from the League when she attacked China, nor had Italy been expelled when she attacked Ethiopia. But when the Soviets attacked Finland, they were promptly ousted from the League.

One of the instruments of formal Soviet diplomacy was the so-called nonaggression pact. This was a mutual guarantee of "the inviolability of the existing frontiers," and an undertaking "to refrain from any act of aggression directed against each other." Beginning in 1926 the Soviet Union signed such pacts with a dozen or more countries, and most of these were renewed at least once. They were further enhanced in the eyes of many by several formal definitions of aggression, and there is no doubt that pacts and definitions contributed toward the reputation of the U.S.S.R. as a peace-loving nation. They proved, however, to have no meaning. The Soviet-Finnish Nonaggression Pact (from which the phrases just above were quoted) was made originally in 1932, and was extended in 1934, ostensibly to the end of 1945. But the U.S.S.R. unilaterally denounced it in 1939. The Soviet nonaggression pledge to Poland was denounced by the U.S.S.R. on the day the Red Army crossed the Polish frontier. On the other hand, the pacts did not protect the U.S.S.R. either. The Germans violated their pact (made in 1939) in June, 1941.

The nonaggression pacts were supplemented and complemented by several "mutual assistance pacts" of which the U.S.S.R. was also fond. These were of two general types. The Soviet-French Mutual Assistance Agreement of 1935 was a defensive alliance of the old-fashioned kind. It provided for consultation between the signatories in case either felt itself in danger of being attacked, and for "aid and assistance" in case an attack was actually made. The 1935 agreement with Czechoslovakia was of the same nature. The other type may be exemplified by the Pact of Mutual Assistance signed in 1936 by the Soviet Union and Outer Mongolia, or by the pacts signed with the Baltic states after the outbreak of war in 1939. The agreements with the little Baltic states were preludes to their annexation by the U.S.S.R. The pact with Outer Mongolia was for the purpose of establishing Soviet mastery over that land as one defense against the expanding power of Japan.

🝧 RELATIONS WITH CHINA AND JAPAN

Soviet foreign policies toward China and Japan were complicated by several special circumstances, which included attempts to use the Chinese Communists for Russian ends, the long-continued Japanese occupation of Soviet soil, the Chinese Eastern Railway, and the Japanese advances on the mainland.

Communism in China began as an intellectual movement which was more in the nature of a series of study clubs than of action groups. These clubs grew in number and in membership during the period of World War I, and were strengthened by contacts with Marxist-Communist groups, which were formed among the Chinese living abroad. (Chou En-lai, for example, founded a Chinese Communist society in Paris, and his wife organized another in Berlin at about the same time that Mao Tse-tung was starting a group in Hunan.) The Bolshevik Revolution gave significant impetus to the Chinese movement, and Chinese Marxists were invited to the founding Congress of the Comintern in 1919. A year later a Comintern agent named Marlin went to Shanghai to assist in the creation of a formal Chinese Communist Party, and this was accomplished in 1921. Thereafter, though intellectuals and students remained strong in the Party, an increasing number of workers and peasants were also brought into the movement. Marlin had suggested that the Communists join with Sun Yat-sen's party, the Kuomintang, in order to use its organization and influence, both of which were far superior to anything that the Communists could immediately create by themselves. The Comintern accepted Marlin's recommendation, and in 1923 ordered the Chinese Communists to join forces with the Kuomintang.

This involved the winning over of Sun, who, though willing to accept individual Communists as members of the Kuomintang, was at first reluctant to agree to a two-party collaboration. Co-operation between the Commissariat of Foreign Affairs and the Comintern was now called into play by the dispatch to China of A. A. Joffe as the official envoy of the Soviet government. Joffe's ostensible purpose was to get diplomatic recognition. His more important task was to win over Sun, and this he was able to do. Joffe readily promised Russian aid against imperialism and for the completion of Sun's revolution, and he also promised not to push Communism in China. One result of this agreement was the sending to Moscow by Sun of Chiang Kai-shek. Chiang was to arrange for specific aid from the Soviets, and one of the Chinese Communists subsequently credited Chiang with the chief responsibility for the Soviet and Kuomintang collaboration. Joffe was now replaced by Karakhan (the same man later accused of Trotskyite treason) and by Michael Borodin. Borodin, an unusually able and astute conspirator, soon became top adviser to the government, in charge of the reorganization of the Kuomintang. His position was that China was not ready for Communism, but that the Kuomintang and the Chinese Communists could profitably co-operate in fighting foreign imperialism and in building Chinese nationalism. His reorganization of Sun's party included the admission of the Chinese Communists to it. They retained their own Party identity, however, and continued to work for their own cause even while assisting certain work of the Kuomintang.

The Kuomintang soon definitely divided into right and left wings, with the leftists in control of the Kuomintang machinery and the Communists in control of the left wing itself. Borodin remained as their chief adviser and link with Moscow. Other Russian and Comintern agents appeared from time to time. After prolonged flirtation with the Communists, Chiang finally turned against them in 1927. A Moscow-directed effort by Borodin to set up a "workers' and peasants' government" in Hankow failed, and he was also unable to carry out the Comintern's orders to form a Communist army and to bring about a confiscation of land under Communist direction. But the fight was a long way from being over. Mao, Chou, and the other Communist leaders loyally maintained their contacts with the Kremlin, built for the future, and waited. The Kremlin did likewise.

The problem of the Chinese Eastern Railway was complicated by several issues. Despite Soviet renunciation in 1919 and 1920 of all the rights and privileges which tsarist Russia had held in China, the Peking government refused to enter into formal diplomatic relations with the Soviets until 1924. In that year formal relations were established through an agreement (signed for Russia by Karakhan) to which were attached specific renunciations of territory and special privileges. Simultaneously there was signed an agreement which provided for joint Sino-Soviet management of the Chinese Eastern Railway as a commercial venture. Because the actual powers of the Peking government did not cover Manchuria, where the line ran, the Soviets also signed a similar agreement with the warlord who controlled that region. The agreement was soon violated by the warlord, and a series of small disputes was climaxed in the partial rupture of diplomatic relations in 1927. The Soviets continued to deal with the virtually independent Manchuria, however, and to share in the operation of the railroad until 1929. By then, three-quarters of the employees of the railroad were Russian, and control was in their hands. The Chinese sought to reverse this situation in the late spring of that year. They drove out the Russians and took control of the line. Soviet consuls were then withdrawn from China, and Soviet troops (a special Far Eastern Army of the U.S.S.R. had been created in 1929) entered Manchuria. The claim was self-defense. The military resistance of Manchuria collapsed, and the Chinese government at Mukden (Manchuria) was constrained to accept a treaty which restored the situation to what it had been before the attack. There matters in general rested until the Japanese took over Manchuria, and set up the puppet state of Manchukuo. Formal Soviet diplomatic relations with China were restored at the end of 1932.

The fall of the Russian Empire and the prolonged revolution had given the Japanese a golden opportunity to advance on the Asiatic mainland. Most of Russia's Far Eastern lands remained under Japanese control until 1922, but northern Sakhalin was not evacuated by the Japanese until 1925. A convention of that year provided for the resumption of diplomatic and consular relations and for the evacuation of northern Sakhalin. In return, the Soviets agreed "to give to Japanese concerns recommended by the Japanese government concessions for the exploitation of 50 per cent of the area of every oil field in Northern Sakhalin." This valuable grant helped oil the Japanese advances. It also marked the height of the Soviet-Japanese *rapprochement,* which continued despite some friction into the 1930's. The Japanese occupation of Manchuria in 1931–32 produced some saber-rattling on both sides and resulted in a definite strengthening of Soviet military power in the Far East. But there was no overt break largely because the Soviets refused to let one occur. They renewed a fishing agreement with the Japanese in 1932, and, though they were rather sharp when Japan refused a nonaggression pact (December, 1932), the Soviets took no action abroad. At home they used the Japanese threat as an added incentive to their people.

The situation continued on this rather unsatisfactory level for some time. The forward drive of Japanese forces brought them to the frontiers of Outer Mongolia, and border clashes between Soviet and Japanese troops became increasingly frequent and furious. Troubles also developed over the Chinese Eastern Railway. The U.S.S.R. did not feel itself able at that moment to resist Japanese pressures, or perhaps did not feel that the situation warranted costly resistance. At any rate, the Soviet leaders repeated a tactic at which they were skillful and experienced. They cut their losses by a figurative retreat. In 1935 they sold the Chinese Eastern Railway to the Japanese for a fraction of its value. But they continued to build up their military and economic strength on the Manchurian border. The border clashes continued until finally they reached in 1937–38 the stage of a full-scale, though undeclared, war, in which the Japanese were repulsed. Meanwhile, what looked like a possible *rapprochement* between the U.S.S.R. and Japan was aborted by the Japanese adherence to the Anti-Comintern Pact in November, 1936.

Germany was actively engaged in trying to embroil Japan with the Soviets during this period. A secret German military mission went to Japan in 1935, and a Nazi company for the exploitation of certain Manchurian resources was also formed in that year. In the year 1936 the Japanese militarists gained ascendency.

These events, combined with some others, brought about a working agreement between the Soviets and Chiang Kai-shek. Professor Max Beloff is of the opinion that this was some sort of a military agreement and that it led to closer co-operation even before the Japanese attack upon China in 1937. Subsequent to that attack, Soviet aid was most certainly given by extensions of credit and by shipments of supplies through Sinkiang (Chinese Turkestan), which, in effect, the Soviets took over.

✹ RELATIONS WITH GERMANY

The relatively good relations established between Russia and Germany at Rapallo had survived Comintern machinations against the Weimar government. A commercial agreement in 1925 had been followed in the next year by a treaty which promised neutrality in case either signatory were attacked, and promised abstention from any economic or financial boycotts which might be invoked by a coalition of powers against either signatory. The 1926 treaty stated that the two governments "shall remain in friendly touch in order to promote an understanding with regard to all political and economic questions jointly affecting the two countries." These agreements and subsequent supplements to them were followed by close financial and commercial relations. Especially under the First Five-Year Plan, Germany seemed well on her way to regaining the economic position she had held in Russia in 1912–13. By 1932 Germany was supplying 46 per cent of Russia's imports—by far the largest single share. There was also co-operation of another sort. The German army had been forbidden by the Versailles Treaty to have certain types of mechanized equipment, including tanks and planes. These items were lacking or relatively undeveloped in the Red Army. So a deal was arranged whereby German equipment and German technicians were tested and trained within the Soviet borders in return for the supplying of materials and training to the Red Army. Rather close co-operation was developed between army officers at this time, as was somewhat inadvertently attested by the Soviet government when it executed Tukhachevski and others on charges of treasonous relations with Germany. These mutually beneficial arrangements probably explain why the rise to power of the author of

Mein Kampf (with its specific plans for expansion at Russian expense) did not seriously disturb Soviet-German relations for some time.

The situation rapidly changed when Germany withdrew from the League (1933), denounced the Versailles Treaty (1935), and reoccupied the Rhineland (1936). The rise of this new and ambitious Power had destroyed the old balance and forced realignments. Professor Beloff, whose excellent pioneer study of Soviet diplomacy has been paraphrased before, made the following comments on this diplomatic shift:

Its unifying factor, in the case of Russia, as in the case of every other European Power, was provided by the rebirth of German military might under the aegis of the Hitler regime. . . .

Considerations of defence thus dominated Soviet policy in the years 1933–1936. . . .

The most obvious and comparatively direct tasks of M. Litvinov . . . were three in number. The first was to prevent the new threat in the West from combining its pressure with the old threat in the East. That meant making concessions to Japan. . . . The second task was to avert the old bugbear of a general capitalist coalition against the Soviet Union. . . . To avoid or at least delay the struggle with Germany was thus the third. . . .[2]

Professor Beloff also observed that Soviet-Nazi relations were quiet at the start, ". . . but grew steadily more strident, reaching in 1936 a pitch of vituperativeness hitherto unknown in the intercourse of civilised nations."

Mr. William Henry Chamberlin [3] made a somewhat different periodic characterization of Soviet foreign policy. Chamberlin called 1917–21 the period of "avowed revolutionary offensive"; 1921–34, "Defensive Isolationism"; and 1934–38, the era of experimental political alliances with capitalist Powers. "Defensive isolationism" was the time of "separate pacts of nonaggression and neutrality." The years 1934–38 saw the Soviet entry into the League and the mutual assistance pacts.

It was the year 1936 in which civil war began in Spain, bringing Franco and his Fascists to power. It was also the year of the formation of the Rome-Berlin Axis (October) and of the German-Japanese Anti-Comintern Pact (November); Italy adhered to this in 1937. Hitler and Mussolini, it will be recalled, furnished material aid—ranging from planes and equipment to trained troops—to the Spanish rebels. Franco, in all probability, would have been unable to triumph without this Nazi-Fascist support. With equal promptness, the Soviets sent money, materials, and men to aid the Spanish government. The French and the British had nothing more to offer than a useless nonintervention agreement to which both the Fascists-Nazis and the Communists paid lip service, but which they both ignored in practice.

Sophisticated opinion at the time held that the battle lines between communism and fascism-naziism were sharply and finally drawn in Spain —a view which was later popularized. It is clear that there was actually a series of battles between the two in Spain, but the Soviets continued to extend commercial agreements with both the Japanese and the Germans. And they lumped fascism and capitalism together as enemies of the Soviet regime. The speeches of Stalin, Molotov, Kalinin, and other Communist leaders in 1937 rang time and again with the phrase "capitalist encirclement." Kalinin declared in a widely publicized speech in January, 1937:

> Our state is socialist, but it is surrounded by capitalist states whose ruling classes are itching to destroy the one bulwark of socialism in the world. They are using the most varied forms of hostility against us—slander, diversion, espionage, and provocation—everything possible is being done to damage the work of socialist construction.

And Kalinin urged a revival of international anticapitalism. Stalin, speaking in March, 1937, was even more forthright:

> The Soviet Union is in a state of capitalist encirclement. . . . Capitalist encirclement is no empty phrase. It is a very real and unpleasant feature. Capitalist encirclement means that here is one country, the Soviet Union, which has established the socialist order within its own territories, and outside this there are many countries, bourgeois countries, which continue to carry on a capitalist mode of life and surround the Soviet Union, waiting for an opportunity to attack it, break it, or at any rate to undermine its power and weaken it. . . . It is precisely this fact which determines the basis of relations between the capitalist encirclers and the Soviet Union.

Eleven months later, Stalin wrote:

> Only blockheads or masked enemies . . . can deny the danger of military intervention . . . as long as capitalist encirclement exists . . . the political assistance of the working class in the bourgeois countries for the working class of our country must be organized.

There was, about that same time, a popular song "If Tomorrow Brings War," which was widely sung in the U.S.S.R. Its lyrics boasted that the whole Soviet nation would rise, strong and mighty, to rout the invader. No nation in the world, declaimed the song, could conquer the U.S.S.R., and it summoned the people to be ready to fight. When this song became generally known in the West—usually in a carefully edited translation—Germany had already invaded Russia, and it was generally supposed that the song forecast that war. This supposition cannot be supported from the original Russian version, which named no specific enemies.

It must be admitted that the Communist leaders could find considerable evidence of capitalist encirclement and of an affinity between fascism and capitalism. There were prominent persons in all the democracies who lauded Mussolini's regime for its alleged efficiencies. There were also persons in all the democracies who were not only quite sure that they could do business with Hitler, but who were also quite ready to try. And there were those who were prepared to say to Hitler and Stalin, "fight each other." Nor is that all. The Western democracies made some show of protest and spoke some harsh words, but they did nothing effective to stop the Japanese rape of China, nor the rearmament of Germany, nor the Italian attack on Ethiopia. Nor did they do anything except to sputter ineffectually about the German annexation of Austria. On the contrary, the governments and nationals—wittingly or not—had often helped the aggressors with credits and materials and in other ways. The surrender of Czechoslovakia to Germany by the agreement made at Munich (September, 1938) did not create a new pattern. It was, on the contrary, a refinement on design of appeasement which had begun long before.

The Soviet Union had no part in the negotiations which led to Munich, nor was she a party to the conference or to the settlement. But her role in the matter is not yet clear. Were the Soviets genuinely prepared to support the Czechs on request? No one can say for sure since the request was never made, and the evidence so far offered is neither conclusive nor convincing. It is clear, however, that Munich convinced the Soviet leaders—if they needed any convincing, which is highly doubtful —that they stood alone in a hostile world. This was largely but by no means all their own doing. But the Soviet championship of collective security—whether made in good faith or in bad faith—had failed. One reason for the failure was the admixture of revolutionary conspiracy with formal Soviet diplomacy.

CHAPTER XXVI

"The Second Great Fatherland War"

🦑 A CAUTION

We are still in the dark concerning much of the history of Soviet foreign policies since Munich, in spite of the publication (by various governments and persons) of numerous documents, memoirs, biographies, autobiographies, and other records. The major outlines seem to be reasonably clear, but details are lacking on many important points. Although we know in general what happened, we do not yet know nor completely understand the whys and wherefores. So many items are still controversial that all conclusions must be regarded as tentative, and even the narrative must be held subject to revision. For example, Soviet propaganda in 1939 began to accuse the Western democracies of trying to foment a war between Germany and Russia. There is no doubt that there were persons and groups in the West who would have been happy to see such a war, and there is no doubt that some of them worked toward that end. But the charge that this was a policy of responsible officials or agencies is unproved. One cannot be sure that the Soviet rulers actually believed these charges themselves. This is an important point, since such belief, even if actually without real foundation, would have been a major determinant of action. One needs to know not only objective reality but also what the participants thought reality to be. In the story of international diplomacy after 1938 we are not sure of either.

🦑 OPPORTUNISM

It would appear that the Soviet rulers after Munich continued to use as one of their guides to foreign policy a dictum laid down by Stalin in 1934. He told the Party's Seventeenth Congress in that year:

We have never had any orientation toward Germany nor have we any orientation toward Poland or France. Our orientation in the past and our orientation at present is toward the U.S.S.R. and toward the U.S.S.R. alone.

And if the interests of the U.S.S.R. demand *rapprochement* with this or that country which is not interested in disturbing the peace, we shall take that step without hesitation.

This was certainly broad and flexible enough to cover any possible contingency. The Soviets were prepared, as Stalin in effect told the Party in 1939, to do business with anyone who would do business with them on Soviet terms, but they continued to gird themselves against attack from any quarter. They were, during these years, in a state of military hostilities (though not technically a state of war) with Japan. These incidents reached a climax in midsummer of 1938, after which the friction began to abate. It did not, however, cease; nor did the Soviets stop their aid to China, which was then engaged in war with Japan. These matters must have had some influence on Soviet policies toward the West.

It would appear that *rapprochement* with Germany began in the autumn of 1938, or perhaps early in 1939 following the extension of the Soviet-German trade agreement. The Soviets did not, however, commit themselves to Germany for some months. Stalin laid down the general directive at the Eighteenth Party Congress in March, 1939, when he told the delegates that one of the tasks of the Party was, "To be cautious and not to allow our country to be drawn into conflicts by warmongers who are accustomed to have others pull the chestnuts out of the fire for them." And cautious they were, accepting overtures from any who wished to make overtures, refusing to deal with one to the exclusion of others, and declining any binding commitments. For example, the day after Stalin's speech on foreign affairs (from which the above quotation was taken) Manuilsky told the congress:

> The plan of the British reactionary *bourgeoisie* is to sacrifice the small states of southeastern Europe to German fascism so as to direct Germany eastward—against the U.S.S.R. . . . to buy off Germany with her imperialist claims on British colonies. At the same time, the British reactionaries would like to use the U.S.S.R. to draw the fangs of German imperialism, to weaken Germany. . . .

But four days later Ivan Maisky, Soviet Ambassador to Britain, declared in London, "Our two countries do not always see eye to eye as to the best methods of securing peace, but it is equally true—and this fact is of highest importance—that at present there is no conflict of interest between the U.S.S.R. and the British Empire in any part of the world." Maisky went on to say that Soviet-British relations would determine the question of peace or war "in our time." This was certainly an invitation to explore the possibilities of closer relations. On the other hand, Soviet sources (during the period of the German alliance) interpreted Stalin's comments as an encouragement to the Germans to pursue the *rapprochement*.

The diplomatic maneuvering that took place in 1939 is still obscure. The Soviet policy was cautious opportunism, in which several events worked to their advantage. The Anglo-French guarantees to Poland and Romania, for instance, helped to protect the U.S.S.R. from any possibility of German attack, since these two smaller nations separated the two large ones. The German advance into what was left of Czechoslovakia finally prodded the French and the British into an abandonment of appeasement. The record of diplomatic dealings between the Soviets on the one side and the French and the British on the other during the spring and summer of 1939 is incomplete. There appears to have been a lack of good faith on both sides. Nor is there any reason to suppose that German-Soviet dealings were marked by any better faith. More important than this—in terms of deciding factors—was the reality of the situation. The best that the French and British could offer the U.S.S.R. was an uncertain alliance with uncertain aid, but with a certainty of involvement in the coming war. It was not a very attractive offer. The Germans were in a better position. They could offer to allow the Soviet Union to annex certain lands and peoples. They could also offer a mutually advantageous economic deal (with certain military overtones). Finally, while a Soviet alliance with the democracies was also sure to lead to war, an alliance with Germany seemed to present some possibility of keeping out of war. This last point may have been decisive. It is clear that the Soviet rulers wanted more time, and it is highly probable that they cherished the illusion (just as many Americans did) that it might be possible to avoid getting into the war at all. That, of course, is supposition. The deals with Germany are matters of published record.

◉ THE SOVIET-GERMAN BARGAIN

The matter was apparently initiated by the Soviets in April, 1939, and was followed up by Molotov who replaced Litvinov as Commissar of Foreign Affairs in May. The Hitler government was receptive, and the conversations went on under cover of negotiations for an economic agreement. An economic agreement was signed on August 19. This provided that Germany would supply large credits to the U.S.S.R. which the Soviets were to use for the purchase in Germany of machinery, machine tools, and various types of war material. In return, the Soviets agreed to ship to Germany such raw materials as petroleum, phosphate, grain, lumber, and cotton. They also agreed to repay previous loans, to pay interest on old and new loans, and to complete shipments promised under the 1938 trade agreement. A "strictly confidential" memorandum of the German Foreign Office noted that, "Apart from the economic import of the treaty, its significance lies in the fact that the negotiations also served to renew political contacts with Russia and that the credit agreement was considered by both sides as the first decisive step in the reshaping of political relations." [1]

The political agreements—the Molotov-Ribbentrop Pacts—were signed in Moscow four days later, on August 23. The first was an open, ten-year nonaggression pact with a provision for the maintenance of "continual contact" between the two governments. Attached to this was a "secret additional protocol" dividing Poland and the Baltic states between Russia and Germany. These political agreements (and the economic bargain as well) were amended and extended by supplementary open and secret treaties. They were, as everyone knows, the immediate forerunners of World War II. That they were so planned and intended by the Germans has been quite generally agreed, but there has been no agreement as to the meaning and intentions of the Soviet actions. At the time of the formal ratification of the nonaggression pact, Molotov explained to the Supreme Soviet:

. . . We have always been of the opinion that a strong Germany is an indispensable condition for durable peace in Europe. . . . Therefore the interests of the peoples of the Soviet Union and Germany do not lie in mutual enmity. On the contrary, the peoples of the Soviet Union and Germany need to live at peace with each other. . . . We have always stood for amity between the peoples of the U.S.S.R. and Germany, for the growth and development of friendship between [them]. . . . Today as far as the European great powers are concerned, Germany is in the position of . . . striving for the earliest termination of war and for peace, whereas Britain and France . . . are in favor of continuing the war, and are opposed to the conclusion of a peace. . . .

Stalin said in a published interview in 1947 that the U.S.S.R. would have continued to co-operate with Germany if the Germans had been willing—a statement which seemed to bear out the assumption that the Soviet leaders hoped to avoid war altogether. The more common official Soviet explanation, repeatedly put forward from 1941 until the Twentieth Party Congress in 1956, was that Stalin knew all along that he could only postpone the conflict and that he was shrewdly playing for time. Khrushchev's famous denunciation of Stalin at that congress officially exploded this myth of Stalin's prophetic genius. Khrushchev thus confirmed what some scholars and commentators had been saying for many years, namely, that the Soviet leaders had taken the pacts at face value until the Nazi invasion.

The Soviet people apparently didn't know any better than the outside world what to make of the sudden change from enmity to amity. The

German ambassador reported from Moscow soon after the agreement was signed that the Soviet people were relieved by the apparent removal of the specter of a Russo-German war, but were baffled by the abrupt transformation of Germany from a dangerous aggressor to a trusted friend and confederate. Perhaps David Low, the famous British cartoonist, most accurately depicted the cynical nature of the Russo-German deal. His cartoon showed Hitler and Stalin bowing graciously to each other over a dead body. Low's Hitler is saying, "The scum of the earth, I believe," and his Stalin responds, "The bloody assassin of the workers, I presume." Mr. Low's one-word caption is entirely adequate. He called his cartoon "Rendezvous."

The two new friends met in Poland. The first suggestion for this came from Germany three days after the war began. The Soviets readily accepted the idea and speeded their military activities in order to keep pace with the advance of the German blitzkrieg. With incredible cynicism the Soviet rulers at first proposed to tell the world that their armed invasion and occupation of Poland was necessary to save Ukrainians and White Russians from German aggression. This was a little too much for the Germans to swallow, so the idea had to be abandoned, but the arrangements for the partition of Poland between the two Great Powers and the final wording of the announcement were no less cynical. Molotov then redefined aggression in such a manner as to place the blame for the war exclusively on the democracies. Later his government and its faithful echoes announced that the war was "an imperialistic conflict" between the "degenerate democracies" and the Fascists. It was, trumpeted the Soviet spokesmen, both "senseless" and "criminal." When, after the first flurry of action, the front remained quietly dull, the same spokesmen then derided the whole thing as "a phony war." It was now the Soviet's turn to chant, "Fight each other." Maisky unofficially and privately explained that his government wanted the war to be fought to a stalemate which would leave the antagonists mutually exhausted. Then the U.S.S.R. could step forth as the arbiter of Europe.

Whether Maisky's explanation was sound or not, his government made important territorial gains as an immediate result of the alliance with Germany. Poland they had to share with their ally, but in 1940 the Soviets took for themselves Estonia, Latvia, Lithuania, Bessarabia, and parts of Finland. The German territorial gains were, of course, much greater, though they proved to be far less lasting. But the situation was changing. Molotov had retorted to news of the German invasion of Norway by wishing his partners complete success, but he very soon warned that Swedish neutrality must be respected. When he was told of the German invasion of the Low Countries, he said only that he had no doubts of German success. The fall of France in May, 1940, was apparently an important turning point for the Soviets. That event made it clear that the war was not likely to end in a stalemate which would permit Stalin to act as arbitrator. The first change noted was an abrupt shift in the Soviet's domestic propaganda. Radio Moscow announced a new propaganda line. The derision and excoriation of the Western democracies disappeared as suddenly as the attacks on Germany had vanished in 1939. The new line was one of praise and encouragement for the "gallant British." Collaboration and co-operation with Germany continued, however, though friction appeared at an increasing number of points. There is some evidence—still scanty, incomplete, and inconclusive—of certain Soviet preparations of a warlike nature along her new western borders. Flying fields and other bases, for example, were prepared in Estonia and elsewhere. But the purpose of these actions is not clear. They may have been preparations for defense against a possible German attack, or for a further Soviet advance westward, or an increase in the Soviet's power-in-being in order to improve her bargaining position. The last possibility seems the most likely.

✾ THE WAR

There was a good deal of diplomatic dispute between Russia and Germany almost from the beginning. There was trouble over German actions in Finland, and over Soviet actions in Lithuania. After the first months, the Germans complained that Soviet demands for war materials and other goods were excessive; and the Soviets complained that German deliveries fell short of promises. Nevertheless, the economic co-operation seems to have been mutually profitable and important. There was also effective naval co-operation, with the Germans supplying naval vessels and equipment in return for port facilities and other help. For example, the German navy in September, 1940, formally thanked the Soviets for the use of "the base on the Murman Coast" which the Germans had used prior to the establishment of their bases in Norway. During the summer, also, Stalin rebuffed an effort by Great Britain to detach the U.S.S.R. from Germany. The signing of the Three Power Pact (Germany, Italy, and Japan) in September, 1940, and the later adherence of Bulgaria to this alliance seriously disturbed the Soviets. A German suggestion of collaboration between the pact nations and the U.S.S.R. and of the creation of spheres of influence was countered by Soviet insistence upon a more precise definition of spheres. Molotov demanded this all through his visit to Berlin in November, 1940, and insisted also upon the paramountcy of Soviet interests in Finland, the Balkans, and Turkey. The climax—and, apparently, the breaking point—came with Molotov's specific demands later that month. He proposed the withdrawal of German troops from Finland which, he said, "belongs to the Soviet Union's sphere of influence"; the recognition that Bulgaria was "inside the security zone" of the U.S.S.R., and the making of a Soviet-Bulgarian mutual assistance pact; the establishment of Soviet naval and military bases on the Bosporus; the acknowledgement of a Soviet sphere "south of Batum and Baku in the general direction of the Persian Gulf"; and the renunciation by Japan of the concessions for the exploitation of coal and oil deposits in northern Sakhalin.

This was more—far more—than Germany was prepared to give. Within less than a month Hitler issued "Directive No. 21, Operation Barbarossa," which began, "The German Armed Forces must be prepared *to crush Soviet Russia in a quick campaign* (Operation Barbarossa) even before the conclusion of the war against England." [2]

The Germans did what they could to forestall any agreement between Russia and Japan. Ribbentrop, in March, 1941, on the occasion of the visit to Berlin of Matsuoka (the Japanese foreign minister), told Matsuoka that Russia was not to be trusted, and that Germany was getting ready to pounce upon the Soviet Union. The German foreign minister also promised his Japanese colleague that Germany would support Japan by attacking Russia from the west, should the Russians ever attack Japan. Ribbentrop told Matsuoka that it would be all right for Japan to make a commercial agreement with Russia, but he warned against making any political deal. To this the Japanese replied that he would have to discuss a nonaggression pact with Russia, since he himself had originally suggested it. Ribbentrop could only agree. As a matter of fact, when Matsuoka visited Moscow in April, the upshot of his negotiations was not a nonaggression treaty, nor a commercial agreement, but a neutrality pact. Meanwhile another contretemps had taken place between the Russians and the Germans when Russia concluded a treaty of friendship and nonaggression with Yugoslavia, literally on the eve of the German invasion of that country.

The evidence on the Soviet side for what happened next is both scanty and suspect. It is, however, clearly established that both the United States and the United Kingdom attempted to warn the Soviets of an impending German attack. These warnings began in March (1941) and continued through April and May. Soviet sources abroad began to report similar warnings at least as early as May. Khrushchev charged in 1956 that, ". . . Stalin took no heed of these warnings." Khrushchev further stated that Stalin ordered the German fire not be returned, even after the invasion had started. "Why? It was because Stalin [said Khrushchev] . . . thought that the war had not yet started, that this was only a provocative action . . . and that our reaction might serve as a reason for the Germans to begin the war."

These charges, part of Khrushchev's down-grading of Stalin, may properly be suspect as polemics. However, they are probably accurate. Anyway, whether the Soviet leaders expected the invasion or not, the Soviet people didn't. News of the German invasion, which began at four o'clock on the morning of June 22, 1941, came as a terrific shock to the Soviet people.

When the German blitzkrieg pulverized Soviet defenses and rolled eastward with apparently inexorable might, the Soviet people were temporarily panic-stricken and embittered. After all, not only had they been hearing for almost two years of their German friend, but they had also been hearing for much longer of the greatness of the Red Army. Molotov, in making the first full-dress announcement of the beginning of the war, had told the people (among other things):

> . . . the Soviet Government has ordered our troops to repulse the preda-
> tory assault and to drive German troops from the territory of our country.
> . . . The government . . . expresses its unshakable conviction that . . .
> [our armed forces] will inflict a crushing blow upon the aggressor. This is
> not the first time that our people have had to deal with an attack of an arro-
> gant foe. At the time of Napoleon's invasion of Russia our people's reply
> was war for the fatherland, and Napoleon suffered defeat and met his doom.
> It will be the same with Hitler. . . .

Twelve days later Stalin had to tell his people, "In spite of heroic resist-ance of the Red Army . . . the enemy continues to push forward. . . ." By then, Lithuania and parts of Latvia, Bielorussia, and western Ukraine were already lost. What the Soviets call—with cavalier disregard of everyone else who was involved—the "Second Great Fatherland War" (or "The Great Patriotic War of the Soviet Union") had begun and be-gun very badly for the Soviets. But the Soviet people and their govern-ment recovered from their initial panic and setbacks, and, with the help of those capitalist nations whom their gospel scorns and hates, finally, in a terribly bitter and costly struggle, beat back the Germans.

THE FIRST YEARS OF THE WAR

Something like 10 per cent of the total Soviet population of 193 million men, women, and children served directly in the armed forces. This was roughly a fifth of the adult population; roughly a third of the male popula-tion of working age. Those who were not directly involved in the armed forces were directly involved in other ways. All males between the ages of sixteen and fifty who were not in the armed forces were required to take military training. All citizens from the ages of eight to sixty were required to take training in civil defense. Very large numbers of Soviet citizens of both sexes and all ages fought as "Civilian Volunteer Guards" or as "Partisans." During the autumn of 1941 the brunt of the gallant attempts to defend their homes fell upon the civilians, to give the armies a chance to regroup, reorganize, and re-equip for a counterattack. The aim was achieved but at terrific cost to the people—most of whom were volunteers.

The people were drafted for labor no less than for military service. This had begun before the war, of course. The workbooks or labor passports, introduced in 1938, were re-enforced in 1940 by decrees which "froze" labor at its jobs and permitted the arbitrary transfer of technicians and skilled laborers from one place of employment to another. Another law of 1940 established a special labor draft for young people from the ages of fourteen through seventeen. The fourteen- and fifteen-year-olds were assigned to trade schools for a two-year course. The sixteen- and seventeen-year-olds were assigned to six months' training for work in metallurgical industries, coal mines, or on construction jobs. These labor draftees, after training, were assigned jobs by the government. The outbreak of war naturally speeded up the drafts on manpower. Martial law was declared for many areas, thus giving the military authorities the right to draft civilians for emergency service of all kinds. A specific mobilization of all workers in war and related industries took place in December, 1941. A later decree mobilized men from sixteen to fifty-five and women from sixteen to fifty years of age, who lived in urban areas, for work in war industries either in their home towns or elsewhere. All able-bodied city people and all high-school students were also mobilized for work on the land as needed. There was even a labor draft for invalids. Workers on railroads, inland waterways, and in the merchant marine were placed under martial law in 1943. Nor was this all. An eight-hour workday plus compulsory overtime of three-and-a-half hours (at time and a half) was established. The legal work week remained six days, but the actual work week was more often seven. This meant that the usual work week was 77 hours, and very many Soviet workers habitually worked much more. Vacations were abolished in war industries, time-and-a-half pay for two weeks being given instead. The conversion of industry to war production was almost complete. Virtually no civilian goods of any kind were produced from June, 1941, until the end of 1945.

Closely related to the mobilization of labor was the large-scale removal of industries from the war zones. Not all plants were removed, nor were all those which were left behind destroyed (as was claimed at the time). The speed of the German advance—as well as panic and confusion and

disloyalty—rendered both the evacuation and the scorched-earth policy
something less than completely effective. But—in accordance with long-
prepared plans—many plants (or, more accurately, their machinery)
were moved bodily from the path of the German advance. Among those
moved were the textile mills of Mozhaisk, the tank and tractor factories
of Kharkov, the aircraft plants of Moscow, the farm-implement factories
of Rostov, the Kirov steel works from Leningrad, the oil-well machinery
from the Maikop fields, and many others. Workers, especially skilled
workers—gunsmiths from Tula, miners from the Ukraine, electrical
workers from Moscow, and so on—were also evacuated. Reports and
information which became available after the war indicated that wartime
claims of the speed, efficiency, and completeness of the transplanting of
industries were often exaggerated. Poor planning, inefficiency of execution, delays, transportation failures, inadequate preparations, and so on,
resulted in the ruining of many machines. But, admitting all the shortcomings and discounting heavily all wartime boasts, the removal of industry under the most adverse conditions was a very considerable accomplishment. For example, over a million carloads of machinery and equipment were moved eastward in the summer and autumn of 1941.

One cannot help reflecting, however, that such feats would have been
unnecessary if the Red Army had been able to live up to prewar and
early war press releases of the Soviet leaders. The Red Army had been
greatly enlarged through the establishment in September, 1939, of the
"Universal Obligation for Military Service," a law which provided for
drafting all males at the ages of eighteen or nineteen. (Women were also
made liable to the draft for certain auxiliary military duties.) The draftee
served a period of from two to five years, depending upon his rank and
the branch of service, and then remained a member of the reserves until
his fiftieth birthday. (The law was altered somewhat after June, 1941.)
Large classes of draftees under this law had entered the armed forces
before the German invasion. (Stalin later complained that the Germans
had invaded before Soviet mobilization had been completed.) And a
number of Soviet soldiers had been blooded in actual combat against
the Japanese and the Finns. Despite this, and despite the official Soviet
claim (made in 1940) that its borders "were girded by a belt of fortified
districts," the Germans penetrated with speed and apparent ease.

There were three main lines and two lesser lines of German advance
in 1941, all of them co-ordinated. One main attack was aimed from
East Prussia at Leningrad; the second was directed from the center to-
ward Moscow; and the third, also from the center, toward Kiev and the
Dnieper Basin. Of less weight were the German-Finnish drive against
Leningrad and the German-Romanian drive toward Odessa and the

Crimea. All were successful in gaining ground, but none succeeded in destroying the Red Army. All along the 1800-mile front—a distance approximately as great as from Denver to either coast—the Germans drove forward. The high tide of the German advance came at the beginning of December. By then, Leningrad was besieged (a siege that lasted sixteen months) and the enemy had penetrated east of the city. The suburbs of Moscow also knew the war at first hand, when German troops attacked the city's outskirts. Kiev fell in September; Kharkov and Odessa, in October; Rostov, in November. Then, to the open-mouthed amazement of the world, the Red Army struck in a counteroffensive which began the day before Pearl Harbor. There had been some changes. Marshals Budyenny and Voroshilov had been removed from field commands in October. All except rear-guard cadres, who were left to organize and direct the civilian defenders, had been withdrawn to the east of Moscow and there had been regrouped and re-enforced. While the ordinary "little people" fought and died in the gallant but hopeless attempts to defend their homes from the invaders—the Red Army was being rebuilt. Its counteroffensive lasted three months and drove the Germans back along about a third of the front. Leningrad remained under siege, but Moscow was relieved, Rostov was recaptured, and Russian troops struck in the Crimea.

Soviet historians up to 1956 credited the counterattack to the "genius of Stalin." He had been announced as chairman of the all-powerful Committee for Defense when that was created in June, 1941. He replaced Timoshenko as Commissar of Defense and became commander-in-chief of all the Soviet armed forces. Later he accepted the titles of Marshal and Generalissimo. The Defense Committee was, with the exception of Voroshilov, composed of Party leaders rather than soldiers, and it seems to have been primarily a policy-making body. Stalin's chief military leaders and advisers were apparently Boris Shaposhnikov, Chief of Staff, who died in 1943; N. N. Voronov, Marshal and artillery specialist; and General (later Marshal) Georgi K. Zhukov.[3] Timoshenko may also have been a member of this select company, though he was removed from active command in August, 1942, for his failure to stem the second great German advance. These are facts of record. Beyond them—as far as the direction of the Soviet military effort at the top levels—lie myth and speculation.

The German offensive of 1942 was concentrated along the southern portion of the front. It sought to reach Moscow from the south and east, but its main weight was thrown toward the oil fields and oil supply lines of the Caucasus. Again the advance was rapid and the penetration was deep. The Kerch peninsula fell and so did the major base of Sevastopol.

German armies entered the Kuban region, capturing Novorossisk and the Maikop oil fields, and moved eastward to threaten the more important Baku-Grozny oil centers. They recaptured Rostov, slammed ahead to the Don from Voronezh to below Stalingrad. Late in August the Germans reached the Volga north of Stalingrad and cut that vital communications line. In September they drove into Stalingrad itself, and then began the defense of that city, which so caught the enthusiasm of the West. It has been generally held that Stalingrad was the turning point of the war and also that its capture became for Hitler an obsession—a matter of prestige for which he threw away a great army. Against this conventional interpretation may be set the suggestion that the turning point was not Stalingrad but the double failure of the Germans to capture Moscow. And without denying its prestige value to Hitler, it may be urged that Stalingrad was no less a matter of prestige to Stalin. Its stubborn and costly defense did not save the Volga supply line.

The portions of the Soviet Union which the Germans had conquered during 1941 and 1942 were (or had been) home to 88 million Soviet citizens, over half the population recorded by the 1939 census. Many of these people continued to live under German rule, some not unhappily, though some suffered terribly and many were killed. From the Krivoi Rog region of Ukraine had come 63 per cent of the iron ore produced in the Soviet Union before the war, and from the Donets basin had come half the coal. The steel mills in the occupied territory had accounted for over half the prewar steel production, and the industries of the area had produced a third of the total Soviet output. A third of the railway mileage lay within the conquered sections as did also the westerly pipelines carrying oil from the Caucasus. And the cutting of the Volga meant that oil could no longer be shipped north along that river. A long detour to the east was necessary. In addition, fully 40 per cent of the sown lands of the U.S.S.R. were lost to the Germans during the first bitter months of the Second Fatherland War.

PEOPLE AND WAR

How did the Soviets keep fighting? How did the people survive? These questions require more in the way of answers than glib statements about heroism and magnificent fighting spirit and great gallantry and extraordinary toughness, though all such statements are true in part. One partial answer has been given in the story of the removal of industries and in the prewar developments of industrial and agricultural centers in the Urals and in the Soviet Middle and Far East. Another partial answer was that the Soviet government had prudently accumulated immense stockpiles of food and raw materials. A third partial answer lay in the calculated deprivation of the people on the ground that it was better for many to perish in order that most might go on existing than to try to save the many at the expense of all. The armed forces had first call on everything—food, clothing, fuel, transportation, goods, medical services, and all else. If there was anything left, the civilians might have it. Rationing was on a basis of inequality, the largest shares going to those whom the rulers held to be the most valuable to the regime and its survival. This meant not only those engaged in the most essential industries but also those who held the most political power. Finally, part of the answer was that millions did not survive hunger, exhaustion, deprivations, and hardships.

It is impossible to describe in a few paragraphs how the Soviet people reacted to the war. Some did all that was demanded of them and more; some did as little as possible. Some served and sacrificed out of pride and conviction and loyalty; others did no more than they were compelled to do. Some shared generously and fairly; others grabbed all they could get. Some were good Samaritans; others were heartless brigands. Some supported the regime; others sought to sabotage it. There were heroes and cowards, loyal citizens and traitors. But for the overwhelming majority of Soviet peoples the war was a cruel ordeal of physical and mental suffering. Acute shortages of food and all necessities were made worse by a roaring inflation produced by the familiar combination of high earnings and short supply. Prices were controlled in government stores; but there were also illicit black markets, as well as the peasants' market, which has sometimes been described (rather inaccurately) as a "government-run black market." (Later—in 1944—the government opened the so-called commercial stores. These were relatively well stocked, but prices were extremely high, although privileged persons were allowed discounts ranging as high as 60 per cent. The purpose of the commercial stores was to get some of the excess currency back in government control.)

As for public morale, it fluctuated from place to place and from time to time. There was at first a sense of shock which was followed by optimism and even by overconfidence. Then came a kind of incredulous dismay which grew into hysterical panic as the Germans encircled Leningrad and approached Moscow. For a brief time, there were mass stampedes, wild disorders, and general looting on a basis of every man for himself. This passed, at least partly because of Stalin's well-publicized refusal to leave the Kremlin, despite the evacuation of many government and all diplomatic offices. Discipline was tightened and morale improved during the Russian counteroffensive, but there was a slump in both as the Germans returned in 1942 and drove deeper. Then the rulers enforced a ruthless "iron discipline" in the army, which included the summary execution of offenders. An officer's orders, said *Pravda* in July, 1942, are "iron laws." And the army's newspaper (*Red Star*) warned that "He who retreats without orders cannot expect mercy." Death was to be regarded as infinitely preferable to capture, and surrender was held tantamount to treason. One factor behind this new campaign was certainly the large-scale desertions of Red Army men, topped off by the defection of Lieutenant General A. A. Vlasov, who had been one of the heroes of the defense of Moscow in 1941. Discipline on the home front (and in the armed forces, also) was re-enforced by an all-out propaganda drive which emphasized love of Russia and hatred of the enemy. Wrote Ilya Ehrenburg, "We must not say, 'Good morning' or 'Good night.' In the morning we must say, 'Kill the Germans' and at night we must say, 'Kill the Germans. . . .' We want to live. And in order to live, we must kill Germans."

✺ THE DIPLOMATIC FRONT: AID FROM THE WEST

Actions and reactions on the diplomatic front were fast and furious after the start of the German invasion of the U.S.S.R. On the evening of June 22, 1941, Churchill broadcast a statement of the British position. "Any man or state who fights against Nazidom will have our aid. . . . we shall give whatever help we can to Russia and to the Russian people. . . . We have offered to the government of Soviet Russia any technical or economic assistance which is in our power. . . ." The next day President Roosevelt and Secretary Hull promised aid to Russia. Steps to implement the promises were taken immediately. Missions scurried back and forth, the first few supplies were processed for transit, and (in July) a mutual aid agreement was entered into by the U.S.S.R. and the United Kingdom. This was followed by a Soviet-Czech pact and by a military alliance between the Soviet Union and the Polish Government-in-Exile. Russia and Britain took, first, joint diplomatic measures and, when these failed, joint military action in Iran to drive out the pro-German Iranian government. Later, a three-way alliance was signed by the Soviets, the British, and the Iranians.

The July agreement between the U.S.S.R. and the United Kingdom was replaced in May, 1942, by a formal alliance. The first part of this agreement bound the two to render each other all aid and support against Germany and her associates and also pledged that no separate peace or armistice would be made. The second part of the alliance dealt with the postwar period and pledged joint action "to render impossible the repetition of aggression" by Germany and her associates in Europe. The two partners also promised that neither would seek territorial gains or interfere in the internal affairs of other states. They further promised "close and friendly collaboration . . . for the organization of security and economic prosperity in Europe." The stated life of the alliance was twenty years, with provision for automatic prolongation.

No such formal alliance was made between the U.S.S.R. and the United States, but the Soviet request for supplies was answered first by the Moscow Protocol (1941), which bound the United States to send goods to the approximate value of a billion dollars to the Soviets. This agreement was later superseded by the master lend-lease agreement of June, 1942. Total American lend-lease to the U.S.S.R. finally amounted to over 11 billion dollars worth of goods, and the Soviets received large quantities of supplies from Britain and Canada under similar agreements. Without attempting to recount the details, two general points need to be kept in mind about this wartime co-operation. The first is that American and British supplies did not begin to reach the Soviets in large quantities until 1943, and *quantitatively* they were far less important than Soviet-made supplies. Roughly four-fifths of the material used by the Red Army was Soviet-made. *Qualitatively,* however, American and British supplies were of vital importance, because they included products, materials, and equipment which the Soviets either lacked completely or had only in very small and inadequate amounts. The second point—one which has too often been forgotten in the postwar years—is that the primary aim and purpose of the democracies in supplying material to the Soviets was to enable the Soviets to fight more effectively against the common enemy. The reverse was also true. The Soviets fought to save themselves, not to save the democracies. The question of gratitude or ingratitude, so often raised in this connection, is irrelevant. The primary aim of Stalin and his associates was to safeguard and advance the interest of the Communist Party of the Soviet Union. This involved, for one thing, the unstinted spending of Soviet lives and treasure. It also involved getting as much as possible from the democracies while giving as little as possible in return. Even before the war was over, they began to tell themselves and the world that the defeat of Germany and Japan was exclusively their doing. This was a lie of gigantic proportions, but no reasonable person can deny that the Soviet share in the defeat of Germany and her European associates was tremendous.

⊕ WAR AND DIPLOMACY, 1943–45

The visible ebbing of the German tide in Russia began with the tremendous surge of Russian forces against the Germans in Stalingrad late in 1942. By June, 1943, a great Soviet offensive had rolled the Germans back all along the line from Leningrad to the Black Sea. The German summer offensive of that year was stopped within a week, and the Red Army then undertook, for the first time, a summer advance of its own, which carried as far as the Dnieper River. By the year's end about three-quarters of the occupied zone had been recovered, and, significantly, there was no German offensive in 1944. The Soviets by that time had some 400 divisions (5 million men—including combat troops and operational reserves) on their western front. Behind them—in the Far East, in various stages of training, in supply and other forces—were perhaps an additional 14 million. The Soviet's own military production had increased, and what had been a trickle of material from the democracies became a good-sized flood. During 1944 Soviet troops completely freed Soviet soil from the Germans and then pressed forward into Axis territory. The Red Army entered East Prussia. Romania, Bulgaria, and Finland were knocked out of the war. All three accepted an armistice. Soviet forces drove forward into Poland and Czechoslovakia. East Prussia fell in 1945, and the Red Army knocked out Hungary, crossed into Austria and entered Vienna. In April the Red Army men met the American GI's who had been waiting for them at Torgau on the Elbe River. And in May Germany signed the "Act of Military Surrender" at Reims and Berlin. V-E Day had come.

Soviet forces in the Far East had taken no part in the war against Japan, and until late in 1944 the Soviet government had scrupulously maintained a formal neutrality in the Pacific war, although it had now and again given some slight assistance to Japan's enemies. But on August 8, 1945, the U.S.S.R. declared war against Japan and Soviet troops promptly occupied Manchuria, the Kurile Islands, southern Sakhalin, Port Arthur, Dairen (Dalny), and parts of Korea. Six days later the Japanese sued for peace and the formal surrender was signed on September 2, 1945. The Soviet claim that this was a cause and effect relationship —that is, that it was the Soviet entry into the war which defeated Japan —is without foundation in fact. The Japanese were already beaten before the Soviets honored their pledge (first made verbally in 1943) to enter the war against Japan.

The diplomatic history of the years 1943 through 1945, even when almost all details are omitted, is still much more complicated than the story of the military campaigns. The comment that Stalin's prime interest was the defense of the Party was based upon his apparent willingness to sacrifice full victory in order to get a negotiated peace on his own. The Soviets began extending peace feelers to Germany early in 1943, but without any success, since the Germans were not then disposed to listen. Their attitude had changed by July, however, and further approaches were then made. Nothing came of these nor of a subsequent Soviet suggestion, put forward in the early autumn. Soviet initiative seems to have stopped at that point. It was now the Germans who talked of a separate peace, and clandestine negotiations were carried on through 1944. Ukraine was the sticking point upon which no deal could be reached, and so the Soviet Union remained in the war. These surreptitious doings were known to the democracies, who bid very high to prevent the making of a separate peace. Much of what Western critics later called "appeasement" was due to those circumstances. It may have been that the Soviets had so calculated; that they talked with Germany not with any genuine intention of making a separate peace but only for the purpose of blackmailing their British ally and their American associates. If that was their plan, it worked. The first peace feelers, incidentally, went by way of Japan; later negotiations were direct.

Another evidence of long-range Soviet planning was their use of German prisoners of war. This began in October, 1941, with the "First Conference of German Prisoners of War" under the leadership of a German Communist. A manifesto to the German people issued by the conferees was the first move in a propaganda campaign which had at least two aims. One was undoubtedly the obvious aim of psychological warfare—the use of German spokesmen in an effort to undermine the will of their countrymen to fight. This was directed both against German soldiers on the Russian front and against civilians in Germany, and was carried on by the skillful and lavish use of broadcasts and printed material. A high point of the campaign was the formation of a "Free Germany Committee" (in July, 1943) and of a "German Officers Corps" (in September, 1943). The two groups worked closely together. The second aim of this move was preparation for the postwar period. Strenuous efforts were made first to indoctrinate and then to train those who joined the groups. (The same tactics were also employed against other prisoners of war, including the Japanese.) The indoctrination and training were carried on both by Soviet Communists and by German Communists. The purpose, of course, was to prepare drilled and disciplined cadres of Communists who would serve Moscow after returning to their homes. A like purpose was served by the treatment accorded the various non-Soviet Communist stalwarts who sat out the war in the U.S.S.R. These people —for example, Thorez of France, Bor of Poland, Pauker of Romania— were groomed to take over the governments of their native lands. The history of the satellites of the Soviets after 1945 shows that these policies paid high dividends.

The story of Soviet relations with Great Britain and the United States during the war centers on two major themes, Russia's efforts to get as much immediate material aid as possible, and her efforts to set up postwar arrangements which would favor the advance of Communist interests. The former not infrequently involved lip service to commitments which would have cut across the latter. Thus Litvinov, who served as the Soviet Ambassador in Washington from December, 1941, to August, 1943, signed the Joint Declaration by the United Nations endorsing the Atlantic Charter. This, it may be recalled, bound its signatories "to seek no aggrandizement, territorial or other," "to respect the right of all peoples to choose the form of government under which they will live," and not to seek any "territorial changes that do not accord with the freely expressed wishes of the people concerned." Thus, also, did the Kremlin announce in May, 1943, the dissolution of the Comintern. Another case in point was the Soviet pledge, made in the Treaty of Alliance with the United Kingdom and repeated in many other documents and on many other occasions, not to enter into separate armistice or peace negotiations. Equally relevant were the agreements among the Soviets and the democracies for joint administration and occupation, free elections, and so on in the "liberated" and conquered countries. Typical was the mutual promise (made at Yalta) for the reorganization of the Lublin (Polish) Government "on a broader democratic basis" and for the holding of "free and unfettered elections as soon as possible on the basis of universal suffrage and secret ballot." There is no need to complete the list of promises, nor to catalogue the points of friction which developed. Note may be made, however, of certain key events (with especial attention to Soviet-American relations).

Concern in 1942 was largely with problems of supply and with the insistent Soviet demand for what they called (with a fine disregard for numerical and other facts) a "second front." They declined to regard the Anglo-American invasion of North Africa as a second front. There was a three-Power military conference (Russia, the United States, and Britain) in August, 1942, and additional formal machinery for the joint effort was placed in operation during that year and the next. There was some exceedingly rough weather in April, 1943, with the revelation that thousands of Polish officers, last seen in Soviet hands, had been massacred in the Katyn Forest. The Polish Government-in-Exile appealed to the Red Cross. The Soviets heatedly denied that the killing had been their work, and blamed it on the Germans. Diplomatic relations between the Kremlin and the exiled (or London) Polish government were broken. There was also a certain awkwardness in Soviet relations with Britain and the United States. The Soviets stood fast on their denial, refused an American offer to mediate between them and the London Poles, and—largely because of the threat of a separate peace—managed to have things their own way. A Conference of Foreign Ministers held at Moscow in October,

1943, resulted in a declaration of full agreement on united action against the enemy, surrender terms, the need of establishing an international organization, and the postwar use of arms and armies. This paved the way for a meeting of Stalin, Churchill, and Roosevelt at Teheran in November–December of the same year. The chief matter of business was the second front. The British wanted to launch the attack against what Churchill called the "soft underbelly" of the enemy—that is, through Italy and the Balkans. Stalin, the American military leaders, and Roosevelt favored a trans-Channel assault on Europe's west coast. There was some inconclusive discussion of a possible postwar dismemberment of Germany and of other matters. Perhaps the most surprising event (and one of the best-kept secrets) was Stalin's unsolicited statement that the Soviet Union would join the United States and Britain in fighting Japan.

The year 1944 saw several formal agreements "in principle" and rather consistent disagreements in detail. The three Great Powers joined in ultimatums to Hungary, Romania, Bulgaria, and Finland to abandon their German ally. This took place in May. During the late summer and early fall, the Big Three, together with lesser Powers, took part in the Dumbarton Oaks Conference. There was disagreement over voting and veto power, but there was agreement on other matters including the principle of an international organization. The Big Three also agreed (in October) to "joint administration" for the defeated Axis associates in eastern and southeastern Europe and (in November) to the future establishment of a co-ordinated military rule of Germany under a Supreme Allied Council. On the other hand, there were great difficulties in co-ordinating military efforts, and there were serious disagreements over the disposition of Romanian oil, the borders to be established for Poland, and other matters. It was partly because of these frictions, but mostly for the purpose of co-ordinating the final drive against Germany, that the Big Three held their meeting at Yalta in February, 1945.

There were half a dozen open agreements and three secret agreements made at Yalta. The open agreements were, with one or two exceptions, on generalities; the secret ones were specific. The first of the open agreements dealt with Germany—the co-ordination of the final attack, the division of Germany into zones with an Allied Control Commission in Berlin, the destruction of naziism and militarism, and the discussion of reparations. The second open agreement set the opening date of the United Nations organizational conference, and registered an agreement previously reached on voting procedures. One of the secret arrangements at Yalta promised the Ukrainian and Bielorussian Soviet Socialist Republics membership and voting power in the to-be-formed United Nations organization. The third open agreement provided for tripartite action in regard to the "liberated countries," and the fourth dealt with Poland. (Some of the provisions of these two sections of agreement have already been mentioned.) The deal over Poland included a promise that Poland would receive "substantial accessions of territory in the north and west." Its eastern border was to follow the Curzon line, with some adjustments. The fifth open agreement recommended the establishment in Yugoslavia of a coalition government to include Tito, who was at that time in excellent favor with the Kremlin. The sixth and final open agreement provided for regular meetings of the foreign ministers in the future.

The first of the secret sections of the Yalta Pact consisted of various military arrangements: the United States was to have airfields in the Budapest area, Russia was to construct air bases for American use in areas around Komsomolsk and Nikolaevsk, and there was to be concerted action against Japan. (The second secret section was noted above.) The third secret agreement bound the U.S.S.R. to go to war against Japan within 90 days after V-E Day. In return for this, the United States and Britain agreed that the Soviets were to get the Kurile Islands, southern Sakhalin, and a lease on Port Arthur. The Chinese Eastern Railway and the Southern Manchurian Railways were to be operated jointly by Russia and China, and the port city of Dairen was to be internationalized. That was the price which the Soviets were able to exact for promised help against the Japanese. It should be noted that the price was set and accepted when it was believed that the defeat of Japan would require several more years of costly war. Since this proved to be entirely wrong—partly because of America's atomic bombs—the Yalta deal turned out to be a great bargain from the Soviet point of view.

There was an international flurry of excitement when the Soviets announced in late March, 1945, that they were sending not Foreign Minister Molotov but a young career diplomat named Andrei Gromyko to represent the U.S.S.R. at the organizational conference of the United Nations. After a direct request from the United States, the Soviets reversed this decision and Molotov did represent them at the San Francisco meeting. There was another flurry when the Soviets demanded that their Polish government be invited to San Francisco. The United States and Britain, and later, the San Francisco Conference itself, refused the demand and the matter was dropped for a time. Late in April, the United States informed the U.S.S.R. of the receipt of German peace offers which excluded the Russians. Britain and the United States, to whom the offers had been extended, flatly rejected the proposals. Despite this demonstration of united action, and despite the success of the San Francisco meeting, which accomplished its major objective, though not without disagreements, there were signs that the wartime coalition was cracking. These signs became more apparent at the Potsdam Conference in July and August. There were serious differences over the unilateral fixing of the Polish-German frontier by the Soviets; reparations; Soviet charges against British actions in Greece; the Soviet request for trusteeship of the Italian colonies in Africa; and various other matters. There were, however, enough agreements—including the establishment of a Council of Foreign Ministers, who were to draft the various peace treaties—to encourage a belief in the democracies that the conference was a success. Perhaps there would have been less confidence and less optimism if the democracies had paid more attention to an article in *Pravda* at the time of V-E Day.

The article was written by the famous Soviet journalist Ilya Ehrenburg. Mr. Ehrenburg admitted that "Shoulder to shoulder with us fought our gallant Allies. . . ." But earlier in his article he wrote (with a complete disregard of facts):

> We long fought single-handed against the colossal forces of Germany. What would have happened to the children of Canadian farmers or Parisian workers if the Russian soldier, who drank the bitter cup on the Don, had not marched to the Spree? We saved not only our own country, but also human culture, the ancient foundations of Europe, its cradles, its workers, its museums, its books.

Single-handed victory was to be a recurrent and increasingly emphasized theme of Soviet propaganda, both domestic and foreign.

There is space here for only the briefest mention of Soviet foreign policies toward the lesser nations during the later war years. The essence of them was the development of Soviet spheres of power, or preparations for the development of such spheres. A "for-the-duration-of-the-war" agreement was reached with the British late in 1944 by which Soviet interests and influence were recognized as dominant in Romania, Bulgaria, and Hungary. The British were to have top position in Greece, and Yugoslavia was to be under both British and Russian influence. This agreement was partially implemented by the armistice terms imposed on Romania (1944), Bulgaria (1944), and Hungary (1945). By these terms, the Soviets gained the dominant place on the Allied Control Commissions for these countries, and broad economic rights, also. The armistice with Finland (1944) gave the U.S.S.R. exclusive political and economic rights there. Before this stage had been reached, the Kremlin had made great progress in the organization and training of Communist-controlled "governments-to-be": the Union of Polish Patriots, which later emerged as the "Lublin Government"; and the "National Liberation" group in Yugoslavia, which later became Tito's regime were both cases in point. Similar preparations had been made for Albania, Greece, Hungary, Romania, Bulgaria, Finland, and Czechoslovakia. Mutual assistance treaties were also signed with Czechoslovakia (1943), the Provisional French Government (1944), Yugoslavia (1945), and Poland (1945). An effort was made to get a similar agreement with Turkey, but the Turks resisted and nothing was accomplished during the war in spite of vigorous Soviet pressures in 1945. As to China, there was signed in August, 1945, a Treaty of Friendship and Alliance (with several supplemental agreements) which, in effect, confirmed the gains made by Russia (at the expense of China) at the Yalta meeting. The Soviet occupation of Manchuria, the subsequent disarming and evacuation of the Japanese, and the seizure of Japanese equipment, factories, and other enterprises there (in blatant violation of agreements) greatly strengthened the Chinese Communists and Moscow's control.

 DOMESTIC CHANGES

There were changes—some real and some only apparent—in the Soviet domestic scene during the last years of the war. Among the former may be noted the postponement of elections; the granting of financial aid for the families of men called to the colors; increased taxes; labor laws (already described); the liquidation of several autonomous republics; and new legislation on marriage, divorce, and the family. The minimum financial aid to dependents of servicemen was one hundred rubles a month, and was scaled up from there. New taxes included a special levy (up to 5 per cent of wages received) for single persons and childless married couples. There were also war taxes on incomes, which raised the tax paid by workers by 50 per cent on wages from 300 to 500 rubles a month; and by 100 per cent on wages above 500 rubles a month. This was later modified by setting up an annual income tax on workers ranging from 120 rubles (for an annual income of 1800 rubles) to 2700 rubles (for an income of 24,000 rubles or over). Servicemen and women and some others were exempted, but those not classed as workers paid double rates. Farm families were assessed a 100 per cent increase on the agricultural tax if they had no one in service; a 50 per cent increase if they had one member in service; and no increase if two or more of the family were in service. Four autonomous republics were abolished between 1941 and 1945. Their total population had been (in 1939) between 2.5 and 3 millions, and many of these people were forcibly transferred from their native regions. This was a significant commentary upon the widely publicized Soviet policy on national minorities. The new marriage and family law (issued in July, 1944) made divorce more difficult and costly, and increased the subsidies for families having more than three children. This —along with the tax on the unmarried and childless—was intended to increase the birth rate.

Other meaningful changes included adjustments in rationing and prices (there were some reductions); the restoration of the eight-hour working day (July, 1945); the partial demobilization of armed forces (September, 1945); changes on the collectives; and the growth in size of the Communist Party. The Party made a strenuous and successful effort to integrate itself and the armed forces by a recruitment campaign designed to bring into the Party all who proved themselves leaders or showed promise of leadership. Admission requirements were relaxed. The result was that Party membership was increased to a new high, despite tremendous war losses. As for the collective farmers, postwar revelations gave the lie to wartime claims of all-out patriotism. Many collective farmers found that the war gave them great bargaining powers in fact, though not in law. In law, new and greater demands for production and the surrender of produce to the state were constantly being made. In fact, many collective farmers used the opportunity illegally to increase the area of their "household plots" and the scope of their individual (as opposed to collective) efforts.

The apparent changes ranged from those which altered only forms and formalities to those which combined some real alterations with purely superficial shifts. An example of the alteration of form was the decree of February, 1944, which allowed each member republic to establish its own Commissariats of Foreign Affairs and of Defense. But full, formal control of Soviet diplomacy and of the Soviet armed forces remained with the federal union, and real control remained with the Politburo. A second example of a superficial change was the formal abolition of the Comintern in 1943. The testimony and corroborating documents brought forth in the "Canadian Spy Case" proved conclusively that all the machinery of the Comintern survived the dissolution unimpaired. A combination of real and superficial changes took place in regard to organized religions.

The official position of the Russian Orthodox Church from the start of the Second Great Fatherland War had been loyally to support the government, and this was apparently also the position of most of the clergy. This demonstration of loyalty, plus the conviction that religious groups were no longer a real threat to the regime, plus the clear realization that concessions to churches would make a most favorable impression upon their democratic allies, resulted in a shift in policy. There was a decrease in active hostility, a cessation of attacks, and then a series of concessions. The Orthodox Church, in 1943, was permitted to reestablish the patriarchate and to elect a patriarch—the first since 1917. Religious books were published and the training of clergy was resumed. A special Council for the Affairs of the Orthodox Church was established

E: Estonia; La: Latvia
L: Lithuania
—o—o—o— Boundaries in 1939
—•—•—•— Boundaries in 1950
—✕✕✕✕— Deepest German penetration
⬚⬚⬚⬚ Soviet conquests, 1939–50

Profit and Loss, 1939–1950

ostensibly to handle all matters of Church-State relationships. (A Council for Affairs of Religious Cults was also set up to handle matters involving religious groups other than the Russian Orthodox. The concessions granted to the Orthodox were generally extended to the other groups also, except the Uniate Church, which was liquidated.) These were genuine concessions. On the other hand, the heads of the councils were Communists to whom religious belief remained anathema; and strenuous antireligious work was continued among the youth. It may further be noted that there were, in 1945, about 16,000 Orthodox churches in the U.S.S.R. as compared to 54,000 in the Russia of 1916. And it was reported in 1945 that only about 15 per cent of the Soviet young people were believers in any religion. Furthermore, freedom of religion continued to mean literally and strictly freedom of formal worship through rituals and liturgies. The Party, of course, continued to control and to use the churches just as it controlled and used all secular groups and organizations.

🏵 LOSSES AND GAINS

There has not yet been—and probably never can be—a complete accounting of the cost of the war to the U.S.S.R. The partial reports, however, are staggering. Over 1700 Soviet towns and cities, over 70,000 villages and hamlets, and over 98,000 collective farms were destroyed—most of them, completely. Thirty-nine thousand miles of railway trackage and some 32,000 shops and factories were also destroyed. Mines were flooded; bridges and dams (including the big dam on the Dnieper—the Soviet's pride) were partially or wholly ruined. Altogether, more than 6 million buildings were destroyed. Crop yields were off by about half between 1940 and 1945; livestock was decreased by from 16 per cent (cattle) to 63 per cent (hogs); and the production of such basic items as pig iron, steel, and petroleum declined by a fifth to a third. Far more dreadful, of course, were the losses in human life—not to mention those in well-being and full health. After the war, Soviet reports spoke of 7 million dead. But during the war, Stalin once remarked privately that at least twice that many soldiers had been killed, and this was before the last big drive. Probably as many as 30 million Soviet citizens died as a result of the war; and untold millions more suffered injuries and illness. It was a terrible price, but the gains it brought were also tremendous.

The Soviet Union emerged from World War II as one of the two Very Great Powers. No longer was there a strong Germany to the west of the U.S.S.R., nor a strong Japanese Empire to the east of it. It had no continental rival either in Europe or in Asia. Moreover, Great Britain —Russia's major rival and competitor for over a century and a half—

had unstintingly spent much of her strength. The victorious Red Army stood on a line from the mouth of the Oder to the head of the Adriatic. Behind that line, to be sure, there were several technically independent states. Their independence, however, was neither real nor lasting—a development to which the presence of the Soviet military might contributed not a little.

The actual territorial gains of the U.S.S.R. measured solely by formal additions of territory were considerably less than the indirect gains suggested above. They were, however, not inconsequential. The Soviets took from Finland the Petsamo (Pechenga) region in the north, and the lands at the northeastern end of the Gulf of Finland (the Karelian Isthmus). They annexed from Germany the area around Koenigsberg (Kaliningrad), and by treaty with Czechoslovakia the Soviets acquired Carpatho-Ukraine (or Ruthenia). In Central Asia, the U.S.S.R. annexed the small state of Tannu-Tuva; and in the Far East, southern Sakhalin and the Kurile Islands.

CHAPTER XXVII

Stalin's Last Years, 1946-53

INTRODUCTION

The Preface referred to history as an air liner of the mind and noted the relative changes in visibility as the flight into the past progressed. When this mental air liner flies through the very recent past, the situation is comparable to that of passengers in a plane just after take-off. They can see the ground quite clearly, but the range of their vision is small. They can see cars on a highway, for example, but they cannot see where the highway leads. This history has now reached the period of the very recent past, a stage comparable to that of a plane immediately after take-off. Furthermore, we find our vision seriously hampered by smog through which we can catch only partial and fleeting glimpses. We cannot look at any object we wish but only at those not concealed by the smog. Because this eddies and shifts with the wind, what we see, or think we see, depends partly on when we look.

The smog is partially our own creation—a function of the tense and troubled times in which we live and our consequent lack of long-range perspective. In the case of recent Russian history, however, another cause is apparent, the deliberate policies of the Soviet rulers in withholding and distorting information. A specific illustration of their reduction in the flow of information may be found in connection with the five-year plans. The First Five-Year Plan was published in such full detail that it required four large volumes. The comparable publication for the Fourth Five-Year Plan was a small pamphlet of about a hundred pages, and for the Fifth Five-Year Plan that was reduced by almost half.

The reduction in the quantity of information published was not the only concealment. The selection of data to be published was equally important, because false impressions are often created by releasing certain items of information while withholding other, relevant items.

Malenkov, for example, told the Nineteenth Party Congress (1952) that the total number of cattle on Soviet farms had been raised by 1948 to the level of 1940. A 1957 Soviet publication corroborated this statement but also gave additional data which completely altered the picture. In choosing 1940 for the comparative figure, Malenkov inflated the apparent recovery. The number of cattle in 1940 was appreciably less than in 1938, 1939, or even 1941. Moreover, the number of cattle on Soviet farms in 1948 was almost 17 million less than it had been in 1928, and 8 million less than the figure for the farms of Imperial Russia in 1916. This puts a very different face on the matter, especially when the figures are seen in relation to the population increases between 1916 or 1928 and 1948.

These comments and examples will show why the materials in these last three chapters are presented tentatively and with diffidence. We do not possess the facts necessary for a full or final story. Much remains unknown to us and, at present, unknowable.

A rigorous revival of discipline and tensions and a vigorous reassertion of Party control characterized the first eight postwar years in the U.S.S.R. There were occasional, calculated relaxations which generally took the form of temporarily releasing one sector in order to grasp another more securely—a modification of the technique of the NEP. The primary aim of the Party bosses was to maintain and to extend their power, using Soviet people and resources, as well as any others they could lay hands on, as their instruments. Unchallenged authority within the U.S.S.R. was and is the *sine qua non* of the Party bosses' main goal: the extension of their power beyond Soviet borders. Achievement of this strategic goal, not consistency in tactics, was the touchstone both in domestic and foreign affairs. Victory brought an end to the casualty lists, but did not bring the relaxations of peace to either the world or to the Soviet people because the Soviet leaders so chose.

There were some peacelike gestures within the Soviet Union and some concessions to the exceedingly war-weary Soviet people. The oldest age groups in the Red Army were demobilized in 1945, and special benefits of various sorts were given to officers, disabled veterans, and families of war dead. The eight-hour day was re-established (but not the five-day work week) and plans were announced for the reconversion of industry to peaceful production. There were price reductions and increases in rations. War taxes were abolished at the end of the year. Publicity was given to plans for the production of automobiles, trucks, and other consumer goods, but capital enterprises and the production of heavy goods were not neglected. It was announced that 31,000 miles of railway trackage had been restored, and that the Baltic–White Sea

Canal, which had been damaged by the German bombings in 1941, would be back in operation by the spring of 1946. It was also reported that the first ball-bearing plant in Ukraine was under construction at Kharkov, and that work had started on "the world's largest reservoir" near Baku.

Efforts were made to enforce the laws and to restore labor discipline, which had become lax during the war, but the immediate and very heavy demand for labor temporarily defeated these attempts. Managers, avid for workers, tended to ignore the regulations concerning workbooks. Some industries were released from martial law, but others were not. During the summer of 1945, all persons over fourteen years of age who lived in rural areas were mobilized for harvest work. This was not voluntary. Preparations, begun by GOSPLAN in August, 1945, for a new five-year plan indicated the intention of the rulers to continue forced-draft industrialization. The respite for which the people longed was once again deferred. However, there were rewards for the great and the near-great. Stalin was elevated to the specially created rank of Generalissimo and awarded the Order of Lenin, the Gold Star, and the Order of Victory. He was also named Hero of the Soviet Union. Beria, boss of the secret police and member of the Politburo, was made a Marshal of the Soviet Union. Some sort of a climax was reached when the embalmer and custodian of Lenin's body was named a Hero of Socialist Labor.

THE 1946 ELECTION

One major event of 1946 was a federal election, the first held for eight years. The order was issued by the Presidium in October, 1945, and preparations were thereafter stepped up week by week. A few changes were noteworthy, especially an increase in electoral districts from 1143 to 1339. The new districts, which included a special type for Soviet troops on duty outside the U.S.S.R., reflected territorial acquisitions since the prewar election. All the members of the Politburo were re-nominated for government office, only one candidate was nominated for each office. The most famous candidate was the new Generalissimo, and his eve-of-election speech (February 9, 1946) was of great importance. It reviewed the immediate past and laid down the general line of future developments.

According to Stalin, World Wars I and II had occurred as ". . . the inevitable result of the world economic and political forces on the basis of monopoly capitalism." He implied that World War III was inevitable ". . . under the present development of world economy." World War II, he said, had been a war for existence—"the most cruel and the hardest of all wars ever experienced in the history of our Motherland." It was also, he added, a test of the Soviet system. "The point is that the Soviet social system has proved to be more capable of life and more stable than a non-Soviet system, that the Soviet social system is a better form of organization for society than any non-Soviet system."

With scant deference to his wartime allies and less regard for truth, Stalin claimed victory for the Soviets alone. "The Red Army heroically withstood all the adversities of the war, routed completely the armies of our enemies, and emerged victoriously from the war." But credit, he was quick to add, was not due the Red Army alone. The victory, Stalin declared, was really a triumph of preparation, accomplished through the five-year plans under the wise and effective leadership of the Communist Party. It was proof that the Party had been correct in insisting that consumer goods and light industry be sacrificed to heavy industry, and it fully justified all the hardships of collectivization and industrialization. The Party, he said, no less than the Soviet system, had been tested by the war and had passed the test magnificently.

The speech also contained some promises—the abolition of rationing and the improvement of living standards through an expanded production of consumer goods—and a statement which most of the outside world dismissed as an empty boast, "I have no doubt that if we render the necessary assistance to our scientists, we will be able not only to overtake, but also, in the very near future, to surpass the achievements of science outside the boundaries of our country." Had the non-Soviet world paid more attention to this sentence in 1946 or given greater credence to it then, there might have been less surprise when the Soviets exploded their first atomic bomb in 1949, their first thermonuclear device in 1953, and tested the first intercontinental ballistic missiles in 1957. But in 1946 the non-Soviet world had no idea of the extent to which Soviet science and industry had penetrated the "secrets" of fission and fusion as well as of rockets and missiles. So it was not really surprising that more attention was paid to other parts of Stalin's speech, especially to his statement that the Party intended ". . . to organize a new, mighty upsurge of the national economy," and to his reference to three new five-year plans which would run until 1960.

The election, to return to 1946, went off smoothly. According to Soviet reports, 99.7 per cent of the 101,717,686 qualified voters went to the polls, and 99.2 per cent of them voted for the official candidates. Almost 85 per cent of the deputies elected to the Union Soviet and over 77 per cent of those elected to the Soviet of Nationalities were Party members. The dominance of the urban proletariat over the peasant majority was also continued—45 per cent of the deputies were urban workers and only about 25 per cent were peasants. The republican, regional, and local elections in 1947 and 1948 followed the same general pattern except that the proportion of Party members elected was much lower.

Following the election, there were some shifts in personnel and some changes in administrative titles, forms, and structures. Generally speaking, the administrative forms and structures of the Soviet government have been continuously in flux, with ministries being dropped, added, or divided to meet immediate needs. For roughly a decade after 1946, announcements of these administrative shifts were one of the few clues to Soviet internal affairs. Specialists therefore watched them closely and used them as a basis for conjectures. For example, the creation in May, 1946, of a Ministry of Labor Reserves strongly suggested stock-piling and other preparations for war. The Minister of Labor Reserves controlled the Labor Reserve (or State Labor) Schools. Boys between the ages of fourteen and eighteen, and girls between the ages of fifteen and eighteen could volunteer to attend such schools or were conscripted to do so. In either case, according to the law, they were ". . . considered as mobilized and are obligated to work four years continuously in state enterprises as directed by the Ministry of Labor Reserves." Soviet reports claimed an enrollment of 800,000 students in these schools in the fall of 1949.

🐦 PERSONALITIES

There were some changes in the leadership. Old "President" Kalinin (as he was usually but incorrectly called in Western accounts) resigned as Chairman of the Presidium of the Supreme Soviet in March, 1946, after having held that post for twenty-seven years. N. M. Shvernick, then an alternate member of the Politburo, took over the chairmanship and retained it until March, 1953, when he was replaced by K. Voroshilov. Lavrentii Beria, who had been made the head of the NKVD [1] in 1938 after the purge of Yezhov, gave up some titles, but surrendered no power. He became a full member of the Politburo, apparently retaining control of the security apparatus, though without portfolio, and was also placed in charge of the development of atomic energy. Georgii Malenkov, another veteran Party official, was also promoted to full membership on the Politburo in 1946. Malenkov had been attached to the Central Committee and to Stalin's personal secretariat in 1925. From 1930 to 1934, he directed the Party organization in Moscow, rising from this to the management of the Party cadres throughout the U.S.S.R. A member of both the Orgburo and the Secburo before the war, Malenkov was made an alternate member of the Politburo in 1941.

During the war he was a member of the State Committee for Defense, a kind of war cabinet to which Beria also belonged. Malenkov's promotion to full Politburo membership and his simultaneous appointment as Vice-Chairman of the Council of Ministers was in recognition of his past work and of his enjoyment of Stalin's favor.

Another favorite of Stalin's was A. A. Zhdanov, once regarded by the outside world as Stalin's probable heir. Zhdanov was Party Secretary for Nizhni-Novgorod from 1922 to 1934, when he was given the more important post of Party Secretary for Leningrad. He was elected to full membership in the Politburo in 1939 and was also a member of both the Orgburo and the Secburo. He appeared to be gaining power after the war, but it was announced early in 1948 that he had been relieved of some responsibilities because of ill health. In August of that year, it was announced that he had died of a heart attack. Zhdanov's chief rival, Malenkov, who had suffered a minor eclipse from 1946 to 1948, began to rise again, and Zhdanov's followers began to disappear. The most spectacular disappearance was that of N. A. Voznesensky, perhaps Zhdanov's most important protégé. Voznesensky had been made the chairman of GOSPLAN (State Planning Commission) in 1938, alternate member of the Politburo and Vice-Premier for Economic Affairs in 1941, and a member of the State Defense Committee in 1942. He was elevated to full membership on the Politburo in 1947. Two years later, after Zhdanov's death, Vosnesensky simply disappeared from all his offices and, indeed, from public view.[2] Lesser Zhdanov protégés suffered lesser disasters.

ISOLATIONISM, MINORITIES, AND NATIONALISM

One of the means used during these years to increase the power of the Party bosses over their subjects was to cut all ties between the Soviet peoples and the West, and to block all channels of possible communication between the Soviet peoples and the non-Communist world. This policy, known in the West by Churchill's striking phrase "The Iron Curtain," went into effect in 1946. It continued throughout Stalin's last years. A stiff censorship was placed on all outgoing news in 1946, and all broadcasts by foreign commentators were banned. Freedom of movement and access to sources of information were steadily restricted. Practically all the populated parts of the U.S.S.R. outside of Leningrad and Moscow were closed to foreigners, and the number of foreign visitors—except those who came from China or the satellites or who were members of "tame" delegations of Communists or fellow travelers—was strictly limited. Social contacts between Soviet citizens and foreigners were officially discouraged, and, from 1947 to 1953,

Soviet citizens were forbidden by law to marry foreigners. An earlier decree which had prohibited any Soviet citizen from discussing his work with foreigners was amplified in June, 1947, by the comprehensive "Decree of State Secrets." State secrets were so defined as to cover almost everything,[3] and the Council of Ministers was authorized to extend the list at any time. Penalties for violation ranged from a minimum of four to a maximum of twenty years at hard labor. These sanctions were apparently not sufficient, because the death penalty for spies, traitors and saboteurs, abolished in 1947, was restored in 1950.

Minority groups continued to be suspect. During the war some 400,-000 Volga Germans, descendants of settlers brought in by Catherine the Great, were deported from their homes to central Siberia and their autonomous republic was abolished. This was explained as a necessary precaution against possible pro-German sabotage. After the war, in the summer of 1946, the Supreme Soviet of the R.S.F.S.R. decreed the extinction of the Crimean and Chechen-Ingush autonomous republics. It subsequently appeared that these peoples, together with others, had been banished from their homes during the war. The Chechens, Ingush, Balkars, and others were "rehabilitated and repatriated" early in 1957. A little later, the Crimean Tatars, who had not even been mentioned in the Soviet press for a dozen years, were again recognized as an ethnic group. They were not, however, repatriated at that time nor have there been any extensive repatriations of the many, many thousands who were deported from the Baltic states, Karelia, and Western Ukraine during these years.

Ethnic and linguistic groups were not the only minorities who felt the heavy hand of despotism. The Uniate Church of Western Ukraine, independent for three and a half centuries, was deprived of its independence and annexed to the Russian Orthodox Church in 1946. The Soviet Union was, for over a generation, praised by many for its alleged eradication of anti-Semitism. Contraindications prior to the war were dismissed as exceptions or fabrications; those which came to light during the war were explained as evil results of German propaganda. German words and deeds played a part in the resurgent anti-Semitism and so did the terrible strains of the war, but these do not explain what happened some years after the end of the war. Incontrovertible evidence of an official anti-Semitic campaign appeared in 1949. Jews and Jewish groups were subjected to discrimination and persecution. Jews were recalled from diplomatic posts, relieved of commands in the armed forces, and removed from other offices. There was a nationwide purge of Jews from administrative and managerial posts in 1952. The Jewish press was liquidated, and the non-Jewish press carried on a somewhat ambiguous but vicious campaign of anti-Semitism. Mass deportations of Jews began in 1952 with most of those deported being sent to Birobidzhan.

There was a tragic irony in this, because a quarter of a century earlier the Soviet regime had been praised for establishing a "Jewish homeland" in the Birobidzhan region of eastern Siberia. Funds and settlers were collected from abroad, as well as from within the Soviet Union, and strenuous efforts were made to encourage Jewish migration to Birobidzhan. In 1934, the area was designated "The Jewish Autonomous Province" (*Raion*). The census of 1939 reported a total population there of 108,000, less than a third of them being Jews. By 1948 the population had increased to 140,000 but the proportion of Jews remained the same. A considerable purge was carried out in Birobidzhan in 1948, and the only Yiddish paper in the U.S.S.R., the *Birobidzhaner Stern,* was liquidated. Forced immigration of Jews, apparently begun in 1947, continued with an estimated twenty-five to thirty thousand being sent in between 1949 and 1952. As of the latter date, much of this "Jewish homeland" consisted of all-Jewish forced-labor camps. No one was allowed to enter or leave Birobidzhan without special permission, and no resident could be absent from his domicile for longer than twenty-four hours.

The anti-Semitic campaign appeared to reach its climax with what *Pravda* in its original announcement on January 13, 1953, headlined as the "Arrest of Group of Saboteur-Doctors." According to the news story, nine doctors and professors had confessed to having murdered Zhdanov and Shcherbakov, two members of the Politburo, and of having attempted "to undermine the health of leading Soviet military personnel." Five of the nine accused were Jews, who were charged with being "connected with the international Jewish bourgeois nationalist organization, 'Joint,' established by American intelligence. . . ." "Joint" (apparently a reference to the Joint Distribution Committee) was identified as "this Zionist espionage organization." The Soviet press seethed with anger against "depraved Jewish bourgeois nationalists," and demanded an increase in vigilance. Other denunciations and arrests followed in February and March. Then, suddenly, early in April, the Soviet press declared that an MVD investigation had proved the whole case against the doctors to be fraudulent. The accusations, said the official report, had been false, the arrests had been "without any lawful basis," and those responsible for this miscarriage of justice had been arrested.

What lay behind this fantasy wrapped in mystery or behind the whole anti-Semitic campaign is not clear. Perhaps the need for a scapegoat played a part. Perhaps it was all connected with struggles for power within the Politburo. One cause may have been the great enthusiasm shown by many Soviet Jews for the new state of Israel. This enthusiasm did not limit itself to ovations before the Israeli legations; it also included flight and emigration. The Soviet rulers may have interpreted these events, especially the clandestine emigration of Jews from the Soviet Union, as proof of the existence of an organization not under Communist control. It is also probable that the anti-Semitic campaign was connected with a marked resurgence of Great Russian nationalism and chauvinism.

The first stirrings of a revival of Great Russian nationalism appeared in some of the literature of the late 1920's in connection with a build-up of Soviet patriotism.[4] The movement continued on a modest scale through the next decade and then burst into full bloom during and after the war. Throughout the 1940's, but more especially after the war, Soviet peoples were told repeatedly that the Great Russians were "first among equals" and "the most outstanding" of all the national groups in the U.S.S.R. Histories written in the early days of the regime which had condemned the expansion of Great Russian power over non-Russian peoples were rewritten in the early 1950's to prove that such expansion was really a blessing in disguise because Great Russian leadership had improved the lot of the non-Russian peoples. The subjugation of non-Russians was held to be a lesser evil than lack of Great Russian leadership.

During Stalin's last years, the Soviet rulers followed a policy of Russification which was strongly reminiscent of that once pursued by the tsars. Immediately after Stalin's death the new regime appeared to reverse this policy. Presumably this reversal was the work of Beria and was thought by some observers to be part of his power struggle against Malenkov. At any rate, after Beria's arrest (June, 1953), he was accused of having "carried out criminal measures in order to revive remnants of the bourgeois nationalist elements," and the policy of favoring Great Russians was resumed.

CONTROLS TIGHTENED

Discipline was reasserted all along the line after the war. The armed forces, which had been subject to "iron discipline" since Stalingrad, were placed under a new and more extensive military code. Political instruction, which had been allowed partially to lapse during the fighting, was vigorously reinstituted among the armed forces and other groups. Repatriated war prisoners and members of the Soviet occupation forces were very carefully screened upon their return to the U.S.S.R. Only those who could completely satisfy the authorities as to their unwavering loyalty to the regime were allowed to return to their homes. Those who were even slightly suspect were resettled in other parts of the Soviet Union, and those who were thought to be tainted by their contacts with the West were sent to forced labor.

The Party leaders found themselves in 1946 with a greatly enlarged list of members, many of whom had entered the Party during the war, when the entrance requirements were greatly relaxed. Many of these new members had never been properly indoctrinated and some were undoubtedly misfits. The Party began to purge itself in 1946. The purges were extensive but with less drastic punishments than the prewar purges. Entrance requirements were again tightened, and strong emphasis was placed on the political "education" of Party members and candidates. Prewar plans for a system of Party schools were expanded and implemented in 1946. The apex of the system was the "Academy of Social Sciences" for the training of top-level teachers, theoreticians, and Party leaders. The Academy offered a "long course" of three years and a "short course" of one year. Next below the Academy was the "Higher Party School" which offered courses ranging from nine months to three years in length. It was designed for second-echelon officials and had about twice the enrollment of the Academy. The third place in the hierarchy was held by two-year Party schools which, in 1947, numbered 177 with a total enrollment of 30,000. The Party also established special training courses which annually enrolled several hundred thousand students. Approximately 500,000 lower-ranking Party members, for example, were graduated from a special eight-month, evening course between 1944 and 1950.

Another aspect of the disciplining and "education" instituted by the Party leaders for both Party and non-Party people was the thought-control campaign launched by Zhdanov, then at the peak of his power, in August, 1946. This was the most intensive and extensive such campaign in the Party's history.[5] The initial targets were two literary journals which were berated for publishing "politically and ideologically obnoxious" prose and poetry. This was only the beginning. Individuals, as well as groups and journals, were attacked. No artistic, literary, scientific, or other cultural, creative or intellectual field escaped attention, although there was much more interference with some than with others. Writers, movie-makers, artists, composers, actors, musicians, doctors, lawyers, teachers, historians, physicists, chemists, and many others came under fire either individually or as groups. The entire science of genetics was overturned after the Party's Central Committee decreed in July, 1948, that the Mendelian-Morgan theories were "bourgeois frauds" which were entirely incompatible with the Marxian laws of environmental determinism. The only theory which a true and loyal Soviet scientist might accept, declared the Committee, was the Lysenko-Michurin doctrine of acquired characteristics. The affair was concisely summed up by Anton Zhebrak, an internationally famous Soviet geneticist who, for fifteen years prior to this decree, had vigorously opposed the Lysenko-Michurin doctrine as unsound. Said Zhebrak after the order was issued, "I, as a Party member, do not consider it possible for me to continue to hold views which have been declared erroneous by the Central Committee of our Party." A similiar reaction came from Soviet specialists in linguistics after Stalin published his *Marxism and Problems of Linguistics* (1950) in which he attacked concepts hitherto accepted by most of these same persons. The thought-control campaign continued unabated in 1953. Pathologists were ordered to rid themselves of "antirevolutionary, idealistic, and antimaterialist" approaches to their subject. Soviet physicists were warned against the "idealistic subjectivism" of the "bourgeois scientist" Einstein's "antiscientific" theory of relativity, and chemists were told to beware of "subjectivist views" in their field, especially the theory of resonance. Matters went so far that writers of science fiction were castigated for "trying to be entertaining" instead of "proceeding from our Soviet reality."

To see all this as merely the evil or as the ridiculous acts of a despotism is to miss a major point. The Communists believe that the goal of an historian is not to seek objective reality; the aim of the scientist is not the pursuit of truth in his field; the purpose of the artist is not the creation of beauty; the ideal of the jurist is not justice. The one and only function of art and science recognized by the Communist as proper is "the Communist education of the masses"—in other words, the advancement of the interests of the rulers. Thought control is an integral part of any system which seeks to enforce its claim to a monopoly upon truth and wisdom.

THE "STALIN FIVE-YEAR PLAN"

Pressures of another sort were maintained by the Fourth or Stalin Five-Year Plan, which was announced in March, 1946. Like its predecessors, this plan continued to stress heavy industry at the expense of consumer goods. To the obvious tasks of reconversion and reconstruction the Soviet rulers chose to add the task of expanding their country's military potential. The choice placed a heavy burden upon the people. It also resulted in the production of a large force of jet-engine fighters (the famous MIGs) and other weapons including fission and fusion bombs. This raises a point sufficiently important to warrant a brief generalization. All economic efforts under the plans are divided by the rulers into areas of high and low priority. To the former, much more is given in funds, labor, managerial skills, materials, and general support; and from it much more is demanded in efficiency, quality, and output. The low-priority areas get what is left in the way of capital, manpower, and support. High priority was given under the Fourth Five-Year Plan to the production of strategic minerals (iron, copper, aluminum, coal, nickel, petroleum), atomic energy, arms and armaments, heavy machinery, and transportation equipment. The effort involved both the rebuilding of war-destroyed industry in the western regions and also the wide dispersal of industry through construction of new plants in the eastern parts of the U.S.S.R. The low-priority areas of the Fourth Plan were the consumer and light-goods industries, and probably agriculture.

By driving their people very hard—the "normal" work week [6] remained forty-eight hours until early 1956, when it was cut to forty-six hours—by drawing very heavily upon the raw materials, finished and semi-finished goods and other resources of areas occupied or dominated by the Soviet armed forces; and by using millions of war prisoners to augment their labor force; the Soviet rulers achieved very substantial successes in the high-priority areas. The production of pig iron, steel, and electric power were all more than doubled; the production of oil was almost doubled; and that of coal was very substantially increased. The output of heavy industry as a whole increased by over 100 per cent between 1947 and 1950. The rebuilding of devastated industries and the dispersal of production were likewise accomplished. For example, coal production in the western area stood at 98 million metric tons in 1940, dropped to 56 million tons in 1945, and was rebuilt to 120 million tons in 1950. The comparable figures for the eastern areas were: 1940, 68 million tons; 1945, 93.3 million tons; and 1950, 140 million tons. The Donets coal fields of Ukraine, which had accounted for about half the total coal output of the U.S.S.R. in 1940, produced only about a third of the total in 1951. The Baku and Caucasus oil fields had produced over four-fifths of the entire Soviet output in 1940. They produced less than half the total output in 1951. Successes in the areas of housing and consumer goods were considerably less.

The amount of housing constructed was greater than the amount called for by the plan, but the planned figure was grossly inadequate. It has been calculated on the basis of Soviet data that the actual living space available in Soviet cities declined between 1940 and 1950. In 1940 the per capita living space was roughly 54 square feet. This had dropped by 1950 to 48 square feet, and there were many millions who had less than this average figure. As Malenkov observed in 1952, ". . . there is still an acute housing shortage everywhere." The overall situation had, however, improved from the low point of 1945, when many millions of Soviet citizens had only tents or caves for shelter. The important thing to the Soviet people was not whether the situation in 1950 was worse than in 1940 but whether it was better than it had been in 1945. Their comparisons were with the immediate past, not with one, two, or three decades earlier. Generally speaking, there has been a steady improvement in living standards since the war. The people are a very long way from having the goods and services they want, and an even longer way from having those to which we are accustomed, but things were better at the end of the Stalin Plan than they had been at its beginning. It mattered less to the ordinary Soviet citizen that about 8 million fewer pairs of shoes were produced in 1950 than in 1940, than that almost 140 million more pairs were made in 1950 than in 1945.

Stalin had promised an end to rationing and the promise had been repeated in the Fourth Five-Year Plan, but a very severe drought in 1946 seriously cut into the supply of foodstuffs and forced a postponement of the end of food rationing. When finally effected in December, 1947, it was coupled with a drastic devaluation of the currency. The people were required to turn in their rubles for new ones at a rate of ten old rubles for each new ruble. The value of ordinary state bonds (which people had long been forced to purchase) was cut by two-thirds; that of the special 1938 bonds by four-fifths. Bank deposits of more than 3000 but less than 10,000 rubles were slashed in value by a third; those over 10,000, by a half. It was announced that these severe measures were necessary to combat inflation and speculation, both of which were admittedly serious. But devaluation was a weapon of political as well as of economic control. The blow fell most heavily on the peasants, because they most frequently kept their savings in cash rather than in bonds or banks. Currency deflation forced the peasants to work harder to make up their losses or to seek jobs in industry, which needed more manpower. Another politico-economic control instituted in 1947 also helped stabilize finances and increased the leverage which the government could use against its people. The piecework system, hitherto very widely used in Soviet industry, was replaced by a system of "progressive norms" under which piecework quotas were automatically increased in step with increases in labor productivity.

Chapter XXIV discussed some of the difficulties of judging what the Soviet standard of living was in the late 1930's. It is perhaps more difficult to make the same judgments for the late 1940's and early 1950's. This is partly because of the suppression and distortion at the source of relevant information. The paucity of data and unresolved questions as to its reliability leave much room for debate on such key items, for example, as earnings and real wages.[6] Since the ruble is not an international currency (its value was arbitrarily set by the Soviet government at four to an American dollar until mid-1957 when it was changed to ten to a dollar) it is almost impossible to arrive at satisfactory comparisons between wages, costs, and prices in the Soviet Union and those in other countries. Differences in socio-economic patterns and in habits of family spending also make it hard to draw meaningful comparisons. For example, in comparison with American families, Soviet families pay only a very small percentage of their incomes—roughly 5 per cent—for hous-

TABLE 6

Item and Unit	Hours of Work Required							
	1947				1950			
	U.S.S.R.		U.S.A.		U.S.S.R.		U.S.A.	
	hrs.	mins.	hrs.	mins.	hrs.	mins.	hrs.	mins.
bread (1 lb.)	0	31	0	07	0	19	0	06
milk (1 qt.)	1	18	0	10	0	52	0	07
eggs (1 dz.)	4	57	0	39	4	00	0	24
sugar (1 lb.)	2	34	0	06	2	00	0	04
beef (1 lb.)	5	15	0	50	3	00	0	42
tea (1 lb.)	11	00	0	40	22	00	0	40
soap (1 bar)	1	39	0	06	0	41	0	03
woman's dress (cotton)	31	51	2	22	23	00	1	57
woman's suit (wool)	252	00	12	54	176	00	11	31
woman's shoes (1 pr.)	107	30	5	32	72	00	3	30
man's shoes (1 pr.)	104	30	7	15	112	00	5	20
man's suit (wool)	580	15	28	04	376	00	24	24

ing. They also pay very little directly for doctors or dentists because these expenses are covered by their tax payments. Very few Soviet families have cars upon which to spend their rubles. (A bicycle still rated as a luxury in the U.S.S.R. in 1957.) An even more striking contrast was the absence of installment buying in the Soviet Union up through 1957. For these reasons, it doesn't mean much to report that, as of 1950, a pound of black bread cost $0.25 in Moscow or that men's shoes cost from $50.00 to $117.00 a pair. It is not much more meaningful to report that, as of the same year, the same quality man's suit which could be bought in New York for $31.95 cost $254.75 in Moscow. In an effort to circumvent this sort of difficulty, specialists have worked out comparisons of the amount of work required to earn certain commodities. Tables 6 and 7 compare the figures for the U.S.S.R. and the U.S.A. for 1947, 1950, and 1951.[7]

TABLE 7

| Item and Unit | Hours of Work Required (April, 1951) | | | |
| | U.S.S.R. | | U.S.A. | |
	hrs.	mins.	hrs.	mins.
pocket watch	95	14	1	39
eggs (10)	4	00	00	21
fish (2.2 lbs.)	07	00	00	36
man's shoes (1 pr.)	67	00	04	00

Even after the series of six price cuts (1948–53) a Soviet worker still had to work about three times as long as his American counterpart to earn a pound of bread; six times as long to earn a pound of meat. On the other hand, the tables show that the Soviet worker had made a substantial advance.

AGRICULTURE

The problem of a low agricultural production bore directly on the living standards of all Soviet citizens. It directly affected the peasants, who were the producers; the workers, who were the most numerous consumers; the bureaucracy, and the managers. It also affected the overall strength of the Soviet system and state. Chapter XXIV noted that there had been widespread violations of the Collective-Farm Code during and after the war. Moreover, lacking sufficient inducements to production, such as consumer goods, the Soviet rulers had continually to extend their controls over the peasants in order to assure maximum deliveries of foodstuffs to the state. Measures designed to halt the violations of the code were decreed in September, 1946. Various officials of the government and of the Party were convicted of mismanagement, malfeasance, and gross corruption. A new Council of Collective Farms was established in October, 1946, under the chairmanship of A. A. Andreyev, a member of the Politburo and a vice-chairman of the Council of Ministers. The announcement bluntly stated that the council had been created to take action against "grafters and parasites who avoid productive work." It was given supervisory powers over all collectives, charged with drafting revisions to the code and with "inspiring" collective farmers to higher productivity.

The "inspiration" took the familiar and well-tested form of alternating offers of the carrot and applications of the stick. Collective farms which had fulfilled their required grain deliveries to the state in 1946 were temporarily allowed in 1947 to engage in the free sale of any surplus grain. But a little later the Party announced that the obligatory deliveries of grain and technical crops would thereafter be calculated not on the basis of the total land cultivated by each farm, as heretofore, but on the total arable land of each farm. This order was designed, of course, to force the farms to bring more land under cultivation. This particular pressure was continued and others were added. The number of collective farms was increased from about 222,000 (1947) to over 254,000 (1950). Responsibility for seeing that the obligatory grain deliveries were made was shifted from the Machine Tractor Stations to an "Inspectorate of Harvest Yields." This body, connected with GOSPLAN, was set up in June, 1947, and was charged not only with overseeing deliveries, but also with increasing yields per acre and with various disciplinary matters. The decree which created the Inspectorate implied that the M.T.S. had become too friendly with and too easy on the peasants. Simultaneously with this decree, others were issued which provided much severer punishments for the theft, embezzlement, or damage of state property. State property in the U.S.S.R. includes collective-farm property, and the new decrees made special reference to crimes against state property by collective farmers. Reports of pilfering, large thefts, corruption, and mismanagement continued to appear in the Soviet press (despite the new decrees) until after Stalin's death. Then such reports ceased, though it seems unlikely that this chronic problem could have vanished overnight.

There were sudden reversals in the collective-farm program during 1950. For years prior to that time, including the period of Andreyev's chairmanship, labor on collective farms had been organized and operated as small teams, called "links" (*zvenya*). This had been hailed as a tremendous advance over the earlier system, which used large gangs (*"brigades"*) of workers. Then in February, 1950, Andreyev was severely censured and deprived of most of his power, and the small links were replaced by the large brigades. Khrushchev, who took over from Andreyev, then announced that small collective farms were to be merged to form larger units. Within less than a year, the almost a quarter of a million collective farms had been reduced to 123,000 and, by October, 1952, the number had been further reduced to 97,000. The official explanations were that the mergers would increase efficiency, decrease costs, improve production, and better the position of the collective farmers. Presumably as part of the improvement of the farmers' lot, Khrushchev proposed (March, 1951) the creation of huge farm cities (*agrogorods*). The prospectus he offered was beguiling, but the peasants soon realized that Khrushchev's plan would reduce their individual allotments. Any such reduction would have made the peasants more dependent on the collective and, therefore, more susceptible to control. This appears to have been the true intention of the whole movement—to transform the partially independent collective farmers into a landless, agricultural proletariat directly employed by and completely under the control of the state. Peasant resistance to the *agrogorod* scheme forced its abandonment (or postponement at least), but the mergers were continued so that by September, 1953, there were only 94,000 collective farms in the whole U.S.S.R. This was subsequently reduced and in 1955 the official reports listed 85,700 collective farms.

Neither amalgamations nor increased controls solved the problems of agricultural production. Articles in the Soviet press through the late spring and early summer of 1953 called for improvements in direction and guidance in order to overcome a variety of shortcomings. In August, Malenkov told the Supreme Soviet of "the intolerable lag" in animal husbandry and of the need "to secure a further, more rapid increase in the production of grain." (This contrasted strangely with his sanguine report to the Party congress in the preceding year. At that time Malenkov had emphasized the recovery of animal husbandry and of the total agricultural output to the prewar level, or better. "The grain problem," he said, ". . . has been solved definitely and finally.") The Party and the government, he told the Supreme Soviet in 1953, had decided upon concessions to the peasants. Higher prices were to be paid for farm products, the "quotas of obligatory deliveries" were to be cut, and taxes on private allotments and the earnings therefrom were to be reduced substantially. These grants were balanced by arrangements to increase Party "guidance" of the collectives.

Shortly thereafter (September, 1953), a series of reports, resolutions, and decrees gave evidence of the continuing seriousness of the farm problem. Khrushchev informed the Party's Central Committee that agricultural production had failed wholly to keep pace with the growth of industry or with the growth of population. Industrial production, he said, had increased 2.3 times between 1940 and 1952 while there had only been a 10 per cent increase in the farm output during that period. He called the general level of agricultural production "inadequate," spoke of a chronic lag in animal husbandry, and demanded strenuous efforts to produce more grain, more vegetables, and more livestock. He did not, however, suggest changing the system of collectivized agriculture. On the contrary, he was explicit in his support both of the system and of the

continuing amalgamation of collectives. Elimination of the private allotments was still the goal, he declared, though it could and would be
reached only by gradual steps. Khrushchev, in other words, speaking in
1953 announced no change in the proposed destination but only in the
timetable. This was also true of the resolutions and decrees by which his
recommendations were implemented.

🎗 SOME POLITICAL AND DEMOGRAPHIC CHANGES

Political and administrative shifts continued to take place frequently.
Sometimes the aim appears to have been a greater centralization of authority, as when all state farms were placed under a single ministry. At
other times the aim seems to have been decentralization as, for example,
when the Ministry of the Armed Forces was divided into a Ministry of
the Army and a Ministry of the Navy. Some shifts were apparently due
to intra-Party politics and rivalries. Whatever the reasons, this sort of
tinkering with the machinery of government was almost continuous both
before and after Stalin's death.

The legal term of the Second Supreme Soviet having run out, the Third
Supreme Soviet was elected in March, 1950. The elections followed the
customary pattern. The Soviet press reported that 99.8 per cent of all
who held the suffrage exercised it, and that 99.73 per cent of all votes
cast went to the official candidates. The report on election districts and
on the number of voters excited considerable interest among specialists
on Soviet affairs because both indicated a very considerable growth in
population. Taken together, they implied a total population of over 201
million. It appears on the basis of data released bit by bit through 1956
that the 1950 figures were greatly exaggerated. There has been no census
taken in the U.S.S.R. between 1939 and the time of this writing so that
all population figures are uncertain at best. The best guesses so far are
that the Soviet Union had a population of roughly 192 million in 1940,
that this had dropped to under 180 million by 1945, gone back up to
184 million by 1950, and reached 200 million in 1956. Specialists have
warned that even these figures may be off by several millions.

Though precise figures are lacking, it is clear that a marked urban
growth took place during the 1940's and 1950's. As of 1939, the twenty
largest Soviet cities ranged from Moscow, with a population of 4,137,-
000 to Molotov (once again renamed Perm in 1957 after Molotov's fall
from power) with a population of 255,000. As of 1956, the same cities
composed the list of the top twenty, but the population range was from
4,839,000 (Moscow) to 525,000 (Stalingrad). Many smaller cities,
especially those in the Urals and Siberia, grew considerably between
1939 and 1956. For example, Magnitogorsk, founded in 1931, grew from

146,000 to about 284,000, and Komsomolsk, founded in 1932, more than doubled its population. All in all, the number of cities increased from 923 (1939) to 1569 (1956) and the urban population rose from 56 million to 87 million. This exacerbated the always present housing shortage.

An effort to alleviate the shortage was made in 1948 through a decree which permitted Soviet citizens to buy or to build houses on plots of land which would be granted in perpetuity to the owner. This was a major departure from former practice, which had forbidden the private ownership of homes. Some houses have been built under this law, but difficulties over permits, materials, and labor have seriously hampered the operation and the number of such houses has remained small.

"REMAKING NATURE"

It was also in 1948 that Soviet newspapers announced with much fanfare "The Stalin Plan for Remaking Nature." The plan called for the afforestation of four belts of land in south central Russia, and for the construction by 1965 of 45,000 reservoirs and ponds on collective farms. The total length of the proposed forest belts was to be 3000 miles and the Soviet people were told that no capitalist country could or would undertake such a venture. This brazen mendacity was characteristic. Eighteen thousand miles of such forest belts had been planted in the United States between 1930 and 1948, and 680,000 ponds and reservoirs had been constructed on American farms within that same time. It should not be forgotten that the Iron Curtain has operated fully as much to exclude information from the U.S.S.R. as to prevent information from leaving it. There is, in fact, some reason to suppose that the Soviet rulers have really been more interested in keeping their people from learning about the Free World than in keeping us from learning about the Soviet Union. To return to the Stalin plans, other grandiose canal and hydroelectric projects, including draining the Pripet marshes, were subsequently announced. The Volga-Don Canal—a major and impressive job involving irrigation, shipping, and hydroelectric power—was partially completed in 1952 and was opened to navigation. Two other major canal projects, a Turkman and a Volga-Ural canal system, were undertaken before Stalin's death. Work on them and on other ambitious projects was apparently suspended by the new regimes.

Soviet boasts of the "millions and millions" of workers employed on these various projects did not mention that many of them were slave labor. Awards made in September, 1952, to top MVD officials for their "outstanding contributions to the completion of the Volga-Don Canal" perhaps revealed more than was intended. The West awoke belatedly and only after World War II to the facts of slave labor in the Soviet system. The system had been in use for years, but much of the West's knowledge of it was acquired after 1945. The full story is not yet available, but certain points are clear. Forced (or slave) labor has long been an integral part of the Soviet economic system. It has not been, as Soviet apologists have urged, just "a corrective measure for offenders" nor a punitive action against "wreckers, saboteurs, and traitors," though it doubtless served both those functions. Its victims have included members of all groups, classes, and occupations: Party people, non-Party people; men, women, and children. The one thing they have all had in common was that someone in a position of power considered them either dangerous or simply available for slave labor. Slave workers have been employed in almost every phase of Soviet production. They have cut and hauled timber; grown grains and other crops; mined coal, iron, and nonferrous metals; worked in the oil fields; built and maintained roads, railroads, canals, and air fields; manufactured furniture, clothing, and other goods. At least until Stalin's death, all these manifold operations were run by the MVD, to which was assigned a larger share of capital construction than given to any other ministry. The millions under MVD control accounted for shares of the total Soviet production ranging from 10 to 50 per cent of the whole output of the various enterprises involved. Some of these slave laborers were released from custody and other punishments by an amnesty which the first post-Stalin regime granted in March, 1953. Stated exclusions from this amnesty caused most Western observers to believe that the supply of slave labor had not been seriously depleted by it.

THE FIFTH FIVE-YEAR PLAN

The directives governing the Fifth Five-Year Plan were not published until August, 1952, but the plan became operative in January, 1951. The general line was the same as before. High priorities were assigned to capital goods and to armaments (which were not listed in the published directives) and consumer goods remained low-priority items. There were large increases in the production of coal, oil, electric power, iron and steel, and military equipment during 1951. Some of the gains in military equipment were achieved by diverting efforts from civilian production. For example, tractor production dropped by 17,000 units between 1950 and 1951, despite the obvious needs of the farmers for more machinery. As late as 1954, the production of locomotives, freight cars, and combines remained below the 1950 level, and the production of trucks only approximated that level. Incidentally, the 1951 budget for military expenditures was about 20 per cent higher than it had been in 1950. Of course, this was the period of the Korean War and the Soviets were supplying military items to both the North Koreans and the Chinese, as well as building up their own armaments. The same general trends continued through 1952 with coal, steel, petroleum, chemicals, military equipment and similar items reaching new high levels of production. Table 8 shows the overall developments, and the contrasts between heavy and consumer goods. The year 1940 is taken as the base year and assigned an arbitrary value of 100.

TABLE 8

Year	Total Industrial Output	Output of Heavy Industry	Output of Consumer Goods
1940	100	100	100
1945	92	112	59
1946	77	82	67
1947	93	101	82
1948	118	130	99
1949	141	163	107
1950	173	205	123
1951	202	239	143
1952	225	268	158
1953	252	299	177
1954	285	340	200
1955	320	389	216

It will be noted that in Stalin's last year heavy industry was producing almost twenty-seven times as much as in 1940 whereas light industry had increased by less than sixteen times during the same period. (The figures are carried beyond the chronological scope of this chapter in order to show the continuity of policy despite the flurry about consumer goods in 1953—a subject which will be considered in the final chapter.)

Excluding the 1952 Party Congress and the continuing emphasis on military preparations, domestic affairs in the U.S.S.R. continued generally along the lines already described. The Iron Curtain was re-enforced by banning the export of most Soviet technical journals and by publishing deliberately obscurantist reports. Thought control was expanded into new areas, and the campaign against "bourgeois nationalism" among minorities was extended to include the Moslems. Discipline and indoctrination were insisted upon within the Party as well as outside of it. Upwards of thirty national and provincial Party secretaries and about a thousand other responsible Party officials were dismissed from their posts during the last half of 1951. Party membership continued to grow, despite the purges, and so did the membership of the Party's two major ancillaries, the Young Communist League and the Pioneers. The league, which is officially described as the Party's direct agent and is also the chief source for new members, grew from 9 million to over 13 million members between March, 1949, and November, 1951. During the same period the Pioneers, an organization for children from the ages of nine through thirteen, jumped from 13 million to 19 million members. These two groups, plus the parent Party and a children's organization called the Octobrists (ages eight through eleven) included well over a quarter of the total population of the U.S.S.R. by the end of 1951. This meant that the Party bosses had wider contacts with the masses than before, but it did not mean that the bosses were sharing their power or preparing to do so. In fact, they complained (in the words of Malenkov) of "a certain deterioration of the qualitative composition of the Party." Concern over this, and, more importantly, intra-Party struggles at the top levels, apparently led to the summoning of the first Party congress to be called in more than thirteen years.

THE NINETEENTH PARTY CONGRESS

The congress, announced in August, 1952, met from October 4 to 14.[8] The weeks between the summons and the sitting were taken up with the election of delegates, the publicizing of draft directives for the Fifth Five-Year Plan and for a revision of the Party statutes. The press reported public "discussions" of these drafts. So far as the public record shows, neither during these preliminaries nor at the sessions did the discussions touch the fundamentals of policy nor question the complete and absolute authoritarianism of the Party bosses. The congress ended, after listening to 86 reports and speeches, by giving unanimous approval to everything which the bosses had recommended. This was a "consent-building" session, not a policy-making one. Prominent parts were played at the congress by Malenkov (who delivered the major report), Khrushchev, and Saburov (who dealt with the five-year plan and who became a member of the new Presidium which the congress created). The congress, however, was dominated by Stalin, even though to outward appearances his was only a minor role. Three days before the congress opened, Stalin published what proved to be his final article. Entitled "The Economic Problems of Socialism in the U.S.S.R.," it was, in effect, the keynote of the session. Together with his brief remarks at the close of the congress, Stalin's article set basic policy lines which were still visible five years later.

The congress elected a new Central Committee of 125 members and 110 alternates, and appointed a few commissions. It dropped the word

"Bolshevik" from the Party's name and the Orgburo and the Secburo from the organizational structure. It replaced the Politburo with a new and larger body called the "Presidium of the Central Committee of the Communist Party of the Soviet Union." The new Presidium had 25 members and 11 alternates. The Secretariat of the Committee, which replaced the Secburo, was doubled in size. There were a few changes in personnel and the functions of the Presidium were changed slightly (at least on paper) from those formerly exercised by the old Politburo. The latter had been described in law as existing "for the political work" of the Central Committee. The Presidium was formally charged with directing the work of the Central Committee between sessions just as the committee was to direct the work of the Party between the meetings of the Party congress. The Party Statutes were also revised, mainly in the direction of ensuring tighter discipline and surer controls from the top. A resolution recognized that many propositions and tasks set forth in the Party program (which had been adopted in 1919 and never modified) "no longer corresponded to modern conditions and the Party's new tasks." But—and there always seems to be a but when analyzing Soviet developments—the 1919 program was left unchanged. And within the new, large Presidium there was created secretly an inner group, known as the Bureau of the Presidium, and apparently composed of six to ten of the old guard—Stalin, Molotov, Malenkov, Beria, Voroshilov, Khrushchev, and others. This, until the end of Stalin's life, was the real seat of power.

Neither the Bureau of the Presidium nor the new Presidium survived Stalin by more than a day. The bureau disappeared as an organized group, and the Presidium was cut back to ten members and four alternates. The Secretariat was also reduced to the size of the pre-Congress Secburo. There were two new faces among the full members—Saburov and Pervukhin—but essentially this was the old Politburo under a new label. It was, of course, minus Stalin, but its powers were more fully spelled out and were publicly acknowledged. Its size varied somewhat between 1953 and mid-1957, but, until Khrushchev successfully appealed from it to the Central Committee in June, 1957, its powers appeared unchanged.

We are still (in 1958) not sure about either the time or the manner of Stalin's death. It was officially announced as having occurred on the evening of March 5, 1953. The announcements were accompanied by the plea, "Let there be no panic and no disorder." Perhaps this was merely the Kremlin's version of, "The king is dead. Long live the king," or perhaps it indicated the apprehension with which Stalin's associates faced the unprecedented problems of succession.

CHAPTER XXVIII

World War to Cold War: Foreign Affairs After 1945

 THE GUIDE TO ACTION

Repeated public-opinion surveys during the war showed that from 40 to 50 per cent of the American people expected that the Soviet Union would co-operate in running a peaceful world after the war.[1] The Soviet's postwar obstructionism and aggressiveness therefore came as a continuing series of rude shocks to many. Even those who had not been so optimistic in their estimates of Soviet postwar behavior were puzzled by the Kremlin's willingness to dissipate the very considerable reservoir of good will which its publicized wartime actions had earned for it. The shock and puzzlement might have been less had people taken more seriously the reiterated Soviet declaration that "The science of Marxism-Leninism is the solid foundation of Soviet foreign policy." But this was either ignored entirely or dismissed as mere lip service to Communist doctrine. It still seems incredible to many that the leaders of Soviet communism believe their doctrinal professions and act, at least in large part, on the basis of such beliefs. Yet the weight of accumulated evidence indicates that this is so. In fact, Soviet foreign affairs in the postwar period make sense only when examined against their doctrinal background.

Over the years, the Communist leaders of the U.S.S.R. have abandoned most of the analytical and rational parts of what they misleadingly call "the science of Marxism-Leninism." What remains are tenets which must be accepted on faith alone, because they are not susceptible of any objective or rational proof. They are, in essence, dogmatic assertions—unproven and unprovable.

Underlying all other tenets is the assumption that there are ascertainable "laws of social development" which control the actions and the lives of men and nations. Next is the indispensable belief that the masters of Communism, and they alone, know and understand these so-called laws and their workings. This is the Communists' fig-leaf, concealing their lust for power. It is also the excuse for their claim to hold a monopoly upon truth—truth being whatever they declare it to be at any given moment. If you concede them this monopoly then you also concede the right to leadership, because obviously the sole possessor of the truth is the only proper leader. Communists believe that human actions affect the course of history. They also believe that these actions are controlled by a mysterious force which they call "historic necessity." But they hold that men will act in accordance with "historic necessity" only if given proper leadership. Proper leadership can be given solely by those who understand the "laws of social development" and the functioning of "historic necessity." By their definitions, this means that the leadership must be by the Communist bosses. This is a neat bit of circular reasoning, and there is also a concentric circle.

If men behave according to "historic necessity," the Communists say, there will inevitably be a tremendous revolution which will destroy the old order and establish a new order run by the Communists. This is what is meant by talk of the inevitability of revolution and of a Communist victory. "Inevitable" is not used by the Communists in this context as it is in our cliché about death and taxes. Communists believe that the revolution and their triumph will inevitably happen if—and only if—the Communists can guide, persuade, or coerce men into doing what the Communists wish. This means that Communists must act in order to bring about what they call inevitable.

It is also a basic tenet of Communism that all human and social growth and progress are functions only of conflict. In every situation there is competition and conflict between two main groups. This competition and conflict results in change and progress. It also results in the triumph of one group over the other. Over a century ago, Marx and Engels declared that there are two major forces (or systems), traditionally designated as capitalism and communism, which are inextricably locked in a titanic conflict; and that between these two there is and must be an implacable hostility which can end only when one destroys the other. There is no Communist who does not still hold to this view, and none who does not believe that his system will do the destroying. Marx-Engels thought of this primarily in terms of the class struggle. Their successors have expanded the concept to apply to whole nations and groups of nations. That the Communists were able, for about a generation, to seize and hold power only in one country forced them to refine this theory to fit that fact. Out of that grew the two doctrines of "capitalist encirclement" and "peaceful coexistence."

🎴 "CAPITALIST ENCIRCLEMENT" AND "PEACEFUL COEXISTENCE"

"Capitalist encirclement" conceives of the whole non-Soviet world as being unrelentingly hostile to the Soviet or Soviet-controlled states. This hostile world, it is held, constantly menaces the Soviet Union and its associates both by possible armed attack and by efforts to foment internal revolution. Stalin told his Central Committee in 1937:

Capitalist encirclement means that there is one country, the Soviet Union, which has established the socialist order on its own territories and besides this there are many countries, bourgeois countries, which continue to carry on a capitalist mode of life and surround the Soviet Union, waiting for an opportunity to attack it, to break it, or at any rate to undermine its power and weaken it.

Stalin also declared on many occasions that this danger would remain as long as capitalist encirclement continued. In this he might well have been echoing Lenin, who warned his colleagues of ". . . the *inevitable* attack against the Soviet state on the part of capitalist encirclement." Soviet leaders since Lenin, though regarding the danger as always present, have not always felt that an outside attack upon them was imminent. They have credited their diplomacy with having checkmated the danger by skillful exploitation of "contradictions" among the capitalist countries. Such exploitation has naturally been one major purpose of their foreign policies.

"Coexistence" was not a Communist creation, though their statements have often implied that it was. As Lenin told his Party in 1919, "We are living not only in a state, but in a system of states. . . ." That was (and still is) simply a statement of fact, a fact which successive Soviet rulers have been unable to change completely, though they have succeeded in making partial alterations. The partial alterations were the wartime and postwar expansion of Soviet Communist power by annexations, the creation of satellites, and the Communist victories in China and elsewhere. Kremlin spokesmen of the postwar period referred to this as "a favorable alteration in the relation of forces" resulting in the U.S.S.R. being surrounded by "friendly socialist states—the people's democracies." Mention of capitalist encirclement gradually became less frequent, and another theme, officially proclaimed by Zhdanov in 1947, took its place for a time. Zhdanov's statement was that World War II had divided ". . . the political forces operating in the international arena into two major camps: the imperialist and antidemocratic camp on the one hand, and the anti-imperialist and democratic camp, on the other." (By the latter, Zhdanov meant the Soviet Union and its associates; by the former, the non-Soviet, non-Communist nations.) This was not actually a new theme. Stalin in 1919 had talked of a decisive and unalterable split into "the camp of imperialism and the camp of socialism," but the theme was not emphasized until after 1947.

Soviet propagandists made profitable use before Stalin's death of the peaceful-coexistence theme and continued to employ it successfully thereafter, citing it as proof of the essential virtuousness and peaceful intentions of the Soviet Union. Optimists have habitually overlooked and enthusiasts have deliberately ignored contraindications inherent in the statements themselves or immediately relevant to them. The remainder of Lenin's 1919 statement which was quoted in the preceding paragraph illustrates this point:

> We are living not only in a state but in a system of states and the existence of the Soviet republic side by side with imperialist states for a prolonged period is unthinkable. At the end, either one or the other will win. And before this happens a series of the most frightful collisions between the Soviet republic and the bourgeois states is inevitable.

Stalin, whose comment on Lenin's pronouncement was, "Clear, one would think!" frequently restated Lenin's theme and referred to a "current streak" of peaceful coexistence as resulting from a "temporary balance of forces." *Pravda*, in 1952, told its readers that "The fate of the world will ultimately be decided by the outcome of the inevitable struggle between the two worlds."

The world was somewhat cheered early in 1956 when Khrushchev, addressing the Twentieth Congress of the Communist Party of the Soviet Union, said, "There is, of course, a Marxist-Leninist precept that wars are inevitable as long as imperialism exists. This precept was evolved at a time when . . . the social and political forces which did not want war . . . [were] unable to compel the imperialists to renounce war. . . . But war is not fatalistically inevitable." This appeared, at first hearing, to constitute a major break with the traditional doctrine and was so headlined throughout the world. More careful reading and analysis, however, convinced many specialists that Khrushchev had not reversed the doctrine on war between Communist and non-Communist states, but had rejected a different theory, advocated by Lenin and Stalin, that war between the "imperialist" (i.e., non-Communist) countries was inevitable.[2] The "social and political forces" which had once been too weak to prevent the imperialists from making war, said Khrushchev, had by 1956 acquired sufficient power "to prevent the imperialists from unleashing war, and, if they actually try to start it, to give a smashing rebuff to the aggressors and frustrate their adventurist plans. To be able to do this, all antiwar forces must be vigilant and prepared; they must act as a united front and never relax their efforts in the battle for peace." The reader will recognize in this a specific application of the Communist tenet that Communist action and leadership are the indispensable components of "inevitability." The applications of other tenets will appear as the history of Soviet foreign policy after 1945 is reviewed.

✠ BREAKDOWN OF CO-OPERATION

One of the most important consequences of World War II was the emergence of the U.S.S.R. as one of the two Very Great Powers. Most of the changes in the postwar distribution and balance of power favored the Soviet Union. So did the postwar domestic situations in Europe and the increasing nationalism in Asia, Africa, and the Near and Middle East. The Kremlin sought to exploit these advantages, and used novel tactics and maneuvers, but there were also strong elements of continuity. It was not new, for example, for the Kremlin to have interests, contacts, and agents all over the world. Lenin's policies had had some of the characteristics of *Weltpolitik*. What was new after 1945 was the very favorable position which enabled the Kremlin to promote its interests and to expand its contacts with hitherto unparalleled success. The goals of Soviet policies were not new, and as the story of the war years became more widely known the public learned that disagreements, suspicions, and open enmities did not suddenly appear after the war. Consider, as an illustration, the problem of Poland.

The Soviets had broken relations with the Polish Government-in-Exile (located in London) following the revelations and recrimination of the Katyn Forest murders. London and Washington continued to recognize the Polish Government-in-Exile, but Moscow set up a creature of its own, the Lublin Government. In the face of Anglo-American requests that such action be postponed, the Soviets extended formal recognition to the Lublin Government in January, 1945. Then, while the London Government-in-Exile talked of an interallied government for Poland, the Lublin Poles followed the advancing Red Army and established civil administration as Poland was "liberated"—that is, occupied by Soviet forces. The conferees at Yalta discussed this problem, and the West believed that an equitable settlement had been reached. They could not have been more mistaken. In essence, the West had the promises; the Soviets had Poland. And the West subsequently discovered that it had also had a preview of the direction of Soviet postwar policy. Another such preview was the cession to the U.S.S.R. by Czechoslovakia of the Trans-Carpathian Ukraine. It cannot be asserted that Czecholovakia was a free agent when the treaty accomplishing the cession was made in June, 1945. The Potsdam Conference, though it reached enough apparent agreement to sustain Western hopes for a real peace, also gave indications of what was to come. Professor Philip Mosely summed up the situation revealed at Potsdam in the following sentences: [3]

> But it was at Potsdam that the Soviet leaders gave frank expression to a program of expansion which, if achieved, would have made their power supreme in Europe and in the eastern Mediterranean. The Potsdam demands . . . added up to a very substantial program: a stranglehold on the Ruhr and on the entire German economy; an uncontested domination of the one hundred million people of eastern Europe; domination of the eastern Mediterranean through control of Greece, Turkey, and Tripolitania; and domination of Iran.

Simultaneously a symptom and a part of the postwar relations was the breakdown of the machinery for co-operation. It had been agreed at Potsdam there should be regular meetings of a Council of Foreign Ministers to draft the various peace treaties and to act in concert on other problems of joint interest. The West had assumed at the time that the Soviet agreement on this was prima facie evidence of the Soviet intention to co-operate and of willingness to negotiate and conclude the peace treaties. The first meeting of the Council of Foreign Ministers was held in London in September and October of 1945. It lasted twenty-two days and ended in complete failure. The second meeting of the council, held in Moscow later in 1945, was able to announce the establishment of a joint commission to set up international control of atomic energy and another joint American-Russian commission to unify Korea. There were also other agreements announced, but as the then Secretary of State of the United States told the American people, the meeting was not a complete success. He added that the situation could have been much better but it could also have been far worse. Perhaps that is as good a general characterization of postwar relations as could be made.

A third session of the Council of Foreign Ministers met in Paris in the spring of 1946 and recessed without reaching any agreements on the peace treaties. A "peace conference," also in Paris that same year, tried to accomplish what the foreign ministers had failed to do, but the conference closed without agreement after eleven weeks of bitter wrangling. The New York meeting of the Council of Foreign Ministers (December, 1946) was more successful. It drafted peace treaties for Italy, Hungary, Bulgaria, Romania, and Finland. These five nations signed their treaties in February, 1947. In general, the treaties exacted reparations, restricted the armies allowed to the defeated states, and left those nations with somewhat limited sovereignty. The foreign ministers, however, got nowhere with peace treaties for Germany and Austria either at New York or at their meeting in Moscow in 1947.

At the end of November, 1947, the Council of Foreign Ministers again met in London. The first item on the agenda was to draft a peace treaty for Austria, but Mr. Molotov, representing the U.S.S.R., at once derailed this by raising the question of Germany. There was a certain realism about his question, because Germany was truly the central problem, but it quickly became apparent that Molotov's purpose in raising the question first was not to secure a settlement but to ensure disagreement. The Soviets demanded a Four-Power control of the Ruhr, and the creation of a strong, central government for Germany. They also sought to break up the economic merger of the American and British zones of Germany—a merger which they had refused to join—and again demanded reparations from Germany to the value of 10 billion dollars. (The Soviets had already taken about one and a quarter billion dollars worth out of the current production of their zone of Germany and were continuing to bleed it at the rate of approximately half a billion dollars a year. They refused to count these gains as part of the reparations.) The London meeting broke down over these issues. Waves of Communist-led strikes in France and Italy during the London meetings did not increase feeling of mutual trust and co-operation among the conferees.

The Austrian peace treaty came up again at the Council of Foreign Ministers in 1948. The Soviets proposed that they would waive all financial claims against Austria provided Austria paid 200 million dollars and turned over two-thirds of her oil production to the U.S.S.R. The proposal was rejected both in its first form and in a modified version. At their Paris meeting in 1949, the foreign ministers agreed to discuss the German problem first. That was about the only agreement reached. The Soviets proposed a return to the Four-Power rule over Germany. This was rejected by Britain, France, and the United States. Mr. Vishinsky, speaking for the U.S.S.R., then rejected a Western proposal to unify all Germany under the constitution which had been set up for Western Germany. He also renewed the Soviet demand for 10 billion dollars in reparations. This was refused once more and the council recessed without having reached any settlement of the German problem. Nor did they get beyond generalities on a peace treaty for Austria. Complete failure, later in 1949, to come to terms on an Austrian peace treaty, and a general deterioration of relations caused a hiatus in the meetings of the foreign ministers. The council did not meet again until 1954, when it held a session in Berlin. Mr. Molotov took essentially the same positions on Germany and Austria as had

Mr. Vishinsky in 1949. A peace treaty for Austria was finally concluded in May of 1955 but no final settlement of the German problem had been reached by the summer of 1958.

Looking back over the past dozen years—a brief moment indeed in terms of historical perspective—it appears that 1947 formed a dividing line, at least in one respect. Soviet communism was aggressive and expansionistic throughout the period, but prior to 1947 its aggressions and expansions were largely self-generating. After 1947, when the United States and other free nations began to take a firmer stand, the Soviets could readily convince themselves and could argue with some degree of plausibility that certain of their actions were necessary responses to the actions of others. Their arguments were often specious and sometimes completely false, but some had more than a little truth. There was a difference, to give one illustration, between Soviet pressure on Turkey in 1945 and in 1957. The pressure in 1945 was intended to persuade or frighten the Turks into ceding a portion of their Black Sea coast to the Soviet Union. The Turks, though standing alone and obviously much weaker than their huge neighbor, refused to be either persuaded or frightened. The Soviet action was a gratuitous attempt at aggression. The pressures in 1957 were intended to frighten the Turks into getting out of the North Atlantic Treaty Organization (NATO) or at least into reducing its NATO activities. These also failed, but in 1957 Turkey was no longer alone. She was a full-fledged member of an alliance system and a close associate of the United States. Neither the alliance nor the United States had aggressive intentions toward the U.S.S.R., but the Soviet leaders might understandably have felt a need to counter moves on their borders. Both in 1945 and in 1957, the Soviets were probing for weak spots which could be exploited to their advantage. Such probing was a constant of their policy after 1945. So, as has been noted, were their aggressiveness and their determination to wring every possible advantage from every situation. An early example which commanded much attention at the time was the Iranian crisis.

✺ THE IRANIAN AFFAIR

Soviet and American troops had been stationed in Iran during the war. The Soviets rejected an American proposal that all foreign troops be withdrawn early in 1946. While discussions were in progress on this point, an uprising, allegedly in behalf of autonomy, broke out in the Iranian province of Azerbaijan, which was under Soviet occupation. A revolutionary government was established in the province, and Iran complained that the Soviets had aided the insurrectionists. Iran asked the United Nations Security Council to investigate alleged Soviet interference in Iranian domestic affairs. The Soviet reaction was to bring charges before the Security Council alleging British interference in Greece and Indonesia. The British promptly announced that they would welcome an investigation of their actions in Greece and Indonesia. Moscow did not make a similar offer in regard to Iran. Instead the Soviets argued that the Iranian affair was not the proper business of the Security Council. The Council heard the charges despite Soviet opposition and ruled that Iran and the U.S.S.R. might settle their differences by direct negotiation subject to UN supervision and review.

There was fighting in Iranian Azerbaijan between government troops and insurgents, and Moscow announced that not all the Soviet troops would be withdrawn, as had been previously agreed. The Iranian government protested and the United States rather sharply reminded the Kremlin of its pledges to take the troops out. The crisis again came before the UN and the Soviet tactics form an interesting and revealing case history. First, Moscow tried and failed to get a postponement of the UN meeting. Then the Soviets proposed a change in the rules of the Security Council so that the major Powers could prevent any other state from naming them as party to a dispute. This also failed, and Mr. Gromyko, representing the U.S.S.R., then tried to keep the Iranian question off the agenda. When it was placed on the agenda despite his efforts, he threatened to walk out of the session unless the questions were postponed. They were not postponed and he carried out his threat, thus creating an important precedent. The Security Council sought explanations from both Moscow and Teheran. After some maneuvering, Moscow promised to remove the Soviet troops. The matter was then tabled by the council. Later the Soviet Union again attempted in vain to get the Security Council to drop the Iranian question from its agenda, and Gromyko again staged a walkout. The dispute dragged on.

Other aspects of Soviet policy which engaged the UN at this period were the Greek and Indonesian affairs, already mentioned, and the problem of international control of atomic energy. A Soviet veto prevented the Security Council from clearing the British in regard to Greece, and threat of a British veto choked off a Soviet attempt to investigate Anglo-Dutch actions in Indonesia. In the meantime, the UN had appointed an International Commission on Atomic Energy. The vote to create this commission was unanimous—a noteworthy event because it proved to be almost the only point concerning atomic energy upon which the Soviets and the West were able to agree in a decade. The American plan for the international control of atomic energy provided for severe sanctions in cases of violation, outlawed the use of the veto in the Security Council to prevent action, and depended upon a system of thorough inspections to ensure adherence to any agreement. The Soviet plan allowed the major Powers to use the veto and depended upon the various nations to police themselves without any outside inspection. It also called for the immediate destruction of all stocks of atomic weapons. No agreements were reached, either inside or outside of the UN, on these two rival plans. During the next eleven years, international control of atomic energy and the problem of disarmament were discussed intermittently, but at length, at all the upper levels of governments through the usual diplomatic channels, in connection with the UN, and at special conferences. No agreement was reached.

One or two other events of 1946 created quite a stir and affected the Soviet relations with the West. In February, 1946, an extensive Soviet spy ring was uncovered in Canada. Moscow sought to minimize the importance of the affair and later complained that the West had played it up in order to increase hostility to the Soviet Union. The Soviets admitted, however, that they had obtained secret data on atomic energy and other matters through the ring. (It subsequently appeared that the Soviets had apparently gotten much more significant information from spies operating in the United States and Great Britain.) There was a violent Soviet reaction—in words, at least—to Churchill's famous speech at Fulton, Missouri, in which, in the presence of President Truman, Churchill introduced the phrase, "the Iron Curtain," and suggested confronting the U.S.S.R. with an Anglo-American association. Stalin retorted by comparing Churchill to Hitler and by calling the former prime minister a warmonger. Finally, late in 1946, the Greek government asked the UN to investigate violations of the Greek frontiers by Soviet satellites. The investigation was ordered despite Soviet objections. The results proved beyond a doubt that the Soviet satellites were guilty as charged and that Moscow had been seeking, with considerable prospect of success, to achieve the goal of domination of the eastern Mediterranean, which she had revealed at Potsdam.

🏵 1947

The events which made 1947 a dividing point were, in a sense, Soviet inspired but were in no sense Soviet actions. In March, President Truman enunciated the doctrine which bears his name. It was, in essence, a promise of American economic and military aid to any nation which would resist Communist aggression. The President's announcement was less bluntly worded, but this was its meaning, as Moscow clearly recognized. The Truman Doctrine was followed in June by the Marshall Plan for giving American economic aid to European nations. The plan would have permitted the Soviets and their satellites to have shared in the aid, but the Soviets would neither have any part of it for themselves nor permit their satellites to participate in it. The Kremlin excoriated the plan (and the European Recovery Program which implemented it) as a thinly veiled American attempt to dominate the world, and later offered as a counterproposal a "Molotov Plan." The Molotov Plan found few takers and none among those nations who were free to choose. Another Soviet countermove was the announcement in September, 1947, of the formation of the Communist Information Bureau (the Cominform).

The announcement claimed that this new instrument of Soviet policy had just been established at a meeting in Warsaw attended by the Communist leaders of nine European countries; and that the purpose of the organization was to facilitate the exchange of information among its members. It appears, however, that the Cominform was established not at Warsaw in 1947 but at Prague in December, 1945. Its chief function was less an exchange of information than the dissemination through its publications of directives from Moscow. Although there were some major differences between them, the Cominform performed essentially the same functions as had the Comintern during the 1930's. The Cominform was abolished by Moscow's action in 1956.

The Greek Communists, to return to 1947, proclaimed the formation of "The First Provisional Democratic Government of Free Greece," dedicated to "liberating Greece from the American imperialists." This action had Moscow's tacit blessing, at least. So did the forced abdication of King Michael of Romania and the establishment by the Romanian Communists of a "People's Republic" under their control. One of the major propaganda lines put forth by Moscow was the promise of the coming victory of Communism. ("In our age," boasted Molotov in November, 1947, "all roads lead to Communism.") The other major line was that the U.S.S.R. and its satellites were the only "peace-loving nations" in the world, whereas the capitalist Powers, paced by the United States, were bent on war and aggression. The torrents of self-praise and abuse of the West mounted simultaneously. This was not a novelty, but both praise and vituperation reached new, sustained heights in 1948. Not all the name-calling nor all the actions were Soviet. The United States Mediterranean Fleet opened the year 1948 with maneuvers in the eastern Mediterranean. Official and private spokesmen in both the United States and Britain became sharper in their criticism of the U.S.S.R. Tensions mounted, with Germany one of the main focal points.

✇ THE BERLIN BLOCKADE

The Soviet-controlled East German press, attacking the Anglo-American economic merger of their zones, suggested in January of 1948 that the

Russians would soon seek to force the Western Powers out of Berlin. The war of nerves mounted steadily thereafter, but despite threats and name-calling, the British and Americans put their new bizonal arrangement into operation in February. The Soviets at once announced the creation of a new economic advisory commission for their zone. All of its members were appointed by the Soviet authorities. In March, the Soviet members of the Allied Control Commission in Berlin walked out of a meeting. They charged that conversations among the Americans, British, French, and West Germans had violated the quadripartite agreements.

A far more serious action began in April, when the Soviet authorities interfered with rail and air transportation into Berlin. Sporadic interference developed into a Soviet blockade of Berlin, which was offset by the famous Berlin Airlift. The Western Powers refused to budge from the onetime German capital, and they refused to permit the blockade to strangle the Berliners. The Western governments also continued their plan for setting up a federal government for western Germany. The blockade became tighter as the weeks went by. This was matched by increasing the airlift and by a counterblockade of eastern Germany. It is not necessary to trace the full story of protests and counterprotests, of actions and reactions, or of the diplomatic jockeying which took place. There were conferences in Berlin and in Moscow and there was a voluminous diplomatic correspondence, but the blockades and the airlift continued, and the tension wound tighter and tighter.

The Berlin problem was brought before the Security Council in October, 1948, and there were furious arguments when the Soviet delegates challenged the council's right to consider any part of the German question. Smaller Powers on the council sought a formula to end the crisis, but their efforts, which went on for weeks, were futile. The Soviets declined to lift their blockade until the Western nations both withdrew the complaint which had been lodged with the council, and also accepted a new, Soviet-sponsored currency for all Berlin. Stalin charged that the Anglo-American actions in regard to Berlin were "a policy of aggression, a policy of unleashing a new war." The Western Powers, on their side, refused to hold further direct talks with the Soviets until the Soviet blockade had been lifted. They also rejected the Soviet currency proposal and an earlier Soviet demand for complete control of all air and land travel into Berlin. There the matter rested at the end of 1948 with a tight Soviet ring around Berlin and with American, British, and French aircraft arriving in increasing numbers at Tempelhof, Gatow, and Tegel airfields inside the ring.

Austria was almost as potentially explosive a problem as Germany. Like Germany, Austria was divided into occupation zones and its capital was jointly patrolled by Soviet and Western troops. Early in 1948 the Soviet commander in Vienna charged that the Americans and British were plotting to make their zones in western Austria into a base from which to launch "imperialist aggression." A little later, as was noted in the discussion of the Council of Foreign Ministers, Soviet proposals for an Austrian peace treaty were rejected as unacceptable. Linked with the question of an Austrian settlement was a dispute over navigation on the Danube. The Soviets in 1946 had taken over the assets and equipment of the Danube Shipping Company, the main carrier on that waterway. The United States favored an internationalization of navigation on the Danube, but this was brusquely refused by the Soviets at a conference in Belgrade during the summer of 1948. That meeting was unusually acrimonious even for that year. The tone was set when Mr. Vishinsky told the Western delegates that they must either accept the Soviet proposal or get out. "The door is open," he said, "for you to leave." They did not leave, and the Soviet proposal—which would have excluded France, Britain, Austria, and the United States from any control of the navigation of the Danube—was rejected by the American State Department.

✇ RIVAL COALITIONS

Both sides were actively building coalitions. A Soviet-Polish trade agreement, which promised Poland almost half a billion dollars worth of industrial equipment in return for an increase in Polish production, was concluded in January, 1948. The next month, the U.S.S.R. signed treaties of friendship and mutual co-operation with Romania and Hungary. Poland, Romania, and Hungary were already wholly subservient to Moscow, so that it was relatively easy for the Soviets to complete these agreements. Other tactics, however, had to be employed against Czechoslovakia, which still retained a little independence. A carefully planned and boldly executed coup was carried out at Prague in late February. President Beneš, after several days of intense pressure, was forced to yield, and full political control was seized by the Moscow-dominated Czech Communist Party. Beneš was forced into retirement, and Jan Masaryk, well and favorably known in the West, was literally harried to his death. Britain, France, and the United States all protested, with no result other than to place their feelings on record. A Soviet veto blocked an effort to set up a UN inquiry into the affair. Czechoslovakia, by mid-June, formally as well as factually had a new master. With this victory and with a military alliance which she forced on Finland in April, the Soviet Union completed a protective cordon along its western borders.

The coup in Prague spurred Moscow's opponents to greater action. Delegates from Belgium, the Netherlands, and Luxembourg—conferring at Brussels—accepted an Anglo-French proposal for a Western European Union. An economic merger of the American, British, and French zones of Germany was arranged; and a fifty-year military and economic pact was signed by the five western European nations. Substantial progress was made in implementing the European Recovery Program, and both military and economic support flowed from the United States to Greece and Turkey. One counteraction attempted by Moscow was an effort to persuade the United States to enter into bilateral discussions and agreements. The United States reiterated its willingness to engage in multilateral talks and settlements but rejected the Soviet suggestion that Moscow and Washington settle matters without reference to others. The Soviet offer was renewed from time to time during the next decade and always with the same result. A second counteraction by Moscow was the announcement in late January, 1949, of the formation of a "Council of Mutual Economic Aid." Its members were Bulgaria, Czechoslovakia, Romania, Hungary, and Poland. This was the implementation of the so-called Molotov Plan. Yugoslavia was pointedly excluded from the council.

A few days after the announcement by Moscow of this council, news came from London of a Council of Europe and of a proposal for a North Atlantic pact. The Soviet Foreign office immediately denounced the proposed pact as an Anglo-American plot to undermine the UN. Washington and London, Moscow charged, were about to embark upon "an openly aggressive course" aimed at world domination. Washington and London paid no attention, but such complete independence was difficult for the small neighbors of the U.S.S.R. An attempt by Norway, Sweden, and Denmark to form a Scandinavian mutual defense alliance was defeated by Soviet pressures. Norway was warned that the U.S.S.R. would regard Norwegian adherence to a North Atlantic pact as an unfriendly act, and then was invited to sign a nonaggression pact with the Soviet Union. The Norwegians courageously refused the Soviet offer and aligned themselves with the Council of Europe. Discussions in this council resulted in the draft of the North Atlantic Pact. Essentially this was a defensive alliance, which pledged that any armed attack against any signatory of the pact would be regarded as an attack against all. The Soviets protested that the pact violated the Charter of the UN, and that it was aimed against the U.S.S.R. Twelve nations rejected both protests and signed the pact in April, 1949, thus bringing into being the North Atlantic Treaty Organization (NATO). A Soviet attempt to have the UN General Assembly consider a charge that the pact violated the UN Charter was blocked. The Soviets suffered another reverse when the UN Security Council rejected a Soviet resolution which would have required the major Powers to reveal complete data on their armed forces and armaments, including the atomic bomb. Meanwhile steps had been taken which led to an ending of the Berlin blockade.

Late in January, 1949, Stalin indicated through a newspaper inter-view—a way of by-passing regular diplomatic channels which Stalin often used between 1945 and 1951 and which his successors also used, though less frequently—that Russia was ready, on certain conditions, to end her blockade of Berlin. Stalin also suggested a meeting between President Truman and himself—another effort at bilateral negotiations. The President refused a bilateral settlement, but had the State Department renew negotiations on Berlin. A number of secret talks between Mr. Philip C. Jessup, for the United States, and Mr. Joseph A. Malik, for the U.S.S.R., brought results. American, British, French, and Soviet representatives met in New York in May and agreed to an ending of the blockades. The Soviet blockade, which had lasted 328 days; and the Western counter-blockade, which had lasted almost as long, were lifted simultaneously at daybreak on March 12. But the foreign ministers, whose meeting at Paris had been arranged by the representatives in New York, failed to agree on any settlement of the larger problem of Germany. The West thereafter went ahead with its plans to form a west German state, and the Federal Republic of Western Germany, with its capital at Bonn, was proclaimed in September, 1949. The following month, a Soviet-sponsored "German Democratic Republic in Eastern Germany" was announced, and the deadlock continued.

🏛 SATELLITES

Meanwhile the Soviets had been having a variety of more or less serious troubles with some of their satellites. By far the most serious was their trouble with Yugoslavia. The Communist Party and its regime in Yugoslavia were unique in that they had been developed with a minimum of help and supervision from Moscow. This worried the Kremlin which can never tolerate for long any hint of independence among its underlings. In addition, there had been some friction between Tito and Stalin over the Soviet efforts to exploit the Yugoslav economy for Soviet benefit and over Tito's objections to Soviet policies in the Balkans. The final straw, apparently, was Tito's order to the Yugoslav secret police to keep under surveillance the secret police and other officials whom Moscow had sent into the country. At any rate, Moscow, acting through the Cominform, suddenly denounced Tito in June of 1948 and accused him of several crimes against Communism. Soviet technicians and other specialists were withdrawn from Yugoslavia and so was Soviet assistance. Presumably Moscow expected that some of Tito's followers and the people of Yugoslavia would respond by throwing Tito out of power. On the contrary, with some exceptions, they rallied to Tito and enabled him to withstand the economic and other pressures which the Cominform countries brought to bear. The economic pressures, after some months, brought Tito to accept economic and military aid from the United States. Neither Tito nor his associates, however, ceased to be or to call themselves Communists. They insisted, on the contrary, that they were the true Communists and that it was the Soviet Communists who had deviated from orthodoxy. They declined to accept a subordinate position to Moscow, and, thanks largely to American support, were able to hold to this position to the date of this writing, despite several post-Stalin attempts to win them back.

The significance of this event to the Soviets was not that Tito broke with or defected from their rule, because he did not. They expelled him. The significance is that he continued in power despite the expulsion. It was this which gave the affair the appearance of a successful revolt to which was attached the label of Titoism. The Soviet attempt to discipline Tito not only failed, it also cost Moscow its control of a strategically important area (at least from 1948 to 1957) and created what the Kremlin must have regarded as a dangerous precedent. Perhaps that lay behind the purges which took place in some of the satellites in 1949 and thereafter.

The vice-premier of Bulgaria was arrested in 1949 "for gross Party errors" and for having been unfriendly toward the U.S.S.R. His boss, Premier George Dimitrov, head of the Bulgarian Communist Party and an old friend of Stalin's, was suddenly given a leave of absence and sent to the Soviet Union for medical treatment. He died while there, and his place in Bulgaria was taken by a veteran revolutionary whose loyalty to Moscow was beyond question. Subsequent purges struck at the top leaders in some of the other satellites. Xoxe of Albania, Gomulka of Poland, Rajk of Hungary, Pauker of Romania, and Slansky of Czechoslovakia were all removed from their positions. Rajk and Xoxe and Slansky were executed. So were thirteen other Czech and Slovak Communists. Moscow steadily increased its controls, using all possible means, and successfully integrated the economic and military systems of the satellites with those of the U.S.S.R. Moscow's intentions and one of its methods were illustrated in November, 1949, when Marshal of the Soviet

Union K. K. Rokossovsky was allowed to resume his Polish citizenship in order to act as Poland's Minister of Defense and commander-in-chief, a post he held until November, 1956. Numerous trade agreements and joint Soviet-satellite companies were other means used to bind the satellites more tightly to Moscow. For example, joint Soviet-Romanian companies were created in 1949 to control the building industry and the production of coal and metals in Romania. The usual contrast between Soviet words and Soviet deeds often appeared in their relations with their satellites. The words were promises of noninterference in the internal affairs of other states. The actions may be exemplified by the use of Soviet armed forces to crush the anti-Communist risings which took place in Czechoslovakia and Eastern Germany in June, 1953.[4]

It is only fair to note that coalition building also continued on the other side. Parts of the armed forces of the signatories of the North Atlantic Pact were pooled to form the NATO Defense Forces under a special command, the Supreme Headquarters of the Allied Powers in Europe (SHAPE). This command was established in December, 1950, with General Dwight D. Eisenhower as the first NATO commander. Greece and Turkey joined NATO, thus extending its range into Asia Minor. The NATO Defense Forces were woefully weak and divided at the outset, but were steadily strengthened and woven together. At the beginning of 1953, however, NATO forces numbered, exclusive of Greece and Turkey, only about 28 divisions with perhaps 4000 aircraft. The Soviets at that date were maintaining in the satellites between 30 and 40 Soviet divisions and 60 to 70 satellite divisions with about 2500 aircraft. It was perhaps this disparity in forces which led the Western Powers to plan the creation of a European Defense Community which would include West German troops. This plan failed because France was unwilling to ratify the treaties which would have established the EDC. Sovereignty, including the right to maintain armed forces, was restored to the Federal Republic of West Germany in 1955, and that nation was added to the membership of NATO. Meanwhile, both the United States and the Soviet Union continued to build air bases and other military installations; the former in the NATO countries and elsewhere; the latter in the satellites, Manchuria, and Tibet. Also, six western European nations adopted the Schuman Plan, which created the European Coal and Steel Community (1952).

The various steps toward a tighter unity among the free nations of the West were countered by various Soviet moves. The U.S.S.R. and its seven satellites—Poland, Albania, Czchoslovakia, East Germany, Hungary, Romania, and Bulgaria—signed a "Treaty of Friendship, Co-operation and Mutual Aid" in May of 1955. This so-called Warsaw Pact provided for the immediate establishment of a unified military force, whose first commander was Marshal I. S. Konev of the Soviet Union. This meant the integration of satellite armies into the Soviet forces. According to Soviet statements, the Warsaw Pact (unlike NATO) was ". . . based on the doctrine of mutual respect and nonintervention in each other's internal affairs, and on respect for the national independence of countries great and small." The relatively gentle handling of riotous unrest and rather extensive changes in Poland in 1956 seemed to lend credibility to this announcement. The Stalinist faction of the Polish Communist Party was forced into a temporary eclipse, and Gomulka, who had previously been purged from the Party and jailed, returned as its leader. He became something of a Polish national hero when he appeared to defy the Soviet rulers, and there was a wave of limited freedom within Poland. However, the barely veiled threat of forceful intervention by the Soviets at the time of the Polish elections in 1957, plus the reappearance in key spots of the "Stalinists" and the curbing of liberties indicated that the change was more superficial than real. Prior to that, more convincing proof of the Kremlin's determination to keep its satellites was given in tragic abundance by the Soviet's brutal suppression of an anti-Communist, anti-Soviet revolt in Hungary (1956). The Soviet's outrageous behavior there was too much even for many veteran non-Soviet Communists to stomach. Yet the U.S.S.R. retained its firm control over its satellites.

✸ ATOMIC WEAPONS AND PEACE OFFENSIVES

The events described in the last several pages took place against a background of happenings which must now be added to the story. The first of these was the explosion by the Soviet Union in 1949 of its first atomic weapon. This ended the American monopoly of such weapons and profoundly altered the strategic situation. From 1949 forward, the Soviets built up their stock piles of atomic weapons and added to them in 1953 thermonuclear devices. Henceforward, thoughtful people could never exclude from their thinking the possibility not only that the United States and the U.S.S.R. might destroy each other by fission and fusion weapons, but also that humanity might be destroyed in the process.

The second background happening was the Soviet's so-called Peace Offensive, which was launched as a full-scale enterprise at a "Scientific and Cultural Congress for World Peace" held in New York in March, 1949. A month later, two "World Congresses of Partisans of Peace" were held, one in Paris and one in Prague. These became an annual feature in 1950 with "Peace Congresses" in Stockholm and Warsaw. The chief instruments of the Peace Offensive, aside from the various Communist Parties, were the World Federation of Trade Unions, the Women's International Democratic Federation, and the World Federation of Democratic Youth—all three under Moscow's control. Many non-Communist individuals and groups, sincerely desirous of peace, were from time to time persuaded to support this movement. The Soviet Union and its satellites spent literally billions of dollars in promoting the Peace Offensive, a clear indication of the Kremlin's judgment of its value as an instrument of Soviet foreign policy.

🐦 KOREAN CRISIS AND WAR

The other part of the background cannot be so briefly described. Back in December of 1945 when the foreign ministers met in Moscow they had reached several agreements concerning the Far East. They agreed that General Douglas MacArthur should remain as the Supreme Commander in Japan, but that Russia, Britain, and China were to share in the control of that country. They also agreed that both Soviet and American troops should be withdrawn from China as soon as a unified government under Chiang Kai-shek was established there. Finally, the foreign ministers agreed that the United States and the U.S.S.R. were to form a joint commission to unify Korea, which was to be governed by a trusteeship of the Big Four until the Koreans were able to govern themselves.

Friction developed in Korea almost at once, but that seemed to be a side issue. There were also troubles in China, including some fighting in Manchuria with Chou En-lai, the Chinese Communist leader of record at that date, demanding a share in the government of Manchuria—a demand which Chiang's government rejected. There were also complaints by Chiang and some Americans that Soviet troops were still in Manchuria in 1946 despite a Soviet promise that they would be removed. On the other side was Moscow's complaint that American ships were being used to transport Chiang's Nationalist forces to Manchuria. A new element was added to the disputes when, in February, 1946, the Soviet commander in Mukden admitted that the U.S.S.R. had removed machinery from Manchurian mines and factories. The Soviet officer said that this had been done in accordance with the Yalta agreements, but the United States promptly denied that there had been any such arrangement. Formal American protests against the Soviet removal of war booty from Manchuria were filed in March. The State Department said that Moscow's reply to the protest was unsatisfactory, but that the United States would drop the matter. There is no published record of Moscow's reaction to this, but there is no reason to think that the Soviets were displeased with the outcome. They had acquired millions of dollars worth of machinery and materials at the cost of nothing more than transportation and an ineffective diplomatic protest. The Chinese reported the departure of Soviet forces from Mukden in March, and the U.S.S.R. announced in May that all its troops had been removed from Manchuria except a garrison which, under the terms of a Sino-Soviet treaty, had been left to defend Port Arthur. However, Chinese Communist troops took over in Manchuria from the departing Russians so that Soviet Communism continued to profit at a minimum of expense to itself. The Chinese Communists attacked Mukden in 1947 and continued their advances in Manchuria in 1948 while the power of Chiang's Nationalist government continued to wane. The conflict in Korea also sharpened.

It will be recalled that Korea had in the nineteenth century been contended for by the imperial Russian and the imperial Japanese governments, and had fallen to Japan in the early twentieth century. For more than a generation, Korea had been part of the Japanese Empire. This was changed by World War II. After the surrender of Japan, Soviet troops occupied northern Korea and American forces occupied southern Korea with the dividing line set at the 38th parallel. The United States assumed that this was no more than a temporary division which would end as soon as a provisional government could be created by and for the Koreans. The creation in 1945 of the joint Soviet-American commission to assist in the creation of a provisional government seemed to bear out this American assumption. The commission was instructed to consult with Korean social and political groups, and to work out measures for the improvement of economic, social, and political conditions within the country. The final decisions on the commission's actions were reserved to the Big Four—in this case, the Soviet Union, China, Great Britain, and the United States.

The whole arrangement turned sour almost immediately. The American and Soviet members of the commission could not agree on what groups to consult nor upon what steps to take to co-ordinate the two zones. The Americans blamed these failures on the Soviet's refusal to consult any but Communists and fellow travelers. The Soviet countercharge was that the Americans insisted on ignoring all "democratic" groups. Meanwhile (February, 1946) the Soviet set up in its zone an interim "People's Committee." Months later, the United States established an interim government in its zone.

After an exchange of diplomatic notes between Moscow and Washington, the joint commission was again put to work in 1947 but found itself still unable to agree on anything. The United States then suggested that the problem be submitted to the Big Four. When the Soviet Union rejected this proposal, the United States took the Korean affair before the

UN. The General Assembly, by a vote of 43 to 0, the U.S.S.R. not voting, accepted an American-sponsored resolution calling for national elections in Korea before the end of March, 1948. After the elections, both occupying Powers were to hand over all controls to the Koreans and withdraw from the country. A UN commission was created to supervise the elections and the transfer of authority.

The Soviet Union flatly refused the UN commission access to north Korea to arrange the election or for any other purpose. Instead, the Soviet news agency *Tass* announced that a constitution and a government for all Korea had been proclaimed by the government of northern Korea. A conference of northern and southern Koreans, held in the north in April (1948), urged the immediate withdrawal of both the Soviets and the Americans. The conference, which was under North Korean sponsorship but which included some non-Communists, also condemned the UN commission for holding elections in southern Korea. The commission went ahead, nonetheless, and supervised the election of an assembly. The north Koreans ignored the new assembly's invitation to join it, adopted a constitution modeled on that of the U.S.S.R., and chose an assembly of its own. The United States ended its military occupation of Korea south of the 38th parallel in August (1948), handing over the government to American civilians for transfer as soon as possible to the Koreans.

There were soon two governments in Korea—a North Korean government supported and recognized by the U.S.S.R.; and a Republic of Korea, under the presidency of Syngman Rhee, which had the support and recognition of the United Nations, Great Britain, and the United States. Soviet troops were said to have been withdrawn from the northern zone in December, 1948, and the last American troops left the southern zone in September, 1949. By that time there were a good many Americans who were ready to get out of Korea. Only strong pressure from the administration persuaded Congress to give financial aid to Korea, which both the President and his Secretary of State declared to be outside of the American "defense perimeter" (January, 1950). Besides, Korea was still somewhat overshadowed by events in China.

The Chinese Communists flowed south from their successes in Manchuria, and, in 1949, wrested control of the mainland of China from Chiang Kai-shek. A "People's Republic of China," Communist-dominated of course, was proclaimed in September, and in December, Chiang and his supporters retired to Formosa. In February, 1950, Chou En-lai, for "Red China," and Mr. Vishinsky, for the Soviet Union, signed a thirty-year treaty of friendship, alliance, and mutual assistance. It was further agreed that Outer Mongolia should be "independent"; that the

Soviet Union would loan the Chinese Communists 300 million dollars at very low interest for the purchase of Soviet industrial and railroad equipment; and that Port Arthur, Darien, and all the Manchurian properties seized by the Soviets, including the Manchurian railroad, should be returned to China not later than 1952. Other agreements set up Sino-Soviet companies for the development of aviation and for the exploitation of the oil and nonferrous metal resources of Sinkiang. Subsequent events suggest the possibility that other arrangements may have been concluded between Moscow and Peiping, but, if so, these have remained unpublished.[5]

The "Supreme People's Assembly" of the North Korean government, on June 20, 1950, decreed that there must be only one constitution, one army, and one government for all Korea; that an all-Korean election must be held under specified conditions; and that the UN commission must be completely withdrawn from the country. Five days later, North Korean troops attacked in force across the 38th parallel. Secretary General of the UN Trygve Lie, acting on a report from the UN commission in Korea, ruled that it was the duty of the Security Council to take immediate action. The Soviet Union was not at that juncture represented on the Security Council because Mr. Jacob Malik, the Soviet representative there, had walked out of the council in January, 1950, after that body had refused a Soviet demand for the expulsion of the representative of the Chinese Nationalists. This Soviet boycott was still in effect when the North Koreans attacked. The Security Council was thus able to act promptly. It asked for an immediate ending of hostilities and for the immediate withdrawal of the North Korean forces. It also asked all members of the UN to support that organization and to refrain from aiding the North Koreans. North Korea condemned the Security Council's actions as illegal on the ground that they were taken in the absence of representatives of the Soviet Union and Communist China.

On June 27, 1950, President Truman ordered American air and naval forces to defend the Republic of Korea and the free nations of the world. Three days later, he authorized the use of American ground forces in Korea. This action followed a request from the Security Council for assistance from the members of the UN in carrying out the council's resolutions. It preceded by one day a further request from the council that all necessary aid be given to the Republic of Korea, and it preceded by ten days a Security Council resolution which placed the UN forces under a commander to be named by the United States. Finally, President Truman's actions antedated by nearly three months the report of the UN commission on Korea, which placed the blame for the war squarely on the aggression committed by the North Koreans.

The Soviet version of events was quite different. The war was provoked, according to Soviet spokesmen, by the totally unjustified attack which forces under the command of the Republic of Korea made upon North Korean troops. The Soviets charged that the resolutions of the Security Council were entirely illegal, and that the council itself was nothing more than the pliant tool of the aggressive rulers of the United States. Later the Soviets shifted their ground to argue that the actions in Korea were really a civil war in which neither the United States nor the United Nations had any right to intervene. To the charge that North Korean troops were equipped with Soviet-made weapons, the Soviet rulers and their followers responded with the patent falsehood that any Soviet-made equipment found in North Korean hands must be left over from 1945. Captured equipment proved conclusively that the North Koreans used Soviet arms and equipment which had been made in 1950.

The military history of the Korean War cannot be told here in detail. The UN forces were nearly swept off the peninsula before they could recover from the initial assault. But during the fall of 1950 they drove the North Koreans back well beyond the 38th parallel, almost to the Yalu River. While the members of the UN and the citizens of the United States debated whether UN forces should cross that river, the North Koreans gathered new strength in arms and men. The arms were mainly Soviet; the men were predominantly Chinese. These greatly augmented and strengthened forces mounted an offensive which, between November, 1950, and January, 1951, carried far south of the 38th parallel. This Communist drive was finally checked and reversed. It required nearly six months for the UN troops to drive the Communist armies out of South Korea. Armistice talks were then begun, but these dragged on month after month while a bloody stalemate was fought out on the battle lines.

The armistice talks broke down entirely in October, 1952, because of the Communist demand that all prisoners of war be returned whether they wished repatriation or not. The UN negotiators were adamant in demanding that POW's should be allowed to decide upon their own repatriation. The breakdown in negotiations lasted until April, 1953, when they were resumed on the initiative of the U.S.S.R. Since the Soviets were not legally a party to the negotiations, their ability to reopen the talks pretty well confirmed what had been an open secret from the beginning—that Moscow was the real master on the Communist side. The negotiators quickly arranged an exchange of sick and wounded prisoners, but it required many more weeks to reach an armistice agreement. The armistice was concluded on July 27, 1953. The repatriation of prisoners was completed in January, 1954, but the establishment of a demarcation line and a neutral zone between the two Koreas did not solve the basic problem nor provide a final settlement.

Two other Soviet policies of the period remain to be mentioned. One —primarily a domestic matter in some ways but with very significant overtones for foreign relations—was the calculated and virulent "Hate-America" campaign which the Kremlin conducted especially within its own borders but also, to a lesser extent, beyond them. This campaign reached a stage of full crescendo in 1951 and remained at that level until after Stalin's death. It was then soft-pedaled for several years, but was gradually restored to full shrillness in 1957. One of its reiterated themes within the Soviet Union was that the United States was preparing to launch an aggressive war against the Soviet peoples and their country. The other policy sought to promote trade between the U.S.S.R. and the rest of the world. This was not a new policy but the reinvigoration of an old one. Foreign trade has been an instrument of Soviet foreign policy since Lenin's time. It has been a means of making friends, of dividing and confounding enemies, and of supplying the Soviet system with needed goods, materials, and foodstuffs. Stalin told the Sixteenth Party Congress in 1930, "Our policy is the policy of peace and of the development of trading relations with all countries." This was echoed at the Nineteenth Party Congress, and repeated by Malenkov after Stalin died. It was also implemented by widely advertised promotional schemes (such as the International Economic Conference, held at Moscow in 1952) and by equally well-publicized trade agreements between the Soviet regime and various non-Soviet firms and countries.

CHAPTER XXIX

"Unfinished Business"

🔥 THE PROBLEM OF SUCCESSION

". . . the most important task of the Party and the government is to ensure uninterrupted and correct leadership of the entire life of the country, which demands the greatest unity of leadership and the prevention of any kind of disorder and panic." Thus ran the joint communiqué of the Party's Central Committee, the Council of Ministers, and the Presidium of the Supreme Soviet after Stalin's death. It may be noted that the Party was mentioned first, and that "correct leadership" is Party jargon for the rule by the Party bosses. Their major difficulty at the moment was that, Stalin having died, no one of his aides was able to step immediately into his place, nor was any of the group willing for a colleague to do so. Two of the major themes of the post-Stalin period were a determination by the clique of Party bosses to retain the full authority which Stalin had exercised, and a struggle within the clique for mastery.

It appeared at first that the second issue might have been settled before Stalin's death. For the space of about a week thereafter, Malenkov was addressed as Chairman of the Council of Ministers of the U.S.S.R. and Secretary of the Central Committee of the Communist Party of the Soviet Union. Then, following some byplay, it was announced that Comrade Malenkov's request to be relieved of the secretaryship had been granted. The post—a key spot because from it the Party organization could be controlled, as Stalin had demonstrated—was taken by Khrushchev. Malenkov continued as premier (more properly, Chairman of the Council of Ministers) until February, 1955, when he "resigned" that position with the explanation that he was incapable of handling it properly. Meanwhile, several significant shifts had taken place. First, Premier Malenkov was not allowed to go it alone. Four First Deputy Premiers (Beria, Molotov, Bulganin, and Kaganovich) and one Deputy

Premier (Mikoyan) were named to share the responsibility with him. Second, it was publicly emphasized that the regime was now operating under a committee government. And, third, Beria made a bid for supreme power, failed, and paid the penalty for failure in a monolithic system.

Beria appeared to have been losing place and power as far back as 1952, and to have been on the verge of disaster when Stalin died. (The infamous "Doctors' plot" may have had as one of its purposes the discrediting of Beria. At any rate, shortly after Beria regained power following Stalin's death, the plot was declared to be a frame-up for which certain anti-Beria men were responsible. They were punished.) He quickly regained his footing, taking back into his own grasp both the Ministry of the Interior (MVD) and the Ministry of State Security (MGB). Outsiders can only speculate as to what happened in the next several months. It was announced in July, 1953, that Beria had been arrested for several heinous crimes; and it was announced in the following December that he and some associates had been convicted and shot. Presumably, Beria had tried in June to make himself the ruler of the clique. After his failure, all publicity releases stressed that the new regime was collective leadership, par excellence. This continued throughout 1955 (and, indeed for some time thereafter), although it seemed that one man, Khrushchev, was gradually emerging at least as "first among equals" if not as something more.

TABLE 9

Change and Continuity in Personnel

Date	Premier	Defense	Police	Foreign Affairs	GOSPLAN
Feb. 1953	Stalin	Bulganin	Ignatiev	Vishinsky	Saburov
March 1953	Malenkov	Bulganin	Beria	Molotov	Saburov
July 1953	Malenkov	Bulganin	Kruglov	Molotov	Saburov
Feb. 1955	Bulganin	Zhukov	Kruglov	Molotov	Saburov
June 1956	Bulganin	Zhukov	Dudorov	Shepilov	Saburov & Baibakov
June 1957	Bulganin	Zhukov	Dudorov	Shepilov	Pervukhin & Baibakov
July 1957	Bulganin	Zhukov	Dudorov	Gromyko	Kuzmin

The machinery of the government-in-law continued to operate throughout this period with perhaps a few more changes than usual. The Supreme Soviet, summoned into special session in March of 1953, required a session of about an hour to approve the most sweeping changes to be made in the government since Lenin's time. This gives a fair measure of the Soviet's power and of some of its functions. The Fourth Supreme Soviet was elected a year later (March, 1954). The published records reached new highs—99.989 per cent of all eligible voters voted, and 99.79 per cent of them voted for the official candidates. (Voters in the local elections in early 1957 did not perform quite as well in one respect, but did better in another. Only 99 per cent of those eligible voted, but from 98.9 per cent to 99.9 per cent voted for the official candidates.) There were also many shifts in administrative divisions and in the government structure. Ministries were frequently divided or combined or redivided or recombined. Table 9, which shows the continuity and the change in five key positions, will serve as an illustration of what happened.

🌐 "DE-STALINIZATION"

The changes and development in the ruler-in-fact continued to be more significant. Local and regional Party conferences and congresses were held during 1954 and 1955 leading up to the Twentieth Party Congress, which was held in February of 1956. The congress chose a new and slightly larger Central Committee. Eighty persons were re-elected to full membership, and fifty-three were so elected for the first time. Seventy-six of the 122 alternate or candidate members were freshmen. It was noticeable that the majority of those elected were supporters of Khrushchev. The new Central Committee subsequently chose eleven full and six candidate members to make up its Presidium. The Congress, as usual, listened to lengthy speeches and reports, applauded "spontaneously" at the proper moments, and voted unanimously in favor of whatever the Party bosses recommended. The congress, in short, was packed, rigged, and well disciplined. Some of the leaders' statements made headlines around the world as, for example, the pronouncement about the inevitability of war. The congress made the expected announcements about peaceful coexistence; issued instructions to representatives of foreign Communist Parties about reviving the "united front" and using parliamentary means to defeat parliamentary ends; instructed the Central Committee to prepare a new Party program for the Twenty-first Congress; and approved the Sixth Five-Year Plan. The various speakers also continued to eulogize "collective leadership" and decry the "cult of the individual." This was not unexpected, but Khrushchev's secret speech condemning Stalin for many crimes was sensational.[1]

It was a long speech—25,000 words, more or less—and it branded Stalin as a virtual paranoid who was responsible for all the excesses and most of the errors of the regime. Khrushchev accused Stalin of arbitrary behavior, administrative violence, mass repressions, terror, brutality, unreasonableness, falsification, slander, gross illegalities, the use of torture, and vicious behavior in general. The old leader was also accused of costly errors in foreign affairs and military policy. Khrushchev, in short, confirmed and corroborated what free men having access even to limited information had long known and long said about Stalin.

Though it must have been the subject of much word-of-mouth reporting, and, although excerpts and paraphrases and somewhat expurgated versions of the Khrushchev speech appeared in the Soviet Union, the first full publication of it was made by the United States Department of State on June 4, 1956. It had literally revolutionary effects on many non-Soviet Communists and Communist Parties. Meanwhile, it had set off in the U.S.S.R. a wave of "de-Stalinization." Throughout the spring and early summer of 1956, the Soviet people heard from their new leaders that Stalin had been the reverse of all-wise, all-generous, and infallible. The charges that Stalin had falsely accused and viciously punished many individuals and groups were substantiated by the "rehabilitation" (usually, but not always posthumous) of such persons as Rykov, Rajk, and Bela Kun of Hungary and of such groups as Jewish writers and artists and peoples like the Chechens. Lenin's "will," in which he condemned certain of Stalin's characteristics, was published in the U.S.S.R. for the first time in May, 1956. (It had long been known in the West.) Stalin was blamed for the heavy losses in World War II and for starting the Cold War.

It is impossible to say with certainty how this drastic reversal of the "Stalin personality cult," which had amounted to virtual deification, affected the Soviet people. That they were initially shocked, partly incredulous, and badly shaken is a matter of record. It also appears from the actions of Khrushchev and his associates after midsummer of 1956 that they felt that de-Stalinization had perhaps gone too far too fast. Zhukov, for example, sternly pointed out the necessity for leadership and discipline in the army. And Khrushchev, particularly in his speeches in 1957, attempted to redress the balance by saying that, although Stalin had made errors, he had also been a great man and a great leader. It is impossible at this stage not to feel that the effects of the down-grading of Stalin have not yet run their full course.

✸ PALACE REVOLUTION, 1957

One other major development in government and administration remains to be noted. There were intermittent signs both during and after the Twentieth Party Congress that struggles were still in process at the highest levels. We do not know exactly what happened, but Khrushchev appeared to lose his majority in the Presidium late in 1956, then to regain it as the new year proceeded. His position was precarious during

USSR and Satellites
July, 1957

Satellites : POLAND
Free Nations : Italy

EAST GERMANY

POLAND

U S S R

West Germany

CZECHOSLOVAKIA

Austria

HUNGARY

ROMANIA

Yugoslavia

Italy

BULGARIA

ALBANIA

Greece

Turkey

the spring and worsened in the early summer. The challenge and the showdown took place in June (1957), with Malenkov, Molotov, and Kaganovich presumably the principal challengers. The meeting of the Presidium on June 17–18 found Khrushchev clearly in the minority, but he refused to acknowledge his colleagues' authority to remove him and engineered an emergency session of the Central Committee. There his long and patient building of a personal following within the Party machinery (à la Stalin, it may be added) paid handsome dividends. ". . . Not a single person in the plenary meeting of the Central Committee," reported the Party's magazine *Party Life* "supported the anti-Party [i.e., the anti-Khrushchev] group." Table 10 summarizes the changes in the composition of the Presidium from October, 1952, to October, 1957. The fourth and fifth columns record the result of Khrushchev's triumph in June. The Presidium of July, 1957, with fifteen full members—only five of whom held that rank in January, 1957—and nine candidate members—seven of them newcomers—appeared to be Khrushchev-dominated.

❦ ECONOMIC CHANGES

During Malenkov's brief tenure as premier, there was a considerable to-do about emphasis on consumer goods and an improvement in living standards. Retail prices, rural taxes, compulsory deliveries of foodstuffs, and forced buying of government bonds were all reduced. Prices for farm produce and some wages were increased. The export of foodstuffs almost ceased and the import of them was increased more than threefold. Great fanfares announced production increases—modest but increases nonetheless—in radios, refrigerators, television sets, and other consumer goods. But as early as January, 1955, stress was again being placed on heavy industry at the expense of consumer goods, and, as has been noted, Malenkov, who had been identified with the new stress on satisfying the consumers, ceased to be premier shortly thereafter. The "correctness" of emphasizing heavy industry was reasserted at the Party congress, in the Sixth Five-Year Plan and discussions thereof, and in public announcements throughout 1956 and 1957.

The Sixth Five-Year Plan, for the years 1956–60, was published in January, 1956, and formally approved in February. The plan aimed, as before, at industrial and agricultural increases, though at a somewhat lower rate than previously; and at the speedier and more nearly complete relocation of major industrial centers in the eastern parts of the U.S.S.R. It appeared in the late summer of 1956 that considerable progress was being made in heavy industry at least. The production of steel was raised in the first half of 1956, but the new total was only

TABLE 10

Changes in the Membership of the Party Presidium

October, 1952	March, 1953	March, 1956	January, 1957	July, 1957
Aristov	—	?	?	Aristov *
—	Bagirov	—	—	—
—	—	—	—	Belyaev *
Beria *	Beria *	—	—	—
—	—	—	—	Brezhnev *
Bulganin *	Bulganin *	Bulganin *	Bulganin *	Bulganin *
—	—	Furtseva	Furtseva	Furtseva *
—	—	—	—	Ignatov *
Kaganovich *	Kaganovich *	Kaganovich *	Kaganovich *	—
—	—	—	—	Kalnberzin
Khrushchev *	Khrushchev *	Khrushchev *	Khrushchev *	Khrushchev *
—	—	Kirichenko *	Kirichenko *	Kirichenko *
—	—	—	—	Kirilenko
—	—	—	—	Korochenko
Kosygin *	—	—	—	Kosygin
—	—	—	Kozlov	Kozlov *
Kuusinen	—	—	?	Kuusinen *
Malenkov *	Malenkov *	Malenkov *	Malenkov *	—
—	—	—	—	Mazurov
—	Melnikov	—	—	—
Mikoyan *	Mikoyan *	Mikoyan *	Mikoyan *	Mikoyan *
Molotov *	Molotov *	Molotov *	Molotov *	—
—	—	—	Mukhitdinov	Mukhitdinov
—	—	—	—	Mzhavanadze
Pervukhin	Pervukhin	Pervukhin	Pervukhin *	Pervukhin
—	Ponomarenko	—	—	—
—	—	—	—	Pospelov
Saburov	Saburov	Saburov *	Saburov *	—
Shvernik	Shvernik	?	Shvernik	Shvernik *
Stalin *	—	—	—	—
Suslov	Suslov	?	Suslov	Suslov *
Voroshilov *	Voroshilov *	Voroshilov *	Voroshilov *	Voroshilov *
—	Zhukov	Zhukov	Zhukov *	

* indicates full member; ? indicates missing or conflicting information; —— indicates not a member

about 40 per cent of the United States production for the same period. However, only a very small part of the Soviet steel production went into automobiles, television sets, refrigerators and the other consumer goods which ate up a large share of American steel production. (In the first six months of 1956, the Soviets produced only about as many cars as American automobile manufacturers were producing in one week.)

A slowing down in the ratio of Soviet industrial advance—the second such slowdown in fourteen months—was announced early in 1957. In March of that year the arbitrary value of the ruble was effectively (but not technically) reduced in dollar terms from twenty-five cents to ten cents. And in April, the government announced that it was suspending for twenty to twenty-five years all payments of interest and principal on 260 billion rubles worth of government bonds. No real explanations were forthcoming from Khrushchev, who made the announcement, but presumably such drastic action would not have been taken for minor causes. Equally drastic, and productive of much discussion among the managerial group in the Soviet Union, was the "decentralization" of industry. Khrushchev had announced the general plan in February, elaborated on it at length in March and April, and presented it to the Supreme Soviet for adoption in May. The final authority for all production was retained by the Kremlin, and control over work relating to national defense was retained by central (or "federal") ministries. Twenty-five of the central ministries were abolished, however, and four more were merged into two. Administrative controls over industrial and construction enterprises, with the exceptions noted, were handed over to ninety-two regional or district bodies. The announced purpose of the reform was to cut down the wastage and inefficiencies inherent in an overly large organization and to stimulate local initiative.

It was noted in July (1957) that the revision of the five-year plan and the slowing down of the economy, both of which the Central Committee had called for in December, 1956, had not been accomplished. They were a few months later. Radio Moscow announced on September 26, 1957, that the Sixth Five-Year Plan was to be cut off at the end of 1959 and replaced by a seven-year plan. The reason given was that the decentralization necessitated a basic change in planning.

AGRICULTURE

The agricultural problem continued to be bothersome. Khrushchev had taken this as his special responsibility as early as 1950 and had fostered the amalgamation of collective farms. His next cure-all was to bring virgin lands in Central Asia (especially Kazakstan) and Siberia under the plow. The Soviet press reported in July, 1957, that 86 million acres had been cultivated for the first time within the past four years. The press had previously reported the resettlement on the virgin lands of several hundred thousands of persons, mostly young people. The program had some success in 1954, failed because of drought in 1955, and scored a major triumph in 1956. Khrushchev's other panacea, the conversion of much Soviet agriculture to the growing of corn, had a more limited success. Khrushchev, however, remained fully confident of success. In mid-1957, he promised that the U.S.S.R. would, within four or five years, surpass the United States in the production of milk and meat.

The familiar "carrot and stick" technique was continued throughout the period. For example, in March, 1956, it was announced that collective farmers were to be given greater autonomy in planning crops, setting wage scales, and controlling membership in the collective. (New legislation in August, 1957, empowered local groups to exile "loafers and parasites.") Provision was made to advance cash payments to farmers every month instead of forcing them to wait until the end of harvest for their cash income. Simultaneously, it was announced that more work was to be done on the collective operations and less on the private plots. Privately owned livestock were no longer required because needs could be supplied from the collective herds. By the same token, farmers need no longer depend on their private allotments for foodstuffs other than vegetables, fruits, and berries "to decorate the life of the farmer" (as the announcement from the Central Committee and the Council of Ministers phrased it). The ultimate goal of the new program was the elimination of the private plots, an end long sought by the regime and consistently opposed by the peasants. The new program aroused opposition enough so that the rulers sought to placate the peasants by a new ruling (July, 1956) that the government would pay free-market prices for produce grown on private plots.

🦅 SOCIAL NORMS

There were various concessions to the Soviet peoples and some relaxations of controls during the first four and a half years after Stalin died. It is not possible to state precisely the effectiveness, permanence, or real meanings of these reforms. Some concessions were only temporary as, for example, the granting of greater freedom to artists, composers, and writers. A general tightening up of controls was reported in January, 1957, and a few months later those concerned pledged their talents to the service of the Party. Other concessions seemed more genuine and probably more lasting. A new pension law went into effect in October, 1956, which raised the minimum pensions from 150 to 350 rubles per month. This was enthusiastically received as was also a new minimum-wage law, which became effective in January, 1957. This raised minimum wages in rural areas from 200 to 270 rubles per month, and in urban areas from 260 to 300 rubles per month. The Soviet government estimated that over eight million persons would benefit from these increases—a revelation which may be interpreted as evidence of the magnitude of the concession or of the desperate state of a sizable segment of the population before the raise. The promise that installment buying would be introduced (1957) and the legalization of abortions (1954) were also tangible concessions. It is harder to be sure of concessions and relaxations which bore on personal freedom. A partial amnesty was announced in 1954; special powers of the MVD to deal extrajudicially with certain crimes were abolished in 1956; and a promise, made at the same time, to abolish slave-labor camps, was partially implemented a year later. American and other visitors to the U.S.S.R. in 1956 and 1957 reported that there had been a definite easing of security restrictions on the Soviet people.

We lack adequate measurements to support a full description of the social norms of the past several years. A few such measures may, however, be added to those already given. Food was generally plentiful and most Soviet citizens ate well. Variety was limited and prices were high by American standards. In Moscow, in the fall of 1956, beef sold at six rubles a pound, butter at 13 rubles a pound, sugar at four rubles a pound, and a man's suit cost 1500 rubles. A year later, vacuum cleaners were selling at from 320 to 650 rubles, and small washing machines (51-ounce capacity) cost 750 rubles. The washing machines had no wringers and no hoses for filling or emptying. These deficiencies were the result of deliberate choice and not of incompetency or backwardness.

The Soviet population was still predominantly agrarian and rural in 1956, though by a narrower margin than before. Of the Soviet labor force, 50 million were in agriculture; 49 million in nonagricultural pursuits; and close to 4 million in the armed forces. (The comparable figures for the United States were 6.4 million in agriculture; 57.6 in nonagricultural lines; and 2.8 million in the armed forces.) The Soviets maintained throughout the period the largest army and biggest submarine force in the world. Their army in 1956 had from 175 to 200 divisions and from 2 million to 2.3 million men. Their armed forces, including the army, numbered between 3.6 million and 4.1 million men. Force reductions in 1955 and 1956 reduced the total under arms by about 1.8 million, but Western specialists believed that these cuts did not appreciably alter the Soviet's military position.

SCIENCE AND TECHNOLOGY

A great deal of attention and a very high priority were given by the Soviets to scientific and technical advances, with special attention to rockets, missiles, aircraft, and nuclear weapons. There was a tremendous expansion and improvement in scientific and technical education, and in stimulating research. The following figures provide a measure of the magnitude of the advance: As of 1941, there were 908,000 "specialists with higher education" at work in the national economy. The figure for 1956 was 2,340,000. The number of professional engineers rose from 290,000 to 586,000 in about the same period. And the number of scientific workers increased from 162,500 to 223,900 between 1950 and 1955.[2]

There were also other pragmatic evidences of the Soviet progress in certain lines. The range and variety were wide—a huge and very efficient radio communications center outside of Moscow, tremendous hydroelectric power stations and extensive power grids, the partial electrification of the Trans-Siberian Railroad, supersonic jet aircraft, and many tests of nuclear weapons. Two developments, at least, merit specific mention. Khrushchev announced publicly in April, 1956, that the Soviet Union would soon have an intercontinental ballistic missile to add to its growing store of weapons. Two such missiles were test-fired—one in the late summer and the second in the early fall of 1957. It was announced by Moscow in June, 1957, that the Soviets had ready the necessary rockets and instruments to launch an earth satellite. Early in the following October, the Soviet Union successfully put into outer space the first earth satellite in human history. These were, in one sense, domestic developments, but they also had tremendous impacts on foreign affairs.

FOREIGN AFFAIRS

Whereas Stalin, in his later years at least, had followed in general a hard policy, his successors skillfully employed alternating hard and soft policies. They were for the most part, soft with the so-called former colonial or dependent nations (China, India, Burma, Indonesia, Egypt, and others) whom they assiduously wooed with sweet words and tangible aid. They were now hard and now soft with the "imperialist nations" (France, the United Kingdom, and the United States) and their Western associates (Norway, Turkey, Western Germany, and others). During 1954, for example, the Soviets participated with greater outward courtesy and geniality (but with no real concessions) in renewed meetings of the Council of Foreign Ministers. They also participated fulsomely in the fifth anniversary of the Communist triumph in China, and flirted (diplomatically speaking) with India, Indonesia, and Burma. The following year, they evacuated Port Arthur and Porkkala (in Finland), established diplomatic relations with the West German Federal Republic, and concluded a joint peace treaty with Austria. They also re-established trade relations with Yugoslavia; arranged an arms deal with Egypt; made friendly approaches to India, Afghanistan, and Yemen; and took part in the famous Summit Conference at Geneva.

For eight years, the Soviets had consistently blocked a peace treaty with Austria. The motivation and the character of the Soviet "new look" were shown less accurately by Soviet claims to have reduced international tension than by the Soviet's comment to the Austrian chancellor, who had gone to Moscow at their invitation, for preliminary negotiations. "We are not motivated," said his hosts to Chancellor Raab, "by any love for Austria." And, indeed, they drove a hard bargain. Austria regained its sovereign independence and a pledge of its territorial integrity together with a removal of all occupation troops. Austria promised to pay to the Soviet Union one million tons of oil annually plus goods to the value of 150 million dollars, over and above what the departing Soviets took with them. French, British, and American troops withdrew beyond the western borders of Austria. Soviet troops withdrew to the east, also beyond the borders but still within fifty miles of Vienna.[3]

During the spring of 1955, the Soviets let it be known that they would welcome a "meeting at the summit." The governments of the United States, the United Kingdom, and France responded with an invitation to a meeting of the heads of states to be held at Geneva in July. "There," as Secretary Dulles put it in his formal report, "President Eisenhower met for six days with the heads of the three other governments in an effort to create a better atmosphere and a new impulse toward the solution of the problems that divide us." There was born— in the warmth of Molotov's newly found geniality and the Eisenhower smile—the temporarily famous "spirit of Geneva." There the Soviets agreed, among other things, that international security and the reunification of Germany must go together, and they promised to consider reunifying Germany by means of free elections. They further agreed to a follow-up meeting of the foreign ministers for the purpose of working out implementation of the general agreements proclaimed in the communiqués of July.

The meeting of the foreign ministers was held in November (1955), also at Geneva. The American Secretary of State summed it up tersely when he reported to the American people, "As I expect most of you know, this Geneva meeting did not reach any agreement." The Kremlin had considered reunifying Germany by means of free elections and had decided against it. In fact, the Kremlin made it clear that the only unified Germany which it would accept had to be a Germany under Communist control. The discussion on disarmament, the second item on the agenda, was, in Secretary Dulles' rather overly mild word, "inconclusive." No serious negotiation of the third item, the improvement and increase of East-West contacts, proved possible. It seemed as the year 1955 closed that the overall situation had been more accurately typified by the Soviet abrogation of its alliance treaties with France and Great Britain (May) and by the Warsaw Pact (May) than by the fanfare which attended the meeting at Geneva.

Soviet policy makers and diplomats continued to ride two horses with great skill and aplomb throughout 1956. Disarmament talks and talks about disarmament talks went on inconclusively. The United States had suggested at Geneva plans for a mutual air-borne inspection of military facilities and an exchange of detailed information. The Soviets sought to tie this to a general reduction of armaments and to an absolute prohibition against nuclear weapons. This was not acceptable to the United States, which continued to insist that mutual inspections and other safeguards must precede all disarmament. The United States also pressed its "atoms for peace" plan which called for a pooling of fissionable materials for peaceful uses under the control of an international agency.

The Soviets continued to exploit nationalist aspirations and anti-Western feelings in the Near, Middle, and Far East. This was partly a matter of rubbing salt in old wounds, partly a matter of profiting from Western difficulties and mistakes, and partly a matter of increasingly generous economic and technical aid to selected countries. Communist-bloc countries, by early 1956, had received Soviet aid to an estimated value of 5.25 billion dollars. Communist China had received the largest share (1.4 billion dollars). North Korea had been given 250 million; East Germany, almost 125 million; and Poland, about half a billion dollars in credits and goods. Yugoslavia, Afghanistan, and India received Soviet loans, credits, and other help to the value of almost 600 million dollars. This foreign-aid program was continued throughout 1956 and into 1957, and presumably was one of the causes of the financial difficulties suggested by the reduction in capital investment and the freezing of bonds. Whether that supposition is accurate or not, the Kremlin made generous commitments—100 million dollars worth of economic aid to Indonesia, military aid to Afghanistan, an offer of aid to Ceylon, and trade agreements with Egypt and Burma. There were also efforts to promote trade with the West, but successes were limited.

Table 11 shows that the rival coalitions continued into 1956, and that the Western coalition managed to survive an extremely grave crisis in the fall of that year. The locale of the crisis was the eastern Mediterranean, and its precipitating cause was the nationalization of the

Suez Canal by Egypt. Complex and prolonged negotiations having proved futile, the British and the French determined to use force to resist this move. They were joined by Israel, which won quick and complete military successes across its frontiers. The Franco-British effort did not go well. Moreover, they incurred opposition instead of receiving support from the United States, whereas Egypt was solidly and effectively backed by the Soviet Union. There are some who feel that only the Soviet threat of a missile attack on France and Britain saved Egypt. The French and the British, unable to continue alone, gave up without achieving any of their objectives. A UN police force occupied the troubled lands and the crisis passed. But in passing, it had demonstrated that the numerically larger Western coalitions were not as closely knit as the Soviet bloc (to which Egypt had, in effect, been added).

The so-called Suez Crisis, which really involved much more than that label suggests, coincided with the revolt in Hungary, which caused a shift in Soviet policies toward its satellites. There was apparently some indecision and a considerable reappraisal of the problem within the Presidium before a course of action was chosen. The new course seemed to permit certain deviations among the satellites but only within clearly defined limits. These limits included support of and obedience to the Soviet Union, the retention of a Communist dictatorship, the liquidation of capitalist enterprises, the establishment of a "socialist" economy, and the defense of these actions.

The alternation of hard and soft policy continued through 1957. The Soviets signed a trade pact with France; announced cuts in its defense budget; suggested an aerial-survey plan which would have opened portions of the satellites, the western Soviet lands, and some of Siberia to Western inspection in return for opening all of western Europe, Alaska, and the United States to Soviet inspection; and ratified the treaty creating an International Atomic Energy Agency. The Kremlin also put forward several proposals for disarmament and engaged in prolonged but unhappily futile discussions with the West on that subject. On the other side, the Soviets continued their testing of atomic and hydrogen weapons (as did Britain and the United States); threatened Norway, West Germany, and Turkey in an effort to persuade those nations to abandon NATO; and continued at home the steady drumfire of the "Hate America" campaign. The Soviets also asked the UN to hear charges of American aggression in the Near and Middle East. The request was rejected as was a Soviet complaint that the Korean truce was being violated by the dispatch of up-to-date weapons to forces still in South Korea. As the fall of 1957 passed, tensions and sore spots remained. If there was any lack of confidence, it was not to be found in the public

TABLE 11

The Rival Coalitions, 1956 *

North Atlantic Treaty Organization		Warsaw Pact
United States	Belgium	Union of Soviet Socialist Republics
United Kingdom	Luxembourg	Poland
Canada	Portugal	Czechoslovakia
France	Italy	East Germany
Norway	Turkey	Hungary
Iceland	Greece	Romania
Denmark		Bulgaria
The Netherlands		Albania
West German Federal Republic		

ANZUS

Australia
New Zealand
United States

Southeast Asia Treaty Organization

Philippines	New Zealand
Thailand	France
Pakistan	United Kingdom
Australia	United States

Middle East Treaty Organization

United Kingdom
Turkey
Iran
Iraq
Pakistan

Bi-Lateral Alliance Treaties

United States and:	U.S.S.R. and:
Japan	Outer Mongolia
South Korea (Republic of Korea)	Communist China
Taiwan (Formosa)	
Philippines	

* The Organization of American States is omitted from this table.

utterances of the rulers of the Soviet Union. "Whether you Western diplomats like it or not, history is on our side. [Said Khrushchev to a group of them in mid-1957] We will bury you."

This final chapter has stressed the twin themes of continuity and change. It has not sought to forecast the results of the changes, but has followed Lincoln's comment in his annual message of 1864: "The result not yet being known, conjecture in regard to it is not here indulged."

NOTES

NOTE TO CHAPTER I

1. Bielorussian is often translated as "White Russian." Though literally accurate, this may be misleading because since 1917 "White Russian" has had a political connotation, that is, anti-Bolshevik or anti-Red. I shall therefore use Bielorussian throughout the book in order to avoid confusion.

   The word *Ukraina,* which is anglicized as Ukraine, dates only from the twelfth century. It originally meant either "at the border" or "the southern border lands," probably the latter. Whichever it was, it was accurately descriptive. Some of the nineteenth- and twentieth-century residents of the area, affected like all the rest of the world by nationalism, grew to feel that their traditional label, "Little Russians," was derogatory and insisted that they be called Ukrainians. "Little Russia" (Malorussia) was, however, the official title of the region throughout the tsarist period.

NOTES TO CHAPTER II

1. Samuel H. Cross, *The Russian Primary Chronicle: Harvard Studies and Notes in Philology and Literature* (Cambridge, Mass.: Harvard Univ. Press, 1930), Vol. XII. The text, which is of the Laurentian version, is preceded by a summary of the findings of previous scholars.
2. *The Chronicle of Novgorod, 1016–1471,* tr. Robert Michell and Nevil Forbes (Camden Third Series; London: The Camden Society, 1914), Vol. XXV.
3. In this account of Russian beginnings I have largely followed Professor George Vernadsky, particularly his volumes entitled *Ancient Russia* and *Kievan Russia* (New Haven, Conn.: Yale Univ. Press, 1948). I have not accepted all of Professor Vernadsky's conclusions, however, and have introduced some modifications of his work.

NOTES TO CHAPTER V

1. *Oprichnina* was the word used in old Russia to describe those portions of lands which were set aside for the life use of widows of princes. It may be translated as "the region set apart" or, simply, as "the apart."
2. There is an excellent discussion of this, as well as a useful evaluation of Ivan, by Mr. Leo Yaresh in *Rewriting Russian History,* ed. Cyril E. Black (N.Y.: Praeger, 1956), chap. 8.

NOTE TO CHAPTER VII

1. The word *nemets* now means "German." Its root is the word *nemet,* "to grow dumb." *Nemetsi* were those who were dumb (*nemoi*), that is, unable to speak Russian; hence, aliens or foreigners.

NOTE TO CHAPTER VIII

1. Ostermann and Münnich were first condemned to death, but this sentence was later commuted to exile in Siberia. The Dolgorukis and Golitsins were brought back from their long exile. So was Bühren.

NOTES TO CHAPTER IX

1. Available in English as *Memoirs of Catherine the Great,* tr. Katherine Anthony (N.Y.: Knopf, 1927). An English translation of the Herzen edition of the memoirs was published in the United States in 1859.
2. An excellent English edition was published in 1931 by the English scholar W. F. Reddaway under the title *Documents of Catherine the Great* (N.Y.: Macmillan, 1931). Quotations from the *Instructions* and data on their authorship are from Mr. Reddaway's work.

NOTES TO CHAPTER XI

1. This part of the story may be quickly summarized. All the secret societies were investigated by the government; their leaders and some hundreds of followers or suspects were arrested. Five hundred and seventy-nine were "tried" by a special court which acquitted 290, gave light sentences to 134, and very stringent punishments to 121. Thirty-six of the 121 were sentenced to death and the remainder were sent to Siberia. Nicholas commuted the death sentences of 26, who then joined the Siberian exiles. Pestel and Muraviev-Apostol were among those executed. In addition, all the privates of the two regiments involved (the Moskovsky and the Chernigovsky) were also exiled, mostly to the Caucasus. Not all the guilty were punished, and not all who were punished were guilty.
2. Nicolai Gogol (1809–52), whose *Revisor* gave a biting description of the bureaucracy and whose *Dead Souls* was a searching condemnation of both bureaucracy and serfdom, had changed his mind and his theme during his later years. In his *Correspondence with Friends,* Gogol had lashed out against the peasants with vicious satire. It was this attack which Belinsky answered in his *Letter to Gogol,* from which the quotation is taken.

NOTES TO CHAPTER XII

1. As a result of a successful revolution in 1830 (the one which Nicholas wished to use Polish troops to suppress) the Kingdom of the Netherlands, established by the Vienna Settlement, had been dissolved and a Kingdom of Belgium created. Franco-British pressure forced the Dutch to accept the situation.
2. The Troppau Protocol (see Chapter X) declared that the Great Powers had the right to intervene in the domestic affairs of states in which revolutions created situations which the Troppau signatories regarded as being against the general interest.

NOTES TO CHAPTER XIII

1. *Mir* also means "peace," "world," and "universe." There is no general agreement over the technical differences, if any, between the meaning of the word *mir* and the word *obshchina,* which also means "community" or "commune." Some have insisted that the two were fundamentally different: *mir* meaning a sort of mythical, corporate personality; and *obshchina* meaning the physical community. *Obshchina* would thus be the manifestation of the *mir.* Others have said that the two were essentially the same, and have used the words interchangeably. Recent Soviet dictionaries define *mir* as "village community (*obshchina*)."

2. For the empire as a whole, the proportion of serfs to the all-peasant population and to the total population was lower.

3. Interior, Public Works, State Property (literally, Imperial Domains), Finance, Justice, Public Instruction, War, Navy, Foreign Affairs, and Imperial Court.

4. Where state or crown serfs were involved, the subdivisions were circles, districts, associated villages, villages.

NOTES TO CHAPTER XIV

1. *Zemstvo* (plural, *zemstva*) is a word derived from *zemlya,* which means land. *Zemstvo* has often been translated as "land" and the zemstva assemblies have often been referred to as "land assemblies." This phrase does not carry a very clear meaning. Sir Donald Wallace, in his justly famous book, *Russia,* renders it as "land-dom" on the analogy of princedom, dukedom, and so on. This is more meaningful to Europeans than to Americans. I shall use the word itself without any further attempt to explain its translation or derivation.

2. Statistics of different authorities do not agree. Miliukov states the percentage divisions as: *dvorianstvo* 48 per cent, peasants 40 per cent, and townsmen 12 per cent. Professor Vinogradoff gave them as, respectively, 43 per cent, 38 per cent, and 18 per cent. Wallace said that 42 per cent of the members were nobles; 38 per cent, peasants. The French historian Leroy-Beaulieu assigned 46 per cent to the nobles and 44 per cent to the peasants. I have used Miliukov's figures.

3. *Narodniki* (singular, *narodnik*) was the name given those who followed Herzen's advice, "Go to the people" (*V narod*). In an effort to make the character of this movement clearer to Westerners, it has often been referred to a "Populism" and its members have been termed "Populists." This unfortunately is likely to be more confusing than clarifying to Americans who recall, however vaguely, the Populist movement in American history. Members of the Russian movement went to the villages in order simultaneously to help, educate, and indoctrinate the peasants. The peak of the movement was reached in 1874.

NOTE TO CHAPTER XV

1. There have been numerous varieties of Pan-Slavism—for example, Russian Pan-Slavism, Polish Pan-Slavism, Serbian Pan-Slavism—all of them mutually antipathetic. We are here concerned only with the Russian variety.

NOTES TO CHAPTER XVI

1. Marx's father was a brother, son, grandson, great-grandson, and so on, of the rabbis of Trier. He had left the faith of his fathers and embraced Christianity in 1816, two years before Karl's birth. Karl was baptized into Christianity in 1824.

2. It hardly seems necessary to point out that these dire predictions have not been fulfilled in capitalist countries. The average real earnings of nonfarm workers in the United States, for example, approximately doubled between 1880–94 and 1945–46. Attention may be called to the fact that Marx-Engels did not say that their prediction would be fulfilled some places but not in others. They stated the prediction as a universal and immutable law. This is also true of many other of their doctrines. Any claim to universality, immutability, or infallibility is invalidated by an exception. Marx-Engels did not admit of exceptions.

3. Bertram Wolfe, *Three Who Made a Revolution* (N.Y.: Dial Press, 1948), p. 63. I am much indebted to Dr. Wolfe for materials on the early history of Marxism in Russia.

NOTES TO CHAPTER XVII

1. Goremykin had previously served in the Department of Justice (which was under the Ministry of the Interior) and as Assistant Minister of the Interior from 1891 to 1895. He was afterwards twice chairman of the Council of Ministers (1906 and 1914–16). He was a bureaucratic timeserver.

2. Professor Lyashchenko, who has been quoted previously in these pages, was born, trained, and reached his academic maturity under the tsars. Although a known Marxist, he was allowed to hold a favored and responsible post in the University of Tomsk, and his published studies were recognized as scholarly works. He survived changes in the Party leadership and in the Party line, and his work remained acceptable to the Party bosses at least down to July, 1957. While rejecting his Marxist-Leninist-Stalinist approach and many of his conclusions, I have borrowed extensively from his data for three reasons: He is the most competent scholar currently working in this field to have full access to Soviet-held sources. His information is therefore more complete than that of earlier writers, such as Mavor. Second, since he was and is a sworn critic of the old regime, he cannot be suspected of depicting it too favorably. Third, I consider such of his data as I have used to be sound. All my references to his work and all quotations from it refer

to the two-volume Russian edition entitled (in translation) *History of the National Economy, USSR,* which was published in 1947–48.

3. The Russo-Chinese Bank was merged with the Northern Bank in 1910 to form the Russo-Asiatic Bank. Of the latter's capital, 72 per cent was non-Russian; 60 per cent of it was French.

4. I shall use this familiar pseudonym from now on, although Lenin did not adopt it until 1901.

5. Though the zemstva were at least quasi-official bodies, the zemstvamen did not consider themselves government officials. They were most jealous of their amateur standing and referred to the zemstva as "public bodies" or as "public service groups," never as government agencies.

6. It is not possible here to more than hint at the extremely interesting and often utterly fantastic relationships of the police and the revolutionaries. Two cases will give some notion of the situation. Yevno Azev, who was the head of the Fighting Organization of the Essars was to some degree responsible for the murders of Sipyagin, the Grand Duke Sergius, Plehve, and others. At the same time, he was also in the pay of the police and was betraying his revolutionary comrades to the tsar's agents. Roman Malinovsky was treasurer and contributing editor of *Pravda* when that newspaper was established in 1912. Later he was chosen by the Bolsheviks to head their small group of members of the Fourth Duma. He had been a police stool pigeon for years, perhaps from 1902, before the police put him on their regular payroll as an informer and *agent provocateur.* He was so employed when Lenin gave him his positions of importance.

NOTES TO CHAPTER XVIII

1. *Out of My Past: The Memoirs of Count Kokovtsov,* ed. H. H. Fisher (Stanford, Calif.: Stanford Univ. Press, 1935), pp. 35 ff.

2. Impartial sources generally agree: (1) that some Social Democrats (Mensheviks and Bolsheviks) took part in the strikes and agitations which preceded Bloody Sunday; (2) that some of them were among the marchers; but (3) that they had neither organized nor initiated the movement or the demonstration. Bolshevik histories, with their customary maltreatment of the truth, claim the whole thing as their own.

3. It is a tribute to the leadership of professional men in forming unions that labor unions in the U.S.S.R. are still called "professional unions."

4. His actual title was President of the Council of Ministers. This body and this office had been created, at Witte's insistence, by the October Manifesto. The office gave its holder responsibility and authority over his ministerial colleagues. The council replaced the Committee of Ministers, which had been created in 1802 by Alexander I, and superseded the Council of Ministers, which Alexander II had created in 1861. The committee, which had only been an advisory body, was formally abolished in 1906.

5. The Soviet secret police are numbered in millions. The *okhrana* never had more than a thousand secret agents in all Russia.

6. Sir Bernard Pares, *The Fall of the Russian Monarchy* (N.Y.: Knopf,

1939), p. 279. This book is indispensable for a detailed study of the period from 1894 to 1917. I have borrowed freely from it, and from my many hours of conversation with Sir Bernard, for the three chapters which I devote to this period.

NOTES TO CHAPTER XIX

1. I am here following a study of this incident made in 1950 by Dr. Kenneth I. Dailey. Dr. Dailey's account was based upon all available Russian, Austrian, German, and British primary sources. Dr. Dailey's services to me while serving as my assistant and associate are too many and too varied to enumerate here. He has helped me to read proof, and to check references, and has relieved me of some of the burdens of teaching and administration. I have also profited from his criticisms and suggestions.

2. Dr. Harold Williams—scholar, linguist of phenomenal versatility—served as the Russian correspondent of the *Manchester Guardian*. Later he became the foreign editor of the London *Times*. The next several pages are paraphrased or quoted from his work *Russia of the Russians* (N.Y.: Scribner, 1915).

NOTES TO CHAPTER XX

1. The name of Lenin's group was officially changed to "Communist Party" in 1918. This change, it will be recalled, was one of the items demanded by Lenin in his April Theses.

2. Oliver H. Radkey, *The Election to the Russian Constituent Assembly of 1917* (Cambridge, Mass.: Harvard Univ. Press, 1950), p. 14. This excellent monograph makes it possible to gauge public opinion and the political sympathies of the Russian people during this crucial period. Professor Radkey is scrupulous in pointing out that there are still gaps in our knowledge and that the image is in a gray monochrome rather than in contrasting colors. But, thanks to his painstaking work, the shapes are reasonably clear.

NOTES TO CHAPTER XXI

1. Sir Bernard Pares, *A Wandering Student* (Syracuse, N.Y.: Syracuse Univ. Press, 1948), pp. 247–56.

2. W. E. D. Allen, *The Ukraine: A History* (Cambridge, Eng.: Univ. Press, 1941), p. 252.

3. Changing terminology is always confusing. Lenin's group started out as the Bolshevik wing or faction of the Russian Social Democratic Party. It broke away and changed its name—but most people continued to refer to it as the Bolshevik Party. The name was formally changed in 1918 to the Russian Communist Party (Bolshevik). This was altered in 1925 to the Communist Party of the Soviet Union (Bolshevik). The word "Bolshevik" is still used in the U.S.S.R. as a synonym for "all-out" or "100 per cent" as "a true Bolshevik effort," but since 1956, Bolshevik has been dropped from the Party's title.

As is probably clear from the context, I have systematically used "Communist" and "Party" (with the initial letters capitalized) in a precise and specific meaning. Communist refers only to the followers of Lenin, Stalin, and their successors; or to their theories, policies, words, actions, or organizations. It is not used in these pages to designate a general philosophical system or anything other than as defined above. "Party" refers only to the Communist Party.

"Soviet," which once meant simply "council," has acquired special meanings. It is the title of legislative bodies in the U.S.S.R. at all levels from villages (village soviets) to the federal union (the Supreme Soviet of the U.S.S.R.). The word also appears in the official title of the federal union (Union of Soviet Socialist Republics), in its abbreviated title (Soviet Union), and also in the titles of members of that union (Russian Socialist Federated Soviet Republic). "Soviet" is commonly used to designate the government, the social and economic systems, the actions, and so on of the U.S.S.R.

Precisionists object to the use of the words "Russia," "Russians," and "Soviet Russia" to describe the U.S.S.R. and its citizens. These objections are technically sound because only the Russian Socialist Federated Soviet Republic and its people are properly spoken of as "Russia" and "Russians." But the R.S.F.S.R. has well over a half of the total population and three-fourths of the lands of the U.S.S.R., which it dominates. The capital of the one is also the capital of the other. Therefore, unless there is a reason to make a clear distinction, the terms Russia, Russian, Soviet, Soviet Union, and so on, have been used in this book as if they were synonymous.

4.   These quotations, all dealing with events in 1918, are a random sample from Soviet sources, taken from James Bunyan, *Intervention, Civil War, and Communism in Russia: April–December, 1918* (Baltimore, Md.: Johns Hopkins Press, 1936), chap. 4. They might be duplicated by hundreds of others.

5.   Quoted in Bunyan, *Intervention,* p. 227.

NOTES TO CHAPTER XXII

1.   Resolution of the First All-Russian Congress of Councils of National Economy (June 3, 1918). This excerpt is quoted from the translation of the document, which was published in James Bunyan, *Intervention, Civil War, and Communism in Russia: April–December, 1918* (Baltimore, Md.: Johns Hopkins Press, 1936), pp. 396–97.

2.   Sir John Maynard, *Russia in Flux,* ed. S. H. Guest (N.Y.: Macmillan, 1948), p. 198.

3.   Bunyan, *Intervention,* pp. 396–97.

4.   A law ordering the end of private trade was issued in November, 1918.

5.   This was also known as the "Regenerated," "Renovated," and "Synodal" Church. One of the best accounts of it is to be found in Paul B. Anderson, *People, Church, and State in Modern Russia* (N.Y.: Macmillan, 1944), pp. 76–88, 97–98. The quotation is from pp. 81–82.

6.   The State Planning Commission was set up in February, 1921. It has usually been known by the abbreviation GOSPLAN.

NOTES TO CHAPTER XXIII

1. The Party claimed 313,000 members in 1919; between 700,000 and 800,000 in 1921. Then came the first general Party purge which reduced the membership to less than 500,000. This was followed by a special membership drive, the "Lenin Enrollment," which brought the total back to 735,000 in 1924. Another decrease was followed by another recruitment so that the Party, by the end of 1927, had a total of 1,125,000 members and candidates (probationary members). Members and candidates totaled almost 2,000,000 in 1930. The figure stood at 2,800,000 in 1934 before the "Great Purges." These—the most intensive, violent, and long-continued purgings so far made—so reduced the number of Communists that, despite a large postpurge recruitment, the total in 1939 was under 2,500,000. The following table shows the combined totals of members and candidates for selected years since 1939. It will be noted that there were tremendous increases throughout the 1940's, but that the totals remained relatively stable from 1950 to 1957.

1940	3,400,000
1941	3,900,000
1942	4,600,000
1944	5,000,000
1945	5,800,000
1946	6,000,000
1947	6,300,000
1950	7,000,000
1952	6,900,000
1957	7,200,000

2. The Twentieth Party Congress was convoked in 1956.
3. Harry Schwartz, *Russia's Soviet Economy* (2d ed.; N.Y.: Prentice-Hall, 1954), p. 122.
4. Cited in Vladimir Gsovski, *Soviet Civil Law* (Ann Arbor, Mich.: Univ. of Michigan Press, 1949), I, 689–90. I am indebted to Dr. Gsovski not only for his translations of the laws on agriculture and the collective farms, but also for his summaries and commentaries (Vol. I, chaps. 19–21; Vol. II, chaps. 30–35). I have drawn freely but not exclusively from his material. He is not, of course, in any way responsible for the manner or content of the story as told here.

NOTES TO CHAPTER XXIV

1. These statistics are from a Soviet source *Narodnoye Khozyaistvo S.S.S.R.* ("People's Economy of the U.S.S.R.") published by the Central Statistical Administration of the Council of Ministers of the U.S.S.R. (Moscow, 1956). I have used both the translation made by the External Research Staff of the Office of Intelligence Research, U.S. Department of State; and the annotated version published by the National Industrial Conference Board Incorporated: *Statistical Handbook*

of the U.S.S.R. with Introduction, Additional Tables and Annotations, ed. Harry Schwartz (Studies in Business Economics, No. 53; N.Y.: The Conference Board, 1957). This is the first statistical handbook published by the Soviets in seventeen years. It opens some peepholes in the Iron Curtain, but it does not raise that curtain. Dr. Schwartz's annotations and supplementary data are particularly useful.

2. Vladimir Gsovski, *Soviet Civil Law* (Ann Arbor, Mich.: Univ. of Michigan Press, 1949), I, 794.

3. The first Supreme Soviet of the U.S.S.R. was elected in December, 1937, and should have ended its term in 1941. It was held, however, that the war made it impossible to hold elections, so the second Supreme Soviet was not elected until 1946. It served its stated term of four years. The third Supreme Soviet was elected in 1950; the fourth, in 1954.

4. An even more dramatic revelation of the real character of the Supreme Soviet was made at the first meeting of that body after Stalin's death. An especially summoned session held on the afternoon of March 15, 1953, lasted just sixty-seven minutes. Within that brief time, "the highest organ of state power" approved the most drastic and sweeping changes to be made for many years in the organization and leadership of the government. It may also be noted that the Supreme Soviet was not even in session in July, 1957, when Molotov, Malenkov, Kaganovich, and others were removed not only from their Party jobs but from their government positions as well.

5. An amendment in 1946 changed this title to "Council of Ministers." It also changed "commissariats" to "ministries" and "commissars" to "ministers." Changes in administrative structure and in governmental forms, as well as in nomenclature, have been frequent. No attempt will be made in this book to recount them all.

NOTES TO CHAPTER XXV

1. Quoted from the petition filed by the U.S. Department of Justice with the Subversive Activities Control Board on November 22, 1950. The Communist Party in the United States was established in 1919. It operated under various names until May, 1944, when it changed its name to "The Communist Political Association." This body, in response to directives from Moscow via Paris, reconstituted the political party in June, 1945, under the title of "The Communist Party of the United States of America."

The American Communist Party accepted the 1921 statute of the Comintern and agreed to abide by the orders and directives of the Comintern and its executive committee. The American Communist Party also accepted and agreed to abide by the 1928 Constitution and Rules of the Comintern. There is abundant evidence to support the attorney-general's charge that the American Communist Party "continues to adhere" to that program in general, and that "it has never knowingly deviated from the views and policies of the Government and Communist party of the Soviet Union. . . ."

2. Max Beloff, *The Foreign Policy of Soviet Russia, 1929–1941* (London: Oxford Univ. Press, 1947 and 1949), I, 89–93, *passim.*
3. William H. Chamberlin, *The Russian Enigma* (N.Y.: Scribner, 1943), pp. 186–87.

NOTES TO CHAPTER XXVI

1. *Nazi-Soviet Relations, 1939–1941: Documents from the Archives of the German Foreign Office,* ed. R. J. Sontag and J. S. Beddie (Wash., D.C.: Department of State, 1948), p. 85.
2. *Ibid.,* p. 260. The italics are in the original. I have used these documents freely but not exclusively in reconstructing the story of Soviet-German relations during this period.
3. Zhukov's military service began in the tsar's army in 1915. He joined the Red Army in 1918 and became a member of the Communist Party in 1919. He became internationally known as the commander-in-chief of the Soviet forces which entered Berlin in 1945. After the war Zhukov was forced into the background by Stalin, but re-emerged most prominently after Stalin's death. Zhukov was elected to candidate membership in the Party Presidium in February, 1956, and to full membership in June, 1957. This attracted much attention abroad because Zhukov was the first professional soldier to attain so high a place in Party ranks. His tenure was short. Zhukov was dismissed from the Presidium and from the Party's Central Committee in October, 1957. He was also removed as Minister of Defense.

NOTES TO CHAPTER XXVII

1. The NKVD (People's Commissariat of Internal Affairs) was divided into the NKVD and the NKGB (People's Commissariat of State Security) in 1943. These became ministries (MVD and MGB) in 1946, MGB having control of the secret police. Three years later, the border guards and internal security troops were transferred from the MVD to the MGB. The two ministries were merged into a new MVD in March, 1953.
2. During the upheavals in the top Party leadership in mid-1957, Khrushchev charged Malenkov with having joined Beria in persecuting Voznesensky, Kuznetsov, Kosygin, and other Zhdanov protégés in the Leningrad Party organization. Previously, in 1954, the Minister of State Security V. S. Abukumov was executed on charges of having fabricated this so-called "Leningrad case."
3. The list of "state secrets" included all data relating to the armed forces, the reserves, transportation, communication, and state administration; equipment for all war industries and suppliers of war industries; imports, exports, current account balances, currency funds; plant capacities, production figures, and production plans.
4. Professor Merle Fainsod observed in his excellent study *How Russia Is Ruled* (Cambridge, Mass.: Harvard Univ. Press, 1953), p. 115, that: "Soviet patriotism in its current manifestation represents a many-sided effort to mobilize support for the regime and to assert state con-

trol over every phase of Soviet life. It relies in part on pure love of country, with particular accent upon the leading position of the Great Russian people in the Soviet family of nations. . . . Soviet patriotism thus operates as an ideological tool to weld the people to the regime.''

5. The general subject of Soviet thought control is excellently treated in detail in George Counts and Nucia Lodge, *The Country of the Blind* (N.Y.: Houghton Mifflin, 1949).

6. The average monthly earnings of Soviet workers from 1953 through 1955 were on the order of 700–750 rubles. A minimum-wage decree of 1956 which raised the minimums to 275–350 rubles per month indicated that maybe as many as eight million workers had been receiving less than 300 rubles per month. At the other extreme were a few favored persons who were paid as much as 10,000 rubles per month. Real wages fell very sharply from 1940 to 1945 and then recovered somewhat more slowly during the next decade. It is a moot point whether real wages in 1955 were as high as they had been in 1928 when the five-year plans began. On the highly technical and controversial subject of the use of Soviet statistics see, for example, "Reliability and Usability of Soviet Statistics: A Symposium," *American Statistician,* reprinted from the April–May and June–July 1953 issues (Washington, D.C.: American Statistical Association, 1953).

7. Table 6 was derived from an article by Mr. Will Lissner, published in the *New York Times* on July 4, 1950. Table 7 was derived from an article by Dr. Harry Schwartz, published in the *New York Times* on May 12, 1951. Scattered data for 1952 and 1953 showed no significant relative changes.

8. For this account of the Nineteenth Party Congress I originally used *Current Soviet Politics: The Documentary Record of the Nineteenth Party Congress and the Reorganization After Stalin's Death,* ed. Leo Gruliow (N.Y.: Praeger, 1953). Mr. Gruliow's editorial comments have, on the whole, proved sound and perspicacious. I have, however, supplemented his 1953 book with a variety of information published since that date in the newspaper and periodical press and in books. Most of my additional sources are listed in the final section of the Suggested Readings.

NOTES TO CHAPTER XXVIII

1. The percentages of those who believed the Soviets would co-operate in making a peaceful world ran from a low of 36 (October, 1943), to a high of 55 (March, 1945). Forty-three per cent in early 1947 thought Russia would co-operate. The percentages of those who believed that the Soviets would not co-operate ranged from 27 to 40 between 1942 and 1945 and stood at the latter figure at the beginning of 1947. See W. B. Walsh, "American Attitudes toward Russia," *Antioch Review,* Summer, 1947, p. 186; and W. B. Walsh, "What the American People Think of Russia," *Public Opinion Quarterly,* VIII (Winter, 1945): 513–23.

2. "The 20th CPSU Congress and the Doctrine of the 'Inevitability of War,'" *Intelligence Report No. 7284* (Unclassified), Division of

Functional Intelligence, Office of Intelligence Research, Department of State, June 22, 1956.

3. Philip E. Mosely, "Soviet-American Relations since the War," *Annals of the American Academy of Political and Social Science,* 263 (May, 1949): 208. Because some have argued that the termination of lend-lease by the United States in August, 1945, provoked the Soviets to retaliation and to a new policy, it should be specifically noted that the Potsdam meeting preceded the ending of lend-lease. Though the manner of termination was brusque, the arrangement for termination was very favorable to the U.S.S.R.

4. Professor Frederick L. Schuman appears to suggest that these Soviet actions were functions of the fears aroused in Moscow by NATO. See Frederick L. Schuman, *Russia Since 1917* (N.Y.: Knopf, 1957), p. 375. Professor Schuman's analyses generally run counter to mine. For an excellent, careful and balanced study of the operations of international communism (including the satellites and Yugoslavia) see Hugh Seton-Watson, *From Lenin to Malenkov* (N.Y.: Praeger, 1953).

5. Some of the details of these agreements are taken from Schuman, op. cit., pp. 388, 389. He is not, however, responsible for the supposition that there may have been additional agreements. Professor Schuman says that the North Korean troops had been armed and trained by the Soviets and adds that "Soviet policy-makers . . . presumably controlled, or believed they controlled, decision-making in Pyongyang [capital of North Korea] as in the capitals of the other Soviet satellites . . . . such 'control' was sometimes fictitious." He also intimates that the Soviet boycott of the Security Council shows that the Kremlin did not directly or indirectly touch off the North Korean attack (*ibid.,* p. 390). I do not find his analysis convincing.

NOTES TO CHAPTER XXIX

1. Accounts of the congress and related events are available in several sources. I have used mainly the following: *Current Soviet Policies: Vol. II, A Documentary Record, 1953–1956, from the Purge of Beria through the Twentieth Communist Party Congress and the Reevaluation of Stalin,* ed. Leo Gruliow (N.Y.: Praeger, 1956); *The Anti-Stalin Campaign and International Communism,* ed. The Russian Institute, Columbia University (N.Y.: Columbia Univ. Press, 1956); *The Crimes of the Stalin Era: Special Report to the 20th Congress of the Communist Party of the Soviet Union by Nikita S. Khrushchev,* annotated by Boris I. Nicolaevsky (N.Y.: the *New Leader,* 1956); *Speech of Party Secretary N. S. Khrushchev . . . "Cult of the Individual" . . . February 25, 1956;* and *Unpublished Documents Distributed among the Delegates to the XXth CPSU Congress* (Wash., D.C.: Department of State, June 4 and 30, 1956).

2. *Statistical Handbook of the U.S.S.R. with Introduction, Additional Tables and Annotations,* ed. Harry Schwartz (Studies in Business Economics, No. 53; N.Y.: The Conference Board, 1957), pp. 12, 91–93. The fullest study so far made of this subject is Nicholas DeWitt,

Soviet Professional Manpower, Its Education, Training and Supply (Wash., D.C.: National Science Foundation, 1955).

3. A contrary interpretation of this affair may be conveniently found in Frederick L. Schuman, *Russia Since 1917* (N.Y.: Knopf, 1957), pp. 436–38.

SUGGESTED READINGS

 FOREWORD

The first purpose of this section is to suggest to the reader where he may find additional information. The second function is to make acknowledgments to those from whom I have learned and borrowed. The third purpose is to provide specialists with a means of checking my work and, possibly, with some assistance in furthering their own studies. These three purposes are, unhappily, not entirely compatible so that it has been necessary to make compromises among them. It has also been necessary to compromise between practical considerations of space and my wish to acknowledge all my debts.

One method of compromise was to divide the notes into two sections. "Section I. General" is intended primarily as a guide to further readings, but it also lists some of my major sources and so acknowledges some of my obligations. "Section II. By Chapters" is intended primarily to show my major sources, but it also serves as a readers' guide. A second compromise applies to both sections. It seemed a fair assumption, on the one hand, that an extensive listing of rare or hard-to-find items and of materials in unfamiliar languages would be of little service to the general reader for whom this book is primarily intended. On the other hand, it is precisely these items which are often of the greatest interest to specialists. The problem was met by listing all major sources, without regard to their availability or language, and omitting most collateral and minor sources. This will, of course, satisfy neither the reader who is looking only for readily usable suggestions nor the searcher for sources, who will find that some are not cited at all.

My choices have been governed by two considerations which are not always consistent: to include all items which I found most useful as well as those which experience indicated might be of the greatest value to the most readers. Inclusion of a work does not imply endorsement or agreement, nor does exclusion imply the reverse. Finally, to conserve space, I have not usually listed here any titles which appear in the footnotes.

 SECTION I. GENERAL

BIBLIOGRAPHIES AND OTHER GUIDES

An extremely useful listing of recent and current publications has been published annually since 1941 in the *Russian Review* (N.Y. and Hanover, N.H.). The exact title has varied slightly over the years, but most recently it has been called "Bibliography: Books, Pamphlets, and Articles on Russia Published in 19 . ." There used to be a comparable listing of books published in Great Britain. The compiler was Mr. Philip Grierson and the listings were published in the *Slavonic and East European Review* (London: School of Slavonic Studies, Univ. of London, 1922–41 and 1945– . .) from 1945 through 1950. This was a continuation of Mr. Grierson's *Books on Soviet Russia, 1917– 1942* (London: Methuen, 1943). W. B. Walsh, *Russia under Tsars and Commissars: A Reader's Guide* (Syracuse, N.Y.: Syracuse Univ. Press, 1946) listed and annotated some 200 titles of interest to the general reader.

A compilation with greater scope than its title indicates is J. T. Dorosh (comp.), *Guide to Soviet Bibliographies* (Wash., D.C.: Library of Congress, 1950); it covers more than the Soviet period and other than Soviet materials. This is also true of M. N. Tikhomirov, *Istochniovednie Istorii SSSR* ("Sources for the History of the U.S.S.R.") (2 vols.; Moscow, 1944). More or less extensive bibliographies will be found in many of the books listed below. S. R. Tompkins, *Russia Through the Ages* (N.Y.: Prentice-Hall, 1940) is particularly good for the old regime; F. L. Schuman, *Russia since 1917* (N.Y.: Knopf, 1957) for recent years.

C. F. Morley, *Guide to Research in Russian History* (Syracuse, N.Y.: Syracuse Univ. Press, 1951) is of particular value to students in the United States because it surveys the major collections on Russian history in American libraries. Among specialized bibliographies, the following are listed partly for their own merit and partly as illustrations: *American Correspondents and Journalists in Moscow, 1917– 1952; Bibliography of Their Books on the U.S.S.R.* (Wash., D.C.: Dept. of State, Division of Library and Reference Sources, 1953); *Bibliography of Soviet Geography* (2 parts; Wash., D.C.: Govt. Printing Office, 1951); H. Schwartz, *Soviet Economy: Selected Bibliography of Materials in English* (Syracuse, N.Y.: Syracuse Univ. Press, 1949); and *Serial Publications of the Soviet Union* (Wash., D.C.: Govt. Printing Office, 1951).

A good guide to the histories and historians of Russia is Pierre Kovalevsky, *Manuel d'histoire Russe: Étude critique des sources* (Paris, 1948). More recent and more readily obtainable is A. G. Mazour, *Modern Russian Historiography* (rev. ed.; Princeton, N.J.: Van Nostrand, 1958). Three excellent bibliographical articles have been published in the professional journals; their coverage is indicated by their titles and dates: M. M. Karpovich, "The Russian Revolution of 1917," *Journal of Modern History,* II (1930): 258–80; Leo Loewenson, "Some Recent Books on Russian History," *History* (London) XXVIII, no. 108, new series (1943): 207–15; and R. D. Warth, "The Russian 'Enigma': Some Recent Studies by Western Writers," *Journal of Modern History,* XXII (1950): 346–55.

ATLASES AND GEOGRAPHIES

The reader will find that use of an historical atlas will increase his understanding of the story of Russia. Unfortunately, "standard" historical atlases give little space to Russian history, and special atlases on the U.S.S.R. emphasize the Soviet period. The most recent and ambitious of such volumes is *The USSR and Eastern Europe, Oxford Regional Economic Atlas,* prepared by the Economist Intelligence Unit and the Cartographic Dept. of the Clarendon Press (London: Oxford Univ. Press, 1956). More compact, less ambitious and much less expensive, but now out of print is George Goodall (ed.), *Soviet Russia in Maps* (Chicago: Denoyer Geppert, 1942). Its maps were better than its comments, which were not always accurate. An inexpensive, Soviet-published *Atlas po Istorii SSSR* ("Atlas for the History of the U.S.S.R.") (3 parts; Moscow, 1949–52) has been readily available in this country. Of course it requires some knowledge of the Russian language. It also follows the official Party line in both maps and commentaries.

Those who wish to learn more about the physical and economic geography of Russia and the U.S.S.R. will find a growing number of works on these subjects. The most comprehensive is Theodore Shabad, *Geography of the U.S.S.R.* (N.Y.: Columbia Univ. Press, 1951). More popularly written are two books by Professor George B. Cressey: *Basis of Soviet Strength* (rev. ed.; N.Y.: McGraw-Hill, 1951); and *How Strong is Russia? A Geographic Appraisal* (Syracuse, N.Y.: Syracuse Univ. Press, 1954). J. S. Gregory and D. W. Shave, *The USSR: Geographical Survey* (N.Y.: Wiley, 1946) pays special attention to the geographical backgrounds of Russian history.

Several studies by Soviet geographers have been translated into English. They are, of course, limited to the officially approved ideology and interpretations, but are useful nonetheless. Among them are: S. S. Balzak, V. F. Vasyutin, and Ya. G. Feigen, *Economic Geography of the USSR,* tr. R. M. Kankin and O. A. Titelbaum (N.Y.: Macmillan, 1949); L. S. Berg, *Natural Regions of the USSR,* tr. O. A. Titelbaum (N.Y.: Macmillan, 1949); Nicholas Mikhailov, *The Russian Story* (N.Y.: Sheridan House, 1945); and N. T. Mirov, *Geography of Russia* (N.Y.: Wiley, 1951). The Mikhailov book is a combination of history and geography and contains a brilliant sketch of the general geography of the U.S.S.R.

ENCYCLOPEDIAS

Those who read the Russian language can find biographical sketches and other information in several Russian/Soviet encyclopedias. Those published during the old regime are generally more scholarly, but have obvious chronological limitations. The Soviet volumes are subject to extensive revisions to keep them in line with changes in the approved interpretations. Beria's downfall and "de-Stalinization"—to mention only two recent examples—were followed by drastic changes. A comparison of the different editions of Soviet encyclopedias and other volumes (such as the *History of the Communist Party of the Soviet Union*) is frequently both instructive and amusing in a macabre sort of way.

The outstanding encyclopedia of the old regime was the Brockhaus-

Efron series, *Entsiklopedicheskii Slovar* (86 vols.; St. Petersburg, 1890–1907). The *Bolshaia Entsiklopediia* ("Great Encyclopedia"), ed. S. N. Iuzhakov (22 vols.; St. Petersburg, 1902–9) is also worth consulting. The *Bolshaia Sovetskaia Entsiklopediia, SSSR* ("Great Soviet Encyclopedia, U.S.S.R.") (Moscow, 1947) has been made available through the *A.C.L.S. Reprints: Russian Series No. 18* (Baltimore, Md., 1949). This encyclopedia has gone through several editions, each with changes appropriate to shifts in the Party's power structure and in the Party line. The Soviets began in 1929 to publish *Sibirskaia Sovetskaia Entsiklopediia* ("Soviet Siberian Encyclopedia"), but only three volumes appeared.

Of considerable value to specialists because they provide summary accounts of the official interpretations of many points are: A. Ia. Vishinsky (ed.), *Diplomaticheskii Slovar* ("Diplomatic Dictionary") (2 vols.; Moscow, 1948 and 1950); and G. Aleksandrov (ed.), *Politicheskii Slovar* ("Political Dictionary") (Moscow, 1950).

PICTURES AND PEOPLE

The best brief account of the origins of the Soviet peoples is the scholarly and reliable *Peoples of the Soviet Union* by A. Hrdlicka (Wash., D.C.: Smithsonian, 1942). Mr. Corliss Lamont used the same title for his book, which was published by Harcourt, Brace of New York in 1946; and Miss Anna L. Strong had previously published under a confusingly similar title, *Peoples of the USSR* (N.Y.: Macmillan, 1944). The books by Lamont and Strong are enthusiastically pro-Soviet. So is George Loukomski, *Face of Russia* (London: Hutchinson, 1944) with its many pictures of minority peoples.

Three rather elaborate "picture books" were published during the years of the wartime "co-operation." The most unusual illustrations are found in Edward Crankshaw, *Russia and Britain* (N.Y.: Hastings House, n.d.). The others are: A. Howard and E. Newman, *Pictorial History of Russia from Rurik to Stalin* (London: Hutchinson, n.d.); and J. S. Martin (ed.), *Picture History of Russia* (N.Y.: Crown, 1945). Their pictures are, in general, far superior to their "history." Since the war, there have been two like efforts: Boris Shub and B. Quint, *Since Stalin, a Photographic History of Our Time* (N.Y.: Swen Publishing, 1951); and Henri Cartier-Bresson, *People of Moscow* (N.Y.: Simon and Schuster, 1954). The former is the more ambitious; the latter, the more artistic.

PAPERS AND STUDIES

To meet the growing needs of students and scholars, several groups have begun to publish collected monographic and scholarly articles in the humanities and in the social studies. Among such publications are the following: *Canadian Slavonic Papers*, Vol. I (Toronto, Ont.: Univ. of Toronto Press, 1956); Michael Ginsburg and J. T. Shaw (eds.), *Indiana Slavic Studies*, Vol. I (Bloomington, Ind.: Indiana Univ., 1956); Serge Konovalov (ed.), *Oxford Slavonic Papers*, Vols. I–V (N.Y.: Oxford Univ. Press, 1951–54); *Slavic and East European*

Studies, Vol. I (Montreal, Que.: Dept. of Slavic Studies, Univ. of Montreal, 1956); and J. Miller and R. A. J. Schlesinger (eds.), *Soviet Studies . . . Univ. of Glasgow* (Oxford, Eng.: Blackwell, 1949– . .). Various viewpoints are represented by these publications, often within a single issue; and the articles are of varying quality and usefulness.

GENERAL HISTORIES

The books listed in this subsection deal with relatively long periods of history. Some are general in the sense that they touch many aspects of Russian development. Others concentrate on a special topic or problem, but carry their discussion over several centuries. Works that are more restricted, either chronologically or topically, are listed under the appropriate chapters in Section II.

A bright and salty book with no major inaccuracies is Nicholas Brian-Chaninov, *History of Russia,* tr. C. J. Hogarth (N.Y.: Dutton, 1930). R. D. Charques, *Short History of Russia* (N.Y.: Dutton, 1956) is a very brief introductory survey. It is in marked contrast to the detailed, scholarly, and full treatment of M. T. Florinsky, *Russia, a History and an Interpretation* (2 vols.; N.Y.: Macmillan, 1953), which can well serve as a textbook for a year's course in Russian and Soviet history. A French study, with the emphasis as indicated by its title is B. Gille, *Histoire économique et sociale de la Russie du moyen age au vingtieme siècle* (Paris: Payot, 1949). Sidney Harcave, *Russia: A History* (Chicago: Lippincott, 1952) is a one-volume text designed for college classes. Otto Hoetzsch, *Grundzuge der Geschichte Russlands* (Stuttgart, 1949) promises more in its title than it delivers in its text. A well-written and clearly organized book is Nina and Fillmore Hyde, *Russia Then and Always* (N.Y.: Coward, McCann, 1944), but it is a thesis history which omits or distorts those facts which do not fit its particular theories.

The next two works are interesting today mainly as curiosities, although both contain considerable primary material not to be had elsewhere: N. M. Karamzin, *Geschichte des Russischen Reiches: Nach der Original-Ausgabe Ubersetst* (11 vols. in 6; Leipzig, 1833). This is, of course, a translation of the famous *Istoriia Gosudarstva Rossiiskogo* ("History of the Russian State"). The second is W. K. Kelley, *History of Russia* (2 vols.; London, 1854–55). Kelley compiled his book from the earlier works of Karamzin, Tooke, Ségur, and others. It covers Russia from early times to 1854.

The great classic of Russian history, though some of its interpretations need revision in the light of later research, is still V. O. Kliuchevskii, *Kurs Russkoi Istorii* ("Course in Russian History"). There have been several editions, including an excellent one published by the Soviets in 1926. The work is available in an English translation by C. J. Hogarth and with the author's name transliterated as Kluchevsky (*History of Russia* [5 vols.; N.Y.: Dutton, 1911–31]). The translation is notoriously poor (even according to the man who made it). The chronological scope covers from early times to 1825, and the emphasis is on domestic developments almost to the exclusion of foreign policies. A handy combination of textual summary and selected readings is provided by Hans Kohn, *Basic History of Modern Russia Political, Cultural, and Social Trends* (Princeton, N.J.: Van Nostrand, 1957). A brief book, it is intended primarily for supplementary reading by college classes.

Brilliant and provocative in its general interpretations, and containing some detailed information not elsewhere available is Anatole Leroy-Beaulieu, *L'Empire des tsars* (Paris, 1890). An English translation of the third French edition was published in 1898 by Putnam of New York under the title *The Empire of the Tsars and the Russians* (3 vols.). Two very important studies, specialized in subject but very broad in time span are P. I. Lyashchenko, *Istoriia Narodnogo Khoziaistva SSSR* ("History of the People's Economy of the U.S.S.R.") (2d ed.; 2 vols. Moscow, 1947–48); and J. Mavor, *An Economic History of Russia* (2d ed.; 2 vols.; N.Y.: Dutton, 1925). An English translation of a 1939 edition of Lyashchenko's book was published by Macmillan in 1949. Mr. L. M. Herman made the translation, which was entitled *History of the National Economy of Russia to the 1917 Revolution.* Lyashchenko made use of materials not available to Mavor, but Mavor was intellectually free, which Lyashchenko was not. (See also note 2 to Chapter XVII.) Mavor's study contains an enormous amount of material, but the work is very poorly organized. Lyashchenko's work is much better organized but it must be used with caution because of its political and ideological bias.

Another single-volume college textbook for Russian history is A. G. Mazour, *Russia Past and Present* (Princeton, N.J.: Van Nostrand, 1951). Much longer and far less useful is an attempt at a specialized history by Mairin Mitchell entitled *Maritime History of Russia, 848–1948* (London: Sidgwick & Jackson, 1949). The veteran Russian liberal politician and historian P. N. Miliukov edited a collaborative, general history of Russia which has considerable merit despite some unevenness: *Histoire de la Russie et de l'U.R.S.S.* (3 vols.; Paris, 1933). A contemporary of Professor Miliukov—a tsarist prince who turned Communist—D. S. Mirsky wrote an interesting social history of his country. The book was edited by C. G. Seligman, and was published as *Russia, A Social History* (N.Y.: Century, 1930). It has many excellent maps and charts. A brief, generalized summary of some distinction is V. V. Nazarevski, *Histoire de Moscou depuis les origines jusqu'à nos jours* (Paris, 1932). The scope is broader than the word "Moscou" might suggest.

For nearly a generation the outstanding one-volume textbook of Russian history has been the *History of Russia,* by the late Sir Bernard Pares. Pares' *History* was, for many of us, a major part of our first introduction to a subject which has fascinated us ever since. The first edition was published in 1926, and the "definitive edition" was published in 1953, after Sir Bernard's death. The publisher of all the editions in this country was Knopf of New York.

A comparison of Western textbooks of Russian history with those published in the U.S.S.R. gives an interesting revelation of Soviet methods and ideologies. The official Soviet history text for secondary schools during the 1940's was A. M. Pankratovoi (and others), *Istoriia SSSR* ("History of the U.S.S.R.") (3 vols.; Moscow, 1940 and later editions, revised). Like most Soviet history texts, this is generously supplied with maps and illustrations. Those who would like to sample Soviet historiography at the textbook level without reading Russian can refer to A. V. Shestakov, *Short History of the USSR* (Moscow, 1938 and later editions, revised).

One of the most distinguished Russian historians of the late nineteenth and early twentieth centuries was S. F. Platonov, the grandson of a serf. Professor Platonov's lectures on Russian history at the University of St. Petersburg were published in 1883–84 in manuscript form as *Lektsii po Russkoi Istorii XVII i XVIII Veka* ("Lectures in Russian History, 17th and 18th Centuries"). These are hard to obtain and difficult to use, but fortunately a part of them was translated by E. Aronsberg and edited by F. A. Golder under the title *History of Russia* (N.Y.: Macmillan, 1929). This volume is still the best available manual on Russian political history up to the nineteenth century.

The leading Marxist historian among the Russians was M. N. Pokrovsky, who was the virtual dictator over Russian historiography and Russian historians during the 1920's, but who was subsequently demoted and damned by the Party as a "Fascist betrayer" and a "Trotskyite traitor." Pokrovsky's major work was *Russkaia Istoriia s Dreveneishikh Vremen* ("History of Russia from the Earliest Times") (4 vols.; Leningrad, 1933). There were also other editions. A part of this, edited and translated by J. D. Clarkson and M. R. M. Griffiths, was published as *History of Russia* by the International Publishers of New York in 1931. The same publisher also brought out in 1933 Mirsky's two-volume translation of Pokrovsky's *Brief History of Russia*. Pokrovsky was a highly competent historian, though his work was cramped within the framework of his ideology.

An older work, outdated in some respects but still valuable for its brilliant sketches of diplomatic and political history is Alfred Rambaud, *Histoire de la Russie depuis les origines jusqu'à nos jours*. First published in Paris in 1879, Rambaud's work was promptly translated into English and went through many editions in both English and French. A pioneer study of distinction and of continuing value because it reproduces many primary-source materials is S. M. Soloviev, *Istoriia Rossii s Dreveneishikh Vremen* ("History of Russia from the Earliest Times") (2d ed.; 7 vols.; St. Petersburg, 1893–97). There is no translation, and the study ends with 1780. The British historian B. H. Sumner, in addition to several valuable monographs on special problems in Russian history, also wrote two general histories: *Short History of Russia* (N.Y.: Reynal & Hitchcock, 1943 and later editions); and *Survey of Russian History* (London, 1947). Both are stimulating and interesting but are better suited to the specialist than to the novice because of nonchronological organization.

Better adapted to the needs of the beginner are two general histories by Professor George Vernadsky: *Political and Diplomatic History of*

Russia (Boston: Houghton Mifflin, 1936); and *History of Russia* (4th rev. ed.; New Haven, Conn.: Yale Univ. Press, 1954). Although it was not intended to be a general history of Russia, W. B. Walsh, *Readings in Russian History* (3d rev. ed.; Syracuse, N.Y.: Syracuse Univ. Press, 1958) has apparently been so used by many. An anthology of materials taken from a wide variety of primary and secondary sources, its time span is virtually the same as this book, to which it might well serve as a supplement.

SPECIAL HISTORIES

The books listed here are "special" by virtue of restriction either in subject or in chronological coverage. The distinction is arbitrary, and some of the titles might have been listed with equal reason elsewhere. This subsection may be regarded as a transition from the first to the second section of these notes.

GENERAL DIPLOMATIC HISTORY

The only work which attempts to survey the whole range of Russian and Soviet diplomatic history is a collaborative effort under the editorship of V. P. Potemkin. It is entitled *Istoriia Diplomatii* ("Diplomatic History") (3 vols.; Moscow, 1945); and is also available in a French translation as *Histoire de la diplomatie* (Paris, 1946–47). It is in no sense an objective study. Very useful for the tsarist period, though its editor was hampered by governmental restrictions is F. Martens, *Sobranie Traktatov i Konventsii Zakluchennykh Rossieu s Inostranym Derzhavachi* or *Recueil des traites et conventions conclus par la Russie avec les puissances étrangères* (15 vols.; St. Petersburg: Ministry of Foreign Affairs, 1874–1900). The documents, together with a helpful running commentary, are printed in both Russian and French.

MARXISM AND COMMUNISM

The literature on these subjects is vast and complicated. However, since one cannot deal with Russian and Soviet history without meeting these subjects head-on, they must at least be introduced, if only cursorily, in these notes. The following titles cover some of the several possible approaches, and other suggestions will be found under the appropriate chapter headings in Section II. Three introductory treatments, all quite dissimilar, are: Franz Borkenau, *European Communism* (N.Y.: Harper, 1953); R. N. Carewe-Hunt, *The Theory and Practice of Communism* (N.Y.: Macmillan, 1950); and M. J. Fisher, *Communist Doctrine and the Free World; the Ideology of Communism According to Marx, Engels, Lenin, and Stalin* (Syracuse, N.Y.: Syracuse Univ. Press, 1952). The last-named book was designed for use in college classes. Varied approaches also mark the next three volumes: Hans Kelsen, *The Political Theory of Bolshevism, A Critical Analysis* (Berkeley, Calif.: Univ. of California Press, 1948); H. B. Mayo, *Democracy and Marxism* (N.Y.: Oxford Univ. Press, 1955); and Jules Monnerot, *The Sociology and Psychology of Communism*

(Boston: Beacon, 1953). Numerous special publications on these subjects have been presented by various branches and agencies of the United States government. These are inexpensive and readily obtainable and some, at least, are very useful. Among the best is a series published for the 84th Congress, 2d Session (House Reports, 2240–43), under the following long and rather forbidding title: *The Communist Conspiracy, Strategy and Tactics of World Communism, Part I, Communism Outside the United States, Foreword, General Introduction, Section A: Marxist Classics; Section B: The U.S.S.R.; Section C: World Congresses of the Communist International; Section D: Communist Activities Around the World; Section E: The Comintern and the CPUSA* (Wash., D.C.: Govt. Printing Office, 1956).

Sidney Hook, *Marx and the Marxists* (Princeton, N.J.: Van Nostrand, 1955) is a combination of introductory text and selected readings designed for use in college classes. Gustav Mayer, *Friedrich Engels* (London, 1935) is the only available biography of Marx's "alter ego." David Mitrany, *Marx Against the Peasant* (Chapel Hill, N.C.: Univ. of North Carolina Press, 1951) is a specialized study with emphasis indicated by the title. C. J. S. Sprigge, *Karl Marx* (N.Y.: Macmillan, 1957) is a re-publication of a very brief biography in popular style, originally published in 1938.

The works of Marx, Engels, Lenin, Stalin, Mao, and others have been published and republished in formats running from pamphlets to multi-volumed "collected works" in many languages. No listing of them is given here because of the ready availability of the works themselves and of bibliographies of them. Professor Mayo's book, for example, has an unusually full, annotated bibliography. There is also a long bibliography in Mitrany's study, and a short one in Professor Hook's volume.

POLAND AND UKRAINE

W. E. D. Allen, *The Ukraine: A History* (Cambridge, Eng.: Cambridge Univ. Press, 1941) is a very careful and completely scholarly account of a highly controversial subject. The views of the Ukrainian nationalists can be found most conveniently in M. S. Hrushevsky, *History of Ukraine,* ed. O. J. Frederiksen (New Haven, Conn.: Yale Univ. Press, 1941). This is a translation of Hrushevsky's popular one-volume *History of Ukraine,* which was published in 1911. Also acceptable to most Ukrainian nationalists is C. A. Manning, *Story of the Ukraine* (N.Y.: Philosophical Library, 1947). Current writings by Ukrainian historians and other specialists will be found in the journal *Ukrainian Quarterly,* published by the Ukrainian Congress Committees of America. A two-volume history of Poland which presents several points of view because it is a collaborative work is W. F. Reddaway and others (eds.), *Cambridge History of Poland* (Cambridge, Eng.: Cambridge Univ. Press, 1941). A concise survey of Russo-Polish relations will be found in Serge Konovalov (ed.), *Russo-Polish Relations: An Historical Survey* (Princeton, N.J.: Princeton Univ. Press, 1945). Mention ought also to be made of V. A. Miakotin, *Ocherki*

Sotsialnoi Istorii Ukrainy ("Outline of the Social History of Ukraine")
(Prague, 1926).

RUSSIAN-AMERICAN RELATIONS

Three general accounts, the second of which is the best-founded,
are: T. A. Bailey, *America Faces Russia* (Ithaca, N.Y.: Cornell Univ.
Press, 1950); F. R. Dulles, *The Road to Teheran The Story of Russia
and America, 1781–1943* (Princeton, N.J.: Princeton Univ. Press,
1944); and W. A. Williams, *American Russian Relations, 1781–1947*
(N.Y.: Rinehart, 1947).

SIBERIA AND THE FAR EAST

Two great sources—largely because they reprint many primary materials which have been lost—are F. G. Muller, *Sammlung Russische
Geschichte* (9 vols.; St. Petersburg, 1732); and his *Opisaniye Sibirskogo
Tsarstva* ("Description of the Siberian Kingdom") (St. Petersburg,
1750). Some of Muller's material was used by E. G. Ravenstein in
his book *The Russians on the Amur* (London, 1861). J. F. Baddely
made extensive use of Russian manuscripts from the Foreign Office
archives for his *Russia, Mongolia, and China* (2 vols.; London, 1919).
Typical of the travelers' accounts which reached the West in the
mid-nineteenth century were two books by T. W. Atkinson: *Oriental
and Western Siberia* (N.Y.: Harpers, 1858); and *Travels in the Regions of the Upper and Lower Amoor and the Russian Acquisitions on
the Confines of India and China* (N.Y.: Harpers, 1860). Much more
important are three monographs by American scholars treating several
aspects of Russian expansion in the Far East (including Siberia and
Alaska). The oldest of these is the monumental work of F. A. Golder,
Russian Expansion on the Pacific, 1641–1850 (Cleveland, Ohio,
1914). R. H. Fisher, *Russian Fur Trade, 1550–1700* (Berkeley, Calif.:
Univ. of California Press, 1943) is a critical, scholarly study touching
on trade routes and settlements as well as other aspects of the fur trade.
The most recent of the three is S. R. Tompkins, *Alaska from Pro-
myshlennik to Sourdough* (Norman, Okla.: Univ. of Oklahoma Press,
1945). All three make extensive use of Russian sources. A Soviet
monograph by S. B. Okun, *Russian-American Company*, has been
translated into English by Carl Ginsburg and published by the Harvard
University Press in 1951. The original Russian edition, *Russo-Ameri-
kanskaia Kompaniia*, was published in Moscow in 1939. There are
also two other recent Soviet monographs dealing with the eastward
expansion of Russia which merit mention: A. S. Berg, *Otkrytie Kam-
chatki i Ekspeditsiia Beringa* ("Discovery of Kamchatka and the
Bering Expedition") (Moscow, 1946); and V. I. Shuykov, *Ocherki
po Istorii Kolonizatsii Sibiri* ("Outline of the History of the Coloniza-
tion of Siberia") (Moscow, 1946).

The best general account for the non-layman is Professor A. A.
Lobanov-Rostovsky, *Russia and Asia* (rev. ed.; Ann Arbor, Mich.:
Wahr, 1951), which touches on the Near East and Middle East as
well as the Far East. An older work, violently Russophobic, is Alexis

Krausse, *Russia in Asia, 1558–1899* (N.Y.: Holt, 1900). Among the more recent accounts is D. J. Dallin, *Rise of Russia in Asia* (New Haven, Conn.: Yale Univ. Press, 1949). Mr. Dallin, a distinguished and irreconcilable foe of the Soviet regime, is more interested in and better informed on the Soviet period than on earlier ones.

SOCIAL AND INTELLECTUAL HISTORY

A recent attempt at an integrated interpretation of religious and intellectual developments in nineteenth-century Russia is Nicolas Arseniev, *La Sainte Moscou* (Paris, 1948). Nicholas Berdayev, a contemporary Russian philosopher who believes that communism and Orthodoxy may be combined, offered a different approach in *The Russian Idea* (N.Y.: Macmillan, 1948). H. Kohn (ed.), *Mind of Modern Russia* (New Brunswick, N.J.: Rutgers Univ. Press, 1955) is a convenient anthology of well-chosen readings. Probably the best history of Russian thought in English is the work of the great Czech statesman and scholar T. G. Masaryk, *The Spirit of Russia* (added chapters by Jan Slavik) (2 vols.; rev. ed.; N.Y.: Macmillan, 1955). Also of high caliber is P. N. Miliukov, *Outlines of Russian Culture*, ed. M. M. Karpovich (3 vols.; Philadelphia: Univ. of Pennsylvania Press, 1941). The emphasis is on the old regime, but there is some material on the Soviet period. S. R. Tompkins, *The Russian Mind from Peter the Great through the Enlightenment* (Norman, Okla.: Univ. of Oklahoma Press, 1953) is more limited chronologically and in approach. The first comprehensive study of its subject to be available in English is G. L. Kline's translation of V. V. Zenkovsky, *History of Russian Philosophy* (2 vols.; N.Y.: Columbia Univ. Press, 1953).

Descriptions and dissertations on Russian and Soviet literature are numerous. The general reader will find the following to be useful introductions to this important subject: Maurice Baring, *An Outline of Russian Literature* (N.Y.: Holt, n.d.)—a brief account which goes only to 1900; Maurice Baring (ed.), *The Oxford Book of Russian Verse* (2d ed.; N.Y.: Oxford Univ. Press, 1949); Babette Deutsch and Avrahm Yarmolinsky (eds.), *Russian Poetry* (N.Y.: International Publishers, 1930)—an anthology from Pushkin to the Soviet period; B. G. Guerney (ed.), *Treasury of Russian Literature* (N.Y.: Vanguard, 1943)—ranges from the ancient chronicles to 1917; N. K. Gudzii, *History of Early Russian Literature*, tr. S. W. Jones (N.Y.: Macmillan, 1949)—a translation of a Soviet text; D. S. Mirsky, *History of Russian Literature*, rev. by F. J. Whitefield (N.Y.: Knopf, 1949); M. L. Slonim, *Epic of Russian Literature from Its Origins through Tolstoy* (N.Y.: Oxford Univ. Press, 1949); M. L. Slonim, *Modern Russian Literature from Chekov to the Present* (N.Y.: Oxford Univ. Press, 1953). The two volumes by Slonim constitute a skilled and careful interpretive history of Russian literature. I. M. Sokolov, *Russian Folklore* (N.Y.: Macmillan, 1950); Avrahm Yarmolinsky (ed.), *Treasury of Great Russian Stories* (N.Y.: Macmillan, 1944)—an anthology with biographical notes from Pushkin to Gorky; and Avrahm Yarmolinsky (ed.), *Treasury of Russian Verse* (N.Y.: Macmillan, 1949) are also helpful.

The following special studies cover a variety of subjects, most of which will be apparent from the titles: M. D. Calvocoressi, *Survey of Russian Music* (N.Y.: Penguin, 1944)—a very brief but helpful introduction; Louis Greenberg, *Jews in Russia*, Vol. I (New Haven, Conn.: Yale Univ. Press, 1944), and M. Wischnitzer, *Jews in Russia*, Vol. II (1951). Volume I deals mainly with the years from 1801 to 1881; Volume II covers from 1881 to 1917. Richard Hare, *Pioneers of Russian Social Thought* (N.Y.: Oxford Univ. Press, 1951) offers a fresh approach to the non-Marxist, Russian thinkers of the nineteenth century. Education under the tsars is examined by W. H. E. Johnson, *Russia's Educational Heritage* (New Brunswick, N.J.: Rutgers Univ. Press, 1950). There is also an earlier study on the same subject by N. Hans, *History of Russian Educational Policy* (London, 1931). Our understanding of meaning of Pan-Slavism has been recently improved by two authoritative studies: Hans Kohn, *Pan-Slavism: Its History and Ideology* (Notre Dame, Ind.: Univ. of Notre Dame Press, 1953); and M. B. Petrovich, *Emergence of Russian Panslavism* (N.Y.: Columbia Univ. Press, 1956). N. V. Riasanovsky, *Russia and the West in the Teaching of the Slavophiles* (Cambridge, Mass.: Harvard Univ. Press, 1952) is a scholarly study of certain aspects of that movement. Because of its subject, Max Laserson, *American Impact on Russia, 1784–1917* (N.Y.: Macmillan, 1950) is of particular interest to Americans. It is also a fresh and useful approach to Russian intellectual history.

The following books are grouped here because their time spans make it difficult to assign them to any single chapter. V. V. Funk and B. Nazerevski, *Histoire des Romanovs, 1613–1918* (Paris, 1930) is well written and generally sound. Its viewpoint is conservative. The best brief introductory summary of the nineteenth and early twentieth centuries is M. M. Karpovich, *Imperial Russia, 1801–1917* (N.Y.: Holt, 1932). A much longer, detailed study of the nineteenth century, strong on domestic affairs, is Alexander Kornilov, *Modern Russian History* (rev. ed.; N.Y.: Knopf, 1943). Kornilov's work was in the best tradition of Russian historical scholarship. The censorship, however, made it difficult for him to deal adequately with events after 1881. A very informative study, which goes far beyond the scope suggested by its title—even to containing material on the medieval laws and courts, is Samuel Kucherow, *Courts, Lawyers, and Trials under the Last Three Tsars* (N.Y.: Praeger, 1953). Although the tsarist censorship seriously hampered Kornilov, it nonetheless permitted the publication of a collaborative work written chiefly by socialist opponents of the regime. With their bias properly discounted, much of the work is valuable. It is titled *Istoriia Rossi v XIX Vek* ("History of 19th-Century Russia") (9 vols.; St. Petersburg, 1909).

Three studies—one pre-Soviet and two Soviet—emphasize the economic and social aspects of nineteenth- and twentieth-century Russian history. The pre-Soviet study is a multi-volumed, collaborative work edited by A. K. Dzhivelegov and others, *Velikaia Reforma* ("The Great Reform") (6 vols.; Moscow, 1911). Its time scope covers from 1861 to its publication. Not all its chapters are equally good. The older Soviet study, containing much information not elsewhere readily available, is C. A. Piontkovskii, *Ocherki Istorii SSSR XIX i XX Vekov* ("Outline of Russian History, 19th and 20th Centuries") (Moscow, 1935). The official interpretation (as of 1948) was presented by V. M. Shtein, *Ocherki Razvitiia Russkoi Obshchestvenno-Ekonomicheskoi mysli XIX–XX Vekov* ("Outline of the Development of Russian Public Economy during the 19th and 20th Centuries") (Leningrad, 1948). An outstanding monograph on a tremendously important socio-economic problem is Professor G. T. Robinson's classic study, *Rural Russia under the Old Regime* (Reprint; N.Y.: Macmillan, 1949).

The following two books are broader in purpose and scope. F. H. Skrine, *Expansion of Russia, 1815–1900* (Cambridge, Eng.: Cambridge Univ. Press, 1904) was long considered a standard account. It now seems rather dated, but it was a careful piece of work which is still worth consulting. It includes more domestic history than its title suggests. Professor Hugh Seton-Watson, *Decline of Imperial Russia, 1855–1914* (N.Y.: Praeger, 1953) divides the period into three parts and each part into three sections—"structure of state and society, political movements, and foreign relations."

There has been a dearth of usable, general histories of the Soviet regime. Most accounts have covered a special area, such as the government or the economy, or a particular problem, wages and prices, for example, or a segment of the period. It is helpful to have now available in English a general historical synthesis, Georg von Rauch, *History of Soviet Russia* (N.Y.: Praeger, 1957).

 SECTION II

PREFACE

The norm and value concept is borrowed from the social psychologists. I am particularly indebted to Hadley Cantril, *Psychology of Social Movements* (N.Y.: Wiley, 1941) and Muzafer Sherif, *Psychology of Social Norms* (N.Y.: Harper, 1936).

CHAPTER I. THE WEDGE AND THE POOL

The geographical description is a synthesis compiled from many sources, old and new, including maps, charts, and pictures as well as verbal accounts. The more important verbal sources are listed under "Atlases and Geographies" in Section I. I have been influenced in regard to the importance of the river systems by R. J. Kerner, *The Urge to the Sea* (Berkeley, Calif.: Univ. of California Press, 1942), although I reject Kerner's main thesis that the urge to the sea along the river routes and portages was the basic force back of Russian expansion.

My main sources on the early peoples, in addition to the titles previously listed, were: S. H. Cross, *Slavic Civilization through the Ages*, ed. L. I. Strakhovsky (Cambridge, Mass.: Harvard Univ. Press, 1948); George Vernadsky, *Ancient Russia* (New Haven, Conn.: Yale Univ. Press, 1943); P. Tretyakov, "Archeological Studies on the

Origins of the Eastern Slavs," *VOKS Bulletin,* no. 6 (Moscow, 1945); and two studies by B. D. Grekov, *Istoriia Kulturi Drevnei Rusi* ("Cultural History of Early Russia") (Moscow, 1948) and *Krestiane na Rusi s Drevneishikh Vremen do XVI Veka* ("Peasants in Rus from the Earliest Times to the Sixteenth Century") (Moscow, 1946). Several of these are also pertinent to the next two chapters as well as to this one.

Frank Nowak, *Medieval Slavdom and the Rise of Russia* (N.Y.: Holt, 1930) is a handy summary.

CHAPTER II. TRADE AND POLITICS: THE FIRST RUS STATES

I used two versions of *The Primary Chronicle:* Louis Paris (ed.), *La chronique de Nestor* (Paris, 1834); and S. H. Cross, *The Russian Primary Chronicle; Harvard Studies and Notes in Philology and Literature,* Vol. XII (Cambridge, Mass.: Harvard Univ. Press, 1930), but I depended mostly upon the latter. For the *Novgorod Chronicle,* I used Robert Michell and Nevil Forbes, *The Chronicle of Novgorod, 1016–1471* (Camden 3d Series; London: Camden Society, 1914), Vol. XXV. A general discussion of the sources of early Russian history will be found in N. K. Chadwick, *The Beginnings of Russian History* (Cambridge, Eng.: Cambridge Univ. Press, 1946).

My interpretation of the first Rus states is largely based upon George Vernadsky, *Ancient Russia* and *Kievan Russia* (New Haven, Conn.: Yale Univ. Press, 1948). The status in recent years of the dispute between the Normanists and anti-Normanists, together with an appraisal of the problem, was well summarized by N. V. Riasanovsky (Riazanovsky) in "The Norman Theory of the Origin of the Russian State," *Russian Review,* VII, no. 1 (1947): 96–110.

What may be called a sociological approach to some aspects of ancient Russian history was taken by Eleanor Elnett, *Historic Origin and Social Development of Family Life in Russia* (N.Y.: Columbia Univ. Press, 1926). Stress is placed on the Asiatic and Byzantine character of pre-Petrine Russia.

CHAPTER III. IN THE DAYS OF KIEVAN RUS

The classic account by Kliuchevskii, as previously noted, has had to be revised. The most scholarly modern account is that of Vernadsky, although Ukrainian nationalists and some other scholars find it unacceptable. The essence of the Ukrainian view was best given by Professor Hrushevsky. The Soviet historian Grekov published prolifically on this subject and a part of his work has been published in English as *Culture of Kievan Rus* (Moscow, 1947). See also his *Kievskaia Rus* ("Kievan Rus") (Moscow, 1944) and his *Kultura Kievskoi Rusi* ("Culture of Kievan Rus") (Moscow, 1944) as well as his previously cited works. Another Soviet study on this period is S. V. Iushkov, *Ocherki po Istorii Feodalizma v Kievskoi Rusi* ("Outline for the History of Feudalism in Kievan Rus") (Moscow, 1939). Some relevant information will also be found in P. P. Melgunov, *Ocherki po*

Istorii Russkoi Torgovli IX–XVIII vv ("Outline for a History of Russian Trade, 9th–18th Centuries") (Moscow, 1905). The material on the Kievan churches is from S. H. Cross (and others), "The Earliest Medieval Churches of Kiev," *Speculum: A Journal of Medieval Studies*, XI, no. 4 (1936): 477–99, and S. H. Cross, *Mediaeval Russian Churches*, ed. K. J. Conant (Cambridge, Eng.: Mediaeval Academy, 1949).

Primary sources used for this chapter included the *Russian Primary Chronicle, the Chronicle of Novgorod,* and the "Lives of the Saints," *Russian Review* (Published by the Univ. of Liverpool), II, no. 3 (1913): 21–44.

CHAPTER IV. TATAR AND MUSCOVITE

The most recent study is George Vernadsky, *Mongols and Russians* (New Haven, Conn.: Yale Univ. Press, 1953) but this does not seem likely immediately to displace Jeremiah Curtin, *The Mongols: A History* (Boston: Little, Brown, 1908) as the classic study of those people. I made extensive use of four monographic articles by British scholars all of which were published in the prewar series of *The Slavonic and East European Review* (London). These were: H. T. Cheshire, "The Great Tartar Invasion of Europe," V, no. 13 (1926): 89–105; A. B. Boswell, "The Kipchak Turks," VI, no. 16 (1927): 68–85; Semen Rappoport, "On the Early Slavs: the Narrative of Irahim-Ibn-Yakub," VIII, no. 23 (1929): 331–41; and A. C. Macartney, "The Petchenegs," VIII, no. 23 (1929): 342–55.

Some primary-source material in English can be found in Richard Hakluyt, *The Principal Navigations, Voyages, Traffiques and Discouveries of the English Nation* (10 vols.; N.Y.: Dutton, 1927).

There is also some relevant information in two recent Soviet studies, although both pertain more to later periods. S. B. Veselovskii, *Feodalnoe Zemlevladanie v Severovostochnoi Rusi* ("Feudal Landownership in Northeastern Rus") Vol. I (Moscow, 1947), and R. Iu. Vipper, *Ivan Grozni.* This book is also available in an English translation by J. Fineburg as: R. Iu. Vipper, *Ivan Grozny* (Moscow, 1947).

CHAPTER V. IVAN GROZNY, AUTOCRAT OF ALL RUSSIA

There is no satisfactory biography of Ivan Grozny. Vipper's study, which is not, strictly speaking, a biography, has certain obvious defects due probably to the system under which he lived and worked. The same may be said of the booklet *Ivan Grozni,* by S. V. Bakhrushin (Moscow, 1945). Hans von Eckardt, *Ivan the Terrible* (N.Y.: Knopf, 1949), first published in German as *Iwan der schreckliche,* is good on Ivan's youth but very weak on the later and more important periods. George Backer, *The Deadly Parallel: Stalin and Ivan the Terrible* (N.Y.: Random House, 1950) has no historical value. Stephen Graham, *Ivan the Terrible* (New Haven, Conn.: Yale Univ. Press, 1933) is also without distinction. The most readable of the older biographies is K. Waliszewski, *Ivan the Terrible,* tr. M. Loyd (Philadelphia: Lippincott, 1904). It is generally sound and fair though marred by some factual inaccuracies.

An unusually large number of primary-source materials on sixteenth-century Russia are available in English. R. H. Major (ed.), *Notes upon Russia: Being a Translation of the Earliest Account of that Country, entitled Rerum Moscovitarum Commentarii by the Baron Sigismund von Herberstein* (2 vols.; London: Hakluyt Society, 1851–52) is the oldest authentic description of Muscovy by a Westerner. Excerpts from it are printed in my *Readings in Russian History* as are also excerpts from various other sources of the period. Hakluyt's *Principal Navigations,* cited above, contains several first-hand accounts by Chancelour, Adams, Napea, Fletcher, and others. The most famous of these observers was Giles Fletcher, and his report, *The Russe Commonwealth,* is available in several versions. I used the Hakluyt version and also E. A. Bond, *Russia at the Close of the 16th Century Comprising the Treatise of the Russe Commonwealth by Dr. Giles Fletcher; and the Travels of Sir Jerome Horsey, Knt., Now for the First Time Printed Entire from His Own Manuscript* (London: Hakluyt Society, 1856). W. R. Morfill made other primary sources available in translation in his book *The Story of Russia* (N.Y.: Putnam, 1891). I borrowed from this work the quotations and paraphrases of the *bylinas.*

An excellent brief summary of the role of the Church is Professor M. M. Karpovich's article "Church and State in Russian History," *Russian Review,* III, no. 3 (1944): 10–20. An introductory summary will also be found in the opening pages of J. S. Curtiss, *Church and State in Russia* (N.Y.: Columbia Univ. Press, 1940). The best study in English of the many dissenting sects in Russia is F. C. Conybeare, *The Russian Dissenters* (Cambridge, Mass.: Harvard Univ. Press, 1921). It is, however, more relevant to later chapters than to this one.

A. Tolstoy's historical novel, *Prince Serebryani,* tr. J. Curtin (N.Y.: Dodd, Mead, 1892) is pertinent to this period.

CHAPTER VI. RELAPSES, RECOVERIES, REBELLIONS AND ROMANOVS

This chapter is based largely on works which have already been listed. To them should be added: R. N. Bain, *The First Romanovs* (London, 1905) and five monographic articles which were published in *The Slavonic and East European Review* (London). The articles are G. Afanasyev, "Boris Godunov and the First Pretender," II, no. 4 (1923): 31–53; B. Alexeyev, "The Restoration of Order and the First Romanovs," II, no. 2 (1923): 14–50; L. R. Lewitter, "Poland, the Ukraine and Russia, in the 17th Century," XXVII, no. 67 (1948): 157–71; and 68 (1948): 414–29; L. Loewenson, "The Moscow Rising of 1648," XXVII, no. 68 (1948): 146–56; and M. Lyubavsky, "The Accession of the Romanovs, 1613," II, no. 1 (1923): 11–31.

CHAPTER VII. THE DYNAMIC PETER

Studies about Peter the Great range all the way from ponderous and pedantic tomes such as B. von Bergmann, *Peter der Grosse als*

Mensch und Regent (6 vols. in 3; Koenigsberg, 1823–29) through literary curiosa such as Daniel Defoe, *An Imperial History of the Life and Actions of Peter Alexowitz, the Present Czar of Muscovy* (London, 1721) to frivolous trivialities such as George Oudard, *Peter the Great,* tr. F. M. Atkinson (N.Y.: Payson and Clarke, 1929). The best biography, though in need of revision, is still Eugene Schuyler, *Peter the Great, Emperor of Russia* (2 vols., N.Y.: Scribner, 1890). A little more readable, but not quite as sound is Kasimir Waliszewski, *Pierre le Grand* (Paris, 1897), which is also available in English as *Peter the Great* (2 vols., N.Y.: Appleton, 1897) and in Russian as *Petr Veliki* (Moscow, 1909). Among the more recent studies are: Constantine de Grunwald, *Peter the Great,* tr. Viola Garvin (N.Y.: Macmillan, 1956); C. B. O'Brien, *Russia Under Two Tsars, 1682– 1689, Regency of Sophia Alekseevna* (Berkeley, Calif.: Univ. of California Press, 1952), which is well documented and well written; and two books by the late B. H. Sumner, *Peter the Great and the Emergence of Russia* (N.Y.: Macmillan, 1951) and *Peter the Great and the Ottoman Empire* (Oxford, Eng.: Blackwell, 1949). Ian Grey, *"Peter the Great in England," History Today* (London), VI, no. 4 (1956): 225–34, is an entertaining and informative account of one of the incidents of Peter's varied career.

Soviet scholars have done much useful spadework and have made available new materials about Peter. Four examples are the excerpts from decrees, proclamations, reports and letters in V. I. Lebedev (comp.), *Reformy Petra I Sbornik Dokumentov* ("Reforms of Peter I Collection of Documents") (Moscow, 1937); M. M. Bogoslovskii, *Petr I Materialy dlia Biografii* ("Peter I Materials for a Biography"), ed. V. I. Lebedev (2 vols.; Moscow, 1940)—the first volume covers 1672–97; the second, 1697–98; *Pisma i Bumagi Imperatora Petra Velikogo* ("Letters and Notes of Emperor Peter the Great") (10 vols.; St. Petersburg, 1887–1956), and A. Iakovlev, *Khlopostvo i Kholopii v Mosvokskom Gosudarstve 17 Veka* ("Slaves and Slavery in Seventeenth-Century Muscovy") (Moscow, 1943), which gives additional data on this aspect of Petrine and pre-Petrine life.

Of the older Russian works, M. M. Shcherbatov's edition of Peter's Journal—very strong on military history—is available in German as *Tagebuch Peters des Grossen vom Jahre 1698 bis zum Schlusse de Neystadter Friedens* (Berlin, 1773) and in French as *Journal de Pierre le Grand, 1698–1721* (Berlin, 1773). More recent are Sieur de Villebois, *Mémoires secret pour servir à l'histoire de la cour de Russie sous les règnes de Pierre le Grand et Catherine I* (Paris, 1853); and E. F. Schmurle (comp.), *Recueil de documents relatifs au règne de l'empereur Pierre le Grand* (Dorpat, Estonia, 1903). More as a literary curiosity than as an historical source, mention may be made of Voltaire, *History of the Russian Empire under Peter the Great.* I used an English edition, published in New York in 1835.

CHAPTER VIII. GUARDSMEN AND EMPRESSES

For this chapter, I followed in the main the excellent secondary accounts written by R. Nisbet Bain: *The Pupils of Peter the Great,*

1697–1740 (London, 1897); *The Daughter of Peter the Great, 1741– 1762* (London, 1899); and *Peter III, Emperor of Russia* (N.Y., 1902). I also used Kasimir Waliszewski's *L'heritage de Pierre le Grand . . . , 1725–1741* (Paris, 1900) and various primary sources. Among the latter were: *La cour de la Russe il y'a cent ans, 1725–1783: Extraits des dépêches des ambassadeurs anglais et français* (Berlin, 1858); General Manstein, *Memoirs of Russia, Historical, Political and Military from the Year MDCCXXVII to MDCCXLIV . . .* (London, 1770); William Tooke, *The Life of Catherine II, Empress of All the Russias* (1st American ed.; 2 vols.; Philadelphia, 1802); A. D. Collyer (ed.), *The Dispatches and Correspondence of John, Second Earl of Buckinghamshire, Ambassador to the Court of Catherine II, 1762–1765* (2 vols.; London: Longmans, Green, 1900– 1901); the *Memoirs of the Empress Catherine II Written by Herself With a Preface by A. Herzen* (N.Y.: Appleton, 1859); and William Tooke, *View of the Russian Empire During the Reign of Catherine the Second, and to the Close of the Present Century* (3 vols.; London, 1799).

The best edition of Catherine's memoirs is D. Maroger (ed.), *The Memoirs of Catherine the Great* (N.Y.: Macmillan, 1955), though it somehow lacks the piquancy of Herzen's version. An excellent collateral reading is an anthology edited by Peter Putnam, *Seven Britons in Imperial Russia* (Princeton, N.J.: Princeton Univ. Press, 1952). An unusual article is Walther Kirchener, "The Death of Catherine I of Russia," *American Historical Review*, LI, no. 2 (1946): 254–61.

CHAPTER IX. MISTRESS OF MEN AND POLITICS

Catherine the Great, like Peter I, has intrigued many writers. One of the better biographies is K. S. Anthony, *Catherine the Great* (Garden City, N.Y., 1925). Miss Anthony also edited the *Memoirs of Catherine the Great* (N.Y.: Knopf, 1927) but her edition is not as good as that by Maroger. W. F. Reddaway published some valuable *Documents of Catherine the Great* (N.Y.: Macmillan, 1931). Two additional biographies, neither of them distinguished, are: E. A. B. Hodgetts, *Life of Catherine the Great of Russia* (N.Y.: Brentano's, 1941), and Gina Kaus, *Catherine, Portrait of an Empress* (N.Y.: Viking, 1935). Very much more useful for its new material and its interpretations is George Soloveytchik, *Potemkin* (N.Y.: Norton, 1947).

I also used the following, additional primary sources, mostly to get the feeling and flavor of Catherine's time: Baron M. D. B. de Borberon, *Un diplomat français à la cour de Catherine II, 1775– 1780 . . .* (2 vols.; Paris, 1901); E. R. Dashkova, *Memoirs of Princess Dashkaw, Lady of Honour to Catherine II*, ed. Mrs. W. Bradford (2 vols.; London, 1840); C. F. P. Masson, *Secret Memoirs of the Court of St. Petersburg* (London, 1895); and Swinton, *Voyage en Norwége, en Danemark, et en Russia dans les années 1788, 89, 90 et 91,* tr. P. Henry (2 vols; Paris, 1798).

Additional secondary accounts of excellent caliber include Walther

Kirchener, "Emigration to Russia," *American Historical Review*, LV, no. 3 (1950): 552–56, which deals mainly with Catherine's period; Andrei Lobanov-Rostovsky, *Russia and Europe, 1789–1825* (Durham, N.C.: Duke Univ. Press, 1947), a straight diplomatic history, which extends through the reign of Alexander I; R. H. Lord, *Second Partition of Poland* (Cambridge, Mass.: Harvard Univ. Press, 1915), which I followed in my account of Catherine's Polish policy; and a brief study by G. S. Thompson, *Catherine the Great and the Expansion of Russia* (N.Y.: Macmillan, 1950).

Two biographies of the great Suvorov are available in English: L. M. P. de Laverne, *The Life of Field Marshal Suvorof* (Baltimore, Md., 1814) and W. L. Blease, *Suvorov* (London: Constable, 1920). The latter, though Blease wrote from memory after the loss of all his papers, is the better. It is based on Russian sources. Some Soviet studies of Suvorov have recently been published but I have not seen them. A part of Suvorov's correspondence was published in Leipzig in 1835 under the title *Correspondentz des Kaus. Russ. Generalissmus, Furst. Italiisch Grafen Alexander Wassiliewich Suworoff.*

CHAPTER X. ALEXANDER, DISCIPLE OF ORDER

Concerning Paul I, the best account is E. S. Shumigorskii, *Imperator Pavel I Zhizn i Tsarstvovanie* ("Emperor Paul I Life and Tsardom") (St. Petersburg, 1907). N. K. Shilder, *Imperator Pavel Pervyi* ("Emperor Paul I") (St. Petersburg, 1901) is also valuable but Shilder was hampered by censorship. Waliszewski's *Paul I,* tr. from the 1913 French edition (London, 1913) is of relatively little use. Also available, though not of great value, is F. Golovkin, *La cour et la règne de Paul I* (Paris, 1905).

On the whole, less light is thrown on Alexander I by his biographers than by the memoirs of his contemporaries. Those of his onetime friend and confidant Czartoryski are of first-rate importance. I used Adam Gielgud (ed.), *Memoirs of Prince Adam Czartoryski and his Correspondence with Alexander I* (2d ed.; 2 vols.; London, 1888). Grand Duke Nicholas Mikhailovich, *Graf, P. A. Stroganov, (1774–1817) Istoricheskoe Issledovanie Epokhi Imperatora Aleksandra I* ("Count P. A. Stroganov [1774–1817] Historical Revelations of the Epoch of Emperor Alexander I") (3 vols.; St. Petersburg, 1903) gives collected correspondence and notes. There is also *Pisma Imperatora Aleksandra I-go i Drugikh osob Tsarstvennago Doma k F. Ts. Lagarpu* ("Letters of Alexander I and Others of the Imperial Court to F. S. LaHarpe") (no publisher, n.d.).

Of lively interest but less importance are Mme. la Comtesse Choiseul-Gouffier, *Historical Memoirs of Alexander I and the Court of Russia,* tr. M. B. Patterson (2d ed.; Chicago: McClurg, 1901); and Richard Metternich (ed.), *Memoirs of Prince Metternich, 1773–1815* (2 vols.; N.Y.: Scribner, 1880). A chatty, informal view of life among the aristocracy in the early nineteenth century may be found in *The Russian Journals of Martha and Catherine Wilmot,* ed. the Marchioness of Londonderry and H. M. Hyde (N.Y.: Macmillan, 1934).

There are two biographies of Alexander I in English—one superficial; the other, highly imaginative. The first is a translation from the French of G. M. Paleologue, *The Enigmatic Czar* (N.Y.: Harper, 1938); and the second is L. I. Strahovsky, *Alexander I* (N.Y.: Norton, 1947). Professor Strahovsky puts forth some amazing assumptions as, for example, that Paul was weak and Alexander was strong because of the ways in which their respective cribs had been fixed.

Much more important and worthy of serious consideration is A. Fateev, *Le Probleme de l'individu et de l'homme d'état dans la personnalité historique d'Alexandre I, empereur de toutes les Russies* (Prague, 1938). There is also some important primary material, as well as other information on Alexander, to be found in an older study, Paul LaCroix, *Histoire de la vie et du règne de Nicholas Ier empereur de Russie* (3 vols.; Paris, 1864–66). LaCroix focuses on the next reign, but deals also with Alexander's last years. J. H. Schnitzler, *Histoire intime de la Russie sous les empereurs Alexandre et Nicholas* (2 vols.; Paris, 1854) is of some value, although it does not live up to the promise of its title.

The legend of Kuzmich, made much of by Strahovsky, is dealt with carefully in G. Vasilich, *Imperator Aleksandr I i Starets Feodor Kuzmich* ("Emperor Alexander I and the Holy Man Fedor Kuzmich") (Moscow, n.d.), and is pretty well disposed of by Anatole Kulomzin in "The Siberian Hermit, Theodore Kuzmich," *Slavonic and East European Review* (London) II, no. 5 (1923): 381–87.

Since I paid scant attention to the military history of the period and since the literature on the French side, at least, is both familiar and voluminous I shall list only three titles. American readers will be interested in the officially sanctioned Soviet view as expressed in Eugene Tarlé, *Napoleon's Invasion of Russia, 1812* (N.Y.: Oxford Univ. Press, 1942). Readers of Russian may wish to compare this with Tarlé's *Otechestvennaia Voina 1812 goda i Razgrom Imperatora Napoleona* ("The Fatherland War of 1812 and the Rout of the Emperor Napoleon") (Moscow, 1941) and readers of English with his *Bonaparte* (N.Y.: Knight, 1937).

An older Russian study still of value for its special information is A. N. Pypin, *Obshchestvennoe Dvizhenie v Rossii pri Aleksandrie I* ("Social Movements in Russia in the Time of Alexander I") (2d ed.; St. Petersburg, 1885).

The slender but very important little volume by Professor G. Mazour, *The First Russian Revolution, 1825* (Berkeley, Calif.: Univ. of California Press, 1937) may be considered either as closing the reign of Alexander I or opening that of Nicholas I. It makes use of most of the new material published by Soviet scholars who have been especially interested in this event. (A special issue of the extremely useful *Krasnyi Arkhiv* ("Red Archives") edited by M. M. Pokrovsky was devoted to the men of December, and there have been many other studies published also. I shall not list them here because, though I consulted some of them, I depended upon Mazour's book.

CHAPTER XI. THE REIGN OF CONTRASTS:
DOMESTIC AFFAIRS, 1825–55

The most recently published biography of Nicholas I is Constantine de Grunwald, *La vie de Nicholas Ier* (Paris, 1946), which is also available in English (Brigit Patmore, tr.) as *Tsar Nicholas I* (N.Y.: Macmillan, 1955). It is, on the whole, a fairly good summary which follows the conventional interpretation. That interpretation is typified both by the title and content of a work by A. E. Presniakov, *Apogei Samoderzhaviia: Nikolai I* ("The Height of Autocracy: Nicholas I") (Leningrad, 1925). Of greater value is: *Materialii dlia Istorii Tsarstvovaniia Imperatora Nikolaia Pavlovicha* ("Materials for the History of the Tsardom of the Emperor Nicholas Pavlovich") (Leipzig, 1880).

The most extensive treatment of the whole reign is Theodor Schiemann, *Geschichte Russlands unter Kaiser Nikolaus I* (3 vols.; Berlin, 1904–13). An older work of some interest, but of no great value is S. M. Schmucker, *Life and Reign of Nicholas of Russia* (Philadelphia, 1856). Of more use, though it covers only to 1830, is N. K. Shilder, *Imperator Nikolai I* ("Emperor Nicholas I") (2 vols.; St. Petersburg, 1903).

New facts and new interpretations about the leading Russian intellectuals of the period are to be found in a work already cited: Max Laserson, *The American Impact on Russia*. More limited in scope is David Hecht, *Russian Radicals Look to America, 1825–1894* (Cambridge, Mass.: Harvard Univ. Press, 1947).

An extremely valuable primary source on Russian conditions in the 1840's is Baron A. von Haxthausen, *The Russian Empire, Its People, Institutions, and Resources,* tr. R. Farie (2 vols.; London, 1856). These volumes are rather rare, but long excerpts from them are reprinted in my *Readings*.

There is a specialized and growing literature concerning the literary-political-intellectual leaders and movements of the nineteenth century. Masaryk, *Spirit of Russia* (listed earlier) is both a good introduction and a good summary. Many of the writings of the leading figures are available in translation and most of them are, of course, quite readily available in Russian. Examples of the latter are V. G. Bielinskii, *Sochineniia* ("Complete Works") (4 vols.; St. Petersburg, 1900); Alexander Gertsen (Herzen), *Byloe i Dumyi* ("Thoughts and Recollections") (5 vols.; Berlin, 1921) and his *Sochineniia* (4 vols.; Geneva, 1875–78).

Translations available (among others) include: Alexander Herzen, *The Memoirs of Alexander Herzen,* ed. J. Duff (New Haven, Conn.: Yale Univ. Press, 1923); I. S. Turgenev, *A Sportsman's Sketches* (N.Y.: Dutton, 1932); Nicholas Gogol, *Taras Bulba* and *Dead Souls* (Everyman's Library); and Sergei Aksakov, *A Russian Gentleman* (N.Y.: Readers Club, 1943).

A fascinating, eyewitness account of the literary circles is Prince Kropotkin, *Memoirs of a Revolutionist* (Boston: Houghton Mifflin,

1899). A recent biography of Kropotkin by G. Woodcock and I. Avakumovic, *The Anarchist Prince* (London: Boardman, 1950) tells his story from within a Marxist framework.

The best-balanced and most informative summary of Slavophilism and Pan-Slavism is to be found in B. H. Sumner, *Russia and the Balkans, 1870–1880* (London: Milford, 1937). The summary serves as an introduction to the main part of that study.

CHAPTER XII. THE OUTWARD POLICIES, 1825–55

The literature on the Eastern question is too full even to be exemplified. However, several works which particularly influenced my interpretations are: H. L. Hoskins, *British Routes to India* (N.Y.: Longmans, Green, 1928); Philip Mosely, *Russian Diplomacy and the Opening of the Eastern Question in 1838 and 1839* (Cambridge, Mass.: Harvard Univ. Press, 1934); V. J. Puryear, *International Economics and Diplomacy in the Near East* (Stanford, Calif.: Stanford Univ. Press, 1935); Harold Temperley, *England and the Near Crimea* (London: Longmans, Green, 1936). I also made considerable use of the documents and comments in the volumes by Martens listed above, and B. E. Schmitt, "The Diplomatic Preliminaries of the Crimean War," *American Historical Review,* XXV, no. 1 (1919): 36–67. A synthesis, mainly of secondary works, which summarizes the narrative diplomatic history of the middle nineteenth century is Andrei Lobanov-Rostovsky, *Russia and Europe, 1825–1878* (Ann Arbor, Mich.: Wahr, 1954).

CHAPTER XIII. THE STATE OF THE NATION AND OTHER MATTERS

The details which were synthesized to form this chapter were dredged from many sources, with not much return from any single one. It is not feasible to list them all and, anyway, most of them have been or will be listed under other chapters. Among those which have been listed are the works of Mavor, Lyaschenko, Rambaud, Pokrovsky, Leroy-Beaulieu, Haxthausen, and Skrine. Among those which will be listed in later chapters are the works of Tatishev, Robinson, Wallace, Kennan, and others. But a few—which might with equal propriety be listed elsewhere—may be set down here because they were in some way particularly useful for this chapter.

For data on population and censuses: Frank Lorimer, *The Population of the Soviet Union: History and Prospects* (Geneva, 1946). For illuminating allusions to the "old" government of Russia, Paul Vinogradoff, *Self-government in Russia* (London: Constable, 1915). For a review of peasant attitudes see S. M. Kravchinskii (Stepniak), *The Russian Peasantry* (London: Routledge, 1905).

Some works by and about Belinsky and Herzen were listed previously. To these may be added: E. H. Carr, *Michael Bakunin* (N.Y.: Macmillan, 1937)—a careful but not unsympathetic study; N. Lerner, *Belinskii* (in Russian) (Moscow, 1922); N. Nekrasov, *Who Can Be Happy and Free in Russia?* (World's Classic Series); and Nicholas Gogol, *The Revisor.*

Two accounts which were influential in forming Western opinions of Russia were: The Marquis de Custine, *Russia* (several editions in French and English); and Count A. de Gurowski, *Russia As It Is* (several editions in French and English). There were American editions of both books in 1854, and some excerpts from the former were reprinted in 1951 under the title *Journey for Our Time,* ed. and tr. P. P. Kohler (N.Y.: Pelligrini & Cudahy).

CHAPTER XIV. REFORMS AND REVOLUTIONARIES

The only biography of Alexander II in English is Stephen Graham, *Tsar of Freedom: Life and Reign of Alexander II* (New Haven, Conn.: Yale Univ. Press, 1935). Unfortunately, it is not a good job. The most extensive treatment in Russian is S. S. Tatishchev, *Imperator Aleksandr II* ("Emperor Alexander II") (2 vols.; St. Petersburg, 1903).

A first-class account, much of it primary in the sense that it was a record of personal observations, is D. Mackenzie Wallace, *Russia* (orig. ed.; London, 1877). Mr. Wallace modified his views as the years went by so that each subsequent, revised edition is somewhat different from its predecessors. Two other interesting eyewitness reports are F. Boyle, *The Narrative of an Expelled Correspondent* (London, 1877); and J. D. Champlain (ed.), *Narrative of the Mission to Russia in 1866 of G. V. Fox from the Journal and Notes of J. F. Loubut* (N.Y.: Appleton, 1873).

Probably the most enlightening single study of the revolutionists of the period is David Footman, *Red Prelude* (New Haven, Conn.: Yale Univ. Press, 1945). There is also a very great deal of information about revolutionists, though mostly of a later period, in the famous work by George Kennan, *Siberia and the Exile System* (2 vols.; N.Y.: Century, 1891). Alice Stone Blackwell edited and published some of Mme. Breshko-Breshkovskaya's letters under the title *The Little Grandmother of the Russian Revolution* (Boston: Little, Brown, 1918). A few items which escaped Miss Blackwell's notice were published in *American Slavic and East Europen Review,* IV, nos. 10–11 (1945): 128–40 (W. B. Walsh, ed.), "Some Breshkovskaya Letters." Also relevant, although it goes beyond the range of this chapter, is Breshko-Breshkovskaya's own book, *Hidden Springs of the Russian Revolution* (Stanford, Calif.: Stanford Univ. Press, 1931).

This period had a special interest for many Russian liberals of the late nineteenth and early twentieth centuries and they frequently referred to it in their works. Examples are P. N. Miliukov, *Russia and Its Crisis* (Chicago: Univ. of Chicago Press, 1906); M. M. Kovalevskii, *Russian Political Institutions* (Chicago: Univ. of Chicago Press, 1902); and S. M. Kravchinski (Stepniak), *Underground Russia* (N.Y.: Scribner, 1883) and *Russia Under the Tzars* (N.Y.: Scribner, 1885).

CHAPTER XV. EXPANSION AND FOREIGN POLICIES
FROM CRIMEA TO KOREA

For information on Russia's Far Eastern policy, in addition to such standard sources as F. Martens, *Sbornik Dogovorov i Diplomaticheskikh Dokumentov po dielam Dalniago Vostoka* ("Collected Agreements and Diplomatic Documents concerning the Far East") (St. Petersburg, 1906), I also used: Hoo Chi-Tsai, *La Chine et la Russie* (Paris, 1918) and F. Martens, *Le conflit entre la Russie et la Chine* (Brussels, 1880). There is some information on the later part of the period covered by this chapter in B. A. Romanov, *Russia in Manchuria, 1892–1906,* tr. S. W. Jones (Ann Arbor, Mich.: Edwards, 1952)—the original Russian edition which I used was published in Leningrad in 1928; S. I. Vitte (Witte), *Vospominaniia* ("Reminiscences") (3 vols.; Berlin, 1922–23); and Avrahm Yarmolinsky (tr. and ed.), *Memoirs of Count Witte* (Garden City, N.Y., 1921).

The article by W. E. Nagengast, "Visit of the Russian Fleet to the United States," *Russian Review,* VIII, no. 1 (1949): 46–55 corrects some long-standing errors. Also important is Hunter Miller, "Russian Opinion on the Cession of Alaska," *American Historical Review,* XLVIII, no. 3 (1949): 521–31.

One of the best short summaries of Russian expansion in Central Asia is found in N. D. Harris, *Europe and the East* (Boston: Houghton Mifflin, 1926). New information of the borderlands is found in the work of Lyashchenko which has previously been cited.

For the story of the rivalries in the Balkans, I followed B. H. Sumner, *Russia and the Balkans 1870–1880* (London: Milford, 1937), in large part, and am indebted to him for some of the materials on Pan-Slavism, though I also borrowed some details from my article, "Pobedonostsev and Panslavism," *Russian Review,* VIII, no. 4 (1949): 316–21. New material was presented by C. W. Clark in "Prince Gorchakov and the Black Sea Question, 1866," *American Historical Review,* XLVIII, no. 1 (1942): 52–60.

My account of the general diplomatic history from 1873 to 1890 rests mainly on standard accounts, somewhat enriched and modified by the seminar work of some of my graduate students. I followed W. L. Langer, *Franco-Russian Alliance, 1890–1894* (Cambridge, Mass.: Harvard Univ. Press, 1929) on that subject. S. Goriainov, *Bosfor i Dardanelly* ("Bosporus and Dardanelles") (St. Petersburg, 1907) is an excellent study for the years from 1798 to 1878. Materials published in *Krasnyi Arkhiv* ("Red Archives") are almost indispensable for a study of this period. Students will find two English-language digests of this publication to be extremely useful. The older is L. S. Rubinchek (comp.), *Digest of the Krasnyi Arkhiv (Red Archives)* Part I, Vols. 1–30 (Cleveland, Ohio: Cleveland Public Library, 1947). The more recent is L. W. Eisele (comp. & annotator), *Digest of the Krasnyi Arkhiv (Red Archives),* Vols. 31–106 (Ann Arbor, Mich.: Univ. of Michigan Press, 1955).

CHAPTER XVI. "PREGNANT WITH MEANING"

Since the reign of Alexander III has not been treated separately by most authors, many of the titles listed for the chapters which precede and follow this one are also relevant here.

The best account of the reign of Alexander III is the work of an archenemy of tsarism, the revolutionary S. M. Kravchinski, who wrote under the pseudonym of Stepniak. His *King Stork and King Log* (2 vols.; London: Downey, 1895) is carefully objective and surprisingly fair. Much less useful is H. von Samson-Himmelstierna, *Russia under Alexander III,* ed. F. Volkhovsky, tr. J. Morrison (N.Y.: Macmillan, 1893).

The most important materials on Pobedonostsev are in Russian. These include: M. N. Pokrovsky (ed.), *K. P. Pobedonostsev i Ego Korrespondenti Pisma i Sapiski* ("K. P. Pobedonostsev and His Correspondence Letters and Notes"), Book I (2 vols.; Leningrad, 1923); "Pisma Pobedonstseva k Aleksandru III" ("Letters of Pobedonostsev to Alexander III"), *Krasnyi Arkhiv,* Vol IV (1923); "Korrespondenti Vitte i Pobedonostsev" ("Witte's Correspondence with Pobedonostsev"), *Krasnyi Arkhiv,* Vol. XXX (1928); and K. P. Pobedonostsev, *Moskovski Sbornik* ("Moscow Collection") (Moscow, 1896). Part of the latter was translated in English by R. C. Long and published as *Reflections of a Russian Statesman* (London: Richards, 1898). There was an excellent, unsigned article, "Pobedonostsev and Alexander III" in *Slavonic and East European Review* (London), VII, no. 19 (1928): 30–54. See also A. F. Tiutcheva, *Pri Dvore Dvukh Imperatov, Dnevnik, 1855–1862* ("At the Courts of Two Emperors, Diary, 1855– 1882") (Moscow, 1929).

An interesting picture of Alexander III is given in Grand Duke Alexander's, *Once a Grand Duke* (N.Y., 1931), and a portrait of the extremist opposition is to be found in Vera Figner, *Memoirs of a Revolutionist* (N.Y.: International Publishers, 1927), an abridged translation of the original. It goes beyond the limits of this chapter.

The voluminous literature on Marx, Engels, and their teachings and followers needs a guide of its own. My account leaned heavily on Leopold Schwarzschild, *Red Prussian* (N.Y.: Scribner, 1947), a well-documented study but with a special thesis which I do not accept. I also owe much to the original edition of an older work by M. M. Bober, *Karl Marx's Interpretation of History* (Cambridge, Mass.: Harvard Univ. Press, 1927). A later edition was published in 1950. A recent pertinent monograph is L. H. Haimson, *Russian Marxists and the Origins of Bolshevism* (Cambridge, Mass.: Harvard Univ. Press, 1955), although its emphasis is on the rise of the Social Democratic Party.

For both facts and interpretations concerning Lenin, Trotsky, Stalin, and the early history of the Party I am much indebted to Dr. Bertram D. Wolfe's outstanding study *Three Who Made a Revolution* (N.Y.: Dial Press, 1945; and Boston: Beacon, 1955). The best biography of Lenin is David Shub, *Lenin, A Biography* (N.Y.: Doubleday, 1948; and Mentor Books, 1950), and the fullest biography of

Stalin is Boris Souvarine, *Stalin, A Critical Survey of Bolshevism* (N.Y.: Longmans, Green, 1939), which is hostile towards its subject. J. T. Murphy, *Stalin, 1879–1944* (London: Lane, 1945) is sympathetic toward Stalin, but not uncritical. I do not hold in high regard Mr. Isaac Deutscher's *Stalin* (N.Y.: Oxford Univ. Press, 1949) nor his later book *The Prophet Armed, Trotsky* (N.Y.: Oxford Univ. Press, 1954); both of which I regard as essentially polemics parading as objective scholarship.

CHAPTER XVII. THE DISTAFF SCEPTER; CHAPTER XVIII. DEVIATION FROM AUTOCRACY; AND CHAPTER XIX. THE FIRST RIDE OF THE FOUR HORSEMEN

The story told by these chapters is so tightly linked that it is realistic to combine the listing of sources into a single subsection.

The leading Western authority on the domestic history of this period was the late Sir Bernard Pares. I am greatly obligated to him for information, interpretations, and probably even for phraseology, since he most generously spent many hours discussing and describing to me the events and persons of this period. His most important study (which he always referred to as "my big book") is *The Fall of the Russian Monarchy* (N.Y.: Knopf, 1939). In addition to its other merits, the volume contains a very helpful critical bibliography. Greater detail concerning the years of "The Liberation Movement" will be found in his *Russia and Reform* (London: Constable, 1907). Sir Bernard also published two volumes of reminiscences: *My Russian Memoirs* (London: Cape, 1931 and 1935), and *A Wandering Student* (Syracuse, N.Y.: Syracuse Univ. Press, 1948). Some of the recollections of Sir Bernard's friend and colleague the late Professor Samuel Harper have been edited by the latter's brother Paul Harper, under the title *The Russia I Believe In* (Chicago: Univ. of Chicago Press, 1945).

The memoirs and commentaries of some of the leading participants are available in English either in whole or in part. Many important excerpts from these and other primary materials will be found in F. A. Golder (ed.), *Documents of Russian History, 1914–1917* (N.Y.: Appleton-Century, 1927). I have reprinted some others in my *Readings* which contains some twenty items—most of them primary sources—on this period. Other documents and materials of value will be found in O. H. Gankin and H. H. Fisher (eds.), *The Bolsheviks and the World War* (Stanford, Calif.: Stanford Univ. Press, 1940).

Among the memoirs of especial value are: Basil Gourko, *War and Revolution in Russia, 1914–1917* (N.Y.: Macmillan, 1919); V. I. Gurko, *Features and Figures of the Past* (Stanford, Calif.: Stanford Univ. Press, 1939); Alexander Izvolski (Iswolsky), *Memoires* (London and Paris, 1921); V. N. Kokovtsov, *Out of My Past,* ed. H. H. Fisher (Stanford, Calif.: Stanford Univ. Press, 1933); F. M. von Ludendorff, *My War Memories, 1914–1918* (2 vols.; London: Hutchinson, n.d.); Baron Rosen, *Forty Years of Diplomacy* (2 vols.; London: Allen and Unwin, 1922); Pierre Gilliard, *Treize années à la cour de Russie* (Paris, 1926), also available in English as *Thirteen Years at the Russian Court* (N.Y.: Doran, n.d.); Sir George Buchanan, *My Mission to Russia* (2 vols.; Boston: Little, Brown, 1923) and Maurice Paleologue, *La Russie des tsars pendant la grande guerre* (3 vols.; Paris: Plon-Nourrit, 1921–22). Also available is V. Sukhomlinov, *Vospominaniia* ("Reminiscences") (Berlin, 1924).

Against Witte's own story (listed earlier) there may be placed: E. de Cyon, *Les finances russes et l'épargne française: Réponse à M. Witte* (Paris, 1895) and *M. Witte et les finances russe* . . . (4th ed.; Paris, 1895). There are also some revelations in V. V. Vodovozov, *Graf S. Iu. Witte i Imperator Nikolai II* ("Count Witte and Emperor Nicholas II") (Leningrad, 1922), and in M. P. Bock, *Vospominaniia o Moem Otse P. A. Stolypine* ("Reminiscences of My Father, P. A. Stolypin") (N.Y.: Chekhov, 1953). Alexander Kerensky's book *The Crucifixion of Liberty* (N.Y.: John Day, 1934), though not a memoir in the formal sense, is a highly personalized history of Russia from 1881 to 1917.

I have also used extensively autobiographical and biographical articles which were published in the University of Liverpool's *Russian Review* and in the *Slavonic and East European Review* (London). A partial list follows. From the *Slavonic Review:* M. Rodichev, "Veteran of Russian Liberalism: Ivan Petrunkevich," VII, no. 20 (1928): 316–27; and F. Rodichev, "The Liberal Movement in Russia," II, no. 5 (1923): 249–62. From the *Russian Review* (Liverpool): S. Shidlovsky, "The Imperial Duma and the Land Settlement," I, no. 1 (1912): 18–26; S. Syromatnikov, "Reminiscences of Stolypin," Vol. I, no. 2 (1912); M. V. Rodzyanko, "The Third Duma," and M. Alexeyenko, "Five Years of Budget Work," I, no. 3 (1912): 3–44; S. N. Harper, "Exceptional Measures in Russia," I, no. 4 (1912): 92–105; G. Khrustalyev-Nosar, "The Council of Workmen Deputies," and Bernard Pares, "Conversations with Stolypin," II, no. 1 (1913): 59–110.

The richest single documentary source for the last years of the old regime is the published stenographic report of the special investigating commission which was set up by the Provisional Government to explore the whole situation. The commission's findings were published by the Soviets under the title *Padenie Tsarskago Rezhima* ("The Fall of the Tsarist Regime") (6 vols.; Leningrad, 1924–26). Many other pertinent materials will be found also in the *Krasny Arkhiv*. Extremely helpful to English-reading students are the two translations previously mentioned: L. S. Rubinchek (comp.), *Digest of the Krasnyi Arkhiv (Red Archives)*, Part I, Vols. 1–30 (Cleveland, Ohio: Cleveland Public Library, 1947) and L. W. Eisele (comp. and annotator), *Digest of the Krasnyi Arkhiv (Red Archives)*, Vols. 31–106 (Ann Arbor, Mich.: Univ. of Michigan Press, 1955).

The diaries and correspondence of the imperial family have also been quite fully exploited. The following are available in Western languages: E. J. Bing (ed.), *Letters of Tsar Nicholas and Empress Marie* (London, 1937); H. Bernstein (ed.), *The Willy-Nicky Correspondence* (N.Y., 1918); Lichnevsky (tr.), *Lettres des grandducs à Nicholas II* (Paris, 1926); and more important, Bernard Pares (ed.), *Letters of the Tsaritsa to the Tsar, 1914–1916* (N.Y., 1924);

and V. Lavarevski (tr. and ed.), *Archives secretes de l'Empereur Nicholas II* (Paris, 1928). Available only in Russian are: *Pisma Imperatrisii Aleksandrii Fedorovnii k Imperatoru Nikolaiu II* ("Letters of the Empress Alexandra Federovna to Emperor Nicholas II") (2 vols.; Berlin, 1922); *Perepiska Nikolai i Aleksandri Romanovikh* ("The Correspondence of Nicholas and Alexandra Romanov") (5 vols.; Moscow, 1925); and *Perepiska Vilgelma II s Nikolaem II, 1894–1914* ("Correspondence of William II with Nicholas II, 1894–1914") (Moscow, n.d.). The last two were edited by Pokrovsky. Nicholas' diary has also been published in Russian: *Dnevnik Imperatora Nikolaia II* ("Diary of Emperor Nicholas II") (Berlin, 1923).

Professor Langer gave a good general coverage of Russian diplomatic history in his books *European Alliances and Alignments* (N.Y.: Knopf, 1931) and *The Diplomacy of Imperialism* (2 vols.; N.Y.: Knopf, 1935). A brief and popularly written account is S. A. Korff, *Russia's Foreign Relations during the Last Half Century* (N.Y.: Macmillan, 1922). Among the more specialized studies are: R. P. Churchill, *The Anglo-Russian Convention of 1907* (Cedar Rapids, Iowa: Torch Press, 1939)—a conventional diplomatic history; Ken Shen Weigh, *Russo-Chinese Diplomacy* (Shanghai, 1922)—valuable because of its materials from the Chinese Repository; Pierre Marc, *Quelques années de politique internationale* (Leipzig, 1914)—containing material from the Witte papers; B. J. Sumner, *Tsardom and Imperialism in the Far and Middle East* (Oxford, Eng.: Oxford Univ. Press, 1940)—a brief historical essay; Pauline Tompkins, *American-Russian Relations in the Far East* (N.Y.: Macmillan, 1949)—chiefly concerned with the period after 1918, but with an excellent introductory summary; V. A. Yakhontoff, *Russia and the Soviet Union in the Far East* (N.Y.: Coward, McCann, 1931)—pro-Soviet, but useful because Yakhontoff had access to archival material; and E. H. Zabriskie, *American-Russian Rivalry in the Far East, 1895–1914* (Philadelphia: Univ. of Pennsylvania Press, 1946)—a conventional monograph.

The fullest account of Russia in the period just prior to and during World War I is found in a multi-volumed, collaborative work published by Yale University Press for the Carnegie Foundation, J. T. Shotwell (ed.), *Economic and Social History of the World War, Russian Series,* Russian Series ed. Sir Paul Vinogradoff and M. T. Florinsky (New Haven, Conn.: Yale Univ. Press, 1928). It is, like all such such works, uneven in quality but is—on the whole—a useful reference. The liveliest account of the military campaigns is Winston Churchill, *The Unknown War* (N.Y.: Scribner, 1931), though it treats the story rather from the German than from the Russian side.

The work of Dr. Harold Williams, from which I used extensive quotations, is adequately identified in the text. Also useful are: Maurice Baring, *The Russian People* (London, 1911) and his *Main Springs of Russia* (London, 1914)—Baring knew Russia well; J. D. Duff (ed.), *Russian Realities and Problems* (Cambridge, Eng.: Cambridge Univ. Press, 1917)—a collection of essays by some of the leading Russian authorities such as Miliukov; Baron A. Heyking, *Practical Guide for Russian Consular Officers* (2d ed.; London, 1916); and *Russia and the*

Imperial Russian Government Economic and Financial (National City Bank of New York, 1916).

One of the most important studies on the Russian agrarian problem is G. T. Robinson, *Rural Russia Under the Old Regime* (Reprint; N.Y.: Macmillan, 1949), which I listed in Section I. There is also another careful and well-founded study by L. A. Owen, *The Russian Peasant Movement, 1906–1917* (London, 1937). A contemporary account in English is H. P. Kennard, *The Russian Peasant* (London, 1907). Considerable information about prerevolutionary Russia is given by Sir John Maynard in his two books *Russia in Flux* and *The Russian Peasant*. These have been skillfully edited and abridged by S. H. Guest under the title *Russia in Flux* (N.Y.: Macmillan, 1948). Sir John's main concern was with the Soviet period. This is also true of Manya Gordon, *Workers Before and After Lenin* (N.Y.: Dutton, 1941), which has a valuable introductory section on Tsarist Russia.

A good deal of trash has been written about Rasputin. The fullest record, but unfortunately not a reliable one, is René Fülöp-Müller, *Rasputin, the Holy Devil,* tr. F. Flint and D. Tait (N.Y.: Viking, 1928). S. M. Trufanoff, *The Mad Monk of Russia* (N.Y.: Century, 1918) manages to get two errors in the title alone—Rasputin was neither mad nor a monk. Two of the most curious accounts of Rasputin were published by two of the men who killed him: V. M. Purishkevich, *Iz Dnevnika . . . Ubiistvo Rasputina* ("From the Diary . . . of the Murderer of Rasputin") (Paris, 1923); and F. Youssoupov, *Rasputin: His Malignant Influence and His Assassination* (London: Cape, 1927). A little-known aspect of Rasputin's behavior was recorded by Avrahm Simanovich, Rasputin's business manager, in *Rasputin i Evrei* ("Rasputin and the Jews") (Riga, n.d.).

Concerning the dumas, there is a monographic study on the Second Duma by Alfred Levin, *The Second Duma* (New Haven, Conn.: Yale Univ. Press, 1940). My working bibliography on the subject may be found in two of my published articles: "The Composition of the Dumas," *Russian Review,* VIII, no. 2 (1949): 111–16; and "Political Parties in the Russian Dumas," *Journal of Modern History,* XXII, no. 2 (1950): 144–50.

Among the various other studies to which these chapters owe something are: J. S. Curtiss, *Church and State in Russia;* V. I. Kovalevskii (ed.), *Rossiia v Kontsie XIX Veka* ("Russia at the Close of the 19th Century") (St. Petersburg, 1900); M. I. Tugan-Baranovskii, *Russkaia Fabrika v Proshlom i Nastoiashchem* ("Russian Factories, Past and Present") (1st ed.; St. Petersburg, 1898; latest ed.; Moscow, 1922); M. M. Kovalevskii, *La crise russe* (Paris, 1906); E. E. Kluge, *Die Russische Revolutionare Presse . . . , 1855–1905* (Zurich, 1948)—a useful though incomplete pioneer study; V. K. Korostovetz, *Seed and Harvest* (London: Faber and Faber, n.d.)—most revealing on the attitudes of some of the Russian upper classes; M. V. Rodzianko, *The Reign of Rasputin* (N.Y., n.d.)—written mostly from memory and therefore not always accurate; and A. T. Vasilev, *The Ochrana* (N.Y.: Harpers, 1930). D. W. Treadgold, *Lenin and His Rivals* (N.Y.: Praeger, 1955) is particularly strong on the period around 1905.

Available documentary and archival collections, in addition to those previously listed, include: *1905 God, Materialy i Dokumenty* ("The year 1905, Materials and Documents") (2 vols.; Leningrad, 1925–27); *Russko-Germanskie Otnosheniia, 1873–1914* ("Russo-German Relations, 1873–1914") (Moscow, 1922); *Materialy po Istorii Franko-Russkikh Otnoshenii za 1910–1914 gg.* ("Materials for a History of Franco-Russian Relations, 1910–1914") (Moscow, 1922); and *Mezhdunarodnye Otnosheniia v Epoku Imperializma* ("International Relations in the Epoch of Imperialism"), Series II, 1900–1913 (20 vols.; Leningrad, 1938–40; Series III, 1914–17 (10 vols.; Moscow, 1931–38).

CHAPTER XX. THE YEAR 1917; CHAPTER XXI. THE SECOND RIDE OF THE FOUR HORSEMEN; CHAPTER XXII. SOME ECONOMIC AND OTHER EXPERIMENTS

The extensive bibliographical aids which are readily available for this period make it superfluous to attempt any general coverage here. In addition to the bibliographies listed in Section I and also those given in many secondary and monographic works, there is a very complete, special bibliography: S. P. Postnikov, *Bibliografiia Russkoi Revoliutsii i Grazhdanskoi Voiny, 1917–1921* ("Bibliography for the Russian Revolution and Civil War, 1917–1921") (Prague, 1938).

These three chapters were written mainly from primary sources. Among those available in English are the following: Henri Barbusse (ed.), *Soviet Union in War and Peace* (N.Y.: International Publishers, n.d.)—documents concerning the "peace proposals" of 1917 to 1929; James Bunyan, *Intervention, Civil War and Communism in Russia, April–December, 1918* (Baltimore, Md.: Johns Hopkins Univ. Press, 1936)—an extremely valuable collection of documents and other materials; James Bunyan and H. H. Fisher (eds.), *Bolshevik Revolution, 1917–1918* (Stanford, Calif.: Stanford Univ. Press, 1934); Jane Degras (ed.), *Soviet Documents on Foreign Policy*, Vol. I, 1917–24; Vol. II, 1925–32; Vol. III, 1933–41 (N.Y.: Oxford Univ. Press, 1951–53); Jane Degras (ed.), *The Communist International, 1919–1943, Documents*, Vol. I, 1919–22 (London: Oxford Univ. Press, 1956); *Soviet Treaty Series, Collection of Bilateral Treaties, Agreements . . . Between the Soviet Union and Foreign Powers*, Vol. I, 1917–28; Vol. II, 1929–39 (Wash., D.C., Georgetown Univ. Press, 1950 and 1955)—these last three items all go beyond the chronological limits of these two chapters and Mrs. Degras' most recent volume became available too late for my use in this book; O. H. Gankin and H. H. Fisher, *Bolsheviks and the World War* (Stanford, Calif.: Stanford Univ. Press, 1940); and F. A. Golder, *Documents of Russian History* (N.Y.: Century, 1927); M. M. Laserson (ed.), *Development of Soviet Foreign Policy, 1917–1942* (Carnegie Endowment for International Peace, January, 1943); and U.S. Dept. of State, *Papers Relating to the Foreign Relations of the United States, 1918, Russia* (3 vols.; Wash., D.C.: Govt. Printing Office, 1932). I also used some of the primary-source materials printed in my *Readings*.

Among the major documentary collections in Russian are: *Arkhiv Grazhdanskoi Voiny* ("Archives of the Civil War") (2 vols.; Berlin, 1922); *Arkhiv Oktiabrskoi Revoliutsii 1917 God v Dokumentakh i Materialalkh* ("Archives of the October Revolution, 1917 . . .") (Moscow and Leningrad, 1930– . . .); J. V. Gessen (ed.), *Arkhiv Russkoi Revoliutsii* ("Archives of the Russian Revolution") (22 vols.; Berlin, 1921–37); *Dokumenty Velikoi Oktiabrskoi Sotsialisticheskoi Revoliutsii* ("Documents of the Great October Socialist Revolution") (Moscow, 1942); I. Mintz and E. Gorodetskii, *Dokumenty po Istorii Grazhdanskoi Voiny v SSSR* ("Documents for the History of the Civil War in the USSR") (Moscow, 1940); I. M. Razgon and E. Gorodetskii, *Dokumenty Velikoi Proletarskoi Revoliutsii* ("Documents Concerning the Great Proletarian Revolution"), Vol. I (Moscow, 1938).

There are numerous histories of the revolutions, ranging in length all the way from E. H. Carr, *Bolshevik Revolution, 1917–1923* (3 vols.; N.Y.: Macmillan, 1950–53) to the small volume of text and documents by J. S. Curtiss, *Russian Revolutions of 1917* (Princeton, N.J.: Van Nostrand, 1957). There is no narrative history in Carr's volumes, which are at least quasi-Marxist in their analyses. Professor Curtiss' book is designed for use in college classes. Still the best on balance is W. H. Chamberlin, *Russian Revolution, 1917–1921* (2 vols.; new ed.; N.Y.: Macmillan, 1952). Two recent, valuable monographs are Richard N. Pipes, *Formation of the Soviet Union* (Cambridge, Mass.: Harvard Univ. Press, 1954) and J. S. Reshetar, *The Ukrainian Revolution, 1917–1920, A Study in Nationalism* (Princeton, N.J.: Princeton Univ. Press, 1952). Among the others are the following apologiae by some of the principal participants: V. M. Chernov, *The Great Russian Revolution,* tr. and ed. P. E. Mosely (New Haven, Conn.: Yale Univ. Press, 1936); A. F. Kerensky, *The Catastrophe, Kerensky's Own Story* (N.Y.: Appleton, 1927) and *Prelude to Bolshevism, The Kornilov Rising* (N.Y., 1919); P. N. Miliukov, *Istorii Vtoroi Russkoi Revoliutsii* ("History of the Second Russian Revolution") (3 parts; Sofia, 1921); P. A. Sorokin, *Leaves from a Russian Diary—and Thirty Years After* (Boston: Beacon, 1950)—the Miliukov and Sorokin volumes are not properly called apologiae; N. N. Sukhanov, *Russian Revolution, 1917,* tr. and ed. J. Carmichael (N.Y.: Oxford Univ. Press, 1955); and Leon Trotsky, *History of the Russian Revolution* (3 vols.; N.Y.: 1932–34; reissued in one volume by the Univ. of Michigan Press, 1957). Brief versions of various Soviet accounts may be found in the *History of the Communist Party of the Soviet Union (Bolshevik) Short Course,* published in many languages and numerous editions. There is also an English translation of M. Gorkii (ed.), *Istoriia Grazhdanskoi Voiny v SSSR* ("History of the Civil War in the USSR") (2 vols.; Moscow, 1938 and 1943). Other important official sources are the stenographic reports of the congresses of the Communist Party and of the Comintern. These have also been published in several languages and editions.

Secondary accounts of Soviet foreign policies are relatively numerous and, like all materials about the Soviets, tremendously varied in worth and in viewpoints. Several of the following cover longer periods than do these three chapters. Max Beloff, *Foreign Policy of Soviet Russia* (2 vols.; N.Y.: Oxford Univ. Press, 1949)—standard, hard to read; R. P. Browder, *Origins of Soviet-American Diplomacy* (Princeton, N.J.: Princeton Univ. Press, 1953)—monographic; A. L. P. Dennis, *Foreign Policies of Soviet Russia* (N.Y.: Dutton, 1924)—a good survey but a little too close to some of the events described to have perspective; Louis Fischer, *Soviets in World Affairs* (2 vols.; 1st ed., 1930; reissued by the Princeton Univ. Press in 1951)—pro-Soviet, but very well informed; G. F. Kennan, *Soviet American Relations, Russia Leaves the War*, Vol. I (Princeton, N.J.: Princeton Univ. Press, 1956) —a professional diplomat turns to scholarship; M. M. Laserson and J. T. Shotwell, *Russia and Poland, 1919–1945* (N.Y.: King's Crown, 1945)—a scholarly presentation of a very controversial subject; Aurelio Palmieri, *La Politica Asiatica dei Bolscevichi* (Bologna, 1924)— monographic; T. A. Taracouzio, *War and Peace in Soviet Diplomacy* (N.Y.: Macmillan, 1940)—an indispensable analysis; B. M. Unterberger, *America's Siberian Expedition, 1918–1920* (Durham, N.C.: Duke Univ. Press, 1956)—monographic; R. D. Warth, *Allied Diplomacy and the Russian Revolution* (Durham, N.C.: Duke Univ. Press, 1953)—highly critical; and J. A. White, *Siberian Intervention* (Princeton, N.J.: Princeton Univ. Press, 1950)—well-balanced study.

I have drawn particular points on Soviet life from 1917 to 1921 from each of the following works. Their titles indicate their special fields. P. B. Anderson, *People, Church and State in Modern Russia* (N.Y.: Macmillan, 1944); E. Boelza, *Handbook of Soviet Musicians* (London, 1943); A. Block, *Changing World in Plays and Theatre* (Boston: Little, Brown, 1939); Jack Chen, *Soviet Arts and Letters* (London, 1944); J. F. Hecker, *Religion and Communism* (London, 1933); Hans Kohn, *Nationalism in the Soviet Union* (N.Y.: Columbia Univ. Press, 1933); Simon Liberman, *Building Lenin's Russia* (Chicago: Univ. of Chicago Press, 1945); M. Spinka, *The Church and the Russian Revolution* (N.Y.: Macmillan, 1927); N. S. Timasheff, *Religion in Soviet Russia, 1917–1942* (N.Y.: Oxford Univ. Press, 1948); and D. F. White, *Growth of the Red Army* (Princeton, N.J.: Princeton Univ. Press, 1944). A more recent study of the Russian army from a different viewpoint is B. H. Liddell Hart, *Red Army* (N.Y.: Harcourt, 1956).

CHAPTER XXIII. PARTY FEUDS AND THE FIRST FIVE-YEAR PLAN; CHAPTER XXIV. COLLECTIVES, PLANS, AND THE "RULER-IN-LAW"; CHAPTER XXV. CONSPIRACY AND DIPLOMACY; CHAPTER XXVI. "THE SECOND GREAT FATHERLAND WAR"; CHAPTER XXVII. STALIN'S LAST YEARS; CHAPTER XXVIII. WORLD WAR TO COLD WAR; CHAPTER XXIX. "UNFINISHED BUSINESS"

There are thousands of books about the Soviet Union—books to suit almost every interest, prejudice, taste, and conviction—books which range from dull pedantry to frivolous chit-chat, from eulogy to abuse, from scholarship seeking to advance truth to scholarship prostituted to the advancement of special interests. It is manifestly impossible to list all these books here. Even a true representative sampling would be too long—my bibliographical files, which are far from complete, contain upwards of 2000 cards. A selected list of "best books" would depend to an unacceptable degree upon subjective judgment. The titles which follow are therefore solely suggestions of where to begin to find further information. The appropriate parts of Section I and the notes to the last ten chapters should also be consulted.

In the writing of these final chapters, I have referred more often to primary sources of a wide variety than to secondary accounts. Memoirs, autobiographies, speeches, reports, testimony, eyewitness accounts—published in books, periodicals, newspapers, pamphlets, and monitored radio broadcasts—have all been used. Yet I certainly have neither seen nor used all available sources. Over the years, for example, I have collected items from *Pravda, Izvestia, Krasnaia Zvezda, Moscow News,* and other Soviet newspapers, but I have not made a systematic, literal day-by-day combing of these sources. The same is true of the *Times* (London), the *New York Times,* the *Manchester Guardian,* the *Christian Science Monitor,* and other Western newspapers; and also of Soviet and Western periodicals. I was very much assisted for a time by the *Soviet Press Translations* (Seattle, Wash.: Univ. of Washington Press, 1946–51) and for a longer period by the *Current Digest of the Soviet Press* (N.Y.: Joint Committee on Slavic Studies, 1949– . . .).

The secondary sources which follow are divided, somewhat arbitrarily, into "analytical tools" and substantive accounts. Of course, the two are not mutually exclusive. The distinction, though mainly a matter of emphasis, is useful in separating studies of the concepts which underlie a system from those which concentrate on describing the system or its parts. R. A. Bauer, Alex Inkeles, and Clyde Kluckhohn, *How the Soviet System Works* (Cambridge, Mass.: Harvard Univ. Press, 1956); R. A. Bauer and Edward Wasiolek, *Nine Soviet Portraits* (N.Y.: Wiley, 1955); F. Beck and W. Godin (pseuds.), *Russian Purge and the Extraction of Confession,* tr. Eyre Mosbacker and David Porter (N.Y.: Viking, 1951); Z. K. Brzezinski, *Permanent Purge, Politics in Soviet Totalitarianism* (Cambridge, Mass.: Harvard Univ. Press, 1956); Milovan Djilas, *The New Class* (N.Y.: Praeger, 1957); Alexander Inkeles, *Public Opinion in Soviet Russia* (Cambridge, Mass.: Harvard Univ. Press, 1950); R. L. Garthoff, *Soviet Military Doctrine* (Glencoe, Ill.: Free Press, 1953); Nathan Leites, *Operational Code of the Politburo* (N.Y.: McGraw-Hill, 1951); Nathan Leites, *Study of Bolshevism* (Glencoe, Ill.: Free Press, 1953); Barrington Moore, *Soviet Politics, Dilemma of Power* (Cambridge, Mass.: Harvard Univ. Press, 1950); Barrington Moore, *Terror and Progress U.S.S.R.* (Cambridge, Mass.: Harvard Univ. Press, 1954); Gerhart Niemeyer and J. S. Reshetar, *Inquiry into Soviet Mentality* (N.Y.: Praeger, 1956); J. S. Reshetar, *Problems of Analysing and Predicting Soviet Behavior* (Garden City, N.Y.: Doubleday, 1955); W. W. Rostow and Alfred Levin, *Dynamics of Soviet Society* (N.Y.: Norton, 1953); and Philip Selznick, *Organizational Weapon, Study of Bolshevik Strategy and Tactics* (N.Y.: McGraw-Hill, 1952) are analytical.

The substantive accounts are subdivided into (1) those which range over many subjects or cover several demi-decades, and (2) those which are specialized as to subject or more limited in time span. The listings in both subdivisions are alphabetical without regard to the nature of the work.

American Federation of Labor, *Slave Labor in Russia* (Wash., D.C.: 1949); D. Iu. Bakhshiev, *Organizatsionnie Osnovy Bolshevistkoi Partii* ("Organizational Principles of the Bolshevik Party") (Moscow, 1945); F. C. Barghoorn, *Soviet Russian Nationalism* (N.Y.: Oxford Univ. Press, 1956); W. R. Batsell, *Soviet Rule in Russia* (N.Y., 1929); Fedor Belov, *History of a Soviet Collective Farm* (N.Y.: Praeger, 1955); H. J. Berman, *Justice in Russia* (Cambridge, Mass.: Harvard Univ. Press, 1950); D. G. Bishop, *Soviet Foreign Relations, Documents and Readings* (Syracuse, N.Y.: Syracuse Univ. Press, 1950); W. H. Chamberlin, *Soviet Russia* (Boston: Little, Brown, 1930); J. S. Curtiss, *Russian Church and Soviet State, 1917–1950* (Boston: Little, Brown, 1953); D. J. Dallin, *Changing World of Soviet Russia* (New Haven, Conn.: Yale Univ. Press, 1956); D. J. Dallin, *Soviet Russia and the Far East* (New Haven, Conn.: Yale Univ. Press, 1948); D. J. Dallin and B. I. Nicolaevsky, *Forced Labor in Soviet Russia* (New Haven, Conn.: Yale Univ. Press, 1947); Margaret Dewar, *Labour Policy in the USSR, 1917–1928* (N.Y.: Royal Institute of International Affairs, 1956); Nicholas DeWitt, *Soviet Professional Manpower* (Wash., D.C.: National Science Foundation, 1955); *Gosudarstvennoe Ustroistvo SSSR i RSFSR* ("Governmental Organization in the USSR and RSFSR") (Moscow, 1939); S. N. Harper, *Civic Training in Soviet Russia* (Chicago: Univ. of Chicago Press, 1929); John Hazard, *Law and Social Change in the USSR* (Toronto, Ont.: Carswell, 1953); O. J. Heilbrunn, *Soviet Secret Service* (N.Y.: Praeger, 1956); A. K. Herling, *Soviet Slave Empire* (N.Y.: Funk, 1951); G. Hilger and A. G. Meyer, *The Incompatible Allies; a Memoir History of German-Soviet Relations, 1918–1941* (N.Y.: Macmillan, 1953); Naum Jasny, *Socialized Agriculture of the USSR* (Stanford, Calif.: Stanford Univ. Press, 1949); J. E. Johnson and Raymond Dennett (eds.), *Negotiating with the Russians* (Boston: World Peace Foundation, 1951); V. A. Karpinsky, *Social and State Structure of the USSR* (Moscow, 1950); Walter Kolarcz, *Russia and her Colonies* (N.Y.: Praeger, 1953); W. W. Kulski, *Soviet Regime* (rev. ed.; Syracuse, N.Y.: Syracuse Univ. Press, 1954); *Land of Socialism Today and Tomorrow* (Moscow, 1939); J. D. Littlepage and Demaree Bess, *In Search of Soviet Gold* (N.Y.: Harcourt Brace, 1938); J. H. Meisal and E. S. Kozera, *Materials for the Study of the Soviet System* (2d ed.; Ann Arbor, Mich.: Wahr, 1953); Boris Meissner, *Communist Party of the Soviet Union* (N.Y.: Praeger, 1956); S. T. Possony, *Century of Conflict* (Chicago: Regnery, 1953); Leonard Schapiro, *Origin of the Communist Autocracy* (Cambridge, Mass.: Harvard Univ. Press, 1956); Rudolf Schlesinger, *Spirit of Postwar Russia: Soviet Ideology, 1917–1946* (N.Y., 1947); G. K. Schueller, *Politburo* (Stanford, Calif.: Stanford Univ. Press, 1951); F. L. Schuman, *Soviet Politics at Home and Abroad* (N.Y.: Knopf, 1946); S. M. Schwarz, *Jews in the Soviet Union* (Syracuse, N.Y.: Syracuse

Univ. Press, 1951); S. M. Schwarz, *Labor in the Soviet Union* (N.Y.: Praeger, 1952); John Scott, *Behind the Urals* (N.Y.: Houghton Mifflin, 1942); E. J. Simmons (ed.), *Continuity and Change in Russian and Soviet Thought* (Cambridge, Mass.: Harvard Univ. Press, 1955); E. J. Simmons (ed.), *Through the Glass of Soviet Literature: Views of Russian Society* (N.Y.: Columbia Univ. Press, 1953); *Soviet Science* (Wash., D.C.: American Assoc. for the Advancement of Science, 1952); Matthew Spinka, *Church in Soviet Russia* (N.Y.: Oxford Univ. Press, 1956); Gleb Struve, *Soviet Russian Literature, 1917–1950* (Norman, Okla.: Univ. of Oklahoma Press, 1951); N. S. Timasheff, *Great Retreat* (N.Y.: Dutton, 1946); Julian Towster, *Political Power in the USSR, 1917–1947* (N.Y.: Oxford Univ. Press, 1950); and B. D. Wolfe, *Six Keys to the Soviet System* (Boston: Beacon, 1956) are substantive accounts of broad range.

The more limited studies are: R. A. Bauer, *New Man in Soviet Psychology* (Cambridge, Mass.: Harvard Univ. Press, 1952); Alexander Baykov, *Development of the Soviet Economic System* (N.Y.: Macmillan, 1947); Max Beloff, *Soviet Policy in the Far East, 1944–1951* (N.Y.: Oxford Univ. Press, 1953); J. S. Berliner, *Factory and Manager in the USSR* (Cambridge, Mass.: Harvard Univ. Press, 1957); E. H. Carr, *History of Soviet Russia, The Interregnum, 1923–1924* (N.Y.: Macmillan, 1954); Edward Crankshaw, *Cracks in the Kremlin Wall* (N.Y.: Viking, 1951), and *Russia without Stalin* (N.Y.: Viking, 1956); D. J. Dallin, *Soviet Russia's Foreign Policy 1939–1942* (New Haven, Conn.: Yale Univ. Press, 1952); J. R. Deane, *Strange Alliance* (N.Y.: Viking, 1946); F. B. Evans (ed.), *Worldwide Communist Propaganda* (N.Y.: Macmillan, 1955); George Fischer, *Soviet Opposition to Stalin* (Cambridge, Mass.: Harvard Univ. Press, 1952); Michel Gordey, *Visa to Moscow,* tr. K. Woods (N.Y.: Knopf, 1952); Maurice Hindus, *Broken Earth* (N.Y., 1926), *Humanity Uprooted* (N.Y., 1929), and *Red Bread* (N.Y., 1931); C. B. Hoover, *Economic Life of Soviet Russia* (N.Y.: Macmillan, 1931); E. M. Kirkpatrick (ed.), *Target the World* (N.Y.: Macmillan, 1956); Robert Magidoff, *Kremlin vs. the People* (N.Y.: Doubleday, 1953); J. T. MacCurdy, *Germany, Russia, and the Future* (Cambridge, Eng.: Cambridge Univ. Press, 1944); J. T. Murphy, *New Horizons* (London: Lane, 1941); William Nelson (ed.), *Out of the Crocodile's Mouth* (Wash., D.C.: Public Affairs Press, 1949); F. W. Notestein (and others), *Future Population of Europe and the Soviet Union* (Geneva, 1944); V. M. and E. Petrov, *Empire of Fear* (N.Y.: Praeger, 1956); *Report on the Soviet Union in 1956,* Institute for the Study of the U.S.S.R. (Munich: The Institute, 1956); H. L. Roberts, *Russia and America* (N.Y.: Harpers, 1956); Andrew Rothstein (tr.), *Soviet Foreign Policy during the Patriotic War, Documents and Materials* (London, n.d.); Frank Rounds, *Window on Red Square* (Boston: Houghton Mifflin, 1953); M. G. Rozanov (pseud., N. Ognyov), *Diary of a Communist Schoolboy* (N.Y., 1928); M. Rush, *Khrushchev and the Stalin Succession* (Santa Monica, Calif.: Rand, 1957); Harrison Salisbury, *American in Russia* (N.Y.: Harpers, 1955); *Second World War, Documents and Materials Relating to the Eve of* (2 vols.;

N.Y.: International Publishers, 1948); Robert Sherwood, *Roosevelt and Hopkins* (N.Y.: Harpers, 1948); J. L. Snell (ed.), *Meaning of Yalta* (Baton Rouge, La.: Univ. of Louisiana Press, 1956); Soviet Information Bureau, *Falsifiers of History* (Moscow, 1948); *Soveshchanie Informatsonnogo Buro Kommunisticheskikh Partii v Vengrii vo Vtoroi Polovine Noviabria 1949 g.* ("Conference of the Information Bureau of the Communist Parties in Hungary in the Latter Half of November, 1949") (Moscow, 1949); W. B. Smith, *My Three Years in Moscow* (Philadelphia: Lippincott, 1950); L. C. Stevens, *Russian Assignment* (Boston: Houghton Mifflin, 1953); L. Street (ed.), *I Married a Russian* (N.Y.: Emerson Books, 1947); Harry and Roberta Timbres, *We Didn't Ask Utopia* (N.Y.: Prentice-Hall, 1939); U.S. Congress, 85th Congress 1st session, Senate Committee on Foreign Relations, *Control and Reduction of Armaments* (Wash., D.C.: Govt. Printing Office, 1957); U.S. Dept. of State, *Austrian State Treaty* (Wash., D.C.: Govt. Printing Office, 1957); U.S. Dept. of State, *Foreign Relations of the United States, Diplomatic Papers, The Soviet Union, 1933–1939* (Wash., D.C.: Govt. Printing Office, 1952); Alexander Werth, *Moscow War Diary* (N.Y., 1942) and *Year of Stalingrad* (N.Y.: Knopf, 1947); N. A. Voznesensky, *Soviet Economy during World War II* (N.Y.: International Publishers, 1949); and Conway Zirkle, *Death of a Science in Russia* (Philadelphia: Univ. of Pennsylvania Press, 1949).

INDEX

"Charley!" Celie said. "That's disgusting!"

Joey furrowed his brow. "He is a wild animal," he said matter-of-factly. "It's not as though he can take a bath."

"I know he can't take a bath," Celie said. How dumb did Joey think she was? She was getting more and more irritated with him. "Oh, never mind," she said. She slammed the book shut. Better not to know too much anyway, she thought, remembering the bit about monkeys getting aggressive. She wouldn't mention that to Ma, either. Besides, they probably meant in the wild, not in captivity.

She put the mammal book down and picked up *Swallows and Amazons*. She was determined not to like it if Joey thought it was that great. But she got so engrossed in the Walker children's adventures in their sailboat, the *Swallow*, that Ma was calling her to wash up for supper before she knew it.

She'd forgotten all about the park. She'd almost forgotten about Joey; she would have if he hadn't kept laughing out loud as he read. They packed up their books and climbed down from the tree house.

"See you tomorrow," Joey said, giving his little wave as he headed toward Mrs. Bentley's.

"Yeah," Celie said, hoisting Charley onto her shoulder. "See ya."

After supper Celie went right to her room and stayed up reading well into the night. What fun, she thought, to have an island all your own, not to mention pirates to battle. She didn't have an island, but she did have a boat! Tomorrow she'd take Joey down to the cove. They'd have their own ocean adventure. If she had to have Joey around, she might as well make use of him. He could be the first mate. She'd be the captain, since it was her boat.

"And you'll be the ship's boy, huh, Charley?" she said, lifting Charley onto her lap. The monkey opened his eyes briefly, then closed them again and went back to sleep. "Oh no you don't," she said. "Ma would kill me if I let you sleep up here." Reluctantly she got out of bed and carried Charley down to the summer kitchen, where he settled into his crate.

Back in her room Celie turned off her light and opened the blackout curtains a bit to let in some cool air. The bell buoy clanged in the harbor. Now and then a searchlight swept across the sky, reminding her, whether she liked it or not, that there was a war on and that enemy planes might be flying overhead that very minute, ready to drop their bombs and destroy her world instantly and forever.

7

Where's your boyfriend?" Ben asked the next morning.

Celie was just finishing her breakfast. She looked up from her oatmeal and growled. "He's not my boyfriend," she said, dropping a piece of crust on the floor for Charley. "I don't even like him."

"If you say so," Ben said, tugging her braid as he walked to the table and took his seat across from her.

Celie felt like kicking him. Why did everyone have to yank her braids all the time?

"Well," Ma said, pulling out a chair and sitting down at the head of the table, "I think it's nice that you've got Joey to spend time with." She folded her hands and looked hard at Celie. "That makes it a lot easier to tell you this."

Celie felt her breakfast pressing its way back up. She swallowed hard. "Tell us what?" Celie asked. "And what's Joey Bentley got to do with it?"

Ma took a deep breath. "I've taken a job as a welder at the shipyard." She paused. "I'm starting a week from Monday."

"What?" Celie and Ben spoke together in a chorus of disbelief.

"Only for the duration," she said. "To help the war effort. You know they need women to work in the plants. There aren't enough men."

Celie felt the way she did when she had eaten too much cotton candy before she got on the Ferris wheel. She pushed her cereal bowl away. "But what about us?" she said. "Who will take care of us?"

"I'll take care of you. And so will Papa." She stopped, then she started again. "You'll take care of each other. And"—she twisted the gold wedding band on her finger—"Mrs. Bentley has promised to help as much as she can."

"Mrs. Bentley?" Celie groaned.

"Ma!" Ben said.

Celie didn't know which was worse, Ma working or Mrs. Bentley baby-sitting.

"I'm too old for a baby-sitter, Ma," Ben said. He jutted his chin out defiantly. "What can Mrs. Bentley do that we can't?"

"You cook now, do you?" asked Ma. Ben turned away and rubbed at a spot on the table with his thumb. "Look," Ma said. "Your little brother is only six years old. He needs to have a grownup around. Someone I can depend on."

"I can watch him," said Celie. She was all mixed up. On the one hand she wanted Ma around to take care of her, but on the other hand she wanted Ma to think she was old enough to take care of herself—and Andy.

Ma held up her hand again. "It's not open to debate," she said. "You two are barely here during the day anyway, and

I'll be home in the evenings—and in the mornings, too, if you get up that early." At that she looked at Ben again, and Celie couldn't keep from smiling. "You'll hardly know I'm gone."

"But, Ma," Celie said, "I don't want you to go to work." How could she make her mother understand? She might not be home all day, but she needed to know that Ma was there. "Does Papa know? I bet Papa doesn't want you to go to work."

"Of course your father knows," Ma said. "And he knows it's what I have to do. The harder we all work, the sooner this war will be over."

Celie had heard the line before. It was on posters in the post office and the train station, and they flashed it on the screen at the movie theater every Saturday. She knew it. But still, she didn't want Ma to go to work.

"It's only for the duration," Ma said again. "It'll be fine."

Celie wondered if her mother was trying to convince herself, as much as them. Her lips were turning white, they were clamped together so tight, and her chin was quivering. She looked around at them once more, then stood up and turned to the sink. The clattering of dishes filled the room.

Celie felt as though she'd been beaned by a fastball. She knew other mothers had gone to work. And she'd seen the pictures in *Life* of Rosie the Riveter, but she couldn't believe her mother was going to be one of those ladies with scarves wrapped around their heads, building war ships. Wendy the Welder? Ma? At least now she knew why Ma had been pushing Joey Bentley so hard. She didn't want Celie to be home alone all summer. But Celie didn't need Joey. She needed Ma.

Finally Ben said, "I don't know about Mrs. Bentley baby-sitting, but I think you're okay, Ma."

Celie looked at her brother. Something was up. He didn't just throw compliments around like that. Not these days.

He paused and then added, "You know, I've been think-ing of doing the same thing, getting a job. Full time, instead of the part-time work I do down at the docks."

Aha, Celie thought.

"I mean, until I'm old enough to join up, that is. Quit school and—"

Ma spun around. "Benjamin Marsh, you will do no such thing!" she shouted. Celie could see tears forming in her mother's eyes. "You will stay in school and get your diploma and that's final." She wiped her hands on her apron. "Why do you think I'm doing this? I'm doing it so that maybe, just maybe, this war will be over before my son is old enough to fight in it. Oh, I know it's a 'necessary war' and all that. But do you have any idea how scared I am?" Her voice broke off and she ran from the room. Celie thought about the picture in the library book of the monkey defending its young. Her mother's eyes had that same fierce look.

She lifted Charley onto her lap. "At least you won't leave me, Charley," she whispered. "At least I've got you."

When Joey showed up shortly after ten, Celie was still

feeling shell-shocked. She wasn't in the mood for the grand adventure she'd planned yesterday.

He was wearing short pants and his brown lace-up shoes. Didn't he even own a pair of sneakers? How could they set sail to their pretend island if he was wearing brown leather shoes? They'd be ruined, and Mrs. Bentley would blame her. It wasn't his fault, she supposed. He didn't know they were going to the cove.

"Look," she said, "you'll have to go home and change. You'll need sneakers. Something that can get wet."

"Wet?" He said the word as though he didn't know what it meant.

"Yeah," said Celie. "Wet. From water? You know, *wet*."

"These are the only shoes I have," he said. "Rationing," he added, as though that explained it, which it didn't, because he could have three pairs of shoes a year and one of them could be sneakers.

Celie rolled her eyes. "Come on," she said, and headed for the stairs. Joey just stood in the doorway. "Come on!" she said again, and started upstairs. Joey followed her.

"Ben must have some old shoes that'll fit you," she said. "Ma never throws anything out." It was true. All Ben's old clothes were tucked away in the attic until Celie or Andy grew into them. Celie always got Ben's hand-me-downs, even though they were boy's clothes, and Andy had been known to wear hers, as long as they weren't too girlie. Celie was sure there would be shoes in the attic that Joey could use.

A large box marked SHOES sat in one corner. Celie opened it. The musty smell of dried sweat mixed with old leather wafted up. It was a safe smell somehow, timeless and unchanging. The smell of things moving from the past to the future in an orderly fashion, undisturbed by war.

"Okay," she said, "there's got to be something in here."

She pulled out several shoes before she found a pair of sneakers that fit Joey. They were worn at the toe and a piece of the rubber was loose on one, but they'd be fine for wading.

Charley had followed them up the stairs and was investigating the various boxes and piles while Joey tried on shoes.

"Come on, Charley," Celie called, after Joey got the sneakers tied and was ready to go.

But Charley had disappeared.

"Charley?" Celie called. She was sure he hadn't gone downstairs. "Charley!"

She heard a muffled squawk and walked toward the sound.

He was scrunched down inside an old blue satchel behind a rack of clothes.

"You goose," she said. "Come on out of there."

Charley squawked and shook his head.

Celie laughed. It was funny how his reactions sometimes made it seem as though he knew what she was saying. "All right," she said, "stay in there, but you're coming with us anyway. We need a ship's boy." She hauled the satchel out. "This can be your bunk," she said.

She carried the satchel, and Joey followed behind, holding his brown shoes in one hand and clomping down the stairs in the sneakers that were, Celie had to admit, just a bit big.

"Where are we going, anyway?" he asked when they got downstairs.

"To the cove," Celie said, sounding more enthusiastic than she felt. "To be adventurers!"

Joey blinked, and Celie wondered if he knew how to have an adventure.

"You know," she said, "like in *Swallows and Amazons*. Only we don't have an island, so we have to pretend."

Joey blinked again.

"But we have a boat," she said triumphantly, raising her free hand in the air and pointing her index finger toward the sky as though she were leading her troops into battle.

Joey still didn't say anything.

"Just come on," she said. "It'll be fun." But she wasn't convinced herself. Ma had just dropped a bomb on her life, and she was beginning to think that Joey wouldn't know fun if it came up and tagged him.

Celie took Charley out of the satchel and filled it with sandwiches and a canteen of water. She made Joey carry the bag. Charley ran along on all fours. People driving by did a double take. Celie laughed. People expected to see a dog at the end of a leash. When they realized Charley wasn't a dog, they turned back around to see exactly what he was. Celie smiled and waved and acted as though it was nothing out of the ordinary, a girl walking her monkey down the street.

Celie was glad to see that the cove was deserted. "Okay,

mate," she said to Joey. "Turn the boat over and let's get aboard."

"You sure it's okay?" he asked.

"Of course it's okay," Celie said. "It's our boat."

He walked over to the boat and grabbed the gunwale with both hands. The boat flipped over and rocked heavily in the sand.

"Where are the oars?" Joey asked, looking about him. "And the life vests?"

"They're locked in the shack along with the motor," Celie said. "We'll have to pretend."

Joey looked at her blankly. You'd think he'd never pretended before.

"We're not really taking the boat out," she explained. "Papa would kill me."

"Oh," Joey said, and he seemed to relax a little.

"Now, mate," she said, "shove off."

"But if we're not really going in the water," Joey said, "why did I need sneakers?"

"Oh for Pete's sake," Celie said. "The water's not very far away, and if we stay here long enough, we just might meet up with it."

"Oh," Joey said again.

"Just jump out and shove us off," Celie said. She kneeled in the bow and held her pretend oar at the ready. She wanted to go, to get away, as far as possible—even if it was only in her imagination. Ma's announcement had swept over her like a tidal wave and washed all firm ground out from under her.

Joey pretended to shove the boat into the cove. Then he climbed back in and they rowed out to the harbor. Charley kept jumping from the boat, no matter how many times Celie told him he'd get eaten by sharks if he wasn't careful. He was worse at pretending than Joey.

"We should keep an eye out for U-boats," Celie called back to Joey.

"Okay," Joey returned. "But I don't think U-boats would be this close to shore, especially with the civilian air corps around."

"Well, planes then," said Celie. "The ones with the big red circles on the wings."

"The Japanese wouldn't be attacking from the Atlantic side," Joey said. "Too far for them to fly. They'd stick to the Pacific. If anyone would attack this side, it'd be the Germans."

Celie wanted to pop him. Of course she knew the Japanese wouldn't attack this side of the country. She had just gotten mixed up. Besides, this was pretend.

"Okay, the Germans then," Celie said, hoping she didn't sound as annoyed as she felt. She tried to remember the pictures she'd seen of German bombers. She knew they'd shown her pictures in school, and she'd seen them in the newsreels at the movie theater. "They're green, right? With swastikas on the wings?"

"Crosses, actually," said Joey. "The swastikas are on their tails."

Celie looked at Joey. "How do you know so much?"

He shrugged. "I read a lot."

She scanned the sky again and wondered whether she'd know a German plane if she saw one. She'd have to tell by the silhouette. They'd shown her that at school, too, how all the planes look different flying overhead. It gave her the chills, just thinking about it. She rubbed her hands over her arms to warm them and to rub down the goose bumps that had risen on her skin.

"It looks all clear to me," she shouted back to Joey. "You, too?" But Joey didn't answer. Celie turned and saw him gazing at the sky, his hand shading his eyes.

"What?" she said. "Do you see something?" The goose bumps were back in an instant.

For a moment, Joey didn't say anything. Then he shook his head and said, "Nope, one of ours."

"Where?" Celie said. She didn't see anything but a few seagulls.

Joey looked puzzled. "Nowhere," he said. "I thought we were pretending."

Celie wanted to slug him. "Joey, you can be so"—she reached for a word and found one of her mother's favorites—"exasperating! No wonder your mother sent you away!" She instantly wanted to take the words back, but it was too late.

Joey blinked. His face was red, and Celie could tell he was trying not to cry. She felt terrible. After all, it wasn't his fault she was angry. He'd been pretending, just the way she'd wanted him to, only pretending too well. He'd scared her was what he'd done. Not that he'd meant to. And she'd been mean, horribly mean, in return. Even though he must know his mother hadn't really sent him away because he was irritating—heck, she probably even liked him!—it had to be tough anyway. A part of him must wonder. She would.

"I'm just kidding," she said, trying to laugh. "Come on, let's go explore the island. Gotta look for the enemy, right?"

She could see that Joey was trying to wipe his eyes without being obvious, but his glasses were in the way. Celie turned around and pretended to be busy unloading the boat. "Okay, Charley," she said, lifting him onto her shoulder and grabbing the satchel, "let's find someplace to set up camp." She climbed up the rocks to the left of the beach and sat down behind a large rock. When she peeked over the top, Joey was slowly climbing out of the boat and heading up the beach toward the road. He was leaving. Celie's stomach flopped. Her cheeks were burning. Joey *was* exasperating, but she hadn't meant to hurt his feelings.

8

Celie leaned back against a cool chunk of granite. Charley climbed up onto her lap. She closed her eyes and let the sun beat down on her face. With the sun shining through, the insides of her eyelids looked red and raw.

"So, is this your hideout?"

Celie practically jumped out of her skin at the unexpected voice. "Joey?"

Joey was standing on the rock above her, looking down.

"I thought you left," she said.

He shrugged, but he didn't say anything. Charley climbed over to him, and Joey reached down and picked him up. Charley put his arms around Joey's neck and looked about contentedly.

"Nah," Celie said, following his lead. "This isn't my hideout. I'm just getting my bearings. There might be a cave over that way." She pointed with her chin. "According to the charts." She pretended to unroll a map.

"Oh," said Joey. "I thought this was an uncharted island."

"Well, it kind of is," Celie said. "But it kind of isn't."

"We'd better find a place to set up camp," Joey said,

climbing down and starting off in the direction in which Celie had pointed. "It'll be getting dark soon. Don't want the enemy to catch us off guard."

Celie looked at him. He really was good at pretending when he put his mind to it. "Right," she said, shouldering the satchel. "Let's go."

They climbed over the rocks, which were covered with sharp barnacles and bits of broken mussel shells. Some were slick with seaweed. They looked as though they'd been heaped there by a giant bulldozer. Finally Joey said, "This looks like a good spot." Celie dropped the satchel, and they sat down to eat.

They ate facing the water, not looking at each other, not talking. They watched as Charley clambered around for a while and explored the tide pools before he sat down next to them, nibbled on some fruit and sandwich scraps, and went to sleep. Then Celie said, "My ma's going to work."

"Yeah," said Joey, "I know."

"So I guess we've both been abandoned."

"Mmm," Joey said. "But it's only—"

"For the duration," Celie finished. "Yeah." It didn't make her feel much better.

They spent the rest of the afternoon exploring the pretend island and looking out for enemy spies. When the sun got too hot, they waded in the cove to cool off. Joey pointed to his wet sneakers and smiled.

Celie laughed. "Told you," she said.

By the time they headed home, Joey was glowing pink

from sunburn. He wasn't complaining, though. And he'd turned out to be a pretty decent spy. In fact, he didn't seem to want to stop.

"We should rig up a system we can use to communicate when we're apart," he said. "Just in case."

"Like what?"

"I don't know," Joey said. "Maybe a pulley system between our houses."

Celie wasn't sure she wanted to be in touch with Joey every minute, but she agreed that it might help them keep an eye out for spies.

After supper she looked around in the attic and found a set of old clothesline pulleys. She was sure Ma wouldn't mind if she put one outside her window, which was at the upstairs back corner of the house just across the driveway from Joey's, but she didn't know how Mrs. Bentley would feel. Finding enough rope to stretch between the houses might be a bigger problem, if they could even get Mrs. Bentley to agree to the plan.

"Ma," Celie said as her mother sat knitting in front of the radio, "don't you think it would be a good idea if we could get in touch with Mrs. Bentley while you're at work?"

"She lives next door," Ma said. "And she has a telephone."

"But what if we couldn't go outside because there were spies, and what if the telephone line had been cut or something?"

"Lucille Marsh," Ma said, "why in heaven's name would anyone cut the telephone line?"

"Germans," Celie said. "Or Japs. Or a bomb even."

Ma rolled her eyes. "The Germans are not going to cut the phone line, Celie. Don't be silly."

"But just in case," Celie said. "You never know. And Joey and I had this idea."

That got her attention. Celie knew it would. Ma liked Joey and she'd do anything to encourage Celie and him to be friends.

"So what have you and Joey thought up?" Ma asked.

"A secret message system," Celie said. "I've got the pulleys; we just need some rope." She paused and waited for Ma's reaction, but she sat there, her knitting needles clacking, and waited for Celie to continue.

"We figured if we put a line between our bedroom windows, we could send messages across," Celie said, adding for emphasis, "in case of an emergency."

"What emergency?" Papa asked. He'd just come in from playing catch with Andy.

"Spies," Ma said, looking as though she were trying not to laugh.

"Or bombs," Celie added hastily, because the way Ma said *spies* made it sound silly, but everyone knew bombs weren't silly.

"Or bombs," Ma added with a nod.

"I see," said Papa. "Did I miss something on the news?"

"No," said Ma. "But Celie and Joey have a plan—for emergencies."

"Great," said Papa. "I'm in favor of plans. What's your idea, Smudge?"

Celie explained about the pulleys and the rope and how it would be especially helpful in case the phone went dead. She left out about German spies cutting the wire.

"Sounds like a good plan," Papa said. "Have you talked to Mrs. Bentley?"

Celie shook her head. "I thought maybe Joey'd have better luck," she said.

"Why don't you let me handle it?" Papa said.

Ma groaned. "Now don't you be frightening that poor woman with talk about spies," she said.

"Poor woman?" Papa laughed, and Ma shushed him with a look.

★

The next day, Celie and Joey had permission to hang the pulley, and they had a good supply of rope as well. Papa said maybe Mrs. Bentley was trying to make up for thirteen years of not being much of a grandma.

Celie and Joey hung the clothesline between their windows. They tied on a basket they thought would be big enough to hold Charley, but he didn't want anything to do with it. It turned out that he preferred to walk back and forth between their rooms on the clothesline itself. Joey had to be careful, though, when Charley was over there. They didn't want Mrs. Bentley to find out he was in the house with her precious Muffin.

Joey decided they had to use a code in case their messages were intercepted. He showed Celie how to use what he called a diffusion cipher. He broke the message into horizontal rows of four letters across, then turned each vertical column into a word. He wrote an example on a pad:

ATTACK AT DAWN

ATTA
CKAT
DAWN

ACD TKA TAW ATN

"It works better with graph paper," Joey said. "But this will have to do."

It took Celie a while to catch on, but by stacking up the code words and reading them vertically, she could decipher the message pretty quickly. The hard part was knowing where the words broke. They agreed that only really important messages would be written in code, though, to save time.

Papa came out around midmorning. "You about ready to go, Smudge?" he asked.

It took Celie a moment to figure out what he was talking about. Then she remembered: fishing. It was Saturday. She looked at Joey, then at Papa. "Um," she said. "Well . . ." She paused. She didn't want to hurt Papa's feelings. "We're kind of busy," she said at last. "Can't you take Andy or something?"

"You sure?" Papa asked. "Joey could come, too. There's plenty of room."

"I'm sure," Celie said.

So Papa took Andy and Rufus out in the boat, which meant there wouldn't be much fish for supper, because those two never sat still long enough to catch anything. It would be franks and beans instead of flounder that night. But Celie didn't care. She and Joey had to finish setting up their communication system. She knew it didn't really make them any safer. They were just pretending. But it made her feel good anyway, to know Joey was only a clothesline away.

9

The next day, Papa announced that they were going to Dogtown Common for a picnic. "It's Father's Day," he said, as though that explained it. But they'd never done anything special for Father's Day before. Hardly anybody did. It wasn't like Mother's Day, when Celie would pick violets and bluets for Ma and make her a pretty card.

Celie guessed this special outing had more to do with Ma's getting a job.

Andy was hopping up and down, he was so excited. He loved to explore Dogtown, which had been a fishing village back in the olden days. But Celie and Ben both groaned. Celie wanted to go to the cove with Joey and look for enemy subs, and Ben wanted to go to the beach with Julie. But Papa wouldn't hear of it.

It was bad enough that they had to spend the whole morning at church, as far as Celie was concerned. That meant the enemy would have the run of the beach for at least three hours. But then Papa said, "We'll take a pass on church today. What better way to show our thanks to the good Lord than to go out and enjoy some of his artwork?"

Celie flashed a look at Ma, who usually didn't appreciate Papa's attempts to get out of church. Today, though, she was smiling. She even decided to do some wash, which she *never* did on Sundays. "It's a shame to waste the sunshine," she said.

It took a few hours to get ready. Ma and Celie washed sheets and a week's worth of Papa's shirts and ran them through the wringer. Then they carried them out back and hung them on the line to dry. They fried the chicken Ma was going to roast for supper and peeled potatoes for potato salad. Ma made a Waldorf salad, too, with apples and celery and walnuts. It was one of Celie's favorites. And finally there were deviled eggs, their sun-yellow middles freckled with paprika. Then, to top it off, five bottles of tonic magically appeared in Papa's hands just as they were leaving the house. And best of all, they were going to take the Packard. They wouldn't have to walk. It was a real Sunday outing, just like in a book. You'd hardly know there was a war on, thought Celie.

Celie went over to tell Joey she'd be gone most of the day, but no one answered the door when she knocked. Mrs. Bentley must have dragged him off to church early, Celie thought. She couldn't imagine being stuck alone with Mrs. Bentley for the whole day. But at least Joey had his library book. He could escape to the tree house if he needed to. Celie went back to her room and sent him a message in the basket so that he wouldn't think she'd been abducted by spies. Even though it wasn't vital to national security, she wrote it in code. Partly to show Joey she could, and partly because she knew he'd like it.

She broke down her message into rows with four letters across.

P I C N

I C B A

C K S U

P P E R

S E E U

Then she followed each row down and carefully printed it across a piece of paper.

PICPS ICKPE CBSEE NAURU

All Joey had to do was line up the code words in four columns. Then he would read them from top to bottom to get Celie's message:

PICNIC BACK SUPPER SEE U

She folded the paper in half six times to make it as secret as possible, and put it inside the can they'd fitted into the basket for the purpose.

She didn't write out *you* because she liked the way the *U* made even rows. And it was more apt to confuse the enemy, she figured, who weren't likely to be fluent in English.

Ma wouldn't let her take Charley on the picnic.

"This is going to be a pleasant family picnic," Ma said.

"But Charley's family," Celie argued.

Ma raised her eyebrow and that ended the discussion. She wasn't going to budge. Celie ran back upstairs and added a second note to the can:

WHR ACL THE CAY

She sure hoped Joey would understand that it said:

WATCH CHARLEY

"Charley," she said as she tied him out back, "behave yourself for Joey, okay?" Charley hunched down in what she'd come to know as his sulking pose. He didn't want to be left behind, she could tell.

She ducked under the clothesline where she and Ma had hung the wet laundry that morning. Papa's shirts and the week's linens were all lined up in gleaming white rows. Celie breathed in their fresh scent as she passed beneath them. The air between the rows was damp and a few degrees cooler, making the hair on her arms stand up.

Papa and Ben were packing up the car when she got back inside. Andy was dancing around, singing, "We're going on a picnic, we're going on a picnic," till Celie thought she might clobber him with a drumstick. But she could understand in a way. It was kind of an adventure. They didn't use the car much since gas rationing, so that alone was something to get excited about—if you weren't one of the ones who had to push it out of the driveway.

The reverse had been broken for about a year and spare parts were hard to come by because of the war, so every time Papa wanted to drive the car, someone had to push until he was out in the street and could go forward. That was another reason they didn't use it much. This time Ma and Ben pushed.

★

Dogtown was little more than stone cellar holes set in a scrubby field. Celie sometimes went there with Ma in the summer to pick the wild berries that had taken over when the last resident was carted off to the poorhouse more than a hundred years ago.

She had heard people talk about seeing the ghosts of the old widows, who lived there before their houses collapsed in ruin. Celie didn't really believe in ghosts, but she knew if they were real, Dogtown was where they'd live.

It was different today, though. The sun was bright and it glinted off the bits of mica dotting the granite boulders, which rose up out of the ground like whales beginning to breach.

The trees that had grown up over the years where cattle used to graze shaded the ground and cooled the air, much like Ma's laundry. Berry bushes grew out of every crack in the old cellar holes, which were the only signs left that people had once lived there. As she climbed out of the car and helped Ma spread the blanket for lunch, Celie couldn't help thinking about those people. There must have been children, just like her and Ben and Andy, who ran over these fields on summer days like this one. Would her house be nothing but a cellar hole one day? It gave her the shivers.

Papa had packed a baseball and gloves for everyone, including Ma. "You should have seen your mother when she was a girl," he said. "She could throw a baseball with the best of them."

Celie looked at Ma. She never knew Ma used to play baseball.

Ma took the glove Papa had handed her and gave him a whack on the shoulder with it. She was smiling, though, and Papa laughed. Celie couldn't remember the last time she had seen her parents goofing around like that.

They had a good game of catch before Ma broke it up, saying she had to set the food out so they could eat before it went bad and they all got ptomaine poisoning. Celie was disappointed that they had to stop. It was true, Ma had a good arm. Who would have guessed.

Lunch was delicious. Food always tasted better after baseball, Celie thought. She didn't know why. Ma had brought a book and Papa was leaning against a rock, reading the Sunday paper. Ben had fallen asleep and was snoring under his cap, which he'd put over his face to block the sun.

Celie licked the fried-chicken grease off her fingers and stuck her glove on. She picked up the ball and tossed it in the air, catching it in her glove with a satisfying thwack. "Come on, Andy," she said. "Let's play catch."

"I want to look for arrowheads," Andy said.

Celie sighed. She knew that there had been Indians here long before it was a fishing village, but she'd never found a single arrowhead. She walked along after Andy, who was intently examining the ground. Now and then she tossed the ball up and caught it.

She was just starting to think they'd wandered a bit too far when she heard dogs barking. She knew the place was named Dogtown for the dogs the women had gotten to protect them when their men were out to sea. For a moment she wondered whether dogs had ghosts. The dogs barked again. There were at least two, maybe more, she figured. Then, piercing the air like a siren, came a blood-curdling scream that lingered and slowly faded.

The hair on Celie's arms stood up. Andy clutched her hand. "What was that?" he whispered.

"I don't know," said Celie, trying not to sound as scared as she was.

"I want to go back," Andy said. His voice was quavering the way it did when he was on the verge of crying.

"It's okay, Andy," she said, though she wasn't at all sure it was. She held his hand tight and started back toward the car. They'd gone so far they couldn't see Ma and Papa anymore. The scream was still echoing in Celie's ears. She started to run. "Come on, Andy," she said, trying to make a game of it. "Last one to the blanket is a rotten egg." But Andy began to shriek at the thought of being left behind, so she had to go back and take his hand. He was too big to carry.

Celie had just caught sight of Ma and Papa and was

opening her mouth to call out to them when a pack of dogs came tearing out of the woods. One held a dead rabbit in its mouth. The rabbit's head was hanging limp on one side of the dog's jaws, its hind legs on the other.

The dogs didn't look like ghosts, and that sure was a real rabbit. She'd read about the death screams of rabbits. That must have been what it was. Still, it had sounded so human. Whoever said animals didn't have feelings had never heard that sound.

Papa laughed when he saw Celie and Andy running toward the car. "Did you think someone had been murdered?" he asked. He reached out and swung Andy onto his shoulders as though he were as light as Charley. Andy screeched and began to giggle. You'd hardly know he'd been crying only moments before.

Celie leaned against the car and caught her breath. The day had been perfect, just perfect, until that scream. It had left a sick feeling in her stomach, a feeling of dread. She wanted to go home.

Once she got there, though, she wanted to be just about anywhere else. They drove into the driveway, and Celie went around back to check on Charley. Rounding the corner, she stopped dead. Charley was up on Ma's clothesline, walking along the ropes, pulling out clothespins. The last of Ma's sheets was about to join Papa's white shirts on the ground.

"Charley, you get down from there," she shouted. But Charley looked over at her as if to say, I'll teach you to leave me home alone, and he pulled the last clothespin. The sheet landed with a gentle *fwump*. That was the moment when Ma came into the yard. Celie heard her yelp, like a dog that's had its tail stepped on.

"What . . ." she sputtered. "How . . ." But she couldn't seem to get out more than one word at a time. Celie knew how she felt.

"I . . ." she began again. "He . . ." That was the best she could do. They both stood there for a moment, staring at their hard work lying in a heap.

Ma finally found her voice. "I'll kill him," she said.

Celie knew Ma meant Charley, but she was thinking about what she was going to do to Joey. He was supposed to have been watching him. She'd told him to. He must have let Charley loose.

Joey would have to wait, though. She was going to spend the rest of that day—and all night, too, probably—washing shirts and sheets.

Charley kept her company in the summer kitchen while she put the laundry through the wringer and hung it on the ropes that crisscrossed the ceiling. The air got hotter and heavier as Celie worked, and droplets of water formed on the windows and ran down in rivulets, puddling on the sills.

Charley watched for a while, then fell asleep in his crate.

"Thanks for keeping me company," Celie growled. "This is all your fault, you know." But Charley just sighed and shifted in his sleep.

"Stupid monkey," she muttered, jamming a clothespin down hard over the corner of a sheet.

Celie began to wonder where Joey was. It wasn't like him to stay away so long. But the Bentley place looked deserted. Maybe they were off doing something for Father's Day. That seemed unlikely, though, since his father was overseas. Then she felt a little sorry that she'd been so angry at him, with his father so far away.

It was pitch dark outside by the time Celie got to bed. She could see light under the door of her parents' room as she went past on her way upstairs. They were talking quietly.

Celie checked for a message from Joey, but the can was empty. He could have taken a minute to answer, she thought, as she dropped the can back into the basket. Maybe he was feeling guilty about letting Charley loose.

She lay in bed for a long time, unable to sleep. When she drifted off at last, she slept fitfully, dreaming she was lost in Dogtown, searching for her mother amid row after row of wet sheets, with German soldiers at her heels. She woke in a cold sweat, only to fall asleep and take up the dream where she'd left off.

It wasn't until the next day that she got to tell Joey off about Charley. But it turned out he hadn't been anywhere near the Marshes' back yard. His grandma had kept him busy all day.

"How'd Charley get loose, then?" Celie asked.

Joey shrugged.

Celie looked at the monkey sitting innocently on the picnic table. Somebody must have come over and unbuckled his belt. There was only one other possibility, and she didn't want to think about that. It would be worse than a nightmare.

10

Ma didn't start her job until the following Monday. Before she could help build ships, she had to spend a week at night school. During that first day she cleaned house and weeded the garden and made supper so Papa would have something to eat when he got home from work. You'd have thought she was going away instead of just to school. She insisted that Celie help. As usual, Ben and Andy got off scot-free.

"Andy's too young," Ma said. "He'll only get in the way."

"What about Ben?" Celie asked, but Ma just looked at her in that way she had, and Celie knew it was time to stop asking. It wasn't fair. At least Charley was tied up in the backyard, and he wouldn't be undoing all her hard work this time.

Celie's fingers were wrinkled as prunes and smelled of furniture wax and onions by the time lunch rolled around. She was tired and grumpy. Joey showed up just as she was putting her plate in the dish drainer.

"Hey," he said, waving his fingers.

"Hey," said Celie. "Don't have time for spies today. The

general's already issued marching orders." She looked back at Ma and rolled her eyes.

"Can I help?" Joey asked.

"I guess," said Celie. "If you want." She couldn't imagine volunteering for chores.

Joey stayed around all afternoon and helped Ma in the garden. He even mowed the front lawn, which Celie thought would have been the least that Ben could have done. But Ben had gotten up and taken off as soon as he saw there were chores. Ben was practically allergic to chores. Papa said he'd have to get over that in a quick hurry if he ever joined up.

By the time Ma left that evening, Celie was exhausted. She was almost glad to see her go. Papa was home, so at least Mrs. Bentley was out of their hair—for the rest of the week, anyway, until Ma finished training and started working days.

Celie was beginning to think that maybe having Ma work wouldn't be so bad. But then Friday came. It was about ten o'clock in the morning and Celie was in the kitchen making a peanut-butter-and-banana sandwich when Ma got up. Celie almost dropped the knife on her foot when she saw her mother. She'd cut off her beautiful braid. Her hair was done up all over in pin curls.

Celie could get used to the idea of her mother wearing pants. She couldn't build ships in a skirt, so she had borrowed trousers from Ben. But this was the last straw. It was awful. Celie hardly recognized her.

"Ma!" Celie said. "What did you do?"

Ma smiled and put her hand up to pat her hair. "Like it?" Ma asked.

"No!" Celie said. How could she even ask?

Ma's smile wavered for a moment, and Celie thought maybe she was forcing it to stay put. Surely Ma couldn't like her hair this way.

"It'll be easier to take care of," she said. "All the girls are getting it done."

"What'd Papa say?" Celie asked. Papa must have hated it.

"He said it made me look younger," Ma said, smiling again.

★

"I don't even know her anymore," she wrote to Joey later. She didn't use code. She was too miserable to think that hard. "I might as well not even have a mother." Then she felt bad because Joey's mother was more of a stranger than her own. Joey might not see his mother until the end of the summer. And he wouldn't see his father even then. But she knew Joey wouldn't say so, which made her feel worse. She pulled Charley onto her lap and rested her cheek against the back of his head.

"I hate it, Charley," she said, not sure whether she meant Ma's hair, or the war, or how nothing was the way it used to be—or ought to be. Or that she was such a lousy friend to Joey. "I just hate it."

★

Once Ma started her day job, Mrs. Bentley practically lived at the Marshes' so she could keep an eye on Andy, even though Andy was usually over at Rufus's. Sometimes Joey ate supper at Celie's. Ma tried to get everything ready before she went off to work. The government posters all said that women working for the war effort still needed to keep their households in order. It was their patriotic duty. So Ma really had two jobs. But sometimes she ran out of time. Then Mrs. Bentley would cook, and the Marshes would have to suffer through a dried-out casserole or an overdone roast. The worst was Mrs. Bentley's disgusting smoked fish cakes. Celie could hardly gag them down, but Mrs. Bentley would purse her wrinkled old lips and say, "A clean plate wins the war," and Joey would look at Celie with those eyes that said, Do it for my dad, so she'd keep on swallowing until her plate was empty. Ben took to eating at Julie's on those days, and somehow Andy got away with having a bowl of oatmeal, which didn't seem fair to Celie. But there was no use complaining.

Things seemed to fall into a routine. And it was too hot and muggy for anyone to get worked up about much, one way or another. The Fourth of July fireworks were canceled and so was the annual St. Peter's Fiesta.

In the middle of July the Allies invaded Sicily, and by the end of the month, Mussolini had been ousted in Italy. The Japanese were taking a pounding in the Pacific, too, which was good, except that was where Joey's father was, and Joey worried about his dad being in the middle of it. Every day they heard about more soldiers missing or killed, and every day they knew Joey's father could be one of them.

They couldn't use baseball to escape from it all, either, because the season was pretty dismal. The high point was the Veterans' Game at Braves Field in Boston, with Babe Ruth managing. Ted Williams even came up from Florida to play.

Celie noticed that Charley was growing. Not getting bigger so much as filling out, the way Ben had when he hit fifteen and Ma said he was going through puberty. Charley looked older somehow. And when he showed his teeth, he looked fierce. He was getting restless, too. A couple of times he got away from her and ended up stuck in trees. Twice they had to call the fire department, but the firefighters refused to come again after Charley hauled off and bit the man who went up to get him the first time.

And Charley wasn't the only one who was growing. Celie was, too—finally. Not for the first time, she wished she had a big sister instead of a brother. She used to receive hand-me-downs from Rita, who was bigger, but now she had to make do with what she had until Ma found time to get her new things. Celie dreaded dressing up for Sunday school.

11

One day near the end of July, Celie was sitting at the kitchen table with Joey eating baked-bean-and-mayonnaise sandwiches for lunch when she saw something streak past the side window. Then she saw it again out the front window and she knew what it was: Charley.

She jumped from her chair and ran to the front door with Joey right behind her.

"Come back here!" Mrs. Bentley called. "You haven't finished your lunch." But Celie and Joey kept on running, down the drive and across the street, following Charley through the cemetery and over the hill to the beach.

By the time they got to him, Charley was up to his waist in the water and splashing around like a seal. There was quite a crowd standing on the beach watching him. Ben was there with Julie, who was dressed to the nines in a skirt and blouse and black pumps. She even had black lines painted up the backs of her legs to make it look as though she were wearing stockings, which you couldn't get anymore because all the nylon was being used to make parachutes for the war. She sure looked elegant. She was wearing makeup, too: mascara and rouge and Victory Red lipstick.

"I guess he was hot," said Celie, taking off her shoes and socks and heading in after Charley.

"Come to think of it," said Julie, "it is rather warm." She took off her shoes and waded into the water. She reached down and splashed some on her face. "Feels good," she said, laughing. "Come on in." She waved to Ben, who was standing on the shore watching her as though she'd slipped a nut.

"No, thanks," Ben said.

"Oh, Ben," Julie said, "loosen up a little, will you?"

Celie laughed. It was about time somebody told Ben off. She was about to say so when she looked at Julie and saw black smears under each of her eyes. She looked like a boxer with matching shiners. Celie laughed even harder. "Your mascara is running," she said.

"Oh well," Julie said with a shrug. "I'm on my way home anyway." She smiled back at Ben. "I got a job. I started a couple of days ago." Then she said, loud enough so Ben could hear, "Your brother doesn't approve."

"No, he wouldn't," Celie said.

"It was just supposed to be for the rest of the summer," Julie said, "but I might keep right on working. I kind of like it."

"Where are you working?" Celie asked.

"I answer the telephone at Dr. Davis's office," she said.

"Dr. Davis? The vet?"

"Mmm," said Julie. "He's a friend of my father's."

"Oh," Celie said.

"He's got a very cute son who's a pilot in the air force," she whispered, this time making sure Ben couldn't hear.

"Oh," Celie said again.

"Not that I'm interested in him or anything," Julie added quickly.

"Uh-huh," said Celie, who was beginning to wonder why Julie was telling her any of this.

"I do like men in uniform, though," Julie went on dreamily.

Celie looked back at Ben and almost felt sorry for him. He was nuts about Julie, even though everyone had told him it wouldn't last, that Julie was just looking for a way out. Jimmy DaSilva had been the first to say so. It was the first time Celie had ever heard her brother swear. After that Ben had started calling Jimmy "that Portagee." Jimmy felt bad, Celie knew. Not because he'd said what he had about Julie, but because Ben didn't talk to him anymore.

Suddenly the water felt cold. Celie picked up Charley and sloshed back to the beach. Julie followed her. The monkey was dripping wet. Celie wished she'd thought to bring his leash, but she'd been in such a hurry.

"How do you think he got loose?" Joey asked.

"I don't know," Celie said. But she did know. Charley had figured out how to undo his belt. That was how he'd gotten loose when they were at Dogtown, and it was what he'd done this time. She only hoped Ma wouldn't find out.

★

Two days later Ben stormed in like a nor'easter. Ma wasn't home from work yet, and Mrs. Bentley was heating up the casserole Ma had left for supper. Celie and Joey were playing cards in the living room.

"What's the matter, Ben?" Papa asked, looking up from his paper. Then he smiled and said with a wink, "Girl trouble?"

Ben scowled. "You could say that." He grabbed a bottle of milk from the icebox and flopped down on the sofa while Mrs. Bentley glared because, first of all, dairy products were rationed and, second, only low-class citizens drank milk from the bottle. Celie had heard the lecture before, and she might have said something herself if it wouldn't have put her in the same camp as Mrs. Bentley. "Julie dumped me."

Celie's mouth dropped open. She wondered if it was the veterinarian's cute son she'd dumped him for.

"I thought you two were forever," Papa said.

"Yeah," said Ben, taking another swig of milk. "So did I. But she's found some new guy."

Papa folded his newspaper and set it on his knee. "So who's the lucky fella?" he asked.

"That's just it," said Ben. "I don't even know him. *She* doesn't even know him. Well, hardly. It's some hotshot pilot named Roger that her brother brought home on leave."

Ben took another long swallow of milk. "She says it was love at first sight," he said. "Can you believe that?"

Maybe Roger has manners, Celie thought, as Ben belched loudly and wiped the dribble of milk off his chin with the back of his hand. "Well, if you ask me, she's crazy," Celie said.

"Thanks, Squirt," said Ben, reaching out and tugging her braid.

Celie shook off his hand. "Don't call me Squirt," she said. "And I didn't mean she was crazy for picking Roger over you. I meant she was crazy for wanting to have a boyfriend at all."

Joey looked up at that, as though he might say something, and Celie felt her cheeks redden.

"Like I said, thanks, Squirt," Ben said. He drained the last of the milk and gave her braid an extra hard yank as he left the room.

★

Ben didn't come down for supper. Papa took a plate up to him after Mrs. Bentley and Joey left, but Ben said he wasn't hungry. Celie couldn't blame him. Ma's codfish casserole wasn't exactly her idea of heaven.

Papa came downstairs carrying the plate, and Ben's door slammed shut, rattling the windows, just as Ma walked in. She looked toward the stairs and then at Papa.

"Julie dumped him," he said. "Some army fella."

Ma dropped her purse onto the chair. "Oh for heaven's sake," she said. She sounded tired, as though it was an effort to get the words out. "Can't say I'm surprised, though. Ben must be crushed."

She hung up her coat and ran her fingers through her curls. "What's for supper?" she asked.

"Don't you remember?" Celie asked. "You made a codfish casserole."

"Oh," Ma said. "Right. I forgot." She sat down heavily on the sofa. "I guess I'm not so hungry, after all."

"Nonsense," said Papa. He put Ben's plate on the kitchen table. "You need your energy."

The defense department had a poster about that, too, Celie remembered. Something about the responsibility of workers to eat right so they could be more productive.

Ma moved to the table and began to eat.

"You shoulda seen Charley today, Ma," Andy began. Celie tried to hush him, but it was too late.

"What'd he do this time?" Ma asked.

"He 'scaped," Andy said.

"Es-caped," Celie corrected. "And that's not true. Or at least we don't know if it's true. Somebody could have let him go."

Ma put down her fork and leaned her forehead against her hand. "From the beginning," she said.

So Celie, with Andy's help, told Ma all about it. "You see," she said. "It was no big thing." She smiled, hoping Ma would buy it.

"Lucille," Ma said after a pause. "You were very lucky. That monkey is a wild animal. Anything could have happened."

"Not anything, Ma," Celie said, and wished she hadn't as soon as Ma looked up at her.

"He bites, Celie," Ma said. "What if he'd bitten someone? A child?"

"But he didn't," Celie said.

"This time," Ma said. She folded her napkin in her lap and looked at Celie. "One of the girls at work has a sister who works for the zoo in Stoneham," she said. "She's sure they'd give Charley a good home. Maybe—"

"Ma!" Celie cut her off before she could finish. How could Ma even think about giving Charley to the zoo? He was one of the family.

"Well, it's good to know," Ma said. "In case."

Papa put his hand on Ma's shoulder. "You're tired, Liz. Come on and listen to the radio and I'll rub your feet, all right?"

Ma stood up and allowed Papa to lead her to the living room. She moved to pick up her knitting, but Papa stopped her.

"Not tonight," he said.

"I ought to go see if Ben's all right," she said.

"I don't think Ben's in the mood for talking," Papa said. "You can check on him in the morning."

But the next morning, Ben didn't want to talk to anyone. He stayed in his room and stomped around.

It was Saturday and Papa had promised to take Celie and Joey fishing, but he changed his mind. "Not today, Smudge," he said, looking at the sky as though the weather was the reason.

Celie knew it was the storm inside Ben that was the matter. She and Joey took Charley to the cove and averted a German invasion.

Ma insisted that Ben join the family for supper. Celie wished she hadn't. He was more disagreeable than ever. He complained about the food, the weather, even the Red Sox game on the radio. After they ate, he sat in front of the radio listening to the war news. He stared at that radio as though he wished he could travel right across the ocean on the sound waves and into battle. The way he'd been acting, Celie almost wished she could give him a boost.

"He'll be better tomorrow," Ma said.

But he wasn't. In the morning, he was gone.

★

Ben was gone and so was all the money in Ma's wallet. There was a note on the table. "I'll pay you back as soon as I can," it said.

"Oh Lord," said Ma. The hand holding the letter dropped to her side and her head tilted up toward the ceiling.

"Did Ben run away from home?" asked Andy. His eyes filled up with tears.

"He'll be back," Celie said. "Where could he go?" But she knew where he'd gone. He'd run off to join the navy.

"Fool kid," Papa said. His jaw was set tight and Celie could see the tendons bulging on either side as he clenched and unclenched his teeth.

"They won't take him," Celie said. "Will they? He's not eighteen." Ma looked at her, and Celie could tell they were both thinking the same thing. Plenty of boys were getting into the service even though they were underage. She knew it. Ma and Papa knew it. And Ben knew it. He'd go to Boston, where no one would recognize him.

Celie wanted to puke. It was her fault. Well, Julie's, but

her fault, too. Maybe if she'd told him Julie would be sorry, or that Roger was a big loser next to him, then he wouldn't have run off to prove what a man he was and maybe get his legs blown off like Billy Jessup, or even killed.

She hated Julie then. She hated herself, too. If only he'd come back. She'd let him call her Squirt. She'd let him pull her braids. She wouldn't even mind if he drank out of the milk bottle.

"We should go after him," Ma said.

Papa shook his head. "He'd just run off again," he said. "We can't lock him in his room."

"He's upset," Ma said. "He doesn't know what he's doing."

"He's got to figure it out for himself," Papa said, and held up his hand to end the discussion.

Celie knew that wouldn't be the end of it. Ma wouldn't let it drop. Would she? And what did Papa think Ben had to figure out? What war was like? Whether he could come home in one piece? What it was like to shoot somebody or be shot at? She didn't want him to figure out any of that. She picked up Charley and carried him outside. What was it about war that made everyone crazy? She gave Charley a quick squeeze before she tied him up under the chestnut tree.

They walked to church that morning. Celie's dress squeezed her chest and her shoes pinched her toes, so she had blisters by the time they got there.

Ma and Papa didn't say a word the whole way. They just walked along grimly while Andy skipped ahead. Ma didn't even scold him for kicking stones and scuffing his good shoes.

Celie didn't feel like going to Sunday school, so Ma let her stay for the service. Celie closed her eyes tight as they sat in the pew. She'd never had to pray for something so important before. She prayed that God wouldn't let Ben join the navy. He drove her nuts most of the time, but she didn't want him hurt. Ma had enough to worry about. She didn't need to be worrying about Ben. And neither did Celie.

Praying didn't make her feel any better. By the time she had finished explaining to God what Ben had done, she was pretty angry. How dare he run off and make them all worry? Wasn't Ma working at the shipyard so that the war would end before he was old enough to fight? It made her so mad she could spit, except she couldn't because she was in church. She had half a mind to go after him and give him a good talking to. Praying was all well and good, but sometimes you needed to take things into your own hands.

On the way home, Celie slipped off her shoes and socks and hooked her fingers through the shoe straps. She felt determined to do something. She wasn't going to let her brother get away with this. She didn't know exactly how, but she was going to find him.

She was so wrapped up in thinking about Ben that she didn't pay much attention to the black car parked in front of Mrs. Bentley's house. And it wasn't until after lunch that thoughts of finding Ben were nearly pushed out of her head altogether.

Andy had gone out back to stash his wagon full of junk

in the shed, but soon he came running back in with Charley's empty leash. "He's gone!" Andy hollered. "Charley's gone!"

"What?" Celie said. She ran outside to look for herself, but Charley was nowhere to be seen. At first she thought maybe Joey had him, but he wouldn't have taken Charley without his leash. No, Charley had run off, all right. Maybe he'd gone to the beach again. Please let him have gone to the beach.

Her stomach felt like a top that had been sent spinning. First Ben, now Charley. Ma always said bad things came in threes, Celie thought. What was next?

12

Celie changed her clothes while Papa called the police to report Charley missing and to see if anyone had found him.

"You call the police about a monkey, but your son disappears and you do nothing?" Ma said.

Papa frowned. "It's not the same thing, Liz," he said. "Ben's not lost; he ran off. And Charley's just a dumb animal. He might not be able to find his way home."

Celie went out the front door and closed it tight behind her to muffle the sound of her parents arguing.

Joey was sitting on Mrs. Bentley's front stoop with his elbows on his knees and his chin resting on his fists.

"Hey, Joey," she called. "You seen Charley? He's run away."

Joey shook his head. He didn't even wave. Celie turned up the walk, past the black car she'd noticed on the way home from church, and sat next to Joey on the stoop. It wasn't until he looked up that she realized he'd been crying.

He sniffed. "My dad," he said. Then he stopped, as though he couldn't say the words.

Celie gasped. "What?" she asked. "Is he—?" But she couldn't say it, either.

Joey shook his head. "No," he said. "Missing." He sniffed and wiped his nose with his shirttail. "He's missing in action."

Celie didn't know what to say. Charley was missing, too, and Ben. But they weren't in the war—even though Ben was trying hard to get there. And she knew that when people went missing in the war there was a good chance they'd never be found—at least not alive. She dug into her pocket and pulled out the old bunched-up handkerchief that she used to wipe the sweat off her hands when she was pitching. It was a little soiled, but it was better than a shirttail.

"Thanks," Joey said, blowing noisily into the handkerchief and handing it back.

"That's okay," Celie said. "You keep it." She forced a smile and pressed her hands between her knees. Joey looked so miserable she thought maybe he could use a distraction. "So I guess you have to hang around here, huh?" she asked. She nodded toward the car. "Company?"

Joey shrugged. "My mom and her brother, Uncle Seth," he said. "They didn't want to tell me over the telephone." He leaned his chin back on his fists and stared at the sidewalk in front of him. Then he swiped at a tear that was starting down his cheek. "Grandma keeps talking about how she never got a chance to say she was sorry. The doctor had to make a house call and give her something to make her sleep. Mom keeps crying. It's awful."

"Well, Charley's escaped and I could really use some

help looking for him," she said. "Ma's in a royal state because Ben ran off in the night to join the navy."

Joey's eyes widened. "Boy," he said, "what else can go wrong?"

"Nothing else," Celie said firmly. "That's three and Ma says bad things come in threes. So now Ben will come home and you and I will find Charley and your dad will stop being missing."

"You think?" Joey said.

The way he said it almost broke Celie's heart. As if she knew. As if anyone knew. It was just one more thing you couldn't control in this world that seemed to be getting crazier by the minute.

"Maybe Mom wouldn't mind if I helped you look for Charley." His voice sounded hopeful, as though he really wished he could get away from everything that was happening inside the house. "I'll go ask," he said.

"I'll meet you back here in two minutes," Celie said. "I've got to get Charley's leash."

She'd hardly gotten in the front door when she heard the air-raid siren start up. It began low and got louder and louder. They all just stood for a moment, looking at one another, feeling the empty space where Ben was supposed to be, ordering them about, telling them what to do.

Finally Celie said, "Get under the table." To her father she said, "Go check the attic for incendiaries."

She climbed under the table with Ma and Andy. Ma hadn't even argued. She was leaning on one hand; the other was around Andy. Her eyes were closed tight, as though that would make it all go away, and when she opened them again the war would be over and Ben would be lying on the sofa in the living room with his muddy feet on the upholstery and a milk bottle in his hand.

They stayed under the table for what seemed like forever.

Celie told Ma about Joey's father and how Mrs. Bentley had to take a pill to make her sleep.

Ma shook her head. "Poor old woman," she said.

"That's the thing," said Celie. "She seems too old to have a son your age."

"She was over forty when Joey Senior was born," Ma said.

"Did you know about him?" Celie asked. "Did you know Mrs. Bentley had a son?"

"Mm-hm," Ma said. "Ben was a baby when Joey Senior married Joey's mother. Mr. Bentley declared he was no longer their son. It broke Mrs. Bentley's heart."

"Why didn't she argue? Why did she let Mr. Bentley decide for her?"

"That's the way some marriages are," Ma said.

"Why didn't she take him back after Mr. Bentley died?"

"I think there was so much pain on both sides," Ma said. "They got used to being angry. They forgot how to forgive each other."

Celie thought about what Joey had said, how Mrs. Bentley didn't get a chance to say she was sorry. It seemed like the saddest thing in the world. No wonder she was so crabby if she was holding in all that hurt.

At last the all-clear blew.

Celie climbed out from under the table. "I'm going over to Joey's," she said. "We're going to look for Charley."

Ma stood up and straightened her skirt. Her hand went up to the back of her head where her bun had been. It was a gesture she used to make all the time, Celie recalled, and she found herself missing Ma's long hair—one more loss in a long list that this war had brought. She blinked back the tears that were threatening and headed out the front door. Joey was waiting for her on the sidewalk.

"Hey," she said.

"Hey," said Joey, raising his hand and waggling his fingers in what she'd come to think of as his barnacle salute. She smiled. At least that hadn't changed.

"I don't see how he could have gotten far," said Joey. But Celie remembered how fast Charley had swung through the trees, and this time he wouldn't have his leash to slow him down.

They went to the beach first, but he wasn't there. It was deserted, except for a few sandpipers chasing the waves in and out. Celie's heart sank. She'd been so sure Charley would be there. Or at least she'd hoped so.

"Charley!" she called, just in case he was behind some rocks and she couldn't see him. "Charley!"

"Lost your monkey?"

Celie turned at the familiar voice. "Hey, Jimmy," she said. "Yeah. You haven't seen him, have you?"

Jimmy shook his head. "Uh-uh," he said. "But don't worry, he'll show up." He tugged Celie's braid. "Like a bad penny, right? Always comes back."

"I guess."

"You're mighty glum," Jimmy said.

"It's not just Charley," Celie said. "Joey's father's missing in action."

"Oh man," Jimmy said. "I'm real sorry to hear that, Joey."

"Thanks," Joey said, and his chin started to quiver as though he might cry again. He turned away and looked out at the water.

"And Ben's run off," Celie said, partly to take the attention off Joey and partly because she thought maybe Jimmy had seen him.

"What?" Jimmy said. "Nah. He's probably just somewhere with Julie."

Celie shook her head. "Nope," she said. "Julie dumped him."

"Oh brother," Jimmy said. "Do you know where he went?"

"To join up, we figure," Celie said.

"Sure," Jimmy said. "Of course." He sat down on a rock and picked up a handful of sand, letting it run through his fingers. Then he said, "Well, if there's anything I can do."

"Yeah," Celie said. "Thanks." She tapped Joey on the

shoulder. "Guess we'd better keep looking," she said. "Charley's not here."

"Yeah," Joey said. "Okay."

"Maybe he was trying to follow us to church," Celie said.

"We can look," said Joey.

It was a fifteen-minute walk to the church. They said goodbye to Jimmy and started off, calling to Charley all along the way. When they arrived, the church and grounds were deserted. Charley was not there.

"Where could he be?" Celie said. Her voice sounded angry, mostly so Joey wouldn't know she was about to cry. She worked the end of her braid into her mouth and bit down hard.

"You know," said Joey, "probably we'll get back to your house and he'll be sitting on the front step waiting for us."

"He won't," she said, sounding even angrier. "And don't go trying to make me feel better," she snapped. "I'm not a baby, you know."

Joey shrugged and looked at his feet. Celie gave a last call for Charley, then she turned sharply, her braids whipping around behind her, and started for home. She turned back to Joey with a scowl on her face. "Are you coming?" she said. Then she hurried on without waiting. She felt embarrassed and cross. She knew she was being horrible—Joey had bigger worries than she did—but she couldn't stop herself. She heard Joey scuffling along behind her and was surprised to find that she felt comforted, knowing he was there.

As Celie had suspected, Charley was not waiting for

them when they got home. Nor was he in the house. It was hopeless. He could be anywhere by now.

It began to drizzle. When they walked in the front door, Ma was fuming.

"Where have you two been?" she shouted.

"We were looking for Charley," said Celie. "I told you."

"All afternoon?" Ma asked.

"We thought he might have gone to the church," said Joey.

"It didn't occur to either of you to tell me where you were going?" She was screaming.

"I'm sorry, Ma," Celie said. And she was. She should have told Ma where she was going. But Ma wasn't the only one with feelings. "I'm worried, too, you know. Charley could be hurt. I know you think he's only a stupid monkey, but he's *my* monkey." She stomped up to her room and slammed the door behind her. She flung herself on her bed, burying her face in her pillow, and cried.

After a while Ma came in. "You are a sight," she said, wiping Celie's cheeks with a corner of the blanket. "Why don't you splash some water on your face and come downstairs. Joey's waiting for you."

At the mention of Joey, Celie groaned. "I'm too embarrassed, Ma," she said, starting to cry all over again. First she'd been rude when he'd tried to help, and then she'd burst into tears over a monkey when Joey's father was missing in action, which was a lot worse. Worse even than Ben's running off, though that was bad enough. "Can't you send him home?"

"I'm not going to send him home," Ma said firmly. "He needs a friend right now. I'll expect you downstairs in five minutes."

"Yes, ma'am," murmured Celie. She got up and went to look in the mirror. Her nose was bright red. So were her eyes. Her freckles stood out in stark contrast to her pale, puffy face.

Ma was right. She was a mess. She loosened her braids and picked up the brush on the bureau. Her hair hung down in orange zigzags. She tossed her head to get all the hair on one side and began brushing. She brushed until her arm ached and the zigzags had turned to soft waves. When she was done, she went into the bathroom and splashed cold water on her face. She put cold water on a facecloth and held it over her eyes. She took one last look in the mirror, grimaced at her reflection, and went downstairs. She wished she had some of Ma's face powder to cover the blotches on her cheeks.

Joey and Ma were sitting on the sofa looking grim. Andy was lying on his stomach on the floor reading comic books. The news blared on the radio.

"Can't we listen to something else?" Celie asked, sitting down next to Ma. "I can't stand any more bad news."

"Pretty soon," Ma said. She reached out and patted Celie's knee. "Shhh."

"Where's Papa?" Celie asked.

"He went out," Ma said, an edge of irritation in her voice.

Celie folded her arms across her chest and sank back into

the cushions. She didn't like to be dismissed as though she were a little girl. She was just so tired of this war, and she was too restless to listen to the news. She was worried about Charley and about Ben. She couldn't stand it much longer. She was going to have to do something.

"I think I'm going to get some air," Joey said suddenly. Celie looked up, and he motioned with a jerk of his head for her to come with him.

They sat on the back porch looking out at the rain, which was falling softly. Celie's hair draped around her shoulders like a shawl, and she was grateful for the warmth.

"You look different with your hair down," Joey said after a while. "It's pretty." He reached up and touched it gently.

Celie felt as though someone had set a match to her cheeks. "If you like bright orange dust mops, I guess," she said, then wished she hadn't. Ma always said she needed to learn to take a compliment. "Sorry I was such a dope before," she added.

"That's okay," said Joey. "You were worried about Charley."

"Yeah," said Celie, tears coming to her eyes.

"He'll be back," Joey said.

She wondered whether he meant Charley or Ben—or his father.

★

Just before dinner, the storm came on in earnest. Jagged Z's of lightning slashed the sky. The weather seemed to match Ma's mood as she stormed around the kitchen. Papa wasn't home yet, and she hadn't heard from him. "That's all we need," she said, tossing a spoon into the sink with an angry clatter. "Another missing person." Ma had made roast beef for Sunday supper. She'd bought it on Saturday, using up a lot of ration stamps, because she'd thought maybe it would cheer Ben up. Now Ben wasn't there to eat it, and Papa wasn't, either.

Ma took one last look out at the rain before she said, "I guess we should eat. No sense in letting good food go to waste. You might as well stay, too, Joey. There's plenty."

"Thank you," Joey said, "but I should be going." Celie didn't blame him. She would have left, too, if she could have.

Ma was just putting the roast on the table when Papa came in, dripping.

Celie thought Ma should have been happy to see him, but she only yelled at him to take off his wet things by the door and not leave water on the wooden floor. He hung his jacket on the doorknob and pried off his boots one at a time. Then he took a dish towel from the sink and ran it through his hair, which had sprung up in a tangle of curls.

"Where were you, Papa?" Andy asked.

"I was looking for Charley," Papa said, pulling out a chair and sitting down at the table. He picked up his fork and stabbed a slice of meat. "And I stopped a few places and asked about Ben."

Ma looked up at that.

"No one's seen him," Papa said before Ma could ask.

Ma turned and looked out the window as another gash

of lightning tore the sky. She was holding tight to the edge of the sink, as though she might fall over if she let go.

Celie was thinking how much Charley hated thunder, and she was about to say so when the phone rang. She and Ma both jumped to answer it. Celie got there first.

"Hello?" she said.

A man's voice, gruff and thickly accented, came over the receiver so loud that Celie had to hold the phone away from her ear. "You the people who own this damn monkey?"

13

"Did you find him?" Celie was so excited she was bouncing from foot to foot.

"Ben?" Ma asked. She was standing over Celie's shoulder trying to listen. Celie shook her head. "Charley," she whispered.

Ma groaned. "Don't tie up the line," she said, and went back to the table.

"You better believe I found him," the man ranted. "Police told me he belonged to you."

Papa must have heard the man yelling because he took the phone.

Celie couldn't stand still.

"He's got Charley," she said, running over to Andy. "I don't know what happened, but he sure sounds angry." She twisted her hands together anxiously.

"I hope Charley didn't bite him," said Ma.

Papa hung up the phone and sat back down at the head of the table. "Well," he said, "it seems our little friend has been busy." Celie could tell he was trying not to laugh in front of Ma.

"Uh-oh," said Celie. "What happened?"

"That was Mr. Skolski. He has a little farm way across town. Somehow Charley made his way over there and holed up in his henhouse."

"Oh no," said Celie. The picture of Charley loose in a henhouse made her wince. "What'd he do?" This wasn't going to make him any more popular with Ma, that was for sure.

"Well," said Papa, "Mr. Skolski heard the chickens squawking and went to see what the problem was. When he looked in the door, Charley got him square on the forehead with a raw egg. By the time he got hold of Charley, he'd been socked with a dozen eggs—the ones he'd been planning to hatch for next year's brood. And when he finally did catch him, Charley bit him."

"Oh gosh," said Celie. She thought about rhesus monkeys getting more aggressive as they got older. "No wonder the man was angry. Can we go get Charley now?"

"Mr. Skolski is going to bring him over in his truck. I told him we'd be by after supper, but he said he was coming this way anyway and he didn't want to have Charley around any longer than necessary."

When Mr. Skolski arrived, it was raining heavily. Charley was hunched miserably in a wooden crate in the back of his truck. He was wet to the bone and shivering—with fear or cold, Celie couldn't tell. She lifted him out of the crate. "You wicked monkey," she said, kissing his wet head. "Don't you ever scare me like that again."

Mr. Skolski still had smears of egg on his face and shirt. He was a short, round man with thinning gray hair and a red face. From the doorway, Ma thanked him and invited him in for coffee, but he refused. "Lucky for you I didn't shoot it," he said.

A clap of thunder drowned out Mr. Skolski's parting remarks, which was just as well, Celie thought. She hurried inside, holding tight to the dripping monkey. Papa followed her in; he folded his wallet and slipped it back into his pocket. Celie wondered how much Papa had had to shell out to get Charley out of hock.

"Let's hope he doesn't do that again soon," he said.

Ma frowned. "He'd better not do it again ever," she said, taking Charley from Celie's arms. She tossed the monkey into the summer kitchen and sent Celie to her room to change into dry clothes. Celie tried to protest—Charley needed drying off more than she did—but Ma would have none of it.

Celie tugged off her soggy shirt and pants, which smelled strongly of wet monkey, and wrung out her hair. She could hear Ma and Papa arguing downstairs.

"I looked everywhere I could think of," Papa was saying. "No one's seen him."

"What about the police?" Ma said.

"This is a private matter, Liz. It's not as though he's lost. He ran off to join up. We both know it."

"Well, you've got to do something," Ma said. From her voice Celie could tell she was crying.

"There's not much more I can do on a Sunday," Papa said. "And we both have to work tomorrow. You know how short they are with the war on. No, Ben's made his bed and he's got to sleep in it."

"He's a boy," Ma said.

"Yes, he is," Papa said, "and there are boys dying over there every day. That's war."

Celie wanted to scream. She wished they'd stop fighting. She went into the bathroom and turned on the shower. When the water was steaming, she stepped into the stream and let it drown out the voices of her parents. She stuck her head into the spray and felt as though the outside world had been washed away. No worries about Ben or Charley or the war. Just heat and steam. She sank down to her knees and let the water pound on her back.

The water was running cold before she got out of the shower and wrapped herself in a towel. Andy was sitting at the top of the stairs with his chin in his hands. "I hate Ben," he said. "He shouldn't'a run away."

"No, he shouldn't have," Celie said, sitting down next to him. It was finally quiet downstairs, but Celie didn't feel like going down. "Come on, Andy," she said. "Let me get my pajamas on and I'll read you a story."

She had to read *The Story of Ferdinand* all the way through three times before Andy fell asleep.

Ma and Papa had stopped shouting, but they were talking quietly in short angry sentences. Celie turned out her bedroom light and opened the window. Ma would have a fit if she knew she was letting rain splatter on the varnished windowsill, but Celie didn't care. She lay there listening to the patter of the rain, which was interrupted now and then by the crackle of lightning and the crashing of thunder and the gonging of the bell buoy in the harbor. Where was Ben now? Was he outside alone in the rain? Maybe he was afraid to come home. If she'd done something as dumb as run away, she would be. Or maybe he wasn't afraid but embarrassed. It must have been pretty humiliating to have Julie dump him the way she did. Celie refused to think about the possibility that he'd actually enlisted and was on his way to boot camp. Not on Sunday, she told herself. The recruiting station wouldn't be open on Sunday. Would it?

Maybe Papa wouldn't go after Ben, but she could. She'd bring him home. She'd take the train. There couldn't be that many places in Boston where he could be, could there? Even if there was more than one recruiting office, Ben would probably look for the one nearest the train station. He didn't know Boston any better than she did. She'd need money, but she had a few dollars in her piggy bank. She could do it. She was sure she could.

Having made the decision, Celie was suddenly exhausted. She rolled over and was about to drift off when she heard the pulley outside her window rattle. Joey was sending a message. She pushed up the screen and stuck her head out the window. She could just make out Joey's silhouette in the darkness. The rain felt good on her face. "Hey," she called in a loud whisper.

"Hey," Joey said.

They were both silent then, and Celie could hear the pulleys squeaking as Joey tugged on the rope, moving the basket with his message closer to her. When she could reach it, she retrieved the message from the can. She was relieved that it wasn't in code but in the telegraph style they'd adopted for their less urgent messages.

GLAD CHARLEY FOUND STOP MOM HERE
INDEFINITELY STOP GRANDMA TOO UP-
SET STOP SEE YOU TOMORROW STOP

Celie picked up the pencil that they kept in the basket.

THANKS STOP SEE YOU TOMORROW STOP
SORRY ABOUT YOUR DAD STOP

She wanted to say something else, something about her plan, but it was too big to fit on a small scrap of paper, so she folded the note and stuck it back in the can and sent it on its way. Then she went back to bed and slept to the steady rhythm of the rain.

★

Celie's first thought in the morning was Ben. But now it hardly seemed likely that her plan would work, not because she was afraid to go but because she couldn't believe that Ben would come back with her. Maybe Papa was right: Ben would have to decide for himself.

The sun was glinting off every rain-washed surface. Celie had to squint when she went outside. Charley had been banished to the backyard, where he was hunched sulkily under the picnic table.

"Andy's staying at Rufus's," Ma said as she headed off to work. "I don't want him bothering Mrs. Bentley today. And you," she said, pointing her finger at Celie and wagging it up and down, "don't let that monkey out of your sight."

"But, Ma—" Celie began.

"No *buts*," Ma said sharply. "Where you go, he goes!"

"Yes, ma'am." Celie swung Charley up onto her shoulder. "You'd think you robbed a bank or something," she said. Charley seemed to nod in agreement and Celie laughed. She started over to Mrs. Bentley's.

Andy was in front of Mrs. Bentley's playing marbles with Rufus. They'd scooped a small hole in the dirt driveway and were shooting moonies.

"Hey, you guys," Celie said.

"Hey," said Rufus.

Andy glanced up and then went right back to the game. Celie noticed that Rufus's marble bag was fuller than Andy's, which meant Rufus had won more rounds. No wonder Andy was so determined.

"I thought you were staying over at Rufus's today," Celie said.

"I am," Andy said, "but Mrs. B. has a better driveway for marbles."

Rufus nodded. "A lot better," he said.

Celie laughed. She wasn't going to ask what made one dirt hole better than another.

As she walked up to Mrs. Bentley's front door, she was surprised to see a banner in the window—white with a blue star and a red border, and gold fringe along the bottom—to show that Mrs. Bentley had a son in the war. It hadn't been there before. She took a deep breath and knocked. Maybe Joey wouldn't be able to do anything today. Maybe he wouldn't want to.

The door opened. Mrs. Bentley peered out at Celie as though she were a stranger. Then something seemed to register, because she said, "Lucille." She sounded as though she had sand in her voice box. "Come in." She didn't seem to notice that Celie had Charley with her. Usually she'd say, "Leave that beast outside."

Mrs. Bentley's house made Celie uncomfortable in the best of times. And one look at Mrs. Bentley, with her hair wrapped in a kerchief and her eyes ringed by dark circles like a raccoon's, would tell you this wasn't the best of times. As always, the house smelled of powder and medicine and old bacon fat, which Mrs. Bentley kept in a crock by the sink and used to cook just about everything, despite the government's wanting people to turn in their fat to be made into bombs. What amazed Celie was that Mrs. Bentley had somehow gotten Andy to keep his mitts off it. It would have been a prize for the Junior Commandos.

Joey's mother and his uncle Seth were sitting at the kitchen table, their hands wrapped around coffee mugs as though to warm them. They looked tired, and Joey's mother's face was blotchy and red. For the first time, Celie noticed photographs on the kitchen wall: one of a man standing next to a swordfish hanging on a hook—that must have been Joey's grandfather; another of a man in a navy uniform—Joey's dad, she figured. She could see the resemblance to Joey right away in both men's faces. Funny, she didn't remember seeing them before. Or maybe Mrs. Bentley had just put them up, like the banner in the window.

"You must be Celie," Joey's mother said.

"Yes, ma'am," said Celie.

"Joey's talked a lot about you—and Charley there."

"Hello, Charley," Uncle Seth said. He put his hands in his pockets. Joey must have told him about Charley's biting.

Celie smiled. She wondered if she should say something about Joey's dad being missing or whether that would be impolite, so she just stood there smiling. Fortunately the sound of Joey clomping down the stairs broke the silence.

He came into the room and Celie could feel his eyes on her. It was a new feeling. She didn't know if she liked it.

"We're going to the beach," Joey said, hustling her out the door as fast as he could.

"What's the hurry?" Celie asked, once they were outside.

"I can't stand it in there," Joey said. "They're all acting as though he's dead already. He's just missing, okay? Missing. Not dead." His jaw was tight and his voice was cracking. Celie had never seen Joey angry.

133

"Of course," she said. "Missing. They'll find him. It'll be okay."

"It'll be okay," Joey repeated. They walked along side by side for a while, neither of them speaking.

Suddenly Celie didn't want to think about the war anymore, or about missing fathers or brothers. She reached up and pulled the ties from her braids. She shook her head hard, letting her hair fly out around her like an orange cloud. "Race you!" she said, and took off over the hill, running with all her might, as though she could leave the whole war behind. Charley jumped down and dashed along ahead of her at the end of his leash. Joey stood there for a moment calling after her. She turned and waved him on. She didn't want to stop.

Celie felt every stone in the path through the thin soles of her worn sneakers. She felt her lungs sucking in air and pushing it out, and she felt the blood pumping through her veins. If she concentrated on all those feelings, she couldn't think about anything else.

By the time she got to the beach, she was winded and sweat was dripping down her neck. She was sitting on an old log trying to catch her breath when Julie walked by. Celie didn't know whether she should say hello or just ignore her, but Julie made the decision for her. She stopped right in front of Celie and smiled. "Hey, Celie," she said.

"Hey," said Celie.

"I almost didn't recognize you with your hair down."

Celie gave her one of those smiles that said, I really don't want to be talking to you. Julie was, after all, the reason her brother had run off to join up and why her parents were fighting all the time. But Julie didn't seem to notice.

"How's Ben?" she said, looking down at her foot with its red-painted toenails. She seemed to be drawing a capital B in the sand with her big toe.

It was really too much. "How's Ben?" Celie asked, her voice rising. "How's Ben? Well, I really wouldn't know, would I, now that he's run off to join up."

Julie stopped drawing the B. She looked at Celie as though she hadn't heard her right. "What?" Now *her* voice was rising. "Ben enlisted? When? How? He's too young."

"Yeah," Celie said, "just like *you're* too young to be dating a pilot."

"Oh that," Julie said, with a giggle that made Celie want to slug her. "That's over. I found out he was dating about ten different girls." She giggled again.

"What?"

"Yeah," said Julie. She was back to drawing in the sand with her toe. "Pretty dumb, huh?"

Celie didn't think she could say what she thought about it. Her ma would make her wash her mouth out with soap. She just sat there looking at Julie with her jaw hanging down. Then she got up and headed back up the hill. "See ya," she said to Julie. By the time she got to the top, she was running. Her plan to bring Ben home might work, after all.

14

When Celie reached the top of the hill, Joey was just coming up the other side. His face was red and he was panting.

"She dumped Roger," Celie told him. "Ben ran away over her and she's dumped Roger."

"Who?" Joey said.

"Julie," said Celie. "She's back there." She pointed over his shoulder toward the beach. "We've got to tell Ben. If he knew, he'd come home."

"How will we ever find him?"

"I don't know," she said, "but we've got to try. You've got to come with me, Joey. You know Boston. Do you know where the navy recruiting station is?"

"Sure," Joey said. "The Fargo Building, downtown. But what if he's not there? Boston's a big place."

"We've got to try," she said again. "Ma's brokenhearted." She fished in her pockets. Nothing but lint. "We'll need money," she said. "And something to put Charley in."

"Charley?" Joey said. "We're going to take the monkey with us?"

"Yeah," Celie said glumly. "I have to. Ma said not to let

him out of my sight. I can't leave him home. If he got into trouble, she'd kill me."

"She'll kill you anyway for running off to Boston to find Ben," Joey said. "She can't kill you twice."

"Never mind," Celie said. "Come on." She started off toward home at a clip. She heard Joey sigh and turn to follow.

★

Celie found the satchel Charley had hidden in when they were in the attic. If she poked some holes in the sides, it'd be perfect for carrying him.

"You can't take a monkey on the train," Joey said.

"People take cats on the train all the time," she said.

"Cats," said Joey, "not monkeys."

"You've got to be more positive," Celie said. "Besides, we don't have a choice. No one else is going to go after Ben." She broke open her piggy bank and counted the money. Four dollars and eighty-six cents. That would be plenty to cover the train ticket, with some left over for food.

Charley wasn't happy about being stuck in the bag, but she held him down and got it zipped up.

"You got any money?" she asked Joey, rubbing the pink welts on her arms where Charley had nipped her in his struggle.

Joey nodded. He had a couple of two-dollar bills in his wallet. Celie rolled her eyes. Leave it to Joey to have a wallet.

"Shouldn't we tell somebody where we're going?" Joey asked.

Celie shook her head. "I want to surprise them. Besides, we'll be back before anyone gets home from work."

"I don't know," Joey said. "My mom—"

"Look, Joey," she said, "you don't have to come if you're chicken."

"I'm not chicken," Joey said, his cheeks turning red. "But remember what your ma said about worrying."

"She won't even know we're gone," Celie said. Ma would be so happy to have Ben back, and she and Papa would stop fighting. It would be all right, Celie told herself. It had to be.

They took turns carrying Charley to the train station, but even so they had to stop three times on the way to rest. It was hot and muggy: a real scorcher, Papa would say. Celie had opened the satchel a bit, and Charley had his head out and was looking about curiously.

"Two tickets to Boston," Celie told the woman at the counter. "Round-trip."

The woman looked at Charley and then at Celie. "You're not taking him on the train." It wasn't a question.

"He'll be in the satchel," she said. "He won't get out. People bring cats on the train, don't they? What's the difference?"

The woman pinched her lips together until a white ring showed around her mouth. "Just a minute," she said. She walked over to a gray-haired man standing across the room holding a clipboard.

The man followed her back to the window and

looked hard at Charley. "Where are your parents?" he asked Celie.

"In Boston," Celie said, crossing her fingers. "That's why we're going there."

The man glared, his eyes narrowed, and he looked them over good. The ticket woman stood behind him with her arms crossed and a smug smile on her face.

"All right," the man said at last. "But he stays in the satchel, and put him in baggage."

"Yes, sir," said Celie. She slid her money across the counter, and the ticket woman grudgingly handed her two tickets.

"You go find our seats," Celie told Joey. "I'll go back to the baggage car and explain to the baggage man about Charley."

The baggage man looked gruff, and when he took off his cap, Celie saw he had a rim of dark hair ringing his shiny bald head. "I don't know about this," he said.

"The man inside said it was okay," Celie said. Then she added, "He's harmless. Really. He won't be any trouble."

"Uh-huh," said the man. He didn't sound convinced.

"Look," said Celie, trying to reassure him, "he's got a leash, see?" She reached into the bag, pulled out the end of Charlie's chain, and zipped the satchel closed again. She looked around the baggage car. "I'll attach it to this handle on the wall," she said. "Then even if he gets out of the bag—which he won't—he can't get loose or anything."

"Well, okay," said the man, straightening his hat. "I guess

if the boss said you could bring him, I haven't got a choice. But don't you go far."

"I won't," Celie said. She heaved a sigh of relief and went to find Joey.

The train had been moving for about ten minutes when the baggage man stormed into the car. "Where is the kid who owns that monkey?" he hollered. He was waving his cap furiously, and his head was shining like a red lightbulb.

Celie wanted to hide under the seat, and she could tell that Joey did, too. But she figured the baggage man would find her one way or another. Besides, if something had happened to Charley, she had to know about it.

"Right here," she said, standing up and stepping out into the aisle.

The baggage man appeared speechless for a moment. He stood there looking at her and spluttering. Finally he bellowed, "Come with me!"

Celie and Joey followed the man back to the baggage compartment. Celie couldn't believe her eyes. The door to the baggage car was open, and there was Charley, flying along outside the train at the end of his chain, flapping his arms like a bird and shrieking, "Waaa, waaaa, waaaaaaa."

The baggage man was yelling and waving his arms and looking a little like Charley.

"How'd he get out of the bag?" Celie asked.

The baggage man looked sheepish as he explained how he'd opened the bag just a bit to let a little air in. Celie knew that was all it took for Charley to work his fingers up and unzip the bag the rest of the way. The man was blaming her when really it was his fault.

"Do something!" he shouted. "I knew we shouldn't have let that animal on the train. I could get fired for this."

Celie wished he would be quiet. He wasn't helping matters by getting hysterical. And what about Charley? He could be hurt. She braced her feet and Joey held her around the waist while she leaned out the door, grabbed Charlie's chain, and reeled him in like a fish on a line.

When she got him into the car, he was still squawking and his eyes were nearly popping out of his head, he was so scared. She didn't see any blood and he seemed to be moving all right, so Celie figured he wasn't injured. She tried to calm him down, but the baggage man wanted him back in the bag.

"Now!" he said.

Joey held the bag open, while Celie tried to stuff Charley in. He put his ears back and bared his teeth. It was going to be a battle. Celie grabbed Charley and held him tight around the middle, pinning his arms to his sides. He kicked and squirmed, but she got his lower end into the satchel. Then she held him down with one hand while Joey zipped the bag. All the while, Charley was biting and squawking as though Celie were trying to kill him. By the time they'd gotten him into the bag and zipped it up again, he'd nipped her arms pretty good. No blood or anything, but some good-sized welts.

The baggage man insisted that they stay in the compartment with him until they got to Boston, so she and Joey pulled up some suitcases and tried to make themselves comfortable. Charley was still squawking inside the satchel. He was jumping and pushing, making the bag hop around on the floor of the car like a Mexican jumping bean. She wished she could let him out. She felt terrible. But all she could do was talk to him.

"It's okay, boy," she said in as soothing a voice as she could muster. "It's going to be all right." But it wasn't really. She knew it. And she wondered if Charley did, too.

15

They got off the train at North Station. Celie was glad to see the last of the baggage man. "Good riddance," she muttered as she climbed down the step lugging the satchel.

"And I'll make sure you can't get on another train with that beast!" the man called after them. Celie had no doubt that he meant it. She turned and darted her tongue out as the door slammed closed behind them.

Celie had been to North Station before, but never without her parents and not for a long time. She'd forgotten how big the train station was, and how many people there were in Boston. She and Joey would never find Ben.

"Maybe we should ask for directions to the recruiting station," Joey said.

"I thought you knew where it was."

"I do. Sort of," he said. "But I need to get my bearings." He pointed across the station. "Look. There's a cop."

Charley was beginning to hop again. "You go ask," Celie said. "I'll stay here with Charley."

Joey walked up to the policeman and Celie watched as the officer pointed and gestured and Joey smiled and nodded. It was funny how different he seemed here on his own turf. He'd been like a fish out of water in Gloucester; now it was her turn.

Joey started toward the exit, beckoning for Celie to follow him. She was glad to be leaving the station. People were beginning to look at her oddly, since Charley was still squawking and bouncing around, and now he was poking his fingers out the air holes she'd made in the satchel. She decided to keep him in the bag for now. She didn't want him getting loose on the streets of Boston.

Joey thought they should take the subway, but Celie wasn't so sure. She'd had enough of trains, and she thought Charley probably had, too. So they hiked it. It was a long walk. Celie was drenched with sweat by the time they got there.

The recruiting station was a tall brick building and there were several young men going in the front door. Some were in uniform, others in civilian clothes, looking a bit nervous.

"You wait here with Charley," she told Joey. "I'll be right back."

It was cool inside the office. A fan was clacking away in one corner. The breeze felt good on her damp face. She looked around for Ben, but she didn't see him.

"I'm looking for my brother," she told a uniformed man at the desk when it was her turn.

"What's his name, honey?" the man asked.

Celie's ears burned. She hated to be called honey, especially by people she didn't know. "Ben Marsh," she said.

"Oh yeah," the man said. He and another fellow nodded knowingly at each other. "He was waiting for us when we opened up this morning. Popular guy, your brother."

"What do you mean?" Celie asked.

"Man called about him this morning. Told him he was gone already."

Celie's stomach did a loop-the-loop. She was too late. "He's gone?" she asked. "Enlisted? Already?"

"Nah, honey," the man said. "Your brother's got feet like pancakes. We can't use a guy with feet like pancakes."

"Say, red," said the second man. She hated that nickname even more than she hated being called honey. "How old is that brother of yours anyway?"

Celie looked him right in the eye and crossed her fingers behind her back. "Eighteen and a half," she said. Then she spun toward the door and left.

She was blowing steam out her ears by the time she got to the door. Who did those guys think they were? They'd obviously known all along that Ben was too young, but they'd played along and then laughed at him behind his back. Some nerve. He did have pancake feet, though, and she'd heard about boys being rejected for that. Still, Ben must be devastated. He'd probably take this worse than the news about Julie.

Celie was out the door before it occurred to her to wonder who had called them. Papa, she thought. It must have been. But Ben had already left. He could be anywhere by now.

"What's the matter?" Joey asked when he saw her. "Were you too late?"

"Yeah," she said. "He's gone. But not to the navy."

"They didn't want him?"

"Nope," Celie said.

"So now what?"

"I don't know," Celie said. "Where would you go if you were Ben?"

Joey shrugged. "I don't know," he said. "Home, I guess."

"Not Ben," Celie said. "He's too proud. I think he'd have to go somewhere to cool down."

"Well, I think Charley needs to get out of this bag. Maybe we should go over to the Common and let him walk around."

The Common was a huge expanse of green in the middle of a maze of buildings so tall that Celie had to crane her neck to see the tops of them.

"See that up there?" Joey said, pointing to an elegant brick building up on a hill beyond the Common.

"Yeah?" Celie said.

"That's the State House."

"I thought the State House had a gold dome," Celie said.

"It does," Joey said. "They painted it gray for the duration. To make it harder to see."

"It's pretty anyway," Celie said.

"Yeah," said Joey.

"And over there"—he pointed down toward the end of the Common—"that's the Public Garden."

Celie nodded. She'd read *Make Way for Ducklings* to

Andy about a million times, all about the mallard ducks that made their home on the pond in the Public Garden. "It's beautiful," she said.

Joey was beaming, as if all this was his and he was sharing it with Celie.

He put Charley's satchel on the ground and unzipped it. Charley scrambled out and instantly let loose a long stream of pee.

Celie laughed. "Oh, poor guy. You were desperate!" He wasn't usually fussy about where he went. He must not have wanted to soil that small space. When he'd finished his business, he clambered up into Celie's arms, then onto her shoulder. Joey grabbed the satchel and they walked over to a bench and sat down.

It seemed that even in Boston, a monkey on a leash was an odd sight. Everyone who passed by pointed and smiled. If she hadn't been so worried about Ben, Celie might have enjoyed the attention.

Now her stomach was grumbling, and she was beginning to wonder whether they'd ever find her brother, not to mention find a way home, since Charley had ruined their chances of taking the train. She closed her eyes and tried to concentrate.

Joey poked her in the ribs with his elbow.

"Ow," she said, giving him her best scowl. Hunger was making her crabby. "What?"

He pointed to a bench across the park where a bum was sleeping. "Isn't that your brother?" he asked.

"What?" she said. "It couldn't be." Could it? But then she

thought about it. Where else would he go? He didn't know Boston. And the Common was close to the recruiting station. It made sense, really. She picked up Charley and started across the park.

It was Ben, all right. His hair was sticking up every which way, his clothes were wrinkled, and his shirttail was hanging out. He looked like someone her mother would steer her well away from if they were walking together.

"Ben!" Celie called.

Ben jerked awake and sat up. He blinked and looked around.

"Ben!" she called again. She grabbed Joey by the arm and started running, clinging to Charley with her other arm.

Ben's bloodshot eyes had finally focused on her. He didn't look awfully glad to see her.

"We thought you'd have shipped out by now," Joey said.

"Nah," Ben said. He leaned over and looked down at his duffel bag, which was planted between his feet. "They didn't want me."

"Well, anyone could have told you you aren't old enough," said Celie.

"It wasn't my age," Ben said. "It's my feet. They're too flat. What are you doing here?" Ben asked. He looked around. "Ma and Pop here somewhere?"

"Uh-uh," Celie said. "Joey and I came to get you, and Ma said I had to keep Charley with me because of him getting into the henhouse . . ."

"Whoa." Ben held up his hand as though he were trying

to stop traffic, like Michael, the police officer in *Make Way for Ducklings*. "Henhouse? What are you talking about?"

"Never mind that," Celie said. "The thing is, Julie's dumped Roger."

"So?" Ben said, but Celie could tell he wanted to know more.

"She found out that Roger guy was dating a bunch of other girls."

Ben sat up straight. "That bum," he said. "If I could get my hands on him—"

"Yeah," Celie said. "So you don't have to join up."

Ben's eyes darkened. "Don't you get it?" he said. "It's not about Julie. Not really. This means I'll never be able to join up. Even when I'm eighteen I won't be able to go. I won't be able to fight for my country. People will think I'm a coward."

"It's not your fault you have flat feet, Ben. People will understand that."

Ben put his face in his hands and Celie stood there watching, not sure what to do. "What now?" she asked.

Ben lifted his shoulders and then dropped them.

She wondered what he would have done if they hadn't found him. Would he have sat there forever? It was up to them, she realized. They had to get him home, she and Joey. And with Charley along, that wasn't going to be easy.

They couldn't take the train. The baggage man had made it clear that he was going to inform the office not to let anyone board with a monkey in a satchel. The bus would cost money; they'd already spent most of theirs on the train tickets, and Ben had spent most of Ma's money on food.

So their choices were limited. They could hitchhike, but Celie knew Ma wouldn't approve of that. They could call Papa at work, which would surely get them into trouble. They could call Mrs. Bentley and see if Joey's uncle could come for them. Or—and this just might work—she could call Jimmy. Charley could ride in the back of the pickup.

Ben didn't care for Jimmy, but that was his tough luck. Jimmy was a good guy, and Celie knew she could count on him. Besides, if Ben was forced to spend an hour in the cab of a truck with Jimmy, maybe he'd learn something.

She didn't know Jimmy's telephone number, but the operator could find it. He'd probably be home, having set his traps early that morning. There was a telephone booth on the street corner. "Here," she said, handing Joey the monkey. "You hold Charley. I'm going to make a phone call."

Jimmy wasn't thrilled—especially since he'd have to use his gas ration—but Celie could tell he wasn't too surprised, either. "Has it occurred to you that that monkey is more trouble than he's worth?" Jimmy said.

Celie tried to explain that it wasn't Charley's fault, but Jimmy wasn't buying it. Celie couldn't say she blamed him. As much as she loved Charley, Jimmy was right—he was trouble. The thing was, he was a wild animal, and wild animals shouldn't ride on trains—or live in houses. Celie knew it now.

"You sure your brother'll take a ride from me?" he asked.

"He will if he wants to get home," Celie said.

Jimmy said he'd meet them at the Swan Boats. He was pretty sure he could find the Public Garden. Celie and Joey took Charley out for a walk. They found a shop where they could buy hot dogs and tonic, and Joey bought three of each with the last of his money. Then they went back and sat on the bench next to Ben to eat.

When they were finished, Celie told Ben they had to walk over to the Swan Boats to wait for their ride.

"Pop's coming?" Ben asked.

"Nope," said Celie. "Jimmy."

"Jimmy DaSilva?" Ben looked disgusted. "I'm not taking a ride from him. The stinking—"

"Hey," Celie said, surprised at the anger in her voice. Ben must have been, too, because he stopped talking. "Jimmy's a friend of mine, so you just be careful."

"Sorry," Ben said. But he didn't sound a bit sorry. He went with them, though, so Celie guessed he was going to accept the ride.

It seemed like forever before Jimmy drove up. He honked his horn and waved them over. "Hurry up," he said. "I don't think I'm supposed to park here." Ben picked up his duffel. He didn't look happy to see Jimmy, but he got into the cab of the truck without a word.

Celie and Joey sat in the bed of the pickup with Charley. He was still out of the satchel and looking about curiously. Celie clutched tight to his leash. It wouldn't do for him to escape now.

The wind blew Charley's fur as they drove along. It was a hard, bumpy ride. Celie felt as though she might rattle to pieces. Her hair whipped around her face, and she wished she'd braided it. By the time they got home, it would be a tangled mess.

They descended into the tunnel that would take them under Boston Harbor and to points north. The tunnel was dark and cool. The sun, when they came out the other side, was brilliant, and Celie had to squeeze her eyes almost shut to see at all.

"Do you miss it?" she asked Joey as the city skyline disappeared in the distance.

"Nah," Joey said.

"Really?" she said. "I would."

"You think?" he asked. He looked at her as though he was trying to see her thoughts, then he said, "I didn't have any friends there." The way he said it made Celie realize he was saying she was his friend and she had to admit, weird as Joey was, he was her best friend. Who else would have gotten on the train with her and Charley to look for her brother in a city the size of Boston? Nobody she could think of. Not even Rita. It was crazy. And him with his own problems. She hadn't even asked him if they'd had any news about his father. But then she figured, if there'd been news, Joey would have said. He wouldn't have waited for her to ask. She smiled at him, and he smiled back.

16

There was a small crowd on the sidewalk in front of the house when Jimmy's truck rolled up and stopped with a squeal of brakes. Ma and Papa were there with Andy, and Mrs. Bentley, and Joey's mother and uncle, too. Jimmy must have told them Celie had called him.

Celie and Joey exchanged a look that said, We're in trouble. They climbed out of the truck and were waiting for the storm to strike when Ben opened the door of the cab, flung his duffel bag onto the sidewalk, then said something to Jimmy that they couldn't hear and waved goodbye as the truck drove off.

Ma's hand went to her mouth. Celie could tell she didn't know whether to hug him or murder him. She figured that was a good break for her and Joey. Maybe they'd escape the wrath of the grownups, who were too busy fussing over Ben. But when Celie motioned to Joey to follow her and tried to sneak past her parents, Ma spun around and grabbed her arm. "Not so fast, young lady," she said.

★

Celie tied Charley out back and went to her room, where Ma had sent her. Ma had been furious. She should have been happy. Hadn't Celie brought her precious Ben home?

There was a sharp rap on the door, and Ma walked in. She sat down on the bed next to Celie and clasped her hands around one knee, leaning back a bit for balance. "What am I going to do with you?" she asked after a long pause.

Celie shrugged. How was she supposed to answer a question like that?

"You've got to start thinking about other people," Ma went on.

"I was thinking about other people," Celie said. "I was thinking about you and how miserable you were. And I was thinking about Ben and how if he knew Julie wasn't engaged, he wouldn't have to join the navy and he could come home."

"But you didn't tell anyone you were going."

"You weren't home to tell," Celie said, and then felt guilty. Ma wasn't working to punish her. "Besides, if I'd told you, you wouldn't have let me go."

"And Ben would still be home, wouldn't he?"

"Maybe," Celie said. She wasn't so sure.

Ma sighed again. "And whatever possessed you to take Charley? I heard about what happened on the train. He could have been killed."

"You told me not to let him out of my sight," Celie said. "I had to take him."

Ma shook her head. "Joey's mother was frantic. She's thinking about taking Joey back to Boston."

"What? She can't!"

"She hasn't decided yet. Maybe after she calms down she'll change her mind," Ma said. "In the meantime, I want you to stay in your room and think hard about your behavior today," Ma said.

Celie lay on her bed and stared at the wall. Nothing had turned out the way it was supposed to. Everyone was supposed to be happy. Ben was home. Julie wasn't getting married. She and Joey and Charley had survived the trip. But instead, everyone was angry. She buried her face in her pillow and cried.

After a while, there was another knock on her door. "Go away!" she shouted.

But the door opened and Ben peeked in. "Hey, Squirt," he said.

"What do you want?" Celie snapped. This was all his fault. All of it. She never would have gone to Boston if it hadn't been for him.

Ben stood just inside the door and stared at his shoes. "I just wanted to say thanks," he said. "For coming after me, I mean." He paused. "I don't know what I would have done. I was pretty low." Celie looked at his face. He was serious. "It was a brave thing to do, going all the way to Boston to bring me home," he went on. "Even if it was kind of dumb."

He just had to add that part, Celie thought.

"I mean, who would ever think of taking a monkey on a train."

Celie flung her pillow at him and Ben ducked behind the door. "Maybe I should have left you there," she said.

Ben smiled, and she smiled back. "I gotta go," he said. "Got a date."

"With Julie?"

"Nope. Jimmy. He's taking me out on his boat."

Celie was speechless. Maybe the day hadn't been a total loss.

She heard Ben drive off with Jimmy, and the house became quiet. She was almost asleep when the squeal of the pulley outside her window woke her. She groaned. What now?

But Joey was tugging on the rope, making the pulley tap against her window, the way he did when he had an urgent message. She rolled over and opened the window.

CHARLEY ESCAPED STOP GOING AFTER STOP DON'T WORRY STOP

"Oh no," Celie grumbled. She stuck her head out the window to see if she could catch a glimpse of Charley. Nothing. She looked at Joey's house. He was straddling the sill of his bedroom window, reaching for the top ledge of the window beneath his with the toe of one of those same stupid brown leather shoes he'd been wearing the day she met him. The day he fell climbing the tree after Charley.

"Joey!" she whispered as loudly as she could. She didn't want to draw Ma's attention. They were in enough trouble already. "What are you doing?"

He turned his head and smiled at her. "I'm going to get Charley."

"No!" she said.

"I'll be okay," he said. "I'll just swing over to that tree." He pointed to the large branch of the maple outside his window.

"No, Joey," Celie said again. But Joey wasn't listening. She wanted to run over and grab him, stop him, but she knew she didn't have time. He was going to fall and break his neck and it would all be her fault. All Charley's fault, she knew.

She squeezed her eyes shut and waited for the crash. But it didn't come. She heard a rustling and a small thud, and when she opened her eyes, Joey was standing under her window smiling up at her as though he'd just climbed Mount Everest. She couldn't help laughing. "Your mother's going to kill you," she said.

Joey just shrugged. He opened his mouth to say something, but his mother came charging out the back door before he could get a word out.

"Joseph W. Bentley, what in heaven's name?" she shouted, marching over to him. "I thought I told you to stay in your room." She took him by the ear, just like in the movies, and dragged him back to the house.

Joey looked back at Celie and grinned. The fingers of his right hand waggled before he disappeared inside.

Celie lay back on her bed and smiled. Joey was fine. He hadn't fallen, in spite of the stupid shoes, which she was going to throw into the ocean the next time he wore them. Still, she knew this wasn't the end of it. He hadn't gotten hurt, but he might have. And who knew what Charley was up to now. He could be anywhere. Doing anything. She felt helpless.

Mickey should never have brought him here, she thought. He was too wild to live with people and too tame to live in the wild. It wasn't fair. Maybe if he'd been a baby when they'd gotten him, it would be different. But he wasn't. And there it was. Tears started down her cheeks and pooled in her ears. She rolled over onto her stomach and buried her face in her pillow. When she couldn't cry any more and her throat ached from the effort, she sat up and picked up the pencil and paper she kept by the window to write to Joey. It was an important message, one that should have been in code, but she was too tired to figure it out.

Dear Joey,

I'm glad you're okay. Sorry I got you in trouble. Don't worry about Charley. I'm sure he'll be back. I've made a decision, though. I'm giving him to the zoo. He's too wild to be a house pet. It's not his fault, but it's what I have to do. Thanks for being my friend. You're the best.

Celie

She put the note in the can and sent the basket over to Joey. When she heard the basket come back to her, she ignored it. Joey would try to talk her out of it, she knew, and she wasn't sure she was strong enough to stick to her guns.

She lay there, staring at the ceiling in her darkening

room, and listened for Charley. It seemed like hours before she heard him squawking at the back door to be let in.

Ma scolded him and shut him up in the summer kitchen. Then she started up the stairs. She opened the door to Celie's room and sat down on the bed. "Charley got loose again, but he came back," she said, reaching over and brushing the hair off Celie's face.

"I know," Celie said. She sat up and took a deep breath. "Ma, remember that lady whose sister works at the zoo?"

"Mmm," Ma said.

Celie took another deep breath. "I think maybe tomorrow we should call her." She barely got it out before she started to sob.

Ma put her arms around Celie and held her tight. She didn't say, I told you so; she just sat on the bed and let Celie cry. After a while she put her finger under Celie's chin and tipped her face up so that their eyes met. "I'm proud of you," she said.

Celie tried to smile, but she couldn't. She wasn't proud.

As though she could read Celie's thoughts, Ma said, "It's not your fault," and Celie nodded, not so much in agreement but because her voice wouldn't work and she knew Ma was waiting for her to say something.

"We'll make arrangements tomorrow," Ma said, and Celie nodded again.

Ma left, and Celie fell asleep to the drone of the radio and her parents' quiet voices floating up from downstairs.

★

Papa took the next day off so he could drive Charley to the zoo. Celie sat in the front seat of the Packard with Charley. Ben pushed the car out of the driveway. Papa waved, and they drove off. It was about an hour's drive. Her father wanted her to put Charley in the satchel, but Celie refused.

"He's going to be in a cage for the rest of his life," she said, trying not to cry. "Let him be out and free one last time."

They were both quiet after that. Celie read the billboards along the roadside:

HITLER SMILES WHEN YOU WASTE MILES.

THE EMPTY SEAT IS A GIFT TO HITLER.

EVERY TIME YOU DECIDE *NOT* TO BUY SOMETHING, YOU
    HELP WIN THE WAR.

"I feel bad about this whole thing, Celie."

Her father's voice startled her. It seemed as though they'd been driving forever in silence, except for a squawk from Charley now and then. She didn't know what to say, so she didn't say anything.

"I never should have brought him home," he said. "Your mother is always telling me I don't think about consequences. I guess she's right."

I guess so, Celie thought. But if Papa had thought about what might happen, she never would have had Charley at all. And what would have happened to him? The problem wasn't that her father had brought him home; it was that someone had captured him in the first place. She thought she should say something to make Papa feel better, but she couldn't think of anything. She felt too awful herself.

"It's going to be all right," she whispered to Charley. He looked up at her with his big brown eyes. She felt terrible, as though she were betraying him. Charley in a cage.

Finally the car stopped. Celie looked up. They were there.

"Let's get it over with," Papa said. "They're expecting us."

Charley held tight to Celie's neck as they followed the signs for the Administration Building. They found it too fast. Before Celie knew it, Papa had signed all the papers and Celie had handed Charley over to a woman in a white coat, who took him to a cage where he'd be examined before being introduced to the general population. Charley hadn't wanted to let go of Celie, and the woman had had to pull him away. It broke Celie's heart.

She stood outside the cage where he sat hunched on a concrete bench. His eyes were wide, like those of a child who'd been left at the sitter's for the first time. Celie started to sob.

"Let's go, Celie," Papa said. He put his arm around her. "No use standing here torturing yourself. Let's go home."

Celie nodded. "Goodbye, Charley," she said. But as she started away, she heard that familiar yelp. She turned. Charley was standing at the bars of the cage, reaching after her. There were tears, real tears just like hers, dripping down his cheeks.

★

Celie was about cried out by the time they got home.

"I made a cherry pie," Ma said. It was an extravagance, with sugar and shortening so scarce, but Celie wasn't hungry.

"I just want to be alone for a while," she said. She went up to her room and closed the door. Then she flopped onto her stomach on her bed. She squeezed her eyes shut, hoping to block out the image of Charley in the cage, but it didn't work. Finally she fell asleep.

When she woke, the sky was in that gray stage between night and day, and she wasn't sure whether it was morning or evening. She lay there a minute trying to get her bearings. She could hear her parents moving about downstairs and the clatter of supper dishes. Evening. Then she heard Andy talking in his room. And Ben. And then she remembered about Charley.

She rubbed the crust from the corners of her eyes and pushed back the curtains. Her whole head felt swollen.

She got out of bed slowly and went to the bathroom to wash her face.

She could still hear Andy talking. He sounded as though he was jumping on his bed as he spoke. She could hear the steady thump, thump, thump. "And the burglars will jump over the wall and open up Charley's cage and then they'll get an airplane and they'll tie a rope to Charley and pull him up into the airplane and fly him back home. And then Celie will stop crying."

"Don't you worry about Celie, pest," Ben said. "She's a strong girl. She's going to be fine." Was that her big brother talking? She could hardly believe it. *Brave*, he'd said earlier. Now *strong*?

Celie looked in the mirror at her puffy face and swollen eyes. Was she really? She washed her face and looked again. She twisted her hair behind her head and held it there. Ma's eyes, she thought. She'd never noticed that before.

Her parents looked up when she walked into the kitchen.

"Hey, Smudge," Papa said. He tried to smile but couldn't quite manage it, and his mouth twisted into a grimace instead.

"Hungry, sweetie?" Ma asked.

Celie shook her head. "He cried, Ma," Celie said. "When we left, he cried."

"Papa told me," she said. "I'm so sorry, Celie."

Her throat was tight and her eyes burned. The smell of cooking onions made her feel sick. She went out to the back porch and sat in the rocking chair. It was getting dark. The air was cool and damp and felt good on her hot cheeks. She curled up in the chair, resting her head on her knees.

After a while, the door opened and her mother came out. She pulled a chair over and sat next to Celie, and they watched the stars. "I should tell you," Ma began slowly. "The Bentleys got some news today."

"Did they find Joey's dad?"

Ma nodded, but from the look on her face Celie could tell the news wasn't good.

"No," Celie said. "Oh, poor Joey." She wouldn't have thought she could find any more tears to shed, but somehow she did. "It's not fair," she said. She hadn't realized it until that moment, but somehow she'd felt that by putting Charley in the zoo she could stop bad things from happening. As though maybe she'd made a deal with God. But it hadn't made any difference. Of course it hadn't.

"No," Ma said, "it's not fair."

"There's nothing we can do, is there?" Celie said.

"No," said Ma. "Except be grateful for the time we have. And love one another."

Love one another. It sounded so simple. Maybe you just had to start with the people next to you and pass it on.

"Mrs. B. didn't get to say she was sorry," Celie said.

"I like to think that he knew," Ma said. "I like to think children know that their mothers love them, even if their mothers forget to tell them as often as they should."

Celie looked up at her mother. In the starlight she could see lines around her mother's eyes and mouth that she'd never noticed before. She'd never thought of her mother as pretty. But she was, pretty and strong. It was in her eyes.

"Come on," Ma said. "I think I hear *I Love a Mystery* coming on."

"Can I have some supper first? I'm starved."

Ma smiled. "I kept it warm," she said.

Later, while they were listening to the radio, Celie felt the hollow place where Charley used to be. She would never stop missing him. One day, after he'd had a chance to get used to the zoo, she'd go visit him. She hadn't taken him out of the wilderness, but still she was responsible for him. She couldn't let him down. Joey, either. Ma said Joey and his mother had decided to stay with Mrs. Bentley. When Joey was up to it she'd take him clamming, Celie thought, and teach him how to throw a baseball.

She picked up the sock she'd started back in June. Her needles clacked in an uneven counterpoint to Ma's steady rhythm. Ben and Andy played checkers, sending up the occasional whoop as one or the other earned a king. In his chair by the fireplace, Papa snored lightly. It was a comfortable sort of harmony, Celie thought, as the foghorn sounded in the harbor. Just like before the world went crazy. Only different. Completely different.